Greens Sheriff Court and Sheriff Appeal Court Rules 2024/2025

Greens Sheriff Court and Sheriff Appeal Court Rules 2024/2025

REPRINTED FROM DIVISION D (COURTS, LOWER)
AND DIVISION S (SHERIFF APPEAL COURT
PRACTICE) OF THE PARLIAMENT HOUSE BOOK

W. Green

Published in 2024 by Thomson Reuters, trading as W. Green.
Thomson Reuters is registered in England & Wales, Company No.1679046
Registered Office and address for service:
5 Canada Square, Canary Wharf, London, E14 5AQ
For further information on our products and services, visit *http://
www.sweetandmaxwell.co.uk.*

ISBN (print) 9780414122819

ISBN (e-book) 9780414122840

ISBN (print and e-book) 9780414122833

Printed and bound by CPI Group (UK) Ltd, Croydon, CR0 4YY
A CIP catalogue record for this book is available from the British Library.
For orders, go to: *http://www.tr.com/uki-legal-contact*; Tel: 0345 600 9355.

FSC
www.fsc.org
MIX
Paper | Supporting
responsible forestry
FSC® C013604

Reprinted from the *Parliament House Book*, published in looseleaf form and updated five times a year by W. Green, the Scottish Law Publisher

The following paperback titles are also available in the series:

Annotated Rules of the Court of Session 2024/2025

Solicitors Professional Handbook 2024/2025

Parliament House Book consists of the following Divisions:

A Fees and Stamps

B Courts, Upper

C Court of Session Practice

D Courts, Lower

E Licensing

F Solicitors

G Legal Aid

H Bankruptcy and other Mercantile

I Companies

J Conveyancing, Land Tenure and Registration

K Family Law

L Landlord and Tenant

M Succession, Trusts, Liferents and Judicial Factors

S Sheriff Appeal Court Practice

Modifications to Court Practice During the COVID-19 Emergency

The Coronavirus (Scotland) Act 2020 came into force on 7 April 2020 and the Coronavirus (Scotland) (No.2) Act 2020 came into force on 27 May 2020. Schedule 4 of both of these Acts contained temporary modifications to the law relating to the justice system (both criminal and civil).

Briefly, the schedules provided that:
- electronic signatures on court documents would be permitted;
- electronic documents could be used in place of the actual documents;
- the requirement to physically attend court no longer applied, and
- anyone excused from personal attendance at court must instead appear by electronic means as directed by the court.

Since the pandemic, the conduct, management and disposal of civil court business has given rise to numerous temporary modifications to practice. In the sheriff court, each sheriffdom has issued guidance and directions to facilitate the continued handling and efficient disposal of business in their sheriffdoms in the light of the prevailing circumstances. These are frequently being reviewed and updated, and reference should be made to the Scottish Courts and Tribunal Services website where all such notices issued during the pandemic are published. See
https://www.scotcourts.gov.uk/coronavirus-orders-and-guidance.

New forms in the Act of Sederunt (Simple Procedure) 2016

The Simple Procedure Rules have been amended by the Act of Sederunt (Simple Procedure Amendment) (Miscellaneous) 2022 (SSI 2022/211). The amendments include the revocation and substitution of multiple forms in Sch.2 and the replacement of various standard orders in Sch.3.

Please note that the following forms, that have been omitted from the new rules, will still be used for actions already raised and proceeding prior to 31 May 2023. The previous version of the forms are available on the SCTS website (*https://www.scotcourts.gov.uk/rules-and-practice/forms/sheriff-court-forms/ simple-procedure-forms*):

- Form 3B (further claimant form)
- Form 3C (further respondent form)
- Form 3E (change of timetable application)
- Form 9A (application to pause)
- Form 9B (application to restart)
- Form 9C (additional respondent application)
- Form 9D (application to amend)
- Form 9E (abandonment notice)
- Form 9F (application to represent)
- Form 9G (incidental orders application)
- Form 10B (recovery of documents application)
- Form 10C (application to open confidential document)
- Form 10D (special recovery of documents application).

MAIN TABLE OF CONTENTS

COURTS, LOWER: STATUTES

SHERIFF COURTS (SCOTLAND) ACT 1907

(7 Edw. 7 c. 51)

D1.1

An Act to regulate and amend the laws and practice relating to the civil procedure in sheriff courts in Scotland, and for other purposes.[1,2]

[28 August 1907]

Preliminary

Short title

1. This Act may be cited for all purposes as the Sheriff Courts (Scotland) Act 1907.

D1.2

2. *[Repealed by the Statute Law Revision Act 1927, (c.42).]*

Interpretation

3. In construing this Act (unless where the context is repugnant to such construction)—

D1.3

(a)[3] "Sheriff principal" includes sheriff;

(b) "Tenant" includes sub-tenant;

(c) "Lease" includes sub-lease;

(d)[4] "Action" or "cause" includes every civil proceeding competent in the ordinary sheriff court;

(e) "Person" includes company, corporation, or association and firm of any description nominate or descriptive, or any Board corporate or unincorporate;

(f) "Sheriff-clerk" includes sheriff-clerk depute;

(g) "Agent" means a law-agent enrolled in terms of the Law Agents (Scotland) Act 1873;

(h) "Final judgment" means an interlocutor which, by itself, or taken along with previous interlocutors, disposes of the subject-matter of the cause, notwithstanding that judgment may not have been pronounced on every question raised, and that the expenses found due may not have been modified, taxed or decerned for;

(i) *[Repealed by the Sheriff Courts (Scotland) Act 1971 (c.58), Sch.2.]*

(j) "Small Debt Acts" means and includes the Small Debt (Scotland) Acts 1887 to 1889, and Acts explaining or amending the same;

(k) "Initial writ" means the statement of claim, petition, note of appeal, or other document by which the action is initiated;

(l) "Procurator-Fiscal" means procurator-fiscal in the sheriff court;

(m) *[Repealed by the Statute Law (Repeals) Act 1989 (c.43), Sch.1, Pt I.]*

(n) "Pursuer" means and includes any person making a claim or demand, or seeking any warrant or order competent in the sheriff court;

---

[1] As amended by the Sheriff Courts (Scotland) Act 1913 (2 & 3 Geo. V c.28). Applied by the Agricultural Holdings (Scotland) Act 1991 (c.55) s.21(4), (5).

[2] For the interpretation of the terms "sheriff" and "sheriff-substitute" throughout this Act, see now the Sheriff Courts (Scotland) Act 1971 (c.58) s.4, and the Interpretation Act 1978 (c.30) Sch.1.

[3] As substituted by the Sheriff Courts (Scotland) Act 1971 (c.58), s.4.

[4] As amended by the Sheriff Courts (Scotland) Act 1913 (c.28), Sch.1.

(o) "Defender" means and includes any person who is required to be called in any action;

(p)[1] "Summary application" means and includes all applications of a summary nature brought under the common law jurisdiction of the sheriff principal, and all applications, whether by appeal or otherwise, brought under any Act of Parliament which provides, or, according to any practice in the sheriff court, which allows that the same shall be disposed of in a summary manner, but which does not more particularly define in what form the same shall be heard, tried, and determined;

(q) *[Repealed by the Law Reform (Miscellaneous Provisions) (Scotland) Act 1980 (c.55), Sch.3.]*

Jurisdiction

D1.4

4.–7. *[Repealed by the Courts Reform (Scotland) Act 2014 (asp 18) Sch.5 para.4 (effective April 1, 2015).]*

D1.5

8.–9. *[Repealed by the Sheriff Courts (Scotland) Act 1971 (c.58) Sch.2.]*

Privilege not to exempt from jurisdiction

D1.6

10. *[Repealed by the Courts Reform (Scotland) Act 2014 (asp 18) Sch.5 para.4 (effective April 1, 2015).]*

Sheriffs

Appointment of sheriffs and salaried sheriffs-substitute

D1.7

11. *[Repealed by the Courts Reform (Scotland) Act 2014 (asp 18) Sch.5 para.4 (effective April 1, 2015).]*

D1.8

12.–13. *[Repealed by the Sheriff Courts (Scotland) Act 1971 (c.58), Sch.2.]*

Salaries of sheriffs and sheriffs-substitute

D1.9

14. *[Repealed by the Courts Reform (Scotland) Act 2014 (asp 18) Sch.5 para.4 (effective April 1, 2015).]*

D1.10

15.–16. *[Repealed by the Sheriff Courts (Scotland) Act 1971 (c.58), Sch.2.]*

Honorary sheriff-substitute

D1.11

17.[2] The sheriff principal may by writing under his hand appoint such persons as he thinks proper to hold the office of honorary sheriff within his sheriffdom during his pleasure, and for whom he shall be answerable. An honorary sheriff, during the subsistence of his commission, shall be entitled to exercise the powers and duties appertaining to the office of sheriff. An honorary sheriff shall hold office, notwithstanding the death, resignation, or removal of the sheriff principal, until his commission shall be recalled by a succeeding sheriff principal. In this section "sheriff principal" does not include sheriff.

D1.12

18.–19. *[Repealed by the Sheriff Courts (Scotland) Act 1971 (c.58), Sch.2.]*

D1.13

20. *[Repealed by the Sheriffs' Pensions (Scotland) Act 1961 (c.42), Sch.2.]*

---

[1] As substituted by the Sheriff Courts (Scotland) Act 1971 (c.58), s.4.
[2] As substituted by the Sheriff Courts (Scotland) Act 1971 (c.58), s.4.

21. *[Repealed by the Sheriff Courts (Scotland) Act 1971 (c.58), Sch.2.]*   **D1.14**

22.–24. *[Repealed by the Sheriff Courts and Legal Officers (Scotland) Act 1927*   **D1.15**
(c.35), Sch.]

25.–26. *[Repealed by the Sheriff Courts (Scotland) Act 1971 (c.58), Sch.2.]*   **D1.16**

Appeals

27.–29. *[Repealed by the Courts Reform (Scotland) Act 2014 (asp 18) Sch.5*   **D1.17**
para.4 1 January 2016; as to savings see SSI 2015/378 art.3).]

30.–31. *[Repealed by the Law Reform (Miscellaneous Provisions) (Scotland)*   **D1.18**
Act 1980 (c.55), Sch.3.]

32. *[Repealed by the Sheriff Courts (Scotland) Act 1913 (2 & 3 Geo. V,*   **D1.19**
c.28),s.1.]

33. *[Repealed by the Juries Act 1949 (c.27), Sch.3.]*   **D1.20**

Removings[1]

Removings

34.[2]   Where lands exceeding two acres in extent are held under a probative lease   **D1.21**
specifying a term of endurance, and whether such lease contains an obligation upon
the tenant to remove without warning or not, such lease, or an extract thereof from
the books of any court of record shall have the same force and effect as an extract
decree of removing obtained in an ordinary action at the instance of the lessor, or
any one in his right, against the lessee or any party in possession, and such lease or
extract shall along with authority in writing signed by the lessor or any one in his
right or by his factor or law agent be sufficient warrant to any sheriff-officer or
messenger-at-arms of the sheriffdom within which such lands or heritages are situated to eject such party in possession, his family, sub-tenants, cottars, and depend-
ants, with their goods, gear, and effects, at the expiry of the term or terms of endurance of the lease: Provided that previous notice in writing to remove shall have been
given—

    (a)   When the lease is for three years and upwards not less than one year and
            not more than two years before the termination of the lease; and

    (b)   In the case of leases from year to year (including lands occupied by tacit
            relocation) or for any other period less than three years, not less than six
            months before the termination of the lease (or where there is a separate ish
            as regards land and houses or otherwise before that ish which is first in
            date):

Provided that if such written notice as aforesaid shall not be given the lease shall
be held to be renewed by tacit relocation for another year, and thereafter from year
to year: Provided further that nothing contained in this section shall affect the right
of the landlord to remove a tenant who has been sequestrated under the Bankruptcy
(Scotland) Act 1913, or against whom a decree of cessio has been pronounced under
the Debtors (Scotland) Act 1880, or who by failure to pay rent has incurred any ir-

---

[1] The provisions of this Act relating to removings are, in the case of an agricultural holding, subject to
the Agricultural Holdings (Scotland) Act 1991 (c.55), s.21: see subs. (4).
[2] Reference to the Bankruptcy (Scotland) Act 1913 inserted by virtue of the Interpretation Act 1889
(c.63), s.38 (1). The 1913 Act was repealed by the Bankruptcy (Scotland) Act 1985 (c.66): see s.5(1)
and Sch.8.

ritancy of his lease or other liability to removal: Provided further that removal or ejectment in virtue of this section shall not be competent after six weeks from the date of the ish last in date: Provided further that nothing herein contained shall be construed to prevent proceedings under any lease in common form; and that the foregoing provisions as to notice shall not apply to any stipulations in a lease entitling the landlord to resume land for building, planting, feuing, or other purposes or to subjects let for any period less than a year.

Letter of removal

D1.22 **35.**[1] Where any tenant in possession of any lands exceeding two acres in extent (whether with or without a written lease) shall, either at the date of entering upon the lease or at any other time, have granted a letter of removal, such letter of removal shall have the same force and effect as an extract decree of removing, and shall be a sufficient warrant for ejection to the like effect as is provided in regard to a lease or extract thereof, and shall be operative against the granter of such letter of removal or any party in his right within the same time and in the same manner after the like previous notice to remove: Provided always that where such letter is dated and signed within twelve months before the date of removal or before the first ish, if there be more than one ish, it shall not be necessary that any notice of any kind shall be given by either party to the other.

Notice to remove

D1.23 **36.** Where lands exceeding two acres in extent are occupied by a tenant without any written lease, and the tenant has given to the proprietor or his agent no letter of removal, the lease shall terminate on written notice being given to the tenant by or on behalf of the proprietor, or to the proprietor by or on behalf of the tenant not less than six months before the determination of the tenancy, and such notice shall entitle the proprietor, in the event of the tenant failing to remove, to apply for and obtain a summary warrant of ejection against the tenant and every one deriving right from him.

Notice of termination of tenancy

D1.24 **37.**[2] In all cases where houses, with or without land attached, not exceeding two acres in extent, lands not exceeding two acres in extent let without houses, mills, fishings, shootings, and all other heritable subjects (excepting land exceeding two acres in extent) are let for a year or more, notice of termination of tenancy shall be given in writing to the tenant by or on behalf of the proprietor or to the proprietor by or on behalf of the tenant: Provided always that notice under this section shall not warrant summary ejection from the subjects let to a tenant, but such notice, whether given to or by or on behalf of the tenant, shall entitle the proprietor to apply to the sheriff principal for a warrant for summary ejection in common form against the tenant and every one deriving right from him: Provided further that the notice provided for by this section shall be given at least forty days before the fifteenth day of May when the termination of the tenancy is the term of Whit-sunday, and at least forty days before the eleventh day of November when the termination of the tenancy is the term of Martinmas.

---

[1] As amended by the Requirements of Writing (Scotland) Act 1995 (c.7) Sch.5 (effective August 1, 1995: s.15(2)).
[2] As substituted by the Sheriff Courts (Scotland) Act 1971 (c.58), s.4.

Exception for certain tenancies

37A.[1, 2]   The provisions of this Act relating to removings (including summary   **D1.25**
removings) shall not apply to or in relation to short limited duration tenancies,
limited duration tenancies, modern limited duration tenancies or repairing tenancies
within the meaning of the Agricultural Holdings (Scotland) Act 2003 (asp 11).

Summary Removings

Summary removing

38.[3, 4]   Where houses or other heritable subjects are let for a shorter period than a   **D1.26**
year, any person by law authorised may present to the sheriff principal a summary
application for removing, and a decree pronounced in such summary cause shall
have the full force and effect of a decree of removing and warrant of ejection. Where
such a let is for a period not exceeding four months, notice of removal therefrom
shall, in the absence of express stipulation, be given as many days before the ish as
shall be equivalent to at least one-third of the full period of the duration of the let;
and where the let exceeds four months, notice of removal shall, in the absence of
express stipulation, be given at least forty days before the expiry of the said period.
Provided that in no case shall notice of removal be given less than twenty-eight days
before the date on which it is to take effect.

Notice of termination in respect of dwelling-houses

38A.[5]   Any notice of termination of tenancy or notice of removal given under   **D1.27**
sections 37 and 38 above in respect of a dwelling-house, on or after the date of the
coming into operation of section 123 of the Housing Act 1974, shall be in writing
and shall contain such information as may be prescribed by virtue of section 131 of
the Rent (Scotland) Act 1971, and Rule 112 of Schedule 1 to this Act shall no longer
apply to any such notice under section 37 above.

Lord Advocate as party to action for divorce

38B.   *[Repealed by the Family Law (Scotland) Act 2006 (asp.2), Sch.3 (effective*   **D1.27.1**
May 4, 2006).]

38C.   *[Repealed by the Children (Scotland) Act 1995 (c.36), Sch.5 (effective*   **D1.27.2**
November 1, 1996).]

---

[1] As inserted by the Agricultural Holdings (Scotland) Act 2003 (asp 11), Sch., para.1 and brought into
force by the Agricultural Holdings (Scotland) Act 2003 (Commencement No.3, Transitional and Savings Provisions) Order 2003 (SSI 2003/548), reg.2(i) (effective November 23, 2003).
[2] As amended by the Land Reform (Scotland) Act 2016 (asp 18) Sch.2(1) para.1(2) (effective 30
November 2017: amendment has effect subject to transitional provision specified in SSI 2017/299
reg.6 as amended by SSI 2017/370 reg.4).
[3] Proviso added by the Rent (Scotland) Act 1971 (c.28), Sch.18.
[4] As substituted by the Sheriff Courts (Scotland) Act 1971 (c.58) s.4. In terms of s.3(a) of the 1907 Act,
the meaning of the term "sheriff principal" includes "sheriff".
[5] As inserted by the Housing Act 1974 (c.44), Sch.13, para.1. For rule 112 read rule 105 of the rules
substituted by SI 1983/747, and rule 34.7 of the rules substituted by SI 1993/1956.

Procedure Rules

Procedure rules

D1.27.3   **39.**   Subject to the provisions of any Act of Parliament in force after the passing of this Act, the procedure in all civil causes shall be conform to the rules of procedure set forth in the First Schedule hereto annexed. Such rules shall be construed and have effect as part of this Act.

Court of Session to regulate fees, etc.

D1.27.4   **40.**   *[Repealed by the Courts Reform (Scotland) Act 2014 (asp 18) Sch.5 para.4 (effective April 1, 2015).]*

Postal Charge

D1.27.5   **41.**   *[Repealed by the Administration of Justice (Scotland) Act 1933 (c.41), Sch.]*

Small Debts Acts

D1.27.6   **42–48.**   *[Repealed by the Sheriff Courts (Scotland) Act 1971 (c.58), Sch.2]*

D1.27.7   **49.**   *[Repealed by the Execution of Diligence (Scotland) Act 1926 (c.16), s.7.]*

Summary Applications

Summary applications

D1.27.8   **50.**[1]   In summary applications (where a hearing is necessary) the sheriff principal shall appoint the application to be heard at a diet to be fixed by him, and at that or any subsequent diet (without record of evidence unless the sheriff principal shall order a record) shall summarily dispose of the matter and give his judgment in writing: Provided that wherever in any Act of Parliament an application is directed to be heard, tried, and determined summarily or in the manner provided by section 52 of the Sheriff Courts (Scotland) Act 1876, such direction shall be read and construed as if it referred to this section of this Act: Provided also that nothing contained in this Act shall affect any right of appeal provided by any Act of Parliament under which a summary application is brought.

The Poor's Roll

D1.27.9   **51.**   *[Repealed by the Statute Law (Repeals) Act 1973 (c.39).]*

Repeal

D1.27.10   **52.**   *[Repealed by the Statute Law Revision Act 1927 (c.42).]*

[THE NEXT PARAGRAPH IS D1.28]

---

[1] As substituted by the Sheriff Courts (Scotland) Act 1971 (c.58) s.4. In terms of s.3(a) of the 1907 Act, the meaning of the term "sheriff principal" includes "sheriff".

FIRST SCHEDULE[1]

ORDINARY CAUSE RULES 1993[2]

Arrangement of Ordinary Cause Rules 1993

---

[1] As substituted by SI 1983/747, affecting any action or proceedings commenced on or after 1 September 1983. New First Schedule substituted in respect of causes commenced on or after 1 January 1994 by SI 1993/1956: see pp.D 44/29 et seq. Please note that we have now removed the pre-1993 Ordinary Cause Rules from this volume.

[2] The Ordinary Cause Rules were amended inter alia by SI 1996/2445, effective 1 November 1996. The amendments made thereby apply equally to causes commenced before that date: see SI 1996/2586.

Initiation and Progress of Causes

Chapter 1

Citation, Interpretation, Representation and Forms

Citation

D1.29   **1.1.**   These Rules may be cited as the Ordinary Cause Rules 1993.

Interpretation

D1.30   **1.2.**—[1](1)[2, 3]   In these Rules, unless the context otherwise requires—

"attend", "attendance" and "attend personally" are construed in accordance with Chapter 4A (mode of attendance at hearings);

"document" has the meaning assigned to it in section 9 of the Civil Evidence (Scotland) Act 1988;

"enactment" includes an enactment comprised in, or in an instrument made under, an Act of the Scottish Parliament;[4]

"Full Case Management Hearing" means a hearing under rules 33.36P or 33A.36P (Full Case Management Hearing), as the case may be;

"Initial Case Management Hearing" means a hearing under rules 33.36J or 33A.36J (Initial Case Management Hearing), as the case may be;

"period of notice" means the period determined under rule 3.6 (period of notice after citation).

"the Act of 2004" means the Vulnerable Witnesses (Scotland) Act 2004.[5]

"the 2014 Act" means the Courts Reform (Scotland) Act 2014;

"the all-Scotland sheriff court" means the sheriff court specified in the All-Scotland Sheriff Court (Sheriff Personal Injury Court) Order 2015(c) so far as the court is constituted by a sheriff sitting in the exercise of the sheriff's all-Scotland jurisdiction for the purpose of dealing with civil proceedings of a type specified in that Order.

(2)   For the purposes of these Rules—

(a)   "affidavit" includes an affirmation and a statutory or other declaration; and

---

[1] As amended by the Act of Sederunt (Rules of the Court of Session 1994 and Sheriff Court Rules Amendment) (No. 2) (Personal Injury and Remits) 2015 r.8 (effective 22 September 2015).

[2] As amended by the Act of Sederunt (Ordinary Cause Rules 1993 Amendment) (Case Management of Defended Family and Civil Partnership Actions) 2022 (SSI 2022/289) r.2(2) (effective 25 September 2023 subject to transitional provision specified in SSI 2022/289 r.3).

[3] As amended by Act of Sederunt (Rules of the Court of Session 1994 and Ordinary Cause Rules 1993 Amendment) (Attendance at Hearings) 2023 (SSI 2023/168) para.3 (effective 3 July 2023).

[4] As inserted by the Act of Sederunt (Ordinary Cause, Summary Application, Summary Cause and Small Claim Rules) Amendment (Miscellaneous) 2007 (SSI 2007/6) para.2(2) (effective 29 January 2007).

[5] As inserted by the Act of Sederunt (Ordinary Cause, Summary Application, Summary Cause and Small Claim Rules) Amendment (Vulnerable Witnesses (Scotland) Act 2004) 2007 (SSI 2007/463) r.2(2) (effective 1 November 2007).

(b) an affidavit shall be sworn or affirmed before a notary public or any other competent authority.

(3) Where a provision in these Rules requires a party to intimate or send a document to another party, it shall be sufficient compliance with that provision if the document is intimated or sent to the solicitor acting in the cause for that party.

(4) Unless the context otherwise requires, anything done or required to be done under a provision in these Rules by a party may be done by the agent for that party acting on his behalf.

(5) Unless the context otherwise requires, a reference to a specified Chapter, Part, rule or form, is a reference to the Chapter, Part, rule, or form in Appendix 1, so specified in these Rules; and a reference to a specified paragraph, sub-paragraph or head is a reference to that paragraph of the rule or form, that sub-paragraph of the paragraph or that head of the sub-paragraph, in which the reference occurs.

(6)[1] In these Rules, references to a solicitor include a reference to a member of a body which has made a successful application under section 25 of the Law Reform (Miscellaneous Provisions) (Scotland) Act 1990 but only to the extent that the member is exercising rights acquired by virtue of section 27 of that Act.

(7) In these Rules—
  (a) references to a sheriff's all-Scotland jurisdiction are to be construed in accordance with section 42(3) of the 2014 Act;
  (b) references to a sheriff's local jurisdiction are to be construed in accordance with section 42(4) of the 2014 Act.

(8)[2] In these Rules, a reference to any document being authenticated, certified, signed, signed and dated, or endorsed by the sheriff, sheriff clerk, the court or the clerk of court includes a reference to that document being authenticated electronically by that person or court, as the case may be.

Representation

1.3.—(1) Subject to paragraph (2), a party to any proceedings arising solely under the provisions of the Debtors (Scotland) Act 1987 shall be entitled to be represented by a person other than a solicitor or an advocate provided that the sheriff is satisfied that such person is a suitable representative and is duly authorised to represent that party.

D1.31

(2) *[Repealed by the Act of Sederunt (Rules of the Court of Session, Sheriff Appeal Court Rules and Sheriff Court Rules Amendment) (Sheriff Appeal Court) 2015 (SSI 2015/419) r.5 (effective 1 January 2016).]*

(3)[3] A party may be represented by any person authorised under any enactment to conduct proceedings in the sheriff court in accordance with the terms of that enactment.

(4)[4] The person referred to in paragraph (3) may do everything for the preparation and conduct of an action as may have been done by an individual conducting his own action.

---

[1] As inserted by the Act of Sederunt (Sheriff Court Rules Amendment) (Sections 25 to 29 of the Law Reform (Miscellaneous Provisions) (Scotland) Act 1990) 2009 (SSI 2009/164) r.2 (effective May 20, 2009).

[2] As inserted by the Act of Sederunt (Sheriff Court Rules Amendment) (Electronic Authentication) 2016 (SSI 2016/415) r.2(2) (effective 15 December 2016).

[3] As inserted by the Act of Sederunt (Ordinary Cause, Summary Application, Summary Cause and Small Claim Rules) Amendment (Miscellaneous) 2007 (SSI 2007/6), para.2(3) (effective January 29, 2007).

[4] As inserted by the Act of Sederunt (Ordinary Cause, Summary Application, Summary Cause and Small Claim Rules) Amendment (Miscellaneous) 2007 (SSI 2007/6), para.2(3) (effective January 29, 2007).

Lay support

1.3A.—[1](1) At any time during proceedings the sheriff may, on the request of a party litigant, permit a named individual to assist the litigant in the conduct of the proceedings by sitting beside or behind (as the litigant chooses) the litigant at hearings in court or in chambers and doing such of the following for the litigant as he or she requires—

    (a)   providing moral support;

    (b)   helping to manage the court documents and other papers;

    (c)   taking notes of the proceedings;

    (d)   quietly advising on—

        (i)   points of law and procedure;

        (ii)   issues which the litigant might wish to raise with the sheriff;

        (iii)   questions which the litigant might wish to ask witnesses.

(2) It is a condition of such permission that the named individual does not receive from the litigant, whether directly or indirectly, any remuneration for his or her assistance.

(3) The sheriff may refuse a request under paragraph (1) only if—

    (a)   the sheriff is of the opinion that the named individual is an unsuitable person to act in that capacity (whether generally or in the proceedings concerned); or

    (b)   the sheriff is of the opinion that it would be contrary to the efficient administration of justice to grant it.

(4) Permission granted under paragraph (1) endures until the proceedings finish or it is withdrawn under paragraph (5); but it is not effective during any period when the litigant is represented.

(5) The sheriff may, of his or her own accord or on the motion of a party to the proceedings, withdraw permission granted under paragraph (1); but the sheriff must first be of the opinion that it would be contrary to the efficient administration of justice for the permission to continue.

(6) Where permission has been granted under paragraph (1), the litigant may—

    (a)   show the named individual any document (including a court document); or

    (b)   impart to the named individual any information,

which is in his or her possession in connection with the proceedings without being taken to contravene any prohibition or restriction on the disclosure of the document or the information; but the named individual is then to be taken to be subject to any such prohibition or restriction as if he or she were the litigant.

(7) Any expenses incurred by the litigant as a result of the support of an individual under paragraph (1) are not recoverable expenses in the proceedings.

---

[1] As inserted by the Act of Sederunt (Sheriff Court Rules) (Miscellaneous Amendments) (No.2) 2010 (SSI 2010/416) r.2 (effective January 1, 2011).

Forms

1.4. Where there is a reference to the use of a form in these Rules, that form in Appendix 1 or Appendix 2, as the case may be, to these Rules, or a form substantially to the same effect, shall be used with such variation as circumstances may require.

D1.33

Chapter 1A[1]

Lay Representation

Application and interpretation

1A.1.—(1) This Chapter is without prejudice to any enactment (including any other provision in these Rules) under which provision is, or may be, made for a party to a particular type of case before the sheriff to be represented by a lay representative.

D1.34

(2) In this Chapter, a "lay representative" means a person who is not—

   (a)   a solicitor;

   (b)   an advocate, or

   (c)   someone having a right to conduct litigation, or a right of audience, by virtue of section 27 of the Law Reform (Miscellaneous Provisions) (Scotland) Act 1990.

Lay representation for party litigants

1A.2.—[2](1) In any proceedings in respect of which no provision as mentioned in rule 1A.1(1) is in force, the sheriff may, on the request of a party litigant, permit a named individual (a "lay representative") to appear, along with the litigant, at a specified hearing for the purpose of representing the litigant at that hearing.

D1.35

(2)   An application under paragraph (1)—

   (a)   is to be made orally on the date of the first hearing at which the litigant wishes a named individual to represent the litigant; and

   (b)   is to be accompanied by a document, signed by the named individual, in Form 1A.2.

(3)   The sheriff may grant an application under paragraph (1) only if the sheriff is of the opinion that it would be in the interests of justice to grant it.

(4)   It is a condition of permission granted by the sheriff that the lay representative does not receive directly or indirectly from the litigant any remuneration or other reward for his or her assistance.

(5)   The sheriff may grant permission under paragraph (1) in respect of one or more specified hearings in the case; but such permission is not effective during any period when the litigant is legally represented.

(6)   The sheriff may, of his or her own accord or on the motion of a party to the proceedings, withdraw permission granted under paragraph (1).

(6A)[3] Where permission is granted under paragraph (1), the lay representative may do anything in the preparation or conduct of the hearing that the litigant may do.

(7)   Where permission has been granted under paragraph (1), the litigant may—

---

[1] As inserted by the Act of Sederunt (Sheriff Court Rules) (Lay Representation) 2013 (SSI 2013/91) r.2 (effective April 4, 2013).

[2] As amended by the Act of Sederunt (Rules of the Court of Session, Sheriff Appeal Court Rules and Sheriff Court Rules Amendment) (Lay Representation) 2017 (SSI 2017/186) r.4(2) (effective 3 July 2017).

[3] As inserted by the Act of Sederunt (Rules of the Court of Session, Sheriff Appeal Court Rules and Sheriff Court Rules Amendment) (Lay Representation) 2017 (SSI 2017/186) r.4(2)(d) (effective 3 July 2017).

(a) show the lay representative any document (including a court document); or

(b) impart to the lay representative any information,

which is in his or her possession in connection with the proceedings without being taken to contravene any prohibition or restriction on the disclosure of the document or the information; but the lay representative is then to be taken to be subject to any such prohibition or restriction as if he or she were the litigant.

(8) Any expenses incurred by the litigant in connection with lay representation under this rule are not recoverable expenses in the proceedings.

Chapter 2

Relief from Compliance with Rules

Relief from failure to comply with rules

D1.36

2.1.—(1) The sheriff may relieve a party from the consequences of failure to comply with a provision in these Rules which is shown to be due to mistake, oversight or other excusable cause, on such conditions as he thinks fit.

(2) Where the sheriff relieves a party from the consequences of a failure to comply with a provision in these Rules under paragraph (1), he may make such order as he thinks fit to enable the cause to proceed as if the failure to comply with the provision had not occurred.

Chapter 3

Commencement of Causes

Form of initial writ

D1.37

3.1.—[1](1)[2] A cause shall be commenced—

(a) in the case of an ordinary cause, by initial writ in Form G1; or

(b) in the case of a commercial action within the meaning of Chapter 40, by initial writ in Form G1A.

or

(c)[3] in the case of a personal injuries action within the meaning of Part AI of Chapter 36, by initial writ in Form PI1.

(d) in the case of a personal injuries action appointed to proceed in accordance with Chapter 36A under rule 36.C1, by initial writ in Form G1 which includes an interlocutor in Form PI4.

(2) The initial writ shall be written, typed or printed on A4 size paper of durable quality and shall not be backed.

(3) Where the pursuer has reason to believe that an agreement exists prorogating jurisdiction over the subject matter of the cause to another court, the initial writ shall contain details of that agreement.

(4) Where the pursuer has reason to believe that proceedings are pending before another court involving the same cause of action and between the same parties as those named in the instance of the initial writ, the initial writ shall contain details of those proceedings.

(5) An article of condescendence shall be included in the initial writ averring—

(a) the ground of jurisdiction; and

---

[1] As amended by the Act of Sederunt (Rules of the Court of Session 1994 and Sheriff Court Rules Amendment) (No. 2) (Personal Injury and Remits) 2015 r.8 (effective September 22, 2015).

[2] As inserted by the Act of Sederunt (Ordinary Cause Rules) Amendment (Commercial Actions) 2001 (SSI 2001/8) (effective March 1, 2001).

[3] As inserted by the Act of Sederunt (Ordinary Cause Rules Amendment) (Personal Injuries Actions) 2009 (SSI 2009/285) r.2 (effective November 2, 2009).

   (b)   the facts upon which the ground of jurisdiction is based.

(5A) Where a personal injuries action within the meaning of Part A1 of Chapter 36 is raised in Edinburgh Sheriff Court the initial writ must include an averment indicating whether the proceedings are for determination in the exercise of the sheriff's all-Scotland jurisdiction or the sheriff's local jurisdiction.

(5B) Where an averment is included indicating that the proceedings are for determination in the exercise of the sheriff's all-Scotland jurisdiction, the heading of the initial writ must state that the action is being raised in the all-Scotland sheriff court.

(6) Where the residence, registered office or place of business, as the case may be, of the defender is not known and cannot reasonably be ascertained, the pursuer shall set out in the instance that the whereabouts of the defender are not known and aver in the condescendence what steps have been taken to ascertain his present whereabouts.

(7) The initial writ shall be signed by the pursuer or his solicitor (if any) and the name and address of that solicitor shall be stated on the back of every service copy of that writ.

Actions relating to heritable property

3.2.—(1) In an action relating to heritable property, it shall not be necessary to call as a defender any person by reason only of any interest he may have as the holder of a heritable security over the heritable property.   **D1.38**

(2) Intimation of such an action shall be made to the holder of the heritable security referred to in paragraph (1)—

   (a)   where the action relates to any heritable right or title; and

   (b)   in any other case, where the sheriff so orders.

(3) *[Repealed by the Act of Sederunt (Sheriff Court Rules) (Enforcement of Securities over Heritable Property) 2010 (SSI 2010/324) para.2 (effective September 30, 2010).]*

Actions relating to regulated agreements

3.2A.[1] In an action which relates to a regulated agreement within the meaning given by section 189(1) of the Consumer Credit Act 1974 the initial writ shall include an averment that such an agreement exists and details of that agreement.   **D1.39**

Warrants of citation

3.3.—[2, 3](1) The warrant of citation in any cause other than—   **D1.40**

   (a)   a family action within the meaning of rule 33.1(1),

   (b)   an action of multiplepoinding,

   (c)   an action in which a time to pay direction under the Debtors (Scotland) Act 1987 or a time order under the Consumer Credit Act 1974 may be applied for by the defender,

---

[1] As inserted by the Act of Sederunt (Sheriff Court Rules) (Miscellaneous Amendments) 2009 (SSI 2009/294) r.2 (effective December 1, 2009) as substituted by the Act of Sederunt (Amendment of the Act of Sederunt (Sheriff Court Rules) (Miscellaneous Amendments) 2009) 2009 (SSI 2009/402) (effective November 30, 2009).

[2] Inserted by the Act of Sederunt (Amendment of Ordinary Cause Rules and Summary Applications, Statutory Applications and Appeals etc. Rules) (Applications under the Mortgage Rights (Scotland) Act 2001) 2002 (SSI 2002/7), para.2(3).

[3] As amended by the Act of Sederunt (Ordinary Cause, Summary Application, Summary Cause and Small Claim Rules) Amendment (Miscellaneous) 2007 (SSI 2007/6), para.2(4) (effective January 29, 2007).

(d) *[Repealed by the Act of Sederunt (Sheriff Court Rules) (Enforcement of Securities over Heritable Property) 2010 (SSI 2010/324) para.2 (effective September 30, 2010).]*

(e)[1] a civil partnership action within the meaning of rule 33A.1(1) shall be in Form O1.

(2) In a cause in which a time to pay direction under the Debtors (Scotland) Act 1987 or a time order under the Consumer Credit Act 1974 may be applied for by the defender, the warrant of citation shall be in Form O2.

(3) In a cause in which a warrant for citation in accordance with Form O2 is appropriate, there shall be served on the defender (with the initial writ and warrant) a notice in Form O3.

(4) *[Repealed by the Act of Sederunt (Sheriff Court Rules) (Enforcement of Securities over Heritable Property) 2010 (SSI 2010/324) para.2 (effective September 30, 2010).]*

Warrants for arrestment to found jurisdiction

D1.41 **3.4.**—(1) Where an application for a warrant for arrestment to found jurisdiction may be made, it shall be made in the crave of the initial writ.

(2) Averments to justify the granting of such a warrant shall be included in the condescendence.

Warrants and precepts for arrestment on dependence

3.5. *[Repealed by the Act of Sederunt (Sheriff Court Rules Amendment) (Diligence) 2008 (SSI 2008/121) r.5(2) (effective April 1, 2008).]*

Period of notice after citation

D1.42 **3.6.**—(1) Subject to rule 5.6(1) (service where address of person is not known) and to paragraph (2) of this rule, a cause shall proceed after one of the following periods of notice has been given to the defender:—

(a) where the defender is resident or has a place of business within Europe, 21 days after the date of execution of service; or

(b) where the defender is resident or has a place of business outside Europe, 42 days after the date of execution of service.

(2) Subject to paragraph (3), the sheriff may, on cause shown, shorten or extend the period of notice on such conditions as to the method or manner of service as he thinks fit.

(3) A period of notice may not be reduced to a period of less than 2 days.

(4) Where a period of notice expires on a Saturday, Sunday, or public or court holiday, the period of notice shall be deemed to expire on the next day on which the sheriff clerk's office is open for civil court business.

Chapter 3A[2]

Personal Injury Pre-action Protocol

Application and interpretation

D1.42.1 **3A.1.**—(1) This Chapter applies to an action of damages for, or arising from, personal injuries.

---

[1] As amended by Act of Sederunt (Ordinary Cause Rules) Amendment (Family Law (Scotland) Act 2006 etc.) 2006 (SSI 2006/207), para.2 (effective May 4, 2006).

[2] As inserted by the Act of Sederunt (Sheriff Court Rules Amendment) (Personal Injury Pre-Action Protocol) 2016 (SSI 2016/215) para.2 (effective 28 November 2016).

(2) In this Chapter "the Protocol" means the Personal Injury Pre-Action Protocol set out in Appendix 4, and references to the "aims of the Protocol", "requirements of the Protocol" and "stages of the Protocol" are to be construed accordingly.

Requirement to comply with the Protocol

3A.2. In any case where the Protocol applies, the court will normally expect parties to have complied with the requirements of the Protocol before proceedings are commenced.

D1.42.2

Consequences of failing to comply with the Protocol

3A.3.—(1) This rule applies where the sheriff considers that a party ("party A")—

D1.42.3

- (a) failed, without just cause, to comply with the requirements of the Protocol; or
- (b) unreasonably failed to accept an offer in settlement which was—
    - (i) made in accordance with the Protocol; and
    - (ii) lodged as a tender during the period beginning with the commencement of proceedings and ending with the lodging of defences.

(2) The sheriff may, on the sheriff's own motion, or on the motion of any party, take any steps the sheriff considers necessary to do justice between the parties, and may in particular—

- (a) sist the action to allow any party to comply with the requirements of the Protocol;
- (b) make an award of expenses against party A;
- (c) modify an award of expenses; or
- (d) make an award regarding the interest payable on any award of damages.

(3) A motion made by a party under paragraph (2) must include a summary of—

- (a) the steps taken by parties under the Protocol with a view to settling the action; and
- (b) that party's assessment of the extent to which parties have complied with the requirements of the Protocol.

(4) In considering what steps (if any) to take under paragraph (2), the sheriff must take into account—

- (a) the nature of any breach of the requirements of the Protocol; and
- (b) the conduct of the parties during the stages of the Protocol.

(5) In assessing the conduct of the parties, the sheriff must have regard to the extent to which that conduct is consistent with the aims of the Protocol.

(6) This rule does not affect any other enactment or rule of law allowing the sheriff to make or modify awards regarding expenses and interest.".

Chapter 4

Caveats

D1.42.4   *[Omitted by Act of Sederunt (Sheriff Court Caveat Rules) 2006 (SI 2006/198), effective April 28, 2006]*

Chapter 4A[1]

Mode of Attendance at Hearings

Application

4A.1. This Chapter is without prejudice to any enactment under which provision has been made regarding the mode of attendance of persons at hearings.

Mode of attendance at hearings – procedural business

D1.42.5   **4A.2.**—(1) Hearings at which only procedural business is to be considered are to be attended by electronic means.

(2) Paragraph (1) does not apply to hearings at which a party is unrepresented or utilising an interpreter.

Alternative mode of attendance at hearings

D1.42.6   **4A.3.**—(1) The sheriff may, at the sheriff's own instance or on the motion of a party on cause shown—

(a)   in relation to hearings to which rule 4A.2(1) applies, order physical attendance at a hearing;

(b)   in relation to any other hearings, order attendance at a hearing by electronic means.

(2) The sheriff may revoke an order granted under paragraph (1) or this paragraph and, where the sheriff does so, the sheriff may make such further order as the sheriff thinks fit.

(3) Before the sheriff makes an order under paragraph (1) or (2), the sheriff is to give parties the opportunity to make representations about the mode of attendance.

Hybrid hearings

D1.42.7   **4A.4.** An order under rule 4A.3(1) or (2) may include provision for a person to attend a hearing—

(a)   both physically and by electronic means;

(b)   by one mode and another person to attend by the other mode,

and at different times or dates.

[THE NEXT PARAGRAPH IS D1.43]

Chapter 5

Citation, Service and Intimation

Signature of warrants

D1.43   **5.1.**—(1)[2] Subject to paragraph (2), a warrant for citation or intimation may be signed by the sheriff or sheriff clerk.

---

[1] Inserted by Act of Sederunt (Rules of the Court of Session 1994 and Ordinary Cause Rules 1993 Amendment) (Attendance at Hearings) 2023 (SSI 2023/168) para.3 (effective 3 July 2023).

[2] As inserted by the Act of Sederunt (Ordinary Cause, Summary Application and Small Claim Rules) Amendment (Miscellaneous) 2004 (SSI 2004/197) para.2(3) (effective 21 May 2004).

(2) The following warrants shall be signed by the sheriff:—

  (a) a warrant containing an order shortening or extending the period of notice or any other order other than a warrant which the sheriff clerk may sign;

  (b)[1,2] a warrant for arrestment to found jurisdiction (including the arrestment of a ship);

  (ba)[3,4] a warrant for arrestment on the dependence;

  (c) a warrant for intimation ordered under rule 33.8 (intimation where alleged association).

  (d)[5] a warrant for intimation ordered under rule 33A.8 (intimation where alleged association).

  (e)[6] a warrant for arrestment of a ship to found jurisdiction;

  (f)[7] a warrant for arrestment of a ship or cargo in rem;

  (g)[8] a warrant for arrestment of cargo.

(3) Where the sheriff clerk refuses to sign a warrant which he may sign, the party presenting the initial writ may apply to the sheriff for the warrant.

Form of citation and certificate

5.2.—[9,10](1) Subject to rule 5.6 (service where address of person is not known), in any cause other than—   **D1.44**

  (a) a family action within the meaning of rule 33.1(1),

  (aa)[11] a civil partnership action within the meaning of rule 33A.1(1);

  (b) an action of multiplepoinding,

  (c) an action in which a time to pay direction under the Debtors (Scotland) Act 1987 or a time order under the Consumer Credit Act 1974 may be applied for by the defender, or

  (d) *[Repealed by the Act of Sederunt (Sheriff Court Rules) (Enforcement of Securities over Heritable Property) 2010 (SSI 2010/324) para.2 (effective September 30, 2010).]*

---

[1] As inserted by the Act of Sederunt (Ordinary Cause, Summary Application and Small Claim Rules) Amendment (Miscellaneous) 2004 (SSI 2004/197) para.2(3) (effective 21 May 2004).

[2] As amended by the Act of Sederunt (Sheriff Court Rules) (Miscellaneous Amendments) 2012 (SSI 2012/188) para.10 (effective 1 August 2012).

[3] As inserted by the Act of Sederunt (Ordinary Cause, Summary Application and Small Claim Rules) Amendment (Miscellaneous) 2004 (SSI 2004/197) para.2(3) (effective 21 May 2004).

[4] As amended by Act of Sederunt (Ordinary Cause Rules) Amendment (Family Law (Scotland) Act 2006 etc.) 2006 (SSI 2006/207) para.2 (effective 4 May 2006).

[5] As inserted by Act of Sederunt (Ordinary Cause Rules) Amendment (Family Law (Scotland) Act 2006 etc.) 2006 (SSI 2006/207) para.2 (effective 4 May 2006).

[6] As inserted by the Act of Sederunt (Sheriff Court Rules) (Miscellaneous Amendments) 2012 (SSI 2012/188) para.10 (effective 1 August 2012).

[7] As inserted by the Act of Sederunt (Sheriff Court Rules) (Miscellaneous Amendments) 2012 (SSI 2012/188) para.10 (effective 1 August 2012).

[8] As inserted by the Act of Sederunt (Sheriff Court Rules) (Miscellaneous Amendments) 2012 (SSI 2012/188) para.10 (effective 1 August 2012).

[9] As amended by SI 1996/2445 (effective 1 November 1996) (clerical error) and further amended by the Act of Sederunt (Amendment of Ordinary Cause Rules and Summary Applications, Statutory Applications and Appeals etc. Rules) (Applications under the Mortgage Rights (Scotland) Act 2001) 2002 (SSI 2002/7) para.2(4).

[10] As amended by the Act of Sederunt (Ordinary Cause, Summary Application, Summary Cause and Small Claim Rules) Amendment (Miscellaneous) 2007 (SSI 2007/6) para.2(5) (effective 29 January 2007).

[11] As inserted by Act of Sederunt (Ordinary Cause Rules) Amendment (Family Law (Scotland) Act 2006 etc.) 2006 (SSI 2006/207) para.2 (effective 4 May 2006).

citation by any person shall be in Form O4 which shall be attached to a copy of the initial writ and warrant of citation and shall have appended to it a notice of intention to defend in Form O7.

(2) In a cause in which a time to pay direction under the Debtors (Scotland) Act 1987 or a time order under the Consumer Credit Act 1974 may be applied for by the defender, citation shall be in Form O5 which shall be attached to a copy of the initial writ and warrant of citation and shall have appended to it a notice of intention to defend in Form O7.

(2A) *[Repealed by the Act of Sederunt (Sheriff Court Rules) (Enforcement of Securities over Heritable Property) 2010 (SSI 2010/324) para.2 (effective September 30, 2010).]*

(3) The certificate of citation in any cause other than a family action within the meaning of rule 33.1(1) or an action of multiplepoinding shall be in Form O6 which shall be attached to the initial writ.

(4) Where citation is by a sheriff officer, one witness shall be sufficient for the execution of citation.

(5) Where citation is by a sheriff officer, the certificate of citation shall be signed by the sheriff officer and the witness and shall state—

    (a) the method of citation; and

    (b) where the method of citation was other than personal or postal citation, the full name and designation of any person to whom the citation was delivered.

(6) Where citation is executed under paragraph (3) of rule 5.4 (depositing or affixing by sheriff officer), the certificate shall include a statement—

    (a) of the method of service previously attempted;

    (b) of the circumstances which prevented such service being executed; and

    (c) that a copy was sent in accordance with the provisions of paragraph (4) of that rule.

Postal service or intimation

D1.45
    5.3.—(1) In any cause in which service or intimation of any document or citation of any person may be by recorded delivery, such service, intimation or citation shall be by the first class recorded delivery service.

(2) Notwithstanding the terms of section 4(2) of the Citation Amendment (Scotland) Act 1882 (time from which period of notice reckoned), where service or intimation is by post, the period of notice shall run from the beginning of the day after the date of posting.

(3) On the face of the envelope used for postal service or intimation under this rule there shall be written or printed the following notice:—

    "This envelope contains a citation to or intimation from (*specify the court*). If delivery cannot be made at the address shown it is to be returned immediately to:— The Sheriff Clerk (*insert address of sheriff clerk's office*)".

(4) The certificate of citation or intimation in the case of postal service shall have attached to it any relevant postal receipts.

Service within Scotland by sheriff officer

D1.46
    5.4.—(1) An initial writ, decree, charge, warrant or any other order or writ following upon such initial writ or decree served by a sheriff officer on any person shall be served—

    (a) personally; or

    (b) by being left in the hands of a resident at the person's dwelling place or an employee at his place of business.

(2) Where service is executed under paragraph (1)(b), the certificate of citation or service shall contain the full name and designation of any person in whose hands the initial writ, decree, charge, warrant or other order or writ, as the case may be, was left.

(3) Where a sheriff officer has been unsuccessful in executing service in accordance with paragraph (1), he may, after making diligent enquiries, serve the document in question—

    (a) by depositing it in that person's dwelling place or place of business; or

    (b)[1] by leaving it at that person's dwelling place or place of business in such a way that it is likely to come to the attention of that person.

(4) Subject to rule 6.1 (service of schedule of arrestment), where service is executed under paragraph (3), the sheriff officer shall, as soon as possible after such service, send a letter containing a copy of the document by ordinary first class post to the address at which he thinks it most likely that the person on whom service has been executed may be found.

(5)[2] Where the firm which employs the sheriff officer has in its possession—

    (a) the document or a copy of it certified as correct by the pursuer's solicitor, the sheriff officer may serve the document upon the defender without having the document or certified copy in his possession, in which case he shall if required to do so by the person on whom service is executed and within a reasonable time of being so required, show the document or certified copy to the person; or

    (b) a certified copy of the interlocutor pronounced allowing service of the document, the sheriff officer may serve the document without having in his possession the certified copy interlocutor if he has in his possession a facsimile copy of the certified copy interlocutor (which he shall show, if required, to the person on whom service is executed).

(6)[3] Where service is executed under paragraphs (1)(b) or (3), the document and the citation or notice of intimation, as the case may be, must be placed in an envelope bearing the notice "This envelope contains a citation to or intimation from (*insert name of sheriff court*)"and sealed by the sheriff officer.

Service on persons furth of Scotland

5.5.—[4](1) Subject to the following provisions of this rule, an initial writ, decree, charge, warrant or any other order or writ following upon such initial writ or decree on a person furth of Scotland shall be served—

    (a) at a known residence or place of business in England, Wales, Northern Ireland, the Isle of Man, the Channel Islands or any country with which the United Kingdom does not have a convention providing for service of writs in that country—

        (i) in accordance with the rules for personal service under the domestic law of the place in which service is to be executed; or

D1.47

---

[1] As substituted by the Act of Sederunt (Sheriff Court Rules) (Miscellaneous Amendments) 2011 (SSI 2011/193) r.2 (effective April 4, 2011).

[2] As inserted by the Act of Sederunt (Ordinary Cause, Summary Application, Summary Cause and Small Claim Rules) Amendment (Miscellaneous) 2003 (SSI 2003/26), para.2(3) (effective January 24, 2003).

[3] As inserted by the Act of Sederunt (Sheriff Court Rules) (Miscellaneous Amendments) 2011 (SSI 2011/193) r.2 (effective April 4, 2011).

[4] As amended by SI 1996/2445 (effective November 1, 1996) and the Act of Sederunt (Ordinary Cause, Summary Application, Summary Cause and Small Claim Rules) Amendment (Miscellaneous) 2003 (SSI 2003/26), para.2(4) (effective January 24, 2003).

(ii) by posting in Scotland a copy of the document in question in a registered letter addressed to the person at his residence or place of business;

(b)[1] in a country which is a party to the Hague Convention on the Service Abroad of Judicial and Extra-Judicial Documents in Civil and Commercial Matters dated 15th November 1965 or the Convention in Schedule 1 or 3C to the Civil Jurisdiction and Judgments Act 1982—

    (i) by a method prescribed by the internal law of the country where service is to be executed for the service of documents in domestic actions upon persons who are within its territory;

    (ii)[2] by or through the central, or other appropriate, authority in the country where service is to be executed at the request of the Scottish Ministers;

    (iii)[3] by or through a British Consular Office in the country where service is to be executed at the request of the Secretary of State for Foreign, Commonwealth and Development Affairs;

    (iv) where the law of the country in which the person resides permits, by posting in Scotland a copy of the document in a registered letter addressed to the person at his residence; or

    (v) where the law of the country in which service is to be executed permits, service by an huissier, other judicial officer or competent official of the country where service is to be executed; or

(c) in a country with which the United Kingdom has a convention on the service of writs in that country other than the conventions mentioned in sub-paragraph (b), by one of the methods approved in the relevant convention.

(d) *[Repealed by the Act of Sederunt (Ordinary Cause, Summary Application, Summary Cause and Small Claim Rules) Amendment (Miscellaneous) 2004 (SSI 2004/197) r.24(a) (effective 21 May 2004).]*

(1A)[4, 5] In a country to which the EC Service Regulation applies, service—

(a) may be effected by the methods prescribed in paragraph (1)(b)(ii) and (iii) only in exceptional circumstances; and

(b) is effected only if the receiving agency has informed the person that acceptance of service may be refused on the ground that the document has not been translated in accordance with paragraph (6).

(2) Any document which requires to be posted in Scotland for the purposes of this rule shall be posted by a solicitor or a sheriff officer; and on the face of the envelope there shall be written or printed the notice set out in rule 5.3(3).

---

[1] As amended by the Act of Sederunt (Ordinary Cause, Summary Application and Small Claim Rules) Amendment (Miscellaneous) 2004 (SSI 2004/197) (effective 21 May 2004), para.2(4).

[2] As substituted by the Act of Sederunt (Sheriff Court Rules) (Miscellaneous Amendments) 2011 (SSI 2011/193) r.6 (effective 4 April 2011).

[3] As amended by the Transfer of Functions (Secretary of State for Foreign, Commonwealth and Development Affairs) Order 2020 (SI 2020/942) Sch.1(1) para.1 (effective 30 September 2020).

[4] As inserted by the Act of Sederunt (Ordinary Cause, Summary Application and Small Claim Rules) Amendment (Miscellaneous) 2004 (SSI 2004/197) (effective 21 May 2004), para.2(4) and substituted by the Act of Sederunt (Sheriff Court Ordinary Cause, Summary Application, Summary Cause and Small Claims Rules) Amendment (Council Regulation (EC) No. 1348 of 2000 Extension to Denmark) 2007 (SSI 2007/440) r.2(2) (effective 9 October 2007).

[5] As substituted by the Act of Sederunt (Sheriff Court Rules) (Miscellaneous Amendments) (No.2) 2008 (SSI 2008/365) r.7 (effective 13 November 2008).

(3)   In the case of service by a method referred to in paragraph (1)(b)(ii) and (iii), the pursuer shall—

(a)[1,2]   send a copy of the writ and warrant for service with citation attached, or other document, as the case may be, with a request for service by the method indicated in the request to the Scottish Ministers or, as the case may be, the Secretary of State for Foreign, Commonwealth and Development Affairs; and

(b)   lodge in process a certificate signed by the authority which executed service stating that it has been, and the manner in which it was, served.

(4)   In the case of service by a method referred to in paragraph (1)(b)(v), the pursuer or the sheriff officer, shall—

(a)   send a copy of the writ and warrant for service with citation attached, or other document, as the case may be, with a request for service by the method indicated in the request to the official in the country in which service is to be executed; and

(b)   lodge in process a certificate of the official who executed service stating that it has been, and the method in which it was, served.

(5)   Where service is executed in accordance with paragraph (1)(a)(i) or (1)(b)(i) other than on another party in the United Kingdom, the Isle of Man or the Channel Islands, the party executing service shall lodge a certificate by a person who is conversant with the law of the country concerned and who practises or has practised law in that country or is a duly accredited representative of the Government of that country, stating that the method of service employed is in accordance with the law of the place where service was executed.

(6)   Every writ, document, citation or notice on the face of the envelope mentioned in rule 5.3(3) shall be accompanied by a translation in—

(a)[3]   an official language of the country in which service is to be executed; or

(b)[4]   in a country to which the EC Service Regulation applies, a language of the member state of transmission that is understood by the person on whom service is being executed.

(7)   A translation referred to in paragraph (6) shall be certified as correct by the person making it; and the certificate shall—

(a)   include his full name, address and qualifications; and

(b)   be lodged with the execution of citation or service.

(8)[5]   In this rule "the EC Service Regulation" means Regulation (EC) No. 1393/ 2007 of the European Parliament and of the Council of 13th November 2007 on the service in the Member States of judicial and extrajudicial documents in civil or commercial matters (service of documents), and repealing Council Regulation (EC) No. 1348/2000, as amended from time to time.

---

[1] As amended by the Act of Sederunt (Sheriff Court Rules) (Miscellaneous Amendments) 2011 (SSI 2011/193) r.7 (effective 4 April 2011).

[2] As amended by the Transfer of Functions (Secretary of State for Foreign, Commonwealth and Development Affairs) Order 2020 (SI 2020/942) Sch.1(1) para.1 (effective 30 September 2020).

[3] As inserted by the Act of Sederunt (Ordinary Cause, Summary Application and Small Claim Rules) Amendment (Miscellaneous) 2004 (SSI 2004/197) (effective 21 May 2004), para.2(4) and substituted by the Act of Sederunt (Sheriff Court Ordinary Cause, Summary Application, Summary Cause and Small Claims Rules) Amendment (Council Regulation (EC) No. 1348 of 2000 Extension to Denmark) 2007 (SSI 2007/440) r.2(2) (effective 9 October 2007).

[4] As substituted by the Act of Sederunt (Sheriff Court Rules) (Miscellaneous Amendments) (No.2) 2008 (SSI 2008/365) r.7 (effective 13 November 2008).

[5] As substituted by the Act of Sederunt (Sheriff Court Rules) (Miscellaneous Amendments) (No.2) 2008 (SSI 2008/365) r.7 (effective 13 November 2008).

Service where address of person is not known

D1.48

5.6.—(A1)[1] Subject to rule 6.A7 this rule applies to service where the address of a person is not known.

(1) Where the address of a person to be cited or served with a document is not known and cannot reasonably be ascertained, the sheriff shall grant warrant for citation or service upon that person—

(a) by the publication of an advertisement in Form G3 in a specified newspaper circulating in the area of the last known address of that person, or

(b) by displaying on the walls of court a copy of the instance and crave of the initial writ, warrant of citation and a notice in Form G4;

and the period of notice fixed by the sheriff shall run from the date of publication of the advertisement or display on the walls of court, as the case may be.

(2) Where service requires to be executed under paragraph (1), the pursuer shall lodge a service copy of the initial writ and a copy of any warrant of citation with the sheriff clerk from whom they may be uplifted by the person for whom they are intended.

(3) Where a person has been cited or served in accordance with paragraph (1) and, after the cause has commenced, his address becomes known, the sheriff may allow the initial writ to be amended subject to such conditions as to re-service, intimation, expenses, or transfer of the cause as he thinks fit.

(4) Where advertisement in a newspaper is required for the purpose of citation or service under this rule, a copy of the newspaper containing the advertisement shall be lodged with the sheriff clerk by the pursuer.

(5) Where display on the walls of court is required under paragraph (1)(b), the pursuer shall supply to the sheriff clerk for that purpose a certified copy of the instance and crave of the initial writ and any warrant of citation.

Persons carrying on business under trading or descriptive name

D1.49

5.7.—[2](1) A person carrying on a business under a trading or descriptive name may sue or be sued in such trading or descriptive name alone; and an extract—

(a) of a decree pronounced in the sheriff court, or

(b) of a decree proceeding upon any deed, decree arbitral, bond, protest of a bill, promissory note or banker's note or upon any other obligation or document on which execution may proceed, recorded in the sheriff court books,

against such person under such trading or descriptive name shall be a valid warrant for diligence against such person.

(2) An initial writ, decree, charge, warrant or any other order or writ following upon such initial writ or decree in a cause in which a person carrying on business under a trading or descriptive name sues or is sued in that name may be served—

(a) at any place of business or office at which such business is carried on within the sheriffdom of the sheriff court in which the cause is brought; or

(b) where there is no place of business within that sheriffdom, at any place where such business is carried on (including the place of business or office of the clerk or secretary of any company, corporation or association or firm).

---

[1] As inserted by the Act of Sederunt (Sheriff Court Rules Amendment) (Diligence) 2008 (SSI 2008/121) r.5(3) (effective 1 April 2008).

[2] As amended by SI 1996/2445 (effective 1 November 1996).

Endorsation unnecessary

5.8. An initial writ, decree, charge, warrant or any other order or writ following upon such initial writ or decree may be served, enforced or otherwise lawfully executed anywhere in Scotland without endorsation by a sheriff clerk; and, if executed by a sheriff officer, may be so executed by a sheriff officer of the court which granted it or by a sheriff officer of the sheriff court district in which it is to be executed.

D1.50

Re-service

5.9. Where it appears to the sheriff that there has been any failure or irregularity in citation or service on a person, he may order the pursuer to re-serve the initial writ on such conditions as he thinks fit.

D1.51

No objection to regularity of citation, service or intimation

5.10.—(1) A person who appears in a cause shall not be entitled to state any objection to the regularity of the execution of citation, service or intimation on him; and his appearance shall remedy any defect in such citation, service or intimation.

D1.52

(2) Nothing in paragraph (1) shall preclude a party from pleading that the court has no jurisdiction.

Chapter 6

Interim Diligence[1]

Annotations to Chapter 6 are by Tim Edward.

GENERAL NOTE

The procedure for obtaining warrant to arrest to found jurisdiction is dealt with at rule 3.4.

D1.53

The procedure for obtaining warrant for diligence on the dependence of an action is dealt with by Rule 6.A2, and by Part 1A of the Debtors (Scotland) Act 1987 (as inserted by the Bankruptcy and Diligence etc. (Scotland) Act 2007).

The 1987 Act, as amended, provides that the court may make an order granting warrant for diligence on the dependence of an action if it is satisfied, having had a hearing on the matter, that: the creditor has a prima facie case on the merits of the action; there is a real and substantial risk that enforcement by the creditor of any decree in the action would be defeated or prejudiced by reason of the debtor being insolvent or verging on insolvency or the likelihood of the debtor removing, disposing of, burdening, concealing or otherwise dealing with all or some of his assets; and that it is reasonable in all the circumstances to do so. An application for an order granting warrant for diligence must be intimated to the debtor and any other person having an interest (unless the application is for warrant to be granted before a hearing, as described below). Before making such an order, the court must give an opportunity to be heard to (a) any person to whom intimation of the date of the hearing was made; and (b) any other person the court is satisfied has an interest.

The court may make an order granting warrant for diligence without a hearing if it is satisfied that the creditor has a prima facie case, that it is reasonable to grant such an order, and that that there is a real and substantial risk that enforcement of any decree in the action in favour of the creditor would be defeated or prejudiced (again, due to insolvency or the risk of the debtor removing or otherwise dealing with his assets) if warrant were not granted in advance of a hearing.

In both cases, the onus is on the creditor to satisfy the court that the order should be made.

The 1987 Act now specifically provides that it is competent for the court to grant warrant for arrestment or inhibition on the dependence where the sum concluded for is a future or contingent debt. At common law, there had to be special circumstances justifying diligence in respect of a future or contingent debt, such as that the debtor was at significant risk of insolvency or was contemplating flight from the jurisdiction. However such special circumstances, as set out above, now have to be demonstrated in respect of all debts. Common law cases on future and contingent debts may now be of assistance in interpreting the rules applying to all cases under the new provisions.

Rule 6 sets out the procedure for execution of such arrestments and Rule 6.A4 deals with the recall of an arrestment.

---

[1] Chapter renamed by the Act of Sederunt (Sheriff Court Rules Amendment) (Diligence) 2008 (SSI 2008/121) r.5(4) (effective 1 April 2008).

Interpretation

D1.54   **6.A1.**[1] In this Chapter—

"the 1987 Act" means the Debtors (Scotland) Act 1987; and
"the 2002 Act" means the Debt Arrangement and Attachment (Scotland) Act 2002.

Application for interim diligence

D1.55   **6.A2.**—[2](1) The following shall be made by motion—

(a) an application under section 15D(1) of the 1987 Act for warrant for diligence by arrestment or inhibition on the dependence of an action or warrant for arrestment on the dependence of an admiralty action;

(b) an application under section 9C of the 2002 Act for warrant for interim attachment.

(2) Such an application must be accompanied by a statement in Form G4A.

(3) A certified copy of an interlocutor granting a motion under paragraph (1) shall be sufficient authority for the execution of the diligence concerned.

Effect of authority for inhibition on the dependence

D1.56   **6.A3.**—[3](1) Where a person has been granted authority for inhibition on the dependence of an action, a certified copy of the interlocutor granting the motion may be registered with a certificate of execution in the Register of Inhibitions and Adjudications.

(2)[4] A notice of a certified copy of an interlocutor granting authority for inhibition under rule 6.A2 may be registered in the Register of Inhibitions and Adjudications; and such registration is to have the same effect as registration of a notice of inhibition under section 155(2) of the Titles to Land Consolidation (Scotland) Act 1868.

Recall etc. of arrestment or inhibition

D1.57   **6.A4.**—[5](1) An application by any person having an interest—

(a) to loose, restrict, vary or recall an arrestment or an interim attachment; or

(b) to recall, in whole or in part, or vary, an inhibition,

shall be made by motion.

(2) A motion under paragraph (1) shall—

(a) specify the name and address of each of the parties;

(b) where it relates to an inhibition, contain a description of the inhibition including the date of registration in the Register of Inhibitions and Adjudications.

Incidental applications in relation to interim diligence, etc

D1.58   **6.A5.**[6] An application under Part 1A of the 1987 Act or Part 1A of the 2002 Act other than mentioned above shall be made by motion.

---

[1] As inserted by the Act of Sederunt (Sheriff Court Rules Amendment) (Diligence) 2008 (SSI 2008/121) r.5(5) (effective April 1, 2008).
[2] As inserted by the Act of Sederunt (Sheriff Court Rules Amendment) (Diligence) 2008 (SSI 2008/121) r.5(5) (effective April 1, 2008).
[3] As inserted by the Act of Sederunt (Sheriff Court Rules Amendment) (Diligence) 2008 (SSI 2008/121) r.5(5) (effective April 1, 2008).
[4] As substituted by the Act of Sederunt (Sheriff Court Rules Amendment) (Diligence) 2009 (SSI 2009/107) r.3 (effective April 22, 2009).
[5] As inserted by the Act of Sederunt (Sheriff Court Rules Amendment) (Diligence) 2008 (SSI 2008/121) r.5(5) (effective April 1, 2008).
[6] As inserted by the Act of Sederunt (Sheriff Court Rules Amendment) (Diligence) 2008 (SSI 2008/121) r.5(5) (effective April 1, 2008).

Form of schedule of inhibition on the dependence

6.A6. *[Revoked by the Act of Sederunt (Sheriff Court Rules Amendment) (Diligence) 2009 (SSI 2009/107) r.3 (effective April 22, 2009).]*

Service of inhibition on the dependence where address of defender not known

6.A7.—[1](1) Where the address of a defender is not known to the pursuer, an **D1.59** inhibition on the dependence shall be deemed to have been served on the defender if the schedule of inhibition is left with or deposited at the office of the sheriff clerk of the sheriff court district where the defender's last known address is located.

(2) Where service of an inhibition on the dependence is executed under paragraph (1), a copy of the schedule of inhibition shall be sent by the sheriff officer by first class post to the defender's last known address.

Form of schedule of arrestment on the dependence[2]

6.A8.—(1) An arrestment on the dependence shall be served by serving the **D1.60** schedule of arrestment on the arrestee in Form G4B.

(2) A certificate of execution shall be lodged with the sheriff clerk in Form G4C.

Service of schedule of arrestment

6.1 If a schedule of arrestment has not been personally served on an arrestee, the **D1.61** arrestment shall have effect only if a copy of the schedule is also sent by registered post or the first class recorded delivery service to—

   (a)   the last known place of residence of the arrestee, or

   (b)   if such place of residence is not known, or if the arrestee is a firm or corporation, to the arrestee's principal place of business if known, or, if not known, to any known place of business of the arrestee;

and the sheriff officer shall, on the certificate of execution, certify that this has been done and specify the address to which the copy of the schedule was sent.

"SCHEDULE OF ARRESTMENT"

What is delivered to the arrestee is the "schedule" of arrestment. This is a short copy of the warrant. The sheriff officer will then return an "execution" or report of arrestment which states that the arrestment was duly executed.

Both the schedule and the execution narrate the warrant for the arrestment, (giving its date and the designation of the parties), the arrestee, the sum or subjects arrested and the date of execution. These must conform to the warrant and craves of the initial writ (*Mactaggart v MacKillop* , 1938 S.L.T. 100).

A high degree of precision is required in the schedule. By statute, the schedule must be signed by the officer, and must contain such information as the date and time of the execution and the name, occupation and address of the witness: Citation Acts 1592 and 1693.

Erroneous or defective execution, if in the essentials, can be fatal. Misnaming the pursuer, for example, may be fatal: *Richards & Wallington (Earthmoving) Limited v Whatlings Limited* , 1982 S.L.T. 66. Here the Lord Ordinary (Maxwell) held that "(a) trivial spelling mistake, for example, might not invalidate, but ... I think that a high degree of accuracy in this field is required."

The same rule applies to naming the arrestee (*Henderson's Trs* (1831) 9 S. 618) and to the description of the capacity in which the funds or subjects are due to the common debtor: *Wilson v Mackie* (1875) 3 R. 18. So too does it apply to ambiguity in the description of the funds intended to be attached: *Lattimore v Singleton, Dunn & Co.* , 1911 2 S.L.T. 360.

It has been held that misnomer of the common debtor is not fatal if there is no risk of misunderstanding: *Pollock, Whyte & Waddell v Old Park Forge Limited* (1907) 15 S.L.T. 3. Similarly, misdescription of the capacity in which the arrestee holds any sum arrested need not be fatal if there is no difficulty in identifying the sums in the hands of the arrestee: *Huber v Banks* , 1986 S.L.T. 58.

Furthermore, a defective execution to a summons can be replaced by a correct one before being produced in judgement: *Henderson v Richardson* (1848) 10 D. 1035; *Hamilton v Monkland Iron & Steel Co.* (1863) 1 M. 672.

---

[1] As inserted by the Act of Sederunt (Sheriff Court Rules Amendment) (Diligence) 2008 (SSI 2008/121) r.5(5) (effective April 1, 2008).

[2] As inserted by the Act of Sederunt (Sheriff Court Rules Amendment) (Diligence) 2009 (SSI 2009/107) r.3 (effective April 22, 2009).

Where an arrestment has been made on the dependence of an action and subsequently decree is granted in favour of the arresting creditor, the arrestment is automatically transformed into an arrestment in execution and no further service of a schedule of arrestment is required: *Abercrombie v Edgar and Crerar Ltd.* , 1923 S.L.T. 271. In contrast to the diligence of poinding and sale, and arrestment against earnings, an arrestment on the dependence of an action or in execution proceeds without a charge having been served on the debtor.

"...PERSONALLY SERVED..."

(i)   Where the arrestee is an individual, the schedule of arrestment need not be served personally; it may also be served at his dwelling-place: *Campbell v Watson Trustees* (1898) 25 R. 690. Rule 6.1 provides that if the latter course is taken then the arrestment shall have effect only if a copy of the schedule of arrestment is also sent by registered post or the first class recorded delivery service to the last known place of residence of the arrestee, or, if such place of residence is not known, or if the arrestee is a firm or corporation, to the arrestee's principal place of business if known, or, if not known, to any known place of business of the arrestee. Postal service alone is incompetent, except in summary cause actions: Execution of Diligence (S) Act 1926, s.2 and *Dick Bros v Thomas C Gray Ltd* , 1958 S.L.T. (Sh. Ct.) 66.

(ii)   If the arrestee is a bank, the service of the arrestment should be made at its registered office, or the schedule should be delivered to an official at head office (see Macphail, *Sheriff Court Practice*, at 11.21. He also states that in all cases, notice by way of another schedule should be served at the branch where the account of the common debtor is kept).

(iii) Where the arrestee is a corporation, the arrestment should name the corporation, and can be delivered to the hands of an employee: *Campbell v Watson's Trustees* (1898) 25 R. 690; *Gall v Stirling Water Commissioners* (1901) 9 S.L.T. (Sh. Ct.) 13. Service on a superior officer of a company does not appear to be essential, although it is a proper precaution according to Lord Young in *Campbell v Watson's Trustees* (1898) 25 R. 690. Delivery to the registered office is certainly competent, by virtue of the Companies Act 2006 s.1139(1).

In *McIntyre v Caledonian Railway Co.* (1909), 25 Sh. Ct Rep. 529, it was held that an arrestment by handing a schedule to a servant of a corporation within one of its branch offices was effectual, and rendered unnecessary the posting of a schedule to the corporation. However, this is authority only for the proposition that service at a branch office is only good in respect of subjects held at that branch.

It should be noted that in *Corson v Macmillan* , 1927 S.L.T. (Sh. Ct.) 13 it was found that service on a director at a place that was not a place of business was bad. This tends to suggest service at the registered office is the safest option. This should also attach subjects at branch offices.

(iv)   For a firm with a social name the arrestment should name the firm and be served at the place of business in the hands of an employee. Should the firm have a descriptive name then the arrestment should be served at its place of business and personally on or at the dwelling- places of three partners, should there be as many.

(v)   Where the arrestees are trustees, the schedule should be served on such trustees as are entitled to act (*Gracie v Gracie* , 1910 S.C. 899). The schedule should also state that the arrestment is served on each as a trustee and not as an individual: *Burns v Gillies* (1906) 8 F. 460.

Where the arrestment is not executed personally, and the arrestee in justifiable ignorance of it has paid away the arrested fund, he cannot be called upon to refund the money (*Laidlaw v Smith* 1838, 16 S. 367, aff'g. 2 Rob. App. 490; *Leslie v Lady Ashburton* , 1827, 6 S. 165)

D1.62   **Arrestment on dependence before service**

6.2.   *[Repealed by the Act of Sederunt (Sheriff Court Rules Amendment) (Diligence) 2008 (SSI 2008/121) r.5(6) (effective April 1, 2008).]*

RULE 6.2

D1.63   Rule 6.2 dealt with arrestment on the dependence of an action before service of the initial writ. This was repealed by the Act of Sederunt (Sheriff Court Rules Amendment) (Diligence) 2008 (SSI 2008/121) r.5(6) (effective 1 April 2008) and this area is now dealt with by Section 15G of the Debtors (Scotland) Act 1987.

D1.64   **Movement of arrested property**

6.3.   [Omitted by the Act of Sederunt (Sheriff Court Rules) (Miscellaneous Amendments) 2012 (SSI 2012/188) para.10 (effective August 1, 2012).]

RULE 6.3

Rule 6.3, which allowed for an application to be made for a warrant authorising the movement of a vessel or cargo which is the subject of an arrestment, was omitted by the Act of Sederunt (Sheriff Court

Rules) (Miscellaneous Amendments) 2012 (SSI 2012/188) para.10 (effective 1 August 2012). Admiralty Actions are now dealt with by Rule 49 and section 47 of the Administration of Justice Act 1956.

Chapter 7

D1.65

Undefended Causes

Application of this Chapter

7.1. This Chapter applies to any cause other than an action in which the sheriff may not grant decree without evidence.

D1.66

Minute for granting of decree without attendance

7.2.—(1)[1] Subject to the following paragraphs, where the defender—

D1.67

(a) does not lodge a notice of intention to defend,

(b) does not lodge an application for a time to pay direction under the Debtors (Scotland) Act 1987 or a time order under the Consumer Credit Act 1974,

(c) has lodged such an application for a time to pay direction or time order and the pursuer does not object to the application or to any recall or restriction of an arrestment sought in the application,

the sheriff may, on the pursuer endorsing a minute for decree on the initial writ, at any time after the expiry of the period for lodging that notice or application, grant decree in absence or other order in terms of the minute so endorsed without requiring the attendance of the pursuer in court.

(2) The sheriff shall not grant decree under paragraph (1)—

(a) unless it appears ex facie of the initial writ that a ground of jurisdiction exists under the Civil Jurisdiction and Judgments Act 1982; and

(b) the cause is not a cause—

(i) in which decree may not be granted without evidence;

(ii) to which paragraph (4) applies; or

(iii)[2] to which rule 33.31 (procedure in undefended family action for a section 11 order) applies.

(3) Where a defender is domiciled in another part of the United Kingdom or in another Contracting State, the sheriff shall not grant decree in absence until it has been shown that the defender has been able to receive the initial writ in sufficient time to arrange for his defence or that all necessary steps have been taken to that end; and for the purposes of this paragraph—

(a) the question whether a person is domiciled in another part of the United Kingdom shall be determined in accordance with sections 41 and 42 of the Civil Jurisdiction and Judgments Act 1982;

(b) the question whether a person is domiciled in another Contracting State shall be determined in accordance with Article 52 of the Convention in Schedule 1 or 3C to that Act; and

(c) the term "Contracting State" has the meaning assigned in section 1 of that Act.

(4) Where an initial writ has been served in a country to which the Hague Convention on the Service Abroad of Judicial and Extra-Judicial Documents in Civil or Commercial Matters dated 15th November 1965 applies, decree shall not be

---

[1] As amended by the Act of Sederunt (Ordinary Cause, Summary Application, Summary Cause and Small Claim Rules) Amendment (Miscellaneous) 2007 (SSI 2007/6) r.2(6) (effective January 29, 2007).

[2] As amended by SI 1996/2167 (effective November 1, 1996) and SI 1996/2445 (effective November 1, 1996).

granted until it is established to the satisfaction of the sheriff that the requirements of Article 15 of that Convention have been complied with.

Applications for time to pay directions or time orders in undefended causes

D1.68

7.3.—(1) This rule applies to a cause in which—

    (a)[1] a time to pay direction may be applied for under the Debtors (Scotland) Act 1987; or

    (b) a time order may be applied for under the Consumer Credit Act 1974.

(2) A defender in a cause which is otherwise undefended, who wishes to apply for a time to pay direction or time order, and where appropriate, to have an arrestment recalled or restricted, shall complete and lodge with the sheriff clerk the appropriate part of Form O3 before the expiry of the period of notice.

(2A)[2] As soon as possible after the application of the defender is lodged, the sheriff clerk shall send a copy of it to the pursuer by first class ordinary post.

(3) Where the pursuer does not object to the application of the defender made in accordance with paragraph (2), he shall minute for decree in accordance with rule 7.2; and the sheriff may grant decree or other order in terms of the application and minute.

(4)[3] Where the pursuer objects to the application of the defender made in accordance with paragraph (2) he shall on the same date—

    (a) complete and lodge with the sheriff clerk Form O3A;

    (b) minute for decree in accordance with rule 7.2; and

    (c) send a copy of Form O3A to the defender.

(4A)[4] The sheriff clerk shall then fix a hearing on the application of the defender and intimate the hearing to the pursuer and the defender.

(4B)[5] The hearing must be fixed for a date within 28 days of the date on which the Form O3A and the minute for decree are lodged.

(5) The sheriff may determine an application in which a hearing has been fixed under paragraph (4) whether or not any of the parties appear.

Decree for expenses

D1.69

7.4.—[6](1) On granting decree in absence or thereafter, the sheriff may grant decree for expenses.

(2) Where the pursuer elects, in the minute for decree, to claim expenses comprising—

    (a) the inclusive charges set out in Part 1 of Table 1 in schedule 4 of the Act of Sederunt (Taxation of Judicial Expenses Rules) 2019; and

    (b) outlays comprising only—

        (i) the court fee for warranting the initial writ;

---

[1] As amended by the Act of Sederunt (Ordinary Cause, Summary Application, Summary Cause and Small Claim Rules) Amendment (Miscellaneous) 2007 (SSI 2007/6) r.2(7) (effective January 29, 2007).

[2] As inserted by the Act of Sederunt (Sheriff Court Rules) (Miscellaneous Amendments) 2009 (SSI 2009/294) r.2 (effective December 1, 2009).

[3] Para.(4) substituted for paras (4)–(4B) by the Act of Sederunt (Sheriff Court Rules) (Miscellaneous Amendments) 2009 (SSI 2009/294) r.2 (effective December 1, 2009).

[4] Para.(4) substituted for paras (4)–(4B) by the Act of Sederunt (Sheriff Court Rules) (Miscellaneous Amendments) 2009 (SSI 2009/294) r.2 (effective December 1, 2009).

[5] Para.(4) substituted for paras (4)–(4B) by the Act of Sederunt (Sheriff Court Rules) (Miscellaneous Amendments) 2009 (SSI 2009/294) r.2 (effective December 1, 2009).

[6] As amended by Act of Sederunt (Rules of the Court of Session, Sheriff Appeal Court Rules and Ordinary Cause Rules Amendment) (Taxation of Judicial Expenses) 2019 (SSI 2019/74) r.3(2) (effective 29 April 2019).

    (ii)   postal charges incurred in effecting, or attempting to effect, service of the initial writ by post; and

    (iii) where applicable, a sheriff officer's fee for service of the initial writ, the sheriff may grant decree for payment of such expenses without the necessity of taxation.

Finality of decree in absence

7.5.[1] Subject to section 9(7) of the Land Tenure Reform (Scotland) Act 1974 (decree in action of removing for breach of condition of long lease to be final when extract recorded in Register of Sasines), a decree in absence which has not been recalled or brought under review by suspension or by reduction shall become final and shall have effect as a decree *in foro contentioso*—

    (a)   on the expiry of six months from the date of the decree or from the date of a charge made under it, as the case may be, where the service of the initial writ or of the charge has been personal; and

    (b)   in any event, on the expiry of 20 years from the date of the decree.

                              D1.70

Amendment of initial writ

7.6.—(1) In an undefended cause, the sheriff may—

    (a)   allow the pursuer to amend the initial writ in any way permitted by rule 18.2 (powers of sheriff to allow amendment); and

    (b)   order the amended initial writ to be re-served on the defender on such period of notice as he thinks fit.

(2) The defender shall not be liable for the expense occasioned by any such amendment unless the sheriff so orders.

(3) Where an amendment has been allowed under paragraph (1), the amendment—

    (a)   shall not validate diligence used on the dependence of a cause so as to prejudice the rights of creditors of the party against whom the diligence has been executed who are interested in defeating such diligence; and

    (b)   shall preclude any objection to such diligence stated by a party or any person by virtue of a title acquired or in right of a debt contracted by him subsequent to the execution of such diligence.

                              D1.71

Disapplication of certain rules

7.7[2] The following rules in Chapter 15 (motions) shall not apply to an action in which no notice of intention to defend has been lodged or to any action in so far as it proceeds as undefended—

rule 15.2 (intimation of motions),
rule 15.3 (opposition to motions),
rule 15.5 (hearing of motions).

                              D1.72

Chapter 8

Reponing

Reponing

8.1.—(1) In any cause other than—

                              D1.73

---

[1] As amended by SI 1996/2445 (effective November 1, 1996).
[2] Inserted by SI 1996/2445 (effective November 1, 1996).

(a)[1] a cause mentioned in rule 33.1(a) to (h) or (n) to (p), (certain family actions), or

(aa)[2] a cause mentioned in rule 33A.1(a), (b) or (f) (certain civil partnership actions);

(b) a cause to which Chapter 37 (causes under the Presumption of Death (Scotland) Act 1977) applies,

the defender or any party with a statutory title or interest may apply to be reponed by lodging with the sheriff clerk, before implement in full of a decree in absence, a reponing note setting out his proposed defence or the proposed order or direction and explaining his failure to appear.

(2) A copy of the note lodged under paragraph (1) shall be served on the pursuer and any other party—

(3) The sheriff may, on considering the reponing note, recall the decree so far as not implemented subject to such order as to expenses as he thinks fit; and the cause shall thereafter proceed as if—

(a) the defender had lodged a notice of intention to defend and the period of notice had expired on the date on which the decree in absence was recalled; or

(b)[3] the party seeking the order or direction had lodged the appropriate application on the date when the decree was recalled.

(4) A reponing note, when duly lodged with the sheriff clerk and served upon the pursuer, shall have effect to sist diligence.

(4A)[4] Where an initial writ has been served on a defender furth of the United Kingdom under rule 5.5(1)(b) (service on persons furth of Scotland) and decree in absence has been pronounced against him as a result of his failure to enter appearance, the court may, on the defender applying to be reponed in accordance with paragraph (1) above, recall the decree and allow defences to be received if—

(a) without fault on his part, he did not have knowledge of the initial writ in sufficient time to defend;

(b) he has disclosed a prima facie defence to the action on the merits; and

(c) the reponing note is lodged within a reasonable time after he had knowledge of the decree or in any event before the expiry of one year from the date of decree.

(5) Any interlocutor or order recalling, or incidental to the recall of, a decree in absence shall be final and not subject to appeal.

Chapter 9

Standard Procedure in Defended Causes

Notice of intention to defend

D1.74 **9.1.**—[5](1)[6, 7] Subject to rule 35.8 (lodging of notice of appearance in action of multiplepoinding), where the defender intends to—

---

[1] As amended by Act of Sederunt (Ordinary Cause Rules) Amendment (Family Law (Scotland) Act 2006 etc.) 2006 (SSI 2006/207) r.2 (effective 4 May 2006) and by the Act of Sederunt (Sheriff Court Rules) (Miscellaneous Amendments) (No.2) 2010 (SSI 2010/416) r.8 (effective 1 January 2011).

[2] Inserted by Act of Sederunt (Ordinary Cause Rules) Amendment (Family Law (Scotland) Act 2006 etc.) 2006 (SSI 2006/207) r.2 (effective 4 May 2006).

[3] Inserted by the Act of Sederunt (Ordinary Cause, Summary Application and Small Claim Rules) Amendment (Miscellaneous) 2004 (SSI 2004/197) r.2(5) (effective 21 May 2004).

[4] Inserted by SSI 2000/239 (effective 2 October 2000).

[5] As amended by the Act of Sederunt (Ordinary Cause Rules 1993 Amendment) (Case Management of Defended Family and Civil Partnership Actions) 2022 (SSI 2022/289) r.2(3) (effective 25 September 2023 subject to transitional provision specified in SSI 2022/289 r.3).

    (a)   challenge the jurisdiction of the court,

    (b)   state a defence, or

    (c)   make a counterclaim,

he shall, before the expiry of the period of notice, lodge with the sheriff clerk a notice of intention to defend in Form O7 and, at the same time, send a copy to the pursuer.

(2) The lodging of a notice of intention to defend shall not imply acceptance of the jurisdiction of the court.

(3)[1] This Chapter shall not apply to a commercial action within the meaning of Chapter 40 or a family or civil partnership action within the meaning of Chapters 33 and 33A.

Fixing date for Options Hearing

9.2.—[2](1)[3] on the lodging of a notice of intention to defend, the sheriff clerk shall fix a date and time for an Options Hearing which date shall be on the first suitable court day occurring not sooner than 10 weeks after the expiry of the period of notice.   **D1.75**

(2) On fixing the date for the Options Hearing, the sheriff clerk shall—

    (a)   forthwith intimate to the parties in Form G5—

        (i)   the last date for lodging defences;

        (ii)   the last date for adjustment; and

        (iii)   the date of the Options hearing; and

    (b)   prepare and sign an interlocutor recording those dates.

(3)[4] The fixing of the date for the Options Hearing shall not affect the right of a party to make any incidental application to the court.

Alteration of date for Options Hearing

9.2A.—[5](1) Subject to paragraph (2), at any time before the date and time fixed under rule 9.2 (fixing date for Options Hearing) or under this rule, the sheriff—   **D1.76**

    (a)   may, of his own motion or on the motion of any party—

        (i)   discharge the Options Hearing; and

        (ii)   fix a new date and time for the Options Hearing; or

    (b)   shall, on the joint motion of the parties—

        (i)   discharge the Options Hearing; and

        (ii)   fix a new date and time for the Options Hearing.

(2) The date and time to be fixed—

---

[6] As amended by the Act of Sederunt (Family Proceedings in the Sheriff Court) 1996 (SI 1996/2167) (effective 1 November 2000).

[7] As amended by Act of Sederunt (Ordinary Cause Rules) Amendment (Family Law (Scotland) Act 2006 etc.) 2006 (SSI 2006/207) r.2 (effective 4 May 2006).

[1] Inserted by the Act of Sederunt (Ordinary Cause Rules) Amendment (Commercial Actions) 2001 (SSI 2001/8) (effective 1 March 2001).

[2] As amended by the Act of Sederunt (Ordinary Cause Rules 1993 Amendment) (Case Management of Defended Family and Civil Partnership Actions) 2022 (SSI 2022/289) r.2(4) (effective 25 September 2023 subject to transitional provision specified in SSI 2022/289 r.3).

[3] As amended by the Act of Sederunt (Sheriff Court Ordinary Cause Rules Amendment) (Miscellaneous) 2000 (SSI 2000/239) (effective 2 October 2000).

[4] As amended by the Act of Sederunt (Sheriff Court Ordinary Cause Rules Amendment) (Miscellaneous) 1996 (SI 1996/2445) (effective 1 November 1996).

[5] Inserted by the Act of Sederunt (Sheriff Court Ordinary Cause Rules Amendment) (Miscellaneous) 1996 (SI 1996/2445) (effective 1 November 1996) and substituted by the Act of Sederunt (Ordinary Cause and Summary Application Rules) Amendment (Miscellaneous) 2006 (SI 2006/410) (effective 18 August 2006).

(a)   under paragraph (1)(a)(ii) may be earlier or later than the date and time fixed for the discharged Options Hearing;

(b)   under paragraph (1)(b)(ii) shall be earlier than the date and time fixed for the discharged Options Hearing.

(3) Where the sheriff is considering making an order under paragraph (1)(a) of his own motion and in the absence of the parties, the sheriff clerk shall—

(a)   fix a date, time and place for the parties to be heard; and

(b)   inform the parties of that date, time and place.

(4) The sheriff may discharge a hearing fixed under paragraph (3) on the joint motion of the parties.

(5) On the discharge of the Options Hearing under paragraph (1), the sheriff clerk shall forthwith intimate to all parties—

(a)   that the Options Hearing has been discharged under paragraph (1)(a) or (b), as the case may be;

(b)   the last date for lodging defences, if appropriate;

(c)   the last date for adjustment, if appropriate; and

(d)   the new date and time fixed for the Options Hearing under paragraph (1)(a) or (b), as the case may be.

(6) Any reference in these Rules to the Options Hearing or a continuation of it shall include a reference to an Options Hearing for which a date and time has been fixed under this rule.

Return of initial writ

D1.77

9.3. Subject to rule 9.4 (lodging of pleadings before Options Hearing), the pursuer shall return the initial writ, unbacked and unfolded, to the sheriff clerk within 7 days after the expiry of the period of notice.

Lodging of pleadings before Options Hearing

D1.78

9.4. Where any hearing, whether by motion or otherwise, is fixed before the Options Hearing, each party shall lodge in process a copy of his pleadings, or, where the pleadings have been adjusted, the pleadings as adjusted, not later than 2 days before the hearing.

Process folder

D1.79

9.5.—(1) On receipt of the notice of intention to defend, the sheriff clerk shall prepare a process folder which shall include—

(a)   interlocutor sheets;

(b)   duplicate interlocutor sheets;

(c)   a production file;

(d)   a motion file; and

(e)   an inventory of process.

(2) Any production or part of process lodged in a cause shall be placed in the process folder.

Defences

D1.80

9.6.—[1](1) Where a notice of intention to defend has been lodged, the defender shall lodge defences within 14 days after the expiry of the period of notice.

---

[1] As amended by the Act of Sederunt (Ordinary Cause Rules 1993 Amendment) (Case Management of Defended Family and Civil Partnership Actions) 2022 (SSI 2022/289) r.2(5) (effective 25 September 2023 subject to transitional provision specified in SSI 2022/289 r.3).

(2) Subject to rule 19.1(3) (form of defences where counterclaim included), defences shall be in the form of answers in numbered paragraphs corresponding to the articles of the condescendence, and shall have appended a note of the pleas-in-law of the defender.

Implied admissions

9.7. Every statement of fact made by a party shall be answered by every other party, and if such a statement by one party within the knowledge of another party is not denied by that other party, that other party shall be deemed to have admitted that statement of fact.

D1.81

Adjustment of pleadings

9.8.—(1) Parties may adjust their pleadings until 14 days before the date of the Options Hearing or any continuation of it.

D1.82

(2) Any adjustments shall be exchanged between parties and not lodged in process.

(3) Parties shall be responsible for maintaining a record of adjustments made during the period for adjustment.

(4) No adjustments shall be permitted after the period mentioned in paragraph (1) except with leave of the sheriff.

Effect of sist on adjustment

9.9.—(1) Where a cause has been sisted, any period for adjustment before the sist shall be reckoned as a part of the period for adjustment.

D1.83

(2) On recall of the sist of a cause, the sheriff clerk shall—

   (a) fix a new date for the Options Hearing;

   (b) prepare and sign an interlocutor recording that date; and

   (c) intimate that date to each party.

Open record

9.10. The sheriff may, at any time before the closing of the record in a cause to which this Chapter applies, of his own motion or on the motion of a party, order any party to lodge a copy of the pleadings in the form of an open record containing any adjustments and amendments made as at the date of the order.

D1.84

Record for Options Hearing

9.11.—(1) The pursuer shall, at the end of the period for adjustment referred to in rule 9.8(1), and before the Options Hearing, make a copy of the pleadings and any adjustments and amendments in the form of a record.

D1.85

(2) Not later than 2 days before the Options Hearing, the pursuer shall lodge a certified copy of the record in process.

(3)[1] Where the Options Hearing is continued under rule 9.12(5), and further adjustment or amendment is made to the pleadings, a copy of the pleadings as adjusted or amended, certified by the pursuer, shall be lodged in process not later than 2 days before the Options Hearing so continued.

Options Hearing

9.12.—[2](1) At the Options Hearing the sheriff shall seek to secure the expeditious progress of the cause by ascertaining from parties the matters in dispute and information about any other matter referred to in paragraph (3).

D1.86

---

[1] Inserted by SI 1996/2445 (effective 1 November 1996).

[2] As amended by the Act of Sederunt (Ordinary Cause Rules 1993 Amendment) (Case Management of Defended Family and Civil Partnership Actions) 2022 (SSI 2022/289) r.2(6) (effective 25 September 2023 subject to transitional provision specified in SSI 2022/289 r.3).

(2)   It shall be the duty of parties to provide the sheriff with sufficient information to enable him to conduct the hearing as provided for in this rule.

(3)   At the Options Hearing the sheriff shall, except where the cause is ordered to proceed under the procedure in Chapter 10 (additional procedure), close the record and—

   (a)   appoint the cause to a proof and make such orders as to the extent of proof, the lodging of a joint minute of admissions or agreement, or such other matter as he thinks fit;

   (b)   after having heard parties and considered any note lodged under rule 22.1 (note of basis of preliminary plea), appoint the cause to a proof before answer and make such orders as to the extent of proof, the lodging of a joint minute of admissions or agreement, or such other matter as he thinks fit; or

   (c)[1]   after having heard parties and considered any note lodged under rule 22.1, appoint the cause to debate if satisfied that there is a preliminary matter of law which if established following debate would lead to decree in favour of any party, or to limitation of proof to any substantial degree.

   (d)[2]   consider any child witness notice or vulnerable witness application that has been lodged where no order has been made, or

   (e)[3]   ascertain whether there is or is likely to be a vulnerable witness within the meaning of section 11(1) of the Act of 2004 who is to give evidence at any proof or hearing and whether any order under section 12(1) of the Act of 2004 requires to be made.

(4)   At the Options Hearing the sheriff may, having heard parties—

   (a)   of his own motion or on the motion of any party, and

   (b)   on being satisfied that the difficulty or complexity of the cause makes it unsuitable for the procedure under this Chapter,

order that the cause proceed under the procedure in Chapter 10 (additional procedure).

(5)   The sheriff may, on cause shown, of his own motion or on the motion of any party, allow a continuation of the Options Hearing on one occasion only for a period not exceeding 28 days or to the first suitable court day thereafter.

(6)   On closing the record—

   (a)   where there are no adjustments made since the lodging of the record under rule 9.11(2), that record shall become the closed record; and

   (b)   where there are such adjustments, the sheriff may order that a closed record including such adjustments be lodged within 7 days after the date of the interlocutor closing the record.

(7)   For the purposes of rule 16.2 (decrees where party in default), an Options Hearing shall be a diet in accordance with those rule.

---

[1]   As amended by the Act of Sederunt (Ordinary Cause, Summary Application and Small Claim Rules) Amendment (Miscellaneous) 2004 (SSI 2004/197) (effective 21 May 2004).

[2]   As inserted by the Act of Sederunt (Ordinary Cause, Summary Application, Summary Cause and Small Claim Rules) Amendment (Vulnerable Witnesses (Scotland) Act 2004) 2007 (SSI 2007/463) r.2(3) (effective 1 November 2007).

[3]   As inserted by the Act of Sederunt (Ordinary Cause, Summary Application, Summary Cause and Small Claim Rules) Amendment (Vulnerable Witnesses (Scotland) Act 2004) 2007 (SSI 2007/463) r.2(3) (effective 1 November 2007).

(8)[1] Where the cause is appointed, under paragraph (3), to a proof or proof before answer, the sheriff shall consider whether a pre-proof hearing should be fixed under rule 28A.1.

9.13.–9.15. *[Omitted by the Act of Sederunt (Ordinary Cause, Summary Application and Small Claim Rules) Amendment (Miscellaneous) 2004 (SSI 2004/197) (effective May 21, 2004), r.2(7).]*

Chapter 9A[2]

Documents and Witnesses

Application of this Chapter

9A.1. This Chapter applies to any cause proceeding under Chapters 9 and 10.   **D1.87**

Inspection and recovery of documents

9A.2.—(1) Each party shall, within 14 days after the date of the interlocutor al-   **D1.88**
lowing proof or proof before answer, intimate to every other party a list of the documents, which are or have been in his possession or control and which he intends to use or put in evidence at the proof, including the whereabouts of those documents.

(2) A party who has received a list of documents from another party under paragraph (1) may inspect those documents which are in the possession or control of the party intimating the list at a time and place fixed by that party which is reasonable to both parties.

(3) A party who seeks to use or put in evidence at a proof a document not on his list intimated under paragraph (1) shall, if any other party objects to such document being used or put in evidence, seek leave of the sheriff to do so; and such leave may be granted on such conditions, if any, as the sheriff thinks fit.

(4) Nothing in this rule shall affect—

    (a) the law relating, or the right of a party to object, to the inspection of a document on the ground of privilege or confidentiality; or

    (b) the right of a party to apply under rule 28.2 for a commission and diligence for recovery of documents or an order under section 1 of the Administration of Justice (Scotland) Act 1972.

Exchange of lists of witnesses

9A.3.—(1) Within 28 days after the date of the interlocutor allowing a proof or   **D1.89**
proof before answer, each party shall—

    (a) intimate to every other party a list of witnesses, including any skilled witnesses, on whose evidence he intends to rely at proof; and

    (b) lodge a copy of that list in process.

(2) A party who seeks to rely on the evidence of a person not on his list intimated under paragraph (1) shall, if any other party objects to such evidence being admitted, seek leave of the sheriff to admit that evidence whether it is to be given orally or not; and such leave may be granted on such conditions, if any, as the sheriff thinks fit.

---

[1] Inserted by the Act of Sederunt (Ordinary Cause and Summary Application Rules) Amendment (Miscellaneous) 2006 (SSI 2006/410) (effective 18 August 2006).

[2] Inserted by the Act of Sederunt (Ordinary Cause, Summary Application and Small Claim Rules) Amendment (Miscellaneous) 2004 (SSI 2004/197) (effective May 21, 2004) and substituted by the Act of Sederunt (Ordinary Cause, Summary Application, Summary Cause and Small Claim Rules) Amendment (Miscellaneous) 2007 (SSI 2007/6) (effective January 29, 2007).

(3)[1] The list of witnesses intimated under paragraph (1) shall include the name, occupation (where known) and address of each intended witness and indicate whether the witness is considered to be a vulnerable witness within the meaning of section 11(1) of the Act of 2004 and whether any child witness notice or vulnerable witness application has been lodged in respect of that witness.

Applications in respect of time to pay directions, arrestments and time orders

D1.90

9A.4. An application for—

(a) a time to pay direction under section 1(1) of the Debtors (Scotland) Act 1987;

(b) the recall or restriction of an arrestment under section 2(3) or 3(1) of that Act; or

(c) a time order under section 129 of the Consumer Credit Act 1974,

in a cause which is defended, shall be made by motion lodged before the sheriff grants decree.

Chapter 10

Additional Procedure

Additional period for adjustment

D1.91

10.1.—(1) Where, under rule 9.12(4) (order at Options Hearing to proceed under Chapter 10), the sheriff orders that a cause shall proceed in accordance with the procedure in this Chapter, he shall continue the cause for adjustment for a period of 8 weeks.

(2) Paragraphs (2) and (3) of rule 9.8 (exchange and record of adjustments) shall apply to a cause in which a period for adjustment under paragraph (1) of this rule has been allowed as they apply to the period for adjustment under that rule.

Effect of sist on adjustment period

D1.92

10.2. Where a cause has been sisted, any period for adjustment before the sist shall be reckoned as part of the period for adjustment.

Variation of adjustment period

D1.93

10.3.—(1) At any time before the expiry of the period for adjustment the sheriff may close the record if parties, of consent or jointly, lodge a motion seeking such an order.

(2) The sheriff may, if satisfied that there is sufficient reason for doing so, extend the period for adjustment for such period as he thinks fit, if any party—

(a) lodges a motion seeking such an order; and

(b) lodges a copy of the record adjusted to the date of lodging of the motion.

(3) A motion lodged under paragraph (2) shall set out—

(a) the reasons for seeking an extension of the period for adjustment; and

(b) the period for adjustment sought.

Order for open record

D1.94

10.4. The sheriff may, at any time before the closing of the record in a cause to which this of his own motion or on the motion of a party, order any party to lodge a copy of the pleadings in the form of an open record containing any adjustments and amendments made as at the date of the order.

---

[1] As amended by the Act of Sederunt (Ordinary Cause, Summary Application, Summary Cause and Small Claim Rules) Amendment (Vulnerable Witnesses (Scotland) Act 2004) 2007 (SSI 2007/463) r.2(4) (effective November 1, 2007).

Closing record

10.5.—(1) On the expiry of the period for adjustment, the record shall be closed and, without the attendance of parties, the sheriff clerk shall forthwith— **D1.95**

    (a) prepare and sign an interlocutor recording the closing of the record and fixing the date of the Procedural Hearing under rule 10.6, which date shall be on the first suitable court day occurring not sooner than 21 days after the closing of the record; and

    (b) intimate the date of the hearing to each party.

(2) The pursuer shall, within 14 days after the date of the interlocutor closing the record, lodge a certified copy of the closed record in process.

(3) The closed record shall contain only the pleadings of the parties.

Procedural Hearing

10.6.—[1](1) At the Procedural Hearing, the sheriff shall seek to secure the expeditious progress of the cause by ascertaining from parties the matters in dispute and information about any other matter referred to in paragraph (3). **D1.96**

(2) It shall be the duty of parties to provide the sheriff with sufficient information to enable him to conduct the hearing as provided for in this rule.

(3) At the Procedural Hearing the sheriff shall—

    (a) appoint the cause to a proof and make such orders as to the extent of proof, the lodging of a joint minute of admissions or agreement, or such other matter as he thinks fit;

    (b) after having heard the parties and considered any note lodged under rule 22.1 (note of basis of preliminary plea), appoint the cause to a proof before answer and make such orders as to the extent of proof, the lodging of a joint minute of admissions or agreement, or such other matter as he thinks fit; or

    (c)[2] after having heard parties and considered any note lodged under rule 22.1, appoint the cause to a debate if satisfied that there is a preliminary matter of law which if established following debate would lead to decree in favour of any party, or to limitation of proof to any substantial degree.

    (d)[3] consider any child witness notice or vulnerable witness application that has been lodged where no order has been made, or

    (e)[4] ascertain whether there is or is likely to be a vulnerable witness within the meaning of section 11(1) of the Act of 2004 who is to give evidence at any proof or hearing and whether any order under section 12(1) of the Act of 2004 requires to be made.

(4)[5] For the purposes of rules 16.2 (decrees where party in default), 33.37 (decree by default in family action) and 33A.37 (decree by default in civil partnership action), a Procedural Hearing shall be a diet in accordance with those rules.

---

[1] As amended by the Act of Sederunt (Ordinary Cause Rules 1993 Amendment) (Case Management of Defended Family and Civil Partnership Actions) 2022 (SSI 2022/289) r.2(7) (effective 25 September 2023 subject to transitional provision specified in SSI 2022/289 r.3).

[2] As amended by the Act of Sederunt (Ordinary Cause, Summary Application and Small Claim Rules) Amendment (Miscellaneous) 2004 (SSI 2004/197) r.2(9) (effective 21 May 2004).

[3] As inserted by the Act of Sederunt (Ordinary Cause, Summary Application, Summary Cause and Small Claim Rules) Amendment (Vulnerable Witnesses (Scotland) Act 2004) 2007 (SSI 2007/463) r.2(5) (effective 1 November 2007).

[4] As inserted by the Act of Sederunt (Ordinary Cause, Summary Application, Summary Cause and Small Claim Rules) Amendment (Vulnerable Witnesses (Scotland) Act 2004) 2007 (SSI 2007/463) r.2(5) (effective 1 November 2007).

[5] As amended by the Act of Sederunt (Ordinary Cause and Summary Application Rules) Amendment (Miscellaneous) 2006 (SSI 2006/410) (effective 18 August 2006).

(5)[1]   Where the cause is appointed, under paragraph (3), to a proof or proof before answer, the sheriff shall consider whether a pre-proof hearing should be fixed under rule 28A.1.

Chapter 11

The Process

Form and lodging of parts of process

D1.97

11.1.   All parts of process shall be written, typed or printed on A4 size paper of durable quality and shall be lodged, unbacked and unfolded, with the sheriff clerk.

Custody of process

D1.98

11.2.—(1)   The initial writ, and all other parts of process lodged in a cause, shall be placed by the sheriff clerk in the process folder.

(2)   The initial writ, interlocutor sheets, borrowing receipts and the process folder shall remain in the custody of the sheriff clerk.

(3)   The sheriff clerk may, on cause shown, authorise the initial writ to be borrowed by the pursuer, his solicitor or the solicitor's authorised clerk.

Borrowing and returning of process

D1.99

11.3.—(1)   Subject to paragraph (3), a process, or any part of a process which may be borrowed, may be borrowed only by a solicitor or by his authorised clerk.

(2)   All remedies competent to enforce the return of a borrowed process may proceed on the warrant of the court from the custody of which the process was obtained.

(3)   A party litigant—

(a)   may borrow a process only—

(i)   with leave of the sheriff; and

(ii)   subject to such conditions as the sheriff may impose; or

(b)   may inspect a process and obtain copies, where practicable, from the sheriff clerk.

(4)   The sheriff may, on the motion of any party, ordain any other party who has borrowed a part of process to return it within such time as the sheriff thinks fit.

Failure to return parts of process

D1.100

11.4.—(1)   Where a solicitor or party litigant has borrowed any part of process and fails to return it for any diet or hearing at which it is required, the sheriff may impose on such solicitor or party litigant a fine not exceeding £50, which shall be payable to the sheriff clerk; but an order imposing a fine may, on cause shown, be recalled by the sheriff.

(2)   An order made under this rule shall not be subject to appeal.

Replacement of lost documents

D1.101

11.5.   Where any part of process is lost or destroyed, a copy of it, authenticated in such manner as the sheriff thinks fit, may be substituted for and shall, for the purposes of the cause to which the process relates, be treated as having the same force and effect as the original.

Intimation of parts of process and adjustments

D1.102

11.6.—[2](1)   After a notice of intention to defend has been lodged, any party lodging a part of process or making an adjustment to his pleadings shall, at the same

---

[1] As amended by the Act of Sederunt (Ordinary Cause and Summary Application Rules) Amendment (Miscellaneous) 2006 (SSI 2006/410) (effective 18 August 2006).

[2] As amended by SI 1996/2445 (effective 1 November 1996).

time, intimate such lodging or adjustment to every other party who has entered the process by delivering to every other party a copy of each part of process or adjustment, including, where practicable, copies of any documentary production.

(2) Unless otherwise provided in these Rules, the party required to give intimation under paragraph (1) shall deliver to every other party who has entered the process a copy of the part of process or adjustment or other document, as the case may be, by—

    (a) any of the methods of service provided for in Chapter 5 (citation, service and intimation); or

    (b) where intimation is to a party represented by a solicitor—

        (i) personal delivery,

        (ii) facsimile transmission,

        (iii) first class ordinary post,

        (iv) delivery to a document exchange,

        to that solicitor.

(3) Subject to paragraph (4), where intimation is given under—

    (a) paragraph (2)(b)(i) or (ii), it shall be deemed to have been given—

        (i) on the day of transmission or delivery where it is given before 5.00 p.m. on any day; or

        (ii) on the day after transmission or delivery where it is given after 5.00 p.m. on any day; or

    (b) paragraph (2)(b)(iii) or (iv), it shall be deemed to have been given on the day after posting or delivery.

(4) Where intimation is given or, but for this paragraph, would be deemed to be given on a Saturday, Sunday or public or court holiday, it shall be deemed to have been given on the next day on which the sheriff clerk's office is open for civil court business.

Retention and disposal of parts of process by sheriff clerk

11.7.—[1](1) Where any cause has been finally determined and the period for making an appeal has expired without an appeal having been made, the sheriff clerk shall—

D1.103

    (a) retain—

        (i) the initial writ;

        (ii) any closed record;

        (iii) the interlocutor sheets;

        (iv) any joint minute;

        (v) any offer and acceptance of tender;

        (vi) any report from a person of skill;

        (vii) any affidavit; and

        (viii) any extended shorthand notes of the proof; and

    (b) dispose of all other parts of process (except productions) in such a manner as seems appropriate.

(2) Where an appeal has been made on the final determination of the cause, the sheriff clerk shall exercise his duties mentioned in paragraph (1) after the final disposal of the appeal and any subsequent procedure.

---

[1] As amended by the Act of Sederunt (Rules of the Court of Session, Sheriff Appeal Court Rules and Sheriff Court Rules Amendment) (Sheriff Appeal Court) 2015 (SSI 2015/419) r.5 (effective 1 January 2016).

Uplifting of productions from process

D1.104   **11.8.**—(1)[1,2] Where a party has lodged productions in a cause, that party must uplift the productions from process within the period specified in paragraph (1A).

(1A) The period is within 14 days after—

(a) the expiry of the period within which an appeal may be made following final determination of the cause, if no appeal is made; or

(b) the date on which such an appeal is finally disposed of.

(2) Where any production has not been uplifted as required by paragraph (1), the sheriff clerk shall intimate to—

(a) the solicitor who lodged the production, or

(b) where no solicitor is acting, the party himself or such other party as seems appropriate,

that if he fails to uplift the production within 28 days after the date of such intimation, it will be disposed of in such a manner as the sheriff directs.

Chapter 12

Interlocutors

Signature of interlocutors by sheriff clerk

D1.105   **12.1.** In accordance with any directions given by the Sheriff Principal, any interlocutor other than a final interlocutor may be written and signed by the sheriff clerk and—

(a) any interlocutor written and signed by a sheriff clerk shall be treated for all purposes as if it had been written and signed by the sheriff; and

(b) any extract of such an interlocutor shall not be invalid by reason only of its being written and signed by a sheriff clerk.

Further provisions in relation to interlocutors

D1.106   **12.2.**—[3](1) The sheriff may sign an interlocutor when outwith his or her sheriffdom.

(2) At any time before extract, the sheriff may correct any clerical or incidental error in an interlocutor or note attached to it.

(3) Paragraphs (4) and (5) apply in any cause other than—

(a) an undefended family action within the meaning of rule 33.1(1); or

(b) an undefended civil partnership action within the meaning of rule 33A.1(1).

(4) At the conclusion of any hearing in which evidence has been led, the sheriff shall either—

(a) pronounce an extempore judgment in accordance with rule 12.3; or

(b) reserve judgment in accordance with rule 12.4.

(5) In circumstances other than those mentioned in paragraph (4), the sheriff may, and must when requested by a party, append to the interlocutor a note setting out the reasons for the decision.

(6) A party must make a request under paragraph (5) in writing within 7 days of the date of the interlocutor.

---

[1] As amended by the Act of Sederunt (Rules of the Court of Session, Sheriff Appeal Court Rules and Sheriff Court Rules Amendment) (Sheriff Appeal Court) 2015 (SSI 2015/419) r.5 (effective 1 January 2016).

[2] As substituted by the Act of Sederunt (Sheriff Appeal Court Rules 2015 and Sheriff Court Rules Amendment) (Miscellaneous) 2016 (SSI 2016/194) r.3 (effective 7 July 2016).

[3] As substituted by the Act of Sederunt (Sheriff Court Rules) (Miscellaneous Amendments) 2012 (SSI 2012/188) para.2 (effective 1 August 2012).

(7) Where a party requests a note of reasons other than in accordance with paragraph (6), the sheriff may provide such a note.

Extempore judgments

12.3.—[1](1) This rule applies where a sheriff pronounces an extempore judgment in accordance with rule 12.2(4)(a).

D1.107

(2) The sheriff must state briefly the grounds of his or her decision, including the reasons for his or her decision on any questions of fact or law or of admissibility of evidence.

(3) The sheriff may, and must if requested to do so by a party, append to the interlocutor a note setting out the matters referred to in paragraph (2) and his or her findings in fact and law.

(4) A party must make a request under paragraph (3) in writing within 7 days of the date of the extempore judgment.

(5) Where a party requests a note of reasons other than in accordance with paragraph (4), the sheriff may provide such a note.

Reserved judgments

12.4.—[2](1) This rule applies where a sheriff reserves judgment in accordance with rule 12.2(4)(b).

D1.108

(2) The sheriff must give to the sheriff clerk—

(a) an interlocutor giving effect to the sheriff's decision and incorporating findings in fact and law; and

(b) a note stating briefly the grounds of his or her decision, including the reasons for his or her decision on any questions of fact or law or of admissibility of evidence.

(3) The date of the interlocutor is the date on which it is received by the sheriff clerk.

(4) The sheriff clerk must forthwith send a copy of the documents mentioned in paragraph (2) to each party.

Chapter 13

Party Minuter Procedure

Annotations to Chapters 13 to 18 by Sheriff Iain Peebles.

Person claiming title and interest to enter process as defender

13.1.—(1) A person who has not been called as a defender or third party may apply by minute for leave to enter a process as a party minuter and to lodge defences.

D1.109

(2) A minute under paragraph (1) shall specify—

(a) the applicant's title and interest to enter the process; and

(b) the grounds of the defence he proposes to state.

(3) Subject to paragraph (4), after hearing the applicant and any party, the sheriff may—

(a) if he is satisfied that the applicant has shown title and interest to enter the process, grant the applicant leave to enter the process as a party minuter and to lodge defences; and

(b) make such order as to expenses or otherwise as he thinks fit.

---

[1] As inserted by the Act of Sederunt (Sheriff Court Rules) (Miscellaneous Amendments) 2012 (SSI 2012/188) para.2 (effective 1 August 2012).

[2] As inserted by the Act of Sederunt (Sheriff Court Rules) (Miscellaneous Amendments) 2012 (SSI 2012/188) para.2 (effective 1 August 2012).

(4)[1] Where an application under paragraph (1) is made after the closing of the record or in a personal injuries action subject to personal injuries procedure after the date upon which the record is required to be lodged, the sheriff shall only grant leave under paragraph (3) if he is satisfied as to the reason why earlier application was not made.

Procedure following leave to enter process

D1.110
13.2.—(1)[2] Where a party minuter lodges answers, the sheriff clerk shall fix a date and time under rule 9.2 for a hearing under rule 9.12 (Options Hearing) as if the party minuter had lodged a notice of intention to defend and the period of notice had expired on the date for lodging defences.

(2) At the Options Hearing, or at any time thereafter, the sheriff may grant such decree or other order as he thinks fit.

(3) A decree or other order against the party minuter shall have effect and be extractable in the same way as a decree or other order against a defender.

(4)[3] Paragraphs (1), (2) and (3) shall not apply to a personal injuries action which is subject to personal injuries procedure.

(5)[4] Where the sheriff grants an application under rule 13.1 in a personal injuries action which is subject to personal injuries procedure, the sheriff may make such further order as he thinks fit.

GENERAL NOTE

D1.111
The procedure set out in this rule is appropriate where a person believes he has title and interest to defend an action but he has not been called as a defender or introduced as a third party by a defender using third party procedure. This rule allows a minute to be lodged setting forth their title, interest and proposed ground of defence.

It is a matter of discretion for the court whether a person who establishes title and interest should be granted leave to enter the process in terms of this Rule of Court. If allowed to enter the process, defences are lodged in the usual form.

It may not be appropriate to allow the party to be sisted where no defence which has a reasonable chance of success has been stated (see: *Glasgow Corporation v Regent Oil Company Ltd* , 1971 S.L.T. (Sh.Ct) 61 per Sheriff Principal Sir Allan Walker at 62). It is important that a reasonably full statement of the proposed defence is set forth in the minute. For examples of situations where it was held not to be appropriate to grant see: *Laing's Sewing Machine Company v Norrie & Sons* , 1877 5 R. 29 and *Aberdeen Grit Company Ltd v The Corporation of the City of Aberdeen* , 1948 S.L.T. (N.) 44 (although the latter case may have been decided on a question of title and interest).

"after closing of the record'.

before leave is granted to enter the process the court must in addition be satisfied that there is a proper reason why an earlier application was not made.

---

[1] As amended by the Act of Sederunt (Ordinary Cause Rules Amendment) (Personal Injuries Actions) 2009 (SSI 2009/285) r.2 (effective 2 November 2009).
[2] As amended by SI 1996/2445 (effective 1 November 1996).
[3] As inserted by the Act of Sederunt (Ordinary Cause Rules Amendment) (Personal Injuries Actions) 2009 (SSI 2009/285) r.2 (effective November 2, 2009).
[4] As inserted by the Act of Sederunt (Ordinary Cause Rules Amendment) (Personal Injuries Actions) 2009 (SSI 2009/285) r.2 (effective November 2, 2009).

"procedure following leave to enter".

broadly follows that set out in Chapter 9.

Chapter 13A[1]

Interventions by the Commission for Equality and Human Rights

Interpretation

13A.1. In this Chapter "the CEHR" means the Commission for Equality and Human Rights.

D1.112

Interventions by the CEHR

13A.2.—(1) The CEHR may apply to the sheriff for leave to intervene in any cause in accordance with this Chapter.

D1.113

(2) This Chapter is without prejudice to any other entitlement of the CEHR by virtue of having title and interest in relation to the subject matter of any proceedings by virtue of section 30(2) of the Equality Act 2006 or any other enactment to seek to be sisted as a party in those proceedings.

(3) Nothing in this Chapter shall affect the power of the sheriff to make such other direction as he considers appropriate in the interests of justice.

(4) Any decision of the sheriff in proceedings under this Chapter shall be final and not subject to appeal.

Applications to intervene

13A.3.—(1) An application for leave to intervene shall be by way of minute of intervention in Form O7A and the CEHR shall—

D1.114

    (a) send a copy of it to all the parties; and

    (b) lodge it in process, certifying that subparagraph (a) has been complied with.

(2) A minute of intervention shall set out briefly—

    (a) the CEHR's reasons for believing that the proceedings are relevant to a matter in connection with which the CEHR has a function;

    (b) the issue in the proceedings which the CEHR wishes to address; and

    (c) the propositions to be advanced by the CEHR and the CEHR's reasons for believing that they are relevant to the proceedings and that they will assist the sheriff.

(3) The sheriff may—

    (a) refuse leave without a hearing;

    (b) grant leave without a hearing unless a hearing is requested under paragraph (4);

    (c) refuse or grant leave after such a hearing.

(4) A hearing, at which the applicant and the parties may address the court on the matters referred to in paragraph (6)(c), may be held if, within 14 days of the minute of intervention being lodged, any of the parties lodges a request for a hearing.

(5) Any diet in pursuance of paragraph (4) shall be fixed by the sheriff clerk who shall give written intimation of the diet to the CEHR and all the parties.

(6) The sheriff may grant leave only if satisfied that—

    (a) the proceedings are relevant to a matter in connection with which the CEHR has a function;

    (b) the propositions to be advanced by the CEHR are relevant to the proceedings and are likely to assist him; and

---

[1] As inserted by the Act of Sederunt (Sheriff Court Rules) (Miscellaneous Amendments) 2008 (SSI 2008/223) r.4(2) (effective July 1, 2008).

(c) the intervention will not unduly delay or otherwise prejudice the rights of the parties, including their potential liability for expenses.

(7) In granting leave the sheriff may impose such terms and conditions as he considers desirable in the interests of justice, including making provision in respect of any additional expenses incurred by the parties as a result of the intervention.

(8) The sheriff clerk shall give written intimation of a grant or refusal of leave to the CEHR and all the parties.

Form of intervention

D1.115
13A.4.—(1) An intervention shall be by way of a written submission which (including any appendices) shall not exceed 5000 words.

(2) The CEHR shall lodge the submission and send a copy of it to all the parties by such time as the sheriff may direct.

(3) The sheriff may in exceptional circumstances—

(a) allow a longer written submission to be made;

(b) direct that an oral submission is to be made.

(4) Any diet in pursuance of paragraph (3)(b) shall be fixed by the sheriff clerk who shall give written intimation of the diet to the CEHR and all the parties.

Chapter 13B[1]

Interventions by the Scottish Commission for Human Rights

Interpretation

D1.116
13B.1. In this Chapter—

"the Act of 2006" means the Scottish Commission for Human Rights Act 2006; and

"the SCHR" means the Scottish Commission for Human Rights.

Application to intervene

D1.117
13B.2.—(1) An application for leave to intervene under section 14(2)(a) of the Act of 2006 shall be by way of minute of intervention in Form O7B and the SCHR shall—

(a) send a copy of it to all the parties; and

(b) lodge it in process, certifying that subparagraph (a) has been complied with.

(2) In granting leave the sheriff may impose such terms and conditions as he considers desirable in the interests of justice, including making provision in respect of any additional expenses incurred by the parties as a result of the intervention.

(3) The sheriff clerk shall give written intimation of a grant or refusal of leave to the SCHR and all the parties.

(4) Any decision of the sheriff in proceedings under this Chapter shall be final and not subject to appeal.

Invitation to intervene

D1.118
13B.3.—(1) An invitation to intervene under section 14(2)(b) of the Act of 2006 shall be in Form O7C and the sheriff clerk shall send a copy of it to the SCHR and all the parties.

(2) An invitation under paragraph (1) shall be accompanied by—

(a) a copy of the pleadings in the proceedings; and

---

[1] As inserted by the Act of Sederunt (Sheriff Court Rules) (Miscellaneous Amendments) 2008 (SSI 2008/223) r.4(2) (effective July 1, 2008).

(b) such other documents relating to those proceedings as the sheriff thinks relevant.

(3) In issuing an invitation under section 14(2)(b) of the Act of 2006, the sheriff may impose such terms and conditions as he considers desirable in the interests of justice, including making provision in respect of any additional expenses incurred by the parties as a result of the intervention.

Form of intervention

13B.4.—(1) An intervention shall be by way of a written submission which (including any appendices) shall not exceed 5000 words.   **D1.119**

(2) The SCHR shall lodge the submission and send a copy of it to all the parties by such time as the sheriff may direct.

(3) The sheriff may in exceptional circumstances—

(a) allow a longer written submission to be made;

(b) direct that an oral submission is to be made.

(4) Any diet in pursuance of paragraph (3)(b) shall be fixed by the sheriff clerk who shall give written intimation of the diet to the SCHR and all the parties.

Chapter 14

Applications by Minute

Application of this Chapter

14.1.—(1) Where an application may be made by minute, the form of the minute and the procedure to be adopted shall, unless otherwise provided in these Rules, be in accordance with this Chapter.   **D1.120**

(2)[1] This Chapter shall not apply to—

(a) a minute of amendment;

(b) a minute of abandonment; or

(c) a joint minute.

GENERAL NOTE

The procedure set out in this rule is appropriate where a party is applying to the court for a decision on matters which cannot be dealt with by motion, and require a crave, supporting averments and plea-in-law.   **D1.120.1**

Form of minute   **D1.121**

14.2. A minute to which this Chapter applies shall contain—

(a) a crave;

(b) where appropriate, a condescendence in the form of a statement of facts supporting the crave; and

(c) where appropriate, pleas-in-law.

GENERAL NOTE

"Form of Minutes" In all essential matters a minute will be in the same form as an Initial Writ.   **D1.121.1**

Lodging of minutes   **D1.122**

14.3.—[2](1) Before intimating any minute, the minuter shall lodge the minute in process.

(2) On the lodging of a minute, and any document under rule 21.1(1)(b) (lodging documents founded on or adopted), the sheriff—

(a) may make an order for answers to be lodged;

(b) may order intimation of the minute without making an order for answers; or

---

[1] As amended by SI 1996/2445 (effective 1 November 1996).
[2] Substituted by SI 1996/2445 (effective 1 November 1996).

    (c) where he considers it appropriate for the expeditious disposal of the minute or for any other specified reason, may fix a hearing.

(3) Any answers ordered to be lodged under paragraph (2)(a) shall, unless otherwise ordered by the sheriff, be lodged within 14 days after the date of intimation of the minute.

(4) Where the sheriff fixes a hearing under paragraph (2)(c), the interlocutor fixing that hearing shall specify whether—

    (a) answers are to be lodged;

    (b) the sheriff will hear evidence at that hearing; and

    (c) the sheriff will allow evidence by affidavit.

(5) Any answers or affidavit evidence ordered to be lodged under paragraph (4) shall be lodged within such time as shall be specified in the interlocutor of the sheriff.

(6) The following rules shall not apply to any hearing fixed under paragraph (2)(c):—

    rule 14.7 (opposition where no order for answers made),

    rule 14.8 (hearing of minutes where no opposition or no answers lodged),

    rule 14.10 (notice of opposition or answers lodged).

(7) The sheriff clerk shall forthwith return the minute to the minuter with any interlocutor pronounced by the sheriff.

GENERAL NOTE

D1.122.1   *"Lodging of Minutes"* After the lodging of the minute in process, depending on the nature of the decision sought and the whole circumstances as set out in the minute, the sheriff will make one of three orders regarding further procedure. If a hearing is fixed by the sheriff at this stage the interlocutor fixing this will further state (a) if evidence is to be heard at the hearing and (b) if evidence will be allowed in the form of affidavits. The normal reason for fixing a hearing at this stage is urgency in having the matter dealt with.

D1.123   **Intimation of minutes**

    14.4.—[1](1) The party lodging a minute shall, on receipt from the sheriff clerk of the minute, intimate to every other party including any person referred to in rule 14.13(1)—

    (a) a notice in Form G7A, G7B or G7C, as the case may be, by any of the methods provided for in rule 14.5 (methods of intimation); and

    (b) a copy of—

      (i) the minute;

      (ii) any interlocutor; and

      (iii) any document referred to in the minute.

(2) The sheriff may, on cause shown, dispense with intimation.

GENERAL NOTE

D1.123.1   *"Intimation of Minutes"* Intimation only occurs following the sheriff pronouncing an interlocutor in terms of 14.3(2).

D1.124   **Methods of intimation**

    14.5.—[2](1) Intimation of a minute may be given by—

    (a) any of the methods of service provided for in Chapter 5 (citation, service and intimation); or

    (b) where intimation is to a party represented by a solicitor, by—

      (i) personal delivery,

      (ii) facsimile transmission,

---

[1] Inserted by SI 1996/2445 (effective 1 November 1996).
[2] Inserted by SI 1996/2445 (effective 1 November 1996).

(iii) first class ordinary post, or

(iv) delivery to a document exchange, to that solicitor.

(2) Where intimation is given—

(a) under paragraph (1)(b)(i) or (ii), it shall be deemed to have been given—

(i) on the day of transmission or delivery where it is given before 5.00 p.m. on any day; or

(ii) on the day after transmission or delivery where it is given after 5.00 p.m. on any day; or

(b) under paragraph 1(b)(iii) or (iv), it shall be deemed to have been given on the day after the date of posting or delivery.

GENERAL NOTE

"Method of Intimation" The methods of intimation are the same as in respect to motions.   **D1.124.1**

Return of minute with evidence of intimation   **D1.125**

14.6.[1] Where intimation of any minute has been given, the minute and a certificate of intimation in Form G8 shall be returned to the sheriff clerk within 5 days after the date of intimation.

Opposition where no order for answers made

14.7.—[2](1) Where a party seeks to oppose a minute lodged under rule 14.3   **D1.126** (lodging of minutes) in which no order for answers has been made under paragraph (2)(a) of that rule, that party shall, within 14 days after the date of intimation of the minute to him—

(a) complete a notice of opposition in Form G9;

(b) lodge the notice with the sheriff clerk; and

(c) intimate a copy of that notice to every other party.

(2) Rule 14.5 (methods of intimation) and rule 14.6 (return of minute with evidence of intimation) shall apply to intimation of opposition to a minute under paragraph (1)(c) of this rule as they apply to intimation of a minute.

(3) The sheriff may, on cause shown, reduce or dispense with the period for lodging the notice mentioned in paragraph (1)(b).

GENERAL NOTE

The procedure to be followed where a minute is opposed and the sheriff has pronounced an interlocu-   **D1.126.1** tor in terms of paragraph 2(a) of the Rule is as set out in 14.7.

Hearing of minutes where no opposition or no answers lodged   **D1.127**

14.8.—[3](1) Where no notice of opposition is lodged or where no answers have been lodged to the minute within the time allowed, the minute shall be determined by the sheriff in chambers without the attendance of parties, unless the sheriff otherwise directs.

(2) Where the sheriff requires to hear a party on a minute, the sheriff clerk shall—

(a) fix a date, time and place for the party to be heard; and

(b) inform that party—

(i) of that date, time and place; and

(ii) of the reasons for the sheriff wishing to hear him.

In the same way as with an unopposed motion an unopposed minute may be determined by the sheriff without the necessity of parties attending. As with an

---

[1] Inserted by SI 1996/2445 (effective 1 November 1996).
[2] Inserted by SI 1996/2445 (effective 1 November 1996).
[3] Inserted by SI 1996/2445 (effective 1 November 1996).

unopposed motion, if the sheriff believes it necessary he may order the attendance of parties to hear from them in relation to the minute.

Intimation of interlocutor

D1.128 **14.9.**[1] Where a minute has been determined in accordance with rule 14.8 (hearing of minutes where no opposition or no answers lodged), the sheriff clerk shall intimate the interlocutor determining that minute to the parties forthwith.

Notice of opposition or answers lodged

D1.129 **14.10.—**[2](1) Where a notice of opposition has, or answers have, been lodged to the minute, the sheriff clerk shall—

> (a) assign a date, time and place for a hearing on the first suitable court day after the date of the lodging of the notice of opposition or answers, as the case may be; and
>
> (b) intimate that date, time and place to the parties.

(2) The interlocutor fixing a hearing under paragraph (1) shall specify whether the sheriff will hear evidence at the hearing or receive evidence by affidavit.

GENERAL NOTE

D1.129.1 *"Notice of Opposition or Answers Lodged"*. If a hearing is fixed and a notice of opposition or answers are lodged then, as with a hearing ordered in terms of paragraph 2(c), the sheriff will specify whether evidence will be heard and if so whether affidavit evidence will be allowed. If answers have been lodged, this interlocutor will normally also allow an adjustment period. Usually adjustment will be allowed until 2 weeks before the date of the hearing. The interlocutor may also direct the lodging of a record, however, the lodging thereof is not mandatory in terms of this rule. If a case proceeds to a hearing in which evidence is to be led the procedure will be the same as at a proof.

Orders under section 11 of the Children (Scotland) Act 1995

D1.130 **14.10A.—**[3, 4](1) This rule applies where a notice of opposition or answers are lodged in respect of a minute including a crave for an order under section 11 of the Children (Scotland) Act 1995 (court orders relating to parental responsibilities etc.).

(2) The sheriff, having regard to the measures referred to in rules 33.36J or 33A.36J (Initial Case Management Hearing), may make such orders as the sheriff considers appropriate to ensure the expeditious resolution of the issues in dispute.

Procedure for hearing

D1.131 **14.11.—**[5](1) A certified copy of the interlocutor assigning a hearing under this Chapter and requiring evidence to be led shall be sufficient warrant to a sheriff officer to cite a witness on behalf of a party.

(2) At the hearing, the sheriff shall hear parties on the minute and any answers lodged, and may determine the minute or may appoint such further procedure as he considers necessary.

Consent to minute

D1.132 **14.12.**[6] Subject to paragraph (2) of rule 14.8 (hearing of minutes where no opposition or no answers lodged), where all parties to the action indicate to the sheriff,

---

[1] Inserted by SI 1996/2445 (effective 1 November 1996).

[2] Inserted by SI 1996/2445 (effective 1 November 1996).

[3] As amended by the Act of Sederunt (Ordinary Cause Rules 1993 Amendment) (Case Management of Defended Family and Civil Partnership Actions) 2022 (SSI 2022/289) r.2(8) (effective 25 September 2023 subject to transitional provision specified in SSI 2022/289 r.3).

[4] As inserted by the Act of Sederunt (Sheriff Court Rules) (Miscellaneous Amendments) (No.2) 2013 (SI 2013/139) para.2 (effective 3 June 2013).

[5] Inserted by SI 1996/2445 (effective 1 November 1996).

[6] Inserted by SI 1996/2445 (effective 1 November 1996).

by endorsement of the minute or otherwise in writing, their intention to consent to the minute, the sheriff may forthwith determine the minute in chambers without the appearance of parties.

Procedure following grant of minute

14.13.—[1](1) Where the minute includes a crave seeking leave—   **D1.133**
    (a) for a person—
        (i) to be sisted as a party to the action, or
        (ii) to appear in the proceedings, or
    (b) for the cause to be transferred against the representatives of a party who has died or is under a legal incapacity,
the sheriff, on granting the minute, may order a hearing under rule 9.12 (Options Hearing) to be fixed or may appoint such further procedure as he thinks fit.

(2) Where an Options Hearing is ordered under paragraph (1), the sheriff clerk shall—
    (a) fix a date and time for such hearing, which date, unless the sheriff otherwise directs, shall be on the first suitable court day occurring not sooner than 10 weeks after the date of the interlocutor of the sheriff ordering such hearing be fixed;
    (b) forthwith intimate to the parties in Form G5—
        (i) where appropriate, the last date for lodging defences;
        (ii) where appropriate, the last date for adjustment; and
        (iii) the date of the Options Hearing; and
    (c) prepare and sign an interlocutor recording those dates.

(3) For the purpose of fixing the date for the Options Hearing referred to in paragraph (1), the date of granting the minute shall be deemed to be the date of expiry of the period of notice.

GENERAL NOTE

"Expenses". If expenses are sought the sheriff will deal with the issue in accordance with the general   **D1.133.1**
rules in respect of the awarding of expenses.

Chapter 15[2]   **D1.134**

Motions

Application of this Chapter

15.A1.—[3](1) This Chapter applies to any cause other than a cause to which   **D1.134.1**
Chapter 15A applies.

Lodging of motions

15.1.—(1) A motion may be made—   **D1.134.2**
    (a) orally with leave of the court during any hearing of a cause; or
    (b) by lodging a written motion in Form G6.

(2) Subject to paragraph (3), a written motion shall be lodged with the sheriff clerk within 5 days after the date of intimation of the motion required by rule 15.2 (intimation of motions) with—
    (a) a certificate of intimation in Form G8; and

---

[1] Inserted by SI 1996/2445 (effective 1 November 1996).
[2] Substituted by SI 1996/2445 (effective 1 November 1996).
[3] As amended by the Act of Sederunt (Rules of the Court of Session 1994 and Sheriff Court Rules Amendment) (No. 2) (Personal Injury and Remits) 2015 (SSI 2015/227) para.8 (effective 22 September 2015).

(b) so far as practicable any document referred to in the written motion and not already lodged in process.

(3) Where the period for lodging opposition to the motion is varied under rule 15.2(4) (variation of and dispensing with period of intimation) to a period of 5 days or less, the written motion and certificate to be lodged in terms of paragraph (2) shall be lodged no later than the day on which the period for lodging opposition expires.

GENERAL NOTE

D1.134.3   A motion is the means by which the court is requested to make an order either procedural or substantive in the course of a depending action.

"*Orally with Leave of the Court*". The vast majority of motions are made by lodging a written motion. However, it is competent to make an oral motion at the bar. Such motions most frequently occur in the course of a debate or proof when a party seeks leave to amend. Motions made during the course of a hearing may only be made with the leave of the court. The court will normally only allow such a motion to be made where there is firstly a good reason why a written motion was not lodged and secondly where there is no prejudice to the other party. Given the issue of prejudice to the other party it is often only with the consent of the other party that such a motion is allowed to be made. Where allowed to be made at the bar, such motions are often continued by the court in order to allow the other party time to prepare a reply and by this means the issue of possible prejudice to the other party is obviated.

Intimation of motions

D1.135   **15.2.**—(1) Subject to paragraphs (4) and (7), a party intending to lodge a motion in accordance with rule 15.1(1)(b) (lodging written motion) shall intimate the motion in Form G7, and a copy of any document referred to in the motion, to every other party.

(2) Intimation of a motion may be given by—

(a) any of the methods of service provided for in Chapter 5 (citation, service and intimation); or

(b) where intimation is to a party represented by a solicitor, by—

(i) personal delivery,

(ii) facsimile transmission,

(iii) first class ordinary post, or

(iv) delivery to a document exchange, to that solicitor.

(3) Where intimation is given—

(a) under paragraph (2)(b)(i) or (ii), it shall be deemed to have been given—

(i) on the day of transmission or delivery where it is given before 5.00 p.m. on any day; or

(ii) on the day after transmission or delivery where it is given after 5.00 p.m. on any day; or

(b) under paragraph (2)(b)(iii) or (iv), it shall be deemed to have been given on the day after posting or delivery.

(4) The sheriff may, on the application of a party intending to lodge a written motion, vary the period of 7 days specified in rule 15.3(1)(c) for lodging opposition to the motion or dispense with intimation.

(5) An application under paragraph (4) shall be made in the written motion, giving reasons for such variation or dispensation.

(6) Where the sheriff varies the period within which notice of opposition is to be lodged under rule 15.3(1)(c), the form of intimation required under rule 15.2(1) (intimation of motion in Form G7) shall state the date by which such notice requires to be lodged.

(7) A joint motion by all parties lodged in Form G6 need not be intimated.

GENERAL NOTE

D1.135.1   "*Copy of any Document Referred to in the Motion*". Such a copy shall be intimated to every party and where practicable lodged in court.

"*Intimation of Motion and Intimation of Opposition to a Motion*". The method and timing of the intimation is the same in relation to both (see: 15.2(2) and (3)).

"*Intimation of Motion*". Intimation is in accordance with Chapter 5 except where the other party is represented by a solicitor where the forms of intimation are considerably widened.

Where such variation or dispensation is sought it should be sought in the written motion and must be supported by reasons. It should be noted that although lengthening of the period for lodging opposition is competent this is very rarely sought. Where shortening of the period is sought the usual reason given is urgency in having the matter dealt with by the court. The test as to whether the court will grant such shortening will be whether it is in the interests of justice to grant it, i.e. whether on balance the need for the matter being dealt with urgently outweighs any prejudice to the other party in shortening the period for lodging opposition.

"*Vary the Period for Lodging Opposition...or Dispense with Intimation*". As regards dispensing with intimation, this will only be granted on the basis of the most cogent of reasons. In terms of 15.5(7) where intimation has been dispensed with, the sheriff shall make such order as he thinks fit for intimation of his determination on those parties to whom intimation was dispensed with.

Opposition to motions

15.3.—(1) Where a party seeks to oppose a motion made in accordance with rule 15.1(1)(b) (written motion), he shall—

    (a)   complete a notice of opposition in Form G9;

    (b)   intimate a copy of that notice to every other party; and

    (c)   lodge the notice with the sheriff clerk within 7 days after the date of intimation of the motion or such other period as the sheriff may have determined under rule 15.2(6).

(2) Paragraphs (2) and (3) of rule 15.2 (methods and time of intimation of motions) shall apply to the intimation of opposition to a motion under paragraph (1)(b) of this rule as they apply to intimation under that rule.

D1.136

Consent to motions

15.4. Where a party consents to a written motion, he shall endorse the motion, or give notice to the sheriff clerk in writing, of his consent.

D1.137

Hearing of motions

15.5.—(1) Subject to paragraph (2), where no notice of opposition is lodged with the sheriff clerk within the period specified in rule 15.3(1)(c), or ordered by virtue of rule 15.2(4), the motion shall be determined by the sheriff in chambers without the appearance of parties, unless the sheriff otherwise directs.

(2) In accordance with any directions given by the sheriff principal, the sheriff clerk may determine any motion other than a motion which seeks a final interlocutor.

(3) Where the sheriff clerk considers that a motion dealt with by him under paragraph (2) should not be granted, he shall refer that motion to the sheriff who shall deal with it in accordance with paragraph (1).

(4) Where the sheriff requires to hear a party on a motion which is not opposed, the sheriff clerk shall—

    (a)   fix a date, time and place for the party to be heard, and

    (b)   inform that party—

        (i)   of that date, time and place; and

        (ii)   of the reasons for the sheriff wishing to hear him.

(5) Where a notice of opposition is lodged in accordance with rule 15.3(1), the sheriff clerk shall—

    (a)   assign a date, time and place, on the first suitable court day after the lodging of the notice of opposition, for the motion to be heard; and

    (b)   intimate that date, time and place to the parties.

(6) Where a motion has been determined under paragraph (1) or (2), the sheriff clerk shall intimate the interlocutor determining that motion to all parties forthwith.

(7) Where the sheriff, under paragraph (4) of rule 15.2, dispenses with intimation required by paragraph (1) of that rule, he shall make such order as he thinks fit

D1.138

for intimation of his determination of the motion to every party to the action in respect of whom intimation has been so dispensed with.

(8) Subject to paragraph (4), where all parties consent to a written motion, the sheriff may determine the motion in chambers without the appearance of parties.

(9) Subject to paragraph (4) where a joint motion of all parties in Form G6 is lodged with the sheriff clerk, the sheriff may determine the motion in chambers without the appearance of parties.

GENERAL NOTE

D1.138.1
"*Hearing of Motions*". Unlike in the Court of Session all unopposed motions may be granted without a hearing at which the appearance of counsel, solicitor or party litigant is necessary.

A sheriff principal may by direction delegate to the sheriff clerk the determination of any motions other than those which seek a final interlocutor. In practice the sheriffs principal have exercised this power in the same way and the list of motions which may be determined by the sheriff clerk is the same in each Sheriffdom. The motions which may be dealt with by the sheriff clerk are all minor and procedural.

An unopposed motion may be put out by a sheriff for a hearing. The sheriff will also give reasons for so ordering. Such a hearing may be procedural in nature or relate to the substance of the motion.

Lengthy Hearings. Where parties believe that an opposed motion is likely to require a lengthy hearing it is good practice to advise the sheriff clerk of the likelihood in order that necessary practical arrangements can be made for the hearing thereof.

Motions to sist

D1.139
15.6.—[1](1) Where a motion to sist is made, either orally or in writing in accordance with rule 15.1(1)(a) or (by—

    (a)   the reason for the sist shall be stated by the party seeking the sist; and

    (b)   that reason shall be recorded in the interlocutor.

(2) Where a cause has been sisted, the sheriff may, after giving parties an opportunity to be heard, recall the sist.

"*Expenses*". Often the issue of expenses is not raised at the stage which the motion is dealt with by the court. If the issue is raised then the sheriff will deal with it in accordance with the general rules in respect of the awarding of expenses.

Dismissal of action due to delay

D1.140
15.7.—[2](1) Any party to an action may, while that action is depending before the court, apply by written motion for the court to dismiss the action due to inordinate and inexcusable delay by another party or another party's agent in progressing the action, resulting in unfairness.

(2) A motion under paragraph (1) shall—

    (a)[3] include a statement of the grounds on which it is proposed that the motion should be allowed; and

    (b)   be lodged in accordance with rule 15.1.

(3) A notice of opposition to the motion in Form G9 shall include a statement of the grounds of opposition to the motion.

(4) In determining an application made under this rule, the court may dismiss the action if it appears to the court that—

    (a)   there has been an inordinate and inexcusable delay on the part of any party or any party's agent in progressing the action; and

    (b)   such delay results in unfairness specific to the factual circumstances, including the procedural circumstances, of that action.

---

[1] Inserted by SSI 2000/239 (effective 2 October 2000).

[2] As inserted by the Act of Sederunt (Sheriff Court Rules) (Miscellaneous Amendments) 2009 (SSI 2009/294) r.14 (effective 1 October 2009).

[3] As amended by the Act of Sederunt (Sheriff Court Rules) (Miscellaneous Amendments) 2010 (SSI 2010/279) r.7(1) (effective 29 July 2010).

(5)   In determining whether or not to dismiss an action under paragraph (4), the court shall take account of the procedural consequences, both for the parties and for the work of the court, of allowing the action to proceed.

Chapter 15A[1]

Motions Intimated and Lodged by Email

Application of this Chapter

15A.1.   This Chapter applies—

    (a)   to a personal injuries action within the meaning of Part A1 of Chapter 36 proceeding in the all-Scotland sheriff court;

    (b)   where each party to such an action has provided to the sheriff clerk an email address for the purpose of transacting motion business.

D1.140.1

Interpretation of this Chapter

15A.1A.—[2](1)   In this Chapter—

    "court day" means a day on which the sheriff clerk's office is open for civil court business;

    "court day 1" means the court day on which a motion is treated as being intimated under rule 15A.4;

    "court day 3" means the second court day after court day 1;

    "court day 4" means the third court day after court day 1;

    "lodging party" means the party lodging the motion;

    "receiving party" means a party receiving the intimation of the motion from the lodging party; and

    "transacting motion business" means—

        (a)   intimating and lodging motions;

        (b)   receiving intimation of motions;

        (c)   intimating consent or opposition to motions;

        (d)   receiving intimation of or opposition to motions.

(2)   In this Chapter, a reference to—

    (a)   the address of a party is a reference to the email address of—

        (i)   that party's solicitor; or

        (ii)   that party,

    included in the list maintained under rule 15A.2(4);

    (b)   the address of the court is a reference to the email address of the court included in that list under rule 15A.2(5).

D1.140.2

Provision of email addresses to sheriff clerk

15A.2.—(1)   A solicitor representing a party in an action of the sort mentioned in rule 15A.1(a) must provide to the sheriff clerk an email address for the purpose of transacting motion business.

(2)   A solicitor who does not have suitable facilities for transacting motion business by email may make a declaration in writing to that effect, which must be—

    (a)   sent to the sheriff clerk; and

D1.140.3

---

[1] As inserted by the Act of Sederunt (Rules of the Court of Session 1994 and Sheriff Court Rules Amendment) (No.2) (Personal Injury and Remits) 2015 (SSI 2015/227) para.8 (effective 22 September 2015).

[2] As re-numbered by the Act of Sederunt (Rules of the Court of Session 1994 and Sheriff Court Rules Amendment) (No.2) (Personal Injury and Remits) 2015 (SSI 2015/227) para.8 (effective 22 September 2015), as amended by the Act of Sederunt (Ordinary Cause Rules 1993 Amendment and Miscellaneous Amendments) 2015 (SSI 2015/296) r.4(2) (effective 22 September 2015).

(b)   intimated to each of the other parties to the cause.

(3)   A party to an action of the sort mentioned in rule 15A.1(a) who is not represented by a solicitor may provide to the sheriff clerk an email address for the purpose of transacting motion business.

(4)   The sheriff clerk must maintain a list of the email addresses provided for the purpose of transacting motion business, which must be published in up to date form on the website of the Scottish Courts and Tribunals Service.

(5)   The sheriff clerk must also include on that list an email address of the court for the purpose of lodging motions.

Making of motions

D1.140.4   **15A.3.**   A motion may be made—

(a)   orally with leave of the court during any hearing; or

(b)   by lodging it in accordance with this Chapter.

Intimation of motions by email

D1.140.5   **15A.4.**—(1)   Where—

(a)   a defender has lodged a notice of intention to defend under rule 9.1;

(b)   a party has lodged a minute or answers; or

(c)   provision is made in these Rules for the intimation of a motion to a party in accordance with this Part,

the lodging party must give intimation of his or her intention to lodge the motion, and of the terms of the motion, to every such party by sending an email in Form G6A (form of motion by email) to the addresses of every party.

(2)   The requirement under paragraph (1) to give intimation of a motion to a party by email does not apply where that party—

(a)   having lodged a notice of intention to defend, fails to lodge defences within the period for lodging those defences;

(b)   has not lodged answers within the period of notice for lodging those answers; or

(c)   has withdrawn or is deemed to have withdrawn the defences, minute or answers, as the case may be.

(3)   A motion intimated under this rule must be intimated not later than 5 p.m. on a court day.

Opposition to motions by email

D1.140.6   **15A.5.**—(1)   A receiving party must intimate any opposition to a motion by sending an email in Form G9A (form of opposition to motion by email) to the address of the lodging party.

(2)   Any opposition to a motion must be intimated to the lodging party not later than 5 p.m. on court day 3.

(3)   Late opposition to a motion must be sent to the address of the court and may only be allowed with the leave of the court, on cause shown.

Consent to motions by email

D1.140.7   **15A.6.**   Where a receiving party seeks to consent to a motion, that party may do so by sending an email confirming the consent to the address of the lodging party.

Lodging unopposed motions by email

D1.140.8   **15A.7.**—(1)   This rule applies where no opposition to a motion has been intimated.

(2)   The motion must be lodged by the lodging party not later than 12.30 p.m. on court day 4 by sending an email in Form G6A headed "Unopposed motion" to the address of the court.

(3) A motion lodged under paragraph (2) is to be determined by the court by 5 p.m. on court day 4.

(4) Where for any reason it is not possible for a motion lodged under paragraph (2) to be determined by 5 p.m. on court day 4, the sheriff clerk must advise the parties or their solicitors of that fact and give reasons.

Lodging opposed motions by email

15A.8.—(1) This rule applies where opposition to a motion has been intimated.　　**D1.140.9**

(2) The motion must be lodged by the lodging party not later than 12.30 p.m. on court day 4 by—

(a) sending an email in Form G6A headed "Opposed motion", to the address of the court;

(b) attaching to that email the opposition in Form G9A intimated by the receiving party to the lodging party.

(3) Where a motion is lodged under paragraph (2), the sheriff clerk must advise parties of the date on which the motion will be heard, which will be on the first suitable court day after court day 4.

Issuing of interlocutor by email

15A.9. Where the court pronounces an interlocutor determining a motion, the　**D1.140.10** sheriff clerk must email a copy of the interlocutor to the addresses of the lodging party and every receiving party.

Other periods of intimation etc. under these Rules

15A.10.—(1) Where a provision of these Rules, other than Chapter 15 (mo-　**D1.140.11** tions), provides for a period of intimation of—

(a) a motion;

(b) opposition to a motion; or

(c) consent to a motion,

other than the period mentioned in this Chapter, that period will apply instead of the period mentioned in this Chapter.

(2) Paragraph (1) applies whether or not the intimation period mentioned elsewhere in these Rules is referred to by a specific number of days.

(3) Where—

(a) every receiving party in a cause consents to a shorter period of intimation; or

(b) the court shortens the period of intimation,

the motion may be lodged by the lodging party, or heard or otherwise determined by the court at an earlier time and date than that which is specified in this Part.

Motions to sist

15A.11.—(1) Where a motion to sist is made—　　**D1.140.12**

(a) the reason for the sist must be stated by the party seeking the sist; and

(b) that reason must be recorded in the interlocutor.

(2) Where a cause has been sisted, the sheriff may, after giving parties an opportunity to be heard, recall the sist.

Dismissal of action due to delay

15A.12.—(1) Any party to an action may, while that action is depending before　**D1.140.13** the court, apply by motion for the court to dismiss the action due to inordinate and inexcusable delay by another party or another party's solicitor in progressing the action, resulting in unfairness.

(2) A motion under paragraph (1) must—

(a)   include a statement of the grounds on which it is proposed that the motion should be allowed; and

(b)   be lodged in accordance with rule 15A.3(b) (lodging of motions).

(3)   A notice of opposition to the motion in Form G9 (form of notice of opposition to motion or minute) or Form G9A (form of opposition to motion by email) must include a statement of the grounds of opposition to the motion.

(4)   In determining an application made under this rule, the sheriff may dismiss the action if it appears to the sheriff that—

(a)   there has been an inordinate and inexcusable delay on the part of any party or any party's solicitor in progressing the action; and

(b)   such delay results in unfairness specific to the factual circumstances, including the procedural circumstances, of that action.

(5)   In determining whether or not to dismiss an action under paragraph (4), the sheriff must take account of the procedural consequences, both for the parties and for the work of the court, of allowing the action to proceed.

[THE NEXT PARAGRAPH IS D1.141]

Chapter 16

Decrees by Default

Application of this Chapter

D1.141   **16.1.**[1]   This Chapter applies to any cause other than—

(a)   an action to which rule 33.37 (decree by default in family action) applies;

(aa)   an action to which rule 33A.37 (decree by default in a civil partnership action) applies;

(b)   an action of multiplepoinding;

(c)   a cause under the Presumption of Death (Scotland) Act 1977; or

(d)   a commercial action within the meaning of Chapter 40.

Decrees where party in default

D1.142   **16.2.**—(1)   In a cause to which this Chapter applies, where a party fails—

(a)   to lodge, or intimate the lodging of, any production or part of process within the period required under a provision in these Rules or an order of the sheriff,

(b)   to implement an order of the sheriff within a specified period,

(c)   to appear or be represented at any diet, or

(d)[2]   otherwise to comply with any requirement imposed upon that party by these Rules;

that party shall be in default.

(2)   Where a party is in default the sheriff may, as the case may be—

(a)   grant decree as craved with expenses;

(b)   grant decree of absolvitor with expenses;

(c)   dismiss the cause with expenses; or

(d)   make such other order as he thinks fit to secure the expeditious progress of the cause.

(3)   Where no party appears at a diet, the sheriff may dismiss the cause.

(4)   In this rule, "diet" includes—

---

[1] As amended by SSI 2001/8 (effective 1 March 2001).

[2] Inserted by the Act of Sederunt (Ordinary Cause and Summary Application Rules) Amendment (Miscellaneous) 2006 (SSI 2006/410) (effective 18 August 2006).

(a)   a hearing under rule 9.12 (Options Hearing);
(b)   a hearing under rule 10.6 (Procedural Hearing);
(c)   a proof or proof before answer; and
(d)   a debate.

Prorogation of time where party in default

16.3.   In an action to which this Chapter applies, the sheriff may, on cause shown, prorogate the time for lodging any production or part of process or for giving intimation or for implementing any order.

D1.143

GENERAL NOTE.

The purpose of the rule is to provide a discretionary remedy to the court in the event that a party to a defended action (being one in which a notice to defend has been lodged) prevents its proper progress by a failure to act in any of the ways specified in the rule.

D1.143.1

NATURE OF DECREE.

A decree by default is (a) a final judgment and (b) if granted after the lodging of defences, and if other than a decree of dismissal, is a decree *in foro* founding a plea of res judicata. If granted prior to the lodging of defences it will not found a plea of res judicata (see: *Esso Petroleum Company Ltd v Law* , 1956, S.C. 33). A decree by default may be obtained prior to the lodging of defences in the event that defences are not lodged timeously (see: OCR 9.6(1)); namely, on the failure to comply with the foregoing rule.

It is a matter for the discretion of the court whether it is appropriate to grant absolvitor or dismissal. In considering whether to grant *absolvitor* or dismissal it is suggested that the court has to consider the issue of whether a decree of *absolvitor* is proportionate to the default and thus in all the circumstances in the interests of justice (see further below).

Where the pursuer is in default decree of *absolvitor* would normally be pronounced. However, in the case of *Group 4 Total Security v Jaymarke Developments Ltd* , 1995 S.C.L.R. 303 where a closed record was lodged late the court held it appropriate to grant only decree of dismissal, thus leaving it open for the action to be re-raised.

Where the defender is in default, the decree normally granted is that craved for.

"*Where no party appears at a diet*" the appropriate decree is a decree of dismissal with a finding of no expenses due to or by either party (pronounced on the basis of want of insistence).

DISCRETION.

In the exercise of discretion whether to grant decree by default, it is for the court in exercising said discretion to see that the interests of justice are met. The court should have regard to the following broad guidelines laid down by the Inner House in considering the interests of justice.

(a)   The court should have regard to whether there is a proper claim or defence. See *McKelvie v Scottish Steel Scaffolding* , 1938 S.C. 278 per Lord Moncrieffe at 281:

> "I would be most reluctant, in any case in which prima facie there appeared to be a proper defence put forward to allow decree to pass against the defender without investigation of that defence. Even if carelessness on the part of the defender or others for whom he had been responsible had delayed the course of the procedure of the action, I should, in such a case, always be willing to entertain an application of relief."

(b)   The court should have regard to whether the default has arisen as a result of the behaviour of the party to the action or his agent. If the default is due to his agent this should not normally result in decree by default. The appropriate finding would be an adverse award of expenses, and perhaps an adverse award of expenses against the agent personally.

(c)   The court should have regard to the seriousness of the default.

"PROROGATION OF TIME WHERE PARTY IN DEFAULT".

The court is given the specific power to prorogate. Cause must be shown and again the court will apply the test of what is in the interests of justice.

Apart from the specific power of prorogation in the rule the court may also be moved to exercise the dispensing power in OCR 2.1.(1).

Generally, if a party fails to appear at a calling of a case, the court will be slow to grant decree unless it can be satisfied that there is likely to be no acceptable reason for the failure (see: *Canmore Housing Association v Scott*, 2003 G.W.D. 9-243). No matter how nominally or informally a party is represented at a diet it is not appropriate for the court to grant decree by default (see: *Samson v Fielding*, 2003 S.L.T. (Sh. Ct) 48).

Solicitor withdraws from acting. in these circumstances the court must fix a peremptory diet (OCR 24.2(1)).

Appeal against decree by default can be made without leave. (See: *GAS Construction Co Ltd v Schrader*, 1992 S.L.T. 528). Appeal against refusal of a decree by default is only competent with the leave of the court.

D1.144

Chapter 17

Summary Decrees

Application of this Chapter

17.1. This Chapter applies to any action other than—

(a) a family action within the meaning of rule 33.1(1);

(aa)[1] a civil partnership action within the meaning of rule 33A.1(1);

(ab)[2] an action of proving the tenor;

(b) an action of multiplepoinding; or

(c) an action under the Presumption of Death (Scotland) Act 1977.

Applications for summary decree

D1.145

17.2.—[3,4](1) Subject to paragraphs (2) to (4), a party to an action may, at any time after defences have been lodged, apply by motion for summary decree in accordance with rule 15.1(1)(b) (lodging of motions) or rule 15A.7 (lodging unopposed motions by email) or rule 15A.8 (lodging opposed motions by email) as the case may be.

(2) An application may only be made on the grounds that—

(a) an opposing party's case (or any part of it) has no real prospect of success; and

(b) there exists no other compelling reason why summary decree should not be granted at that stage.

(3) The party enrolling the motion may request the sheriff—

(a) to grant decree in terms of all or any of the craves of the initial writ or counterclaim;

(b) to dismiss a cause or to absolve any party from any crave directed against him or her;

(c) to pronounce an interlocutor sustaining or repelling any plea-in-law; or

(d) to dispose of the whole or part of the subject-matter of the cause.

(4) The sheriff may—

(a) grant the motion in whole or in part, if satisfied that the conditions in subparagraph (2) are met,

(b) ordain any party, or a partner, director, officer or office-bearer of any party—

(i) to produce any relevant document or article; or

(ii) to lodge an affidavit in support of any assertion of fact made in the pleadings or at the hearing of the motion.

(5) Notwithstanding the refusal of all or part of a motion for summary decree, a subsequent motion may be made where there has been a change in circumstances.

---

[1] Inserted by Act of Sederunt (Ordinary Cause Rules) Amendment (Family Law (Scotland) Act 2006 etc.) 2006 (SSI 2006/207) r.2 (effective 4 May 2006).

[2] As inserted by the Act of Sederunt (Ordinary Cause Rules 1993 Amendment and Miscellaneous Amendments) 2015 (SSI 2015/296) para.2(2) (effective 21 September 2015).

[3] As substituted by the Act of Sederunt (Sheriff Court Rules) (Miscellaneous Amendments) 2012 (SSI 2012/188) para.3 (effective August 1, 2012).

[4] As amended by the Act of Sederunt (Rules of the Court of Session 1994 and Sheriff Court Rules Amendment) (No. 2) (Personal Injury and Remits) 2015 (SSI 2015/227) para.8 (effective September 22, 2015).

The rule may flow from comments made by Lord Stewart in *Ellon Castle Estates Company Ltd v MacDonald*, 1975 S.L.T. (News) 66. Although this case considerably predates the rule it is frequently founded upon as setting forth a definition of the type of defences the rule is intended to strike at.

D1.145.1

The purpose of the introduction of this rule of court was summarised by Lord McDonald in an unreported decision of March 26, 1985: *McAlinden v Bearsden & Milngavie District Council* as follows:

> "I have no doubt it is intended to deal with the regrettable situation where there is no valid stateable defence but procedural technicalities are founded upon to delay prompt settlement of an unanswerable claim."

In his judgment, in *McAlinden v Bearsden & Milngavie District Council* supra, Lord McDonald further stated—

> "It (the summary decree motion) is not in my view intended to provide an opportunity on the motion roll for legal debate appropriate to the procedure roll."

This opinion has been followed in a number of cases (see example: *Mitchell v H A T Contracting Services Ltd (No. 2)* 1993 S.L.T. 734; and *Rankin v Reid* , 1987 S.L.T. 352). Thus a summary decree motion is not the appropriate forum for a decision on relevancy and if such an issue arises in the course of such a motion it should be sent to debate. However, Sheriff Principal Nicholson, Q.C., held in *Matthews v SLAB & Henderson* , 1995 S.C.L.R. 184 that where the sole issue in the course of the summary decree motion was whether there was a legal basis for the defence then it is not inappropriate for a sheriff to approach that issue in a manner which is not entirely different from that which would be appropriate at a debate. See also *Royal Bank of Scotland Ltd v Dinwoodie* , 1987 S.L.T. 82 and *McKays Stores Ltd v City Wall (Holdings) Ltd* , 1989 S.L.T. 835 at 836E per Lord McCluskey "The test which I have to apply at this stage: I have to ask myself if the question of law which is raised admits of a clear and obvious answer". If the answer to that question is yes then the matter can be appropriately dealt with by way of a summary decree motion.

It should not, however, be thought that a summary decree motion is a narrower procedure than a debate. Rather as Lord Caplan stated in *Frimobar v Mobile Technical Plant (International) Ltd* , 1990 S.L.T. 180 at 181L "A hearing in a summary decree motion is more far reaching (than a debate) because the rules of court specifically admit material extraneous to the pleadings such as affidavits or productions. Thus the court is concerned not only to test the relevancy of the defence but the authenticity of the defence."

"at any time after a defender has lodged defences".

A motion for summary decree may be moved at any time up to final decree. Such motions are due to their nature most commonly enrolled shortly after the lodging of defences.

"no defence to the action".

In considering whether no defence is disclosed the court should have regard to the pleadings before it at the time of the motion. Although, in exceptional cases, the court may have regard to a minute of amendment presented but not yet part of the pleadings (see: *Robinson v Thomson* , 1987 S.L.T. 120). The court is further entitled to have regard to documents extraneous to the pleadings which have been lodged together with the history of the case and any relevant background information (see: *Spink & Son Ltd v McColl* , 1992 S.L.T. 470).

What the court should have regard to is the substance of the defence and not the manner in which it is pled. The issue for the court is to decide whether there is a genuine issue to try raised by the defences. The court is not confined to merely considering the narrow issue of relevancy (see: *Frimobar UK Ltd v Mobile Tech Plant (International) Ltd* supra). In considering the defence the court should consider whether by adjustment or minute of amendment a case can be improved to enable a genuine defence to be stated. In that event summary decree should not be pronounced.

Before the court can properly grant a summary decree it must be satisfied that no defence is disclosed. The test should be applied at the time that the motion is made (see: *Frimobar* supra). The standard of satisfaction has been defined by the court as being one of more than probability but less than complete certainty (see: *Watson-Towers Ltd v McPhail* , 1986 S.L.T. 617) or as put by Lord Prosser in *P and M Sinclair v The Bamber Gray Partnership* , 1987 S.C. 203 at 206 near certainty was required in order to fulfil the test.

Personal Injury Actions.

Generally courts have been slow to grant summary decrees in personal injury actions. It has been made clear that the putting forward of such a motion merely on the basis that the defender has lodged skeletal defences would not of itself be sufficient to obtain a summary decree (see: *McManus v Speirs Dick & Smith Ltd* , 1989 S.L.T. 806 per Lord Caplan at 807L). However, summary decree has been granted (see *Campbell v Golding* , 1992 S.L.T. 889) where the pursuer was able to found on an extract conviction relative to the defender. In *Struthers v British Alcan Rolled Products Ltd* , 1995 S.L.T. 142 summary decree was granted where the pursuer was able to found on a report lodged by the defenders indicating fault on their part.

Order to produce a document or lodge an affidavit.

The court may order the production of a document or the lodging of an affidavit which it considers may be of assistance in deciding the issue of whether there is a genuine defence.

It has been held that the court is entitled on the basis of evidence contained in an affidavit to hold itself satisfied that a certain state of fact exists although a denial of that state of facts is contained within the defences. (See: *Ingram Coal Co. v Nugent*, 1991 S.L.T. 603).

"Change of circumstances" giving rise to a subsequent motion.

Such a change of circumstances may arise from, for example, on an alteration in the pleadings; the lodging of certain documents in process; and the production of an affidavit.

Appeal.

If as a result of a summary decree motion a final judgment is pronounced (see: s.27 of the 1907 Act) then such decree is appealable without leave. Otherwise any other decision made in the course of a motion for summary decree with the exception of an interlocutor making an order *ad factum praestandum*, for example the lodging of a document requires leave to appeal.

Counterclaim.

The above points are equally applicable where an application for summary decree is made by a defender in terms of a counterclaim.

D1.146

Chapter 18

Amendment of Pleadings

Alteration of sum sued for

18.1.—(1)[1]   In a cause in which all other parties have lodged defences or answers, the pursuer may, before the closing of the record, alter any sum sued for by amending the crave of the initial writ, and any record.

(2)   The pursuer shall forthwith intimate any such amendment in writing to every other party.

Powers of sheriff to allow amendment

D1.147

18.2.—(1)   The sheriff may, at any time before final judgment, allow an amendment mentioned in paragraph (2).

(2)   Paragraph (1) applies to the following amendments:—

    (a)   an amendment of the initial writ which may be necessary for the purpose of determining the real question in controversy between the parties, notwithstanding that in consequence of such amendment—

        (i)   the sum sued for is increased or restricted after the closing of the record; or

        (ii)   a different remedy from that originally craved is sought;

    (b)   an amendment which may be necessary—

        (i)   to correct or supplement the designation of a party to the cause;

        (ii)   to enable a party who has sued or has been sued in his own right to sue or be sued in a representative capacity;

        (iii)   to enable a party who has sued or has been sued in a representative capacity to sue or be sued in his own right or in a different representative capacity;

        (iv)   to add the name of an additional pursuer or person whose concurrence is necessary;

        (v)   where the cause has been commenced or presented in the name of the wrong person, or it is doubtful whether it has been commenced

---

[1] As amended by SI 1996/2445 (effective November 1, 1996).

or presented in the name of the right person, to allow any other person to be sisted in substitution for, or in addition to, the original person; or

(vi) to direct a crave against a third party brought into an action under Chapter 20 (third party procedure);

(c) an amendment of a condescendence, defences, answers, pleas-in-law or other pleadings which may be necessary for determining the real question in controversy between the parties; and

(d) where it appears that all parties having an interest have not been called or that the cause has been directed against the wrong person, an amendment inserting in the initial writ an additional or substitute party and directing existing or additional craves, averments and pleas-in-law against that party.

GENERAL NOTE.

Before this rule amendment procedure in the Sheriff Court was governed by Rules 79 and 80 of Schedule 1 to the 1970 Act which were in wholly different terms from Rule 18.2. Cases decided in terms of the old Sheriff Court Rules are no longer of relevance. **D1.147.1**

Rule 18 is now in broadly similar terms to Rule 24 in the Court of Session and cases decided in terms of said latter rule are accordingly of relevance.

The power to allow amendment given by this rule is a wide one. However, amendment cannot cure fundamental nullity (see: *Rutherford v Vertue* , 1993 S.C.L.R. 886).

Test as to allowing of Minute of amendment.

In terms of para.8.2(2)(a) and (c) the test as to whether a minute of amendment should be allowed is a two-part one.

"necessary for...determining the real question in controversy":

Firstly, is the minute of amendment necessary to determine the real question in controversy between the parties.

Secondly, should the court in the exercise of its discretion allow the minute of amendment? In other words, is it in the interests of justice to allow the minute of amendment? (See: *Thomson v Glasgow Corporation* , 1962 S.C. (HL) 36 per Thomson LJC at 51).

The decision as to whether to allow a minute of amendment is a matter for the discretion of the court, even when the amendment required to determine the real question in controversy is radical in nature and even if presented outwith the triennium (see: *Sellars v IMI Yorkshire Imperial Ltd* , 1986 S.L.T. 629).

In terms of the first test the court must consider inter alia:

1. Is the minute of amendment relevant?
2. Does the minute of amendment cure or at least to a material extent cure the identified defect or defects in the party's case?

Turning to the second part of the test, in seeking to apply the test of whether it is fair and in the interests of justice to allow the minute of amendment the court will have regard to inter alia the following broad factors—

1. The whole procedural history of the case.
2. The extent to which the amendment seeks to alter the case already pled.
3. The procedural stage at which the amendment is sought.
4. The extent and nature of the prejudice to the other party by the allowance of the amendment.
5. The extent to which such prejudice can be ameliorated/obviated by the awarding of expenses against the party seeking to amend or by the attachment of any other conditions to the granting of the minute of amendment. The most common condition attached is the discharge of a diet of proof in order to allow the party who is required to answer the minute of amendment to prepare to meet the amendment.

Stage in Procedure when minute of Amendment is Presented

General Rule. "before final Judgment".

A minute of amendment may be competently moved at any time before final judgment.

It can be broadly stated that the later in an action leave is sought the more likely it is that prejudice to the other side will not be capable of amelioration by an award of expenses or otherwise.

Specific Stages at Which Leave to Amend May be Sought

(a) Where leave to amend is sought at or before a diet of debate it will often be allowed as it is unlikely that at that stage any prejudice to the other party will be of such a nature or extent that it cannot properly be compensated by an appropriate award of expenses. Where leave to amend is sought at the commencement of or during the course of a debate then it will be necessary for the party seeking leave to be in a position to satisfy the court that he can or will be able to answer the points set forth in the Rule 22 Note which it is accepted require to be answered.

(b) Where leave to amend is sought sufficiently prior to the proof not to require any adjournment it is likely to be allowed. On the other hand, if amendment is sought so close to the diet of proof as to require a discharge in order to allow investigation by the other side then leave to amend is more likely to be refused on the basis that it is not in the interests of justice that the other side should lose their diet of proof (see: *Dryburgh v NCB* 1962 S.C. 485 at 492 per Lord Guthrie). It will be of particular importance in persuading the court that leave should be allowed at this stage that there is some very good reason why the minute of amendment comes at such a late stage in the case.

(c) Where minute of amendment is tendered in the course of proof. In considering whether leave should be granted at this stage of a case, the court will consider a number of factors:

    (i) whether it has been presented at the first opportunity (see: *Cameron v Lanarkshire Health Board*, 1997 S.L.T. 1040 at 1043D to Eper Lord Gill and *Rafferty v Weir*, 1966 S.L.T. (News) 23).

    (ii) whether there is a good explanation as to why the minute of amendment is presented at such a late stage.

    (iii) prejudice to the other party.

At this stage it is often difficult to see how an award of expenses or any other condition could compensate for the prejudice which has arisen to the other side by the late stage at which leave to amend is being sought. However, it should be borne in mind in relation to the issue of countering any prejudice to the other party that witnesses can be recalled.

Circumstances requiring an amendment during the course of a proof. If it is sought to advance a ground not covered by the record (see: *Gunn v John McAdam & Son*, 1949 S.C. 31) then a minute of amendment is required.

A ground is not covered by record where it can be described as being other than a "variation, modification or development" of the case on record. (See Thompson LJC in *Burns v Dixon's Ironworks Ltd*, 1961 S.C. 102 at 107).

Such a motion to seek leave to amend will almost always arise on an objection of no record being made by the other side. Should the other side fail to object timeously to a line of evidence for which there is in fact no record and there should have been then amendment is not required (see: *McGlone v BRB*, 1966 S.C. (HL) 1).

(d) Where a minute of amendment is presented after proof. Such a minute of amendment although competent would only be granted in the rarest of situations given the almost inevitable material prejudice to the other side by allowing it. An example of where such a minute of amendment has been allowed is *Moyes v Burntisland Shipping Company*, 1952 S.L.T. 417. Here a minute of amendment was allowed following a jury trial. In that case the circumstances were described as exceptional and in order to deal to some extent with the prejudice caused by the lateness of the minute of amendment a proof before answer was ordered rather than a further jury trial.

(e) Where amendment is sought after the marking of an appeal. Frequently such amendment is allowed by the party which has lost at debate and then appeals. The considerations as to whether such an amendment should be allowed are broadly similar to those which are relevant where leave to amend is sought shortly before or at a diet of debate. However, following upon a hearing at which evidence has been led the granting of leave to appeal at this stage will be extremely rare. The factors referred to at (c) will again apply, however, with even more force.

(f) Where amendment is sought after expiry of the time limit. The court will not, in general, allow a pursuer by amendment to substitute the right defender for the wrong defender, or to cure a radical incompetence in his action, or to change the basis of his case if he only seeks to make such amendments after the expiry of a time limit which would have prevented him at that stage from raising fresh proceedings: see *Pompa's Trustees v The Magistrates of Edinburgh*, 1942 S.C. 119 at 125 per Cooper LJC.

The question which most frequently arises is what amounts to changing the basis of the case. Lord President Cooper in *McPhail v Lanarkshire County Council*, 1951 S.C. 301 at 309 elaborated on what he had said in *Pompa's Trustees v The Magistrates of Edinburgh supra* and gives the clearest statement of what amounts to the changing of the basis of the case:

I think the pursuer may well claim, not to have offered a new but only to have presented the old case but from a new angle, not to have changed the foundation of his action but only to have made certain alterations to the superstructure.

The appropriate time to consider the issue of time bar/prescription where it is raised in answer to the presentation of a minute of amendment is when the motion to allow the record to be amended is being heard (see: *Greenhorn v Smart*, 1979 S.C. 427 per Lord Cameron at 432 and *Stewart v Highlands & Islands Development Board*, 1991 S.L.T. 787).

The courts will not allow a new pursuer to be added by amendment post expiry of the relevant period of time bar or prescriptive period (see *MacLean v BRB*, 1966 S.L.T. 39).

"the sum sued for is increased:" Such amendment can be competently made following the expiry of a time limit in terms of the law of prescription or time bar (see *Mackie v Glasgow Corporation* , 1924 S.L.T. 510).

"a different remedy from that originally craved is sought:" A fundamental change in the form of the action is not competent see e.g. *Sleigh v City of Edinburgh District Council* , 1988 S.L.T. 253, in which a motion for leave to amend a petition for interdict to a petition for judicial review was refused under reference to Lord Cooper's opinion in *Pompa's Trustees supra.*

Applications to amend

D1.148

18.3.—(1) A party seeking to amend shall lodge a minute of amendment in process setting out his proposed amendment and, at the same time, lodge a motion—

(a) to allow the minute of amendment to be received; and

(b) to allow—

(i) amendment in terms of the minute of amendment and, where appropriate, to grant an order under rule 18.5(1)(a) (service of amendment for additional or substitute party); or

(ii) where the minute of amendment may require to be answered, any other person to lodge answers within a specified period.

(2) Where the sheriff has pronounced an interlocutor allowing a minute of amendment to be received and answered, he may allow a period of adjustment of the minute of amendment and answers and, on so doing, shall fix a date for parties to be heard on the minute of amendment and answers as adjusted.

(3)[1] Any adjustment to any minute of amendment or answers shall be exchanged between parties and not lodged in process.

(4)[2] Parties shall be responsible for maintaining a record of adjustment made and the date of their intimation.

(5)[3] No adjustments shall be permitted after the period of adjustment allowed, except with leave of the sheriff.

(6)[4] Each party shall, no later than 2 days before the hearing fixed in terms of paragraph (2), lodge in process a copy of their minute of amendment or answers with all adjustments made thereto in italic or bold type, or underlined.

"to add the name of an additional pursuer." The courts will allow this even when the pursuers title has been defective during the course of the action (see: *Donaghy v Rollo* , 1964 S.C. 278). A minute of sist is not required (see: Macphail, Sheriff Court Practice para. 10.09).

"Lodge a motion." The procedure as set out in OCR 15 should be followed.

"shall fix a date for parties to be heard on the minute of amendment." If there is opposition to the minute of amendment this is the appropriate stage for opposition to be made to the minute of amendment. Broadly, the only exception to this would be if the lodging of the minute of amendment due to the stage at which it is lodged gives rise to the issue of possible discharge of a proof or a debate. In such circumstances it would be appropriate to lodge opposition to the motion to have the minute of amendment received. The motion made at the hearing in terms of 18.3(2) for the record to be amended in terms of the minute of amendment and answers (if necessary as adjusted) is made orally as to do it by written motion would require the whole of OCR 15 to be followed.

"Each party shall no later than 2 days before the hearing—lodge in process a copy of their minute of amendment or answers with all adjustments made thereto in italics." It is important that this rule is complied with in that non compliance results in the court being unable to prepare for and conduct the hearing properly as in terms of 18.3(3) no copy of adjustments is lodged in court when adjustments are exchanged.

"Form of Minute of Amendment." It should begin with the instance and be followed by a preamble.

... for the pursuer/defender craved and hereby craves leave of the court to amend the initial writ/ defence or to open the closed record and to amend the same as follows—

Thereafter in numbered paragraphs the amendments should be set out.

At the end IN RESPECT WHEREOF should appear.

---

[1] Inserted by SSI 2000/239 (effective October 2, 2000).

[2] Inserted by SSI 2000/239 (effective October 2, 2000).

[3] Inserted by SSI 2000/239 (effective October 2, 2000).

[4] Inserted by SSI 2000/239 (effective October 2, 2000).

"Form of Answers:" It should begin with the instance and be followed by a preamble—

... for the pursuer/defender craved and hereby craves leave of the court to answer the minute of amendment number...of process as follows—

Thereafter in numbered paragraphs the answers should be set out.

At the end IN RESPECT WHEREOF should appear.

D1.149

Applications for diligence on amendment

18.4.—(1) Where a minute of amendment is lodged by a pursuer under rule 18.2(2)(d) (all parties not, or wrong person, called), he may apply by motion for warrant to use any form of diligence which could be used on the dependence of a separate action.

(2) A copy certified by the sheriff clerk of the interlocutor granting warrant for diligence on the dependence applied for under paragraph (1) shall be sufficient authority for the execution of that diligence.

Service of amended pleadings

D1.150

18.5.—(1)[1] Where an amendment under rule 18.2(2)(b)(iv), (v) or (vi) (additional or substitute defenders added by amendment) or rule 18.2(2)(d) (all parties not, or wrong person, called) has been made—

    (a)   the sheriff shall order that a copy of the initial writ or record, as the case may be, as so amended be served by the party who made the amendment on that additional or substitute party with—

        (i)[2] in a cause in which a time to pay direction under the Debtors (Scotland) Act 1987 or a time order under the Consumer Credit Act 1974 may be applied for, a notice in Form 08 specifying the date by which a notice of intention must be lodged in process, a notice in Form 03 and a notice of intention to defend in Form 07; or

        (ii) in any other cause, a notice in Form 09 specifying the date by which a notice of intention to defend must be lodged in process and a notice of intention to defend in Form 07; and

    (b)   the party who made the amendment shall lodge in process—

        (i)   a copy of the initial writ or record as amended;

        (ii) a copy of the notice sent in Form 08 or Form 09; and

        (iii) a certificate of service.

(2) When paragraph (1) has been complied with, the cause as so amended shall proceed in every respect as if that party had originally been made a party to the cause.

(3) Where a notice of intention to defend is lodged by virtue of paragraph (1)(a), the sheriff clerk shall fix a date for a hearing under rule 9.12 (Options Hearing).

General Note

D1.150.1

Where in terms of the minute of amendment the parties to the action are intended to be altered then service of the writ or record as amended will be ordered. Service will require to conform to OCR 5.

D1.151

Expenses and conditions of amendment

18.6. The sheriff shall find the party making an amendment liable in the expenses occasioned by the amendment unless it is shown that it is just and equitable that the expenses occasioned by the amendment should be otherwise dealt with, and may attach such other conditions as he thinks fit.

---

[1] As amended by SI 1996/2445 (effective November 1, 1996).

[2] As amended by the Act of Sederunt (Ordinary Cause, Summary Application, Summary Cause and Small Claim Rules) Amendment (Miscellaneous) 2007 (SSI 2007/6), para.2(9) (effective January 29, 2007).

This rule specifically directs that the party amending will be found liable in the expenses occasioned by the amendment, unless it is just and equitable, to make any other type of award. The most common instance of where a party amending will not be found liable in expenses is where the other party adjusted shortly before the closing of the record not allowing adjustments in answer to be made timeously and thus requiring a minute of amendment to deal with these adjustments. **D1.151.1**

expenses occasioned by the amendment

will include the expenses of preparing answers (see: *Campbell v Henderson* , 1949 S.C. 172). Such awards of expenses may also cover more than merely the cost of preparing answers. If the lodging of the minute of amendment has resulted in either the procedure which has gone before in its entirety or to some specific prior stage for eg. the closing of the record being rendered worthless then the party amending may be found liable for either the whole of the procedure or to that specific stage (see: *Campbell v Henderson supra*). Further, where the lodging of a minute of amendment has resulted in the discharge of a debate or proof the party amending is likely to be found liable for the costs of the discharge (see e.g. *Mackenzie v Mackenzie* , 1951 S.C. 163 at 165–166).

Effect of amendment on diligence

D1.152

18.7. Where an amendment has been allowed, the amendment—

(a) shall not validate diligence used on the dependence of a cause so as to prejudice the rights of creditors of the party against whom the diligence has been executed who are interested in defeating such diligence; and

(b) shall preclude any objection to such diligence stated by a party or any person by virtue of a title acquired or in right of a debt contracted by him subsequent to the execution of such diligence.

Preliminary pleas inserted on amendment

18.8.—(1) Where a party seeks to add a preliminary plea by amendment or answers to an amendment, or by adjustment thereto, a note of the basis for the plea shall be lodged at the same time as the minute, answers or adjustment, as the case may be. **D1.153**

(2) If a party fails to comply with paragraph (1), that party shall be deemed to be no longer insisting on the preliminary plea and the plea shall be repelled by the sheriff.

If the minute of amendment or answers thereto seeks to add a preliminary plea, a note of the basis of that plea must be lodged at the same time as the minute, answers or adjustments thereto which introduces the plea (OCR 18.8(1))

"Appeal." Leave to appeal is required both in relation to a grant and refusal of a motion for leave to amend. **D1.153.1**

Chapter 19 **D1.154**

Counterclaims

Annotations to Chapters 19 to 29 by Simon Di Rollo, Q.C.

Counterclaims

19.1.—(1)[1] In any action other than a family action within the meaning of rule 33.1(1), a civil partnership action within the meaning of rule 33A.1(1) or an action of multiplepoinding, a defender may counterclaim against a pursuer—

(a) where the counterclaim might have been made in a separate action in which it would not have been necessary to call as defender any person other than the pursuer; and

---

[1] As amended by Act of Sederunt (Ordinary Cause Rules) Amendment (Family Law (Scotland) ct 2006 etc.) 2006 (SSI 2006/207) r.2 (effective May 4, 2006).

    (b)   in respect of any matter—
- (i)   forming part, or arising out of the grounds, of the action by the pursuer;
- (ii)   the decision of which is necessary for the determination of the question in controversy between the parties; or
- (iii)   which, if the pursuer had been a person not otherwise subject to the jurisdiction of the court, might have been the subject-matter of an action against that pursuer in which jurisdiction would have arisen by reconvention.

(2) A counterclaim shall be made in the defences—
- (a)   when the defences are lodged or during the period for adjustment;
- (b)   by amendment at any other stage, with the leave of the sheriff and subject to such conditions, if any, as to expenses or otherwise as the sheriff thinks fit.

(3) Defences which include a counterclaim shall commence with a crave setting out the counterclaim in such form as, if the counterclaim had been made in a separate action, would have been appropriate in the initial writ in that separate action and shall include—
- (a)   answers to the condescendence of the initial writ as required by rule 9.6(2) (form of defences);
- (b)   a statement of facts in numbered paragraphs setting out the facts on which the counterclaim is founded, incorporating by reference, if necessary, any matter contained in the defences; and
- (c)   appropriate pleas-in-law.

GENERAL NOTE

The Ordinary Cause Rules 1993 made several important changes to sheriff court counterclaim procedure. Care is required in relation to earlier sheriff court decisions made under the old rules. The terms of the sheriff court rule are now practically identical to the current Court of Session rule (see RCS 1994, Chapter 25). The language of the latter is in similar terms to the earlier Court of Session rule. The older Court of Session cases remain of value.

The purpose of the counterclaim procedure is to allow the defender to obtain a decree (apart from absolvitor or dismissal) against the pursuer where he has a claim against him which is connected with the grounds of the pursuer's action. It is expedient to permit the parties to resolve the whole of their dispute in one process. Family actions have their own discrete rules (see Chapter 33) and are excluded from Chapter 19 as are, for obvious reasons, actions of multiplepoinding. In all other actions under the Ordinary Cause Rules a counterclaim is competent under this chapter. Provided the requirements of the rules are otherwise satisfied, it is competent to counterclaim for interdict (*Mclean v Marwhirn Developments Ltd*, 1976 S.L.T. (Notes) 47) or delivery (*Borthwick v Dean Warwick Ltd*, 1985 S.L.T. 269) and presumably in an appropriate case for other types of non-pecuniary decree.

A counterclaim is often (but not exclusively) used in response to an action for payment of the contract price where the defender seeks damages for breach of contract, or in the converse situation. It is important not to confuse two questions. The first question is whether in an action for debt it is relevant to plead in defence that a debt is due by the pursuer to the defender. The answer to that question is a matter of the substantive law (see Wilson, *Debt* (2nd ed., 1991), Chap.13 and McBryde, *Contract* (2nd ed., 2001), pp.499–501). For a detailed and comprehensive review of the authorities on the substantive law see *Inveresk Plc v Tullis Russell Papermakers Ltd*, 2010 S.L.T. 941; 2010 SC (UKSC) 106. The second question is in an action what types of claim can form the basis of a counterclaim under the rule in this chapter? That is a question to be answered by the terms of this rule. In this context if the defender seeks to withhold the price on the ground of the pursuer's breach of contract then it may not be necessary to lodge a counterclaim (see Macphail, *Sheriff Court Practice* (2nd ed., 1998), p.390 footnote 37), but he still requires to give fair notice in his defences of the precise basis upon which payment is withheld and to make adequate relevant averments (including specification of the amount of the damage) to permit the equitable doctrine of retention (see *Inveresk Plc* (above) at paras [60] to [107]) to be operated.

OCR, r.19.1(1)(a), (b)(i), (ii) and (iii) define the scope of the connection required between the pursuer's action and the defender's response which permit the latter to lodge a counterclaim.

RULE 19.1(1)(A)

First, it is essential that the counterclaim could have been brought by the same defender as a separate action against the same pursuer without having to call any other party as defender (*Tods Murray W.S. v Arakin Ltd*, 2001 S.C. 840, IH).

RULE 19.1(1)(B)(I) OR (II) OR (III)

Secondly, the subject matter of the counterclaim must either (i) form part of the pursuer's action, or (ii) arise out of its grounds, or (iii) be a matter the decision of which is necessary for the determination of the question in controversy between the parties, or (iv) arise from the common law principle of reconvention (in so far as that has not been swept away by the Civil Jurisdiction and Judgements Act 1982).

RULE 19.1(1)(B)(I)—"FORM PART OF THE PURSUER'S ACTION", OR "ARISE OUT OF ITS GROUNDS"

In the contractual context when a contract is one and indivisible, a counterclaim arising out of one item can be competently pursued in answer to a claim for payment on the whole contract. Often there is a series of transactions between the parties with each transaction or group representing a separate contract. In that event if the pursuer sues upon one contract the defender's counterclaim has to relate to that contract in order to be said to form part of the pursuer's action or arise out of its grounds (see *JW Chafer (Scotland) Ltd v Hope* , 1963 S.L.T. (Notes) 11). Nevertheless, the defender may be able to bring himself within rule 19.1(1)(b)(ii).

RULE 19.1(1)(B)(II)—"NECESSARY FOR THE DETERMINATION OF THE QUESTION IN CONTROVERSY BETWEEN THE PARTIES"

This permits a counterclaim to be maintained even though the defender is not allowed under the substantive law of contract to retain a sum in defence to the pursuer's claim for payment. In *Fulton Clyde Ltd v JF McCallum & Co. Ltd* , 1960 S.C. 78; 1960 S.L.T. 253 the pursuer sought payment of the price of goods delivered. The defenders did not dispute that the goods had been delivered or the contract price. They sought to retain the price in respect of a failure to deliver goods on an earlier occasion. It was held that the earlier failure in delivery was a separate contract and so the defender was not entitled to retain the contract price in respect of the later delivery. Decree was granted for the sum sought by the pursuer. However, the court allowed the counterclaim to proceed on the basis that the questions in controversy between the parties on the whole pleadings included whether the defender was entitled to damages for breach of contract due to the failure to make an earlier delivery (see also *Borthwick v Dean Warwick Ltd* , 1985 S.L.T. 269 where the court considered that on the pleadings it could not be said that the counterclaim did not arise out of the same contract).

RULE 19.1(1)(B)(III)

This only applies where the common law doctrine of reconvention can be invoked. Reconvention is a common law equitable doctrine that permits a pursuer who raises an action against the defender to be counterclaimed against where he would not otherwise be subject to the jurisdiction of the court. The basic principles involved are illustrated in *Thompson v Whitehead* (1862) 24 D. 331, and for a modern example where it was held to apply, see e.g. *MacKenzie v Macleod's Executor* , 1988 S.L.T. 207, OH. In the sheriff court the doctrine had statutory sanction by virtue of section 6(h) of the Sheriff Courts (Scotland) Act 1907 which provided that the sheriff had jurisdiction "where the party sued is the pursuer in any action pending within [his] jurisdiction against the party suing". Section 20 of the Civil Jurisdiction and Judgements Act 1982 provides that section 6 of the 1907 Act ceases to have effect to the extent that it determines jurisdiction in relation to any matter to which Schedule 8 applies. Paragraph 2(15)(c) of Schedule 8 to the 1982 Act provides that there is jurisdiction on a counterclaim arising from the same contract or facts on which the original claim was based, in the court in which the original claim is pending. The common law doctrine of reconvention can only be invoked in relation to those matters in Schedule 9 of the 1982 Act (see Anton, *Private International Law* (3rd ed., 2011), paras 8.331 and 8.332).

RULE 19.1(2)(A) AND (B)

Leave is required to lodge a counterclaim after the record has closed. Before that stage is reached, provided the counterclaim meets the requirement of the rules, there is no discretion to it being included in the defences.

RULE 19.1(3)

This prescribes how to set out the defences and counterclaim and should be followed in every case. The order is crave, answers to each article of condescendence, pleas-in-law relating to the answers, statement of facts and pleas in law relating to the statement of facts.

Warrants for diligence on counterclaims

19.2.—[1](1) A defender who makes a counterclaim may apply for a warrant for interim diligence which would have been permitted had the warrant been sought in an initial writ in a separate action.

(2)–(4) *[Repealed by the Act of Sederunt (Sheriff Court Rules) (Miscellaneous Amendments) 2009 (SSI 2009/294) r.10 (effective October 1, 2009).]*

D1.155

---

[1] As amended by the Act of Sederunt (Sheriff Court Rules) (Miscellaneous Amendments) 2009 (SSI 2009/294) r.10 (effective October 1, 2009).

See OCR 1993 Chapter 6 Interim Diligence. The law is codified in the Debtors (Scotland) Act 1987 ss.15A to 15N.

D1.156

Form of record where counterclaim lodged

19.2A.[1]   Where, under rule 9.10 (open record), 9.11 (record for Options Hearing), 10.4 (open record), or 10.5 (closed record), a record requires to be lodged in an action in which a counterclaim is included in the defences, the pleadings of the parties shall be set out in the record in the following order:—

   (a)   the crave of the initial writ;

   (b)   the condescendence and answers relating to the initial writ;

   (c)   the pleas-in-law of the parties relating to the crave of the initial writ;

   (d)   the crave of the counterclaim;

   (e)   the statement of facts and answers relating to the counterclaim; and

   (f)   the pleas-in-law of the parties relating to the counterclaim.

GENERAL NOTE

This rule helpfully provides the correct format of the record where there is a counterclaim, and should be followed in every case.

D1.157

Effect of abandonment of cause

19.3.—(1)   The right of a pursuer to abandon a cause under rule 23.1 shall not be affected by a counterclaim; and any expenses for which the pursuer is found liable as a condition of, or in consequence of, such abandonment shall not include the expenses of the counterclaim.

(2)   Notwithstanding abandonment by the pursuer, a defender may insist in his counterclaim; and the proceedings in the counterclaim shall continue in dependence as if the counterclaim were a separate action.

GENERAL NOTE

The counterclaim, once it is born, has an existence independent of the principal action. It can proceed in conjunction with the principal action or on its own should that be abandoned.

D1.158

Disposal of counterclaims

19.4.   The sheriff may—

   (a)   deal with a counterclaim as if it had been stated in a separate action;

   (b)   regulate the procedure in relation to the counterclaim as he thinks fit; and

   (c)   grant decree for the counterclaim in whole or in part or for the difference between it and the sum sued for by the pursuer.

GENERAL NOTE

Usually the counterclaim will be subject to the same procedure as the main action but there is scope for having separate enquires or debates. The parties should make it clear what procedure they desire in relation to both the principal action and the counterclaim and any interlocutor should be specific to each in relation to any procedure to take place. The court has the same powers in relation to the disposal of the counterclaim as it does with regard to the principal action.

D1.159

Chapter 20

Third Party Procedure

Applications for third party notice

20.1.—(1)   Where, in an action, a defender claims that—

   (a)   he has in respect of the subject-matter of the action a right of contribution, relief or indemnity against any person who is not a party to the action, or

---

[1] Inserted by SI 1996/2445 (effective November 1, 1996).

    (b)   a person whom the pursuer is not bound to call as a defender should be made a party to the action along with the defender in respect that such person is—

        (i)   solely liable, or jointly or jointly and severally liable with the defender, to the pursuer in respect of the subject-matter of the action, or

        (ii)   liable to the defender in respect of a claim arising from or in connection with the liability, if any, of the defender to the pursuer,

he may apply by motion for an order for service of a third party notice upon that other person in Form O10 for the purpose of convening that other person as a third party to the action.

    (2)[1] Where—

    (a)   a pursuer against whom a counterclaim has been made, or

    (b)   a third party convened in the action,

seeks, in relation to the claim against him, to make against a person who is not a party, a claim mentioned in paragraph (1) as a claim which could be made by a defender against a third party, he shall apply by motion for an order for service of a third party notice in Form O10 in the same manner as a defender under that paragraph; and rules 20.2 to 20.6 shall, with the necessary modifications, apply to such a claim as they apply in relation to such a claim by a defender.

GENERAL NOTE

    Like the counterclaim procedure (see Chapter 19) the purpose of the third party procedure is to permit matters arising out of a dispute to be resolved in one process. Where a defender considers that responsibility for the pursuer's claim lies ultimately in whole or in part with another person, he may introduce that person into the action as a third party. The procedure is available when a defender claims: (1) a right of contribution, relief or indemnity against a third party; or (2) that the third party is either solely liable or jointly or jointly and severally liable with him to the pursuer. Again like counterclaim procedure the rule is purely procedural (see *National Coal Board v Knight Bros* , 1972 S.L.T. (Notes) 24, OH; *R and Watson Ltd v David Traill & Sons Ltd* , 1972 S.L.T. (Notes) 38). The terms "contribution, relief or indemnity" in the rule are to be interpreted in a broad way and it is not essential that any separate action against the third party would be put into any particular pigeon-hole (see, e.g. *Nicol Homeworld Contractors Ltd v Charles Gray Builders Ltd* , 1986 S.L.T. 317, OH). Thereafter the rights of the parties must be worked out under reference to the substantive law. A pursuer in a counterclaim may also lodge a third party notice. A third party may counterclaim against a defender or lodge a further third party notice himself. In that event the further third party is referred to as "second third party".

    Application to lodge a third party notice is made by motion for an order for service of a notice in Form O10. The notice requires specification of the basis upon which the third party is to be convened to the action, but the terms of any such notice do not prevent the defender from altering the pleadings against the third party from one of joint liability to sole fault or vice versa (*Beedie v Norrie* , 1966 S.C. 207; 1966 S.L.T. 295).

Averments where order for service of third party notice sought   D1.160

    20.2.—(1) Where a defender intends to apply by motion for an order for service of a third party notice before the closing of the record, he shall, before lodging the motion, set out in his defences, by adjustment to those defences, or in a separate statement of facts annexed to those defences—

    (a)   averments setting out the grounds on which he maintains that the proposed third party is liable to him by contribution, relief or indemnity or should be made a party to the action; and

    (b)   appropriate pleas-in-law.

    (2) Where a defender applies by motion for an order for service of a third party notice after the closing of the record, he shall, on lodging the motion, lodge a minute of amendment containing—

---

[1] As amended by SI 1996/2445 (effective November 1, 1996).

(a) averments setting out the grounds on which he maintains that the proposed third party is liable to him by contribution, relief or indemnity or should be made a party to the action, and

(b) appropriate pleas-in-law,

unless those grounds and pleas-in-law have been set out in the defences in the closed record.

(3) A motion for an order for service of a third party notice shall be lodged before the commencement of the hearing of the merits of the cause.

General Note

Rule 20.2(3)

Until the commencement of the hearing on the merits it is entirely a matter for the discretion of the court whether a motion to introduce a third party is granted or not. The length of time that a case has been in dependence, the inevitable delay caused by allowing a motion and the requirement to discharge a proof may each be important factors weighing against allowing a motion to allow an order for service of a third party notice being granted. It is not competent to lodge a third party notice after the commencement of the hearing on the merits.

D1.161

Warrants for diligence on third party notice

20.3.—[1](1) A defender who applies for an order for service of a third party notice may apply for—

(a) a warrant for arrestment to found jurisdiction;

(b) a warrant for interim diligence,

which would have been permitted had the warrant been sought in an initial writ in a separate action.

(2) Averments in support of the application for a warrant under paragraph (1)(a) shall be included in the defences or the separate statement of facts referred to in rule 20.2(1).

(3) An application for a warrant under paragraph (1)(a) shall be made by motion—

(a) at the time of applying for the third party notice; or

(b) if not applied for at that time, at any stage of the cause thereafter.

(4) A certified copy of the interlocutor granting warrant for diligence applied for under paragraph (2) shall be sufficient authority for execution of the diligence.

General Note

A warrant for diligence may be sought (see generally OCR 1993 Chapter 6 Interim Diligence). The law is codified in the Debtors (Scotland) Act 1987 ss.15A to 15N) but an explanation for seeking it has to be made expressly in the pleadings.

D1.162

Service on third party

20.4.—(1) A third party notice shall be served on the third party within 14 days after the date of the interlocutor allowing service of that notice.

(2) Where service of a third party notice has not been made within the period specified in paragraph (1), the order for service of it shall cease to have effect; and no service of the notice may be made unless a further order for service of it has been applied for and granted.

(3)[2] There shall be served with a third party notice—

(a) a copy of the pleadings (including any adjustments and amendments); and

(b) where the pleadings have not been amended in accordance with the minute of amendment referred to in rule 20.2, a copy of that minute.

---

[1] As amended by the Act of Sederunt (Sheriff Court Rules) (Miscellaneous Amendments) 2009 (SSI 2009/294) r.10 (effective October 1, 2009).
[2] As amended by SSI 2003/26, r.2 (effective from January 24, 2003).

(4) A copy of the third party notice, with a certificate of service attached to it, shall be lodged in process by the defender.

GENERAL NOTE

Rule 20.4(1), (2)

It is essential to serve the third party notice within 14 days of the order for service. This prevents a defender from delaying bringing in the third party once an order for service has been made. If service is not effective during that period the defender must return to court and obtain a fresh order.

Rule 20.4(3)

The pleadings served with the third party notice must contain the averments anent the basis of the claim made by the defender against the third party.

Answers to third party notice

D1.163

20.5.—(1) An order for service of a third party notice shall specify 28 days, or such other period as the sheriff on cause shown may specify, as the period within which the third party may lodge answers.

(2) Answers for a third party shall be headed "Answers for [E.F.], Third Party in the action at the instance of [A.B.], Pursuer against [C.D.], Defender" and shall include—

(a) answers to the averments of the defender against him in the form of numbered paragraphs corresponding to the numbered articles of the condescendence annexed to the summons and incorporating, if the third party so wishes, answers to the averments of the pursuer; or

(b) where a separate statement of facts has been lodged by the defender under rule 20.2(1), answers to the statement of facts in the form of numbered paragraphs corresponding to the numbered paragraphs of the statement of facts; and

(c) appropriate pleas-in-law.

GENERAL NOTE

It is important that the answers for the third party are organised in such a way so as to make clear the response in relation to the pursuer's averments and thereafter the defenders averments. The answers should be headed "Answers to condescendence and answers to averments for the defender". The third party is entitled to be heard in relation to the pursuer's claim against the defender, including any plea to the relevancy or other preliminary plea.

Consequences of failure to amend pleadings

D1.164

20.5A.[1] Where the pleadings have not been amended in accordance with the minute of amendment referred to in rule 20.2, no motion for a finding, order or decree against a third party may be enrolled by the defender unless, at or before the date on which he enrols the motion, he enrols a motion to amend the pleadings in accordance with that minute.

Procedure following answers

D1.165

20.6.—(1) Where a third party lodges answers, the sheriff clerk shall fix a date and time under rule 9.2 for a hearing under rule 9.12 (Options Hearing) as if the third party had lodged a notice of intention to defend and the period of notice had expired on the date for lodging answers.

(2) At the Options Hearing, or at any time thereafter, the sheriff may grant such decree or other order as he thinks fit.

(3) A decree or other order against the third party shall have effect and be extractable in the same way as a decree or other order against a defender.

---

[1] As inserted by SSI 2003/26 r.2 (effective January 24, 2003).

A final date for adjustment should be specified. The pursuer and the defender may require to adjust their pleadings in the light of the answers for the third party. The pursuer requires to consider whether or not to adopt the defender's case against the third party and/or whether or not to adopt the third party's case against the defender. If the pursuer wishes to adopt a case against the third party he requires to insert a crave for decree against the third party (which he must do by amendment) and to insert an appropriate plea in law. In any such amendment for the pursuer it is competent (but not essential) to redesign the third party as a second defender. The original defender may develop his case against the third party beyond what is stated as the ground of action in the third party notice.

RULE 20.6(2)

This rule is expressed in exceedingly wide terms and at first sight appears to permit the sheriff to deal with the merits of the whole case at the options hearing. It is thought, however, that the intention is to permit as much flexibility as possible in regulating further procedure as between all of the parties. It is possible to have separate debates or proofs depending on whether there are separate issues between the parties that may be advantageously resolved at different stages.

D1.166

Chapter 21

Documents Founded on or Adopted in Pleadings

Lodging documents founded on or adopted

21.1.—(1) Subject to any other provision in these Rules, any document founded on by a party, or adopted as incorporated, in his pleadings shall, so far as in his possession or within his control, be lodged in process as a production by him—

  (a)[1] when founded on or adopted in an initial writ, at the time of returning the initial writ under rule 9.3 or, in the case of a personal injuries action raised under Part AI of Chapter 36, when the initial writ is presented for warranting in accordance with rule 5.1;

  (b) when founded on or adopted in a minute, defences, counterclaim or answers, at the time of lodging that part of process; and

  (c) when founded on or adopted in an adjustment to any pleadings, at the time when such adjustment is intimated to any other party.

  (2) Paragraph (1) shall be without prejudice to any power of the sheriff to order the production of any document or grant a commission and diligence for recovery of it.

GENERAL NOTE

A document founded upon (by reference to it) or incorporated in the pleadings (by the use of a form of words expressly incorporating it) must be lodged. It is the original that must be lodged. A document is founded on if it is a document that forms the basis at least to some extent of the action. Typically, a contract, lease, title deed, will or invoice is apt to form the basis of an action. A document is incorporated in the pleadings if that is expressly stated, the traditional form of words being "The [the title of the document] is held as repeated herein *brevitatis causa*". A more modern form is "The [document] is held as incorporated here in full". Documents that contain assertions of fact or expressions of opinion from witnesses in relation to the issues in the case (such as expert reports or medical reports) should not under any circumstances be founded on in pleadings, nor should such items be incorporated in the pleadings. The pleader should extract from such documents the material required to make specific averments based on that material. Otherwise difficulties can arise (see e.g. *Reid v Shetland Sea Ferries* , 1999 S.C.C.R. 735). At a debate on relevancy or specification the court can only look at the pleadings. If the document has been incorporated then the document forms part of the pleadings and the court may have regard to it. If it has not been incorporated then even if the document is referred to and founded upon the court may not consider the document (although it must have regard to such parts of it as actually form part of the pleadings).

By virtue of OCR, rule 1.2(1), "document" has the meaning assigned to it in section 9 of the Civil Evidence (Scotland) Act 1988 (i.e. it includes maps, plans, graphs or drawings, photographs, discs, film, negatives, tapes, sound tracks or other devices from which sounds or other data or visual images are recorded so as to be capable (with or without the aid of some other equipment) of being reproduced).

A party may be penalised in expenses if there has been any wasted procedure through failure to lodge a document founded upon or incorporated.

---

[1] As amended by the Act of Sederunt (Ordinary Cause Rules Amendment) (Personal Injuries Actions) 2009 (SSI 2009/285) r.2 (effective 2 November 2009).

Rule 21.1(2)

The sheriff has residuary power (presumably on the motion of a party or ex propio motu) to order production of a document at any stage of the cause (see Macphail, *Sheriff Court Practice* (3rd ed.), para.15.48).

Consequences of failure to lodge documents founded on or adopted

21.2. Where a party fails to lodge a document in accordance with rule 21.1(1), he may be found liable in the expenses of any order for production or recovery of it obtained by any other party.

D1.167

General Note

This is without prejudice to other sanctions available to secure compliance with OCR.

Objection to documents founded on

21.3.—(1) Where a deed or writing is founded on by a party, any objection to it by any other party may be stated and maintained by exception without its being reduced.

D1.168

(2) Where an objection is stated under paragraph (1) and an action of reduction would otherwise have been competent, the sheriff may order the party stating the objection to find caution or give such other security as he thinks fit.

(3)[1] An objection may not be stated by exception if the sheriff considers that the objection would be more conveniently disposed of in a separate action of reduction.

General Note

A document that has a patent defect that renders it void or *ipso jure* null (such as a document that is executed without the necessary statutory solemnities or is unstamped) will simply not be given effect in any proceedings. If a defect is not of that type or there is room for doubt then the document has to be set aside by reduction. An action of reduction is not competent in the sheriff court but it is competent in certain circumstances to state an objection *ope exceptionis*. If a deed or writing (not decree) founded upon by a party in a sheriff court action is objected to then that objection may be stated and maintained, i.e. insisted upon (see Macphail, *Sheriff Court Practice* (3rd ed.), paras 12.66 to 12.72). Fair notice of the objection is required by averments and a plea in law.

Chapter 22

D1.169

Preliminary Pleas

Note of basis of preliminary plea

22.1.—[2](1) A party intending to insist on a preliminary plea shall, not later than 3 days before the Options Hearing under rule 9.12, the Procedural Hearing under rule 10.6 or the Full Case Management Hearing under rule 33.36P or rule 33A.36P—

    (a) lodge in process a note of the basis for the plea; and

    (b) intimate a copy of it to every other party.

(2) Where the Options Hearing or Full Case Management Hearing is continued under rules 9.12(5) or 33.36P(7) and a preliminary plea is added by adjustment, a party intending to insist on that plea shall, not later than 3 days before the date of the Options Hearing or Full Case Management Hearing so continued—

    (a) lodge in process a note of the basis for the plea; and

    (b) intimate a copy of it to every other party.

---

[1] As inserted by the Act of Sederunt (Ordinary Cause Rules Amendment) (Proving the Tenor and Reduction) 2015 (SSI 2015/176) para.2 (effective 25 May 2015).

[2] As amended by the Act of Sederunt (Ordinary Cause Rules 1993 Amendment) (Case Management of Defended Family and Civil Partnership Actions) 2022 (SSI 2022/289) r.2(9) (effective 25 September 2023 subject to transitional provision specified in SSI 2022/289 r.3).

(3) If a party fails to comply with paragraph (1) or (2), the party is deemed to be no longer insisting on the preliminary plea; and the plea shall be repelled by the sheriff at the Options Hearing, Procedural Hearing or Full Case Management Hearing.

(4)[1] At any proof before answer or debate, parties may on cause shown raise matters in addition to those set out in the note mentioned in paragraph (1) or (2).

(5) Where a note of the basis of a preliminary plea has been lodged under paragraph (1), and the Options Hearing is continued under rule 9.12(5), unless the basis of the plea has changed following further adjustment, it shall not be necessary for a party who is insisting on the plea to lodge a further note before the Options Hearing so continued.

GENERAL NOTE

Rule 22.1(1)

One of the most useful innovations of OCR 1993 was the removal of the automatic right to debate together with the requirement to provide notice of the basis of a preliminary plea. At the options hearing the court requires to make an informed decision as to further procedure. To do that in addition to studying the pleadings the sheriff must have a clear indication of the basis upon which any preliminary plea is stated. Accordingly any party that has a preliminary plea must lodge a note under this rule three days before the hearing. Failure to comply means that the preliminary plea must be repelled at the options hearing (or continued options hearing)—although it may just be possible in certain circumstances to invoke the dispensing power under OCR, rule 2.1 (see *Colvin v Montgomery Preservations Ltd* , 1995 S.L.T. (Sh. Ct) 14—that case involved sending the case for additional procedure in terms of Chapter 10 and was an early decision (less latitude might be shown now)). See also *Humphrey v Royal Sun Alliance Plc* , 2005 S.L.T. (Sh. Ct) 31.

Rule 22.1(2)

Where a preliminary plea is added by adjustment between an options hearing and a continued options hearing a note of the basis of the plea must be lodged failing which it will be repelled. Likewise, where a preliminary plea is added by amendment (or answers thereto) it is necessary to lodge a note of argument failing which the plea must be repelled (see OCR, rule 18.8) (cf. *Sutherland v Duncan* , 1996 S.L.T. 428—another early case and where the sheriff's exercise of the dispensing power was not interfered with on appeal).

Rule 22.1(4)

On cause shown it is competent to make an argument in support of a preliminary plea not foreshadowed in the rule 22 note but if the argument is new, separate or distinct from the note of the basis of the plea as intimated it might, if successful, result in a penalty in expenses at least to some extent. On the other hand it is not competent to attempt at debate or by amendment to introduce a new or different plea (in relation to the same pleadings that have already been considered at the options hearing) or to reintroduce a plea that has been repelled already (see *George Martin (Builders) Ltd v Jamal* , 2001 S.L.T. (Sh. Ct) 119; see also *Bell v John Davidson (Pipes)* , 1995 S.L.T. (Sh. Ct) 15).

D1.170

Chapter 23

Abandonment

Abandonment of causes

23.1.—(1) A pursuer may abandon a cause at any time before decree of absolvitor or dismissal by lodging a minute of abandonment and—

 (a) consenting to decree of absolvitor; or

 (b) seeking decree of dismissal.

(2)[2] The sheriff shall not grant decree of dismissal under paragraph (1)(b) unless full judicial expenses have been paid to the defender, and any third party against whom the pursuer has directed any crave, within 28 days after the date of taxation.

---

[1] As amended by the Act of Sederunt (Sheriff Court Ordinary Cause Rules Amendment) (Miscellaneous) 2000 (SSI 2000/239) (effective 2 October 2000).
[2] As amended by SSI 2003/26, reg. 2 (effective from January 24, 2003).

(3) If the pursuer fails to pay the expenses referred to in paragraph (2) to the party to whom they are due within the period specified in that paragraph, that party shall be entitled to decree of absolvitor with expenses.

GENERAL NOTE

A pursuer has a right to abandon an action against one or more defenders without reserving the ability to raise a fresh action against the same defender in respect of the same subject matter. Such abandonment without reservation will result in decree of absolvitor being pronounced in favour of the defender who will have the benefit of the plea of res judicata should the same pursuer raise the same action against him. The minute is in the following terms "[Name of Solicitor] for the pursuer stated and hereby stated to the court that the pursuer abandons the cause and consents to decree of absolvitor in terms of rule 23.2(1)(a) of the Ordinary Cause Rules". It is usual for the minute also to concede expenses, although this is not a prerequisite. The pursuer should enrol a motion to abandon in terms of the minute (*Walker v Walker* , 1995 S.C.L.R. 187). If the minute is silent as to expenses the defender should oppose the motion to abandon *quaod* the matter of expenses. Expenses as taxed will ordinarily be pronounced in favour of the defender unless, for example, the defender has wrongly misled the pursuer into raising an action against him in which case the pursuer may be able to persuade the court to award him expenses despite the abandonment.

The pursuer may want to reserve the right to raise a fresh action. To achieve that he must ensure that the court pronounces dismissal as opposed to absolvitor, and to do that he must comply with the peremptory terms of the rule. The court will not grant dismissal unless full judicial expenses are paid to the defender within 28 days of the date of taxation. The procedure is for a motion to be lodged for dismissal together with a minute stating "[Name of Solicitor] for the pursuer stated and hereby states to the court that the pursuer abandons the cause and seeks decree of dismissal in terms of rule 23.1(1)(b) of the Ordinary Cause Rules". The court allows the minute to be received, appoints the defender to lodge an account of expenses (within such period as the court may specify) and remits the same when lodged to the auditor of court to tax and to report. The pursuer has 28 days from the date of taxation in order to pay the account if he seeks dismissal as opposed to absolvitor. If he pays he should lodge the receipt in process together with a motion for dismissal in respect that the expenses as taxed due to the defender have been paid (or consigned) and the court then pronounces an interlocutor allowing the pursuer to abandon the cause and dismisses the action. If the expenses are not paid within the 28-day period the defender can enrol for absolvitor with expenses (see *VP Packaging Ltd v The ADF Partnership* , 2002 S.L.T. 1224; see also *Anderson v Hardie* , 1997 S.L.T. (Sh. Ct) 70), but the court still has a discretion to allow a pursuer to withdraw a minute of abandonment at any time before the final decree disposing of the action (subject to such conditions as to expenses as seem appropriate (see *Lee v Pollock's Trustees* (1906) F. 857)). Rule 23.1 makes no provision for the situation where parties agree on the amount of expenses without the account being taxed, and if that is done it has been held that the pursuer may be presumed to have abandoned any right to ask for dismissal in terms of the rule (see *VP Packaging* (above) but for a contrary view see *Beattie v The Royal Bank of Scotland Plc* , 2003 S.L.T. 564 which suggests that the dispensing power may be used in these circumstances).

Application of abandonment to counterclaims

D1.171

23.2. Rule 23.1 shall, with the necessary modifications, apply to the abandonment by a defender of his counterclaim as it applies to the abandonment of a cause.

Chapter 24

Withdrawal of Solicitors

Intimation of withdrawal to court

24.1.—(1)[1] Subject to paragraph (3), where a solicitor withdraws from acting on behalf of a party, he shall intimate his withdrawal by letter to the sheriff clerk and to every other party.

D1.172

(2)[2] The sheriff clerk shall forthwith lodge such letter in process.

(3)[3] Where a solicitor withdraws from acting on behalf of a party in open court and in the presence of the other parties to the action or their representatives, paragraph (1) shall not apply.

---

[1] As amended by the Act of Sederunt (Sheriff Court Ordinary Cause Rules Amendment) (Miscellaneous) 2000 (SSI 2000/239) (effective 2 October 2000).
[2] As amended by the Act of Sederunt (Sheriff Court Ordinary Cause Rules Amendment) (Miscellaneous) 2000 (SSI 2000/239) (effective 2 October 2000).
[3] Inserted by the Act of Sederunt (Sheriff Court Ordinary Cause Rules Amendment) (Miscellaneous) 2000 (SSI 2000/239) (effective October 2, 2000).

An agent is entitled to withdraw from acting without asking for leave from the court but must intimate the withdrawal by letter to the sheriff clerk and every other party. The agent also has a duty to furnish the agents for the other parties with the address of his former client, if it is known to him (see *Sime, Sullivan & Dickson's Trustee v Adam* , 1908 S.C. 32). Of course, notwithstanding the requirements of this rule the court still has discretion to pronounce decree by default if a party is unrepresented at a diet (see Chapter 16 and for an example see *Munro & Miller (Pakistan) Ltd v Wyvern Structures Ltd* , 1997 S.C. 1).

D1.173 **Intimation to party whose solicitor has withdrawn**

24.2.—(1)[1] Subject to paragraph (1A), the sheriff shall, of his own motion, or on the motion of any other party, pronounce an interlocutor ordaining the party whose solicitor has withdrawn from acting to appear or be represented at a specified diet fixed by the sheriff to state whether or not he intends to proceed, under certification that if he fails to do so the sheriff may grant decree or make such other order or finding as he thinks fit.

(1A)[2] Where any previously fixed diet is to occur within 14 days from the date when the sheriff first considers the solicitor's withdrawal, the sheriff may either—

(a) pronounce an interlocutor in accordance with paragraph (1);
or
(b) consider the matter at the previously fixed diet.

(2) The diet fixed in the interlocutor under paragraph (1) shall not be less than 14 days after the date of the interlocutor unless the sheriff otherwise orders.

(3) The party who has lodged the motion under paragraph (1), or any other party appointed by the sheriff, shall forthwith serve on the party whose solicitor has withdrawn a copy of the interlocutor and a notice in Form G10; and a certificate of service shall be lodged in process.

It is very important that the requirements of intimation, notice and certification are complied with to ensure the peremptory nature of the diet at which the now unrepresented party is required to appear.

D1.174 **Consequences of failure to intimate intention to proceed**

24.3. Where a party on whom a notice and interlocutor has been served under rule 24.2(2) fails to appear or be represented at a diet fixed under rule 24.2(1) and to state his intention as required by that paragraph, the sheriff may grant decree or make such other order or finding as he thinks fit.

If the requirements of intimation, notice and certification are followed then, ordinarily, decree will be pronounced (see, e.g. *Connelly v Lanarkshire Health Board* , 1999 S.C. 364). The decree could be *de plano* in favour of a pursuer or dismissal in favour of a defender. It is competent to pronounce absolvitor in favour of a defender but generally the court will pronounce decree of dismissal. The decree is a decree *in foro*. If the requirements are followed then appeal though competent is unlikely to succeed (see *Connelly*).

D1.175 Chapter 25

Minutes of Sist and Transference

Minutes of sist

25.1. Where a party dies or comes under legal incapacity while a cause is depending, any person claiming to represent that party or his estate may apply by minute to be sisted as a party to the cause.

---

[1] As amended by the Act of Sederunt (Sheriff Court Ordinary Cause Rules Amendment) (Miscellaneous) 2000 (SSI 2000/239) (effective 2 October 2000).
[2] Inserted by the Act of Sederunt (Sheriff Court Ordinary Cause Rules Amendment) (Miscellaneous) 2000 (SSI 2000/239) (effective October 2, 2000).

Death of a party suspends all procedure in the cause at whatever stage it is at (including appeal) and any further procedure is inept unless the representatives of the deceased sist themselves to the cause, or the action is transferred (by amendment) against such representatives. Where a party becomes bankrupt during the dependence of the action the trustee has power (section 39(2)(b) of the Bankruptcy (Scotland) Act 1985) to carry it on (or continue to defend it) and if he so wishes he should sist himself as a party. By so doing he renders himself liable to the opposite party in the whole expenses of the action. If the trustee declines to sist himself as a party then the bankrupt, if he continues to have title to sue, may continue the action. If the bankrupt is a pursuer the court (if asked) will ordain him to find caution but not if he is a defender (see *William Dow (Potatoes) Ltd v Dow* , 2001 S.L.T. (Sh. Ct) 37). Where a party becomes insane the cause should be sisted so that a guardian may be appointed. Once appointed the guardian is entitled to sist himself as a party. If the guardian fails to sist himself as a party then the other party may apply for and obtain decree and expenses against the incapax (provided of course that proper intimation is made to the guardian).

In the case of corporate bodies, if a company is struck from the register under s.1000 of the Companies Act 2006 during the dependence of the action, the action should be sisted to allow an application to restore it to the register (see *Steans Fashions Ltd v General Assurance Society* [1995] B.C.C. 510—a decision of the English Court of Appeal). If a defender company goes into liquidation during the dependence of the action the permission of the court (in the liquidation process) is required to continue the proceedings against it (see section 130(2) of the Insolvency Act 1986). If the company is a pursuer then the liquidator has power to carry it on (see section 169(2) of the Insolvency Act 1986) and if he wishes to do so he should sist himself as a party to the action. In the case of a company in administration it is essential to obtain the permission of the administrator or the court (in the administration process) to continue proceedings against the company (see s.8 of the Insolvency Act 1988; Schedule B1 para.43(b)). It is unnecessary for an administrator or receiver to sist himself as a party to the action but the instance should be amended to narrate the position.

Minutes of transference

D1.176

25.2.[1] Where a party dies or comes under legal incapacity while a cause is depending and the provisions of rule 25.1 are not invoked, any other party may apply by minute to have the cause transferred in favour of or against, as the case may be, any person who represents that party or his estate.

If the representatives of a deceased or incapax do not sist themselves to the cause, then any other party may apply by minute of transference to have it transferred in favour of or against the person who represents the estate. Decree *cognitionis causa tantum* should be sought so as to constitute the debt against a deceased's estate. If no one comes to represent a pursuer then decree of absolvitor may be obtained.

Chapter 26

D1.177

Transfer and Remit of Causes

Transfer to another sheriff court

26.1.—(1)[2] The sheriff may, on cause shown, transfer any cause to another sheriff court.

(2) Subject to paragraph (4), where a cause in which there are two or more defenders has been brought in the sheriff court of the residence or place of business of one of them, the sheriff may transfer the cause to any other sheriff court which has jurisdiction over any of the defenders.

(3) Subject to paragraph (4), where a plea of no jurisdiction is sustained, the sheriff may transfer the cause to the sheriff court before which it appears to him the cause ought to have been brought.

(4) The sheriff shall not transfer a cause to another sheriff court under paragraph (2) or (3) except—

---

[1] As amended by the Act of Sederunt (Sheriff Court Ordinary Cause Rules Amendment) (Miscellaneous) 1996 (SI 1996/2445) (effective 1 November 1996).

[2] As amended by the Act of Sederunt (Rules of the Court of Session 1994 and Sheriff Court Rules Amendment) (No. 2) (Personal Injury and Remits) 2015 (SSI 2015/227) para.7 (effective 22 September 2015).

    (a)   on the motion of a party; and

    (b)   where he considers it expedient to do so having regard to the convenience of the parties and their witnesses.

  (5) On making an order under paragraph (1), (2) or (3), the sheriff—

    (a)   shall state his reasons for doing so in the interlocutor; and

    (b)   may make the order on such conditions as to expenses or otherwise as he thinks fit.

  (6) The court to which a cause is transferred under paragraph (1), (2) or (3) shall accept the cause.

  (7) A transferred cause shall proceed in all respects as if it had been originally brought in the court to which it is transferred.

  (8) *[Repealed by the Act of Sederunt (Rules of the Court of Session, Sheriff Appeal Court Rules and Sheriff Court Rules Amendment) (Sheriff Appeal Court) 2015 (SSI 2015/419) r.5 (effective 1 January 2016).]*

GENERAL NOTE

The convenience of the parties and witnesses is the paramount consideration determining whether to transfer a cause from one sheriff court to another. The ability of the court to transfer rather than dismiss an action where it has no jurisdiction is based on expediency (see *Wilson v Ferguson* , 1957 S.L.T. (Sh. Ct) 52). It is necessary that either the transferring court or the court to which the cause is transferred otherwise has jurisdiction over the defender. It is essential that the sheriff sets out the reasons for the transfer in the interlocutor.

D1.177.1   **Remit and transfer of summary cause proceedings to all-Scotland sheriff court**

    26.1A.—[1](1) This rule applies where the sheriff directs that a summary cause is to be treated as an ordinary cause and, at the same time, makes an order transferring the action to the all-Scotland sheriff court.

  (2) The pursuer must lodge an initial writ and intimate it to every other party within 14 days of the date of the order.

  (3) The defender must lodge defences within 28 days after the date of the order.

  (4) Following the making of a direction and order mentioned in paragraph (1), the action is to be treated as a personal injuries action within the meaning of Part A1 of Chapter 36.

[THE NEXT PARAGRAPH IS D1.178]

D1.178   **Remit to the Court of Session: proceedings to which section 39 of the 2014 Act does not apply**

    26.2.—[2](1) An application under section 92(2) of the 2014 Act (remit of cases to the Court of Session) is to be made by motion.

  (2) Within 4 days after the sheriff has pronounced an interlocutor remitting a cause to the Court of Session under section 92(2), the sheriff clerk must—

    (a)   send written notice of the remit to each party;

    (b)   certify on the interlocutor sheet that subparagraph (a) has been complied with;

    (c)   transmit the process to the Deputy Principal Clerk of Session.

  (3) Failure by a sheriff clerk to comply with paragraph (2)(a) or (b) does not affect the validity of a remit.

---

[1] As inserted by the Act of Sederunt (Rules of the Court of Session 1994 and Sheriff Court Rules Amendment) (No. 2) (Personal Injury and Remits) 2015 (SSI 2015/227) para.7 (effective September 22, 2015).

[2] As substituted by the Act of Sederunt (Rules of the Court of Session 1994 and Sheriff Court Rules Amendment) (No. 2) (Personal Injury and Remits) 2015 (SSI 2015/227) para.7 (effective September 22, 2015).

General Note

The general power to remit to the Court of Session is contained in section 37(1)(b) of the Sheriff Courts (Scotland) Act 1971, which provides:

"In the case of any ordinary cause brought in the sheriff court the sheriff—

(b)   may, subject to section 7 of the Sheriff Courts (Scotland) Act 1907, on the motion of any of the parties to the cause, if he is of the opinion that the *importance or difficulty* of the cause make it appropriate to do so, remit the cause to the Court of Session."

"Importance or difficulty"

The leading case is the five judge decision in *Mullan v Anderson* , 1993 S.L.T. 835. Despite the divergence of opinions it is submitted that there should not be much difficulty in practice in recognising a case that is suitable to be remitted to the Court of Session. In assessing the matter, the sheriff has a wide discretion and should consider the importance of the cause to the parties and weigh up the procedural implications as well as the expense and delay involved. He should also consider the public interest. In *Mullan* it was clearly appropriate that an allegation of murder be tried in the Supreme Court. In the personal injury field it is insufficient merely to assert that the claim is a substantial one to justify a remit (see *Butler v Thom* , 1982 S.L.T. (Sh. Ct) 57) but other considerations may justify a remit—see *Gallagher v Birse* , 2003 S.C.L.R. 623.

A decision to remit or not to remit may be appealed to the Court of Session without leave (see section 37(3)(b) of the Sheriff Courts (Scotland) Act 1971).

Section 37 of the Sheriff Courts (Scotland) Act 1971 also contains specific powers to remit in family actions and there are specific provisions under section 1 of the Presumption of Death (Scotland) Act 1977 and section 44 of the Crown Proceedings Act 1947.

If a remit is granted, the Sheriff Clerk must send the process to the Court of Session within four days. Once the process is received by him the Deputy Principal Clerk of Session writes the date of receipt on the interlocutor sheet and intimates that date to each party. Within 14 days after such intimation the party on whose motion the remit was made, or if the cause was remitted by the sheriff at his own instance, the pursuer makes up and lodges a process incorporating the sheriff court process in the General Department and makes a motion for such further procedure as he desires and thereafter the cause proceeds as though it had been initiated in the Court of Session (see RCS 1994, rr.32.3 and 32.4).

The other party is entitled to insist on the remit (RCS 1994, r.32.6), but if neither party enrols for further procedure the remit will be deemed to have been abandoned and the cause transmitted back to the sheriff clerk (RCS 1994, r.32.7).

The Court of Session also has power in terms of section 33 of the Court of Session Act to order transmission of a sheriff court process to it on the ground of contingency (see RCS 1994, r.32.2).

Once a cause is before the Court of Session it is incompetent (see *Baird v Scottish Motor Traction Co* , 1948 S.C. 526) to remit it back to the sheriff to consider questions relating to expenses (such as certification of the cause as suitable for the employment of counsel). There is no reason why such matters cannot be dealt with before a remit is granted. But if they have not been, then it is a matter for the Auditor of the Court of Session upon taxation to consider such issues relating to expenses relative to the whole action.

Remit to the Court of Session: proceedings to which section 39 of the 2014 Act applies   D1.178.1

26.2A.—[1](1)   An application under section 92(4) of the 2014 Act (request for remit to the Court of Session) is to be made by motion.

(2)   The decision of a sheriff on an application made under section 92(4) is to be recorded in an interlocutor, and a note of the sheriff's reasons for that decision must be appended to that interlocutor.

(3)   Following receipt of an interlocutor from the Court of Session allowing the proceedings to be remitted the sheriff must issue an interlocutor remitting the proceedings under section 92(6).

(4)   Within 4 days after the sheriff has pronounced an interlocutor remitting a cause to the Court of Session under section 92(6), the sheriff clerk must—

(a)   send written notice of the remit to each party;

(b)   certify on the interlocutor sheet that subparagraph (a) has been complied with;

---

[1] As inserted by the Act of Sederunt (Rules of the Court of Session 1994 and Sheriff Court Rules Amendment) (No. 2) (Personal Injury and Remits) 2015 (SSI 2015/227) para.7 (effective September 22, 2015).

(c)   transmit the process to the Deputy Principal Clerk of Session.

(5)   Failure by a sheriff clerk to comply with paragraph (4)(a) or (b) does not affect the validity of a remit.

D1.178.2   **Remit to the Court of Session: remits under other enactments**

26.2B.—[1](1)   This rule applies where the sheriff has pronounced an interlocutor remitting a cause to the Court of Session under an enactment other than section 92 of the 2014 Act.

(2)   Within 4 days after the sheriff has pronounced that interlocutor, the sheriff clerk must—

(a)   send written notice of the remit to each party;

(b)   certify on the interlocutor sheet that subparagraph (a) has been complied with;

(c)   transmit the process to the Deputy Principal Clerk of Session.

(3)   Failure by a sheriff clerk to comply with paragraph (2)(a) or (b) does not affect the validity of a remit.

[THE NEXT PARAGRAPH IS D1.179]

D1.179   **Remit from Court of Session**

26.3.[2]   On receipt of the process in an action which has been remitted from the Court of Session under section 93 of the 2014 Act (remit of cases from the Court of Session), the sheriff clerk shall—

(a)   record the date of receipt on the interlocutor sheet;

(b)   fix a hearing to determine further procedure on the first court day occurring not earlier than 14 days after the date of receipt of the process; and

(c)   forthwith send written notice of the date of the hearing fixed under subparagraph (b) to each party.

GENERAL NOTE

The provision under section 14 of the Law Reform (Miscellaneous Provisions) (Scotland) Act 1985 (to allow the Court of Session to remit a cause to the sheriff, "where, in the opinion of the court the nature of the action makes it appropriate to do") was not introduced to effect a general redistribution of work between the courts but to meet the needs of particular cases (see *McIntosh v British Railways Board (No.1)* , 1990 S.L.T. 637 (see also *Gribb v Gribb* , 1993 S.L.T. 178). The power to remit should be exercised on grounds particular to the case concerned (see *Bell v Chief Constable of Strathclyde* , 2011 S.L.T. 244). For an example where a remit was granted see *Colin McKay v Lloyd's TSB Mortgages Ltd* , 2005 S.C.L.R. 547.

D1.180   Chapter 27

                                   Caution and Security

Application of this Chapter

27.1.   This Chapter applies to—

(a)   any cause in which the sheriff has power to order a person to find caution or give other security; and

(b)   security for expenses ordered to be given by the election court or the sheriff under section 136(2)(i) of the Representation of the People Act 1983 in an election petition.

---

[1] As inserted by the Act of Sederunt (Rules of the Court of Session 1994 and Sheriff Court Rules Amendment) (No. 2) (Personal Injury and Remits) 2015 (SSI 2015/227) para.7 (effective September 22, 2015).

[2] As amended by the Act of Sederunt (Rules of the Court of Session 1994 and Sheriff Court Rules Amendment) (No. 2) (Personal Injury and Remits) 2015 (SSI 2015/227) para.7 (effective September 22, 2015).

Caution or other security (usually but not necessarily consignation) may be ordered as a condition of recall of arrestment on the dependence. It may also be sought as an alternative to sisting a mandatary where the other party is not resident in an EU country (see *Deiter Rossmeier v Mounthooly Transport* , 2000 S.L.T. 208). Moreover, the court has power to order that a party find caution or consign a sum as security for expenses and/or the sum sought. There are certain particular provisions where caution consignation may be ordered, such as under OCR r.21.3(2) or section 100 of the Bills of Exchange Act 1882. Apart from these, the court has a general power within its discretion to make an order. In relation to natural persons, however, the court will generally not order that caution or security be found unless the party is an undischarged bankrupt, is a nominal pursuer or there are exceptional circumstances justifying an order. Being poor is not of itself a sufficient reason to require caution or security to be found since that would deprive a large section of the community of access to the court (see *Stevenson v Midlothian D.C.* , 1983 S.C. (H.L.) 50 and *McTear's Exr v Imperial Tobacco Ltd* , 1997 S.L.T. 530). If the case is patently without merit then an order may be granted, but such a situation is rare since agents have a professional duty not to prosecute or defend unstateable cases. Defenders are not generally required to find caution, nevertheless the terms of the defence will be scrutinised with care (and a defender with a counter claim falls to be treated in the same way as a pursuer: see *William Dow (Potatoes) Ltd v Dow* , 2001 S.L.T. (Sh Ct) 37). Limited companies as pursuers are required to find security under s.726(2) of the Companies Act 1985 (this is still in force; see Companies Act 2006 (Consequential Amendments Transitional Provisions and Savings) Order 2009 (SI 2009/1941)) if it appears by credible testimony that there is reason to believe that the company will be unable to pay the defender's expenses if successful in his defence. Absence of trading and the failure to comply with the requirements to lodge accounts or annual returns are relevant.

Form of applications

D1.181

27.2.—(1)   An application for an order for caution or other security or for variation or recall of such an order, shall be made by motion.

(2)   The grounds on which such an application is made shall be set out in the motion.

It is important to provide detail in the motion as to the reason for seeking security and any supporting documents should be lodged.

Orders

D1.182

27.3.   Subject to section 726(2) of the Companies Act 1985 (expenses by certain limited companies), an order to find caution or give other security shall specify the period within which such caution is to be found or such security given.

Section 726(2) of the Companies Act 1985 permits the action to be sisted pending the finding of security, but the court is also entitled to impose a time limit within which caution should be found in relation to which failure to comply would amount to default. At common law it is competent to ordain a defender company to find caution. A defender company with a counterclaim falls to be treated in the same way as a pursuer under section 726(2): see *William Dow (Potatoes) Ltd v Dow* , 2001 S.L.T. (Sh Ct) 37.

Methods of finding caution or giving security

D1.183

27.4.—(1)   A person ordered—

   (a)   to find caution, shall do so by obtaining a bond of caution; or
   (b)   to consign a sum of money into court, shall do so by consignation under the Sheriff Court Consignations (Scotland) Act 1893 in the name of the sheriff clerk.

(2)   The sheriff may approve a method of security other than one mentioned in paragraph (1), including a combination of two or more methods of security.

(3)   Subject to paragraph (4), any document by which an order to find caution or give other security is satisfied shall be lodged in process.

(4)   Where the sheriff approves a security in the form of a deposit of a sum of money in the joint names of the agents of parties, a copy of the deposit receipt, and not the principal, shall be lodged in process.

(5)   Any document lodged in process, by which an order to find caution or give other security is satisfied, shall not be borrowed from process.

GENERAL NOTE

Joint deposit receipt is another form of security.

D1.184
Cautioners and guarantors[1]

27.5.[2] A bond of caution or other security shall be given only by a person who is an "authorised person" within the meaning of section 31 of the Financial Services and Markets Act 2000.

GENERAL NOTE

See *Greens Annotated Rules of the Court of Session* (W.Green, 2002) and the annotation to RCS 1994, r.33.5.

D1.185
Form of bonds of caution and other securities

27.6.—(1) A bond of caution shall oblige the cautioner, his heirs and executors to make payment of the sums for which he has become cautioner to the party to whom he is bound, as validly and in the same manner as the party, his heirs and successors, for whom he is cautioner, are obliged.

(2)[3] A bond of caution or other security document given by a person shall state whether that person is an "authorised person" within the meaning of section 31 of the Financial Services and Markets Act 2000.

Sufficiency of caution or security and objections

D1.186
27.7.—(1) The sheriff clerk shall satisfy himself that any bond of caution, or other document lodged in process under rule 27.4(3), is in proper form.

(2) A party who is dissatisfied with the sufficiency or form of the caution or other security offered in obedience to an order of the court may apply by motion for an order under rule 27.9 (failure to find caution or give security).

GENERAL NOTE

Clearly it is in the interest of the party in whose favour the order has been granted to satisfy himself that the security is in proper form.

D1.187
Insolvency or death of cautioner or guarantor

27.8. Where caution has been found by bond of caution or security has been given by guarantee and the cautioner or guarantor, as the case may be—

  (a)[4] becomes apparently insolvent within the meaning assigned by section 16 of the Bankruptcy (Scotland) Act 2016 (meaning of apparent insolvency),

  (b) calls a meeting of his creditors to consider the state of his affairs,

  (c) dies unrepresented, or

  (d) is a company and—

      (i)[5] an administration, bank administration or building society special administration order or a winding up, bank insolvency or building society insolvency order has been made, or a resolution for a voluntary winding up has been passed, with respect to it,

---

[1] As substituted by the Act of Sederunt (Sheriff Court Ordinary Cause Rules Amendment) (Miscellaneous) 1996 (SI 1996/2445) r.3(31) (effective November 1, 1996).
[2] As amended by the Act of Sederunt (Ordinary Cause Rules) Amendment (Caution and Security) 2005 (SSI 2005/20) r.2(2) (effective February 1, 2005).
[3] As amended by the Act of Sederunt (Ordinary Cause Rules) Amendment (Caution and Security) 2005 (SSI 2005/20) r.2(3) (effective February 1, 2005).
[4] As amended by the Act of Sederunt (Rules of the Court of Session, Sheriff Appeal Court Rules and Sheriff Court Rules Amendment) (Bankruptcy (Scotland) Act 2016) 2016 (SSI 2016/312) para.5 (effective 30 November 2016).
[5] As substituted by the Act of Sederunt (Sheriff Court Rules) (Miscellaneous Amendments) 2009 (SSI 2009/294) r.16 (effective October 1, 2009).

> (ii) a receiver of all or any part of its undertaking has been appointed, or
>
> (iii) a voluntary arrangement (within the meaning assigned by section 1(1) of the Insolvency Act 1986) has been approved under Part I of that Act,
>
> the party entitled to benefit from the caution or guarantee may apply by motion for a new security or further security to be given.

Failure to find caution or give security

27.9. Where a party fails to find caution or give other security (in this rule referred to as "the party in default") any other party may apply by motion—

D1.188

(a) where he party in default is a pursuer, for decree of absolvitor; or

(b) where the party in default is a defender or a third party, for decree by default or for such other finding or order as the sheriff thinks fit.

GENERAL NOTE

See Chapter 16. A decree whether absolvitor or by default is in foro and is res judicata between the parties. A successful motion to award caution cannot be appealed without leave (see sections 27 and 28 of the Sheriff Courts (Scotland) Act 1907), but a decree of absolvitor or default can be and the earlier interlocutor ganting security will be opened up as a result: see *McCue v Scottish Daily Record and Sunday Mail*, 1998 S.C. 811.

Chapter 27A[1]

Pursuers' Offers

Interpretation of this Chapter

27A.1.[2] In this Chapter—

D1.188.1

"appropriate date" means the date by which a pursuer's offer could reasonably have been accepted;

"charges" means charges for work carried out by the pursuer's solicitor, and includes any additional charge;

"pursuer's offer" means an offer by a pursuer to settle a claim against a defender made in accordance with this Chapter;

"relevant period" means the period from the appropriate date to the date of acceptance of the pursuer's offer or, as the case may be, to the date on which judgment was given, or on which the verdict was applied.

Pursuers' offers

27A.2.—(1) A pursuer's offer may be made in any cause where the initial writ includes a crave for an order for payment of a sum or sums of money, other than an order—

D1.188.2

(a) which the sheriff may not make without evidence; or

(b) the making of which is dependent on the making of another order which the sheriff may not make without evidence.

(2) This Chapter has no effect as regards any other form of offer to settle.

Making of offer

27A.3.—(1) A pursuer's offer is made by lodging in process an offer in the terms specified in rule 27A.4.

D1.188.3

---

[1] Chapter 27A added by the Act of Sederunt (Rules of the Court of Session 1994 and Ordinary Cause Rules 1993 Amendment) (Pursuers' Offers) 2017 (SSI 2017/52) r.3(2) (effective 3 April 2017).

[2] As amended by the Act of Sederunt (Rules of the Court of Session, Sheriff Appeal Court Rules and Ordinary Cause Rules Amendment) (Taxation of Judicial Expenses) 2019 (SSI 2019/74) r.3 (effective 29 April 2019).

(2) A pursuer's offer may be made at any time before—

    (a) the sheriff makes avizandum or, if the sheriff does not make avizandum, gives judgment; or

    (b) in a jury trial, the jury retires to consider the verdict.

(3) A pursuer's offer may be withdrawn at any time before it is accepted by lodging in process a minute of withdrawal.

Form of offer

D1.188.4   **27A.4.** A pursuer's offer must—

    (a) state that it is made under this Chapter;

    (b) offer to accept—

        (i) a sum or sums of money, inclusive of interest to the date of the offer; and

        (ii) the taxed expenses of process; and

    (c) specify the crave or craves of the initial writ in satisfaction of which the sum or sums and expenses referred to in paragraph (b) would be accepted.

Disclosure of offers

D1.188.5   **27A.5.**—(1) No averment of the fact that a pursuer's offer has been made may be included in any pleadings.

(2) Where a pursuer's offer has not been accepted—

    (a) the sheriff must not be informed that an offer has been made until—

        (i) the sheriff has pronounced judgment; or

        (ii) in the case of a jury trial, the jury has returned its verdict; and

    (b) a jury must not be informed that an offer has been made until it has returned its verdict.

Acceptance of offers

D1.188.6   **27A.6.**—(1) A pursuer's offer may be accepted any time before—

    (a) the offer is withdrawn;

    (b) the sheriff makes avizandum or, if the sheriff does not make avizandum, gives judgment; or

    (c) in the case of a jury trial, the jury retires to consider its verdict.

(2) A pursuer's offer is accepted by lodging in process an acceptance of the offer in the form of a minute of acceptance.

(3) A minute of acceptance must be unqualified other than as respects any question of contribution, indemnity or relief.

(4) On acceptance of a pursuer's offer either the pursuer or the defender may apply by motion for decree in terms of the offer and minute of acceptance.

(5) Where a pursuer's offer includes an offer to accept a sum of money in satisfaction of a crave for decree jointly and severally against two or more defenders, the offer is accepted only when accepted by all such defenders.

(6) However, the sheriff may, on the motion of the pursuer, and with the consent of any defender who has lodged a minute of acceptance, grant decree in terms of the offer and minute of acceptance.

Late acceptance of offers

D1.188.7   **27A.7.**—(1) This rule applies to the determination of a motion under rule 27A.6(4) where the sheriff is satisfied that a defender lodged a minute of acceptance after the appropriate date.

(2) On the pursuer's motion the sheriff must, except on cause shown—

    (a) allow interest on any sum decerned for from the date on which the pursuer's offer was made; and

(b)   find the defender liable for payment to the pursuer of a sum calculated in accordance with rule 27A.9.

(3)   Where the sheriff is satisfied that more than one defender lodged a minute of acceptance after the appropriate date the sheriff may find those defenders liable to contribute to payment of the sum referred to in paragraph (2)(b) in such proportions as the sheriff thinks fit.

(4)   Where the sheriff makes a finding under paragraph (2)(b), the pursuer may apply for decerniture for payment of the sum as so calculated no later than the granting of decree for expenses as taxed.

Non-acceptance of offers

27A.8.—(1)   This rule applies where—   **D1.188.8**

    (a)   a pursuer's offer has been made, and has not been withdrawn;

    (b)   the offer has not been accepted;

    (c)   either—

        (i)   the sheriff has pronounced judgment; or

        (ii)   in the case of a jury trial, the verdict of the jury has been applied;

    (d)   the judgment or verdict, in so far as relating to the craves specified in the pursuer's offer, is at least as favourable in money terms to the pursuer as the terms offered; and

    (e)   the sheriff is satisfied that the pursuer's offer was a genuine attempt to settle the proceedings.

(2)   For the purpose of determining if the condition specified in paragraph (1)(d) is satisfied, interest awarded in respect of the period after the lodging of the pursuer's offer is to be disregarded.

(3)   On the pursuer's motion the sheriff must, except on cause shown, decern against the defender for payment to the pursuer of a sum calculated in accordance with rule 27A.9.

(4)   Such a motion must be lodged no later than the granting of decree for expenses as taxed.

(5)   Where more than one defender is found liable to the pursuer in respect of a crave specified in the offer, the sheriff may find those defenders liable to contribute to payment of the sum referred to in paragraph (3) in such proportions as the sheriff thinks fit.

Extent of defender's liability

27A.9.[1]   The sum that may be decerned for under rule 27A.7(2)(b) or rule   **D1.188.9**
27A.8(3) is a sum corresponding to half the charges allowed on taxation of the pursuer's account of expenses, in so far as those charges are attributable to the relevant period, or in so far they can reasonably be attributed to that period.

[THE NEXT PARAGRAPH IS D1.189]

Chapter 28   **D1.189**

Recovery of Evidence

Application and interpretation of this Chapter

28.1.—(1)   This Chapter applies to the recovery of any evidence in a cause depending before the sheriff.

---

[1] As amended by the Act of Sederunt (Rules of the Court of Session, Sheriff Appeal Court Rules and Ordinary Cause Rules Amendment) (Taxation of Judicial Expenses) 2019 (SSI 2019/74) r.3 (effective 29 April 2019).

(2) In this Chapter, "the Act of 1972" means the Administration of Justice (Scotland) Act 1972.

GENERAL NOTE

An application for recovery under Chapter 28 refers to a cause depending before the sheriff. Before the commencement of an action, the court may grant applications to recover documents, inspect and preserve property, etc. (under the Administration of Justice (Scotland) Act 1972 (as amended)). Such applications require to be brought by summary application (see Act of Sederunt (Summary Applications, Statutory Applications and Appeals etc. Rules) 1999 (SI 1999/929) (reproduced at page D 488) and Part I, rules 3.1.1 and 3.1.2 (page D 513)).

D1.190   **Applications for commission and diligence for recovery of documents or for orders under section 1 of the Act of 1972**

28.2.—(1) An application by a party for—

    (a)   a commission and diligence for the recovery of a document, or

    (b)   an order under section 1 of the Act of 1972,

shall be made by motion.

(2) At the time of lodging a motion under paragraph (1), a specification of—

    (a)   the document or other property sought to be inspected, photographed, preserved, taken into custody, detained, produced, recovered, sampled or experimented with or upon, as the case may be, or

    (b)   the matter in respect of which information is sought as to the identity of a person who might be a witness or a defender,

shall be lodged in process.

(3)[1] A copy of the specification lodged under paragraph (2) and the motion made under paragraph (1) shall be intimated by the applicant to—

    (a)   every other party;

    (b)   in respect of an application under section 1(1) of the Act of 1972, any third party haver; and

    (c)[2]   where necessary—

        (i)   the Advocate General for Scotland (in a case where the document or other property sought is in the possession of either a public authority exercising functions in relation to reserved matters within the meaning of Schedule 5 to the Scotland Act 1998, or a cross-border public authority within the meaning of section 88(5) of that Act); or

        (ii)   the Lord Advocate (in any other case),

        and, if there is any doubt, both.

(4) Where the sheriff grants a motion under paragraph (1) in whole or in part, he may order the applicant to find such caution or give such other security as he thinks fit.

(5) The Advocate General for Scotland or the Lord Advocate or both, as appropriate, may appear at the hearing of any motion under paragraph (1).

GENERAL NOTE

Rule 28.2(1)(a)

The common law process whereby evidence can be recovered and preserved for use in an action is termed commission and diligence. The commission is the written authority of the court to a person (normally a solicitor in practice at the sheriff court where the order is granted) to take the evidence of the

---

[1] As substituted by SI 1996/2445 (effective November 1, 1996).

[2] As substituted by the Act of Sederunt (Ordinary Cause, Summary Application, Summary Cause and Small Claim Rules) Amendment (Miscellaneous) 2007 (SSI 2007/6) r.2(10) (effective January 29, 2007).

witness (or haver) as to the existence or whereabouts of the document; and the diligence is the warrant to cite such witnesses or haver to appear before the commissioner.

Rule 28.2(1)(b)

Apart from the power to order recovery and inspection before the action is raised, the Administration of Justice (Scotland) Act 1972 also augments the common law powers of the court to order inspection, photographing, preservation, custody and detention of documents and other property which appear to be property as to which any question may relevantly arise in any existing civil proceedings before that court. Section 1A of the 1972 Act also gives power to the court to require any person to disclose such information as he has as to the identity of witnesses to the proceedings. The general rule that a litigant will not normally be permitted to recover or inspect property until after the closing of the record is thus modified, and cases, such as *Boyle v Glasgow Royal Infirmary and Associated Hospitals Board of Management* , 1969 S.C. 72, decided before this provision came into force, require to be read in the light of it. The judicial climate and the background culture has altered significantly not least because of the passing into law of the Freedom of Information (Scotland) Act 2002 and there is now no reason why there should be any difference between the test for recovery before and after the closing of the record (cf. *Moore v Greater Glasgow Health Board* , 1978 S.C. 123—it is unthinkable now that an application of the type made in *Moore* could be opposed successfully).

Whether the application for recovery is at common law or under the statute it must satisfy the test of relevancy. A call is relevant if it is designed to recover documents or items which would permit a party to make more detailed or specific averments that are already in the pleadings (including responding to the other side's pleadings). Further a call is relevant if it is designed to recover a document the purpose of which is to prove an averment. Fishing (that is, looking for documents in the hope that material will be obtained to make a case not yet pled) is not permitted.

Rule 28.2(2)

The application is made by motion (see Chapter 15) and at the same time a specification of document(s) or, as the case may be, specification of property or matter requires to be lodged in process. If the application is made before the options hearing the pleadings as adjusted to date should be lodged in process (see OCR, rule 9.4).

"Specification"

A specification is in the form of written calls specifying precisely the document or items sought. There are two types of call. The first is a named description of the document or item. This is appropriate where the document or item is known to exist or at least to have been in existence and can be readily identified by a verbal description. The second type seeks a range of documents which may contain an entry relevant to the case. There is a tendency for practitioners to favour the second type of call. Nevertheless it is advantageous, wherever possible, to use the first type since that minimises the work of the haver in locating the particular document sought and thereafter of the commissioner in excerpting from the documents produced to him the relevant entries falling within the terms of the call. It is not necessary in any specification to identify the name of the haver, but it is helpful to all concerned if it is frequently done. Of course, frequently the haver is unknown and a series of diets of commission require to take place before the document or item is traced to any person.

"Intimated"

It is necessary to intimate the motion to every other party and to the Lord Advocate and/or the Advocate General where what is sought is in the possession of the Crown. Intimation to the Lord Advocate of an application to recover medical records is not necessary; see e.g. Practice Note No.2 of 2006 for Grampian, Highland and Islands (all the other Sherrifdoms have issued practice notes). It is also now necessary to intimate to the haver where what is sought is an order under section 1 of the Administration of Justice (Scotland) Act 1972. It is important therefore that the applicant is clear which of the court's powers is being invoked.

In the case of documents held by the Scottish Government, United Kingdom government departments or other public authorities an objection may be raised that recovery would be contrary to public policy. In that event the court, while accepting a statement to the effect that production would be contrary to the public interest, has to decide whether nevertheless justice requires that the order be granted in the interests of the individual party (*Glasgow Corporation v Central Land Board* , 1956 S.C. (H.L.) 1; *Rogers v Orr* , 1939 S.C. 492; *AB v Glasgow West of Scotland Blood Transfusion Service* , 1993 S.L.T. 36). The objection is frequently taken to protect information gathered by the Police, the Crown Office and Procurator Fiscal service. Whether the objection (which may be at the instance of a party or the haver or both) is successful depends upon the circumstances of the case, the nature of the application and the document sought to be recovered. (See generally, Walker, *Evidence* (3rd ed.), pp.193–198).

It is also the case that by virtue of art.8 of ECHR the Court may require the motion to other persons who may be affected; see *M v A Scottish Local Authority* , 2012 S.L.T. 6.

D1.191   **Optional procedure before executing commission and diligence**

28.3.—[1](1) Subject to rule 28.3A (optional procedure where there is a party litigant), this rule applies where a party has obtained a commission and diligence for the recovery of a document on an application made under rule 28.2(1)(a).

(2) Such a party may, at any time before executing the commission and diligence against a haver, serve on the haver an order in Form G11 (in this rule referred to as "the order").

(3) The order and a copy of the specification referred to in rule 28.2(2), as approved by the sheriff, must be served on the haver or his known agent and must be complied with by the haver in the manner and within the period specified in the order.

(4) Not later than the day after the date on which the order, and any document recovered, is received from a haver by the party who obtained the order, that party—

    (a)   must give written intimation of that fact in Form G11A to the sheriff clerk and every other party; and

    (b)   must—

        (i)   if the document has been sent by post, send a written receipt for the document in Form G11B to the haver; or

        (ii)   if the document has been delivered by hand, give a written receipt in Form G11B to the person delivering the document.

(5) Where the party who has recovered any such document does not lodge it in process within 14 days of receipt of it, that party must—

    (a)   give written intimation to every party that that party may borrow, inspect or copy the document within 14 days after the date of that intimation; and

    (b)   in so doing, identify the document.

(6) Where a party who has obtained any document under paragraph (5) wishes to lodge the document in process, that party must—

    (a)   lodge the document within 14 days after receipt of it; and

    (b)   at the same time, send a written receipt for the document in Form G11C to the party who obtained the order.

(7) Where—

    (a)   no party wishes to lodge or borrow any such document under paragraph (5), the document is to be returned to the haver by the party who obtained the order within 14 days after the expiry of the period specified in paragraph (5)(a); or

    (b)   any such document has been uplifted by another party under paragraph (5) and that party does not wish to lodge it in process, the document shall be returned to the haver by that party within 21 days after the date of receipt of it by him.

(8) Any such document lodged in process is to be returned to the haver by the party lodging it within 14 days after the expiry of any period allowed for appeal or, where an appeal has been marked, from the disposal of any such appeal.

(9) If any party fails to return any such document as provided for in paragraph (7) or (8), the haver may apply by motion (whether or not the cause is in dependence) for an order that the document be returned to him and for the expenses occasioned by that motion.

---

[1] As substituted by the Act of Sederunt (Rules of the Court of Session, Ordinary Cause Rules and Summary Cause Rules Amendment) (Miscellaneous) 2014 (SSI 2014/152) r.3 (effective July 7, 2014).

(10) The party holding any such document (being the party who last issued a receipt for it) is responsible for its safekeeping during the period that the document is in his custody or control.

(11) If the party who served the order is not satisfied that—

(a) full compliance has been made with the order, or

(b) adequate reasons for non-compliance have been given,

he may execute the commission and diligence under rule 28.4.

(12) Where an extract from a book of any description (whether the extract is certified or not) is produced under the order, the sheriff may, on the motion of the party who served the order, direct that that party may inspect the book and take copies of any entries falling with the specification.

(13) Where any question of confidentiality arises in relation to a book directed to be inspected under paragraph (12), the inspection shall be made, and any copies shall be taken, at the sight of the commissioner appointed in the interlocutor granting the commission and diligence.

(14) The sheriff may, on cause shown, order the production of any book (not being a banker's book or book of public record) containing entries falling under a specification, notwithstanding the production of a certified extract from that book.

General Note

The vast majority of commissions proceed under the optional procedure and a diet of commission is not required. The procedure is designed to ensure that all documents falling within the terms of the calls of the specification are produced to the sheriff clerk so that all parties are aware of all of the documents recovered, giving all parties an opportunity of lodging them in process and in the event that they are not lodged ensuring their safe return to the haver. A demand for production (within seven days) in Form G11 (or "order") is served on the haver or his known solicitor together with the specification as approved by the court. The haver produces to the sheriff clerk the certificate appended to the Form G11 together with all documents in his possession falling within the specification. The haver certifies (1) that he has produced all documents in his possession sought under the specification; (2) a list of any other documents that are believed to be in the hands of other named persons; and (3) that there are no other documents falling within the terms of the calls of the specification. No later than the day after the order and documents are produced, the sheriff clerk intimates the returned Form G11 and any document to each party. The party seeking the documents may or may not choose to uplift them from the sheriff clerk within seven days. If he does not then the sheriff clerk must inform every other party of this to enable it to uplift the documents. If a party uplifts the document but decides not to lodge it, the document must be returned to the sheriff clerk within 14 days. The sheriff clerk must intimate the return to all parties and after 14 days of that intimation return the document to the haver.

Optional procedure where there is a party litigant   D1.191.1

28.3A.—[1](1) This rule applies where any of the parties to the action is a party litigant.

(2) The party who has obtained a commission and diligence for the recovery of a document on an application under rule 28.2(1)(a) may, at any time before executing it against a haver, serve on the haver an order in Form G11D (in this rule referred to as "the order").

(3) The order and a copy of the specification referred to in rule 28.2(2), as approved by the sheriff, must be served on the haver or his known agent and must be complied with by the haver in the manner and within the period specified in the order.

(4) Not later than the day after the date on which the order, and any document recovered, is received from a haver by the sheriff clerk, the sheriff clerk shall give written intimation of that fact to each party.

---

[1] As inserted by the Act of Sederunt (Rules of the Court of Session, Ordinary Cause Rules and Summary Cause Rules Amendment) (Miscellaneous) 2014 (SSI 2014/152) r.3 (effective July 7, 2014).

(5) No party, other than the party who served the order, may uplift any such document until after the expiry of 7 days after the date of intimation under paragraph (4).

(6) Where the party who served the order fails to uplift any such document within 7 days after the date of intimation under paragraph (4), the sheriff clerk must give written intimation of that failure to every other party.

(7) Where no party has uplifted any such document within 14 days after the date of intimation under paragraph (6), the sheriff clerk must return it to the haver.

(8) Where a party who has uplifted any such document does not wish to lodge it, he must return it to the sheriff clerk who must—

(a) give written intimation of the return of the document to every other party; and

(b) if no other party uplifts the document within 14 days after the date of intimation, return it to the haver.

(9)[1] Any such document lodged in process is to be returned to the haver by the party lodging it within 14 days after the expiry of any period allowed for appeal or, where an appeal has been made, from the disposal of any such appeal.

(10) If any party fails to return any such document as provided for in paragraph (8) or (9), the haver may apply by motion (whether or not the cause is in dependence) for an order that the document be returned to him and for the expenses occasioned by that motion.

(11) The party holding any such document (being the party who last issued a receipt for it) is responsible for its safekeeping during the period that the document is in his custody or control.

(12) If the party who served the order is not satisfied that—

(a) full compliance has been made with the order, or

(b) adequate reasons for non-compliance have been given,

he may execute the commission and diligence under rule 28.4.

(13) Where an extract from a book of any description (whether the extract is certified or not) is produced under the order, the sheriff may, on the motion of the party who served the order, direct that that party shall be allowed to inspect the book and take copies of any entries falling within the specification.

(14) Where any question of confidentiality arises in relation to a book directed to be inspected under paragraph (13), the inspection shall be made, and any copies shall be taken, at the sight of the commissioner appointed in the interlocutor granting the commission and diligence.

(15) The sheriff may, on cause shown, order the production of any book (not being a banker's book or book of public record) containing entries falling under a specification, notwithstanding the production of a certified extract from that book.

[THE NEXT PARAGRAPH IS D1.192]

D1.192 **Execution of commission and diligence for recovery of documents**

28.4.—(1) The party who seeks to execute a commission and diligence for recovery of a document obtained under rule 28.2(1)(a) shall—

(a) provide the commissioner with a copy of the specification, a copy of the pleadings (including any adjustments and amendments) and a certified copy of the interlocutor of his appointment; and

---

[1] As amended by the Act of Sederunt (Rules of the Court of Session, Sheriff Appeal Court Rules and Sheriff Court Rules Amendment) (Sheriff Appeal Court) 2015 (SSI 2015/419) r.5 (effective 1 January 2016).

(b) instruct the clerk and any shorthand writer considered necessary by the commissioner or any party; and

(c) be responsible for the fees of the commissioner and his clerk, and of any shorthand writer.

(2) The Commissioner shall, in consultation with the parties, fix a diet for the execution of the commission.

(3) The interlocutor granting such a commission and diligence shall be sufficient authority for citing a haver to appear before the commissioner.

(4)[1] A citation in Form G13 shall be served on the haver with a copy of the specification and, where necessary for a proper understanding of the specification, a copy of the pleadings (including any adjustments and amendments) and the party citing the haver shall lodge a certificate of citation in Form G12.

(5) The parties and the haver shall be entitled to be represented by a solicitor or person having a right of audience before the sheriff at the execution of the commission.

(6)[2] At the commission, the commissioner shall—

(a) administer the oath de fideli administratione to any clerk and any shorthand writer appointed for the commission; and

(b) administer to the haver the oath in Form G14, or, where the haver elects to affirm, the affirmation in Form G15.

(7) The report of the execution of the commission and diligence, any document recovered and an inventory of that document, shall be sent by the commissioner to the sheriff clerk.

(8) Not later than the day after the date on which such a report, document and inventory, if any, are received by the sheriff clerk, he shall intimate to the parties that he has received them.

(9) No party, other than the party who served the order, may uplift such a document until after the expiry of 7 days after the date of intimation under paragraph (8).

(10) Where the party who served the order fails to uplift such a document within 7 days after the date of intimation under paragraph (8), the sheriff clerk shall intimate that failure to every other party.

(11) Where no party has uplifted such a document within 14 days after the date of intimation under paragraph (10), the sheriff clerk shall return it to the haver.

(12) Where a party who has uplifted such a document does not wish to lodge it, he shall return it to the sheriff clerk who shall—

(a) intimate the return of the document to every other party; and

(b) if no other party uplifts the document within 14 days of the date of intimation, return it to the haver.

GENERAL NOTE

This rule provides the standard procedure to be followed where a party decides not to use the optional procedure or is not satisfied that there has been full compliance with the G11 order or that adequate reasons for non-compliance have been given. The commissioner may or may not have been appointed in the original interlocutor allowing the commission and diligence. If he has not been appointed then it is necessary to ask the sheriff to make an appointment before the commission can proceed. As well as the commissioner it is necessary to instruct the clerk and any shorthand writer. It is not essential to instruct a shorthand writer, but it is very unwise to proceed without one. Normally the clerk to the commission is the shorthand writer who takes the oath de fideli administratione "to faithfully discharge the duties of clerk and shorthand writer at this commission". The haver is cited to the diet of commission by the party seeking to recover the documents. Failure to obtemper a citation is dealt with in the same way as with any witness citation (see OCR, rules 28.15 and 29.10). If the haver is not a natural person a responsible official or representative should be cited. Usually the organisation will identify a suitable person, if not then

---

[1] As amended by SI 1996/2445 (effective November 1, 1996).
[2] As amended by SI 1996/2445 (effective November 1, 1996).

the managing director or chief executive of the organisation may require to be cited. At a commission the haver is placed on oath but the questions that may be asked is very limited (see JA Maclaren, *Court of Session Practice* (1916), 1079). Legitimate questions are (1) whether the witness has the document or item; (2) whether he has had the document or item at any time; (3) whether he has disposed of it; (4) whether he knows or suspects where it is or has been; (5) whether he is aware of whether anyone else has had, has or has disposed of the document or item; (6) whether the document or item has been destroyed and, if so, when by whom, why and how; and (7) any question designed to ascertain the whereabouts of the document or item or facilitate its recovery. It is illegitimate to use the commission to inquire into the merits of the cause and any such question clearly having that purpose as opposed to a legitimate purpose should simply be disallowed by the commissioner. The haver's representative and any other party (if they have decided to attend) may ask questions to clarify any ambiguities in relation to the answers given to the restricted permissible questions but again must not stray into the merits of the cause.

The clerk will prepare the report which will include a transcript of the proceedings together with an inventory of the documents recovered. These items are transmitted to the sheriff clerk and may be uplifted and lodged, failing which, returned to the haver.

D1.193 Execution of orders for production or recovery of documents or other property under section 1(1) of the Act of 1972

28.5.—(1)   An order under section 1(1) of the Act of 1972 for the production or recovery of a document or other property shall grant a commission and diligence for the production or recovery of that document or other property.

(2)   Rules 28.3 (optional procedure before executing commission and diligence) and 28.4 (execution of commission and diligence for recovery of documents) shall apply to an order to which paragraph (1) applies as they apply to a commission and diligence for the recovery of a document.

General Note

This rules makes it clear that an order for production or recovery of documents or other items under the 1972 Act is for a commission and diligence and that the optional procedure and standard procedure apply mutatis mutandis.

D1.194 Execution of orders for inspection etc. of documents or other property under section 1(1) of the Act of 1972

28.6.—(1)   An order under section 1(1) of the Act of 1972 for the inspection or photographing of a document or other property, the taking of samples or the carrying out of any experiment thereon or therewith, shall authorise and appoint a specified person to photograph, inspect, take samples of, or carry out any experiment on or with, any such document or other property, as the case may be, subject to such conditions, if any, as the sheriff thinks fit.

(2)   A certified copy of the interlocutor granting such an order shall be sufficient authority for the person specified to execute the order.

(3)   When such an order is executed, the party who obtained the order shall serve on the haver a copy of the interlocutor granting it, a copy of the specification and, where necessary for a proper understanding of the specification, a copy of the pleadings (including any adjustments and amendments).

General Note

Rules 28.6 and 28.7 make specific provision where what is sought is inspection or preservation or documents or other property in terms of the 1972 Act as opposed to production and recovery.

D1.195 Execution of orders for preservation etc. of documents or other property under section 1(1) of the Act of 1972

28.7.—[1](1)   An order under section 1(1) of the Act of 1972 for the preservation, custody and detention of a document or other property shall grant a commission and diligence for the detention and custody of that document or other property.

(2)   The party who has obtained an order under paragraph (1) shall—

(a)   provide the commissioner with a copy of the specification, a copy of the

---

[1] As amended by SI 1996/2445 (effective November 1, 1996).

pleadings (including any adjustments and amendments) and a certified copy of the interlocutor of his appointment;

(b) be responsible for the fees of the commissioner and his clerk; and

(c) serve a copy of the order on the haver.

(3) The report of the execution of the commission and diligence, any document or other property taken by the commissioner and an inventory of such property, shall be sent by the commissioner to the sheriff clerk for the further order of the sheriff.

Confidentiality

28.8.—[1](1) Where confidentiality is claimed for any evidence sought to be recovered under any of the following rules, such evidence shall, where practicable, be enclosed in a sealed packet:—

28.3 (optional procedure before executing commission and diligence),

[2]rule 28.3A (optional procedure where there is a party litigant),

28.4 (execution of commission and diligence for recovery of documents),

28.5 (execution of orders for production or recovery of documents or other property under section 1(1) of the Act of 1972),

28.7 (execution of orders for preservation etc. of documents or other property under section 1(1) of the Act of 1972).

(2) A motion to have such a sealed packet opened up or such recovery allowed may be lodged by—

(a) the party who obtained the commission and diligence; or

(b)[3] any other party after the date of intimation under rule 28.3(5), 28.3A(8) or 28.4(10).

(3) In addition to complying with rule 15.2 (intimation of motions) or rule 15A.4 (intimation of motions by email), the party lodging such a motion shall intimate the terms of the motion to the haver by post by the first class recorded delivery service.

(4) The person claiming confidentiality may oppose a motion made under paragraph (2).

D1.196

GENERAL NOTE

Confidentiality can be claimed at the stage when a commission and diligence is sought and if successful will prevent the application being granted. Confidentiality can be claimed where the document (1) is a communication between a party and his solicitor (but the client that can plead or waive confidentiality and where the subject matter of the dispute involves an examination of the comunings between the client and agent there is no confidentiality (see *Micosta SA v Shetland Islands Council* , 1983 S.L.T. 483); (2) came into existence *post litam motam* (that is to say, material that a party has made in preparing his case but not otherwise; see *Komori v Tayside Health Board* , 2010 S.L.T. 387)—the full rigour of the *post litam motam* rule has been undermined by OCR, rule 9A.2 (entitlement to inspection and recovery of documents to be put in evidence at proof) and OCR, rule 36.17C (requirement to lodge medical reports to be relied on the action); (3) is a communication between a party or agents in an attempt to negotiate settlement; and (4) where art.8 of ECHR may be engaged see *M v A Scottish Local Authority* , 2012 S.L.T. 6. Where a party or the court has reason to anticipate that an issue of confidentiality may arise it is sensible to intimate the motion for a commission and diligence to the haver so that the issue may be dealt with at that stage. If confidentiality is claimed before the commission and diligence is granted the court may require all documents falling within the terms of the call to be produced to it so that it can determine the issue and it may (if there is a lot of material to be examined) appoint a commissioner for that purpose. Where a commissioner is appointed it remains for the court to determine whether or not any material identified by him as potentially confidential should be produced to the party seeking the recovery.

---

[1] As amended by SI 1996/2445 (effective November 1, 1996).

[2] As amended by the Act of Sederunt (Rules of the Court of Session, Ordinary Cause Rules and Summary Cause Rules Amendment) (Miscellaneous) 2014 (SSI 2014/152) r.3 (effective July 7, 2014).

[3] As amended by the Act of Sederunt (Rules of the Court of Session and Sheriff Court Rules Amendment) (Miscellaneous) 2014 (SSI 2014/201) r.3 (effective August 1, 2014).

Frequently the first time that a haver will be in a position to claim confidentiality will be at a stage after he has been ordered to produce the documents or item. In that event the documents or item should, where practicable, be produced in a sealed packet. A motion is then made to open up the sealed packet which motion may be opposed by the haver.

D1.197 **Warrants for production of original documents from public records**

28.9.—(1) Where a party seeks to obtain from the keeper of any public record production of the original of any register or deed in his custody for the purposes of a cause, he shall apply to the sheriff by motion.

(2) Intimation of a motion under paragraph (1) shall be given to the keeper of the public record concerned at least 7 days before the motion is lodged.

(3) In relation to a public record kept by the Keeper of the Registers of Scotland or the Keeper of the Records of Scotland, where it appears to the sheriff that it is necessary for the ends of justice that a motion under this rule should be granted, he shall pronounce an interlocutor containing a certificate to that effect; and the party applying for production may apply by letter (enclosing a copy of the interlocutor duly certified by the sheriff clerk), addressed to the Deputy Principal Clerk of Session, for an order from the Court of Session authorising the Keeper of the Registers or the Keeper of the Records, as the case may be, to exhibit the original of any register or deed to the sheriff.

(4) The Deputy Principal Clerk of Session shall submit the application sent to him under paragraph (3) to the Lord Ordinary in chambers who, if satisfied, shall grant a warrant for production or exhibition of the original register or deed sought.

(5) A certified copy of the warrant granted under paragraph (4) shall be served on the keeper of the public record concerned.

(6) The expense of the production or exhibition of such an original register or deed shall be met, in the first instance, by the party who applied by motion under paragraph (1).

GENERAL NOTE

It may sometimes be necessary to obtain the original public record (for instance a coloured plan annexed to a deed, although any extract should also be in colour). If it is, then this rule provides the procedure. Normally an official extract of public record will suffice, and such a document is admissible (see Walkers, *Evidence* (1st ed.), para.227). Another approach is provided by s.6 of the Civil Evidence (Scotland) Act 1988.

D1.198 **Commissions for examination of witnesses**

28.10.—(1)[1] This rule applies to a commission—

    (a)   to take the evidence of a witness who—

        (i)   is resident beyond the jurisdiction of the court;

        (ii)   although resident within the jurisdiction of the court, resides at some place remote from that court; or

        (iii)   by reason of age, infirmity or sickness, is unable to attend the diet of proof;

    (b)   in respect of the evidence of a witness which is in danger of being lost, to take the evidence to *lie in retentis*; or

    (c)   on special cause shown, to take evidence of a witness on a ground other than one mentioned in sub-paragraph (a) or (b).

(2) An application by a party for a commission to examine a witness shall be made by motion; and that party shall specify in the motion the name and address of at least one proposed commissioner for approval and appointment by the sheriff.

[1] As amended by SI 1996/2445 (effective November 1, 1996).

(2A)[1] A motion under paragraph (2) may include an application for authority to record the proceedings before the commissioner by video recorder.

(3) The interlocutor granting such a commission shall be sufficient authority for citing the witness to appear before the commissioner.

(4)[2] At the commission, the commissioner shall—

(a) administer the oath *de fideli administratione* to any clerk and any shorthand writer appointed for the commission; and

(b) administer to the witness the oath in Form G14, or where the witness elects to affirm, the affirmation in Form G15.

(5) Where a commission is granted for the examination of a witness, the commission shall proceed without interrogatories unless, on cause shown, the sheriff otherwise directs.

GENERAL NOTE

The recovery of evidence for use in an action is termed commission and diligence. The commission is the written authority of the court to the person appointed commissioner (either a solicitor or advocate but there is no reason why the Sheriff hearing the proof should not appoint himself commissioner) to take the evidence of the witness and the diligence is the warrant to cite the witness to appear before the commissioner.

A commission to take the evidence of a witness may be granted where a party wishes evidence that is in danger of being lost (through death or serious illness or prolonged absence abroad) to be taken to *lie in retentis* pending a proof or where the witness is unable to attend through age or infirmity or sickness or is resident beyond the jurisdiction or because of a special cause (such as holiday or important professional commitments). There has been an increased willingness to use the procedure so as not to cause disproportionate inconvenience to witnesses.

Commissions on interrogatories   D1.199

28.11.—(1) Where interrogatories have not been dispensed with, the party who obtained the commission to examine a witness under rule 28.10 shall lodge draft interrogatories in process.

(2) Any other party may lodge cross-interrogatories.

(3) The interrogatories and any cross-interrogatories, when adjusted, shall be extended and returned to the sheriff clerk for approval and the settlement of any dispute as to their contents by the sheriff.

(4) The party who has obtained the commission shall—

(a) provide the commissioner with a copy of the pleadings (including any adjustments and amendments), the approved interrogatories and any cross-interrogatories and a certified copy of the interlocutor of his appointment;

(b) instruct the clerk; and

(c) be responsible, in the first instance, for the fee of the commissioner and his clerk.

(5) The commissioner shall, in consultation with the parties, fix a diet for the execution of the commission to examine the witness.

(6) The executed interrogatories, any document produced by the witness and an inventory of that document, shall be sent by the commissioner to the sheriff clerk.

(7) Not later than the day after the date on which the executed interrogatories, any document and an inventory of that document, are received by the sheriff clerk, he shall intimate to each party that he has received them.

(8) The party who obtained the commission to examine the witness shall lodge in process—

(a) the report of the commission; and

---

[1] As inserted by the Act of Sederunt (Sheriff Court Rules) (Miscellaneous Amendments) 2008 (SSI 2008/223) para.11 (effective July 1, 2008).

[2] As amended by SI 1996/2445 (effective November 1, 1996).

    (b)   the executed interrogatories and any cross-interrogatories.

GENERAL NOTE

Unless dispensed with a commission proceeds upon interrogatories, that is a series of approved questions in writing for the witness to answer. This procedure is derived from the Court of Session where it was often used in divorce cases where the subject matter was exceedingly straightforward. Interrogatories are not ideal for anything but the simplest of cases. The exception is now the rule so that interrogatories are almost always dispensed with. See OCR r.28.10(5).

D1.200   **Commissions without interrogatories**

    28.12.—(1) Where interrogatories have been dispensed with, the party who has obtained a commission to examine a witness under rule 28.10 shall—

    (a)   provide the commissioner with a copy of the pleadings (including any adjustments and amendments) and a certified copy of the interlocutor of his appointment;

    (b)   fix a diet for the execution of the commission in consultation with the commissioner and every other party;

    (c)   instruct the clerk and any shorthand writer; and

    (d)[1] be responsible in the first instance for the fees of the commissioner, his clerk and any shorthand writer.

    (2) All parties shall be entitled to be present and represented at the execution of the commission.

    (3) The report of the execution of the commission, any document produced by the witness and an inventory of that document, shall be sent by the commissioner to the sheriff clerk.

    (4) Not later than the day after the date on which such a report, any document and an inventory of that document are received by the sheriff clerk, he shall intimate to each party that he has received them.

    (5) The party who obtained the commission to examine the witness shall lodge the report in process.

GENERAL NOTE

The standard commission takes place without interrogatories. The party whose commission it is fixes the diet and should also instruct a shorthand writer who will act as clerk. A shorthand writer is not compulsory but it is unwise to proceed without one. The commissioner should place the shorthand writer ("I do swear that I will faithfully discharge the duties of clerk and shorthand writer to this commission. So help me God") and witness ("I swear by almighty God that I will tell the truth, the whole truth and nothing but the truth") on oath. If the witness affirms then it is "I solemnly, sincerely and truly declare and affirm that I will tell the truth, the whole truth and nothing but the truth". Productions to be put to the witness should be borrowed from process in advance for that purpose. A commission can take place at any location. The party whose commission it is examines the witness and cross-examination and reexamination follows in the usual way. Objections to questions or to the line of evidence are normally dealt with by allowing the evidence to be heard subject to competency and relevancy. The evidence thus heard should be noted on a paper apart so that it is easily identifiable for determination as to its admissibility by the sheriff due course. Once the commission has been completed, a written transcript and report will be made up by the clerk (and shorthand writer) and signed by him and the commissioner. The report of the commission must be lodged in process.

D1.201   **Evidence taken on commission**

    28.13.—(1) Subject to the following paragraphs of this rule and to all questions of relevancy and admissibility, evidence taken on commission under rule 28.11 or 28.12 may be used as evidence at any proof of the cause.

    (2) Any party may object to the use of such evidence at a proof; and the objection shall be determined by the sheriff.

---

[1] As amended by the Act of Sederunt (Ordinary Cause, Summary Application, Summary Cause and Small Claim Rules) Amendment (Vulnerable Witnesses (Scotland) Act 2004) 2007, r.2(7) (effective November 1, 2007).

(3)   Such evidence shall not be used at a proof if the witness becomes available to attend the diet of proof.

(4)   A party may use such evidence in accordance with the preceding paragraphs of this rule notwithstanding that it was obtained at the instance of another party.

GENERAL NOTE

If the evidence is to be relied upon it must be tendered before the party relying upon it closes its case. Any of the parties may do so. Although there is no modern reported decision there seems no reason in principle why a witness who gives evidence at a proof having made a statement at a commission may not be examined as to consistencies or cross examined as to inconsistencies (see section 3 of the Civil Evidence (Scotland) Act 1988; cf. *Forrests v Low's Trs* , 1907 S.C. 1240).

Letters of request   D1.202

28.14.—[1](1)   Subject to paragraph (7), this rule applies to an application for a letter of request to a court or tribunal outside Scotland to obtain evidence of the kind specified in paragraph (2), being evidence obtainable within the jurisdiction of that court or tribunal, for the purposes of a cause depending before the sheriff.

(2)[2]   An application to which paragraph (1) applies may be made in relation to a request—

  (a)   for the examination of a witness,
  (b)   for the inspection, photographing, preservation, custody, detention, production or recovery of, or the taking of samples of, or the carrying out of any experiment on or with, a document or other property, as the case may be,
  (c)   for the medical examination of any person,
  (d)   for the taking and testing of samples of blood from any person, or
  (e)   for any other order for obtaining evidence,

for which an order could be obtained from the sheriff.

(3)   Such an application shall be made by minute in Form G16 together with a proposed letter of request in Form G17.

(4)[3]   It shall be a condition of granting a letter of request that any solicitor for the applicant, or a party litigant, as the case may be, shall be personally liable, in the first instance, for the whole expenses which may become due and payable in respect of the letter of request to the court or tribunal obtaining the evidence and to any witness who may be examined for the purpose; and he shall consign into court such sum in respect of such expenses as the sheriff thinks fit.

(5)   Unless the court or tribunal to which a letter of request is addressed is a court or tribunal in a country or territory—

  (a)   where English is an official language, or
  (b)   in relation to which the sheriff clerk certifies that no translation is required,

then the applicant shall, before the issue of the letter of request, lodge in process a translation of that letter and any interrogatories and cross-interrogatories into the official language of that court or tribunal.

(6)[4]   The letter of request when issued; any interrogatories and cross-interrogatories adjusted as required by rule 28.11 and the translations (if any), shall be forwarded by the sheriff clerk to the Scottish Ministers or to such person and in such manner as the sheriff may direct.

---

[1] As amended by the Act of Sederunt (Taking of Evidence in the European Community) 2003 (SSI 2003/601).
[2] As amended by SI 1996/2445 (effective November 1, 1996).
[3] As amended by SI 1996/2445 (effective November 1, 1996).
[4] As substituted by the Act of Sederunt (Sheriff Court Rules) (Miscellaneous Amendments) 2011 (SSI 2011/193) r.8 (effective April 4, 2011).

(7) This rule does not apply to any request for the taking of evidence under Council Regulation (EC) No. 1206/2001 of 28th May 2001 on cooperation between the courts of the Member States in the taking of evidence in civil or commercial matters.

GENERAL NOTE

There is no power to enforce the attendance of witnesses who are furth of Scotland but an application may be made to apply for evidence to be taken on commission or by letter of request. A commission still relies on co-operation of the witness outwith the jurisdiction. A letter of request enables the foreign court or tribunal to compel the witness to give evidence. In relation to witnesses in other parts of the United Kingdom, the sheriff appoints a commissioner to take the evidence and the attendance of that witness at a commission is compelled by the High Court in England and Wales and Northern Ireland (see Evidence (Proceedings in Other Jurisdictions) Act 1975, ss.1–4). Witnesses beyond the United Kingdom require to be considered under reference to the Hague Convention on the Taking of Evidence Abroad in Civil or Commercial Matters, March 18, 1970. OCR r.28.14 is for all practical purposes identical to the rule in the equivalent rule in the Court of Session (see *Greens Annotated Rules of the Court of Session* (W.Green, 2002), pp.C250–C253).

D1.203

Taking of evidence in the European Community
28.14A.—[1](1) This rule applies to any request—
- (a) for the competent court of another Member State to take evidence under Article 1.1(a) of the Council Regulation; or
- (b) that the court shall take evidence directly in another Member State under Article 1.1(b) of the Council Regulation.

(2) An application for a request under paragraph (1) shall be made by minute in Form G16, together with the proposed request in form A or I (as the case may be) in the Annex to the Council Regulation.

(3) In this rule, "the Council Regulation" means Council Regulation (EC) No. 1206/2001 of 28th May 2001 on cooperation between the courts of the Member States in the taking of evidence in civil or commercial matters.

Citation of witnesses and havers
D1.204

28.15. The following rules shall apply to the citation of a witness or haver to a commission under this Chapter as they apply to the citation of a witness for a proof:—

rule 29.7 (citation of witnesses) except paragraph 4,

rule 29.9 (second diligence against a witness,

rule 29.10 (failure of witness to attend).

---

[1] As amended by the Act of Sederunt (Taking of Evidence in the European Community) 2003 (SSI 2003/601).

GENERAL NOTE

A witness is cited for a commission as he would be for a proof and his attendance may likewise be enforced.

Chapter 28A[1]   **D1.205**

Pre-Proof Hearing

Pre-proof hearing

28A.1.—[2](1)[3] Subject to paragraph (1A) the appointment of a cause to a proof or proof before answer or thereafter on the motion of any party or of his own motion, the sheriff may appoint the cause to a pre-proof hearing.

(1A) In a family action which must follow the procedure set out in Part III of Chapter 33 or 33A (defended family actions), the sheriff will fix a pre-proof hearing at the Full Case Management Hearing.

(2) It shall be the duty of the parties to provide the sheriff with sufficient information to enable him to conduct the hearing as provided for in this rule.

(3) At a pre-proof hearing the sheriff shall ascertain, so far as is reasonably practicable, whether the cause is likely to proceed to proof on the date fixed for that purpose and, in particular—

    (a)   the state of preparation of the parties; and

    (b)   the extent to which the parties have complied with their duties under rules 9A.2, 9A.3, 29.11 and 29.15 and any orders made by the sheriff under—

        (i)   rules 9.12(3)(a), (b), (d) or (e);

        (ii)   rules 10.6(3)(a) or (b);

        (iii)   rules 33.36P(4)(a), (b), (d) or (6); or

        (iv)   rules 33A.36P(4)(a), (b), (d) or (6); and

    (c)[4]   consider any child witness notice or vulnerable witness application that has been lodged where no order has been made, or ascertain whether there is or is likely to be a vulnerable witness within the meaning of section 11(1) of the 2004 Act who is to give evidence at any proof or hearing and whether any order under section 12(1) of the Act of 2004 requires to be made.

(4) At a pre-proof hearing the sheriff may—

    (a)   discharge the proof or proof before answer and fix a new date for such proof or proof before answer;

    (b)   adjourn the pre-proof hearing; or

    (c)   make such other order as he thinks fit to secure the expeditious progress of the cause.

(5) For the purposes of rules 16.2 (decrees where party in default), 33.37 (decree by default in family action) and 33A.37 (decree by default in civil partnership action), a pre-proof hearing shall be a diet in accordance with those rules.

---

[1] Inserted by the Act of Sederunt (Ordinary Cause and Summary Application Rules) Amendment (Miscellaneous) 2006 (SSI 2006/410) (effective 18 August 2006).

[2] As amended by the Act of Sederunt (Ordinary Cause Rules 1993 Amendment) (Case Management of Defended Family and Civil Partnership Actions) 2022 (SSI 2022/289) r.2(10) (effective 25 September 2023 subject to transitional provision specified in SSI 2022/289 r.3).

[3] As inserted by the Act of Sederunt (Sheriff Court Rules)(Miscellaneous Amendments) (No.2) 2013 (SI 2013/139) para.2 (effective 3 June 2013).

[4] As inserted by the Act of Sederunt (Ordinary Cause, Summary Application, Summary Cause and Small Claim Rules) Amendment (Vulnerable Witnesses (Scotland) Act 2004) 2007 (SSI 2007/463) r.2(6)(b) (effective 1 November 2007).

GENERAL NOTE

This is a particularly useful rule designed to allow effective management of court resources. The Sheriff is directed to find out whether parties are in a position to proceed and to check that they have complied with their obligations under the rules. There is sufficient flexibility to allow, if so advised, for the scope of the proof to be confined or restricted if appropriate.

Chapter 29

Proof

Reference to oath

D1.206

29.1.—(1) Where a party intends to refer any matter to the oath of his opponent he shall lodge a motion to that effect.

(2) If a party fails to appear at the diet for taking his deposition on the reference to his oath, the sheriff may hold him as confessed and grant decree accordingly.

GENERAL NOTE

The procedure is described in Walker's *Evidence*, Chapter 25. The Requirements of Writing (Scotland) Act 1995 has rendered the procedure of reference to oath of no practical importance although it remains theoretically possible that it could still be used in relation to events prior to the coming into force of that Act (see e.g. *McEleveen v McQuiilan's Executors* , 1997 S.L.T. (Sh Ct) 46.

D1.207

Remit to person of skill

29.2.—(1) The sheriff may, on a motion by any party or on a joint motion, remit to any person of skill, or other person, to report on any matter of fact.

(2) Where a remit under paragraph (1) is made by joint motion or of consent of all parties, the report of such person shall be final and conclusive with respect to the subject-matter of the remit.

(3) Where a remit under paragraph (1) is made—

(a) on the motion of one of the parties, the expenses of its execution shall, in the first instance, be met by that party; and

(b) on a joint motion or of consent of all parties, the expenses shall, in the first instance, be met by the parties equally, unless the sheriff otherwise orders.

GENERAL NOTE

There are no modern reported examples of the use of this procedure but there may well be cases where it could be usefully employed, particularly now that many issues of disputed fact are spoken to by experts. Perhaps if the sheriff were able to remit to a man of skill *ex proprio motu* the procedure would be used more often. The rule does not prevent a remit being made before the record has closed but it is normally better to know what the parties' final position is in relation to the dispute before a remit is made as it offends against OCR r.29.17.

D1.208

Written statements

29.3.[1] Where a statement in a document is admissible under section 2(1)(b) of the Civil Evidence (Scotland) Act 1988, any party who wishes to have that statement received in evidence shall—

(a) docquet that document as follows:—

"*(Place and date)*
This document contains a statement admissible under section 2(1)(b) of the Civil Evidence (Scotland) Act 1988.
(Signed)
(Designation and address)";

(b) lodge that document in process; and

(c) provide all other parties with a copy of that document.

---

[1] As inserted by the Act of Sederunt (Ordinary Cause, Summary Application and Small Claim Rules) Amendment (Miscellaneous) 2004 (SSI 2004/197) (effective May 21, 2004), para.2(11).

General Note

Rule 29.3 addresses a *lacuna* in the Ordinary Cause Rules by providing for receiving into evidence written statements.

Renouncing probation

D1.209

29.4.—[1](1) Where, at any time, the parties seek to renounce probation, they shall lodge in process a joint minute to that effect with or without a statement of admitted facts and any productions.

(2) On the lodging of a joint minute under paragraph (1), the sheriff may make such order as he thinks fit to secure the expeditious progress of the cause.

General Note

Once a joint minute is lodged renouncing probation, both parties are contractually barred from leading evidence. Any attempt to amend is likely to be refused. The renunciation of probation is rare but does happen from time to time where parties are in agreement as to the material facts. If necessary a separate statement of agreed facts can be lodged. The diet of proof may be converted into a diet of debate.

Orders for proof

D1.210

29.5. Where proof is necessary in any cause, the sheriff shall fix a date for taking the proof and may limit the mode of proof.

General Note

In terms of OCR r.9.12(3), a proof will be ordered at the options hearing; but if after additional procedure, debate or amendment a proof is required, then this rule authorises that to be done at any procedural hearing or debate. This rule is also without prejudice to OCR r.28A(4).

The interlocutor allowing proof should make it clear whose averments are admitted to probation, and if any averments are not the subject of proof that should also be made clear. If the proof is a preliminary proof then the subject matter of the proof should be specified precisely in the interlocutor. Where there is a counter-claim the interlocutor should indicate whether the averments in the counterclaim are admitted to probation.

Proof by writ or oath has been abolished (see section 11 of the Requirements of Writing (Scotland) Act 1995) so the mode of proof will not be limited; but this is subject to section 14(3) which provides that the 1995 Act does not apply to anything done before the commencement of that Act.

Hearing parts of proof separately

D1.211

29.6.—(1)[2] In any cause, the sheriff may—

    (a) of his own motion, or

    (b) on the motion of any party,

order that proof on liability or any specified issue be heard separately from proof on the question of the amount for which decree may be pronounced and determine the order in which the proofs shall be heard.

(2) The sheriff shall pronounce such interlocutor as he thinks fit at the conclusion of the first proof of any cause ordered to be heard in separate parts under paragraph (1).

General Note

This rule is designed to allow a certain amount of flexibility and to avoid wasted procedure.

The obvious examples are preliminary proof on the question of limitation or prescription and separation of proof on liability and quantum. Whether to split a proof is a matter for the discretion of the sheriff in the circumstances of any particular case. See also OCR r.28A(4).

Citation of witnesses

D1.212

29.7.—(1) A witness shall be cited for a proof—

    (a) by registered post or the first class recorded delivery service by the solicitor for the party on whose behalf he is cited; or

    (b) by a sheriff officer—

---

[1] As amended by the Act of Sederunt (Ordinary Cause and Summary Application Rules) Amendment (Miscellaneous) 2006 (SI 2006/410) (effective August 18, 2006).
[2] As amended by SI 1996/2445 (effective November 1, 1996).

    (i)   personally;

    (ii) by a citation being left with a resident at the person's dwelling place or an employee at his place of business;

    (iii) by depositing it in that person's dwelling place or place of business;

    (iv) by affixing it to the door of that person's dwelling place or place of business; or

    (v) by registered post or the first class recorded delivery service.

(2) Where service is executed under paragraph (1)(b)(iii) or (iv), the sheriff officer shall, as soon as possible after such service, send, by ordinary post to the address at which he thinks it most likely that the person may be found, a letter containing a copy of the citation.

(3) A certified copy of the interlocutor allowing a proof shall be sufficient warrant to a sheriff officer to cite a witness on behalf of a party.

(4) A witness shall be cited on a period of notice of 7 days in Form G13 and the party citing the witness shall lodge a certificate of citation in Form G12.

(5) A solicitor who cites a witness shall be personally liable for his fees and expenses.

(6) In the event of a solicitor intimating to a witness that his citation is cancelled, the solicitor shall advise him that the cancellation is not to affect any other citation which he may have received from another party.

GENERAL NOTE

This rule is without prejudice to OCR r.9A.3 (exchange of list of witnesses). It is not necessary to cite a witness to lead him in evidence as the purpose of citation is to compel attendance, but it is wise to cite any witness that it is intended to call. The methods of citation are similar to the citation of parties. As soon as a proof is allowed the witnesses should be informed of its date and they should be cited with as much notice as possible. The seven-day period in the rule is a minimum period of notice. Parties should communicate with each other in order to minimise the inconvenience to witnesses. Fees of witnesses are set out in Act of Sederunt (Fees of Witnesses and Shorthand Writers in the Sheriff Court) 1992.

D1.213   **Citation of witnesses by party litigants**

    29.8.—(1) Where a party to a cause is a party litigant, he shall—

    (a) not later than 4 weeks before the diet of proof, apply to the sheriff by motion to fix caution in such sum as the sheriff considers reasonable having regard to the number of witnesses he proposes to cite and the period for which they may be required to attend court; and

    (b) before instructing a sheriff officer to cite a witness, find caution for such expenses as can reasonably be anticipated to be incurred by the witness in answering the citation.

(2) A party litigant who does not intend to cite all the witnesses referred to in his application under paragraph (1)(a), may apply by motion for variation of the amount of caution.

GENERAL NOTE

The sheriff clerk has a duty to assist party litigants to comply with the requirements of this rule.

D1.214   **Second diligence against a witness**

    29.9.—(1) The sheriff may, on the motion of a party, grant a second diligence to compel the attendance of a witness under pain of arrest and imprisonment until caution can be found for his due attendance.

(2) The warrant for a second diligence shall be effective without endorsation and the expenses of such a motion and diligence may be decerned for against the witness.

Where there is reason to think in advance of the proof that a witness will not attend, then a motion for second diligence to compel attendance may be made. The procedure is described in Maclaren *Court of Session Practice*, pp.343–344. The letters are issued by the sheriff clerk in the name of the sheriff principal and addressed to the sheriff officer, requiring him to apprehend the witness and imprison him within a named prison. Once caution is found the witness must be released. The appropriate sum as a penalty should now be £250 and the sheriff should fix the amount of caution. Letters of second diligence will not be granted unless the witness is essential, there has been effective citation failing which a clear attempt to evade it and that there is a real risk that the witness will not attend.

Failure of witness to attend
29.10.—(1) Where a witness fails to answer a citation after having been duly cited, the sheriff may, on the motion of a party and on production of a certificate of citation, grant warrant for the apprehension of the witness and for bringing him to court; and the expenses of such a motion and apprehension may be decerned for against the witness.

(2) Where a witness duly cited and after having demanded and been paid his travelling expenses, fails to attend a diet, either before the sheriff or before a commissioner, the sheriff may—

  (a) ordain the witness to forfeit and pay a penalty not exceeding £250 unless a reasonable excuse be offered and sustained; and

  (b) grant decree for that penalty in favour of the party on whose behalf the witness was cited.

D1.215

GENERAL NOTE

Decree for the penalty is enforceable by civil diligence.

Lodging productions
29.11.—(1)[1,2] Where a proof has been allowed, all productions and affidavits which are intended to be used at the proof shall be lodged in process not later than 28 days before the diet of proof.

(2) A production which is not lodged in accordance with paragraph (1) shall not be used or put in evidence at a proof unless—

  (a) by consent of parties; or

  (b) with leave of the sheriff on cause shown and on such conditions, if any, as to expenses or otherwise as the sheriff thinks fit.

D1.216

GENERAL NOTE

This rule is without prejudice to OCR r.9A.2 (inspection and recovery of documents); OCR r.21.1 (lodging of documents founded on or adopted); or OCR r.36.17C (lodging of medical reports in actions of damages). It is not necessary to lodge under this rule a document used (usually in cross-examination) only to test the credibility of a witness (see *Paterson & Sons v Kit Coffee Co. Ltd* (1908) 16 S.L.T. 180) whether or not the witness is a party (Macphail, *Sheriff Court Practice* (2nd ed.), para.16.25, and see *Robertson v Anderson* , May 15, 2001 Unreported, OH Lord Carloway paras [64] to [68]).

Copy productions
29.12.—(1)[3] A copy of every documentary production, marked with the appropriate number of process of the principal production, shall be lodged for the use of the sheriff at a proof not later than 48 hours before the diet of proof.

(2) Each copy production consisting of more than one sheet shall be securely fastened together by the party lodging it.

D1.217

---

[1] As amended by SSI 2000/239 (effective October 2, 2000).
[2] As amended by the Act of Sederunt (Ordinary Cause and Summary Application Rules) Amendment (Miscellaneous) 2006 (SSI 2006/410) (effective August 18, 2006).
[3] As amended by SSI 2000/239 (effective October 2, 2000).

Copy productions should be legible and have the same page numbers as the principal.

D1.218
Returning borrowed parts of process and productions before proof

29.13. All parts of process and productions which have been borrowed shall be returned to process before 12.30 pm on the day preceding the diet of proof.

GENERAL NOTE

This rule is without prejudice to OCR rr.11.3, 11.4 and 11.5. Failure to return a borrowed production may result in liability for expenses if any procedure is wasted.

D1.219
Notices to admit and notices of non-admission

29.14.—(1)[1] At any time after the record has closed, a party may intimate to any other party a notice or notices calling on him to admit for the purposes of that cause only—

    (a)   such facts relating to an issue averred in the pleadings as may be specified in the notice;

    (b)   that a particular document lodged in process and specified in the notice is—

        (i)   an original and properly authenticated document; or

        (ii)   a true copy of an original and properly authenticated document.

  (2) Where a party on whom a notice is intimated under paragraph (1)—

    (a)   does not admit a fact specified in the notice, or

    (b)   does not admit, or seeks to challenge, the authenticity of a document specified in the notice,

he shall, within 21 days after the date of intimation of the notice under paragraph (1), intimate a notice of non-admission to the party intimating the notice to him under paragraph (1) stating that he does not admit the fact or document specified.

  (3) A party who fails to intimate a notice of non-admission under paragraph (2) shall be deemed to have admitted the fact or document specified in the notice intimated to him under paragraph (1); and such fact or document may be used in evidence at a proof if otherwise admissible in evidence, unless the sheriff, on special cause shown, otherwise directs.

  (4) [Repealed by the Act of Sederunt (Sheriff Court Rules) (Miscellaneous Amendments) (No.2) 2008 (SSI 2008/365) para.4 (effective December 1, 2008).]

  (5) The party serving a notice under paragraph (1) or (2) shall lodge a copy of it in process.

  (6) A deemed admission under paragraph (3) shall not be used against the party by whom it was deemed to be made other than in the cause for the purpose for which it was deemed to be made or in favour of any person other than the party by whom the notice was given under paragraph (1).

  (7)[2] The sheriff may, at any time, allow a party to amend or withdraw an admission made by him on such conditions, if any, as he thinks fit.

  (8)[3] A party may, at any time, withdraw in whole or in part a notice of non admission by intimating a notice of withdrawal.

GENERAL NOTE

The record is supposed to be the place where parties identify with precision what is truly in dispute between them. Each fact averred requires to be carefully considered by the other party and if appropriate admitted. Frequently the parties respond with a general denial which covers at least some averments that are not in dispute. The whole system of written pleading proceeds on trust that parties will honestly

---

[1] As amended by SSI 2000/239 (effective October 2, 2000).
[2] Inserted by SSI 2000/239 (effective October 2, 2000).
[3] Inserted by SSI 2000/239 (effective October 2, 2000).

answer averments by an opponent on matters within their knowledge and a party must admit averments that he knows to be true. Unfortunately for one reason or another parties do not always live up to these expectations. Furthermore, it is often the case that facts even not strictly speaking within the knowledge of the other party should be identified as not being in dispute. Sometimes there are facts (and there may well be documents) that are not necessarily the subject of averment but which may be relevant to the proof of a parties case that can be usefully identified as being capable of agreement.

This rule provides a mechanism apart from the written pleadings whereby a party can call upon the other to admit certain facts including the originality or authenticity of a document. A failure to respond results in a deemed admission and a response that turns out to be unjustified ought to result at the very least in liability in expenses for any unnecessary procedure. Admissions can be withdrawn and departed from on special cause being shown.

Instruction of shorthand writer

D1.220

29.15. Where a shorthand writer is to record evidence at a proof, the responsibility for instructing a shorthand writer shall lie with the pursuer.

GENERAL NOTE

Failure to instruct the shorthand writer means that the proof cannot proceed unless recording of the evidence by mechanical means is available or recording is dispensed with under r.29.18. Another option may be to seek to have the cause treated as a summary cause (under section 37(1)(a) of the Sheriff Courts (Scotland) Act 1971) but that will restrict any decree accordingly.

Administration of oath or affirmation to witnesses

D1.221

29.16. The sheriff shall administer the oath to a witness in Form G14 or, where the witness elects to affirm, the affirmation in Form G15.

GENERAL NOTE

"I swear by Almighty God that I will tell the truth, the whole truth and nothing but the truth"

"I solemnly sincerely and truly declare and affirm that I will tell the truth, the whole truth and nothing but the truth"

Children under 12 do not have the oath administered but are admonished to tell the truth. Between these ages whether to administer the oath is at the discretion of the Sheriff. The oath (or affirmation) should be administered where the child is 14 or over. It is unlawful to ask questions of a witness before he gives evidence intended to establish that he does not understand the duty to give truthful evidence or the difference between truth and lies (see Vulnerable Witnesses (Scotland) Act 2004 s.24).

Proof to be taken continuously

D1.222

29.17. A proof shall be taken continuously so far as possible; but the sheriff may adjourn the diet from time to time.

GENERAL NOTE

It is important that proof should proceed continuously so as to save time and expense and any adjournment for any period should be arranged with this rule in mind.

Proof management hearing

D1.222.1

29.17A.—[1](1) Where a proof diet has been—
  (a) discharged;
  (b) adjourned, whether under rule 29.17 (proof to be taken continuously) or otherwise; or
  (c) continued to a later date,
the sheriff may, of the sheriff's own motion, fix a proof management hearing.

(2) It is the duty of the parties to provide the sheriff with sufficient information to enable the sheriff to conduct the hearing as provided for in this rule.

(3) At a proof management hearing the sheriff is to ascertain, so far as is reasonably practicable, whether the cause can proceed to proof or, as the case may be, continued proof and in particular—
  (a) when the parties expect to be able to proceed to proof or continued proof;
  (b) the likely availability of witnesses;

---

[1] As inserted by the Act of Sederunt (Rules of the Court of Session 1994 and Sheriff Court Rules Amendment) (Miscellaneous) 2020 (SSI 2020/166) para.3 (effective 2 June 2020).

    (c)   the extent to which the proof or continued proof, and the attendance of witnesses, may be conducted remotely and how that might be achieved; and

    (d)   the extent to which affidavit evidence may be used.

(4) At a proof management hearing the sheriff may—

    (a)   discharge the proof or continued proof;

    (b)   fix a date for the proof diet or, as the case may be, a new date for the continued proof;

    (c)   continue the proof management hearing to a later date;

    (d)   make such other order as the sheriff thinks fit to secure the expeditious progress of the cause.

D1.223   **Recording of evidence**

29.18.—[1](1)[2] Evidence in a cause shall be recorded by—

    (a)   a shorthand writer, to whom the oath *de fideli administratione* in connection with the sheriff court service generally shall have been administered, or

    (b)   tape recording or other mechanical means approved by the court, unless the parties, by agreement and with the approval of the sheriff, dispense with the recording of evidence.

(2) Where a shorthand writer is employed to record evidence, he shall, in the first instance, be paid by the parties equally.

(3) Where evidence is recorded by tape recording or other mechanical means, any fee payable shall, in the first instance, be paid by the parties equally.

(4) The solicitors for the parties shall be personally liable for the fees payable under paragraph (2) or (3), and the sheriff may make an order directing payment to be made.

(5) The record of the evidence at a proof shall include—

    (a)   any objection taken to a question or to the line of evidence;

    (b)   any submission made in relation to such an objection; and

    (c)   the ruling of the court in relation to the objection and submission.

(6) A transcript of the record of the evidence shall be made only on the direction of the sheriff; and the cost shall, in the first instance, be borne—

    (a)   in an undefended cause, by the solicitor for the pursuer; and

    (b)   in a defended cause, by the solicitors for the parties in equal proportions.

(7) The transcript of the record of the evidence provided for the use of the court shall be certified as a faithful record of the evidence by—

    (a)   the shorthand writer who recorded the evidence; or

    (b)   where the evidence was recorded by tape recording or other mechanical means, by the person who transcribed the record.

(8) The sheriff may make such alterations to the transcript of the record of the evidence as appear to him to be necessary after hearing the parties; and, where such alterations are made, the sheriff shall authenticate the alterations.

(9) Where a transcript of the record of the evidence has been made for the use of the sheriff, copies of it may be obtained by any party from the person who transcribed the record on payment of his fee.

(10) Except with leave of the sheriff, the transcript of the record of the evidence may be borrowed from process only for the purpose of enabling a party to consider whether to appeal against the interlocutor of the sheriff on the proof.

---

[1] As amended by SI 1996/2445 (effective November 1, 1996).

[2] As amended by SI 1996/2445 (effective November 1, 1996).

(11)   Where a transcript of the record of the evidence is required for the purpose of an appeal but has not been directed to be transcribed under paragraph (6), the appellant—

    (a)   may request such a transcript from the shorthand writer or as the case may be, the cost of the transcript being borne by the solicitor for the appellant in the first instance; and

    (b)   shall lodge the transcript in process; and copies of it may be obtained by any party from the shorthand writer or as the case may be, on payment of his fee.

(12)   Where the recording of evidence has been dispensed with under paragraph (1), the sheriff, if called upon to do so, shall—

    (a)   in the case of an objection to—

        (i)   the admissibility of evidence on the ground of confidentiality, or

        (ii)   the production of a document on any ground,

    note the terms in writing of such objections and his decision on the objection; and

    (b)   in the case of any other objection, record, in the note to his interlocutor disposing of the merits of the cause, the terms of the objection and his decision on the objection.

(13)   This rule shall, with the necessary modifications, apply to the recording of evidence at a commission as it applies to the recording of evidence at a proof.

GENERAL NOTE

In the sheriff court the principal method of recording evidence remains the shorthand writer. It may seem curious that this superior form of recording the evidence should be retained in the ordinary sheriff court when it has disappeared from the Court of Session, High Court of Justiciary and solemn sheriff court procedure. Only in the ordinary sheriff court did (do) the parties pay for the shorthand writer. Further, if there was no shorthand writer then the clerk would have to remain in the court room to operate the tape recording equipment. This would have manning implications, particularly in the smaller courts.

Rule 29.18(5)

Parties themselves should keep a note of these matters as it is necessary to ask the sheriff to deal with reserved matters at the hearing on evidence. One of the advantages of a shorthand writer is that one can always ask for a note of these matters before they disappear at the end of the evidence.

Rule 29.18(8)

If the sheriff considers that the transcript is inaccurate he may correct it after hearing the parties and he may hear the witness again (see e.g. *Wilson v MacQueen* , 1925 S.L.T. (Sh Ct) 130.

Rulings on admissibility of evidence: leave to appeal   D1.224

29.19.—[1](1)   This rule applies where a party or any other person objects to—

    (a)   the admissibility of oral or documentary evidence on the ground of confidentiality;

    (b)   the production of a document on any ground.

(2)   An application for leave to appeal against the decision of the sheriff on the objection must be made immediately.

GENERAL NOTE

This is the only competent method of review as to the admissibility of evidence or production of a document during a proof. It would only be in exceptional circumstances that a sheriff would grant leave under this rule as any decision on admissibility can also be challenged following the final interlocutor (see section 27 of the Sheriff Courts (Scotland) Act 1907). Appeal from the sheriff principal also requires leave in terms of section 28 of the Sheriff Courts (Scotland) Act 1907.

---

[1] As substituted by the Act of Sederunt (Rules of the Court of Session, Sheriff Appeal Court Rules and Sheriff Court Rules Amendment) (Sheriff Appeal Court) 2015 (SSI 2015/419) r.5 (effective 1 January 2016).

D1.225

Parties to be heard at close of proof

29.20. At the close of the proof, or at an adjourned diet if for any reason the sheriff has postponed the hearing, the sheriff shall hear parties on the evidence and thereafter shall pronounce judgment with the least possible delay.

General Note

Parties should tell the court in precise terms what order they require. They should bear in mind that in terms of OCR r.12.2(3)(a) the sheriff is required to make findings in fact and law. Accordingly, parties should indicate what pleas-in-law are to be sustained and repelled and under reference to the pleadings, what averments of fact have been proved. Care should be taken to concentrate on findings necessary to resolve the issues (see *B v G* , 2012 S.L.T. 840 at para.48). If objection has been taken to evidence and the evidence allowed to be heard subject to competency and relevancy, then the party who has taken the objection should indicate whether he insists on the objection and if so justify such a position. Interest, the remuneration of witnesses attending but not called, the expenses of skilled witnesses and certification of the cause as suitable for the employment of counsel should be addressed at this stage. The question of expenses and any motion relating to modification or enhancement is normally better left until the outcome of the case is known.

D1.226

Chapter 30

Decrees, Extracts and Execution

Interpretation of this Chapter

30.1. In this Chapter, "decree" includes any judgment, deliverance, interlocutor, act, order, finding or authority which may be extracted.

Taxes on funds under control of the court

D1.227

30.2.—(1) Subject to paragraph (2), in a cause in which money has been consigned into court under the Sheriff Court Consignations (Scotland) Act 1893, no decree, warrant or order for payment to any person shall be granted until there has been lodged with the sheriff clerk a certificate by an authorised officer of the Inland Revenue stating that all taxes or duties payable to the Commissioners of Inland Revenue have been paid or satisfied.

(2) In an action of multiplepoinding, it shall not be necessary for the grant of a decree, warrant or order for payment under paragraph (1) that all of the taxes or duties payable on the estate of a deceased claimant have been paid or satisfied.

Decrees for payment in foreign currency

D1.228

30.3.—(1) Where decree has been granted for payment of a sum of money in a foreign currency or the sterling equivalent, a party requesting extract of the decree shall do so by minute endorsed on or annexed to the initial writ stating the rate of exchange prevailing on the date of the decree sought to be extracted or the date, or within 3 days before the date, on which the extract is ordered, and the sterling equivalent at that rate for the principal sum and interest decerned for.

(2) A certificate in Form G18, from the Bank of England or a bank which is an institution authorised under the Banking Act 1987 certifying the rate of exchange and the sterling equivalent shall be lodged with the minute requesting extract of the decree.

(3) The extract decree issued by the sheriff clerk shall mention any certificate referred to in paragraph (2).

When decrees extractable

D1.229

30.4.—(1)[1] Subject to the following paragraphs:—

    (a) subject to sub-paragraph (c), a decree in absence may be extracted after the expiry of 14 days from the date of decree;

    (b) subject to sub-paragraph (c), any decree pronounced in a defended cause

---

[1] As amended by SI 1996/2445 (effective November 1, 1996).

may be extracted at any time after whichever is the later of the following:—

    (i)   the expiry of the period within which an application for leave to appeal may be made and no such application has been made;

    (ii) the date on which leave to appeal has been refused and there is no right of appeal from such refusal;

    (iii)[1] the expiry of the period within which an appeal may be made and no appeal has been made; or

    (iv) the date on which an appeal has been finally disposed of; and

  (c) where, the sheriff has, in pronouncing decree, reserved any question of expenses, extract of that decree may be issued only after the expiry of 14 days from the date of the interlocutor disposing of the question of expenses unless the sheriff otherwise directs.

(2) The sheriff may, on cause shown, grant a motion to allow extract to be applied for and issued earlier than a date referred to in paragraph (1).

(3) In relation to a decree referred to in paragraph (1)(b) or (c), paragraph (2) shall not apply unless—

  (a) the motion under that paragraph is made in the presence of parties; or

  (b) the sheriff is satisfied that proper intimation of the motion has been made in writing to every party not present at the hearing of the motion.

(4) Nothing in this rule shall affect the power of the sheriff to supersede extract.

Extract of certain awards notwithstanding appeal

30.5.[2] The sheriff clerk may issue an extract of an order under section 11 of the Children (Scotland) Act 1995 or in respect of aliment notwithstanding that an appeal has been made against an interlocutor containing such an award unless an order under rule 31.5 (appeals in connection with orders under section 11 of the Children (Scotland) Act 1995 or aliment) has been made excusing obedience to or implement of that interlocutor.   **D1.230**

Form of extract decree

30.6.—(1) The extract of a decree mentioned in Appendix 2 shall be in the appropriate form for that decree in Appendix 2.   **D1.231**

(2) In the case of a decree not mentioned in Appendix 2, the extract of the decree shall be modelled on a form in that Appendix with such variation as circumstances may require.

Form of warrant for execution

30.7. An extract of a decree on which execution may proceed shall include a warrant for execution in the following terms:— "This extract is warrant for all lawful execution hereon.".   **D1.232**

---

[1] As amended by the Act of Sederunt (Rules of the Court of Session, Sheriff Appeal Court Rules and Sheriff Court Rules Amendment) (Sheriff Appeal Court) 2015 (SSI 2015/419) r.5 (effective 1 January 2016).

[2] As substituted by the Act of Sederunt (Sheriff Court Rules) (Miscellaneous Amendments) (No.2) 2010 (SSI 2010/416) r.6 (effective January 1, 2011).

Date of decree in extract

D1.233   **30.8.**—(1)[1]   Where the Sheriff Appeal Court has adhered to the decision of the sheriff following an appeal, the date to be inserted in the extract decree as the date of decree shall be the date of the decision of the Sheriff Appeal Court.

(2)   Where a decree has more than one date it shall not be necessary to specify in an extract what was done on each date.

Service of charge where address of defender not known

D1.234   **30.9.**—(1)   Where the address of a defender is not known to the pursuer, a charge shall be deemed to have been served on the defender if it is—

  (a)   served on the sheriff clerk of the sheriff court district where the defender's last known address is located; and

  (b)   displayed by the sheriff clerk on the walls of court for the period of the charge.

(2)   On receipt of such a charge, the sheriff clerk shall display it on the walls of court and it shall remain displayed for the period of the charge.

(3)   The period specified in the charge shall run from the first date on which it was displayed on the walls of court.

(4)   On the expiry of the period of charge, the sheriff clerk shall endorse a certificate on the charge certifying that it has been displayed in accordance with this rule and shall thereafter return it to the sheriff officer by whom service was executed.

Expenses

D1.235   **30.10.**[2]   A party who—

  (a)   is or has been represented by a person authorised under any enactment to conduct proceedings in the sheriff court; and

  (b)   would have been found entitled to expenses if he had been represented by a solicitor or an advocate,

may be awarded any expenses or outlays to which a party litigant may be found entitled under the Litigants in Person (Costs and Expenses) Act 1975 or any enactment under that Act.

Chapter 31

Appeals

Time limit for appeal

D1.236   **31.1.**   [Repealed by the Act of Sederunt (Rules of the Court of Session, Sheriff Appeal Court Rules and Sheriff Court Rules Amendment) (Sheriff Appeal Court) 2015 (SSI 2015/419) r.5 (effective 1 January 2016).]

Applications for leave to appeal

D1.237   **31.2.**—(1)   Where leave to appeal is required, applications for leave to appeal against an interlocutor of a sheriff shall be made within 7 days after the date of the interlocutor against which it is sought to appeal unless the interlocutor has been extracted following a motion under rule 30.4(2) (early extract).

---

[1] As amended by the Act of Sederunt (Rules of the Court of Session, Sheriff Appeal Court Rules and Sheriff Court Rules Amendment) (Sheriff Appeal Court) 2015 (SSI 2015/419) r.5 (effective 1 January 2016).

[2] As inserted by the Act of Sederunt (Ordinary Cause, Summary Application, Summary Cause and Small Claim Rules) Amendment (Miscellaneous) 2007 (SSI 2007/6), para.2(11) (effective January 29, 2007).

(2)   [Repealed by the Act of Sederunt (Rules of the Court of Session, Sheriff Appeal Court Rules and Sheriff Court Rules Amendment) (Sheriff Appeal Court) 2015 (SSI 2015/419) r.5 (effective 1 January 2016).]

(3)[1]   An application for leave to appeal from a decision in relation to—
(a)   a time to pay direction under section 1 of the Debtors (Scotland) Act 1987;
(b)   the recall or restriction of an arrestment made under section 3(4) of that Act; or
(c)   a time order under section 129 of the Consumer Credit Act 1974, shall specify the question of law on which the appeal is made.

Appeals in connection with interim diligence
31.2A.   *[Repealed by the Act of Sederunt (Rules of the Court of Session, Sheriff Appeal Court Rules and Sheriff Court Rules Amendment) (Sheriff Appeal Court) 2015 (SSI 2015/419) r.5 (effective 1 January 2016).]*   D1.238

Form of appeal to Court of Session
31.3.   *[Repealed by the Act of Sederunt (Rules of the Court of Session, Sheriff Appeal Court Rules and Sheriff Court Rules Amendment) (Sheriff Appeal Court) 2015 (SSI 2015/419) r.5 (effective 1 January 2016).]*   D1.239

Form of appeal to the sheriff principal
31.4.   *[Repealed by the Act of Sederunt (Rules of the Court of Session, Sheriff Appeal Court Rules and Sheriff Court Rules Amendment) (Sheriff Appeal Court) 2015 (SSI 2015/419) r.5 (effective 1 January 2016).]*   D1.240

Transmission of process and notice to parties   D1.241
31.5.   *[Repealed by the Act of Sederunt (Rules of the Court of Session, Sheriff Appeal Court Rules and Sheriff Court Rules Amendment) (Sheriff Appeal Court) 2015 (SSI 2015/419) r.5 (effective 1 January 2016).]*

Record of pleadings etc.
31.6   *[Repealed by the Act of Sederunt (Rules of the Court of Session, Sheriff Appeal Court Rules and Sheriff Court Rules Amendment) (Sheriff Appeal Court) 2015 (SSI 2015/419) r.5 (effective 1 January 2016).]*   D1.242

Determination of appeal
31.7.   *[Repealed by the Act of Sederunt (Rules of the Court of Session, Sheriff Appeal Court Rules and Sheriff Court Rules Amendment) (Sheriff Appeal Court) 2015 (SSI 2015/419) r.5 (effective 1 January 2016).]*   D1.243

Fixing of Options Hearing or making other order following appeal
31.8.   *[Repealed by the Act of Sederunt (Rules of the Court of Session, Sheriff Appeal Court Rules and Sheriff Court Rules Amendment) (Sheriff Appeal Court) 2015 (SSI 2015/419) r.5 (effective 1 January 2016).]*   D1.244

Appeals in connection with orders under section 11 of the Children (Scotland) Act 1995 or aliment
31.9.[2, 3]   Where an appeal is marked against an interlocutor making an order under section 11 of the Children (Scotland) Act 1995 (court orders relating to   D1.245

---

[1] As substituted by the Act of Sederunt (Ordinary Cause, Summary Application, Summary Cause and Small Claim Rules) Amendment (Miscellaneous) 2007 (SSI 2007/6), para.2(12) (effective January 29, 2007).
[2] Inserted by SI 1996/2445 (effective 1 November 1996).

parental responsibilities etc.) or in respect of aliment, the marking of that appeal shall not excuse obedience to or implement of that order unless by order of the sheriff or the Sheriff Appeal Court.

Interim possession etc. pending appeal

D1.246 **31.10.**—[1, 2](1) Notwithstanding an appeal, the sheriff from whose decision an appeal has been taken shall have power—

(a)   to regulate all matters relating to interim possession;

(b)   to make any order for the preservation of any property to which the action relates or for its sale if perishable;

(c)   to make provision for the preservation of evidence; or

(d)   to make any interim order which a due regard to the interests of the parties may require.

(2)   An order made under paragraph (1) may be reviewed by the Sheriff Appeal Court.

D1.247 ### Abandonment of appeal

31.11.[3] *[Repealed by the Act of Sederunt (Rules of the Court of Session, Sheriff Appeal Court Rules and Sheriff Court Rules Amendment) (Sheriff Appeal Court) 2015 (SSI 2015/419) r.5 (effective 1 January 2016).]*

Chapter 31A[4]

Qualified One-Way Costs Shifting

Application and interpretation of this Chapter

D1.247.1 **31A.1.**—(1) This Chapter applies in civil proceedings, where either or both—

(a)   an application for an award of expenses is made to the sheriff;

(b)   such an award is made by the sheriff.

(2)   Where this Chapter applies—

(a)   rules 23.1(2) and (3) (abandonment of causes);

(b)   any common law rule entitling a pursuer to abandon a cause, to the extent that it concerns expenses,

are disapplied.

(3)   In this Chapter—

"the Act" means the Civil Litigation (Expenses and Group Proceedings) (Scotland) Act 2018;

"the applicant" has the meaning given in rule 31A.2(1), and "applicants" is construed accordingly;

"civil proceedings" means civil proceedings to which section 8 of the Act (restriction on pursuer's liability for expenses in personal injury claims) applies.

---

[3] As amended by the Act of Sederunt (Rules of the Court of Session, Sheriff Appeal Court Rules and Sheriff Court Rules Amendment) (Sheriff Appeal Court) 2015 (SSI 2015/419) r.5 (effective 1 January 2016).

[1] Former rule 31.6 renumbered by SI 1996/2445 (effective November 1, 1996).

[2] As amended by the Act of Sederunt (Rules of the Court of Session, Sheriff Appeal Court Rules and Sheriff Court Rules Amendment) (Sheriff Appeal Court) 2015 (SSI 2015/419) r.5 (effective 1 January 2016).

[3] Former rule 31.7 renumbered by SI 1996/2445 (effective November 1, 1996).

[4] Inserted by Act of Sederunt (Rules of the Court of Session 1994, Sheriff Appeal Court Rules and Sheriff Court Rules Amendment) (Qualified One-Way Costs Shifting) 2021 (SSI 2021/226) (effective 30 June 2021).

Application for an award of expenses

31A.2.—(1) Where civil proceedings have been brought by a pursuer, another party to the action ("the applicant") may make an application to the sheriff for an award of expenses to be made against the pursuer, on one or more of the grounds specified in either or both— **D1.247.2**

    (a)   section 8(4)(a) to (c) of the Act;

    (b)   paragraph (2) of this rule.

(2) The grounds specified in this paragraph, which are exceptions to section 8(2) of the Act, are as follows—

    (a)   failure by the pursuer to obtain an award of damages greater than the sum offered by way of a tender lodged in process;

    (b)   unreasonable delay on the part of the pursuer in accepting a sum offered by way of a tender lodged in process;

    (c)   decree of absolvitor or decree of dismissal has been granted against the pursuer in terms of rule 17.2(3)(b) (applications for summary decree);

    (d)   abandonment of the cause in terms of rule 23.1(1), or at common law.

Award of expenses

31A.3.—(1) Subject to paragraph (2), the determination of an application under rule 31A.2(1) is at the discretion of the sheriff. **D1.247.3**

(2) Where, having determined an application made under rules 31A.2(1), the sheriff makes an award of expenses against the pursuer on the ground specified in rule 31A.2(2)(a) or (b)—

    (a)   the pursuer's liability is not to exceed the amount of expenses the applicant has incurred after the date of the tender;

    (b)   the liability of the pursuer to the applicant, or applicants, lodging the tender is to be limited to an aggregate sum, payable to all applicants (if more than one) of 75% of the amount of damages awarded to the pursuer and that sum is to be calculated without offsetting against those expenses any expenses due to the pursuer by the applicant, or applicants, before the date of the tender;

    (c)   the sheriff must order that the pursuer's liability is not to exceed the sum referred to in sub-paragraph (b), notwithstanding that any sum assessed by the Auditor of Court as payable under the tender procedure may be greater or, if modifying those expenses to a fixed amount in terms of rule 32.1 (taxation before decree for expenses), that such amount does not exceed that referred to in sub-paragraph (b);

    (d)   where the award of expenses is in favour of more than one applicant the sheriff, failing agreement between the applicants, is to apportion the award of expenses recoverable under the tender procedure between them.

(3) In the event that the sheriff makes an award of expenses against the pursuer on the ground specified in rule 31A.2(2)(d), the sheriff may make such orders in respect of expenses, as it considers appropriate, including—

    (a)   making an award of decree of dismissal dependant on payment of expenses by the pursuer within a specified period of time;

    (b)   provision for the consequences of failure to comply with any conditions applied by the court.

Procedure

31A.4.—(1) An application under rule 31A.2(1)— **D1.247.4**

(a) must be made by written motion, and Chapters 15 (motions) and 15A (motions intimated and lodged by email) otherwise apply to motions made under this Chapter;

(b) may be made at any stage in the case prior to the granting of an order disposing of the expenses of the cause.

(2) Where an application under rule 31A.2(1) is made, the sheriff may make such orders as the sheriff thinks fit for dealing with the application, including an order—

(a) requiring the applicant to intimate the application to any other person;

(b) requiring any party to lodge a written response;

(c) requiring the lodging of any document;

(d) fixing a hearing.

Award against legal representatives

D1.247.5   **31A.5.** Section 8(2) of the Act does not prevent the sheriff from making an award of expenses against a pursuer's legal representative in terms of section 11 (awards of expenses against legal representatives) of the Act.

Chapter 32

Taxation of Expenses

Taxation before decree for expenses

D1.248   **32.1.**—[1](1) Expenses allowed in any cause, whether in absence or *in foro contentioso*, unless modified at a fixed amount, shall be taxed before decree is granted for them.

(2) Paragraph (1) applies subject to rule 7.4(2).

Time for lodging account of expenses

D1.249   **32.1A.**—[2, 3](1) A party found entitled to expenses must lodge an account of expenses in process—

(a) not later than four months after the final judgment; or

(b) at any time with permission of the sheriff, but subject to such conditions, if any, as the sheriff thinks fit to impose.

(2) Where an account of expenses is lodged by the Scottish Legal Aid Board in reliance on regulation 39(2)(a) of the Civil Legal Aid (Scotland) Regulations 2002, paragraph (1)(a) applies as if the period specified there is 8 months.

(3) In this rule, "final judgment" has the meaning assigned by section 136(1) of the Courts Reform (Scotland) Act 2014.

Decree for expenses in name of solicitor

D1.250   **32.2.** The sheriff may allow a decree for expenses to be extracted in the name of the solicitor who conducted the cause.

---

[1] As amended by the Act of Sederunt (Rules of the Court of Session, Sheriff Appeal Court Rules and Ordinary Cause Rules Amendment) (Taxation of Judicial Expenses) 2019 (SSI 2019/74) r.3 (effective 29 April 2019).

[2] Inserted by the Act of Sederunt (Ordinary Cause, Summary Application and Small Claim Rules) Amendment (Miscellaneous) 2004 (SSI 2004/197) (effective May 21, 2004), para.2(12).

[3] As substituted by the Act of Sederunt (Rules of the Court of Session, Sheriff Appeal Court Rules and Ordinary Cause Rules Amendment) (Taxation of Judicial Expenses) 2019 (SSI 2019/74) r.3 (effective 29 April 2019).

Diet of taxation

32.3.—[1](1)   Where an account of expenses awarded in a cause is lodged for taxa-   **D1.251**
tion, the sheriff clerk must transmit the account and the process to the auditor of
court.

(2)   Subject to paragraph (3), the auditor of court must fix a diet of taxation on
receipt of—

(a)   the account of expenses;

(b)   the process;

(c)   vouchers in respect of all outlays claimed in the account, including
counsel's fees; and

(d)   a letter addressed to the auditor of court—

    (i)   confirming that the items referred to in sub-paragraph (c) have
been intimated to the party found liable in expenses; and

    (ii)   providing such information as is required to enable the auditor of
court to give intimation to the party found liable in expenses in accordance with paragraph (4)(b).

(3)   The auditor of court must fix a diet of taxation where paragraph (2)(c) or (d),
or both, have not been complied with.

to every other party.

(4)   The auditor of court shall intimate the diet of taxation to—

(a)   the party found entitled to expenses; and

(b)   the party found liable in expenses.

(5)   The party found liable in expenses may, not later than 4.00 pm on the fourth
business day before the diet of taxation, intimate to the auditor of court and to the
party found entitled to expenses particular points of objection, specifying each item
objected to and stating concisely the nature and ground of objection.

(6)   Subject to paragraph (7), if the party found liable in expenses fails to intimate
points of objection under paragraph (5) within the time limit set out there, the auditor of court must not take account of them at the diet of taxation.

(7)   Where a failure to comply with the requirement contained in paragraph (5)
was due to mistake, oversight or other excusable cause, the auditor of court may
relieve a party of the consequences of such failure on such conditions, if any, as the
auditor thinks fit.

(8)   At the diet of taxation, or within such reasonable period of time thereafter as
the auditor of court may allow, the party found entitled to expenses must make
available to the auditor of court all documents, drafts or copies of documents sought
by the auditor and relevant to the taxation.

(9)   In this rule, "business day" means any day other than a Saturday, Sunday or
public or court holiday.

Diet of taxation

32.3A.—[2](1)   The auditor of court must—   **D1.251.1**

(a)   prepare a statement of the amount of expenses as taxed;

(b)   transmit the process, the taxed account and the statement to the sheriff
clerk; and

---

[1] As substituted by the Act of Sederunt (Rules of the Court of Session, Sheriff Appeal Court Rules and
Ordinary Cause Rules Amendment) (Taxation of Judicial Expenses) 2019 (SSI 2019/74) r.3 (effective
29 April 2019).

[2] As inserted by the Act of Sederunt (Rules of the Court of Session, Sheriff Appeal Court Rules and
Ordinary Cause Rules Amendment) (Taxation of Judicial Expenses) 2019 (SSI 2019/74) r.3 (effective
29 April 2019).

(c) on the day on which the documents referred to in sub-paragraph (b) are transmitted, intimate that fact and the date of the statement to each party to whom the auditor intimated the diet of taxation.

(2) The party found entitled to expenses must, within 7 days after the date of receipt of intimation under paragraph (1)(c), send a copy of the taxed account to the party found liable in expenses.

(3) Where no objections are lodged under rule 32.4 (objections to taxed account), the sheriff may grant decree for the expenses as taxed.

Objections to taxed account

D1.252

32.4.—[1](1) A party to a cause who has appeared or been represented at a diet of taxation may object to the auditor of court's statement by lodging in process a note of objection within 14 days after the date of the statement.

(2) The party lodging a note of objection is referred to in this rule as *"the objecting party"*.

(3) On lodging the note of objection the objecting party must apply by motion for an order—

(a) allowing the note of objection to be received; and

(b) allowing a hearing on the note of objection.

(4) On the granting of the order mentioned in paragraph (3), the objecting party must intimate to the auditor of court—

(a) the note of objection; and

(b) the interlocutor containing the order.

(5) Within 14 days after receipt of intimation of the items mentioned in paragraph (4) the auditor of court must lodge in process a statement of reasons in the form of a minute stating the reasons for the auditor's decision in relation to the items to which objection is taken in the note.

(6) On the lodging of the statement of reasons the sheriff clerk must fix a hearing on the note of objection.

(7) At the hearing, the sheriff may—

(a) sustain or repel any objection or remit the account of expenses to the auditor of court for further consideration; and

(b) find any party liable in the expenses of the procedure on the note of objection.

Interest on expenses

D1.252.1

32.5.—[2](1) Paragraph (2) applies where the sheriff grants decree for payment of—

(a) expenses as taxed; and

(b) interest thereon.

(2) Without prejudice to the sheriff's other powers in relation to interest, the decree pronounced may require the party decerned against to pay interest on the

---

[1] As substituted by the Act of Sederunt (Rules of the Court of Session, Sheriff Appeal Court Rules and Ordinary Cause Rules Amendment) (Taxation of Judicial Expenses) 2019 (SSI 2019/74) r.3 (effective 29 April 2019).

[2] As inserted by the Act of Sederunt (Rules of the Court of Session, Sheriff Appeal Court Rules and Ordinary Cause Rules Amendment) (Taxation of Judicial Expenses) 2019 (SSI 2019/74) r.3 (effective 29 April 2019).

taxed expenses, or any part thereof, from a date no earlier than 28 days after the date on which the account of expenses was lodged.

Chapter 32A

Live Links

[Chapter 32A revoked by Act of Sederunt (Rules of the Court of Session 1994 and Ordinary Cause Rules 1993 Amendment) (Attendance at Hearings) 2023 (SSI 2023/168) para.3 (effective 3 July 2023), subject to transitional provisions in SSI 2023/168 para.4.]   **D1.253**

SPECIAL PROVISIONS IN RELATION TO PARTICULAR CAUSES

Chapter 33

Family Actions

Part I – General Provisions

Interpretation of this Chapter

33.1.—[1](1)   In this Chapter, "family action" means—   **D1.254**

    (a)   an action of divorce;

    (b)   an action of separation;

    (c)   an action of declarator of legitimacy;

    (d)   an action of declarator of illegitimacy;

    (e)   an action of declarator of parentage;

    (f)   an action of declarator of non-parentage;

    (g)   an action of declarator of legitimation;

    (h)   an action or application for, or in respect of, an order under section 11 of the Children (Scotland) Act 1995 (court orders relating to parental responsibilities etc.), except—

        (i)   an application for the appointment of a judicial factor mentioned in section 11(2)(g) of the Act of 1995 to which Part I of the Act of Sederunt (Judicial Factors Rules) 1992 applies;

        (ii) *[Repealed by the Act of Sederunt (Sheriff Court Rules) (Miscellaneous Amendments) 2011 (SSI 2011/193) r.13 (effective 4 April 2011).]*

    (i)   an action of affiliation and aliment;

    (j)   an action of, or application for or in respect of, aliment;

    (k)   an action or application for financial provision after a divorce or annulment in an overseas country within the meaning of Part IV of the Matrimonial and Family Proceedings Act 1984;

    (l)   an action or application for an order under the Act of 1981;

    (m) an application for the variation or recall of an order mentioned in section 8(1) of the Law Reform (Miscellaneous Provisions) (Scotland) Act 1966.

    (n)[2] an action of declarator of marriage;

    (o)[3] an action of declarator of nullity of marriage.

---

[1] As amended by SI 1996/2167 (effective 1 November 1996).

[2] Inserted or substituted by Act of Sederunt (Ordinary Cause Rules) Amendment (Family Law (Scotland) Act 2006 etc.) 2006 (SSI 2006/207) (effective 4 May 2006).

[3] Inserted or substituted by Act of Sederunt (Ordinary Cause Rules) Amendment (Family Law (Scotland) Act 2006 etc.) 2006 (SSI 2006/207) (effective 4 May 2006).

(p)[1] an action for declarator of recognition, or non-recognition, of a relevant foreign decree within the meaning of section 7(9) of the Domicile and Matrimonial Proceedings Act 1973.

(q)[2] an application under section 28 or 29 of the Act of 2006 (financial provision for former co-habitants).

(r)[3] an action for declarator of recognition, or non-recognition, of a relevant foreign decree within the meaning of paragraph 1 of Schedule 1B to the Domicile and Matrimonial Proceedings Act 1973, or of a judgment to which paragraph 2(1)(b) of that Schedule refers.

(2) In this Chapter, unless the context otherwise requires—

"the Act of 1975" means the Children Act 1975;

"the Act of 1976" means the Divorce (Scotland) Act 1976;

"the Act of 1981" means the Matrimonial Homes (Family Protection) (Scotland) Act 1981;

"the Act of 1985" means the Family Law (Scotland) Act 1985;

"the Act of 1995" means the Children (Scotland) Act 1995;

"the Act of 2006" means the Family Law (Scotland) Act 2006;

"contact order" has the meaning assigned in section 11(2)(d) of the Act of 1995;

"full gender recognition certificate" and "interim gender recognition certificate" mean the certificates issued as such under section 4 or 5 of the Gender Recognition Act 2004;[4]

"Gender Recognition Panel" is to be construed in accordance with Schedule 1 to the Gender Recognition Act 2004;

"incapable" means incapable, by reason of mental disorder, of—

    (a) acting;

    (b) making decisions;

    (c) communicating decisions;

    (d) understanding decisions; or

    (e) retaining the memory of decisions,

but a person is not incapable by reason only of a lack of deficiency in a faculty of communication where that lack or deficiency can be made good by human or mechanical aid (whether of an interpretative nature or otherwise);[5]

"local authority" means a council constituted under section 2 of the Local Government etc. (Scotland) Act 1994;

"mental disorder" has the meaning assigned in section 328 of the Mental Health (Care and Treatment) (Scotland) Act 2003;[6]

---

[1] As inserted by the Act of Sederunt (Sheriff Court Rules) (Miscellaneous Amendments) (No.2) 2010 (SSI 2010/416) r.8 (effective 1 January 2011).

[2] As inserted by the Act of Sederunt (Sheriff Court Rules) (Miscellaneous Amendments) 2012 (SSI 2012/188) para.5 (effective 1 August 2012).

[3] As inserted by the Act of Sederunt (Rules of the Court of Session and Sheriff Court Rules Amendment No.2) (Marriage and Civil Partnership (Scotland) Act 2014) 2014 (SSI 2014/302) para.5 (effective 16 December 2014).

[4] Inserted by the Act of Sederunt (Ordinary Cause Rules) Amendment (Gender Recognition Act 2004) 2005 (SSI 2005/189) (effective 4 April 2005).

[5] As inserted by the Act of Sederunt (Rules of the Court of Session 1994 and Sheriff Court Rules Amendment) (Curators ad litem) (SSI 2017/132) r.2(2) (effective 1 June 2017 subject to saving specified in SSI 2017/132 r.4).

[6] Inserted or substituted by Act of Sederunt (Ordinary Cause Rules) Amendment (Family Law (Scotland) Act 2006 etc.) 2006 (SSI 2006/207) (effective 4 May 2006).

"order for financial provision" means, except in Part VII of this Chapter (financial provision after overseas divorce or annulment), an order mentioned in section 8(1) of the Act of 1985;

"parental responsibilities" has the meaning assigned in section 1(3) of the Act 1995;

"parental rights" has the meaning assigned in section 2(4) of the Act of 1995;

"residence order" has the meaning assigned in section 11(2)(c) of the Act of 1995;

"section 11 order" means an order under section 11 of the Act of 1995.

(3) For the purposes of rules 33.2 (averments in actions of divorce or separation about other proceedings) and 33.3 (averments where section 11 order sought) and, in relation to proceedings in another jurisdiction, Schedule 3 to the Domicile and Matrimonial Proceedings Act 1973 (sisting of consistorial actions in Scotland), proceedings are continuing at any time after they have commenced and before they are finally disposed of.

Averments in certain family actions about other proceedings

33.2.—[1](1) This rule applies to an action of divorce, separation, declarator of marriage or declarator of nullity of marriage.

D1.255

(2) In an action to which this rule applies, the pursuer shall state in the condescendence of the initial writ—

(a) whether to his knowledge any proceedings are continuing in Scotland or in any other country in respect of the marriage to which the initial writ relates or are capable of affecting its validity or subsistence; and

(b) where such proceedings are continuing—

  (i) the court, tribunal or authority before which the proceedings have been commenced;

  (ii) the date of commencement;

  (iii) the names of the parties;

  (iv) the date, or expected date of any proof (or its equivalent) in the proceedings; and

  (v)[2,3] such other facts as may be relevant to the question of whether or not the action before the sheriff should be sisted under Schedule 3 to the Domicile and Matrimonial Proceedings Act 1973 for the 1996 Convention on Jurisdiction, Applicable Law, Recognition, Enforcement and Co-operation in Respect of Parental Responsibility and Measures for the Protection of Children, signed at the Hague on 19th October 1996.

(3) Where—

(a) such proceedings are continuing;

(b) the action before the sheriff is defended; and

(c) either—

  (i) the initial writ does not contain the statement referred to in paragraph (2)(a), or

---

[1] As amended by Act of Sederunt (Ordinary Cause Rules) Amendment (European Matrimonial and Parental Responsibility Jurisdiction and Judgments) 2001 (SSI 2001/144) (effective 2 April 2001).

[2] As amended by the Act of Sederunt (Sheriff Court Rules) (Miscellaneous Amendments) (No.2) 2012 (SSI 2012/221) para.3 (effective 1 August 2012).

[3] As amended by the Act of Sederunt (Rules of the Court of Session 1994 and Sheriff Court Rules Amendment) (Miscellaneous) 2021 (SSI 2021/75) r.3(2) (effective 1 March 2021).

           (ii)   the particulars mentioned in paragraph (2)(b) as set out in the initial writ are incomplete or incorrect,

any defences or minute, as the case may be, lodged by any person to the action shall include that statement and, where appropriate, the further or correct particulars mentioned in paragraph (2)(b).

Averments where section 11 order sought

D1.256   33.3.—[1](1) A party to a family action, who makes an application in that action for a section 11 order in respect of a child shall include in his pleadings—

      (a)   where that action is an action of divorce, separation or declarator of nullity of marriage, averments giving particulars of any other proceedings known to him, whether in Scotland or elsewhere and whether concluded or not, which relate to the child in respect of whom the section 11 order is sought;

      (b)   in any other family action—

           (i)   the averments mentioned in paragraph (a); and

          (ii)   averments giving particulars of any proceedings known to him which are continuing, whether in Scotland or elsewhere, and which relate to the marriage of the parents of that child.

      (c)[2] where the party seeks an order such as is mentioned in any of paragraphs (a) to (e) of subsection (2) of that section, an averment that no permanence order (as defined in section 80(2) of the Adoption and Children (Scotland) Act 2007) is in force in respect of the child.

    (2) Where such other proceedings are continuing or have taken place and the averments of the applicant for such a section 11 order—

      (a)   do not contain particulars of the other proceedings, or

      (b)   contain particulars which are incomplete or incorrect,

any defences or minute, as the case may be, lodged by any party to the family action shall include such particulars or such further or correct particulars as are known to him.

    (3) In paragraph (1)(b)(ii), "child" includes a child of the family within the meaning assigned in section 42(4) of the Family Law Act 1986.

Averments where identity or address of person not known

D1.257   33.4. In a family action, where the identity or address of any person referred to in rule 33.7 as a person in respect of whom a warrant for intimation requires to be applied for is not known and cannot reasonably be ascertained, the party required to apply for the warrant shall include in his pleadings an averment of that fact and averments setting out what steps have been taken to ascertain the identity or address, as the case may be, of that person.

Averments about maintenance orders

D1.258   33.5. In a family action in which an order for aliment or periodical allowance is sought, or is sought to be varied or recalled, by any party, the pleadings of that party shall contain an averment stating whether and, if so, when and by whom, a maintenance order (within the meaning of section 106 of the Debtors (Scotland) Act 1987) has been granted in favour of or against that party or of any other person in respect of whom the order is sought.

---

[1] As amended by SI 1996/2167 (effective 1 November 1996) and SI 1996/2445 (effective 1 November 1996) (clerical error).
[2] As inserted by the Act of Sederunt (Sheriff Court Rules Amendment) (Adoption and Children (Scotland) Act 2007) 2009 (SSI 2009/284) (effective 28 September 2009).

Averments where aliment or financial provision sought

33.6.—[1](1)   In this rule—   D1.259

"the Act of 1991" means the Child Support Act 1991;

"child" has the meaning assigned in section 55 of the Act of 1991;

"crave relating to aliment" means—

(a)   for the purposes of paragraph (2), a crave for decree of aliment in relation to a child or for recall or variation of such a decree; and

(b)   for the purposes of paragraph (3), a crave for decree of aliment in relation to a child or for recall or variation of such a decree or for the variation or termination of an agreement on aliment in relation to a child;

"maintenance calculation" has the meaning assigned in section 54 of the Act of 1991.

(2)   A family action containing a crave relating to aliment and to which section 8(6), (7), (8) or (10) of the Act of 1991 (top up maintenance orders) applies shall—

(a)   include averments stating, where appropriate—

(i)   that a maintenance calculation under section 11 of that Act (maintenance calculations) is in force;

(ii)   the date of the maintenance calculation;

(iii)   the amount and frequency of periodical payments of child support maintenance fixed by the maintenance calculation; and

(iv)   the grounds on which the sheriff retains jurisdiction under section 8(6), (7), (8) or (10) of that Act; and

(b)   unless the sheriff on cause shown otherwise directs, be accompanied by any document issued by the Secretary of State to the party intimating the making of the maintenance calculation referred to in sub-paragraph (a).

(3)   A family action containing a crave relating to aliment, and to which section 8(6), (7), (8) or (10) of the Act of 1991 does not apply, shall include averments stating—

(a)   that the habitual residence of the absent parent, person with care or qualifying child, within the meaning of section 3 of that Act, is furth of the United Kingdom;

(b)   that the child is not a child within the meaning of section 55 of that Act; or

(c)   where the action is lodged for warranting before 7th April 1997, the grounds on which the sheriff retains jurisdiction.

(4)   In an action for declarator of non-parentage or illegitimacy—

(a)   the initial writ shall include an article of condescendence stating whether the pursuer previously has been alleged to be the parent in an application for a maintenance calculation under section 4, 6 or 7 of the Act of 1991 (applications for maintenance calculation); and

(b)   where an allegation of paternity has been made against the pursuer, the Secretary of State shall be named as a defender in the action.

(5)   A family action involving parties in respect of whom a decision has been made in any application, review or appeal under the Act of 1991 relating to any child of those parties, shall—

---

[1]   As amended by the Act of Sederunt (Ordinary Cause, Summary Application, Summary Cause and Small Claim Rules) Amendment (Miscellaneous) 2003 (SSI 2003/26) r.2(8) (effective 24 January 2003).

(a) include averments stating that such a decision has been made and giving details of that decision; and

(b) unless the sheriff on cause shown otherwise directs, be accompanied by any document issued by the Secretary of State to the parties intimating that decision.

Averments where divorce sought on ground of issue of interim gender recognition certificate

D1.259A   **33.6ZA.**—[1](1) This rule applies to an action of divorce in which divorce is sought on the ground that an interim gender recognition certificate has been issued to either party.

(2) In an action to which this rule applies, the pursuer shall state in the condescendence of the initial writ—

(a) where the pursuer is the party to whom the interim gender recognition certificate was issued, whether or not the Gender Recognition Panel has issued a full gender recognition certificate to the pursuer, and

(b) where the defender is the party to whom the interim gender recognition certificate was issued, whether—

(i) since the issue of the interim gender recognition certificate, the pursuer has made a statutory declaration consenting to the marriage continuing, and

(ii) the Gender Recognition Panel has given the pursuer notice of the issue of a full gender recognition certificate to the defender.

Application by survivor for provision on intestacy

D1.260   **33.6A.**—[2](1) In an action for an order under section 29(2) of the Act of 2006 (application by survivor for provision on intestacy), the pursuer shall call the deceased's executor as a defender.

(2) An application under section 29(9) of the Act of 2006 for variation of the date or method of payment of the capital sum shall be made by minute in the process of the action to which the application relates.

(3) Words and expressions used in this rule shall have the same meaning as in section 29 of the Act of 2006.

Warrants and forms for intimation

D1.261   **33.7.**—[3](1) Subject to paragraph (5) and rule 33.7A (warrants and forms for intimation to a child and for seeking a child's views), in the initial writ in a family action, the pursuer shall include a crave for a warrant for intimation—

(a) in an action where the address of the defender is not known to the pursuer and cannot reasonably be ascertained, to—

---

[1] As inserted by the Act of Sederunt (Rules of the Court of Session and Sheriff Court Rules Amendment No.2) (Marriage and Civil Partnership (Scotland) Act 2014) 2014 (SSI 2014/302) para.5 (effective 16 December 2014).

[2] As inserted by the Act of Sederunt (Sheriff Court Rules) (Miscellaneous Amendments) 2012 (SSI 2012/188) para.5 (effective 1 August 2012).

[3] As amended by SI 1996/2167 (effective 1 November 1996) and SI 1996/2445 (effective 1 November 1996).

As amended by the Act of Sederunt (Rules of the Court of Session 1994 and Ordinary Cause Rules 1993 Amendment) (Views of the Child) 2019 (SSI 2019/123) para.3 (effective 24 June 2019).

(i)[1,2]   every person who is a child of the family (as defined in section 12(4)(a) of the Act of 1995) who has reached the age of 16 years; and

(ii)   one of the next-of-kin of the defender who has reached that age,

unless the address of such a person is not known to the pursuer and cannot reasonably be ascertained, and a notice of intimation in Form F1 shall be attached to the copy of the initial writ intimated to any such person;

(b)[3]   in an action of divorce where the pursuer alleges that the defender has committed adultery with another person, to that person, unless—

(i)   that person is not named in the initial writ and, if the adultery is relied on for the purposes of section 1(2)(a) of the Act of 1976 (irretrievable breakdown of marriage by reason of adultery), the initial writ contains an averment that his or her identity is not known to the pursuer and cannot reasonably be ascertained; or

(ii)   the pursuer alleges that the defender has been guilty of rape upon or incest with, that named person,

and a notice of intimation in Form F2 shall be attached to the copy of the initial writ intimated to any such person;

(c)   in an action where the defender is a person who is suffering from a mental disorder, to—

(i)[4]   those persons mentioned in sub-paragraph (a)(i) and (ii), unless the address of such person is not known to the pursuer and cannot reasonably be ascertained;

(ii)   the curator bonis to the defender, if one has been appointed,

and a notice of intimation in Form F3 shall be attached to the copy of the initial writ intimated to any such person;

(iii)[5]   any person holding the office of guardian or continuing or welfare attorney to the defender under or by virtue of the Adults with Incapacity (Scotland) Act 2000,

(d)   in an action relating to a marriage which was entered into under a law which permits polygamy where—

(i)   one of the decrees specified in section 2(2) of the Matrimonial Proceedings (Polygamous Marriages) Act 1972 is sought; and

(ii)   either party to the marriage in question has any spouse additional to the other party,

to any such additional spouse, and a notice of intimation in Form F4 shall be attached to the initial writ intimated to any such person;

(e)[6]   in an action of divorce, separation or declarator of nullity of marriage where the sheriff may make a section 11 order in respect of a child—

---

[1] As amended by the Act of Sederunt (Sheriff Court Rules) (Miscellaneous Amendments) 2012 (SSI 2012/188) para.5 (effective 1 August 2012).

[2] As amended by the Act of Sederunt (Sheriff Court Rules) (Miscellaneous Amendments) (No.2) 2012 (SSI 2012/221) para.3 (effective 1 August 2012).

[3] As amended by the Act of Sederunt (Sheriff Court Rules) (Miscellaneous Amendments) 2012 (SSI 2012/188) para.5 (effective 1 August 2012).

[4] As amended by Act of Sederunt (Ordinary Cause Rules) Amendment (Family Law (Scotland) Act 2006 etc.) 2006 (SSI 2006/207) r.2 (effective 4 May 2006).

[5] Inserted or substituted by Act of Sederunt (Ordinary Cause Rules) Amendment (Family Law (Scotland) Act 2006 etc.) 2006 (SSI 2006/207) r.2 (effective 4 May 2006).

[6] As amended by Act of Sederunt (Ordinary Cause Rules) Amendment (Family Law (Scotland) Act 2006 etc.) 2006 (SSI 2006/207) r.2 (effective 4 May 2006).

(i) who is in the care of a local authority, to that authority and a notice of intimation in Form F5 shall be attached to the initial writ intimated to that authority;

(ii) who, being a child of one party to the marriage, has been accepted as a child of the family by the other party to the marriage and who is liable to be maintained by a third party, to that third party, and a notice of intimation in Form F5 shall be attached to the initial writ intimated to that third party; or

(iii) in respect of whom a third party in fact exercises care and control, to that third party, and a notice of intimation in Form F6 shall be attached to the initial writ intimated to that third party;

(f) in an action where the pursuer craves a section 11 order, to any parent or guardian of the child who is not a party to the action, and a notice of intimation in Form F7 shall be attached to the initial writ intimated to any such parent or guardian;

(g) *[Repealed by the Act of Sederunt (Sheriff Court Rules) (Miscellaneous Amendments) (No.2) 2010 (SSI 2010/416) r.7 (effective 1 January 2011).]*

(h) *[Repealed by the Act of Sederunt (Rules of the Court of Session 1994 and Ordinary Cause Rules 1993 Amendment) (Views of the Child) 2019 (SSI 2019/123) r.3(2) (effective 24 June 2019).]*

(i) in an action where the pursuer makes an application for an order under section 8(1)(aa) of the Act of 1985 (transfer of property) and—

(i) the consent of a third party to such a transfer is necessary by virtue of an obligation, enactment or rule of law, or

(ii) the property is subject to a security,

to the third party or creditor, as the case may be, and a notice of intimation in Form F10 shall be attached to the initial writ intimated to any such person;

(j) in an action where the pursuer makes an application for an order under section 18 of the Act of 1985 (which relates to avoidance transactions), to—

(i) any third party in whose favour the transfer of, or transaction involving, the property is to be or was made, and

(ii) any other person having an interest in the transfer of, or transaction involving, the property,

and a notice of intimation in Form F11 shall be attached to the initial writ intimated to any such person;

(k) in an action where the pursuer makes an application for an order under the Act of 1981—

(i) where he is a non-entitled partner and the entitled partner has a spouse, to that spouse; or

(ii) where the application is under section 2(1)(e), 2(4)(a), 3(1), 3(2), 4, 7, 13 or 18 of that Act, and the entitled spouse or entitled partner is a tenant or occupies the matrimonial home by permission of a third party, to the landlord or the third party, as the case may be,

and a notice of intimation in Form F12 shall be attached to the initial writ intimated to any such person;

(l) in an action where the pursuer makes an application for an order under section 8(1)(ba) of the Act of 1985 (orders under section 12A of the Act of 1985 for pension lump sum), to the person responsible for the pension arrangement, and a notice of intimation in Form F12A shall be attached to the initial writ intimated to any such person;

(m)[1] in an action where a pursuer makes an application for an order under section 8(1)(baa) of the Act of 1985 (pension sharing orders), to the person responsible for the pension arrangement and a notice of intimation in Form F12B shall be attached to the initial writ intimated to any such person;

(n)[2] in an action where a pursuer makes an application for an order under section 8(1)(bab) of the Act of 1985 (pension compensation sharing order), to the Board of the Pension Protection Fund, and a notice of intimation in Form F12C shall be attached to the initial writ intimated to that Board; and

(o)[3] in an action where a pursuer makes an application for an order under section 8(1)(bb) of the Act of 1985 (an order under section 12B(2) of the Act of 1985 for pension compensation), to the Board of the Pension Protection Fund and a notice of intimation in Form F12D shall be attached to the initial writ intimated to that Board.

(p)[4] in an action where a pursuer makes an application for an order under section 29(2) of the Act of 2006 (application by survivor for provision on intestacy) to any person having an interest in the deceased's net estate, and a notice of intimation in Form F12E shall be attached to the initial writ intimated to any such person.

(2)[5] Expressions used in—

(a) paragraph (1)(k) which are also used in the Act of 1981; and

(b) paragraph (1)(p) which are also used in section 29 of the Act of 2006, shall have the same meanings as in that Act or section, as the case may be.

(3) A notice of intimation under paragraph (1) shall be on a period of notice of 21 days unless the sheriff otherwise orders; but the sheriff shall not order a period of notice of less than 2 days.

(4) *[Repealed by the Act of Sederunt (Sheriff Court Rules) (Miscellaneous Amendments) (No.2) 2010 (SSI 2010/416) r.7 (effective 1 January 2011).]*

(5)[6,7] Where the address of a person mentioned in paragraph (1)(b), (d), (e), (f), (i), (j), (k), (l), (m) or (p) or a child mentioned in rule 33.7A(1) is not known and cannot reasonably be ascertained, the pursuer shall include a crave in the initial writ to dispense with intimation; and the sheriff may grant that crave or make such other order as he thinks fit.

(6) Where the identity or address of a person to whom intimation of a family action is required becomes known during the course of the action, the party who would have been required to insert a warrant for intimation to that person shall lodge a motion for a warrant for intimation to that person or to dispense with such intimation.

---

[1] Inserted by the Act of Sederunt (Ordinary Cause Rules) Amendment (No.2) (Pension Sharing on Divorce etc.) 2000 (SSI 2000/408) r.2(2)(b)(ii).

[2] As inserted by the Act of Sederunt (Sheriff Court Rules) (Miscellaneous Amendments) 2011 (SSI 2011/193) r.15 (effective 6 April 2011).

[3] As inserted by the Act of Sederunt (Sheriff Court Rules) (Miscellaneous Amendments) 2011 (SSI 2011/193) r.15 (effective 6 April 2011).

[4] As inserted by the Act of Sederunt (Sheriff Court Rules) (Miscellaneous Amendments) 2012 (SSI 2012/188) para.5 (effective 1 August 2012).

[5] As substituted by the Act of Sederunt (Sheriff Court Rules) (Miscellaneous Amendments) 2012 (SSI 2012/188) para.5 (effective 1 August 2012).

[6] As amended by Act of Sederunt (Ordinary Cause Rules) Amendment (Family Law (Scotland) Act 2006 etc.) 2006 (SSI 2006/207) r.2 (effective 4 May 2006).

[7] As amended by the Act of Sederunt (Sheriff Court Rules) (Miscellaneous Amendments) 2012 (SSI 2012/188) para.5 (effective 1 August 2012).

(7) *[Repealed by the Act of Sederunt (Rules of the Court of Session 1994 and Ordinary Cause Rules 1993 Amendment) (Views of the Child) 2019 (SSI 2019/123) r.3(2) (effective 24 June 2019).]*

Warrants and forms for intimation to a child and for seeking a child's views

D1.261.1   **33.7A.**—[1](1)   Subject to paragraph (2), in an action which includes a crave for a section 11 order in respect of a child who is not a party to the action, the pursuer must—

(a)   include in the initial writ a crave for a warrant for intimation and the seeking of the child's views in Form F9;

(b)   when presenting the initial writ for warranting, submit a draft Form F9, showing the details that the pursuer proposes to include when the form is sent to the child.

(2)   Where the pursuer considers that it would be inappropriate to send Form F9 to the child (for example, where the child is under 5 years of age), the pursuer must include in the initial writ—

(a)   a crave to dispense with intimation and the seeking of the child's views in Form F9;

(b)   averments setting out the reasons why it is inappropriate to send Form F9 to the child.

(3)   The sheriff must be satisfied that the draft Form F9 submitted under paragraph (1)(b) has been drafted appropriately.

(4)   The sheriff may dispense with intimation and the seeking of views in Form F9 or make any other order that the sheriff considers appropriate.

(5)   An order granting warrant for intimation and the seeking of the child's views in Form F9 under this rule must—

(a)   state that the Form F9 must be sent in accordance with rule 33.7A(6);

(b)   be signed by the sheriff.

(6)   The Form F9 must be sent in accordance with—

(a)   rule 33.19 (views of the child – undefended actions), where the action is undefended;

(b)   rule 33.19A (views of the child – section 11 order sought by pursuer only), where the action is defended and a section 11 order is sought by the pursuer only;

(c)   rule 33.19B (views of the child – section 11 order sought by defender only), where a section 11 order is sought by the defender only; or

(d)   rule 33.19C (views of the child – section 11 orders sought by both pursuer and defender), where a section 11 order is sought by both parties.

Intimation where alleged association[2]

D1.262   **33.8.**—(1)[3]   In a family action where the pursuer founds upon an association between the defender and another named person, the pursuer shall, immediately after the expiry of the period of notice, lodge a motion for an order for intimation to that person or to dispense with such intimation.

(2)   In determining a motion under paragraph (1), the sheriff may—

(a)   make such order for intimation as he thinks fit; or

---

[1] As inserted by the Act of Sederunt (Rules of the Court of Session 1994 and Ordinary Cause Rules 1993 Amendment) (Views of the Child) 2019 (SSI 2019/123) para.3 (effective 24 June 2019).

[2] As amended by Act of Sederunt (Ordinary Cause Rules) Amendment (Family Law (Scotland) Act 2006 etc.) 2006 (SSI 2006/207) r.2 (effective 4 May 2006).

[3] As amended by Act of Sederunt (Ordinary Cause Rules) Amendment (Family Law (Scotland) Act 2006 etc.) 2006 (SSI 2006/207) r.2 (effective 4 May 2006).

(b)   dispense with intimation; and

(c)   where he dispenses with intimation, order that the name of that person be deleted from the condescendence of the initial writ.

(3)   Where intimation is ordered under paragraph (2), a copy of the initial writ and an intimation in Form F13 shall be intimated to the named person.

(4)[1]   In paragraph (1), "association" means sodomy, incest or any homosexual relationship.

Productions in action of divorce or where a section 11 order or order for financial provision may be made

33.9.[2, 3]   Unless the sheriff otherwise directs—   **D1.263**

(a)[4]   in an action of divorce or declarator of nullity of marriage, a warrant for citation shall not be granted without there being produced with the initial writ an extract of the relevant entry in the register of marriages or an equivalent document; and

(b)   in an action which includes a crave for a section 11 order, a warrant for citation shall not be granted without there being produced with the initial writ an extract of the relevant entry in the register of births or an equivalent document.

(c)[5]   in an action which includes a crave for an order for financial provision, the pursuer must lodge a completed Form F13A signed by the pursuer with the initial writ or minute of amendment as the case may be.

Productions in action of divorce on ground of issue of interim gender recognition certificate

33.9A.—[6](1)   This rule applies where, in an action of divorce, the ground on   **D1.264** which decree of divorce may be granted is that an interim gender recognition certificate has, after the date of the marriage, been issued to either party to the marriage.

(2)   Unless the sheriff otherwise directs, a warrant for citation shall not be granted without there being produced with the initial writ—

(a)   where the pursuer is the subject of the interim gender recognition certificate, the interim gender recognition certificate or, failing that, a certified copy of the interim gender recognition certificate; or

(b)   where the pursuer is the spouse of the person who is the subject of the interim gender recognition certificate, a certified copy of the interim gender recognition certificate.

(3)   For the purposes of this rule, a certified copy of an interim gender recognition certificate shall be a copy of that certificate sealed with the seal of the Gender Recognition Panels and certified to be a true copy by an officer authorised by the President of Gender Recognition Panels.

---

[1] As amended by Act of Sederunt (Ordinary Cause Rules) Amendment (Family Law (Scotland) Act 2006 etc.) 2006 (SSI 2006/207) r.2 (effective 4 May 2006).

[2] As amended by Act of Sederunt (Family Proceedings in the Sheriff Court) 1996 (SI 1996/2167) (effective 1 November 1996).

[3] As amended by the Act of Sederunt (Sheriff Court Rules) (Miscellaneous Amendments) 2012 (SSI 2012/188) para.4 (effective 1 August 2012).

[4] As amended by Act of Sederunt (Ordinary Cause Rules) Amendment (Family Law (Scotland) Act 2006 etc.) 2006 (SSI 2006/207) (effective 4 May 2006).

[5] As amended by the Act of Sederunt (Sheriff Court Rules) (Miscellaneous Amendments) 2012 (SSI 2012/188) para.4 (effective 1 August 2012).

[6] Inserted by the Act of Sederunt (Ordinary Cause Rules) Amendment (Gender Recognition Act 2004) 2005 (SSI 2005/189) r.2 (effective 4 April 2005).

Application for corrected gender recognition certificate

D1.265 **33.9B.**[1] An application for a corrected gender recognition certificate under section 6 of the Gender Recognition Act 2004 by—

    (a) the person to whom a full gender recognition certificate has been issued; or

    (b) the Secretary of State,

shall be made by minute in the process of the action pursuant to which the full gender recognition certificate was issued.

Warrant of citation

D1.266 **33.10.** The warrant of citation in a family action shall be in Form F14.

Form of citation and certificate

D1.267 **33.11.**—(1) Subject to rule 5.6 (service where address of person is not known), citation of a defender shall be in Form F15, which shall be attached to a copy of the initial writ and warrant of citation and shall have appended to it a notice of intention to defend in Form F26.

    (2) The certificate of citation shall be in Form F16 which shall be attached to the initial writ.

Intimation to local authority

D1.268 **33.12.**—[2](1) In any family action where the pursuer craves a residence order in respect of a child, the sheriff may, if the sheriff thinks fit, order intimation to the local authority in which area the pursuer resides; and such intimation shall be in Form F8.

    (2) Where an order for intimation is made under paragraph (1), intimation to that local authority shall be given within 7 days after the date on which an order for intimation has been made.

Service in cases of mental disorder of defender

D1.269 **33.13.**—(1) In a family action where the defender suffers or appears to suffer from mental disorder and is resident in a hospital or other similar institution, citation shall be executed by registered post or the first class recorded delivery service addressed to the medical officer in charge of that hospital or institution; and there shall be included with the copy of the initial writ—

    (a) a citation in Form F15;

    (b) any notice required by rule 33.14(1);

    (c) a request in Form F17;

    (d) a form of certificate in Form F18 requesting the medical officer to—

        (i) deliver and explain the initial writ, citation and any notice or form of notice of consent required under rule 33.14(1) personally to the defender; or

        (ii) certify that such delivery or explanation would be dangerous to the health or mental condition of the defender; and

    (e) a stamped envelope addressed for return of that certificate to the pursuer or his solicitor, if he has one.

    (2) The medical officer referred to in paragraph (1) shall send the certificate in Form F18 duly completed to the pursuer or his solicitor, as the case may be.

---

[1] Inserted by the Act of Sederunt (Ordinary Cause Rules) Amendment (Gender Recognition Act 2004) 2005 (SSI 2005/189) r.2 (effective 4 April 2005).

[2] As substituted by the Act of Sederunt (Sheriff Court Rules) (Miscellaneous Amendments) (No.2) 2010 (SSI 2010/416) r.7 (effective January 1, 2011).

(3)   The certificate mentioned in paragraph (2) shall be attached to the certificate of citation.

(4)   Where such a certificate bears that the initial writ has not been delivered to the defender, the sheriff may, at any time before decree—

    (a)   order such further medical inquiry, and

    (b)   make such order for further service or intimation,

as he thinks fit.

Notices in certain actions of divorce or separation

33.14.—(1)   In the following actions of divorce or separation there shall be attached to the copy of the initial writ served on the defender—   **D1.270**

    (a)[1]   in an action relying on section 1(2)(d) of the Act of 1976 (no cohabitation for one year with consent of defender to decree)—

        (i)   which is an action of divorce, a notice in Form F19 and a notice of consent in Form F20;

        (ii)   which is an action of separation, a notice in Form F21 and a form of notice of consent in Form F22;

    (b)[2]   in an action relying on section 1(2)(e) of the Act of 1976 (no cohabitation for two years)—

        (i)   which is an action of divorce, a notice in Form F23;

        (ii)   which is an action of separation, a notice in Form F24.

    (c)[3]   in an action relying on section 1(1)(b) of the Act of 1976 (grounds for divorce: interim gender recognition certificate), a notice in Form F24A

(2)[4]   The certificate of citation of an initial writ in an action mentioned in paragraph (1) shall state which notice or form mentioned in paragraph (1) has been attached to the initial writ.

Orders for intimation

33.15.—[5](1)   Except in relation to intimation to a child in Form F9, in any family action, the sheriff may, at any time—   **D1.271**

    (a)   order intimation to be made on such person as he thinks fit;

    (b)   postpone intimation, where he considers that such postponement is appropriate and, in that case, the sheriff shall make such order in respect of postponement of intimation as he thinks fit; or

    (c)   dispense with intimation, where he considers that such dispensation is appropriate.

[Repealed by the Act of Sederunt (Rules of the Court of Session 1994 and Ordinary Cause Rules 1993 Amendment) (Views of the Child) 2019 (SSI 2019/123) r.3(4) (effective 24 June 2019).]

(3)   Where a party makes a crave or averment in a family action which, had it been made in an initial writ, would have required a warrant for intimation under rule 33.7, that party shall include a crave in his writ for a warrant for intimation or to

---

[1] As amended by Act of Sederunt (Ordinary Cause Rules) Amendment (Family Law (Scotland) Act 2006 etc.) 2006 (SSI 2006/207) r.2 (effective 4 May 2006).

[2] As amended by Act of Sederunt (Ordinary Cause Rules) Amendment (Family Law (Scotland) Act 2006 etc.) 2006 (SSI 2006/207) r.2 (effective 4 May 2006).

[3] Inserted or substituted by Act of Sederunt (Ordinary Cause Rules) Amendment (Family Law (Scotland) Act 2006 etc.) 2006 (SSI 2006/207) r.2 (effective 4 May 2006).

[4] As amended by SI 1996/2445 (effective 1 November 1996).

[5] As amended by the Act of Sederunt (Rules of the Court of Session 1994 and Ordinary Cause Rules 1993 Amendment) (Views of the Child) 2019 (SSI 2019/123) r.3 (effective 24 June 2019).

dispense with such intimation; and rule 33.7 shall, with the necessary modifications, apply to a crave for a warrant under this paragraph as it applies to a crave for a warrant under that rule.

Appointment of curators ad litem to defenders

D1.272

33.16.—[1,2](1)[3,4] This rule applies to a family action where it appears to the court that the defender has a mental disorder.

(2) In an action to which this rule applies, the sheriff shall, after the expiry of the period for lodging a notice of intention to defend—

    (a) appoint a curator ad litem to the defender;

    (b) make an order requiring the curator *ad litem* to lodge in process a report, based on medical evidence, stating whether or not, in the opinion of a suitably qualified medical practitioner, the defender is incapable of instructing a solicitor to represent the defender's interests.

(3)[5] Within 7 days after the appointment of a curator ad litem under paragraph (2)(a), the pursuer shall send to him—

    (a) a copy of the initial writ and any defences (including any adjustments and amendments) lodged; and

    (b) a copy of any notice in Form G5A sent to the curator *ad litem* by the sheriff clerk.

(4) On lodging a report under paragraph (2)(b), the curator *ad litem* must intimate that this has been done to—

    (a) the pursuer; and

    (b) the solicitor for the defender, if known.

(5) Within 14 days after the report required under paragraph (2)(b) has been lodged, the curator *ad litem* must lodge in process one of the writs mentioned in paragraph (6).

(6) The writs referred to in paragraph (5) are—

    (a) a notice of intention to defend;

    (b) defences to the action;

    (c) a minute adopting defences already lodged; and

    (d) a minute stating that the curator ad litem does not intend to lodge defences.

(7) Notwithstanding that he has lodged a minute stating that he does not intend to lodge defences, a curator ad litem may appear at any stage of the action to protect the interests of the defender.

(8)[6] At such intervals as the curator *ad litem* considers reasonable having regard to the nature of the defender's mental disorder, the curator *ad litem* must review

---

[1] As amended by the Act of Sederunt (Ordinary Cause Rules 1993 Amendment) (Case Management of Defended Family and Civil Partnership Actions) 2022 (SSI 2022/289) r.2(11) (effective 25 September 2023 subject to transitional provision specified in SSI 2022/289 r.3).

[2] As amended by the Act of Sederunt (Rules of the Court of Session 1994 and Sheriff Court Rules Amendment) (Curators ad litem) 2017 (SSI 2017/132) r.2(3) (effective 1 June 2017 subject to saving specified in SSI 2017/132 r.4).

[3] As amended by Act of Sederunt (Ordinary Cause Rules) Amendment (Family Law (Scotland) Act 2006 etc.) 2006 (SSI 2006/207) r.2 (effective 4 May 2006).

[4] As amended by the Act of Sederunt (Sheriff Court Rules) (Miscellaneous Amendments) 2012 (SSI 2012/188) para.5 (effective 1 August 2012).

[5] As amended by SI 1996/2445 (effective 1 November 1996).

[6] As substituted by the Act of Sederunt (Rules of the Court of Session 1994 and Sheriff Court Rules Amendment) (Curators ad litem) 2017 (SSI 2017/132) r.2(3)(e) (effective 1 June 2017 subject to saving specified in SSI 2017/132 r.4).

whether there appears to have been any change in the defender's capacity to instruct a solicitor, in order to ascertain whether it is appropriate for the appointment to continue.

(8A)[1] If it appears to the curator *ad litem* that the defender may no longer be incapable, the curator *ad litem* must by motion seek the sheriff's permission to obtain an opinion on the matter from a suitably qualified medical practitioner.

(8B)[2] If the motion under paragraph (8A) is granted, the curator *ad litem* must lodge in process a copy of the opinion as soon as possible.

(8C)[3] Where the opinion concludes that the defender is not incapable of instructing a solicitor, the curator *ad litem* must seek discharge from appointment by minute.

(9) The pursuer shall be responsible, in the first instance, for payment of the fees and outlays of the curator ad litem incurred during the period from his appointment until—

(a) he lodges a minute stating that he does not intend to lodge defences;
(b) he decides to instruct the lodging of defences or a minute adopting defences already lodged; or
(c) being satisfied after investigation that the defender is not incapable of instructing a solicitor, he is discharged.

Applications for sist

33.17. An application for a sist, or the recall of a sist, under Schedule 3 to the Domicile and Matrimonial Proceedings Act 1973 shall be made by written motion.

D1.273

Notices of consent to divorce or separation

33.18.—(1)[4] Where, in an action of divorce or separation in which the facts in section 1(2)(d) of the Act of 1976 (no cohabitation for one year with consent of defender to decree) are relied on, the defender wishes to consent to the grant of decree of divorce or separation he shall do so by giving notice in writing in Form F20 (divorce) or Form F22 (separation), as the case may be, to the sheriff clerk.

D1.274

(2) The evidence of one witness shall be sufficient for the purpose of establishing that the signature on a notice of consent under paragraph (1) is that of the defender.

(3) In an action of divorce or separation where the initial writ includes, for the purposes of section 1(2)(d) of the Act of 1976, an averment that the defender consents to the grant of decree, the defender may give notice by letter sent to the sheriff clerk stating that he has not so consented or that he withdraws any consent which he has already given.

(4) On receipt of a letter under paragraph (3), the sheriff clerk shall intimate the terms of the letter to the pursuer.

---

[1] As inserted by the Act of Sederunt (Rules of the Court of Session 1994 and Sheriff Court Rules Amendment) (Curators ad litem) 2017 (SSI 2017/132) r.2(3)(e) (effective 1 June 2017 subject to saving specified in SSI 2017/132 r.4).

[2] As inserted by the Act of Sederunt (Rules of the Court of Session 1994 and Sheriff Court Rules Amendment) (Curators ad litem) 2017 (SSI 2017/132) r.2(3)(e) (effective 1 June 2017 subject to saving specified in SSI 2017/132 r.4).

[3] As inserted by the Act of Sederunt (Rules of the Court of Session 1994 and Sheriff Court Rules Amendment) (Curators ad litem) 2017 (SSI 2017/132) r.2(3)(e) (effective 1 June 2017 subject to saving specified in SSI 2017/132 r.4).

[4] As amended by Act of Sederunt (Ordinary Cause Rules) Amendment (Family Law (Scotland) Act 2006 etc.) 2006 (SSI 2006/207) r.2 (effective 4 May 2006).

(5) On receipt of any intimation under paragraph (4), the pursuer may, within 14 days after the date of the intimation, if none of the other facts mentioned in section 1(2) of the Act of 1976 is averred in the initial writ, lodge a motion for the action to be sisted.

(6) If no such motion is lodged, the pursuer shall be deemed to have abandoned the action and the action shall be dismissed.

(7) If a motion under paragraph (5) is granted and the sist is not recalled or renewed within a period of 6 months from the date of the interlocutor granting the sist, the pursuer shall be deemed to have abandoned the action and the action shall be dismissed.

Views of the child – undefended actions

D1.275
33.19.—[1](1) This rule applies to undefended actions in which a section 11 order is sought and warrant has been granted for intimation and the seeking of the child's views in Form F9.

(2) The pursuer must—

(a) following the expiry of the period of notice, send the child the Form F9 that was submitted and approved under rule 33.7A (warrants and forms for intimation to a child and for seeking a child's views);

(b) lodge with the minute for decree a certificate of intimation in Form F9A;

(c) not send the child a copy of the initial writ.

(3) Except on cause shown, the sheriff must not grant decree in the period of 28 days following the date on which the Form F9 was sent to the child.

Views of the child – section 11 order sought by pursuer only

D1.275.1
33.19A.—[2](1) This rule applies to defended actions in which only the pursuer seeks a section 11 order and warrant has been granted for intimation and the seeking of the child's views in Form F9.

(2) The pursuer must—

(a) no later than 14 days after the notice of intention to defend is lodged, send the child the Form F9 that was submitted and approved under rule 33.7A (warrants and forms for intimation to a child and for seeking a child's views);

(b) on the same day, lodge a certificate of intimation in Form F9A;

(c) not send the child a copy of the initial writ, the notice of intention to defend or the defences.

Views of the child – section 11 order sought by defender only

D1.275.2
33.19B.—[3](1) This rule applies to defended actions in which only the defender seeks a section 11 order and warrant has been granted for intimation and the seeking of the child's views in Form F9.

(2) The defender must—

(a) no later than 14 days after the notice of intention to defend is lodged, send the child the Form F9 that was submitted and approved under rule 33.34 (notice of intention to defend and defences etc.);

(b) on the same day, lodge a certificate of intimation in Form F9A;

---

[1] As substituted by the Act of Sederunt (Rules of the Court of Session 1994 and Ordinary Cause Rules 1993 Amendment) (Views of the Child) 2019 (SSI 2019/123) para.3 (effective 24th June 2019).

[2] As inserted by the Act of Sederunt (Rules of the Court of Session 1994 and Ordinary Cause Rules 1993 Amendment) (Views of the Child) 2019 (SSI 2019/123) para.3 (effective 24th June 2019).

[3] As inserted by the Act of Sederunt (Rules of the Court of Session 1994 and Ordinary Cause Rules 1993 Amendment) (Views of the Child) 2019 (SSI 2019/123) para.3 (effective 24th June 2019).

(c)   not send the child a copy of the initial writ, the notice of intention to defend or the defences.

Views of the child – section 11 orders sought by both pursuer and defender

33.19C.—[1](1)   This rule applies to defended actions in which section 11 orders are sought by both the pursuer and the defender and warrant has been granted for intimation and the seeking of the child's views in Form F9.

  (2)   The pursuer must—

    (a)   no later than 14 days after the notice of intention to defend is lodged, send the child the Form F9 that was submitted and approved under rule 33.7A (warrants and forms for intimation to a child and for seeking a child's views), amended so as also to narrate the section 11 order sought by the defender;

    (b)   on the same day—

       (i)   lodge a certificate of intimation in Form F9A;

      (ii)   send the defender a copy of the Form F9 that was sent to the child;

    (c)   not send the child a copy of the initial writ, the notice of intention to defend or the defences.

Views of the child – the sheriff's role

33.19D.—[2](1)   In a family action, in relation to any matter affecting a child, where that child has—

    (a)   returned a Form F9 to the sheriff clerk; or

    (b)   otherwise indicated to the court a wish to express views,

the sheriff must not grant any order unless an opportunity has been given for the views of that child to be obtained or heard.

  (2)   Where the sheriff is considering making an interim section 11 order before the views of the child have been obtained or heard, the sheriff must consider whether, and if so how, to seek the child's views in advance of making the order.

  (3)   Where a child has indicated a wish to express views, the sheriff must order any steps to be taken that the sheriff considers appropriate to obtain or hear the views of that child.

  (4)   The sheriff must not grant an order in a family action, in relation to any matter affecting a child who has expressed views, unless the sheriff has given due weight to the views expressed by that child, having regard to the child's age and maturity.

  (5)   In any action in which a section 11 order is sought, where Form F9 has not been sent to the child concerned or where it has been sent but the sheriff considers that the passage of time requires it to be sent again, the sheriff may at any time order either party to—

    (a)   send the Form F9 to that child within a specified timescale;

    (b)   on the same day, lodge—

       (i)   a copy of the Form F9 that was sent to the child;

      (ii)   a certificate of intimation in Form F9B.

D1.275.3

D1.275.4

[THE NEXT PARAGRAPH IS D1.276]

---

[1] As inserted by the Act of Sederunt (Rules of the Court of Session 1994 and Ordinary Cause Rules 1993 Amendment) (Views of the Child) 2019 (SSI 2019/123) para.3 (effective 24th June 2019).

[2] As inserted by the Act of Sederunt (Rules of the Court of Session 1994 and Ordinary Cause Rules 1993 Amendment) (Views of the Child) 2019 (SSI 2019/123) para.3 (effective 24th June 2019).

Recording of views of the child

D1.276   **33.20**—[1,2](1) This rule applies where a child expresses a view on a matter affecting him whether expressed personally to the sheriff or to a person appointed by the sheriff for that purpose or provided by the child in writing.

(2) The sheriff, or the person appointed by the sheriff, shall record the views of the child in writing; and the sheriff may direct that such views, and any written views, given by a child shall—

(a) be sealed in an envelope marked "Views of the child—confidential";

(b) be kept in the court process without being recorded in the inventory of process;

(c) be available to a sheriff only;

(d) not be opened by any person other than a sheriff; and

(e) not form a borrowable part of the process.

Child welfare reporters

D1.277   **33.21.**—[3,4](1) At any stage of a family action the sheriff may, in relation to any matter affecting a child, appoint a person (referred to in this rule as a "child welfare reporter")—

(a) to seek the views of the child and to report any views expressed by the child to the court; or

(b) to undertake enquiries and to report to the court.

(2) A child welfare reporter may only be appointed under paragraph (1)(b) where the sheriff is satisfied that the appointment—

(a) is in the best interests of the child; and

(b) will promote the effective and expeditious determination of an issue in relation to the child.

(3) An interlocutor appointing a child welfare reporter must—

(a) specify a date by which the report is to be submitted to the court;

(b) include a direction as to the fees and outlays of the child welfare reporter;

(c) where the appointment is under paragraph (1)(a), specify the issues in respect of which the child's views are to be sought and include a direction as to whether a copy of the report is to be provided to the parties under paragraph (9)(d);

(d) where the appointment is under paragraph (1)(b), specify the enquiries to be undertaken, and the issues requiring to be addressed in the report; and

(e) where the appointment is under paragraph (1)(b) and seeking the views of the child forms part of the enquiries to be undertaken, include a direction as to whether the views of the child should be recorded in a separate report and, if so, whether a copy of that report is to be provided to the parties under paragraph (9)(d).

(4) An interlocutor complies with subparagraph (c) or (d) of paragraph (3) if the issues or, as the case may be the enquiries, referred to in that subparagraph are specified in an annex to the interlocutor in Form F44.

---

[1] As substituted by the Act of Sederunt (Family Proceedings in the Sheriff Court) 1996 1996 (SI 1996/2167) (effective 1 November 1996).

[2] As amended by the Act of Sederunt (Rules of the Court of Session 1994 and Ordinary Cause Rules 1993 Amendment) (Views of the Child) 2019 (SSI 2019/123) para.3 (effective 24th June 2019).

[3] As substituted by the Act of Sederunt (Rules of the Court of Session 1994 and Ordinary Cause Rules 1993 Amendment) (Child Welfare Reporters) 2015 (SSI 2015/312) para.4 (effective 26 October 2015).

[4] As amended by the Act of Sederunt (Rules of the Court of Session 1994 and Ordinary Cause Rules 1993 Amendment) (Views of the Child) 2019 (SSI 2019/123) para.3 (effective 24th June 2019).

(5) Where the sheriff has appointed a child welfare reporter with a view to the report being considered at an assigned hearing, the date specified in accordance with paragraph (3)(a) must be a date no less than three clear days before that hearing, excluding any day on which the sheriff clerk's office is not open for civil court business, unless cause exists for specifying a later date.

(6) On appointing a child welfare reporter the sheriff may also—

(a) make such further order as may be required to facilitate the discharge of the child welfare reporter's functions;

(b) direct that a party to the proceedings is to be responsible for providing the child welfare reporter with copies of such documents lodged in the process as may be specified; and

(c) give the child welfare reporter directions.

(7) The direction referred to in paragraph (3)(b) must assign liability for payment of the child welfare reporter's fees and outlays in the first instance, and require that liability to be borne—

(a) in equal shares by—

(i) the pursuer,

(ii) any defender who has lodged a notice of intention to defend, and

(iii) any minuter who has been granted leave to enter the process; or

(b) by one or more parties to the proceedings on such other basis as may be justified on cause shown.

(8) On the granting of an interlocutor appointing a child welfare reporter the sheriff clerk must—

(a) give the child welfare reporter—

(i) a certified copy of the interlocutor, and

(ii) sufficient information to enable the child welfare reporter to contact the solicitor for each party to the proceedings, or any party not represented by a solicitor; and

(b) intimate the name and address of the child welfare reporter to any local authority to which intimation of the proceedings has been made.

(9) A child welfare reporter appointed under this rule must—

(a) where the appointment is under paragraph (1)(a)—

(i) seek the child's views on the specified issues, and

(ii) prepare a report for the court reporting any such views;

(b) where the appointment is under paragraph (1)(b)—

(i) undertake the specified enquiries, and

(ii) prepare a report for the court having regard to the specified issues;

(c) send the report to the sheriff clerk by the date specified; and

(d) unless otherwise directed, send a copy of the report to each party to the proceedings by that date.

(10) A child welfare reporter may—

(a) apply to the sheriff clerk to be given further directions by the sheriff;

(b) bring to the attention of the sheriff clerk any impediment to the performance of any function arising under this rule.

(11) Where a child welfare reporter acts as referred to in paragraph (10), the sheriff may, having heard parties, make any order or direction that could competently have been made under paragraph (6).

Appointment of local authority to report on a child

D1.277.1 **33.21A.**—[1](1) This rule applies where the sheriff appoints a local authority to investigate and report to the court on the circumstances of a child and on the proposed arrangements for the care and upbringing of the child.

(2) The following provisions of rule 33.21 apply as if the reference to the child welfare reporter was a reference to the local authority appointed by the sheriff—

(a) paragraph (3)(a) and (b);

(b) paragraph (6)(a) and (b);

(c) paragraph (7); and

(d) paragraph (8).

(3) On completion of the report referred to in paragraph (1), the local authority must—

(a) send the report to the sheriff clerk; and

(b) unless otherwise directed by the sheriff, send a copy of the report to each party to the proceedings.

[THE NEXT PARAGRAPH IS D1.278]

Referral to family mediation

D1.278 **33.22.**[2,3](1) In any family action, where the sheriff considers it appropriate to do so, the sheriff may, at any stage of the action, refer the action, or part thereof, to a mediator accredited to a specified family mediation organisation.

(2) The sheriff must have particular regard to any averments of domestic abuse when considering the appropriateness of referring the action, or part thereof, to a mediator under paragraph (1).

(3) In this rule "any family action" means any action to which the Civil Evidence (Family Mediation) (Scotland) Act 1995 applies.

Child Welfare Hearing

D1.279 **33.22A.**—[4,5](1) Where—

(a) on the lodging of a notice of intention to defend in a family action in which the initial writ seeks or includes a crave for a section 11 order, a defender wishes to oppose any such crave or order, or seeks the same order as that craved by the pursuer,

(b) on the lodging of a notice of intention to defend in a family action, the defender seeks a section 11 order which is not craved by the pursuer, or

(c) in any other circumstances in a family action, the sheriff considers that a Child Welfare Hearing should be fixed and makes an order (whether at his own instance or on the motion of a party) that such a hearing shall be fixed,

---

[1] As inserted by the Act of Sederunt (Rules of the Court of Session 1994 and Ordinary Cause Rules 1993 Amendment) (Child Welfare Reporters) 2015 (SSI 2015/312) para.4 (effective 26 October 2015).

[2] Substituted by the Act of Sederunt (Ordinary Cause Rules 1993 Amendment) (Case Management of Defended Family and Civil Partnership Actions) 2022 (SSI 2022/289) r.2(12) (effective 25 September 2023 subject to transitional provision specified in SSI 2022/289 r.3).

[3] As inserted by the Act of Sederunt (Family Proceedings in the Sheriff Court) 1996 (SI 1996/2167) (effective 1 November 1996).

[4] As amended by the Act of Sederunt (Ordinary Cause Rules 1993 Amendment) (Case Management of Defended Family and Civil Partnership Actions) 2022 (SSI 2022/289) r.2(13) (effective 25 September 2023 subject to transitional provision specified in SSI 2022/289 r.3).

[5] As inserted by the Act of Sederunt (Family Proceedings in the Sheriff Court) 1996 (SI 1996/2167) (effective 1 November 1996).

the sheriff clerk shall fix a date and to be heard either at the same time as the Initial Case Management Hearing or on the first suitable court date occurring not sooner than 21 days and not later than 49 days after the last date for lodging of the notice of intention to defend, unless the sheriff directs the hearing to be held on an earlier date.

(2) On fixing the date for the Child Welfare Hearing, the sheriff clerk must—

(a) if the Child Welfare Hearing is to be heard at the same time as the Initial Case Management Hearing, intimate the date on which both hearings will take place to the parties in Form G5A; or

(b) if the Child Welfare Hearing is to be heard at a different time from the Initial Case Management Hearing, intimate the date of the Child Welfare Hearing to the parties in Form F41.

(3) The fixing of the date of the Child Welfare Hearing shall not affect the right of a party to make any other application to the court whether by motion or otherwise.

(4)[1] At the Child Welfare Hearing (which may be held in private), the sheriff shall seek to secure the expeditious resolution of disputes in relation to the child by ascertaining from the parties the matters in dispute and any information relevant to that dispute, and may—

(a) order such steps to be taken, make such order, if any, or order further procedure, as he thinks fit, and

(b) ascertain whether there is or is likely to be a vulnerable witness within the meaning of section 11(1) of the Act of 2004 who is to give evidence at any proof or hearing and whether any order under section 12(1) of the Act of 2004 requires to be made.

(5) All parties (including a child who has indicated his wish to attend) shall, except on cause shown, attend the Child Welfare Hearing personally.

(6) It shall be the duty of the parties to provide the sheriff with sufficient information to enable him to conduct the Child Welfare Hearing.

Applications for orders to disclose whereabouts of children

33.23.—(1) An application for an order under section 33(1) of the Family Law Act 1986 (which relates to the disclosure of the whereabouts of a child) shall be made by motion.

D1.280

(2) Where the sheriff makes an order under section 33(1) of the Family Law Act 1986, he may ordain the person against whom the order has been made to appear before him or to lodge an affidavit.

Applications in relation to removal of children

33.24.—[2](1) An application for leave under section 51(1) of the Act of 1975 (authority to remove a child from the care and possession of the applicant for a residence order) or for an order under section 35(3) of the Family Law Act 1986 (application for interdict or interim interdict prohibiting removal of child from jurisdiction) shall be made—

D1.281

(a) by a party to the action, by motion; or

(b) by a person who is not a party to the action, by minute.

(2) An application under section 35(3) of the Family Law Act 1986 need not be served or intimated.

---

[1] As substituted by the Act of Sederunt (Ordinary Cause, Summary Application, Summary Cause and Small Claim Rules) Amendment (Vulnerable Witnesses (Scotland) Act 2004) 2007 (SSI 2007/463) r.2(9) (effective 1 November 2007).

[2] As amended by Act of Sederunt (Family Proceedings in the Sheriff Court) 1996 (SI 1996/2167) (effective 1 November 1996).

(3) An application under section 23(2) of the Child Abduction and Custody Act 1985 (declarator that removal of child from United Kingdom was unlawful) shall be made—

    (a) in an action depending before the sheriff—

        (i) by a party, in the initial writ, defences or minute, as the case may be, or by motion; or

        (ii) by any other person, by minute; or

    (b) after final decree, by minute in the process of the action to which the application relates.

Intimation to local authority before supervised contact order

D1.282   **33.25.**[1] Where the sheriff, at his own instance or on the motion of a party, is considering making a contact order or an interim contact order subject to supervision by the social work department of a local authority, he shall ordain the party moving for such an order to intimate to the Chief Executive of that local authority (where not already a party to the action and represented at the hearing at which the issue arises)—

    (a) the terms of any relevant motion;

    (b) the intention of the sheriff to order that the contact order be supervised by the social work department of that local authority; and

    (c) that the local authority shall, within such period as the sheriff has determined—

        (i) notify the sheriff clerk whether it intends to make representations to the sheriff; and

        (ii)[2] where it intends to make representations in writing, do so within that period.

Joint minutes

D1.283   **33.26.**[3] Where any parties have reached agreement in relation to—

    (a) a section 11 order,

    (b) aliment for a child,

    (c) an order for financial provision, or

    (d)[4] an order under section 28 or 29 of the Act of 2006

a joint minute may be entered into expressing that agreement; and, subject to rule 33.19(3) (no order before views of child expressed), the sheriff may grant decree in respect of those parts of the joint minute in relation to which he could otherwise make an order, whether or not such a decree would include a matter for which there was no crave.

Affidavits

D1.284   **33.27.** The sheriff may accept evidence by affidavit at any hearing for an order or interim order.

---

[1] As amended by the Act of Sederunt (Family Proceedings in the Sheriff Court) (Marriage and Civil Partnership 1996 (SI 1996/2167) (effective 1 November 1996).

[2] As amended by Act of Sederunt (Ordinary Cause Rules) Amendment (Family Law (Scotland) Act 2006 etc.) 2006 (SSI 2006/207) r.2 (effective 4 May 2006).

[3] As amended by Act of Sederunt (Family Proceedings in the Sheriff Court) 1996 (SI 1996/2167) (effective 1 November 1996).

[4] As inserted by the Act of Sederunt (Sheriff Court Rules) (Miscellaneous Amendments) 2012 (SSI 2012/188) para.5 (effective 1 August 2012).

Applications for postponement of decree under section 3A of the Act of 1976

33.27A.[1]   An application under section 3A(1) (application for postponement of decree where impediment to religious marriage exists) or section 3A(4) (application for recall of postponement) of the Act of 1976 shall be made by minute in the process of the action to which the application relates.

D1.285

Part II – Undefended Family Actions

Evidence in certain undefended family actions

33.28.—[2](1)   This rule—

D1.286

   (a) subject to sub-paragraph (b), applies to all family actions in which no notice of intention to defend has been lodged, other than a family action—

       (i)   for a section 11 order or for aliment;

       (ii) of affiliation and aliment;

     (iii) for financial provision after an overseas divorce or annulment within the meaning of Part IV of the Matrimonial and Family Proceedings Act 1984; or

     (iv) for an order under the Act of 1981;

      (v)[3] for declarator of recognition, or non-recognition, of a relevant foreign decree within the meaning of section 7(9) of the Domicile and Matrimonial Proceedings Act 1973;

     (vi)[4] for an order under section 28 or 29 of the Act of 2006;

    (vii)[5] for declarator of recognition, or non-recognition, of a relevant foreign decree within the meaning of paragraph 1 of Schedule 1B to the Domicile and Matrimonial Proceedings Act 1973, or of a judgment to which paragraph 2(1)(b) of that Schedule refers.

   (b) applies to a family action in which a curator ad litem has been appointed under rule 33.16 where the curator ad litem to the defender has lodged a minute intimating that he does not intend to lodge defences;

   (c) applies to any family action which proceeds at any stage as undefended where the sheriff so directs;

   (d) applies to the merits of a family action which is undefended on the merits where the sheriff so directs, notwithstanding that the action is defended on an ancillary matter.

   (2)   Unless the sheriff otherwise directs, evidence shall be given by affidavits.

   (3)   Unless the sheriff otherwise directs, evidence relating to the welfare of a child shall be given by affidavit, at least one affidavit being emitted by a person other than a parent or party to the action.

---

[1] Substituted by Act of Sederunt (Ordinary Cause Rules) Amendment (Family Law (Scotland) Act 2006 etc.) 2006 (SSI 2006/207) r.2 (effective 4 May 2006) and amended by the Act of Sederunt (Ordinary Cause, Summary Application, Summary Cause and Small Claim Rules) Amendment (Miscellaneous) 2007 (SSI 2007/6) r.2(14) (effective 26 February 2007).

[2] As amended by Act of Sederunt (Family Proceedings in the Sheriff Court) 1996 (SI 1996/2167) (effective 1 November 1996).

[3] As inserted by the Act of Sederunt (Sheriff Court Rules) (Miscellaneous Amendments) (No.2) 2010 (SSI 2010/416) r.8 (effective 1 January 2011).

[4] As inserted by the Act of Sederunt (Sheriff Court Rules) (Miscellaneous Amendments) 2012 (SSI 2012/188) para.5 (effective 1 August 2012).

[5] As inserted by the Act of Sederunt (Rules of the Court of Session and Sheriff Court Rules Amendment No.2) (Marriage and Civil Partnership (Scotland) Act 2014) 2014 (SSI 2014/302) r.5 (effective 16 December 2014).

(4) Evidence in the form of a written statement bearing to be the professional opinion of a duly qualified medical practitioner, which has been signed by him and lodged in process, shall be admissible in place of parole evidence by him.

Procedure for decree in actions under rule 33.28

D1.287 **33.29.**—(1) In an action to which rule 33.28 (evidence in certain undefended family actions) applies, the pursuer shall at any time after the expiry of the period for lodging a notice of intention to defend—

    (a) lodge in process the affidavit evidence; and

    (b) endorse a minute in Form F27 on the initial writ.

(2) The sheriff may, at any time after the pursuer has complied with paragraph (1), without requiring the appearance of parties—

    (a) grant decree in terms of the motion for decree; or

    (b) remit the cause for such further procedure, if any, including proof by parole evidence, as the sheriff thinks fit.

Extracts of undefended decree

D1.288 **33.30.**[1] In an action to which rule 33.28 (evidence in certain undefended family actions) applies, the sheriff clerk shall, after the expiry of 14 days after the grant of decree under rule 33.29 (procedure for decree in cases under rule 33.28), issue to the pursuer and the defender an extract decree.

Procedure in undefended family action for section 11 order

D1.289 **33.31.**—[2](1) Where no notice of intention to defend has been lodged in a family action for a section 11 order, any proceedings in the cause shall be dealt with by the sheriff in chambers.

(2) In an action to which paragraph (1) applies, decree may be pronounced after such inquiry as the sheriff thinks fit.

No recording of evidence

D1.290 **33.32.** It shall not be necessary to record the evidence in any proof in a family action which is not defended.

Disapplication of Chapter 15

D1.291 **33.33.**[3] Other than rule 15.1(1), Chapter 15 (motions) shall not apply to a family action in which no notice of intention to defend has been lodged, or to a family action in so far as it proceeds as undefended.

Late appearance and application for recall by defenders

D1.292 **33.33A.**—[4](1)[56] In a cause mentioned in rule 33.1(a) to (g) or (n) to (q) or rule 33.7A(1) (warrants and forms for intimation to a child and for seeking a child's

---

[1] As amended by Act of Sederunt (Ordinary Cause Rules) Amendment (Family Law (Scotland) Act 2006 etc.) 2006 (SSI 2006/207) r.2 (effective 4 May 2006).

[2] As amended by Act of Sederunt (Family Proceedings in the Sheriff Court) 1996 (SI 1996/2167) (effective 1 November 1996).

[3] As amended by SI 1996/2445 (effective November 1, 1996).

[4] As inserted by the Act of Sederunt (Sheriff Court Rules) (Miscellaneous Amendments) 2008 (SSI 2008/223) r.2(2) (effective 1 July 2008).
As amended by the Act of Sederunt (Rules of the Court of Session 1994 and Ordinary Cause Rules 1993 Amendment) (Views of the Child) 2019 (SSI 2019/123) para.3 (effective 24 June 2019).

[5] As amended by the Act of Sederunt (Sheriff Court Rules) (Miscellaneous Amendments) (No.2) 2010 (SSI 2010/416) r.8 (effective 1 January 2011).

[6] As amended by the Act of Sederunt (Sheriff Court Rules) (Miscellaneous Amendments) 2012 (SSI 2012/188) para.5 (effective 1 August 2012).

views), the sheriff may, at any stage of the action before the granting of final decree, make an order with such conditions, if any, as he thinks fit—

    (a)   directing that a defender who has not lodged a notice of intention to defend be treated as if he had lodged such a notice and the period of notice had expired on the date on which the order was made; or

    (b)   allowing a defender who has not lodged a notice of intention to defend to appear and be heard at a diet of proof although he has not lodged defences, but he shall not, in that event, be allowed to lead evidence without the pursuer's consent.

(2)   Where the sheriff makes an order under paragraph (1), the pursuer may recall a witness already examined or lead other evidence whether or not he closed his proof before that order was made.

(3)   Where no order under paragraph (1) has been sought by a defender who has not lodged a notice of intention to defend and decree is granted against him, the sheriff may, on an application made within 14 days of the date of the decree, and with such conditions, if any, as he thinks fit, make an order recalling the decree.

(4)   Where the sheriff makes an order under paragraph (3), the cause shall thereafter proceed as if the defender had lodged a notice of intention to defend and the period of notice had expired on the date on which the decree was recalled.

(4A)   Where the sheriff makes an order under paragraph (1) or (3), the sheriff must order any steps to be taken that the sheriff considers appropriate to obtain or hear the views of the child in relation to any section 11 order sought by the defender.

(5)   An application under paragraph (1) or (3) shall be made by note setting out the proposed defence and explaining the defender's failure to appear.

(6)   An application under paragraph (1) or (3) shall not affect any right of appeal the defender may otherwise have.

(7)   A note lodged in an application under paragraph (1) or (3) shall be served on the pursuer and any other party.

Part III – Defended Family Actions

General provisions

33.33B.—[1](1)   Chapters 9 (standard procedure in defended causes) and 10 (additional procedure) do not apply to a family action in which a notice of intention to defend has been lodged in accordance with rule 33.34 (notice of intention to defend and defences etc.).   **D1.292.1**

(2)   Subject to paragraph (3), a family action in which a notice of intention to defend has been lodged must follow the procedure set out in this Part of this Chapter.

(3)   The sheriff may, in exceptional circumstances, of the sheriff's own motion or on the motion of a party, disapply any rule mentioned in this Part of this Chapter.

Notice of intention to defend and defences etc.[2]

33.34.—[3](1)   This rule applies where the defender in a family action seeks—   **D1.293**

    (a)   to oppose any crave in the initial writ;

    (b)   to make a claim for—

        (i)   aliment;

---

[1] Inserted by the Act of Sederunt (Ordinary Cause Rules 1993 Amendment) (Case Management of Defended Family and Civil Partnership Actions) 2022 (SSI 2022/289) r.2(14) (effective 25 September 2023 subject to transitional provision specified in SSI 2022/289 r.3).

[2] As amended by the Act of Sederunt (Sheriff Court Rules) (Miscellaneous Amendments) 2012 (SSI 2012/188) para.5 (effective 1 August 2012).

[3] As amended by Act of Sederunt (Family Proceedings in the Sheriff Court) 1996 (SI 1996/2167) (effective 1 November 1996).

        (ii)   an order for financial provision within the meaning of section 8(3) of the Act of 1985;

        (iii)   a section 11 order;

        (iv)[1] an order for financial provision under section 28 or 29 of the Family Law (Scotland) Act 2006; or

  (c)   an order—

        (i)   under section 16(1)(b) or (3) of the Act of 1985 (setting aside or varying agreement as to financial provision);

        (ii)   under section 18 of the Act of 1985 (which relates to avoidance transactions); or

        (iii) under the Act of 1981; or

  (d)   to challenge the jurisdiction of the court.

(2) In an action to which this rule applies, the defender shall—

  (a)   lodge a notice of intention to defend in Form F26 before the expiry of the period of notice and, at the same time, send a copy to the pursuer; and

  (b)   make any claim or seek any order referred to in paragraph (1), as the case may be, in those defences by setting out in his defences—

        (i)   craves;

        (ii)   averments in the answers to the condescendence in support of those craves; and

        (iii) appropriate pleas-in-law.

(3) *[Repealed by the Act of Sederunt (Rules of the Court of Session 1994 and Ordinary Cause Rules 1993 Amendment) (Views of the Child) 2019 (SSI 2019/123) r.3(2) (effective 24 June 2019).]*

(4)[2, 3] Where a defender opposes a crave for an order for financial provision or makes a claim in accordance with paragraph (1)(b)(ii), the defender must lodge a completed Form F13A signed by the defender with the defences, minute of amendment or answers as the case may be.

(4A)[4] Subject to paragraph (4B), where a defender intends to make an application for a section 11 order in respect of a child who is not a party to the action the defender must—

  (a)   include in the notice of intention to defend a crave for a warrant for intimation and the seeking of the child's views in Form F9;

  (b)   when lodging the notice of intention to defend, submit a draft Form F9, showing the details that the defender proposes to include when the form is sent to the child.

(4B) Where the defender considers that it would be inappropriate to send Form F9 to the child (for example, where the child is under 5 years of age), the defender must include in the notice of intention to defend—

  (a)   a crave to dispense with intimation and the seeking of the child's views in Form F9;

---

[1] As inserted by the Act of Sederunt (Sheriff Court Rules) (Miscellaneous Amendments) 2012 (SSI 2012/188) para.4,5 (effective 1 August 2012).

[2] As inserted by the Act of Sederunt (Sheriff Court Rules) (Miscellaneous Amendments) 2012 (SSI 2012/188) para.4,5 (effective 1 August 2012).

[3] As amended by the Act of Sederunt (Sheriff Court Rules) (Miscellaneous Amendments) (No.2) 2012 (SSI 2012/221) para.2 (effective 31 July 2012).

[4] As amended by the Act of Sederunt (Ordinary Cause Rules 1993 Amendment) (Case Management of Defended Family and Civil Partnership Actions) 2022 (SSI 2022/289) r.2(15) (effective 25 September 2023 subject to transitional provision specified in SSI 2022/289 r.3).

(b) averments setting out the reasons why it is inappropriate to send Form F9 to the child.

(4C) The sheriff must be satisfied that the draft Form F9 submitted under paragraph (4A)(b) has been drafted appropriately.

(4D) The sheriff may dispense with intimation and the seeking of views in Form F9 or make any other order that the sheriff considers appropriate.

(4E) An order granting warrant for intimation and the seeking of the child's views in Form F9 under this rule must —

(a) state that the Form F9 must be sent to the child in accordance with rule 33.19B (views of the child – section 11 order sought by defender only);

(b) be signed by the sheriff.

Abandonment by pursuer

33.35. Notwithstanding abandonment by a pursuer, the court may allow a defender to pursue an order or claim sought in his defences; and the proceedings in relation to that order or claim shall continue in dependence as if a separate cause.   **D1.294**

Attendance of parties at Options Hearing

33.36.[1] All parties must, except on cause shown, attend personally case management hearings under rules 33.36J (Initial Case Management Hearing) and 33.36P (Full Case Management Hearing).   **D1.295**

Fixing of date and time for Initial Case Management Hearing

33.36A.—[2](1) On the lodging of a notice of intention to defend under rule 33.34   **D1.295.1** (notice of intention to defend and defences etc.), the sheriff clerk must fix a date and time for an Initial Case Management Hearing which date must be on the first suitable court day occurring not sooner than 21 days and not later than 49 days after the last date for the lodging of the notice of intention to defend.

(2) In cases involving a crave for a section 11 order the sheriff must have regard to holding the Initial Case Management Hearing and the Child Welfare Hearing at the same time.

(3) On fixing the date for Initial Case Management Hearing, the sheriff clerk must—

(a) intimate forthwith to the parties in Form G5A—

(i) the last date for lodging defences;

(ii) the date for the return of the initial writ;

(iii) the date of the Initial Case Management Hearing;

(iv) whether the Child Welfare Hearing is to be held at the same time with the Initial Case Management Hearing;

(b) prepare an interlocutor addressing all of the matters in sub-paragraph (a) for the sheriff to sign.

(4) The fixing of the date of the Initial Case Management Hearing does not affect the right of a party to make any incidental application to the court.

---

[1] Substituted by the Act of Sederunt (Ordinary Cause Rules 1993 Amendment) (Case Management of Defended Family and Civil Partnership Actions) 2022 (SSI 2022/289) r.2(16) (effective 25 September 2023 subject to transitional provision specified in SSI 2022/289 r.3).

[2] Inserted by the Act of Sederunt (Ordinary Cause Rules 1993 Amendment) (Case Management of Defended Family and Civil Partnership Actions) 2022 (SSI 2022/289) r.2(17) (effective 25 September 2023 subject to transitional provision specified in SSI 2022/289 r.3).

Alteration of date and time for Initial Case Management Hearing

D1.295.2   **33.36B.**—[1](1)   Subject to paragraph (2), at any time before the date and time fixed under rule 33.36A (fixing of date and time for Initial Case Management Hearing) or under this rule, the sheriff may of the sheriff's own motion, on the motion of any party or on the joint motion of the parties—

 (a)   discharge the Initial Case Management Hearing or, where fixed, the Child Welfare Hearing or both, as the case may be; and

 (b)   fix a new date and time for either the Initial Case Management Hearing or the Child Welfare Hearing or both, as the case may be.

(2)   The date and time of any hearing to be fixed under paragraph (1)(b) may be earlier or later than the date and time fixed for the discharged hearing, but must be fixed for a date within the period specified in rule 33.36A(1) or the first available court date thereafter.

(3)   Where the sheriff is considering making an order under paragraph (1) of the sheriff's own motion and in the absence of the parties, the sheriff clerk must—

 (a)   fix a date, time and place for the parties to be heard;

 (b)   prepare an interlocutor recording those dates, times and places for the sheriff to sign.

(4)   The sheriff may discharge a hearing fixed under paragraph (3) on the joint motion of the parties.

(5)   On the discharge of a hearing under paragraph (1)(a) or paragraph (4), the sheriff clerk must forthwith intimate to all parties—

 (a)   that the hearing has been discharged under paragraph (1)(a) or, as the case may be, paragraph (4);

 (b)   the last date for lodging defences, if appropriate;

 (c)   the last date for adjustment, if appropriate;

 (d)   the new date and time fixed for any hearing under paragraph (1)(b).

(6)   Any reference in these Rules to the Initial Case Management Hearing, the Child Welfare Hearing or a continuation of either, includes a reference to an Initial Case Management Hearing or Child Welfare Hearing for which a date and time has been fixed under this rule.

Return of initial writ

D1.295.3   **33.36C.**[2]   Subject to rule 33.36D (lodging of pleadings before Initial Case Management Hearing) the pursuer must return the initial writ, unbacked and unfolded, to the sheriff clerk within 7 days of the expiry of the period of notice and in accordance with the date intimated on Form G5A.

Lodging of pleadings before Initial Case Management Hearing

D1.295.4   **33.36D.**[3]   Where any hearing, whether by motion or otherwise, is fixed before the Initial Case Management Hearing, each party must lodge in process a copy of the party's pleadings, or, where the pleadings have been adjusted, the pleadings as adjusted, not later than 2 days before the hearing.

---

[1] Inserted by the Act of Sederunt (Ordinary Cause Rules 1993 Amendment) (Case Management of Defended Family and Civil Partnership Actions) 2022 (SSI 2022/289) r.2(17) (effective 25 September 2023 subject to transitional provision specified in SSI 2022/289 r.3).

[2] Inserted by the Act of Sederunt (Ordinary Cause Rules 1993 Amendment) (Case Management of Defended Family and Civil Partnership Actions) 2022 (SSI 2022/289) r.2(17) (effective 25 September 2023 subject to transitional provision specified in SSI 2022/289 r.3).

[3] Inserted by the Act of Sederunt (Ordinary Cause Rules 1993 Amendment) (Case Management of Defended Family and Civil Partnership Actions) 2022 (SSI 2022/289) r.2(17) (effective 25 September 2023 subject to transitional provision specified in SSI 2022/289 r.3).

Process folder

33.36E.—[1](1) On receipt of the notice of intention to defend, the sheriff clerk must prepare a process folder which must include—

    (a)   interlocutor sheets;

    (b)   duplicate interlocutor sheets;

    (c)   a production file;

    (d)   a motion file;

    (e)   an inventory of process.

(2) Any productions or part of process lodged in a cause must be placed in the process folder.

D1.295.5

Defences

33.36F.—[2](1) Where a notice of intention to defend has been lodged, the defender must lodge defences within 14 days after the expiry of the period of notice.

(2) Defences must be in the form of answers in numbered paragraphs corresponding to the articles of the condescendence and must have appended a note of the pleas-in- law of the defender.

(3) Defences which include a counterclaim must commence with a crave setting out the counterclaim in such form as, if the counterclaim had been made in a separate action, would have been appropriate in the initial writ in that separate action and must include—

    (a)   answers to the condescendence of the initial writ;

    (b)   a statement of facts in numbered paragraphs setting out the facts on which the counterclaim is founded, incorporating by reference, if necessary, any matter contained in the defences;

    (c)   appropriate pleas-in-law.

D1.295.6

Implied admissions

33.36G.[3] Every statement of fact made by a party must be answered by every other party, and if such a statement by one party within the knowledge of another party is not denied by that other party, that other party will be deemed to have admitted that statement of fact.

D1.295.7

Sisting

33.36H.—[4](1) The sheriff may, on cause shown, of the sheriff's own motion or on the motion of any party, sist the action until a specified date.

(2) Where the action is sisted, the sheriff clerk must—

    (a)   prepare an interlocutor specifying the reason for the sist and the date specified in paragraph (1) for the sheriff to sign;

    (b)   fix a date for a review of sist hearing for not later than 30 days following the expiration of the sist;

    (c)   intimate the date of the review of sist hearing to each party.

D1.295.8

---

[1] Inserted by the Act of Sederunt (Ordinary Cause Rules 1993 Amendment) (Case Management of Defended Family and Civil Partnership Actions) 2022 (SSI 2022/289) r.2(17) (effective 25 September 2023 subject to transitional provision specified in SSI 2022/289 r.3).

[2] Inserted by the Act of Sederunt (Ordinary Cause Rules 1993 Amendment) (Case Management of Defended Family and Civil Partnership Actions) 2022 (SSI 2022/289) r.2(17) (effective 25 September 2023 subject to transitional provision specified in SSI 2022/289 r.3).

[3] Inserted by the Act of Sederunt (Ordinary Cause Rules 1993 Amendment) (Case Management of Defended Family and Civil Partnership Actions) 2022 (SSI 2022/289) r.2(17) (effective 25 September 2023 subject to transitional provision specified in SSI 2022/289 r.3).

[4] Inserted by the Act of Sederunt (Ordinary Cause Rules 1993 Amendment) (Case Management of Defended Family and Civil Partnership Actions) 2022 (SSI 2022/289) r.2(17) (effective 25 September 2023 subject to transitional provision specified in SSI 2022/289 r.3).

(3)   Where a cause has been sisted, any period for adjustment before the sist is to be reckoned as a part of the period for adjustment.

Open record

D1.295.9 **33.36I.**[1]   The sheriff may, at any time before the closing of the record in a family action, of the sheriff's own motion or on the motion of a party, order any party to lodge a copy of the pleadings in the form of an open record containing any adjustments and amendments made as at the date of the order.

Initial Case Management Hearing

D1.295.10 **33.36J.**—[2](1)   At the Initial Case Management Hearing the sheriff must seek to secure the expeditious progress of the cause by ascertaining from parties the matters in dispute and information about any other matter referred to in paragraph (3).

(2)   It is the duty of the parties to provide the sheriff with sufficient information to enable the sheriff to conduct the hearing as provided for in this rule.

(3)   At the Initial Case Management Hearing each party must address the court on—

    (a)   any matters that are capable of agreement;

    (b)   the matters that are in dispute between the parties;

    (c)   any matters of potential complexity or difficulty;

    (d)   any valuations that are likely to be required;

    (e)   any expert or skilled witness evidence that is likely to be required and the scope for joint instruction;

    (f)   whether additional steps require to be taken to give a child an opportunity to express the child's view;

    (g)   whether steps require to be taken to investigate any facts or circumstances relating to a child;

    (h)   the suitability of the action for referral to mediation;

    (i)   whether special measures will be required for the purposes of taking the evidence of any vulnerable witnesses;

    (j)   the scope for use of affidavits and other documents in place of oral evidence;

    (k)   the extent to which the parties have complied with any orders made by the court;

    (l)   the number and availability of witnesses;

    (m)   the content, volume and form of productions;

    (n)   the requirement for access to IT equipment to view productions;

    (o)   whether sanction is sought for the employment of counsel;

    (p)   the progress of any legal aid application.

(4)   At the Initial Case Management Hearing, the sheriff must fix a date and time for a Full Case Management Hearing which date must be on the first suitable court day occurring—

    (a)   in cases involving a crave for a section 11 order only, not sooner than 16 weeks and not later than 24 weeks after the last date for the lodging of defences;

---

[1] Inserted by the Act of Sederunt (Ordinary Cause Rules 1993 Amendment) (Case Management of Defended Family and Civil Partnership Actions) 2022 (SSI 2022/289) r.2(17) (effective 25 September 2023 subject to transitional provision specified in SSI 2022/289 r.3).

[2] Inserted by the Act of Sederunt (Ordinary Cause Rules 1993 Amendment) (Case Management of Defended Family and Civil Partnership Actions) 2022 (SSI 2022/289) r.2(17) (effective 25 September 2023 subject to transitional provision specified in SSI 2022/289 r.3).

(b) in all other cases, not sooner than 20 weeks and not later than 24 weeks after the last date for the lodging of defences.

(5) Following the Initial Case Management Hearing the sheriff clerk must intimate forthwith to the parties in Form G6B—

(a) the last date for lodging a note of the basis for any preliminary pleas;
(b) the last date for adjustment;
(c) the last date for lodging a copy of the record;
(d) the date of the Full Case Management Hearing.

Alteration of date and time for Full Case Management Hearing

33.36K.—[1](1) Subject to paragraph (2), at any time before the date and time **D1.295.11** fixed under rule 33.36J (Initial Case Management Hearing) or under this rule, the sheriff may, of the sheriff's own motion, on the motion of any party or on the joint motion of the parties—

(a) discharge the Full Case Management Hearing; and
(b) fix a new date and time for a Full Case Management Hearing.

(2) The date and time of any hearing to be fixed under paragraph (1)(b) may be earlier or later than the date and time fixed for the discharged hearing, but must be fixed for a date within the relevant period specified in rule 33.36J(4) or the first available court date thereafter.

(3) Where the sheriff is considering making an order under paragraph (1) of the sheriff's own motion and in the absence of the parties, the sheriff clerk must—

(a) fix a date, time and place for the parties to be heard;
(b) prepare an interlocutor recording those dates, times and places for the sheriff to sign.

(4) The sheriff may discharge a hearing fixed under paragraph (3) on the joint motion of the parties.

(5) On the discharge of a hearing under paragraph (1)(a) or paragraph (4), the sheriff clerk must forthwith intimate to all parties—

(a) that the hearing has been discharged under paragraph (1)(a) or, as the case may be, paragraph (4);
(b) the last date for lodging a note of basis of preliminary pleas, if appropriate;
(c) the last date for adjustment, if appropriate;
(d) the last date for lodging a copy of the record, if appropriate;
(e) the new date and time fixed for the hearing under paragraph (1)(b).

(6) Any reference in these Rules to the Full Case Management Hearing includes a reference to a Full Case Management Hearing for which a date and time has been fixed under this rule.

Pre-Hearing Meeting

33.36L.—[2](1) In advance of the Full Case Management Hearing the parties **D1.295.12** must hold a pre-hearing meeting, at which parties must—

(a) discuss settlement of the action;
(b) agree, so far as is possible, the matters which are not in dispute between them;

---

[1] Inserted by the Act of Sederunt (Ordinary Cause Rules 1993 Amendment) (Case Management of Defended Family and Civil Partnership Actions) 2022 (SSI 2022/289) r.2(17) (effective 25 September 2023 subject to transitional provision specified in SSI 2022/289 r.3).

[2] Inserted by the Act of Sederunt (Ordinary Cause Rules 1993 Amendment) (Case Management of Defended Family and Civil Partnership Actions) 2022 (SSI 2022/289) r.2(17) (effective 25 September 2023 subject to transitional provision specified in SSI 2022/289 r.3).

(c) discuss the information referred to in rule 33.36P(3) (Full Case Management Hearing).

(2) Not later than 2 days before the Full Case Management Hearing the pursuer must lodge with the court a joint minute of the pre-hearing meeting, signed by both parties, addressing the points in rule 33.36P(3) or explain to the sheriff why such a minute has not been lodged.

(3) If a party is not present during the pre-hearing meeting, that party's representative must be able to contact the party during the meeting and be in full possession of all relevant facts.

Adjustment of pleadings

D1.295.13 **33.36M.**—[1](1) Parties may adjust their pleadings until 14 days before the date of the Full Case Management Hearing or any continuation of it.

(2) Any adjustments must be exchanged between parties and not lodged in process.

(3) Parties are responsible for maintaining a record of adjustments made during the period for adjustment.

(4) No adjustments are permitted after the period mentioned in paragraph (1) except with leave of the sheriff.

Record for Full Case Management Hearing

D1.295.14 **33.36N.**—[2](1) The pursuer must, at the end of the period for adjustment referred to in rule 33.36M(1) (adjustment of pleadings) and before the Full Case Management Hearing, make a copy of the pleadings and any adjustments and amendments in the form of a record.

(2) Not later than 2 days before the Full Case Management Hearing, the pursuer must lodge a certified copy of the record in process.

(3) Where the Full Case Management Hearing is continued under rule 33.36P(7), and further adjustment or amendment is made to the record, a copy of the record as adjusted or amended, certified by the pursuer, must be lodged in process not later than 2 days before the Full Case Management Hearing so continued.

Exchange of lists of witnesses

D1.295.15 **33.36O.**—[3](1) Not later than 7 days before the Full Case Management Hearing, each party must—

(a) intimate to every other party a list of witnesses, including any skilled witnesses, on whose evidence they intend to rely at proof;

(b) lodge a copy of that list in process.

(2) A party who seeks to rely on the evidence of a person not on the list intimated under paragraph (1)(a) must, if any other party objects to such evidence being admitted, seek leave of the sheriff to admit that evidence; and such leave may be granted on such conditions, if any, as the sheriff thinks fit.

(3) The list of witnesses intimated under paragraph (1)(a) must include—

(a) the name, occupation (where known) and address of each witness;

---

[1] Inserted by the Act of Sederunt (Ordinary Cause Rules 1993 Amendment) (Case Management of Defended Family and Civil Partnership Actions) 2022 (SSI 2022/289) r.2(17) (effective 25 September 2023 subject to transitional provision specified in SSI 2022/289 r.3).

[2] Inserted by the Act of Sederunt (Ordinary Cause Rules 1993 Amendment) (Case Management of Defended Family and Civil Partnership Actions) 2022 (SSI 2022/289) r.2(17) (effective 25 September 2023 subject to transitional provision specified in SSI 2022/289 r.3).

[3] Inserted by the Act of Sederunt (Ordinary Cause Rules 1993 Amendment) (Case Management of Defended Family and Civil Partnership Actions) 2022 (SSI 2022/289) r.2(17) (effective 25 September 2023 subject to transitional provision specified in SSI 2022/289 r.3).

(b) a summary of up to 50 words on the matters to which each witness is expected to speak;

(c) details of whether the witness is considered to be a vulnerable witness within the meaning of section 11(1) of the Act of 200426 and whether any child witness notice under section 12(2) of that Act or vulnerable witness application under section 12(6) of that Act has been lodged in respect of that witness.

Full Case Management Hearing

33.36P.—[1](1) At the Full Case Management Hearing the sheriff must seek to **D1.295.16** secure the expeditious progress of the cause by ascertaining from the parties the matters in dispute and information about any other matter referred to in paragraph (3).

(2) It is the duty of the parties to provide the sheriff with sufficient information to enable the sheriff to conduct the hearing as provided for in this rule.

(3) At the Full Case Management Hearing each party must address the court on—

(a) any matters that are capable of agreement;

(b) the matters that are in dispute between the parties;

(c) any matters of potential complexity or difficulty;

(d) any valuations that are likely to be required;

(e) any expert or skilled witness evidence that is likely to be required and the scope for joint instruction;

(f) whether additional steps require to be taken to give a child an opportunity to express the child's views;

(g) whether steps require to be taken to investigate any facts or circumstances relating to a child;

(h) the suitability of the action for referral to mediation;

(i) whether special measures will be required for the purposes of taking the evidence of any vulnerable witnesses;

(j) the scope for use of affidavits and other documents in place of oral evidence;

(k) the extent to which the parties have complied with any orders made by the court;

(l) the number and availability of witnesses;

(m) the content, volume and form of productions;

(n) the requirement for access to IT equipment to view productions;

(o) whether sanction is sought for the employment of counsel;

(p) the progress of any legal aid application.

(4) After having heard parties at the Full Case Management Hearing the sheriff must close the record, fix a pre-proof hearing in accordance with Chapter 28A (pre-proof hearing)27 and—

(a) appoint the action to a proof and make such orders as to the extent of proof, the lodging of a joint minute of admissions or agreement, or such matters as the sheriff thinks fit;

(b) consider any note lodged under rule 22.1 (note of basis of preliminary plea)28, appoint the cause to a proof before answer and make such orders

---

[1] Inserted by the Act of Sederunt (Ordinary Cause Rules 1993 Amendment) (Case Management of Defended Family and Civil Partnership Actions) 2022 (SSI 2022/289) r.2(17) (effective 25 September 2023 subject to transitional provision specified in SSI 2022/289 r.3).

as to the extent of the proof, the lodging of a joint minute of admissions or agreement, or such other matters as the sheriff thinks fit; or

    (c)   consider any note lodged under rule 22.1, appoint the cause to a debate if satisfied that there is a preliminary matter of law which if established following debate would lead to decree in favour of any party, or to limitation of proof to any substantial degree.

   (5) The diet fixed under paragraph (4)—

    (a)   is to be assigned for the appropriate number of days for resolution of the issues with reference to the information provided under paragraph (3) and subject to paragraph (6);

    (b)   may only be extended or varied on exceptional cause shown and subject to such orders (including awards of expenses) as the sheriff considers appropriate.

   (6) The sheriff may make such orders as thought fit to ensure compliance with this rule and the expeditious resolution of the issues in dispute, including—

    (a)   restricting the issues for proof;

    (b)   the scope for instruction of a joint expert or a meeting between skilled persons;

    (c)   excluding specified documents, reports or witnesses from proof;

    (d)   fixing other hearings;

    (e)   awarding expenses.

   (7) The sheriff may, on cause shown, of the sheriff's own motion or on the motion of any party, allow a continuation of the Full Case Management Hearing on one occasion only for a period not exceeding 28 days or to the first suitable court day thereafter.

   (8) On closing the record—

    (a)   where there are no adjustments made since the lodging of the record under rule 33.36N (record for Full Case Management Hearing), that record becomes the closed record;

    (b)   where there are such adjustments, the sheriff may order that a closed record including such adjustments be lodged within 7 days after the date of the interlocutor closing the record.

Judicial continuity

D1.295.17   **33.36Q.**—[1] Where possible, the same sheriff is to preside at—

    (a)   the Initial Case Management Hearing;

    (b)   the Full Case Management Hearing;

    (c)   the pre-proof hearing;

    (d)   where fixed, any—

       (i)   Child Welfare Hearing;

      (ii)   proof;

     (iii)   proof before answer;

     (iv)   debate.

Decree by default

D1.296   **33.37.**—(1)[2] In a family action in which the defender has lodged a notice of intention to defend, where a party fails—

---

[1] Inserted by the Act of Sederunt (Ordinary Cause Rules 1993 Amendment) (Case Management of Defended Family and Civil Partnership Actions) 2022 (SSI 2022/289) r.2(17) (effective 25 September 2023 subject to transitional provision specified in SSI 2022/289 r.3).

[2] As amended by Act of Sederunt (Sheriff Court Ordinary Cause Rules Amendment) (Miscellaneous) 1996 (SI 1996/2445) (effective 1 November 1996) (clerical error).

(a)   to lodge, or intimate the lodging of, any production or part of process,

(b)   to implement an order of the sheriff within a specified period,

(c)   to appear or be represented at any diet, or

(d)[1]   otherwise to comply with any requirement imposed upon that party by these Rules;

that party shall be in default.

(2)[2]   Where a party is in default under paragraph (1), the sheriff may—

(a)[3]   where the family action is one mentioned in rule 33.1(a) to (h) or (n) to (p) allow the cause to proceed as undefended under Part II of this Chapter; or

(b)[4]   where the family action is one mentioned in rule 33.1(1)(i) to (m) or (q), grant decree as craved; or

(c)   grant decree of absolvitor; or

(d)   dismiss the family action or any claim made or order sought; or

(da)   make such other order as he thinks fit to secure the expeditious progress of the cause; and

(e)   award expenses.

(3)   Where no party appears at a diet in a family action, the sheriff may dismiss that action.

(4)   In a family action, the sheriff may, on cause shown, prorogate the time for lodging any production or part of process, or for intimating or implementing any order.

Part IV – Applications and Orders Relating to Children in Certain Actions

Application and interpretation of this Part

33.38.[5, 6]   This Part applies to an action of divorce, separation or declarator of nullity of marriage.   **D1.297**

Applications in actions to which this Part applies

33.39.—[7](1)   An application for an order mentioned in paragraph (2) shall be made—   **D1.298**

(a)   by a crave in the initial writ or defences, as the case may be, in an action to which this Part applies; or

(b)   where the application is made by a person other than the pursuer or defender, by minute in that action.

(2)   The orders referred to in paragraph (1) are—

(a)   an order for a section 11 order; and

(b)   an order for aliment for a child.

---

[1] As inserted by the Act of Sederunt (Ordinary Cause and Summary Application Rules) Amendment (Miscellaneous) 2006 (SSI 2006/410) (effective 18 August 2006).

[2] As amended by Act of Sederunt (Ordinary Cause Rules) Amendment (Family Law (Scotland) Act 2006 etc.) 2006 (SSI 2006/207) para.2 (effective 4 May 2006) and the Act of Sederunt (Ordinary Cause and Summary Application Rules) Amendment (Miscellaneous) 2006 (SSI 2006/410) (effective 18 August 2006).

[3] As amended by the Act of Sederunt (Sheriff Court Rules) (Miscellaneous Amendments) (No.2) 2010 (SSI 2010/416) r.8 (effective 1 January 2011).

[4] As amended by the Act of Sederunt (Sheriff Court Rules) (Miscellaneous Amendments) 2012 (SSI 2012/188) para.5 (effective 1 August 2012).

[5] As amended by Act of Sederunt (Family Proceedings in the Sheriff Court) 1996 (SI 1996/2167) (effective 1 November 1996).

[6] As amended by Act of Sederunt (Ordinary Cause Rules) Amendment (Family Law (Scotland) Act 2006 etc.) 2006, para.2 (SSI 2006/207) (effective 4 May 2006).

[7] As amended by Act of Sederunt (Family Proceedings in the Sheriff Court) 1996 (SI 1996/2167) (effective 1 November 1996).

33.40. *[Repealed by the Act of Sederunt (Family Proceedings in the Sheriff Court) 1996 (SI 1996/2167) (effective 1 November 1996).]*

33.41. *[Repealed by the Act of Sederunt (Family Proceedings in the Sheriff Court) 1996 (SI 1996/2167) (effective 1 November 1996).]*

33.42. *[Repealed by the Act of Sederunt (Family Proceedings in the Sheriff Court) 1996 (SI 1996/2167) (effective 1 November 1996).]*

Applications in depending actions by motion

D1.299   **33.43.**[1] An application by a party in an action depending before the court to which this Part applies for, or for variation of, an order for—

    (a)   interim aliment for a child under the age of 18, or

    (b)   a residence order or a contact order,

shall be made by motion.

Applications after decree relating to a section 11 order

D1.300   **33.44.**—[2](1)[3] An application after final decree for, or for the variation or recall of, a section 11 order or in relation to the enforcement of such an order shall be made by minute in the process of the action to which the application relates.

(2)   Where a minute has been lodged under paragraph (1), any party may apply by motion for any interim order which may be made pending the determination of the application.

Warrants for intimation to child and permission to seek views

D1.300.1   **33.44A.**—[4](1)   Subject to paragraph (2), when lodging a minute under rule 14.3 (lodging of minutes)(c) which includes a crave after final decree for, or the variation or recall of, a section 11 order in respect of a child who is not a party to the action, the minuter must—

    (a)   include in the minute a crave for a warrant for intimation and the seeking of the child's views in Form F9;

    (b)   when lodging the minute, submit a draft Form F9, showing the details that the minuter proposes to include when the form is sent to the child.

(2)   Where the minuter considers that it would be inappropriate to send Form F9 to the child (for example, where the child is under 5 years of age), the minuter must include in the minute—

    (a)   a crave to dispense with intimation and the seeking of the child's views in Form F9;

    (b)   averments setting out the reasons why it is inappropriate to send Form F9 to the child.

(3)   The sheriff must be satisfied that the draft Form F9 submitted under paragraph (1)(b) has been drafted appropriately.

(4)   The sheriff may dispense with intimation and the seeking of views in Form F9 or make any other order that the sheriff considers appropriate.

(5)   An order granting warrant for intimation and the seeking of the child's views in Form F9 under this rule must—

    (a)   state that the Form F9 must be sent in accordance with rule 33.44A(6);

---

[1] As amended by Act of Sederunt (Family Proceedings in the Sheriff Court) 1996 (SI 1996/2167) (effective 1 November 1996).

[2] As amended by Act of Sederunt (Family Proceedings in the Sheriff Court) 1996 (SI 1996/2167) (effective 1 November 1996).

[3] As amended by SSI 2000/239 (effective October 2, 2000).

[4] As inserted by the Act of Sederunt (Rules of the Court of Session 1994 and Ordinary Cause Rules 1993 Amendment) (Views of the Child) 2019 (SSI 2019/123) r.3 (effective 24 June 2019).

    (b)   be signed by the sheriff.

  (6) The Form F9 must be sent in accordance with—

    (a)   rule 33.44B (views of the child – unopposed minutes relating to a section 11 order), where the minute is unopposed;

    (b)   rule 33.44C (views of the child – craves relating to a section 11 order sought by minuter only), where the minute is opposed and a section 11 order is sought by the minuter only; or

    (c)   rule 33.44D (views of the child – craves relating to a section 11 order sought by both minuter and respondent), where a section 11 order is sought by both the minuter and the respondent.

Views of the child—unopposed minutes relating to a section 11 order

33.44B.—[1](1) This rule applies to minutes which include a crave after final decree for, or the variation or recall of, a section 11 order in respect of which no notice of opposition or answers are lodged and warrant has been granted for intimation and the seeking of the child's views in Form F9.   **D1.300.2**

  (2) The minuter must—

    (a)   send the child the Form F9 that was submitted and approved under rule 33.44A (warrants for intimation to child and permission to seek views);

    (b)   on the same day, lodge a certificate of intimation in Form F9A;

    (c)   not send the child a copy of the minute.

  (3) Except on cause shown, the sheriff must not determine the minute in the period of 28 days following the date on which the Form F9 was sent to the child.

Views of the child—craves relating to a section 11 order sought by minuter only

33.44C.—[2](1) This rule applies where a notice of opposition or answers have been lodged in respect of a minute after final decree and a crave for, or the variation or recall of, a section 11 order is sought by the minuter only and warrant has been granted for intimation and the seeking of the child's views in Form F9.   **D1.300.3**

  (2) The minuter must—

    (a)   no later than 14 days after the notice of opposition or answers are lodged, send the child the Form F9 that was submitted and approved under rule 33.44A (warrants for intimation to child and permission to seek views);

    (b)   on the same day, lodge a certificate of intimation in Form F9A;

    (c)   not send the child a copy of the minute, the notice of opposition or answers.

Views of the child—craves relating to a section 11 order sought by both minuter and respondent

33.44D.—[3](1) This rule applies where a notice of opposition or answers have been lodged in respect of a minute after final decree and craves for, or the variation or recall of, a section 11 order are sought by both the minuter and the respondent and warrant has been granted for intimation and the seeking of the child's views in Form F9.   **D1.300.4**

  (2) The minuter must—

    (a)   no later than 14 days after the notice of opposition or answers are lodged,

---

[1] As inserted by the Act of Sederunt (Rules of the Court of Session 1994 and Ordinary Cause Rules 1993 Amendment) (Views of the Child) 2019 (SSI 2019/123) r.3 (effective 24 June 2019).

[2] As inserted by the Act of Sederunt (Rules of the Court of Session 1994 and Ordinary Cause Rules 1993 Amendment) (Views of the Child) 2019 (SSI 2019/123) r.3 (effective 24 June 2019).

[3] As inserted by the Act of Sederunt (Rules of the Court of Session 1994 and Ordinary Cause Rules 1993 Amendment) (Views of the Child) 2019 (SSI 2019/123) r.3 (effective 24 June 2019).

send the child the Form F9 that was submitted and approved under rule 33.44A (warrants for intimation to child and permission to seek views), amended so as also to narrate the section 11 order sought by the respondent;

(b) on the same day—

    (i) lodge a certificate of intimation in Form F9A;

    (ii) send the respondent a copy of the Form F9 that was sent to the child;

(c) not send the child a copy of the minute, the notice of opposition or answers.

[THE NEXT PARAGRAPH IS D1.301]

Applications after decree relating to aliment

D1.301   **33.45.**—(1) An application after final decree for, or for the variation or recall of, an order for aliment for a child shall be made by minute in the process of the action to which the application relates.

(2) Where a minute has been lodged under paragraph (1), any party may lodge a motion for any interim order which may be made pending the determination of the application.

Applications after decree by persons over 18 years for aliment

D1.302   **33.46.**—(1) A person—

(a) to whom an obligation of aliment is owed under section 1 of the Act of 1985,

(b) in whose favour an order for aliment while under the age of 18 years was made in an action to which this Part applies, and

(c) who seeks, after attaining that age, an order for aliment against the person in that action against whom the order for aliment in his favour was made,

shall apply by minute in the process of that action.

(2) An application for interim aliment pending the determination of an application under paragraph (1) shall be made by motion.

(3) Where a decree has been pronounced in an application under paragraph (1) or (2), any application for variation or recall of any such decree shall be made by minute in the process of the action to which the application relates.

Part V – Orders Relating to Financial Provision

Application and interpretation of this Part

D1.303   **33.47.**—(1) This Part applies to an action of divorce.

(2) In this Part, "incidental order" has the meaning assigned in section 14(2) of the Act of 1985.

Applications in actions to which this Part applies

D1.304   **33.48.**—(1) An application for an order mentioned in paragraph (2) shall be made—

(a) by a crave in the initial writ or defences, as the case may be, in an action to which this Part applies; or

(b) where the application is made by a person other than the pursuer or defender, by minute in that action.

(2) The orders referred to in paragraph (1) are—

(a) an order for financial provision within the meaning of section 8(3) of the Act of 1985;

(b)   an order under section 16(1)(b) or (3) of the Act of 1985 (setting aside or varying agreement as to financial provision);

(c)   an order under section 18 of the Act of 1985 (which relates to avoidance transactions); and

(d)   an order under section 13 of the Act of 1981 (transfer or vesting of tenancy).

Applications in depending actions relating to incidental orders

33.49.—(1) In an action depending before the sheriff to which this Part applies—   **D1.305**

(a)   the pursuer, notwithstanding rules 33.34(2) (application by defender for order for financial provision) and 33.48(1)(a) (application for order for financial provision in initial writ or defences), may apply by motion for an incidental order; and

(b)   the sheriff shall not be bound to determine such a motion if he considers that the application should properly be by a crave in the initial writ or defences, as the case may be.

(2) In an action depending before the sheriff to which this Part applies, an application under section 14(4) of the Act of 1985 for the variation or recall of an incidental order shall be made by minute in the process of the action to which the application relates.

Applications relating to interim aliment

33.50. An application for, or for the variation or recall of, an order for interim   **D1.306**
aliment for the pursuer or the defender shall be made by motion.

Applications relating to orders for financial provision

33.51.—(1) An application—   **D1.307**

(a)   after final decree under any of the following provisions of the Act of 1985—

(i)   section 8(1) for periodical allowance,

(ii)   section 12(1)(b) (payment of capital sum or transfer of property),

(iii) section 12(4) (variation of date or method of payment of capital sum or date of transfer of property), or

(iv)   section 13(4) (variation, recall, backdating or conversion of periodical allowance), or

(v)[1] section 14(1) (incidental orders), or

(b)   after the grant or refusal of an application under—

(i)   section 8(1) or 14(3) for an incidental order, or

(ii)   section 14(4) (variation or recall of incidental order),

shall be made by minute in the process of the action to which the application relates.

(2) Where a minute is lodged under paragraph (1), any party may lodge a motion for any interim order which may be made pending the determination of the application.

(3)[2] An application under—

(a)   paragraph (5) of section 12A of the Act of 1985 (recall or variation of order in respect of a pension lump sum),

---

[1] As inserted by the Act of Sederunt (Sheriff Court Rules) (Miscellaneous Amendments) (No.3) 2011 (SSI 2011/386) para.2 (effective 28 November 28, 2011).

[2] As inserted by SI 1996/2445 (effective 1 November 1996) and as amended by the Act of Sederunt (Ordinary Cause, Summary Application, Summary Cause and Small Claim Rules) Amendment (Miscellaneous) 2003 (SSI 2003/26), para.2(9) (effective 24 January 2003).

(b)   paragraph (7) of that section (variation of order in respect of pension lump sum to substitute trustees or managers),

(ba)[1] section 12B(4) of the Act of 1985 (recall or variation of a capital sum order), or

(c)   section 28(10) or 48(9) of the Welfare Reform and Pensions Act 1999,

shall be made by minute in the process of the action to which the application relates.

Pension Protection Fund notification

D1.308   **33.51A.**—[2](1) In this rule—

"assessment period" shall be construed in accordance with section 132 of the Pensions Act 2004;

"pension arrangement" shall be construed in accordance with the definition in section 27 of the Act of 1985; and

"valuation summary" shall be construed in accordance with the definition in Schedule 2 to the Pension Protection Fund (Provision of Information) Regulations 2005.

(2) This rule applies where a party at any stage in the proceedings applies for an order under section 8 or section 16 of the Act of 1985.

(3) Where the party against whom an order referred to in paragraph (2) is sought has received notification in compliance with the Pension Protection Fund (Provision of Information) Regulations 2005 or does so after the order is sought—

(a)   that there is an assessment period in relation to his pension arrangement; or

(b)   that the Board of the Pension Protection Fund has assumed responsibility for all or part of his pension arrangement,

he shall comply with paragraph (4).

(4) The party shall—

(a)   lodge the notification; and

(b)   obtain and lodge as soon as reasonably practicable thereafter–

(i)   a valuation summary; and

(ii)   a forecast of his compensation entitlement.

(5) Subject to paragraph (6), the notification referred to in paragraph (4)(a) requires to be lodged—

(a)   where the notification is received before the order is sought, within 7 days of the order being sought;

(b)   where the notification is received after the order is sought, within 7 days of receiving the notification.

(6) Where an order is sought against the defender before the defences are lodged, and the notification is received before that step occurs, the notification shall be lodged with the defences.

(7) At the same time as lodging documents under paragraph (4), copies shall be sent to the other party to the proceedings.

Applications after decree relating to agreements and avoidance transactions

D1.309   **33.52.** An application for an order—

(a)   under section 16(1)(a) or (3) of the Act of 1985 (setting aside or varying agreement as to financial provision), or

---

[1] As inserted by the Act of Sederunt (Sheriff Court Rules) (Miscellaneous Amendments) 2011 (SSI 2011/193) r.15 (effective 6 April 2011).

[2] As inserted by the Act of Sederunt (Sheriff Court Rules) (Miscellaneous Amendments) 2008 (SSI 2008/223) para.3(2) (effective 1 July 2008).

(b) under section 18 of the Act of 1985 (which relates to avoidance transactions),

made after final decree shall be made by minute in the process of the action to which the application relates.

Part VI – Applications Relating to Avoidance Transactions

Form of applications

33.53.—(1) An application for an order under section 18 of the Act of 1985 (which relates to avoidance transactions) by a party to an action shall be made by including in the initial writ, defences or minute, as the case may be, appropriate craves, averments and pleas-in-law.   **D1.310**

(2) An application for an order under section 18 of the Act of 1985 after final decree in an action, shall be made by minute in the process of the action to which the application relates.

Part VII – Financial Provision after Overseas Divorce or Annulment

Interpretation of this Part

33.54. In this Part—   **D1.311**

"the Act of 1984" means the Matrimonial and Family Proceedings Act 1984;
"order for financial provision" has the meaning assigned in section 30(1) of the Act of 1984;
"overseas country" has the meaning assigned in section 30(1) of the Act of 1984.

Applications for financial provision after overseas divorce or annulment

33.55.—[1](1) An application under section 28 of the Act of 1984 for an order for financial provision after a divorce or annulment in an overseas country shall be made by initial writ.   **D1.312**

(2) An application for an order in an action to which paragraph (1) applies made before final decree under—

(a) section 13 of the Act of 1981 (transfer of tenancy of matrimonial home),
(b) section 29(4) of the Act of 1984 for interim periodical allowance, or
(c) section 14(4) of the Act of 1985 (variation or recall of incidental order),

shall be made by motion.

(3) An application for an order in an action to which paragraph (1) applies made after final decree under—

(a) section 12(4) of the Act of 1985 (variation of date or method of payment of capital sum or date of transfer of property),
(b) section 13(4) of the Act of 1985 (variation, recall, backdating or conversion of periodical allowance), or
(c) section 14(4) of the Act of 1985 (variation or recall of incidental order),

shall be made by minute in the process of the action to which the application relates.

(4)[2] An application under—

(a) paragraph (5) of section 12A of the Act of 1985 (recall or variation of order in respect of a pension lump sum), or
(b) paragraph (7) of that section (variation of order in respect of pension lump sum to substitute trustees or managers),

shall be made by minute in the process of the action to which the application relates.

---

[1] Heading amended by SI 1996/2445 (effective 1 November 1996).
[2] Inserted by SI 1996/2445 (effective November 1, 1996).

(5) Where a minute has been lodged under paragraph (3), any party may apply by motion for an interim order pending the determination of the application.

Part VIII – Actions of Aliment

Interpretation of this Part

D1.313   **33.56.** In this Part, "action of aliment" means a claim for aliment under section 2(1) of the Act of 1985.

Undefended actions of aliment

D1.314   **33.57.**—(1) Where a motion for decree in absence under Chapter 7 (undefended causes) is lodged in an action of aliment, the pursuer shall, on lodging the motion, lodge all documentary evidence of the means of the parties available to him in support of the amount of aliment sought.

(2) Where the sheriff requires the appearance of parties, the sheriff clerk shall fix a hearing.

Applications relating to aliment

D1.315   **33.58.**—(1) An application for, or for variation of, an order for interim aliment in a depending action of aliment shall be made by motion.

(2) An application after final decree for the variation or recall of an order for aliment in an action of aliment shall be made by minute in the process of the action to which the application relates.

(3) A person—

     (a) to whom an obligation of aliment is owed under section 1 of the Act of 1985,

     (b) in whose favour an order for aliment while under the age of 18 years was made in an action of aliment, or

     (c) who seeks, after attaining that age, an order for aliment against the person in that action against whom the order for aliment in his favour was made,

shall apply by minute in the process of that action.

(4) An application for interim aliment pending the determination of an application under paragraph (2) or (3) shall be made by motion.

(5) Where a decree has been pronounced in an application under paragraph (2) or (3), any application for variation or recall of any such decree shall be made by minute in the process of the action to which the application relates.

Applications relating to agreements on aliment

D1.316   **33.59.**—[1](1) Subject to paragraph (2) and rule 33A.53, an application under section 7(2) of the Act of 1985 (variation or termination of agreement on aliment) shall be made by summary application.

(2) In a family action in which a crave for aliment may be made, an application under section 7(2) of the Act of 1985 shall be made by a crave in the initial writ or in defences, as the case may be.

Part IX – Applications for Orders under Section II of the Children (Scotland) Act 1995

Application of this Part

D1.317   **33.60.**[23] This Part applies to an application for a section 11 order in a family action other than in an action of divorce, separation or declarator of nullity of marriage.

---

[1] As amended by Act of Sederunt (Ordinary Cause Rules) Amendment (Family Law (Scotland) Act 2006 etc.) 2006, para.2 (SSI 2006/207) (effective 4 May 2006).
[2] Substituted by SI 1996/2167 (effective 1 November 1996).

Form of applications

33.61.[1] Subject to any other provision in this Chapter, an application for a sec- **D1.318**
tion 11 order shall be made—

(a) by an action for a section 11 order;

(b) by a crave in the initial writ or defences, as the case may be, in any other family action to which this Part applies; or

(c) where the application is made by a person other than a party to an action mentioned in paragraph (a) or (b), by minute in that action.

Defenders in action for a section 11 order

33.62.[2] In an action for a section 11 order, the pursuer shall call as a defender— **D1.319**

(a) the parents or other parent of the child in respect of whom the order is sought;

(b) any guardian of the child;

(c) any person who has treated the child as a child of his family;

(d) any person who in fact exercises care or control in respect of the child; and

(e) *[Repealed by SSI 2000/239 (effective 2 October 2000).]*

Applications relating to interim orders in depending actions

33.63.[3, 4] An application, in an action depending before the sheriff to which this **D1.320**
Part applies, for, or for the variation or recall of, an interim residence order or an interim contact order shall be made—

(a) by a party to the action, by motion; or

(b) by a person who is not a party to the action, by minute.

33.64. *[Repealed by SI 1996/2167 (effective 1 November 1996).]*

Applications after decree

33.65.—[5](1) An application after final decree for variation or recall of a section **D1.321**
11 order shall be made by minute in the process of the action to which the application relates.

(2) Where a minute has been lodged under paragraph (1), any party may apply by motion for an interim order pending the determination of the application.

(3)[6] Rules 33.44A (warrants for intimation to child and permission to seek views) to 33.44D (views of the child – craves relating to a section 11 order sought by both minuter and respondent) apply (with the necessary modifications) to the seeking of the child's views in relation to a minute lodged in accordance with this rule.

---

[3] As amended by Act of Sederunt (Ordinary Cause Rules) Amendment (Family Law (Scotland) Act 2006 etc.) 2006, para.2 (SSI 2006/207) (effective 4 May 2006).

[1] As amended by Act of Sederunt (Family Proceedings in the Sheriff Court) 1996 (SI 1996/2167) (effective 1 November 1996).

[2] Substituted by SI 1996/2167 (effective 1 November 1996). Clerical error corrected by SI 1996/2445 (effective 1 November 1996).

[3] As amended by Act of Sederunt (Family Proceedings in the Sheriff Court) 1996 (SI 1996/2167) (effective 1 November 1996).

[4] As amended by Act of Sederunt (Ordinary Cause Rules) Amendment (Family Law (Scotland) Act 2006 etc.) 2006, para.2 (SSI 2006/207) (effective 4 May 2006).

[5] As amended by Act of Sederunt (Family Proceedings in the Sheriff Court) 1996 (SI 1996/2167) (effective 1 November 1996).

[6] As inserted by the Act of Sederunt (Rules of the Court of Session 1994 and Ordinary Cause Rules 1993 Amendment) (Views of the Child) 2019 (SSI 2019/123) r.3 (effective 24 June 2019).

Application for leave

D1.322   **33.65A.**—[1](1)   Where leave of the court is required under section 11(3)(aa) of the Act of 1995 for the making of an application for a contact order under that section, the applicant must lodge along with the initial writ a written application in the form of a letter addressed to the sheriff clerk stating—

     (a)   the grounds on which leave is sought;

     (b)   whether or not the applicant has applied for legal aid.

     (2)   Where the applicant has applied for legal aid he must also lodge along with the initial writ written confirmation from the Scottish Legal Aid Board that it has determined, under regulation 7(2)(b) of the Civil Legal Aid (Scotland) Regulations 2002, that notification of the application should be dispensed with or postponed pending the making by the sheriff of an order for intimation under paragraph (4)(b).

     (3)   Subject to paragraph (4)(b), an application under paragraph (1) shall not be served or intimated to any party.

     (4)   The sheriff shall consider an application under paragraph (1) without hearing the applicant and may—

     (a)   refuse the application and pronounce an interlocutor accordingly; or

     (b)   if he is minded to grant the application order the applicant—

         (i)   to intimate the application to such persons as the sheriff considers appropriate; and

         (ii)   to lodge a certificate of intimation in, as near as may be, Form G8.

     (5)   If any person who receives intimation of an application under paragraph (4)(b) wishes to be heard he shall notify the sheriff clerk in writing within 14 days of receipt of intimation of the application.

     (6)   On receipt of any notification under paragraph (5) the sheriff clerk shall fix a hearing and intimate the date of the hearing to the parties.

     (7)   Where an application under paragraph (1) is granted, a copy of the sheriffs interlocutor must be served on the defender along with the warrant of citation.

Part X – Actions under the Matrimonial Homes (Family Protection) (Scotland) Act 1981

Interpretation of this Part

D1.323   **33.66.**   Unless the context otherwise requires, words and expressions used in this Part which are also used in the Act of 1981 have the same meaning as in that Act.

Form of applications

D1.324   **33.67.**—(1)   Subject to any other provision in this Chapter, an application for an order under the Act of 1981 shall be made—

     (a)   by an action for such an order;

     (b)   by a crave in the initial writ or in defences, as the case may be, in any other family action; or

     (c)   where the application is made by a person other than a party to any action mentioned in paragraph (a) or (b), by minute in that action.

     (2)[2]   An application under section 7(1) (dispensing with consent of non-entitled spouse to a dealing) or section 11 (application in relation to attachment) shall, unless made in a depending family action, be made by summary application.

---

[1] As inserted by the Act of Sederunt (Sheriff Court Rules Amendment) (Adoption and Children (Scotland) Act 2007) 2009 (SSI 2009/284) (effective 28 September 2009).
[2] As amended by the Act of Sederunt (Debt Arrangement and Attachment (Scotland) Act 2002) 2002 (SSI 2002/560), art.4, Sch.3 (effective 30 December 2002).

Defenders

33.68. The applicant for an order under the Act of 1981 shall call as a defender—   **D1.325**

  (a) where he is seeking an order as a spouse, the other spouse;

  (b)[1] where he is a third party making an application under section 7(1) dispensing with consent of non-entitled spouse to a dealing), or 8(1) (payment from non-entitled spouse in respect of loan), of the Act of 1981, both spouses;

  (c) where the application is made under section 18 of the Act of 1981 (occupancy rights of cohabiting couples), or is one to which that section applies, the other partner; and

  (d)[2] where the application is made under section 18A of the Act of 1981 (application for domestic interdict), the other partner.

Applications by motion

33.69.—(1) An application under any of the following provisions of the Act of   **D1.326**
1981 shall be made by motion in the process of the depending action to which the application relates:—

  (a) section 3(4) (interim order for regulation of rights of occupancy, etc.);

  (b) section 4(6) (interim order suspending occupancy rights);

  (c) section 7(1) (dispensing with consent of non-entitled spouse to a dealing);

  (d) [Omitted by Act of Sederunt (Ordinary Cause Rules) Amendment (Family Law (Scotland) Act 2006 etc.) 2006, para.2 (SSI 2006/207) (effective 4 May 2006).]; and

  (e) the proviso to section 18(1) (extension of period of occupancy rights).

  (2) Intimation of a motion under paragraph (1) shall be given—

  (a) to the other spouse or partner, as the case may be;

  (b) where the motion is under paragraph (1)(a), (b) or (e) and the entitled spouse or partner is a tenant or occupies the matrimonial home by the permission of a third party, to the landlord or third party, as the case may be; and

  (c) to any other person to whom intimation of the application was or is to be made by virtue of rule 33.7(1)(k) (warrant for intimation to certain persons in actions for orders under the Act of 1981) or 33.15 (order for intimation by sheriff).

Applications by minute

33.70.—(1) An application for an order under—   **D1.327**

  (a) section 5 of the Act of 1981 (variation and recall of orders regulating occupancy rights and of exclusion order), or

  (b) [Omitted by Act of Sederunt (Ordinary Cause Rules) Amendment (Family Law (Scotland) Act 2006 etc.) 2006, para.2 (SSI 2006/207) (effective 4 May 2006).]

shall be made by minute.

  (2) A minute under paragraph (1) shall be intimated—

  (a) to the other spouse or partner, as the case may be;

---

[1] As amended by Act of Sederunt (Ordinary Cause Rules) Amendment (Family Law (Scotland) Act 2006 etc.) 2006, para.2 (SSI 2006/207) (effective 4 May 2006).

[2] Inserted by Act of Sederunt (Ordinary Cause Rules) Amendment (Family Law (Scotland) Act 2006 etc.) 2006, para.2 (SSI 2006/207) (effective 4 May 2006).

(b) where the entitled spouse or partner is a tenant or occupies the matrimonial home by the permission of a third party, to the landlord or third party, as the case may be; and

(c) to any other person to whom intimation of the application was or is to be made by virtue of rule 33.7(1)(k) (warrant for intimation to certain persons in actions for orders under the Act of 1981) or 33.15 (order for intimation by sheriff).

Sist of actions to enforce occupancy rights

D1.328

33.71. Unless the sheriff otherwise directs, the sist of an action by virtue of section 7(4) of the Act of 1981 (where action raised by non-entitled spouse to enforce occupancy rights) shall apply only to such part of the action as relates to the enforcement of occupancy rights by a non-entitled spouse.

Certificates of delivery of documents to chief constable

33.72. [Omitted by Act of Sederunt (Ordinary Cause Rules) Amendment (Family Law (Scotland) Act 2006 etc.) 2006, para.2 (SSI 2006/207) (effective 4 May 2006).]

Part XI – Simplified Divorce Applications

Application and interpretation of this Part

D1.329

33.73.—(1)[1] This Part applies to an application for divorce by a party to a marriage made in the manner prescribed in rule 33.74 (form of applications) if, but only if—

(a) that party relies on the facts set out in section 1(2)(d) (no cohabitation for one year with consent of defender to decree), or section 1(2)(e) (no cohabitation for two years), or section 1(1)(b) (issue of interim gender recognition certificate) of the Act of 1976;

(b) in an application under section 1(2)(d) of the Act of 1976, the other party consents to decree of divorce being granted;

(c) no other proceedings are pending in any court which could have the effect of bringing the marriage to an end;

(d) there are no children of the marriage under the age of 16 years;

(e) neither party to the marriage applies for an order for financial provision on divorce;

(f) neither party to the marriage suffers from mental disorder; and

(g)[2] neither party to the marriage applies for postponement of decree under section 3A of the Act of 1976 (postponement of decree where impediment to religious marriage exists).

(2) If an application ceases to be one to which this Part applies at any time before final decree, it shall be deemed to be abandoned and shall be dismissed.

(3) In this Part "simplified divorce application" means an application mentioned in paragraph (1).

---

[1] As amended by Act of Sederunt (Ordinary Cause Rules) Amendment (Family Law (Scotland) Act 2006 etc.) 2006, para.2 (SSI 2006/207) (effective 4 May 2006).

[2] Inserted by Act of Sederunt (Ordinary Cause Rules) Amendment (Family Law (Scotland) Act 2006 etc.) 2006, para.2 (SSI 2006/207) (effective 4 May 2006) and substituted by the Act of Sederunt (Ordinary Cause, Summary Application, Summary Cause and Small Claim Rules) Amendment (Miscellaneous) 2007 (SSI 2007/6), para.2(15) (effective 26 February 2007).

Form of applications

33.74.—¹(1)² A simplified divorce application in which the facts set out in sec-   **D1.330**
tion 1(2)(d) of the Act of 1976 (no cohabitation for one year with consent of defender
to decree) are relied on shall be made in Form F31 and shall only be of effect if—

   (a)   it is signed by the applicant; and

   (b)   the form of consent in Part 2 of Form F31 is signed by the party to the
marriage giving consent.

   (2)   A simplified divorce application in which the facts set out in section 1(2)(e)
of the Act of 1976 (no cohabitation for two years) are relied on shall be made in
Form F33 and shall only be of effect if it is signed by the applicant.

   (3)³ A simplified divorce application in which the facts set out in section 1(1)(b)
of the Act of 1976 (grounds of divorce: interim gender recognition certificate) are
relied on shall be made in Form F33A and shall only be of effect if signed by the
applicant.

Lodging of applications

33.75.⁴ The applicant shall send a simplified divorce application to the sheriff   **D1.331**
clerk with—

   (a)   an extract or certified copy of the marriage certificate;

   (b)   the appropriate fee; and

   (c)⁵   in an application under section 1(1)(b) of the Act of 1976 (grounds of
divorce: interim gender recognition certificate), the interim gender
recognition certificate or a certified copy within the meaning of rule
33.9A(3).

Citation and intimation

33.76.—(1) This rule is subject to rule 33.77 (citation where address not known).   **D1.332**

   (2)   It shall be the duty of the sheriff clerk to cite any person or intimate any
document in connection with a simplified divorce application.

   (3)   The form of citation—

   (a)⁶   in an application relying on the facts in section 1(2)(d) of the Act of 1976
shall be in Form F34;

   (b)   in an application relying on the facts in section 1(2)(e) of the Act of 1976
shall be in Form F35; and

   (c)⁷   in an application relying on the facts in section 1(1)(b) of the Act of 1976
shall be in Form F35A.

   (4)⁸ The citation or intimation required by paragraph (2) shall be made—

---

¹ —As amended by Act of Sederunt (Ordinary Cause Rules) Amendment (Family Law (Scotland) Act
2006 etc.) 2006, para.2 (SSI 2006/207) (effective 4 May 2006).

² As amended by Act of Sederunt (Sheriff Court Ordinary Cause Rules Amendment) (Miscellaneous)
1996 (SI 1996/2445) (effective 1 November 1996) (clerical error).

³ Inserted by Act of Sederunt (Ordinary Cause Rules) Amendment (Family Law (Scotland) Act 2006
etc.) 2006, para.2 (SSI 2006/207) (effective 4 May 2006).

⁴ As amended by Act of Sederunt (Ordinary Cause Rules) Amendment (Family Law (Scotland) Act
2006 etc.) 2006, para.2 (SSI 2006/207) (effective 4 May 2006).

⁵ Inserted by Act of Sederunt (Ordinary Cause Rules) Amendment (Family Law (Scotland) Act 2006
etc.) 2006, para.2 (SSI 2006/207) (effective 4 May 2006).

⁶ As amended by Act of Sederunt (Ordinary Cause Rules) Amendment (Family Law (Scotland) Act
2006 etc.) 2006, para.2 (SSI 2006/207) (effective 4 May 2006).

⁷ Inserted by Act of Sederunt (Ordinary Cause Rules) Amendment (Family Law (Scotland) Act 2006
etc.) 2006, para.2 (SSI 2006/207) (effective 4 May 2006).

⁸ Substituted by SSI 2000/239 (effective 2 October 2000).

(a) by the sheriff clerk by registered post or the first class recorded delivery service in accordance with rule 5.3 (postal service or intimation);

(b)[1] on payment of an additional fee, by a sheriff officer in accordance with rule 5.4(1) to (4) (service within Scotland by sheriff officer); or

(c) where necessary, by the sheriff clerk in accordance with rule 5.5 (service on persons furth of Scotland).

(5)[2] Where citation or intimation is made in accordance with paragraph (4)(c), the translation into an official language of the country in which service is to be executed required by rule 5.5(6) shall be provided by the party lodging the simplified divorce application.

Citation where address not known

D1.333

33.77.—(1)[3] In a simplified divorce application in which the facts in section 1(2)(e) of the Act of 1976 (no cohabitation for two years) or section 1(1)(b) of the Act of 1976 (grounds of divorce: issue of interim gender recognition certificate) are relied on and the address of the other party to the marriage is not known and cannot reasonably be ascertained—

(a) citation shall be executed by displaying a copy of the application and a notice in Form F36 on the walls of court on a period of notice of 21 days; and

(b) intimation shall be made to—

(i) every child of the marriage between the parties who has reached the age of 16 years, and

(ii) one of the next of kin of the other party to the marriage who has reached that age, unless the address of such person is not known and cannot reasonably be ascertained.

(2) Intimation to a person referred to in paragraph (1)(b) shall be given by intimating a copy of the application and a notice of intimation in Form F37.

Opposition to applications

D1.334

33.78.—(1) Any person on whom service or intimation of a simplified divorce application has been made may give notice by letter sent to the sheriff clerk that he challenges the jurisdiction of the court or opposes the grant of decree of divorce and giving the reasons for his opposition to the application.

(2) Where opposition to a simplified divorce application is made under paragraph (1), the sheriff shall dismiss the application unless he is satisfied that the reasons given for the opposition are frivolous.

(3) The sheriff clerk shall intimate the decision under paragraph (2) to the applicant and the respondent.

(4) The sending of a letter under paragraph (1) shall not imply acceptance of the jurisdiction of the court.

Evidence

D1.335

33.79. Parole evidence shall not be given in a simplified divorce application.

Decree

D1.336

33.80.—(1) The sheriff may grant decree in terms of the simplified divorce application on the expiry of the period of notice if such application has been properly

---

[1] As substituted by the Act of Sederunt (Sheriff Court Rules) (Miscellaneous Amendments) 2010 (SSI 2010/279) r.2 (effective 29 July 2010).

[2] Inserted by SSI 2000/239 (effective 2 October 2000).

[3] As amended by Act of Sederunt (Ordinary Cause Rules) Amendment (Family Law (Scotland) Act 2006 etc.) 2006, para.2 (SSI 2006/207) (effective 4 May 2006).

served provided that, when the application has been served in a country to which the Hague Convention on the Service Abroad of Judicial and Extra-Judicial Documents in Civil and Commercial Matters dated November 15, 1965 applies, decree shall not be granted until it is established to the satisfaction of the sheriff that the requirements of Article 15 of that Convention have been complied with.

(2)   The sheriff clerk shall, not sooner than 14 days after the granting of decree in terms of paragraph (1), issue to each party to the marriage an extract of the decree of divorce in Form F38.

Appeals
33.81.—[1](1)   Any appeal against an interlocutor granting decree of divorce under rule 33.80 (decree) may be made, within 14 days after the date of decree, by sending a letter to the court giving reasons for the appeal.

D1.337

(2)   Within 4 days after receiving an appeal, the sheriff clerk must transmit to the Clerk of the Sheriff Appeal Court—

    (a)   the appeal;

    (b)   all documents and productions in the simplified divorce application.

(3)   On receipt of the appeal, the Clerk of the Sheriff Appeal Court is to fix a hearing and intimate the date, time and place of that hearing to the parties.

Applications after decree
33.82.   Any application to the court after decree of divorce has been granted in a simplified divorce application which could have been made if it had been made in an action of divorce shall be made by minute.

D1.338

Part XII – Variation of Court of Session Decrees

Application and interpretation of this Part
33.83.—(1)   This Part applies to an application to the sheriff for variation or recall of any order to which section 8 of the Act of 1966 (variation of certain Court of Session orders) applies.

D1.339

(2)   In this Part, the "Act of 1966" means the Law Reform (Miscellaneous Provisions) (Scotland) Act 1966.

Form of application and intimation to Court of Session
33.84.—(1)   An application to which this Part applies shall be made by initial writ.

D1.340

(2)   In such an application there shall be lodged with the initial writ a copy of the interlocutor, certified by a clerk of the Court of Session, which it is sought to vary.

(3)   Before lodging the initial writ, a copy of the initial writ certified by the pursuer or his solicitor shall be lodged, or sent by first class recorded delivery post to the Deputy Principal Clerk of Session to be lodged in the process of the cause in the Court of Session in which the original order was made.

(4)   The pursuer or his solicitor shall attach a certificate to the initial writ stating that paragraph (3) has been complied with.

(5)[2]   The sheriff may, on cause shown, prorogate the time for lodging the certified copy of the interlocutor required under paragraph (2).

---

[1] As amended by the Act of Sederunt (Rules of the Court of Session, Sheriff Appeal Court Rules and Sheriff Court Rules Amendment) (Sheriff Appeal Court) 2015 (SSI 2015/419) r.5 (effective 1 January 2016).

[2] As amended by Act of Sederunt (Sheriff Court Ordinary Cause Rules Amendment) (Miscellaneous) 1996 (SI 1996/2445) (effective 1 November 1996) (clerical error).

Defended actions

D1.341   **33.85.**—(1) Where a notice of intention to defend has been lodged and no request is made under rule 33.87 (remit of application to Court of Session), the pursuer shall within 14 days after the date of the lodging of a notice of intention to defend or within such other period as the sheriff may order, lodge in process the following documents (or copies) from the process in the cause in the Court of Session in which the original order was made:—

(a)   the pleadings;

(b)   the interlocutor sheets;

(c)   any opinion of the court; and

(d)   any productions on which he seeks to found.

(2)   The sheriff may, on the joint motion of parties made at any time after the lodging of the documents mentioned in paragraph (1)—

(a)   dispense with proof;

(b)   whether defences have been lodged or not, hear the parties; and

(c)   thereafter, grant decree or otherwise dispose of the cause as he thinks fit.

Transmission of process to Court of Session

D1.342   **33.86.**—(1)[1] Where decree has been granted or the cause otherwise disposed of—

(a)   and the period for making an appeal has elapsed without an appeal being made, or

(b)   after the determination of the cause on any appeal,

the sheriff clerk shall transmit to the Court of Session the sheriff court process and the documents from the process of the cause in the Court of Session which have been lodged in the sheriff court process.

(2)   A sheriff court process transmitted under paragraph (1) shall form part of the process of the cause in the Court of Session in which the original order was made.

Remit of application to Court of Session

D1.343   **33.87.**—(1) A request for a remit to the Court of Session under section 8(3) of the Act of 1966 shall be made by motion.

(2)   The sheriff shall, in respect of any such motion, order that the cause be remitted to the Court of Session; and, within 4 days after the date of such order, the sheriff clerk shall transmit the whole sheriff court process to the Court of Session.

(3)   A cause remitted to the Court of Session under paragraph (2) shall form part of the process of the cause in the Court of Session in which the original order was made.

Part XIII – Child Support Act 1991

Interpretation of this Part

D1.344   **33.88.**[2] In this Part—

"the Act of 1991" means the Child Support Act 1991;

"child" has the meaning assigned in section 55 of the Act of 1991;

---

[1] As amended by the Act of Sederunt (Rules of the Court of Session, Sheriff Appeal Court Rules and Sheriff Court Rules Amendment) (Sheriff Appeal Court) 2015 (SSI 2015/419) r.5 (effective 1 January 2016).

[2] As amended by SI 1996/2445 (effective 1 November 1996) and the Act of Sederunt (Ordinary Cause, Summary Application, Summary Cause and Small Claim Rules) Amendment (Miscellaneous) 2003 (SSI 2003/26), para.2(10) (effective 24 January 2003).

"maintenance calculation" has the meaning assigned in section 54 of the Act of 1991.

Restriction of expenses

33.89. Where the Secretary of State is named as a defender in an action for declarator of non-parentage or illegitimacy, and the Secretary of State does not defend the action, no expenses shall be awarded against the Secretary of State.

D1.345

Effect of maintenance calculations

33.90.—(1)[1] The sheriff clerk shall, on receiving notification that a maintenance calculation has been made, cancelled or has ceased to have effect so as to affect an order of a kind prescribed for the purposes of section 10 of the Act of 1991, endorse on the interlocutor sheet relating to that order a certificate, in Form F39 or F40, as the case may be.

D1.346

Effect of maintenance calculations on extracts relating to aliment

33.91.—(1)[2] Where an order relating to aliment is affected by a maintenance calculation, any extract of that order issued by the sheriff clerk shall be endorsed with the following certificate:—

D1.347

> "A maintenance calculation having been made under the Child Support Act 1991 on (*insert date*), this order, in so far as it relates to the making or securing of periodical payments to or for the benefit of (*insert name(s) of child/children*), ceases to have effect from (*insert date 2 days after the date on which the maintenance calculation was made*)."

(2) Where an order relating to aliment has ceased to have effect on the making of a maintenance calculation, and that maintenance calculation is later cancelled or ceases to have effect, any extract of that order issued by the sheriff clerk shall be endorsed also with the following certificate:—

> "The jurisdiction of the child support officer under the Child Support Act 1991 having terminated on (*insert date*), this order, in so far as it relates to (*insert name(s) of child/children*), again shall have effect as from (*insert date of termination of child support officer's jurisdiction*).".

---

[1] As amended by the Act of Sederunt (Ordinary Cause, Summary Application, Summary Cause and Small Claim Rules) Amendment (Miscellaneous) 2003 (SSI 2003/26), para.2(11) (effective 24 January 2003).

[2] As amended by the Act of Sederunt (Ordinary Cause, Summary Application, Summary Cause and Small Claim Rules) Amendment (Miscellaneous) 2003 (SSI 2003/26), para.2(12) (effective 24 January 2003).

Applications to recall or vary an interdict

D1.348   **33.91A.**[1]   An application under section 32L(11)(b) of the Act of 1991 (orders preventing avoidance) for the variation or recall of an order for interdict is to be made by minute in the process of the action to which the application relates.

Part XIV – Referrals to Principal Reporter

33.92.–33.94.   *[Repealed by the Act of Sederunt (Children's Hearings (Scotland) Act 2011) (Miscellaneous Amendments) 2013 (SI 2013/172) para.5 (effective 24 June 2013).]*

Part XV – Management of Money Payable to Children

D1.349   **33.95.**   Where the sheriff has made an order under section 13 of the Act of 1995 (awards of damages to children), an application by a person for an order by virtue of section 11(1)(d) of that Act (administration of child's property) may be made in the process of the cause in which the order under section 13 of that Act was made.

Part XVI[2] – Action of Declarator of Recognition or Non-recognition of a Foreign Decree

Action of declarator in relation to certain foreign decrees

D1.350   **33.96.**—(1)[3]   This rule applies to an action for declarator of recognition, or non-recognition, of a decree of divorce, nullity or separation granted outwith the United Kingdom, the Channel Islands or the Isle of Man.

(2)   In an action to which this rule applies, the pursuer shall state in the condescendence of the initial writ—

(a)   the court, tribunal or other authority which granted the decree;

(b)   the date of the decree of divorce, annulment or separation to which the action relates;

(c)   the date and place of the marriage to which the decree of divorce, nullity or separation relates;

(d)   the basis on which the court has jurisdiction to entertain the action;

(e)   whether to the pursuer's knowledge any other proceedings whether in Scotland or in any other country are continuing in respect of the marriage to which the action relates or are capable of affecting its validity or subsistence; and

(f)   where such proceedings are continuing—

(i)   the court, tribunal or authority before which the proceedings have been commenced;

(ii)   the date of commencement;

(iii)   the names of the parties; and

(iv)   the date, or expected date of any proof (or its equivalent), in the proceedings.

(3)   Where—

(a)   such proceedings are continuing;

(b)   the action before the sheriff is defended; and

(c)   either—

---

[1] As inserted by the Act of Sederunt (Ordinary Cause Rules) Amendment (Child Maintenance and Other Payments Act 2008) 2010 (SSI 2010/120) r.2 (effective 6 April 2010).

[2] As inserted by the Act of Sederunt (Sheriff Court Rules) (Miscellaneous Amendments) (No.2) 2010 (SSI 2010/416) r.8 (effective 1 January 2011).

[3] Substituted by the Act of Sederunt (Rules of the Court of Session 1994 and Sheriff Court Rules Amendment) (Miscellaneous) 2021 (SSI 2021/75) r.3(3) (effective 1 March 2021).

     (i)   the initial writ does not contain the statement referred to in paragraph (2)(e), or

    (ii) the particulars mentioned in paragraph (2)(f) as set out in the initial writ are incomplete or incorrect,

any defences or minute, as the case may be, lodged by any person to the action shall include that statement and, where appropriate, the further or correct particulars mentioned in paragraph (2)(f).

(4)   Unless the sheriff otherwise directs, a declarator of recognition, or non-recognition, of a decree under this rule shall not be granted without there being produced with the initial writ—

   (a)   the decree in question or a certified copy of the decree;

   (b)   the marriage extract or equivalent document to which the action relates.

(5)   Where a document produced under paragraph (4)(a) or (b) is not in English it shall, unless the sheriff otherwise directs, be accompanied by a translation certified by a notary public or authenticated by affidavit.

(6)   For the purposes of this rule, proceedings are continuing at any time after they have commenced and before they are finally disposed of.

<h3 style="text-align:center">Chapter 33A[1]</h3>

<h3 style="text-align:center">Civil Partnership Actions</h3>

<h3 style="text-align:center">Part I – General Provisions</h3>

Interpretation of this Chapter

33A.1.—(1)   In this Chapter, "civil partnership action" means—   **D1.351**

   (a)   an action of dissolution of civil partnership;

   (b)   an action of separation of civil partners;

   (c)   an action or application for an order under Chapter 3 or Chapter 4 of Part 3 of the Act of 2004;

   (d)   an application for a declarator or other order under section 127 of the Act of 2004;

   (e)   an action or application for financial provision after overseas proceedings as provided for in Schedule 11 to the Act of 2004;

   (f)[2]   an action for declarator of nullity of civil partnership.

(2)   In this Chapter, unless the context otherwise requires—

"the Act of 1985" means the Family Law (Scotland) Act 1985;

"the Act of 1995" means the Children (Scotland) Act 1995;

"the Act of 2004" means the Civil Partnership Act 2004;

"civil partnership" has the meaning assigned in section 1(1) of the Act of 2004;

"contact order" has the meaning assigned in section 11(2)(d) of the Act of 1995;

"Gender Recognition Panel" is to be construed in accordance with Schedule 1 to the Gender Recognition Act 2004;

"interim gender recognition certificate" means the certificate issued under section 4 of the Gender Recognition Act 2004;

"incapable" means incapable, by reason of mental disorder, of—

     (a)   acting;

     (b)   making decisions;

---

[1] Inserted by Act of Sederunt (Ordinary Cause Rules) Amendment (Civil Partnership Act 2004) 2005 (SSI 2005/638), para.2 (effective 8 December 2005).

[2] Inserted by Act of Sederunt (Ordinary Cause Rules) Amendment (Family Law (Scotland) Act 2006 etc.) 2006, para.2 (SSI 2006/207) (effective 4 May 2006).

(c) communicating decisions;

(d) understanding decisions; or

(e) retaining the memory of decisions,

but a person is not incapable by reason only of a lack of deficiency in a faculty of communication where that lack or deficiency can be made good by human or mechanical aid (whether of an interpretative nature or otherwise);[1]

"local authority" means a council constituted under section 2 of the Local Government etc. (Scotland) Act 1994;

"mental disorder" has the meaning assigned in section 328 of the Mental Health (Care and Treatment) (Scotland) Act 2003;

"order for financial provision" means, except in Part VII of this Chapter (financial provision after overseas proceedings as provided for in Schedule 11 to the Act of 2004), an order mentioned in section 8(1) of the Act of 1985;

"parental responsibilities" has the meaning assigned in section 1(3) of the Act of 1995;

"parental rights" has the meaning assigned in section 2(4) of the Act of 1995;

"relevant interdict" has the meaning assigned in section 113(2) of the Act of 2004;

"residence order" has the meaning assigned in section 11(2)(c) of the Act of 1995;

"section 11 order" means an order under section 11 of the Act of 1995.

(3) For the purposes of rules 33A.2 (averments in actions of dissolution of civil partnership or separation of civil partners about other proceedings) and 33A.3 (averments where section 11 order sought) and, in relation to proceedings in another jurisdiction, Part XIII of this Chapter (sisting of civil partnership actions in Scotland), proceedings are continuing at any time after they have commenced and before they are finally disposed of.

Averments in certain civil partnership actions about other proceedings[2]

D1.352   **33A.2.**—(1)[3] This rule applies to an action of dissolution or declarator of nullity of civil partnership or separation of civil partners.

(2) In an action to which this rule applies, the pursuer shall state in the condescendence of the initial writ—

(a) whether to his knowledge any proceedings are continuing in Scotland or in any other country in respect of the civil partnership to which the initial writ relates or are capable of affecting its validity or subsistence; and

(b) where such proceedings are continuing—

(i) the court, tribunal or authority before which the proceedings have been commenced;

(ii) the date of commencement;

(iii) the names of the parties;

(iv) the date, or expected date of any proof (or its equivalent) in the proceedings; and

---

[1] As inserted by the Act of Sederunt (Rules of the Court of Session 1994 and Sheriff Court Rules Amendment) (Curators ad litem) (SSI 2017/132) 2017 r.2(4) (effective 1 June 2017 subject to saving specified in SSI 2017/132 r.4).

[2] As amended by Act of Sederunt (Ordinary Cause Rules) Amendment (Family Law (Scotland) Act 2006 etc.) 2006, para.2 (SSI 2006/207) (effective 4 May 2006).

[3] As amended by Act of Sederunt (Ordinary Cause Rules) Amendment (Family Law (Scotland) Act 2006 etc.) 2006, para.2 (SSI 2006/207) (effective 4 May 2006).

(v)   such other facts as may be relevant to the question of whether or not the action before the sheriff should be sisted under Part XIII of this Chapter.

(3)   Where—

(a)   such proceedings are continuing;

(b)   the action before the sheriff is defended; and

(c)   either—

(i)   the initial writ does not contain the statement referred to in paragraph (2)(a); or

(ii)   the particulars mentioned in paragraph (2)(b) as set out in the initial writ are incomplete or incorrect,

any defences or minute, as the case may be, lodged by any person to the action shall include that statement and, where appropriate, the further or correct particulars mentioned in paragraph (2)(b).

Averments where section 11 order sought

33A.3.—(1)   A party to a civil partnership action who makes an application in that action for a section 11 order in respect of a child shall include in his pleadings—   **D1.353**

(a)[1]   where that action is an action of dissolution or declarator of nullity of civil partnership or separation of civil partners, averments giving particulars of any other proceedings known to him, whether in Scotland or elsewhere and whether concluded or not, which relate to the child in respect of whom the section 11 order is sought;

(b)   (b) in any other civil partnership action—

(i)   the averments mentioned in paragraph (a); and

(ii)   averments giving particulars of any proceedings known to him which are continuing, whether in Scotland or elsewhere, and which relate to the civil partnership of either of the parents of that child.

(c)[2]   where the party seeks an order such as is mentioned in any of paragraphs (a) to (e) of subsection (2) of that section, an averment that no permanence order (as defined in section 80(2) of the Adoption and Children (Scotland) Act 2007) is in force in respect of the child.

(2)   Where such other proceedings are continuing or have taken place and the averments of the applicant for such a section 11 order—

(a)   do not contain particulars of the other proceedings, or

(b)   contain particulars which are incomplete or incorrect,

any defences or minute, as the case may be, lodged by any party to the civil partnership action shall include such particulars or such further or correct particulars as are known to him.

(3)   In paragraph 1(b)(ii), "child" includes a child of the family within the meaning assigned in section 101(7) of the Act of 2004.

Averments where identity or address of person not known

33A.4.   In a civil partnership action, where the identity or address of any person referred to in rule 33A.7 as a person in respect of whom a warrant for intimation requires to be applied for is not known and cannot reasonably be ascertained, the   **D1.354**

---

[1] As amended by Act of Sederunt (Ordinary Cause Rules) Amendment (Family Law (Scotland) Act 2006 etc.) 2006, para.2 (SSI 2006/207) (effective 4 May 2006).

[2] As inserted by the Act of Sederunt (Sheriff Court Rules Amendment) (Adoption and Children (Scotland) Act 2007) 2009 (SSI 2009/284) (effective 28 September 2009).

party required to apply for the warrant shall include in his pleadings an averment of that fact and averments setting out what steps have been taken to ascertain the identity or address, as the case may be, of that person.

Averments about maintenance orders

D1.355
    33A.5. In a civil partnership action in which an order for aliment or periodical allowance is sought, or is sought to be varied or recalled, by any party, the pleadings of that party shall contain an averment stating whether and, if so, when and by whom, a maintenance order (within the meaning of section 106 of the Debtors (Scotland) Act 1987) has been granted in favour of or against that party or of any other person in respect of whom the order is sought.

Averments where aliment or financial provision sought

D1.356
    33A.6.—(1) In this rule—

> "the Act of 1991" means the Child Support Act 1991;
> "child" has the meaning assigned in section 55 of the Act of 1991;
> "crave relating to aliment" means—
>> (a) for the purposes of paragraph (2), a crave for decree of aliment in relation to a child or for recall or variation of such a decree; and
>> (b) for the purposes of paragraph (3), a crave for decree of aliment in relation to a child or for recall or variation of such a decree or for the variation or termination of an agreement on aliment in relation to a child;
> "maintenance calculation" has the meaning assigned in section 54 of the Act of 1991.

(2) A civil partnership action containing a crave relating to aliment and to which section 8(6), (7), (8), or (10) of the Act of 1991 (top up maintenance orders) applies shall—

> (a) include averments stating, where appropriate—
>> (i)   that a maintenance calculation under section 11 of that Act (maintenance calculations) is in force;
>> (ii) the date of the maintenance calculation;
>> (iii) the amount and frequency of periodical payments of child support maintenance fixed by the maintenance calculation; and
>> (iv) the grounds on which the sheriff retains jurisdiction under section 8(6), (7), (8) or (10) of that Act; and
> (b) unless the sheriff on cause shown otherwise directs, be accompanied by any document issued by the Secretary of State to the party intimating the making of the maintenance calculation referred to in sub paragraph (a).

(3) A civil partnership action containing a crave relating to aliment, and to which section 8(6), (7), (8) or (10) of the Act of 1991 does not apply, shall include averments stating—

> (a) that the habitual residence of the absent parent, person with care or qualifying child, within the meaning of section 3 of that Act, is furth of the United Kingdom; or
> (b) that the child is not a child within the meaning of section 55 of that Act.

(4) A civil partnership action involving parties in respect of whom a decision has been made in any application, review or appeal under the Act of 1991 relating to any child of those parties, shall—

> (a) include averments stating that such a decision has been made and giving details of that decision; and

(b)   unless the sheriff on cause shown otherwise directs, be accompanied by any document issued by the Secretary of State to the parties intimating that decision.

Warrants and forms for intimation

33A.7.—[1](1)   Subject to paragraph (5) and rule 33A.7A (warrants and forms for intimation to a child and for seeking a child's views), in the initial writ in a civil partnership action, the pursuer shall include a crave for a warrant for intimation—

D1.357

  (a)   in an action where the address of the defender is not known to the pursuer and cannot reasonably be ascertained, to—

    (i)   every person who was a child of the family (within the meaning of section 101(7) of the Act of 2004) and who has reached the age of 16 years, and

    (ii)   one of the next of kin of the defender who has reached that age,

  unless the address of such a person is not known to the pursuer and cannot reasonably be ascertained, and a notice of intimation in Form CP1 shall be attached to the copy of the initial writ intimated to any such person;

  (b)   in an action where the defender is a person who is suffering from a mental disorder, to—

    (i)   those persons mentioned in sub paragraph (a)(i) and (ii), unless the address of such person is not known to the pursuer and cannot reasonably be ascertained; and

    (ii)   any person who holds the office of guardian, or continuing or welfare attorney to the defender under or by virtue of the Adults with Incapacity (Scotland) Act 2000,

  and a notice of intimation in Form CP2 shall be attached to the copy of the initial writ intimated to any such person;

  (c)[2]   in an action of dissolution or declarator of nullity of civil partnership or separation of civil partners where the sheriff may make a section 11 order in respect of a child—

    (i)   who is in the care of a local authority, to that authority and a notice of intimation in Form CP3 shall be attached to the initial writ intimated to that authority;

    (ii)   who, being a child of one party to the civil partnership, has been accepted as a child of the family by the other party to the civil partnership and who is liable to be maintained by a third party, to that third party, and a notice of intimation in Form CP3 shall be attached to the initial writ intimated to that third party; or

    (iii)   in respect of whom a third party in fact exercises care or control, to that third party, and a notice of intimation in Form CP4 shall be attached to the initial writ intimated to that third party;

  (d)   in an action where the pursuer craves a section 11 order, to any parent or guardian of the child who is not a party to the action, and a notice of intimation in Form CP5 shall be attached to the initial writ intimated to any such parent or guardian;

  (e)   *[Repealed by the Act of Sederunt (Sheriff Court Rules) (Miscellaneous Amendments) (No.2) 2010 (SSI 2010/416) r.7 (effective 1 January 2011).]*

---

[1] As amended by the Act of Sederunt (Rules of the Court of Session 1994 and Ordinary Cause Rules 1993 Amendment) (Views of the Child) 2019 (SSI 2019/123) r.3 (effective 24 June 2019).
[2] As amended by Act of Sederunt (Ordinary Cause Rules) Amendment (Family Law (Scotland) Act 2006 etc.) 2006, para.2 (SSI 2006/207) (effective 4 May 2006).

(f) *[Repealed by the Act of Sederunt (Rules of the Court of Session 1994 and Ordinary Cause Rules 1993 Amendment) (Views of the Child) 2019 (SSI 2019/123) r.3 (effective 24 June 2019).]*

(g) in an action where the pursuer makes an application for an order under section 8(aa) of the Act of 1985 (transfer of property) and—

    (i) the consent of a third party to such a transfer is necessary by virtue of an obligation, enactment or rule of law, or

    (ii) the property is subject to a security,

to the third party or creditor, as the case may be, and a notice of intimation in Form CP8 shall be attached to the initial writ intimated to any such person;

(h) in an action where the pursuer makes an application for an order under section 18 of the Act of 1985 (which relates to avoidance transactions), to—

    (i) any third party in whose favour the transfer of, or transaction involving, the property is to be or was made, and

    (ii) any other person having an interest in the transfer of, or transaction involving, the property,

and a notice of intimation in Form CP9 shall be attached to the initial writ intimated to any such person;

(i) in an action where the pursuer makes an application for an order under Chapter 3 of Part 3 of the Act of 2004, where the application is under section 102(e), 102(4)(a), 103(1), 103(2), 104, 107 or 112 of that Act, and the entitled civil partner is a tenant or occupies the family home by permission of a third party, to the landlord or the third party, as the case may be and a notice of intimation in Form CP10 shall be attached to the initial writ intimated to any such person;

(j) in an action where the pursuer makes an application for an order under section 8(ba) of the Act of 1985 (orders under section 12A of the Act of 1985 for pension lump sum), to the person responsible for the pension arrangement, and a notice of intimation in Form CP11 shall be attached to the initial writ intimated to any such person;

(k) in an action where a pursuer makes an application for an order under section 8(baa) of the Act of 1985 (pension sharing orders), to the person responsible for the pension arrangement and a notice of intimation in Form CP12 shall be attached to the initial writ intimated to any such person.

(l)[1] in an action where a pursuer makes an application for an order under section 8(1)(bab) of the Act of 1985 (pension compensation sharing order), to the Board of the Pension Protection Fund, and a notice of intimation in Form CP12A shall be attached to the initial writ intimated to that Board; and

(m)[2] in an action where a pursuer makes an application for an order under section 8(1)(bb) of the Act of 1985 (an order under section 12B(2) of the Act of 1985 for pension compensation), to the Board of the Pension Protection Fund and a notice of intimation in Form CP12B shall be attached to the initial writ intimated to that Board.

---

[1] As inserted by the Act of Sederunt (Sheriff Court Rules) (Miscellaneous Amendments) 2011 (SSI 2011/193) r.15 (effective 6 April 2011).

[2] As inserted by the Act of Sederunt (Sheriff Court Rules) (Miscellaneous Amendments) 2011 (SSI 2011/193) r.15 (effective 6 April 2011).

(2)   Expressions used in paragraph (1)(i) which are also used in Chapter 3 of Part 3 of the Act of 2004 have the same meaning as in that Chapter.

(3)   A notice of intimation under paragraph (1) shall be on a period of notice of 21 days unless the sheriff otherwise orders; but the sheriff shall not order a period of notice of less than 2 days.

(4)   *[Repealed by the Act of Sederunt (Sheriff Court Rules) (Miscellaneous Amendments) (No.2) 2010 (SSI 2010/416) r.7 (effective 1 January 2011).]*

(5)   Where the address of a person mentioned in paragraph (1)(c), (d), (g), (h), (i), (j) or (k) or a child mentioned in rule 33A.7A(1) is not known and cannot reasonably be ascertained, the pursuer shall include a crave in the initial writ to dispense with intimation; and the sheriff may grant that crave or make such other order as he thinks fit.

(6)   Where the identity or address of a person to whom intimation of a civil partnership action is required becomes known during the course of the action, the party who would have been required to insert a warrant for intimation to that person shall lodge a motion for a warrant for intimation to that person or to dispense with such intimation.

(7)   *[Repealed by the Act of Sederunt (Rules of the Court of Session 1994 and Ordinary Cause Rules 1993 Amendment) (Views of the Child) 2019 (SSI 2019/123) r.3 (effective 24 June 2019).]*

Warrants and forms for intimation to a child and for seeking a child's views

33A.7A.—[1](1)   Subject to paragraph (2), in an action which includes a crave for a section 11 order in respect of a child who is not a party to the action, the pursuer must—

D1.357.1

    (a)   include in the initial writ a crave for a warrant for intimation and the seeking of the child's views in Form F9;

    (b)   when presenting the initial writ for warranting, submit a draft Form F9, showing the details that the pursuer proposes to include when the form is sent to the child.

(2)   Where the pursuer considers that it would be inappropriate to send Form F9 to the child (for example, where the child is under 5 years of age), the pursuer must include in the initial writ—

    (a)   a crave to dispense with intimation and the seeking of the child's views in Form F9;

    (b)   averments setting out the reasons why it is inappropriate to send Form F9 to the child.

(3)   The sheriff must be satisfied that the draft Form F9 submitted under paragraph (1)(b) has been drafted appropriately.

(4)   The sheriff may dispense with intimation and the seeking of views in Form F9 or make any other order that the sheriff considers appropriate.

(5)   An order granting warrant for intimation and the seeking of the child's views in Form F9 under this rule must—

    (a)   state that the Form F9 must be sent in accordance with rule 33A.7A(6);

    (b)   be signed by the sheriff.

(6)   The Form F9 must be sent in accordance with—

    (a)   rule 33A.19 (views of the child – undefended actions), where the action is undefended;

---

[1] As inserted by the Act of Sederunt (Rules of the Court of Session 1994 and Ordinary Cause Rules 1993 Amendment) (Views of the Child) 2019 (SSI 2019/123) r.3 (effective 24 June 2019).

(b) rule 33A.19A (views of the child – section 11 order sought by pursuer only), where the action is defended and a section 11 order is sought by the pursuer only;

(c) rule 33A.19B (views of the child – section 11 order sought by defender only), where a section 11 order is sought by the defender only; or

(d) rule 33A.19C (views of the child – section 11 orders sought by both pursuer and defender), where a section 11 order is sought by both parties.

Intimation where alleged association

D1.358   **33A.8.**—(1) In a civil partnership action where the pursuer founds upon an alleged association between the defender and another named person, the pursuer shall, immediately after the expiry of the period of notice, lodge a motion for an order for intimation to that person or to dispense with such intimation.

(2) In determining a motion under paragraph (1), the sheriff may—

(a) make such order for intimation as he thinks fit; or

(b) dispense with intimation; and

(c) where he dispenses with intimation, order that the name of that person be deleted from the condescendence of the initial writ.

(3) Where intimation is ordered under paragraph (2), a copy of the initial writ and an intimation in Form CP13 shall be intimated to the named person.

(4) In paragraph (1), "association" means sodomy, incest, or any homosexual or heterosexual relationship.

Productions in action of dissolution of civil partnership or where a section 11 order or order for financial provision may be made[1]

D1.359   **33A.9.**—(1) This rule applies unless the sheriff directs otherwise.

(2)[2] In an action of dissolution or declarator of nullity of civil partnership, a warrant for citation shall not be granted without there being produced with the initial writ—

(a) an extract of the relevant entry in the civil partnership register or an equivalent document; and

(b) where the ground of action is that an interim gender recognition certificate has, after the date of registration of the civil partnership, been issued to either of the civil partners—

(i) where the pursuer is the subject of the interim gender recognition certificate, the interim gender recognition certificate or, failing that, a certified copy of the interim gender recognition certificate; or

(ii) where the defender is the subject of the interim gender recognition certificate, a certified copy of the interim gender recognition certificate.

(3) In a civil partnership action which includes a crave for a section 11 order, a warrant for citation shall not be granted without there being produced with the initial writ an extract of the relevant entry in the register of births or an equivalent document.

---

[1] As amended by the Act of Sederunt (Sheriff Court Rules) (Miscellaneous Amendments) 2012 (SSI 2012/188) para.4 (effective 1 August 2012).
[2] As amended by Act of Sederunt (Ordinary Cause Rules) Amendment (Family Law (Scotland) Act 2006 etc.) 2006, para.2 (SSI 2006/207) (effective 4 May 2006).

(4) For the purposes of this rule, a certified copy of an interim gender recognition certificate shall be a copy of that certificate sealed with the seal of the Gender Recognition Panels and certified to be a true copy by an officer authorised by the President of Gender Recognition Panels.

(5)[1] In a civil partnership action which includes a crave for an order for financial provision, the pursuer must lodge a completed Form CP13A signed by the pursuer with the initial writ or minute of amendment as the case may be.

Warrant of citation
33A.10. The warrant of citation in a civil partnership action shall be in Form CP14.

  D1.360

Form of citation and certificate
33A.11.—(1) Subject to rule 5.6 (service where address of person is not known), citation of a defender shall be in Form CP15, which shall be attached to a copy of the initial writ and warrant of citation and shall have appended to it a notice of intention to defend in Form CP16.

  D1.361

(2) The certificate of citation shall be in Form CP17 which shall be attached to the initial writ.

Intimation to local authority
33A.12.—(1) In any civil partnership action where the pursuer craves a residence order in respect of a child, the sheriff may, if the sheriff thinks fit, order intimation to the local authority in which area the pursuer resides; and such intimation shall be in Form CP6.

  D1.362

(2) Where an order for intimation is made under paragraph (1), intimation to that local authority shall be given within 7 days after the date on which an order for intimation has been made.

Service in cases of mental disorder of defender
33A.13.—(1) In a civil partnership action where the defender suffers or appears to suffer from mental disorder and is resident in a hospital or other similar institution, citation shall be executed by registered post or the first class recorded delivery service addressed to the medical officer in charge of that hospital or institution; and there shall be included with the copy of the initial writ—

  D1.363

 (a) a citation in Form CP15;
 (b) any notice required by rule 33A.14(1);
 (c) a request in Form CP18;
 (d) a form of certificate in Form CP19 requesting the medical officer to—
   (i) deliver and explain the initial writ, citation and any notice or form of notice of consent required under rule 33A.14(1) personally to the defender; or
   (ii) certify that such delivery or explanation would be dangerous to the health or mental condition of the defender; and
 (e) a stamped envelope addressed for return of that certificate to the pursuer or his solicitor, if he has one.

(2) The medical officer referred to in paragraph (1) shall send the certificate in Form CP19 duly completed to the pursuer or his solicitor, as the case may be.

(3) The certificate mentioned in paragraph (2) shall be attached to the certificate of citation.

---

[1] As inserted by the Act of Sederunt (Sheriff Court Rules) (Miscellaneous Amendments) 2012 (SSI 2012/188) para.4 (effective 1 August 2012).

(4) Where such a certificate bears that the initial writ has not been delivered to the defender, the sheriff may, at any time before decree—

    (a) order such further medical inquiry, and

    (b) make such order for further service or intimation,

as he thinks fit.

Notices in certain actions of dissolution of civil partnership or separation of civil partners

D1.364

33A.14.—(1) In the following actions of dissolution of civil partnership or separation of civil partners there shall be attached to the copy of the initial writ served on the defender—

    (a)[1] in an action relying on section 117(3)(c) of the Act of 2004 (no cohabitation for one year with consent of defender to decree)—

        (i) which is an action of dissolution of civil partnership, a notice in Form CP20 and a notice of consent in Form CP21;

        (ii) which is an action of separation of civil partners, a notice in Form CP22 and a form of notice of consent in Form CP23;

    (b)[2] in an action relying on section 117(3)(d) of the Act of 2004 (no cohabitation for two years)—

        (i) which is an action of dissolution of civil partnership, a notice in Form CP24;

        (ii) which is an action of separation of civil partners, a notice in Form CP25.

    (c)[3] in an action relying on section 117(2)(b) of the Act of 2004 (grounds of dissolution: interim gender recognition certificate), a notice in Form CP25A.

(2) The certificate of citation of an initial writ in an action mentioned in paragraph (1) shall state which notice or form mentioned in paragraph (1) has been attached to the initial writ.

Orders for intimation

D1.365

33A.15.—[4](1) Except in relation to intimation to a child in Form F9, in any civil partnership action, the sheriff may, at any time—

    (a) order intimation to be made on such person as he thinks fit;

    (b) postpone intimation, where he considers that such postponement is appropriate and, in that case, the sheriff shall make such order in respect of postponement of intimation as he thinks fit; or

    (c) dispense with intimation, where he considers that such dispensation is appropriate.

(3) Where a party makes a crave or averment in a civil partnership action which, had it been made in an initial writ, would have required a warrant for intimation under rule 33.7, that party shall include a crave in his writ for a warrant for intima-

---

[1] As amended by Act of Sederunt (Ordinary Cause Rules) Amendment (Family Law (Scotland) Act 2006 etc.) 2006, para.2 (SSI 2006/207) (effective 4 May 2006).

[2] As amended by Act of Sederunt (Ordinary Cause Rules) Amendment (Family Law (Scotland) Act 2006 etc.) 2006, para.2 (SSI 2006/207) (effective 4 May 2006).

[3] Inserted by Act of Sederunt (Ordinary Cause Rules) Amendment (Family Law (Scotland) Act 2006 etc.) 2006, para.2 (SSI 2006/207) (effective 4 May 2006).

[4] As amended by the Act of Sederunt (Rules of the Court of Session 1994 and Ordinary Cause Rules 1993 Amendment) (Views of the Child) 2019 (SSI 2019/123) r.3 (effective 24 June 2019).

tion or to dispense with such intimation; and rule 33A.7 shall, with the necessary modifications, apply to a crave for a warrant under this paragraph as it applies to a crave for a warrant under that rule.

Appointment of curators ad litem to defenders

33A.16.—[1](1)[2, 3] This rule applies to a civil partnership action where it appears **D1.366** to the court that the defender has a mental disorder.

(2) In an action to which this rule applies, the sheriff shall, after the expiry of the period for lodging a notice of intention to defend—

  (a) appoint a curator ad litem to the defender;
  (b) make an order requiring the curator *ad litem* to lodge in process a report, based on medical evidence, stating whether or not, in the opinion of a suitably qualified medical practitioner, the defender is incapable of instructing a solicitor to represent the defender's interests.

(3)[4] Within 7 days after the appointment of a curator ad litem under paragraph (2)(a), the pursuer shall send to him—

  (a) a copy of the initial writ and any defences (including any adjustments and amendments) lodged; and
  (b) a copy of any notice in Form G5A sent to the curator ad litem by the sheriff clerk.

(4)[5] On lodging a report under paragraph (2)(b), the curator *ad litem* must intimate that this has been done to—

  (a) the pursuer; and
  (b) the solicitor for the defender, if known.

(5)[6] Within 14 days after the report required under paragraph (2)(b) has been lodged, the curator *ad litem* must lodge in process one of the writs mentioned in paragraph (6).

(6) The writs referred to in paragraph (5) are—

  (a) a notice of intention to defend;
  (b) defences to the action;
  (c) a minute adopting defences already lodged; and
  (d) a minute stating that the curator ad litem does not intend to lodge defences.

(7) Notwithstanding that he has lodged a minute stating that he does not intend to lodge defences, a curator ad litem may appear at any stage of the action to protect the interests of the defender.

---

[1] As amended by the Act of Sederunt (Rules of the Court of Session 1994 and Sheriff Court Rules Amendment) (Curators ad litem) (SSI 2017/132) 2017 r.2(5) (effective 1 June 2017 subject to saving specified in SSI 2017/132 r.4).

[2] As amended by Act of Sederunt (Ordinary Cause Rules) Amendment (Family Law (Scotland) Act 2006 etc.) 2006, para.2 (SSI 2006/207) (effective 4 May 2006).

[3] As amended by the Act of Sederunt (Sheriff Court Rules) (Miscellaneous Amendments) 2012 (SSI 2012/188) para.6 (effective 1 August 2012).

[4] As amended by the Act of Sederunt (Ordinary Cause Rules 1993 Amendment) (Case Management of Defended Family and Civil Partnership Actions) 2022 (SSI 2022/289) r.2(18) (effective 25 September 2023 subject to transitional provision specified in SSI 2022/289 r.3).

[5] As substituted by the Act of Sederunt (Rules of the Court of Session 1994 and Sheriff Court Rules Amendment) (Curators ad litem) (SSI 2017/132) 2017 r.2(5)(c) (effective 1 June 2017: subject to saving specified in SSI 2014/132 r.4).

[6] As substituted by the Act of Sederunt (Rules of the Court of Session 1994 and Sheriff Court Rules Amendment) (Curators ad litem) (SSI 2017/132) 2017 r.2(5)(d) (effective 1 June 2017: subject to saving specified in SSI 2014/132 r.4).

(8)[1] At such intervals as the curator *ad litem* considers reasonable having regard to the nature of the defender's mental disorder, the curator *ad litem* must review the defender's capacity to instruct a solicitor, in order to ascertain whether it is appropriate for the appointment to continue.

(8A)[2] If it appears to the curator *ad litem* that the defender may no longer be incapable, the curator *ad litem* must by motion seek the sheriff's permission to obtain an opinion on the matter from a suitably qualified medical practitioner.

(8B)[3] If the motion under paragraph (8A) is granted, the curator *ad litem* must lodge in process a copy of the opinion as soon as possible.

(8C)[4] Where the opinion concludes that the defender is not incapable of instructing a solicitor, the curator *ad litem* must seek discharge from appointment by minute.

(9) The pursuer shall be responsible, in the first instance, for payment of the fees and outlays of the curator ad litem incurred during the period from his appointment until—

   (a) he lodges a minute stating that he does not intend to lodge defences;

   (b) he decides to instruct the lodging of defences or a minute adopting defences already lodged; or

   (c) being satisfied after investigation that the defender is not incapable of instructing a solicitor, he is discharged.

Applications for sist

D1.367   **33A.17.** An application for a sist, or the recall of a sist, under Part XIII of this Chapter shall be made by written motion.

Notices of consent to dissolution of civil partnership or separation of civil partners

D1.368   **33A.18.**—(1)[5] Where, in an action of dissolution of civil partnership or separation of civil partners in which the facts in section 117(3)(c) of the Act of 2004 (no cohabitation for one year with consent of defender to decree) are relied on, the defender wishes to consent to the grant of decree of dissolution of civil partnership or separation of civil partners he shall do so by giving notice in writing in Form CP21 (dissolution) or Form CP23 (separation), as the case may be, to the sheriff clerk.

(2) The evidence of one witness shall be sufficient for the purpose of establishing that the signature on a notice of consent under paragraph (1) is that of the defender.

(3) In an action of dissolution of civil partnership or separation of civil partners where the initial writ includes, for the purposes of section 117(3)(c) of the Act of 2004, an averment that the defender consents to the grant of decree, the defender may give notice by letter sent to the sheriff clerk stating that he has not so consented

---

or that he withdraws any consent which he has already given.

(4) On receipt of a letter under paragraph (3), the sheriff clerk shall intimate the terms of the letter to the pursuer.

(5) On receipt of any intimation under paragraph (4), the pursuer may, within 14 days after the date of the intimation, if none of the other facts mentioned in section 117(3) of the Act of 2004 is averred in the initial writ, lodge a motion for the action to be sisted.

(6) If no such motion is lodged, the pursuer shall be deemed to have abandoned the action and the action shall be dismissed.

(7) If a motion under paragraph (5) is granted and the sist is not recalled or renewed within a period of 6 months from the date of the interlocutor granting the sist, the pursuer shall be deemed to have abandoned the action and the action shall be dismissed.

Views of the child—undefended actions

33A.19.—[1](1) This rule applies to undefended actions in which a section 11 order is sought and warrant has been granted for intimation and the seeking of the child's views in Form F9.   **D1.369**

(2) The pursuer must—
- (a) following the expiry of the period of notice, send the child the Form F9 that was submitted and approved under rule 33A.7A (warrants and forms for intimation to a child and for seeking a child's views);
- (b) lodge with the minute for decree a certificate of intimation in Form F9A;
- (c) not send the child a copy of the initial writ.

(3) Except on cause shown, the sheriff must not grant decree in the period of 28 days following the date on which the Form F9 was sent to the child.

Views of the child—section 11 order sought by pursuer only

33A.19A.—[2](1) This rule applies to defended actions in which only the pursuer seeks a section 11 order and warrant has been granted for intimation and the seeking of the child's views in Form F9.   **D1.369.1**

(2) The pursuer must—
- (a) no later than 14 days after the notice of intention to defend is lodged, send the child the Form F9 that was submitted and approved under rule 33A.7A (warrants and forms for intimation to a child and for seeking a child's views);
- (b) on the same day, lodge a certificate of intimation in Form F9A;
- (c) not send the child a copy of the initial writ, the notice of intention to defend or the defences.

Views of the child—section 11 order sought by defender only

33A.19B.—[3](1) This rule applies to defended actions in which only the defender seeks a section 11 order and warrant has been granted for intimation and the seeking of the child's views in Form F9.   **D1.369.2**

(2) The defender must—
- (a) no later than 14 days after the notice of intention to defend is lodged, send the child the Form F9 that was submitted and approved under rule 33A.34

---

[1] As substituted by the Act of Sederunt (Rules of the Court of Session 1994 and Ordinary Cause Rules 1993 Amendment) (Views of the Child) 2019 (SSI 2019/123) r.3 (effective 24 June 2019).
[2] As inserted by the Act of Sederunt (Rules of the Court of Session 1994 and Ordinary Cause Rules 1993 Amendment) (Views of the Child) 2019 (SSI 2019/123) r.3 (effective 24 June 2019).
[3] As inserted by the Act of Sederunt (Rules of the Court of Session 1994 and Ordinary Cause Rules 1993 Amendment) (Views of the Child) 2019 (SSI 2019/123) r.3 (effective 24 June 2019).

(notice of intention to defend and defences);

    (b)   on the same day, lodge a certificate of intimation in Form F9A;

    (c)   not send the child a copy of the initial writ, the notice of intention to defend or the defences.

Views of the child—section 11 orders sought by both pursuer and defender

D1.369.3   **33A.19C.**—[1](1) This rule applies to defended actions in which section 11 orders are sought by both the pursuer and the defender and warrant has been granted for intimation and the seeking of the child's views in Form F9.

    (2) The pursuer must—

    (a)   no later than 14 days after the notice of intention to defend is lodged, send the child the Form F9 that was submitted and approved under rule 33A.7A (warrants and forms for intimation to a child and for seeking a child's views), amended so as also to narrate the section 11 order sought by the defender;

    (b)   on the same day—

        (i)   lodge a certificate of intimation in Form F9A;

        (ii) send the defender a copy of the Form F9 that was sent to the child;

    (c)   not send the child a copy of the initial writ, the notice of intention to defend or the defences.

Views of the child—the sheriff's role

D1.369.4   **33A.19D.**—[2](1) In a civil partnership action, in relation to any matter affecting a child, where that child has—

    (a)   returned a Form F9 to the sheriff clerk; or

    (b)   otherwise indicated to the court a wish to express views,

the sheriff must not grant any order unless an opportunity has been given for the views of that child to be obtained or heard.

    (2) Where the sheriff is considering making an interim section 11 order before the views of the child have been obtained or heard, the sheriff must consider whether, and if so how, to seek the child's views in advance of making the order.

    (3) Where a child has indicated a wish to express views, the sheriff must order any steps to be taken that the sheriff considers appropriate to obtain or hear the views of that child.

    (4) The sheriff must not grant an order in a civil partnership action, in relation to any matter affecting a child who has expressed views, unless the sheriff has given due weight to the views expressed by that child, having regard to the child's age and maturity.

    (5) In any action in which a section 11 order is sought, where Form F9 has not been sent to the child concerned or where it has been sent but the sheriff considers that the passage of time requires it to be sent again, the sheriff may at any time order either party to—

    (a)   send the Form F9 to that child within a specified timescale;

    (b)   on the same day, lodge—

        (i)   a copy of the Form F9 that was sent to the child;

        (ii) a certificate of intimation in Form F9B.

[THE NEXT PARAGRAPH IS D1.370]

---

[1] As inserted by the Act of Sederunt (Rules of the Court of Session 1994 and Ordinary Cause Rules 1993 Amendment) (Views of the Child) 2019 (SSI 2019/123) r.3 (effective 24 June 2019).

[2] As inserted by the Act of Sederunt (Rules of the Court of Session 1994 and Ordinary Cause Rules 1993 Amendment) (Views of the Child) 2019 (SSI 2019/123) r.3 (effective 24 June 2019).

Recording of views of the child

33A.20.—(1) This rule applies where a child expresses a view on a matter af-   **D1.370**
fecting him whether expressed personally to the sheriff or to a person appointed by
the sheriff for that purpose or provided by the child in writing.

(2) The sheriff, or the person appointed by the sheriff, shall record the views of
the child in writing; and the sheriff may direct that such views, and any written
views, given by a child shall—

(a) be sealed in an envelope marked "Views of the child confidential";

(b) be kept in the court process without being recorded in the inventory of
process;

(c) be available to a sheriff only;

(d) not be opened by any person other than a sheriff; and

(e) not form a borrowable part of the process.

Child welfare reporters

33A.21.—[1, 2](1) At any stage of a civil partnership action the sheriff may, in   **D1.371**
relation to any matter affecting a child, appoint a person (referred to in this rule as a
"child welfare reporter")—

(a) to seek the views of the child and to report any views expressed by the
child to the court; or

(b) to undertake enquiries and to report to the court.

(2) A child welfare reporter may only be appointed under paragraph (1)(b) where
the sheriff is satisfied that the appointment—

(a) is in the best interests of the child; and

(b) will promote the effective and expeditious determination of an issue in
relation to the child.

(3) An interlocutor appointing a child welfare reporter must—

(a) specify a date by which the report is to be submitted to the court;

(b) include a direction as to the fees and outlays of the child welfare reporter;

(c) where the appointment is under paragraph (1)(a), specify the issues in
respect of which the child's views are to be sought and include a direction
as to whether a copy of the report is to be provided to the parties under
paragraph (9)(d);

(d) where the appointment is under paragraph (1)(b), specify the enquiries to
be undertaken, and the issues requiring to be addressed in the report; and

(e) where the appointment is under paragraph (1)(b) and seeking the views of
the child forms part of the enquiries to be undertaken, include a direction
as to whether the views of the child should be recorded in a separate report
and, if so, whether a copy of that report is to be provided to the parties
under paragraph (9)(d).

(4) An interlocutor complies with subparagraph (c) or (d) of paragraph (3) if the
issues or, as the case may be the enquiries, referred to in that subparagraph are
specified in an annex to the interlocutor in Form CP38.

(5) Where the sheriff has appointed a child welfare reporter with a view to the
report being considered at an assigned hearing, the date specified in accordance with
paragraph (3)(a) must be a date no less than three clear days before that hearing,

---

[1] As substituted by the Act of Sederunt (Rules of the Court of Session 1994 and Sheriff Court Rules
Amendment) (Miscellaneous) 2016 (SSI 2016/102) r.3 (effective 21 March 2016).

[2] As amended by the Act of Sederunt (Rules of the Court of Session 1994 and Ordinary Cause Rules
1993 Amendment) (Views of the Child) 2019 (SSI 2019/123) r.3 (effective 24 June 2019).

excluding any day on which the sheriff clerk's office is not open for civil court business, unless cause exists for specifying a later date.

(6)[1] On appointing a child welfare reporter the sheriff may also—

(a) make such further order as may be required to facilitate the discharge of the child welfare reporter's functions;

(b) direct that a party to the proceedings is to be responsible for providing the child welfare reporter with copies of such documents lodged in the process as may be specified; and

(c) give the child welfare reporter directions.

(7) The direction referred to in paragraph (3)(b) must assign liability for payment of the child welfare reporter's fees and outlays in the first instance, and require that liability to be borne—

(a) in equal shares by—

(i) the pursuer,

(ii) any defender who has lodged a notice of intention to defend, and

(iii) any minuter who has been granted leave to enter the process; or

(b) by one or more parties to the proceedings on such other basis as may be justified on cause shown.

(8) On the granting of an interlocutor appointing a child welfare reporter the sheriff clerk must—

(a) give the child welfare reporter—

(i) a certified copy of the interlocutor, and

(ii) sufficient information to enable the child welfare reporter to contact the solicitor for each party to the proceedings, or any party not represented by a solicitor; and

(b) intimate the name and address of the child welfare reporter to any local authority to which intimation of the proceedings has been made.

(9) A child welfare reporter appointed under this rule must—

(a) where the appointment is under paragraph (1)(a)—

(i) seek the child's views on the specified issues, and

(ii) prepare a report for the court reporting any such views;

(b) where the appointment is under paragraph (1)(b)—

(i) undertake the specified enquiries, and

(ii) prepare a report for the court having regard to the specified issues;

(c) send the report to the sheriff clerk by the date specified; and

(d) unless otherwise directed, send a copy of the report to each party to the proceedings by that date.

(10) A child welfare reporter may—

(a) apply to the sheriff clerk to be given further directions by the sheriff;

(b) bring to the attention of the sheriff clerk any impediment to the performance of any function arising under this rule.

(11) Where a child welfare reporter acts as referred to in paragraph (10), the sheriff may, having heard parties, make any order or direction that could competently have been made under paragraph (6).

---

[1] As amended by the Act of Sederunt (Sheriff Appeal Court Rules 2015 and Sheriff Court Rules Amendment) (Miscellaneous) 2016 (SSI 2016/194) r.3 (effective 7 July 2016).

Appointment of local authority to report on a child

33A.21A.—[1](1)   This rule applies where, in a civil partnership action, the sheriff   **D1.372**
appoints a local authority to investigate and report to the court on the circumstances
of a child and on the proposed arrangements for the care and upbringing of a child.

(2)   The following provisions of rule 33A.21 apply as if the reference to the child
welfare reporter was a reference to the local authority appointed by the sheriff—

(a)   paragraph (3)(a) and (b);

(b)   paragraph (6)(a) and (b);

(c)   paragraph (7); and

(d)   paragraph (8).

(3)   On completion of the report referred to in paragraph (1), the local authority
must—

(a)   send the report to the sheriff clerk; and

(b)   unless otherwise directed by the sheriff, send a copy of the report to each
party to the proceedings.

Referral to family mediation

33A.22.—[2](1)   In any civil partnership action, where the sheriff considers it ap-   **D1.372.1**
propriate to do so the sheriff may, at any stage of the action, refer the action, or part
thereof, to a mediator accredited to a specified family mediation organisation.

(2)   The sheriff must have particular regard to any averments of domestic abuse
when considering the appropriateness of referring the action, or part thereof, to a
mediator under paragraph (1).

(3)   In this rule any civil partnership action means an action to which the Civil
Evidence (Family Mediation) (Scotland) Act 1995 applies.

[THE NEXT PARAGRAPH IS D1.373]

Child Welfare Hearing

33A.23.—[3](1)   Where—   **D1.373**

(a)   on the lodging of a notice of intention to defend in a civil partnership action in which the initial writ seeks or includes a crave for a section 11
order, a defender wishes to oppose any such crave or order, or seeks the
same order as that craved by the pursuer,

(b)   on the lodging of a notice of intention to defend in a civil partnership action, the defender seeks a section 11 order which is not craved by the
pursuer, or

(c)   in any other circumstances in a civil partnership action, the sheriff considers that a Child Welfare Hearing should be fixed and makes an order
(whether at his own instance or on the motion of a party) that such a hearing shall be fixed,

the sheriff clerk shall fix a date and time for a Child Welfare Hearing to be heard
either at the same time as the Initial Case Management Hearing or on the first suit-

---

[1] As inserted by the Act of Sederunt (Rules of the Court of Session 1994 and Sheriff Court Rules
Amendment) (Miscellaneous) 2016 (SSI 2016/102) r.3 (effective 21 March 2016).

[2] Substituted by the Act of Sederunt (Ordinary Cause Rules 1993 Amendment) (Case Management of
Defended Family and Civil Partnership Actions) 2022 (SSI 2022/289) r.2(19) (effective 25 September
2023 subject to transitional provision specified in SSI 2022/289 r.3).

[3] As amended by the Act of Sederunt (Ordinary Cause Rules 1993 Amendment) (Case Management of
Defended Family and Civil Partnership Actions) 2022 (SSI 2022/289) r.2(20) (effective 25 September
2023 subject to transitional provision specified in SSI 2022/289 r.3).

able court date occurring not sooner than 21 days and not later than 49 days after the last date for lodging of the notice of intention to defend, unless the sheriff directs the hearing to be held on an earlier date.

(2) On fixing the date for the Child Welfare Hearing the sheriff clerk must—

(a) if the Child Welfare Hearing is to be heard at the same time as the Initial Case Management Hearing, intimate the date on which both hearings will take place to parties in Form G5A; or

(b) if the Child Welfare Hearing is to be heard at a different time from the Initial Case Management Hearing, intimate the date of the Child Welfare Hearing to parties in Form F41.

(3) The fixing of the date of the Child Welfare Hearing shall not affect the right of a party to make any other application to the court whether by motion or otherwise.

(4)[1] At the Child Welfare Hearing (which may be held in private), the sheriff shall seek to secure the expeditious resolution of disputes in relation to the child by ascertaining from the parties the matters in dispute and any information relevant to that dispute, and may—

(a) order such steps to be taken, make such order, if any, or order further procedure, as he thinks fit, and

(b) ascertain whether there is or is likely to be a vulnerable witness within the meaning of section 11(1) of the Act of 2004 who is to give evidence at any proof or hearing and whether any order under section 12(1) of the Act of 2004 requires to be made.

(5) All parties (including a child who has indicated his wish to attend) shall, except on cause shown, attend the Child Welfare Hearing personally.

(6) It shall be the duty of the parties to provide the sheriff with sufficient information to enable him to conduct the Child Welfare Hearing.

Applications for orders to disclose whereabouts of children

D1.374
33A.24.—(1) An application in a civil partnership action for an order under section 33(1) of the Family Law Act 1986 (which relates to the disclosure of the whereabouts of a child) shall be made by motion.

(2) Where the sheriff makes an order under section 33(1) of the Family Law Act 1986, he may ordain the person against whom the order has been made to appear before him or to lodge an affidavit.

Applications in relation to removal of children

D1.375
33A.25.—(1) An application in a civil partnership action for leave under section 51(1) of the Children Act 1975 (authority to remove a child from the care and possession of the applicant for a residence order) or for an order under section 35(3) of the Family Law Act 1986 (application for interdict or interim interdict prohibiting removal of child from jurisdiction) shall be made—

(a) by a party to the action, by motion; or

(b) by a person who is not a party to the action, by minute.

(2) An application under section 35(3) of the Family Law Act 1986 need not be served or intimated.

(3) An application in a civil partnership action under section 23(2) of the Child Abduction and Custody Act 1985 (declarator that removal of child from United Kingdom was unlawful) shall be made—

---

[1] As substituted by the Act of Sederunt (Ordinary Cause, Summary Application, Summary Cause and Small Claim Rules) Amendment (Vulnerable Witnesses (Scotland) Act 2004) 2007 (SSI 2007/463) r.2(10) (effective 1 November 2007).

    (a)   in an action depending before the sheriff—
        (i)   by a party, in the initial writ, defences or minute, as the case may be, or by motion; or
        (ii)   by any other person, by minute; or
    (b)   after final decree, by minute in the process of the action to which the application relates.

Intimation to local authority before supervised contact order

33A.26. Where in a civil partnership action the sheriff, at his own instance or on the motion of a party, is considering making a contact order or an interim contact order subject to supervision by the social work department of a local authority, he shall ordain the party moving for such an order to intimate to the chief executive of that local authority (where not already a party to the action and represented at the hearing at which the issue arises)—   **D1.376**

    (a)   the terms of any relevant motion;
    (b)   the intention of the sheriff to order that the contact order be supervised by the social work department of that local authority; and
    (c)   that the local authority shall, within such period as the sheriff has determined—
        (i)   notify the sheriff clerk whether it intends to make representations to the sheriff; and
        (ii)   where it intends to make representations in writing, do so within that period.

Joint minutes

33A.27. Where any parties in a civil partnership action have reached agreement in relation to—   **D1.377**

    (a)   a section 11 order;
    (b)   aliment for a child; or
    (c)   an order for financial provision,

a joint minute may be entered into expressing that agreement; and, subject to rule 33A.19(3) (no order before views of child expressed), the sheriff may grant decree in respect of those parts of the joint minute in relation to which he could otherwise make an order, whether or not such a decree would include a matter for which there was no crave.

Affidavits

33A.28. The sheriff in a civil partnership action may accept evidence by affidavit at any hearing for an order or interim order.   **D1.378**

Part II – Undefended Civil Partnership Actions

Evidence in certain undefended civil partnership actions

33A.29.—(1) This rule—   **D1.379**

    (a)   subject to sub paragraph (b), applies to all civil partnership actions in which no notice of intention to defend has been lodged, other than a civil partnership action—
        (i)   for financial provision after overseas proceedings as provided for in Schedule 11 to the Act of 2004; or
        (ii)   for an order under Chapter 3 or Chapter 4 of Part 3 or section 127 of the Act of 2004;
    (b)   applies to a civil partnership action in which a curator ad litem has been appointed under rule 33A.16 where the curator ad litem to the defender has lodged a minute intimating that he does not intend to lodge defences;

(c) applies to any civil partnership action which proceeds at any stage as undefended where the sheriff so directs;

(d) applies to the merits of a civil partnership action which is undefended on the merits where the sheriff so directs, notwithstanding that the action is defended on an ancillary matter.

(2) Unless the sheriff otherwise directs, evidence shall be given by affidavits.

(3) Unless the sheriff otherwise directs, evidence relating to the welfare of a child shall be given by affidavit, at least one affidavit being emitted by a person other than a parent or party to the action.

(4) Evidence in the form of a written statement bearing to be the professional opinion of a duly qualified medical practitioner, which has been signed by him and lodged in process, shall be admissible in place of parole evidence by him.

Procedure for decree in actions under rule 33A.29

D1.380

33A.30.—(1) In an action to which rule 33A.29 (evidence in certain undefended civil partnership actions) applies, the pursuer shall at any time after the expiry of the period for lodging a notice of intention to defend—

(a) lodge in process the affidavit evidence; and

(b) endorse a minute in Form CP27 on the initial writ.

(2) The sheriff may, at any time after the pursuer has complied with paragraph (1), without requiring the appearance of parties—

(a) grant decree in terms of the motion for decree; or

(b) remit the cause for such further procedure, if any, including proof by parole evidence, as the sheriff thinks fit.

Extracts of undefended decree

D1.381

33A.31 In an action to which rule 33A.29 (evidence in certain undefended civil partnership actions) applies, the sheriff clerk shall, after the expiry of 14 days after the grant of decree under rule 33A.30 (procedure for decree in actions under rule 33A.29), issue to the pursuer and the defender an extract decree.

No recording of evidence

D1.382

33A.32. It shall not be necessary to record the evidence in any proof in a civil partnership action which is not defended.

Disapplication of Chapter 15

D1.383

33A.33. Other than rule 15.1(1), Chapter 15 (motions) shall not apply to a civil partnership action in which no notice of intention to defend has been lodged, or to a civil partnership action in so far as it proceeds as undefended.

Late appearance and application for recall by defenders

D1.384

33A.33A.—[1,2](1) In a cause mentioned in rule 33A.1(a), (b) or (f), the sheriff may, at any stage of the action before the granting of final decree, make an order with such conditions, if any, as he thinks fit—

(a) directing that a defender who has not lodged a notice of intention to defend be treated as if he had lodged such a notice and the period of notice had expired on the date on which the order was made; or

(b) allowing a defender who has not lodged a notice of intention to defend to

---

[1] As inserted by the Act of Sederunt (Sheriff Court Rules) (Miscellaneous Amendments) 2008 (SSI 2008/223) para.2(3) (effective 1 July 2008).

[2] As amended by the Act of Sederunt (Rules of the Court of Session 1994 and Ordinary Cause Rules 1993 Amendment) (Views of the Child) 2019 (SSI 2019/123) r.3 (effective 24 June 2019).

appear and be heard at a diet of proof although he has not lodged defences, but he shall not, in that event, be allowed to lead evidence without the pursuer's consent.

(2) Where the sheriff makes an order under paragraph (1), the pursuer may recall a witness already examined or lead other evidence whether or not he closed his proof before that order was made.

(3) Where no order under paragraph (1) has been sought by a defender who has not lodged a notice of intention to defend and decree is granted against him, the sheriff may, on an application made within 14 days of the date of the decree, and with such conditions, if any, as he thinks fit, make an order recalling the decree.

(4) Where the sheriff makes an order under paragraph (3), the cause shall thereafter proceed as if the defender had lodged a notice of intention to defend and the period of notice had expired on the date on which the decree was recalled.

(4A) Where the sheriff makes an order under paragraph (1) or (3), the sheriff must order any steps to be taken that the sheriff considers appropriate to obtain or hear the views of the child in relation to any section 11 order sought by the defender.

(5) An application under paragraph (1) or (3) shall be made by note setting out the proposed defence and explaining the defender's failure to appear.

(6) An application under paragraph (1) or (3) shall not affect any right of appeal the defender may otherwise have.

(7) A note lodged in an application under paragraph (1) or (3) shall be served on the pursuer and any other party.

Part III – Defended Civil Partnership Actions

General provisions

33A.33B.—(1) Chapters 9 (standard procedure in defended causes) and 10 (additional procedure) do not apply to a civil partnership action in which a notice of intention to defend has been lodged in accordance with rule 33A.34 (notice of intention to defend and defences etc.). **D1.384.1**

(2) Subject to paragraph (3), a civil partnership action in which a notice of intention to defend has been lodged must follow the procedure set out in this Part of this Chapter.

(3) The sheriff may, in exceptional circumstances, of the sheriff's own motion or on the motion of a party, disapply any rule mentioned in this Part of this Chapter.

Notice of intention to defend and defences

33A.34.—[1,2](1) This rule applies where the defender in a civil partnership action seeks— **D1.385**

    (a)   to oppose any crave in the initial writ;

    (b)   to make a claim for—

        (i)   aliment;

        (ii) an order for financial provision within the meaning of section 8(3) of the Act of 1985; or

        (iii) a section 11 order; or

    (c)   an order—

        (i)   under section 16(1)(b) or (3) of the Act of 1985 (setting aside or varying agreement as to financial provision);

---

[1] As inserted by the Act of Sederunt (Sheriff Court Rules) (Miscellaneous Amendments) 2012 (SSI 2012/188) para.4 (effective 1 August 2012).

[2] As amended by the Act of Sederunt (Rules of the Court of Session 1994 and Ordinary Cause Rules 1993 Amendment) (Views of the Child) 2019 (SSI 2019/123) r.3 (effective 24 June 2019).

(ii)   under section 18 of the Act of 1985 (which relates to avoidance transactions); or

(iii)   under Chapter 3 or Chapter 4 of Part 3 or section 127 of the Act of 2004; or

(d)   to challenge the jurisdiction of the court.

(2) In an action to which this rule applies, the defender shall—

(a)   lodge a notice of intention to defend in Form CP16 before the expiry of the period of notice and, at the same time, send a copy to the pursuer; and

(b)   make any claim or seek any order referred to in paragraph (1), as the case may be, in those defences by setting out in his defences—

(i)   craves;

(ii)   averments in the answers to the condescendence in support of those craves; and

(iii)   appropriate pleas-in-law.

(4)[1,2] Where a defender opposes a crave for an order for financial provision or makes a claim in accordance with paragraph (1)(b)(ii), the defender must lodge a completed Form CP13A signed by the defender with the defences, minute of amendment or answers as the case may be.

(4A)[3] Subject to paragraph (4B), where a defender intends to make an application for a section 11 order in respect of a child who is not a party to the action the defender must—

(a)   include in the notice of intention to defend a crave for a warrant for intimation and the seeking of the child's views in Form F9;

(b)   when lodging the notice of intention to defend, submit a draft Form F9, showing the details that the defender proposes to include when the form is sent to the child.

(4B) Where the defender considers that it would be inappropriate to send Form F9 to the child (for example, where the child is under 5 years of age), the defender must include in the notice of intention to defend—

(a)   a crave to dispense with intimation and the seeking of the child's views in Form F9;

(b)   averments setting out the reasons why it is inappropriate to send Form F9 to the child.

(4C) The sheriff must be satisfied that the draft Form F9 submitted under paragraph (4A)(b) has been drafted appropriately.

(4D) The sheriff may dispense with intimation and the seeking of views in Form F9 or make any other order that the sheriff considers appropriate.

(4E) An order granting warrant for intimation and the seeking of the child's views in Form F9 under this rule must—

(a)   state that the Form F9 must be sent to the child in accordance with rule 33A.19B (views of the child – section 11 order sought by defender only);

(b)   be signed by the sheriff.

---

[1] As inserted by the Act of Sederunt (Sheriff Court Rules) (Miscellaneous Amendments) 2012 (SSI 2012/188) para.4 (effective 1 August 2012).

[2] As amended by the Act of Sederunt (Sheriff Court Rules) (Miscellaneous Amendments) (No.2) 2012 (SSI 2012/221) para.2 (effective 31 July 2012).

[3] As amended by the Act of Sederunt (Ordinary Cause Rules 1993 Amendment) (Case Management of Defended Family and Civil Partnership Actions) 2022 (SSI 2022/289) r.2(22) (effective 25 September 2023 subject to transitional provision specified in SSI 2022/289 r.3).

Abandonment by pursuer

33A.35. Notwithstanding abandonment by a pursuer of a civil partnership action, the court may allow a defender to pursue an order or claim sought in his defences; and the proceedings in relation to that order or claim shall continue in dependence as if a separate cause.

D1.386

Attendance of parties at Options Hearing

33A.36.[1] All parties must, except on cause shown, attend personally case management hearings under rules 33A.36J (Initial Case Management Hearing) and 33A.36P (Full Case Management Hearing).

D1.387

Fixing of date and time for Initial Case Management Hearing

33A.36A.—[2](1) On the lodging of a notice of intention to defend under rule 33A.34 (notice of intention to defend and defences etc.) the sheriff clerk must fix a date and time for an Initial Case Management Hearing which date must be on the first suitable court day occurring not sooner than 21 days and not later than 49 days after the last date for the lodging of the notice of intention to defend.

D1.387.1

(2) In cases involving a crave for a section 11 order the sheriff must have regard to holding the Initial Case Management Hearing and the Child Welfare Hearing at the same time.

(3) On fixing the date for the Initial Case Management Hearing, the sheriff clerk must—

    (a) intimate forthwith to the parties in Form G5A—
        (i) the last date for lodging defences;
        (ii) the date for the return of the initial writ;
        (iii) the date of the Initial Case Management Hearing;
        (iv) whether a Child Welfare Hearing is to be held at the same time as the Initial Case Management Hearing;
    (b) prepare an interlocutor addressing all of the matters in sub-paragraph (a) for the sheriff to sign.

(4) The fixing of the date of the Initial Case Management Hearing does not affect the right of a party to make any incidental application to the court.

Alteration of date and time for Initial Case Management Hearing

33A.36B.—[3](1) Subject to paragraph (2), at any time before the date and time fixed under rule 33A.36A (fixing of date and time for Initial Case Management Hearing) or under this rule, the sheriff may of the sheriff's own motion, on the motion of any party or on the joint motion of the parties—

D1.387.2

    (a) discharge the Initial Case Management Hearing or, where fixed, the Child Welfare Hearing or both, as the case may be; and
    (b) fix a new date and time for either the Initial Case Management Hearing or the Child Welfare Hearing or both, as the case may be.

---

[1] Substituted by the Act of Sederunt (Ordinary Cause Rules 1993 Amendment) (Case Management of Defended Family and Civil Partnership Actions) 2022 (SSI 2022/289) r.2(23) (effective 25 September 2023 subject to transitional provision specified in SSI 2022/289 r.3).

[2] Inserted by the Act of Sederunt (Ordinary Cause Rules 1993 Amendment) (Case Management of Defended Family and Civil Partnership Actions) 2022 (SSI 2022/289) r.2(23) (effective 25 September 2023 subject to transitional provision specified in SSI 2022/289 r.3).

[3] Inserted by the Act of Sederunt (Ordinary Cause Rules 1993 Amendment) (Case Management of Defended Family and Civil Partnership Actions) 2022 (SSI 2022/289) r.2(23) (effective 25 September 2023 subject to transitional provision specified in SSI 2022/289 r.3).

(2)   The date and time of any hearing fixed under paragraph (1)(b) may be earlier or later than the date and time fixed for the discharged hearing but must be fixed for a date within the period specified in rule 33A.36A(1) or the first available court date thereafter.

(3)   Where the sheriff is considering making an order under paragraph (1) of the sheriff's own motion and in the absence of the parties, the sheriff clerk must—

(a)   fix a date, time and place for the parties to be heard;

(b)   prepare and sign an interlocutor recording those dates, times and places for the sheriff to sign.

(4)   The sheriff may discharge a hearing fixed under paragraph (3) on the joint motion of the parties.

(5)   On the discharge of a hearing under paragraph (1)(a) or paragraph (4), the sheriff clerk must forthwith intimate to all parties—

(a)   that the hearing has been discharged under paragraph (1)(a) or, as the case may be, paragraph (4);

(b)   the last date for lodging defences, if appropriate;

(c)   the last date for adjustment, if appropriate;

(d)   the new date and time fixed for any hearing under paragraph (1)(b).

(6)   Any reference in these Rules to the Initial Case Management Hearing, the Child Welfare Hearing or a continuation of either includes a reference to an Initial Case Management Hearing or Child Welfare Hearing for which a date and time has been fixed under this rule.

Return of initial writ

D1.387.3   **33A.3C.**[1]   Subject to rule 33A.36D (lodging of pleadings before Initial Case Management Hearing) the pursuer must return the initial writ, unbacked and unfolded, to the sheriff clerk within 7 days of the expiry of the period of notice in accordance with the date intimated on Form G5A.

Lodging of pleadings before Initial Case Management Hearing

D1.387.4   **33A.36D.**[2]   Where any hearing, whether by motion or otherwise, is fixed before the Initial Case Management Hearing, each party shall lodge in process a copy of the party's pleadings, or where the pleadings have been adjusted, the pleadings as adjusted, not later than 2 days before the hearing.

Process folder

D1.387.5   **33A.36E.**—[3](1)   On receipt of the notice of intention to defend, the sheriff clerk must prepare a process folder which must include—

(a)   interlocutor sheets;

(b)   duplicate interlocutor sheets;

(c)   a production file;

(d)   a motion file;

(e)   an inventory of process.

---

[1] Inserted by the Act of Sederunt (Ordinary Cause Rules 1993 Amendment) (Case Management of Defended Family and Civil Partnership Actions) 2022 (SSI 2022/289) r.2(23) (effective 25 September 2023 subject to transitional provision specified in SSI 2022/289 r.3).

[2] Inserted by the Act of Sederunt (Ordinary Cause Rules 1993 Amendment) (Case Management of Defended Family and Civil Partnership Actions) 2022 (SSI 2022/289) r.2(23) (effective 25 September 2023 subject to transitional provision specified in SSI 2022/289 r.3).

[3] Inserted by the Act of Sederunt (Ordinary Cause Rules 1993 Amendment) (Case Management of Defended Family and Civil Partnership Actions) 2022 (SSI 2022/289) r.2(23) (effective 25 September 2023 subject to transitional provision specified in SSI 2022/289 r.3).

(2) Any production or part of process lodged in cause must be placed in the process folder.

Defences

33A.36F.—[1](1) Where a notice of intention to defend has been lodged, the defender must lodge defences within 14 days after the expiry of the period of notice.

(2) Defences must be in the form of answers in numbered paragraphs corresponding to the articles of the condescendence and must have appended a note of the pleas-in- law of the defender.

(3) Defences which include a counterclaim must commence with a crave setting out the counterclaim in such form as, if the counterclaim had been made in a separate action, would have been appropriate in the initial writ in that separate action and must include—

   (a) answers to the condescendence of the initial writ;

   (b) a statement of facts in numbered paragraphs setting out the facts on which the counterclaim is founded, incorporating by reference, if necessary, any matter contained in the defences;

   (c) appropriate pleas-in-law.

D1.387.6

Implied admissions

33A.33G.[2] Every statement of fact made by a party must be answered by every other party, and if such a statement by one party within the knowledge of another party is not denied by that other party, that other party will be deemed to have admitted that statement of fact.

D1.387.7

Sisting

33A.36H.—[3](1) The sheriff may, on cause shown, of the sheriff's own motion or on the motion of any party, sist the action until a specified date.

(2) Where the action is sisted, the sheriff clerk must—

   (a) prepare an interlocutor specifying the reason for the sist and the date specified in paragraph (1) for the sheriff to sign;

   (b) fix a date for a review of sist hearing not later than 30 days following the expiration of the sist;

   (c) intimate the date of the review of sist hearing to each party.

(3) Where a cause has been sisted, any period for adjustment before the sist is to be reckoned as a part of the period for adjustment.

D1.387.8

Open record

33A.36I.[4] The sheriff may, at any time before the closing of the record in a civil partnership action, of the sheriff's own motion or on the motion of a party, order any party to lodge a copy of the pleadings in the form of an open record containing any adjustments and amendments made as at the date of the order.

D1.387.9

---

[1] Inserted by the Act of Sederunt (Ordinary Cause Rules 1993 Amendment) (Case Management of Defended Family and Civil Partnership Actions) 2022 (SSI 2022/289) r.2(23) (effective 25 September 2023 subject to transitional provision specified in SSI 2022/289 r.3).

[2] Inserted by the Act of Sederunt (Ordinary Cause Rules 1993 Amendment) (Case Management of Defended Family and Civil Partnership Actions) 2022 (SSI 2022/289) r.2(23) (effective 25 September 2023 subject to transitional provision specified in SSI 2022/289 r.3).

[3] Inserted by the Act of Sederunt (Ordinary Cause Rules 1993 Amendment) (Case Management of Defended Family and Civil Partnership Actions) 2022 (SSI 2022/289) r.2(23) (effective 25 September 2023 subject to transitional provision specified in SSI 2022/289 r.3).

[4] Inserted by the Act of Sederunt (Ordinary Cause Rules 1993 Amendment) (Case Management of Defended Family and Civil Partnership Actions) 2022 (SSI 2022/289) r.2(23) (effective 25 September 2023 subject to transitional provision specified in SSI 2022/289 r.3).

Initial Case Management Hearing

D1.387.10   **33A.36J.**—[1](1)   At the Initial Case Management Hearing the sheriff must seek to secure the expeditious progress of the cause by ascertaining from the parties the matters in dispute and information about any other matter referred to in paragraph (3).

(2)   It is be the duty of the parties to provide the sheriff with sufficient information to enable the sheriff to conduct the hearing as provided for in this rule.

(3)   At the Initial Case Management Hearing each party must address the court on—

- (a)   any matters that are capable of agreement;
- (b)   the matters that are in dispute between the parties;
- (c)   any matters of potential complexity or difficulty;
- (d)   any valuations that are likely to be required;
- (e)   any skilled witness evidence that is likely to be required and the scope for joint instruction;
- (f)   whether additional steps require to be taken to give a child an opportunity to express the child's views;
- (g)   whether steps require to be taken to investigate any facts or circumstances relating to a child;
- (h)   the suitability of the action for referral to mediation;
- (i)   whether special measures will be required for the purposes of taking the evidence of any vulnerable witnesses;
- (j)   the scope for use of affidavits and other documents in place of oral evidence;
- (k)   the extent to which the parties have complied with any orders made by the court;
- (l)   the number and availability of witnesses;
- (m)   the content, volume and form of productions;
- (n)   the requirement for access to IT equipment to view productions;
- (o)   whether sanction is sought for the employment of counsel;
- (p)   the progress of any legal aid application.

(4)   At the Initial Case Management Hearing, the sheriff must fix a date and time for a Full Case Management Hearing which date must be on the first suitable court day occurring—

- (a)   in cases involving a crave for a section 11 order only, not sooner than 16 weeks and not later than 24 weeks after the last date for the lodging of defences;
- (b)   in all other cases, not sooner than 20 weeks and not later than 24 weeks after the last date for the lodging of defences.

(5)   Following the Initial Case Management Hearing the sheriff clerk must intimate forthwith to the parties in Form G6B—

- (a)   the last date for lodging a note of the basis for any preliminary pleas;
- (b)   the last date for adjustment;
- (c)   the last date for lodging a copy of the record;
- (d)   the date of the Full Case Management Hearing.

---

[1] Inserted by the Act of Sederunt (Ordinary Cause Rules 1993 Amendment) (Case Management of Defended Family and Civil Partnership Actions) 2022 (SSI 2022/289) r.2(23) (effective 25 September 2023 subject to transitional provision specified in SSI 2022/289 r.3).

Alteration of date and time for Full Case Management Hearing

33A.36K.—[1](1)   Subject to paragraph (2), at any time before the date and time   **D1.387.11**
fixed under rule 33A.36J (Initial Case Management Hearing) or under this rule, the
sheriff may, of the sheriff's own motion, on the motion of any party or on the joint
motion of the parties—

(a)   discharge the Full Case Management Hearing; and

(b)   fix a new date and time for a Full Case Management Hearing.

(2)   The date and time of any hearing to be fixed under paragraph (1)(b) may be
earlier or later than the date and time fixed for the discharged hearing, but must be
fixed for a date within the relevant period specified in rule 33A.36J(4) or the first
available court date thereafter.

(3)   Where the sheriff is considering making an order under paragraph (1) of the
sheriff's own motion and in the absence of the parties, the sheriff clerk must—

(a)   fix a date, time and place for the parties to be heard;

(b)   prepare an interlocutor recording those dates, times and places for the
sheriff to sign.

(4)   The sheriff may discharge a hearing fixed under paragraph (3) on the joint
motion of the parties.

(5)   On the discharge of a hearing under paragraph (1)(a) or paragraph (4), the
sheriff clerk must forthwith intimate to all parties—

(a)   that the hearing has been discharged under paragraph (1)(a) or, as the case
may be, paragraph (4);

(b)   the last date for lodging a note of basis of preliminary pleas, if appropriate;

(c)   the last date for adjustment, if appropriate;

(d)   the last date for lodging a copy of the record, if appropriate;

(e)   the new date and time fixed for the hearing under paragraph (1)(b).

(6)   Any reference in these Rules to the Full Case Management Hearing includes
a reference to a Full Case Management Hearing for which a date and time has been
fixed under this rule.

Pre-Hearing Meeting

33A.36L.—[2](1)   In advance of the Full Case Management Hearing the parties   **D1.387.12**
must hold a pre-hearing meeting, at which parties must—

(a)   discuss settlement of the action;

(b)   agree, so far as is possible, the matters which are not in dispute between
them;

(c)   discuss the information referred to in rule 33A.36P(3) (Full Case Management Hearing).

(2)   Not later than 2 days before the Full Case Management Hearing the pursuer
must lodge with the court a joint minute of the pre-hearing meeting signed by both
parties, addressing the points in rule 33A.36P(3) or explain to the sheriff why such a
minute has not been lodged.

---

[1] Inserted by the Act of Sederunt (Ordinary Cause Rules 1993 Amendment) (Case Management of
Defended Family and Civil Partnership Actions) 2022 (SSI 2022/289) r.2(23) (effective 25 September
2023 subject to transitional provision specified in SSI 2022/289 r.3).

[2] Inserted by the Act of Sederunt (Ordinary Cause Rules 1993 Amendment) (Case Management of
Defended Family and Civil Partnership Actions) 2022 (SSI 2022/289) r.2(23) (effective 25 September
2023 subject to transitional provision specified in SSI 2022/289 r.3).

(3) If a party is not present during the pre-hearing meeting, that party's representative must be able to contact the party during the meeting and be in full possession of all relevant facts.

Adjustment of pleadings

D1.387.13 **33A.36M.**—[1](1) Parties may adjust their pleadings until 14 days before the date of the Full Case Management Hearing or any continuation of it.

(2) Any adjustments must be exchanged between parties and not lodged in process.

(3) Parties are responsible for maintaining a record of adjustments made during the period for adjustment.

(4) No adjustments are permitted after the period mentioned in paragraph (1) except with leave of the sheriff.

Record for Full Case Management Hearing

D1.387.14 **33A.36N.**—[2](1) The pursuer must, at the end of the period for adjustment referred to in rule 33A.36M(1) (adjustment of pleadings) and before the Full Case Management Hearing, make a copy of the pleadings and any adjustments and amendments in the form of a record.

(2) Not later than 2 days before the Full Case Management Hearing, the pursuer must lodge a certified copy of the record in process.

(3) Where the Full Case Management Hearing is continued under rule 33A.36P(7) and further adjustment or amendment is made to the record, a copy of the record as adjusted or amended, certified by the pursuer, must be lodged in process not later than 2 days before the Full Case Management Hearing so continued.

Exchange of lists of witnesses

D1.387.15 **33A.36O.**—[3](1) Not later than 7 days before the Full Case Management Hearing, each party must—

  (a) intimate to every other party a list of witnesses, including any skilled witnesses, on whose evidence they intend to rely at proof;

  (b) lodge a copy of that list in process.

(2) A party who seeks to rely on the evidence of a person not on the list intimated under paragraph (1)(a) must, if any other party objects to such evidence being admitted, seek leave of the sheriff to admit that evidence; and such leave may be granted on such conditions, if any, as the sheriff thinks fit.

(3) The list of witnesses intimated under paragraph (1)(a) must include—

  (a) the name, occupation (where known) and address of each witness;

  (b) a summary of up to 50 words on the matters to which each witness is expected to speak;

  (c) details of whether the witness is considered to be a vulnerable witness within the meaning of section 11(1) of the Vulnerable Witnesses (Scotland) Act 2004 and whether any child witness notice under section 12(2) of that

---

[1] Inserted by the Act of Sederunt (Ordinary Cause Rules 1993 Amendment) (Case Management of Defended Family and Civil Partnership Actions) 2022 (SSI 2022/289) r.2(23) (effective 25 September 2023 subject to transitional provision specified in SSI 2022/289 r.3).

[2] Inserted by the Act of Sederunt (Ordinary Cause Rules 1993 Amendment) (Case Management of Defended Family and Civil Partnership Actions) 2022 (SSI 2022/289) r.2(23) (effective 25 September 2023 subject to transitional provision specified in SSI 2022/289 r.3).

[3] Inserted by the Act of Sederunt (Ordinary Cause Rules 1993 Amendment) (Case Management of Defended Family and Civil Partnership Actions) 2022 (SSI 2022/289) r.2(23) (effective 25 September 2023 subject to transitional provision specified in SSI 2022/289 r.3).

Act or vulnerable witness application under section 12(6) of that Act has been lodged in respect of that witness.

Full Case Management Hearing

33A.36P.—[1](1) At the Full Case Management Hearing the sheriff must seek to secure the expeditious progress of the cause by ascertaining from the parties the matters in dispute and information about any other matter referred to in paragraph (3). **D1.387.16**

(2) It is the duty of the parties to provide the sheriff with sufficient information to enable the sheriff to conduct the hearing as provided for in this rule.

(3) At the Full Case Management Hearing each party must address the court on—

(a) any matters that are capable of agreement;

(b) the matters that are in dispute between the parties;

(c) any matters of potential complexity or difficulty;

(d) any valuations that are likely to be required;

(e) any expert or skilled witness evidence that is likely to be required and the scope for joint instruction;

(f) whether additional steps require to be taken to give a child an opportunity to express the child's views;

(g) whether steps require to be taken to investigate any facts or circumstances relating to a child;

(h) the suitability of the action for referral to mediation;

(i) whether special measures will be required for the purposes of taking the evidence of any vulnerable witnesses;

(j) the scope for use of affidavits and other documents in place of oral evidence;

(k) the extent to which the parties have complied with any orders made by the court;

(l) the number and availability of witnesses;

(m) the content, volume and form of productions;

(n) the requirement for access to IT equipment to view productions;

(o) whether sanction is sought for the employment of counsel;

(p) the progress of any legal aid application.

(4) After having heard parties at the Full Case Management Hearing the sheriff must close the record, fix a pre-proof hearing in accordance with Chapter 28A (pre-proof hearing) and—

(a) appoint the action to a proof and make such orders as to the extent of proof, the lodging of a joint minute of admissions or agreement, or such matter as the sheriff thinks fit;

(b) consider any note lodged under rule 22.1 (note of basis of preliminary pleas), appoint the cause to a proof before answer and make such orders as to the extent of the proof, the lodging of a joint minute of admissions or agreement, or such other matters as the sheriff thinks fit; or

(c) consider any note lodged under rule 22.1, appoint the cause to a debate if satisfied that there is a preliminary matter of law which if established following debate would lead to decree in favour of any party, or to limitation of proof to any substantial degree.

---

[1] Inserted by the Act of Sederunt (Ordinary Cause Rules 1993 Amendment) (Case Management of Defended Family and Civil Partnership Actions) 2022 (SSI 2022/289) r.2(23) (effective 25 September 2023 subject to transitional provision specified in SSI 2022/289 r.3).

(5) The diet fixed under paragraph (4)—

    (a) is to be assigned for the appropriate number of days for resolution of the issues with reference to the information provided under paragraph (3) and subject to paragraph (6);

    (b) may only be extended or varied on exceptional cause shown and subject to such orders (including awards of expenses) as the sheriff considers appropriate.

(6) The sheriff may make such orders as thought fit to ensure compliance with this rule and the expeditious resolution of the issues in dispute, including—

    (a) restricting the issues for proof;

    (b) the scope for instruction of a joint expert or a meeting between skilled persons;

    (c) excluding specified documents, reports or witnesses from proof;

    (d) fixing other hearings;

    (e) awarding expenses.

(7) The sheriff may, on cause shown, of the sheriff's own motion or on the motion of any party, allow a continuation of the Full Case Management Hearing on one occasion only for a period not exceeding 28 days or to the first suitable court day thereafter.

(8) On closing the record—

    (a) where there are no adjustments made since the lodging of the record under rule 33A.36N (record for Full Case Management Hearings), that record becomes the closed record;

    (b) where there are such adjustments, the sheriff may order that a closed record including such adjustments be lodged within 7 days after the date of the interlocutor closing the record.

Judicial continuity

D1.387.17   **33A.36Q.**—[1] Where possible, the same sheriff is to preside—

    (a) the Initial Case Management Hearings;

    (b) the Full Case Management Hearing;

    (c) the pre-proof hearing;

    (d) where fixed, any—

        (i) Child Welfare Hearing;

        (ii) proof;

        (iii) proof before answer;

        (iv) debate.

Decree by default

D1.388   **33A.37.**—(1) In a civil partnership action in which the defender has lodged a notice of intention to defend, where a party fails—

    (a) to lodge, or intimate the lodging of, any production or part of process;

    (b) to implement an order of the sheriff within a specified period; or

    (c) to appear or be represented at any diet,

that party shall be in default.

(2) Where a party is in default under paragraph (1), the sheriff may—

---

[1] Inserted by the Act of Sederunt (Ordinary Cause Rules 1993 Amendment) (Case Management of Defended Family and Civil Partnership Actions) 2022 (SSI 2022/289) r.2(23) (effective 25 September 2023 subject to transitional provision specified in SSI 2022/289 r.3).

(a)[1]   where the civil partnership action is one mentioned in rule 33A.1(1)(a), (b) or (f) allow that action to proceed as undefended under Part II of this Chapter; or

(b)   where the civil partnership action is one mentioned in rule 33A.1(1)(c) to (e), grant decree as craved; or

(c)   grant decree of absolvitor; or

(d)   dismiss the civil partnership action or any claim made or order sought; and

(e)   award expenses.

(3)   Where no party appears at a diet in a civil partnership action, the sheriff may dismiss that action.

(4)   In a civil partnership action, the sheriff may, on cause shown, prorogate the time for lodging any production or part of process, or for intimating or implementing any order.

Part IV – Applications And Orders Relating To Children In Certain Actions

Application and interpretation of this Part

33A.38.[2]   This Part applies to an action of dissolution or declarator of nullity of civil partnership or separation of civil partners.   **D1.389**

Applications in actions to which this Part applies

33A.39.—(1)   An application for an order mentioned in paragraph (2) shall be made—   **D1.390**

(a)   by a crave in the initial writ or defences, as the case may be, in an action to which this Part applies; or

(b)   where the application is made by a person other than the pursuer or defender, by minute in that action.

(2)   The orders referred to in paragraph (1) are:—

(a)   an order for a section 11 order; and

(b)   an order for aliment for a child.

Applications in depending actions by motion

33A.40.   An application by a party in an action depending before the court to which this Part applies for, or for variation of, an order for—   **D1.391**

(a)   interim aliment for a child under the age of 18; or

(b)   a residence order or a contact order,

shall be made by motion.

Applications after decree relating to a section 11 order

33A.41.—(1)   An application after final decree for, or for the variation or recall of, a section 11 order or in relation to the enforcement of such an order shall be made by minute in the process of the action to which the application relates.   **D1.392**

(2)   Where a minute has been lodged under paragraph (1), any party may apply by motion for any interim order which may be made pending the determination of the application.

---

[1] As amended by Act of Sederunt (Ordinary Cause Rules) Amendment (Family Law (Scotland) Act 2006 etc.) 2006 (SSI 2006/207) para.2 (effective 4 May 2006).

[2] As amended by Act of Sederunt (Ordinary Cause Rules) Amendment (Family Law (Scotland) Act 2006 etc.) 2006 (SSI 2006/207) para.2 (effective 4 May 2006).

Warrants for intimation to child and permission to seek views

D1.392.1   **33A.41A.**—[1](1)   Subject to paragraph (2), when lodging a minute under rule 14.3 (lodging of minutes) which includes a crave after final decree for, or the variation or recall of, a section 11 order in respect of a child who is not a party to the action, the minuter must—

(a)   include in the minute a crave for a warrant for intimation and the seeking of the child's views in Form F9;

(b)   when lodging the minute, submit a draft Form F9, showing the details that the minuter proposes to include when the form is sent to the child.

(2)   Where the minuter considers that it would be inappropriate to send Form F9 to the child (for example, where the child is under 5 years of age), the minuter must include in the minute—

(a)   a crave to dispense with intimation and the seeking of the child's views in Form F9;

(b)   averments setting out the reasons why it is inappropriate to send Form F9 to the child.

(3)   The sheriff must be satisfied that the draft Form F9 submitted under paragraph (1)(b) has been drafted appropriately.

(4)   The sheriff may dispense with intimation and the seeking of views in Form F9 or make any other order that the sheriff considers appropriate.

(5)   An order granting warrant for intimation and the seeking of the child's views in Form F9 under this rule must—

(a)   state that the Form F9 must be sent in accordance with rule 33A.41A(6);

(b)   be signed by the sheriff.

(6)   The Form F9 must be sent in accordance with—

(a)   rule 33A.41B (views of the child – unopposed minutes relating to a section 11 order), where the minute is unopposed;

(b)   rule 33A.41C (views of the child – craves relating to a section 11 order sought by minuter only), where the minute is opposed and a section 11 order is sought by the minuter only; or

(c)   rule 33A.41D (views of the child – craves relating to a section 11 order sought by both minuter and respondent), where a section 11 order is sought by both the minuter and the respondent.

Views of the child – unopposed minutes relating to a section 11 order

D1.392.2   **33A.41B.**—[2](1)   This rule applies to minutes which include a crave after final decree for, or the variation or recall of, a section 11 order in respect of which no notice of opposition or answers are lodged and warrant has been granted for intimation and the seeking of the child's views in Form F9.

(2)   The minuter must—

(a)   send the child the Form F9 that was submitted and approved under rule 33A.41A (warrants for intimation to child and permission to seek views);

(b)   on the same day, lodge a certificate of intimation in Form F9A;

(c)   not send the child a copy of the minute.

(3)   Except on cause shown, the sheriff must not determine the minute in the period of 28 days following the date on which the Form F9 was sent to the child.

---

[1] As inserted by the Act of Sederunt (Rules of the Court of Session 1994 and Ordinary Cause Rules 1993 Amendment) (Views of the Child) 2019 (SSI 2019/123) r.3 (effective 24 June 2019).

[2] As inserted by the Act of Sederunt (Rules of the Court of Session 1994 and Ordinary Cause Rules 1993 Amendment) (Views of the Child) 2019 (SSI 2019/123) r.3 (effective 24 June 2019).

Views of the child – craves relating to a section 11 order sought by minuter only

33A.41C.—[1](1)   This rule applies where a notice of opposition or answers have been lodged in respect of a minute after final decree and a crave for, or the variation or recall of, a section 11 order is sought by the minuter only and warrant has been granted for intimation and the seeking of the child's views in Form F9.

(2)   The minuter must—

    (a)   no later than 14 days after the notice of opposition or answers are lodged, send the child the Form F9 that was submitted and approved under rule 33A.41A (warrants for intimation to child and permission to seek views);

    (b)   on the same day, lodge a certificate of intimation in Form F9A;

    (c)   not send the child a copy of the minute, the notice of opposition or answers.

D1.392.3

Views of the child – craves relating to a section 11 order sought by both minuter and respondent

33A.41D.—[2](1)   This rule applies where a notice of opposition or answers have been lodged in respect of a minute after final decree and craves for, or the variation or recall of, a section 11 order are sought by both the minuter and the respondent and warrant has been granted for intimation and the seeking of the child's views in Form F9.

(2)   The minuter must—

    (a)   no later than 14 days after the notice of opposition or answers are lodged, send the child the Form F9 that was submitted and approved under rule 33A.41A (warrants for intimation to child and permission to seek views), amended so as also to narrate the section 11 order sought by the respondent;

    (b)   on the same day—

        (i)   lodge a certificate of intimation in Form F9A;

        (ii)   send the respondent a copy of the Form F9 that was sent to the child;

    (c)   not send the child a copy of the minute, the notice of opposition or answers.

D1.392.4

[THE NEXT PARAGRAPH IS D1.393]

Applications after decree relating to aliment

33A.42.—(1)   An application after final decree for, or for the variation or recall of, an order for aliment for a child shall be made by minute in the process of the action to which the application relates.

(2)   Where a minute has been lodged under paragraph (1), any party may lodge a motion for any interim order which may be made pending the determination of the application.

D1.393

Applications after decree by persons over 18 years for aliment

33A.43—(1)   A person—

    (a)   to whom an obligation of aliment is owed under section 1 of the Act of 1985;

D1.394

---

[1] As inserted by the Act of Sederunt (Rules of the Court of Session 1994 and Ordinary Cause Rules 1993 Amendment) (Views of the Child) 2019 (SSI 2019/123) r.3 (effective 24 June 2019).

[2] As inserted by the Act of Sederunt (Rules of the Court of Session 1994 and Ordinary Cause Rules 1993 Amendment) (Views of the Child) 2019 (SSI 2019/123) r.3 (effective 24 June 2019).

(b)   in whose favour an order for aliment while under the age of 18 years was made in an action to which this Part applies, and

(c)   who seeks, after attaining that age, an order for aliment against the person in that action against whom the order for aliment in his favour was made,

shall apply by minute in the process of that action.

(2)   An application for interim aliment pending the determination of an application under paragraph (1) shall be made by motion.

(3)   Where a decree has been pronounced in an application under paragraph (1) or (2), any application for variation or recall of any such decree shall be made by minute in the process of the action to which the application relates.

Part V – Orders Relating To Financial Provisions

Application and interpretation of this Part

D1.395   **33A.44.**—[1](1)   This Part applies to an action of dissolution or declarator of nullity of civil partnership.

(2)   In this Part, "incidental order" has the meaning assigned in section 14(2) of the Act of 1985.

Applications in actions to which this Part applies

D1.396   **33A.45.**—(1)   An application for an order mentioned in paragraph (2) shall be made—

(a)   by a crave in the initial writ or defences, as the case may be, in an action to which this Part applies; or

(b)   where the application is made by a person other than the pursuer or defender, by minute in that action.

(2)   The orders referred to in paragraph (1) are:—

(a)   an order for financial provision within the meaning of section 8(3) of the Act of 1985;

(b)   an order under section 16(1)(b) or (3) of the Act of 1985 (setting aside or varying agreement as to financial provision);

(c)   an order under section 18 of the Act of 1985 (which relates to avoidance transactions); and

(d)   an order under section 112 of the Act of 2004 (transfer of tenancy).

Applications in depending actions relating to incidental orders

D1.397   **33A.46.**—(1)   In an action depending before the sheriff to which this Part applies—

(a)   the pursuer or defender, notwithstanding rules 33A.34(2) (application by defender for order for financial provision) and 33A.45(1)(a) (application for order for financial provision in initial writ or defences), may apply by motion for an incidental order; and

(b)   the sheriff shall not be bound to determine such a motion if he considers that the application should properly be by a crave in the initial writ or defences, as the case may be.

(2)   In an action depending before the sheriff to which this Part applies, an application under section 14(4) of the Act of 1985 for the variation or recall of an incidental order shall be made by minute in the process of the action to which the application relates.

---

[1] As amended by Act of Sederunt (Ordinary Cause Rules) Amendment (Family Law (Scotland) Act 2006 etc.) 2006, para.2 (SSI 2006/207) (effective 4 May 2006).

Applications relating to interim aliment

33A.47. An application for, or for the variation or recall of, an order for interim   **D1.398**
aliment for the pursuer or defender shall be made by motion.

Applications relating to orders for financial provision

33A.48.—(1) An application—   **D1.399**
- (a) after final decree under any of the following provisions of the Act of
  1985—
  - (i) section 8(1) for periodical allowance;
  - (ii) section 12(1)(b) (payment of capital sum or transfer of property);
  - (iii) section 12(4) (variation of date or method of payment of capital sum or date of transfer of property); or
  - (iv) section 13(4) (variation, recall, backdating or conversion of periodical allowance); or
  - (v)[1] section 14(1) (incidental orders), or
- (b) after the grant or refusal of an application under—
  - (i) section 8(1) or 14(3) for an incidental order; or
  - (ii) section 14(4) (variation or recall of incidental order),

shall be made by minute in the process of the action to which the application relates.

(2) Where a minute is lodged under paragraph (1), any party may lodge a motion for any interim order which may be made pending the determination of the application.

(3) An application under—
- (a) paragraph (5) of section 12A of the Act of 1985 (recall or variation of order in respect of a pension lump sum);
- (b) paragraph (7) of that section (variation of order in respect of pension lump sum to substitute trustees or managers);
- (ba)[2] section 12B(4) of the Act of 1985 (recall or variation of a capital sum order); or
- (c) section 28(10) or 48(9) of the Welfare Reform and Pensions Act 1999,

shall be made by minute in the process of the action to which the application relates.

Pension Protection Fund notification

33A.48A.—[3](1) In this rule—   **D1.400**

"assessment period" shall be construed in accordance with section 132 of the Pensions Act 2004;

"pension arrangement" shall be construed in accordance with the definition in section 27 of the Act of 1985; and

"valuation summary" shall be construed in accordance with the definition in Schedule 2 to the Pension Protection Fund (Provision of Information) Regulations 2005.

(2) This rule applies where a party at any stage in the proceedings applies for an order under section 8 or section 16 of the Act of 1985.

---

[1] As inserted by the Act of Sederunt (Sheriff Court Rules) (Miscellaneous Amendments) (No.3) 2011 (SSI 2011/386) para.2 (effective 28 November 2011).

[2] As inserted by the Act of Sederunt (Sheriff Court Rules) (Miscellaneous Amendments) 2011 (SSI 2011/193) r.15 (effective 6 April 2011).

[3] As inserted by the Act of Sederunt (Sheriff Court Rules) (Miscellaneous Amendments) 2008 (SSI 2008/223) r.3(3) (effective 1 July 2008).

(3)   Where the party against whom an order referred to in paragraph (2) is sought has received notification in compliance with the Pension Protection Fund (Provision of Information) Regulations 2005 or does so after the order is sought—

(a)   that there is an assessment period in relation to his pension arrangement; or

(b)   that the Board of the Pension Protection Fund has assumed responsibility for all or part of his pension arrangement, he shall comply with paragraph (4).

(4)   The party shall—

(a)   lodge the notification; and

(b)   obtain and lodge as soon as reasonably practicable thereafter—

(i)   a valuation summary; and

(ii)   a forecast of his compensation entitlement.

(5)   Subject to paragraph (6), the notification referred to in paragraph (4)(a) requires to be lodged—

(a)   where the notification is received before the order is sought, within 7 days of the order being sought;

(b)   where the notification is received after the order is sought, within 7 days of receiving the notification.

(6)   Where an order is sought against the defender before the defences are lodged, and the notification is received before that step occurs, the notification shall be lodged with the defences.

(7)   At the same time as lodging documents under paragraph (4), copies shall be sent to the other party to the proceedings.

Applications after decree relating to agreements and avoidance transactions

D1.401   **33A.49.**   An application for an order—

(a)   under section 16(1)(a) or (3) of the Act of 1985 (setting aside or varying agreements as to financial provision), or

(b)   under section 18 of the Act of 1985 (which relates to avoidance transactions), made after final decree shall be made by minute in the process of the action to which the application relates.

Part VI – Applications Relating To Avoidance Transactions

Form of applications

D1.402   **33A.50.**—(1)   An application for an order under section 18 of the Act of 1985 (which relates to avoidance transactions) by a party to a civil partnership action shall be made by including in the initial writ, defences or minute, as the case may be, appropriate craves, averments and pleas in law.

(2)   An application for an order under section 18 of the Act of 1985 after final decree in a civil partnership action shall be made by minute in the process of the action to which the application relates.

Part VII – Financial Provision After Overseas Proceedings

Interpretation of this Part

D1.403   **33A.51.**   In this Part—

"order for financial provision" has the meaning assigned in paragraph 4 of Schedule 11 to the Act of 2004;

"overseas proceedings" has the meaning assigned in paragraph 1(1)(a) of Schedule 11 to the Act of 2004.

Applications for financial provision after overseas proceedings

33A.52.—(1) An application under paragraph 2(1) of Schedule 11 to the Act of 2004 for an order for financial provision after overseas proceedings shall be made by initial writ.

D1.404

(2) An application for an order in an action to which paragraph (1) applies made before final decree under—

(a) section 112 of the Act of 2004 (transfer of tenancy of family home);
(b) paragraph 3(4) of Schedule 11 to the Act of 2004 for interim periodical allowance; or
(c) section 14(4) of the Act of 1985 (variation or recall of incidental order), shall be made by motion.

(3) An application for an order in an action to which paragraph (1) applies made after final decree under—

(a) section 12(4) of the Act of 1985 (variation of date or method of payment of capital sum or date of transfer of property);
(b) section 13(4) of the Act of 1985 (variation, recall, backdating or conversion of periodical allowance); or
(c) section 14(4) of the Act of 1985 (variation or recall of incidental order), shall be made by minute in the process of the action to which it relates.

(4) An application under—

(a) paragraph (5) of section 12A of the Act of 1985 (recall or variation of order in respect of a pension lump sum); or
(b) paragraph (7) of that section (variation of order in respect of pension lump sum to substitute trustees or managers), shall be made by minute in the process of the action to which the application relates.

(5) Where a minute has been lodged under paragraph (3), any party may apply by motion for an interim order pending the determination of the application.

Part VIII – Actions In Respect Of Aliment

Applications relating to agreements on aliment

33A.53. In a civil partnership action in which a crave for aliment may be made, an application under section 7(2) of the Act of 1985 shall be made by a crave in the initial writ or in defences, as the case may be.

D1.405

Part IX – Applications For Orders Under Section it Of The Children (Scotland) Act 1995

Application of this Part

33A.54[1] This Part applies to an application for a section 11 order in a civil partnership action other than in an action of dissolution or declarator of nullity of civil partnership or separation of civil partners.

D1.406

Form of applications

33A.55. Subject to any other provision in this Chapter, an application for a section 11 order shall be made—

D1.407

(a) by a crave in the initial writ or defences, as the case may be, in a civil partnership action to which this Part applies; or
(b) where the application is made by a person other than a party to an action mentioned in paragraph (a), by minute in that action.

---

[1] As amended by Act of Sederunt (Ordinary Cause Rules) Amendment (Family Law (Scotland) Act 2006 etc.) 2006, para.2 (SSI 2006/207) (effective 4 May 2006).

Applications relating to interim orders in depending actions

D1.408   **33A.56.** An application, in an action depending before the sheriff to which this Part applies, for, or for the variation or recall of, an interim residence order or an interim contact order shall be made—

     (a)   by a party to the action, by motion; or

     (b)   by a person who is not a party to the action, by minute.

Applications after decree

D1.409   **33A.57.**—(1) An application after final decree for variation or recall of a section 11 order shall be made by minute in the process of the action to which the application relates.

(2) Where a minute has been lodged under paragraph (1), any party may apply by motion for an interim order pending the determination of the application.

(3)[1] Rules 33A.41A (warrants for intimation to child and permission to seek views) to 33A.41D (views of the child – craves relating to a section 11 order sought by both minuter and respondent) apply (with the necessary modifications) to the seeking of the child's views in relation to a minute lodged in accordance with this rule.

Application for leave

D1.410   **33A.57A.**—[2](1) Where leave of the court is required under section 11(3)(aa) of the Act of 1995 for the making of an application for a contact order under that section, the applicant must lodge along with the initial writ a written application in the form of a letter addressed to the sheriff clerk stating—

     (a)   the grounds of which leave is sought; and

     (b)   whether or not the applicant has applied for legal aid.

(2) Where the applicant has applied for legal aid he must also lodge along with the initial writ written confirmation from the Scottish Legal Aid Board that it has determined, under regulation 7(2)(b) of the Civil Legal Aid (Scotland) Regulations 2002, that notification of the application for legal aid should be dispensed with or postponed pending the making by the sheriff of an order for intimation under paragraph (4)(b).

(3) Subject to paragraph (4)(b) an application under paragraph (1) shall not be served or intimated to any party.

(4) The sheriff shall consider an application under paragraph (1) without hearing the applicant and may—

     (a)   refuse the application and pronounce an interlocutor accordingly; or

     (b)   if he is minded to grant the application order the applicant—

         (i)   to intimate the application to such persons as the sheriff considers appropriate; and

         (ii)   to lodge a certificate of intimation in, as near as may be, Form G8.

(5) If any person who receives intimation of an application under paragraph (4)(b) wishes to be heard he shall notify the sheriff clerk in writing within 14 days of receipt of intimation of the application.

(6) On receipt of any notification under paragraph (5) the sheriff clerk shall fix a hearing and intimate the date of the hearing to the parties.

---

[1] As inserted by the Act of Sederunt (Rules of the Court of Session 1994 and Ordinary Cause Rules 1993 Amendment) (Views of the Child) 2019 (SSI 2019/123) r.3 (effective 24 June 2019).

[2] As inserted by the Act of Sederunt (Sheriff Court Rules Amendment) (Adoption and Children (Scotland) Act 2007) 2009 (SSI 2009/284) (effective 28 September 2009).

(7)   Where an application under paragraph (1) is granted, a copy of the sheriffs interlocutor must be served on the defender along with the warrant of citation.

Part X – Actions Relating To Occupancy Rights And Tenancies

Application of this Part

33A.58.   This Part applies to an action or application for an order under Chapter 3 or Chapter 4 of Part 3 or section 127 of the Act of 2004.   **D1.411**

Interpretation of this Part

33A.59.   Unless the context otherwise requires, words and expressions used in this Part which are also used in Chapter 3 or Chapter 4 of Part 3 of the Act of 2004 have the same meaning as in Chapter 3 or Chapter 4, as the case may be.   **D1.412**

Form of application

33A.60.—(1)   Subject to any other provision in this Chapter, an application for an order under this Part shall be made—   **D1.413**
- (a)   by an action for such an order;
- (b)   by a crave in the initial writ or defences, as the case may be, in any other civil partnership action;
- (c)   where the application is made by a person other than a party to any action mentioned in paragraph (a) or (b), by minute in that action.

(2)   An application under section 107(1) (dispensation with civil partner's consent to dealing) or section 127 (application in relation to attachment) of the Act of 2004 shall, unless made in a depending civil partnership action, be made by summary application.

Defenders

33A.61.   The applicant for an order under this Part shall call as a defender—   **D1.414**
- (a)   where he is seeking an order as a civil partner, the other civil partner; and
- (b)   where he is a third party making an application under section 107(1) (dispensation with civil partner's consent to dealing), or 108(1) (payment from non-entitled civil partner in respect of loan) of the Act of 2004, both civil partners.

Applications by motion

33A.62.—(1)   An application under any of the following provisions of the Act of 2004 shall be made by motion in the process of the depending action to which the application relates—   **D1.415**
- (a)   section 103(4) (interim order for regulation of rights of occupancy, etc.);
- (b)   section 104(6) (interim order suspending occupancy rights);
- (c)   section 107(1) (dispensation with civil partner's consent to dealing); and
- (d)   *[Omitted by Act of Sederunt (Ordinary Cause Rules) Amendment (Family Law (Scotland) Act 2006 etc.) 2006, para.2 (SSI 2006/207) (effective May 4, 2006).]*

(2)   Intimation of a motion under paragraph (1) shall be given—
- (a)   to the other civil partner;
- (b)   where the motion is under paragraph (1)(a) or (b) and the entitled civil partner is a tenant or occupies the family home by the permission of a third party, to the landlord or third party, as the case may be; and
- (c)   to any other person to whom intimation of the application was or is to be made by virtue of rule 33A.7(1)(i) (warrant for intimation to certain persons in actions for orders under Chapter 3 of Part 3 of the Act of 2004) or rule 33A.15 (order for intimation by sheriff).

Applications by minute

D1.416   **33A.63.**—(1) An application for an order under section 105 of the Act of 2004 (variation and recall of orders made under section 103 or section 104 of the Act of 2004) shall be made by minute.

(2) A minute under paragraph (1) shall be intimated—

(a) to the other civil partner;

(b) where the entitled civil partner is a tenant or occupies the family home by the permission of a third party, to the landlord or third party, as the case may be; and

(c) to any other person to whom intimation of the application was or is to be made by virtue of rule 33A.7(1)(i) (warrant for intimation to certain persons in actions for orders under Chapter 3 of Part 3 of the Act of 2004) or rule 33A.15 (order for intimation by sheriff).

Sist of actions to enforce occupancy rights

D1.417   **33A.64.** Unless the sheriff otherwise directs, the sist of an action by virtue of section 107(4) of the Act of 2004 (where action raised by non entitled civil partner to enforce occupancy rights) shall apply only to such part of the action as relates to the enforcement of occupancy rights by a non entitled civil partner.

Certificates of delivery of documents to chief constable

33A.65. *[Omitted by Act of Sederunt (Ordinary Cause Rules) Amendment (Family Law (Scotland) Act 2006 etc.) 2006, para.2 (SSI 2006/207) (effective May 4, 2006).]*

Part XI – Simplified Dissolution Of Civil Partnership Applications

Application and interpretation of this Part

D1.418   **33A.66.**—(1) This Part applies to an application for dissolution of civil partnership by a party to a civil partnership made in the manner prescribed in rule 33A.67 (form of applications) if, but only if—

(a)[1] that party relies on the facts set out in section 117(3)(c) (no cohabitation for one year with consent of defender to decree), section 117(3)(d) (no cohabitation for two years), or section 117(2)(b) (issue of interim gender recognition certificate) of the Act of 2004;

(b) in an application under section 117(3)(c) of the Act of 2004, the other party consents to decree of dissolution of civil partnership being granted;

(c) no other proceedings are pending in any court which could have the effect of bringing the civil partnership to an end;

(d)[2] there is no child of the family (as defined in section 12(4)(b) of the Act of 1995) under the age of 16 years;

(e) neither party to the civil partnership applies for an order for financial provision on dissolution of civil partnership; and

(f) neither party to the civil partnership suffers from mental disorder.

(2) If an application ceases to be one to which this Part applies at any time before final decree, it shall be deemed to be abandoned and shall be dismissed.

(3) In this Part "simplified dissolution of civil partnership application" means an application mentioned in paragraph (1).

---

[1] As amended by Act of Sederunt (Ordinary Cause Rules) Amendment (Family Law (Scotland) Act 2006 etc.) 2006, para.2 (SSI 2006/207) (effective 4 May 2006).
[2] As amended by the Act of Sederunt (Sheriff Court Rules) (Miscellaneous Amendments) 2012 (SSI 2012/188) para.9 (effective August 1, 2012).

Form of applications

33A.67.—(1) A simplified dissolution of civil partnership application in which the facts set out in section 117(3)(c) of the Act of 2004 (no cohabitation for two years with consent of defender to decree) are relied on shall be made in Form CP29 and shall only be of effect if—

    (a)   it is signed by the applicant; and

    (b)   the form of consent in Part 2 of Form CP29 is signed by the party to the civil partnership giving consent.

(2) A simplified dissolution of civil partnership application in which the facts set out in section 117(3)(d) of the Act of 2004 (no cohabitation for five years) are relied on shall be made in Form CP30 and shall only be of effect if it is signed by the applicant.

(3) A simplified dissolution of civil partnership application in which the facts set out in section 117(2)(b) of the Act of 2004 (issue of interim gender recognition certificate) are relied on shall be made in Form CP31 and shall only be of effect if it is signed by the applicant.

D1.419

Lodging of applications

33A.68. The applicant shall send a simplified dissolution of civil partnership application to the sheriff clerk with—

    (a)   an extract or certified copy of the civil partnership certificate;

    (b)   the appropriate fee; and

    (c)   in an application under section 117(2)(b) of the Act of 2004, the interim gender recognition certificate or a certified copy, within the meaning of rule 33A.9(4).

D1.420

Citation and intimation

33A.69.—(1) This rule is subject to rule 33A.70 (citation where address not known).

(2) It shall be the duty of the sheriff clerk to cite any person or intimate any document in connection with a simplified dissolution of civil partnership application.

(3) The form of citation—

    (a)   in an application relying on the facts in section 117(3)(c) of the Act of 2004 shall be in Form CP32;

    (b)   in an application relying on the facts in section 117(3)(d) of the Act of 2004 shall be in Form CP33; and

    (c)   in an application relying on the facts in section 117(2)(b) of the Act of 2004 shall be in Form CP34.

(4) The citation or intimation required by paragraph (2) shall be made—

    (a)   by the sheriff clerk by registered post or the first class recorded delivery service in accordance with rule 5.3 (postal service or intimation);

    (b)[1]   on payment of an additional fee, by a sheriff officer in accordance with rule 5.4(1) to (4) (service within Scotland by sheriff officer); or

    (c)   where necessary, by the sheriff clerk in accordance with rule 5.5 (service on persons furth of Scotland).

(5) Where citation or intimation is made in accordance with paragraph (4)(c), the translation into an official language of the country in which service is to be executed required by rule 5.5(6) shall be provided by the party lodging the simplified dissolution of civil partnership application.

D1.421

---

[1] As substituted by the Act of Sederunt (Sheriff Court Rules) (Miscellaneous Amendments) 2010 (SSI 2010/279) r.3 (effective July 29, 2010).

Citation where address not known

D1.422   **33A.70.**—(1)[1] In a simplified dissolution of civil partnership application in which the facts in section 117(3)(d) (no cohabitation for two years) or section 117(2)(b) (issue of interim gender recognition certificate) of the Act of 2004 are relied on and the address of the other party to the civil partnership is not known and cannot reasonably be ascertained—

    (a) citation shall be executed by displaying a copy of the application and a notice in Form CP35 on the walls of court on a period of notice of 21 days; and

    (b) intimation shall be made to—

        (i)[2] every person who was a child of the family (within the meaning of section 101(7) of the Act of 2004) who has reached the age of 16 years, and

        (ii) one of the next of kin of the other party to the civil partnership who has reached that age, unless the address of such person is not known and cannot reasonably be ascertained.

(2) Intimation to a person referred to in paragraph (1)(b) shall be given by intimating a copy of the application and a notice of intimation in Form CP36.

Opposition to applications

D1.423   **33A.71.**—(1) Any person on whom service or intimation of a simplified dissolution of civil partnership application has been made may give notice by letter sent to the sheriff clerk that he challenges the jurisdiction of the court or opposes the grant of decree of dissolution of civil partnership and giving the reasons for his opposition to the application.

(2) Where opposition to a simplified dissolution of civil partnership application is made under paragraph (1), the sheriff shall dismiss the application unless he is satisfied that the reasons given for the opposition are frivolous.

(3) The sheriff clerk shall intimate the decision under paragraph (2) to the applicant and the respondent.

(4) The sending of a letter under paragraph (1) shall not imply acceptance of the jurisdiction of the court.

Evidence

D1.424   **33A.72.** Parole evidence shall not be given in a simplified dissolution of civil partnership application.

Decree

D1.425   **33A.73.**—(1) The sheriff may grant decree in terms of the simplified dissolution of civil partnership application on the expiry of the period of notice if such application has been properly served provided that, when the application has been served in a country to which the Hague Convention on the Service Abroad of Judicial and Extra Judicial Documents in Civil or Commercial Matters dated 15 November 1965 applies, decree shall not be granted until it is established to the satisfaction of the sheriff that the requirements of article 15 of that Convention have been complied with.

---

[1] As amended by Act of Sederunt (Ordinary Cause Rules) Amendment (Family Law (Scotland) Act 2006 etc.) 2006, para.2 (SSI 2006/207) (effective 4 May 2006).

[2] As amended by the Act of Sederunt (Sheriff Court Rules) (Miscellaneous Amendments) 2012 (SSI 2012/188) para.9 (effective August 1, 2012).

(2) The sheriff clerk shall, not sooner than 14 days after the granting of decree in terms of paragraph (1), issue to each party to the civil partnership an extract of the decree of dissolution of civil partnership in Form CP37.

Appeals

33A.74.—[1](1) Any appeal against an interlocutor granting decree of dissolution of civil partnership under rule 33A.73 (decree) may be made, within 14 days after the date of decree, by sending a letter to the court giving reasons for the appeal.

D1.426

(2) Within 4 days after receiving an appeal, the sheriff clerk must transmit to the Clerk of the Sheriff Appeal Court—

(a) the appeal;

(b) all documents and productions in the simplified dissolution of civil partnership application.

(3) On receipt of the appeal, the Clerk of the Sheriff Appeal Court is to fix a hearing and intimate the date, time and place of that hearing to the parties.

Applications after decree

33A.75. Any application to the court after decree of dissolution of civil partnership has been granted in a simplified dissolution of civil partnership application which could have been made if it had been made in an action of dissolution of civil partnership shall be made by minute.

D1.427

Part XII – Referrals To Principal Reporter

33A.76.–33A.78. *[Repealed by the Act of Sederunt (Children's Hearings (Scotland) Act 2011) (Miscellaneous Amendments) 2013 (SI 2013/172) para.5 (effective June 24, 2013).]*

Part XIII – Sisting Of Civil Partnership Actions

Application and interpretation of this Part

33A.79.—(1) This Part applies to any action for—

D1.428

dissolution of civil partnership;

separation of civil partners.

(2) In this Part—

"another jurisdiction" means any country outside Scotland.

"related jurisdiction" means any of the following countries, namely, England and Wales, Northern Ireland, Jersey, Guernsey and the Isle of Man (the reference to Guernsey being treated as including Alderney and Sark).

(3) For the purposes of this Part—

(a) neither the taking of evidence on commission nor a separate proof relating to any preliminary plea shall be regarded as part of the proof in the action; and

(b) an action is continuing if it is pending and not sisted.

(4) Any reference in this Part to proceedings in another jurisdiction is to proceedings in a court or before an administrative authority of that jurisdiction.

Duty to furnish particulars of concurrent proceedings

33A.80. While any action to which this Part applies is pending in a sheriff court and proof in that action has not begun, it shall be the duty of the pursuer, and of any other person who has entered appearance in the action, to furnish, in such manner

D1.429

---

[1] As amended by the Act of Sederunt (Rules of the Court of Session, Sheriff Appeal Court Rules and Sheriff Court Rules Amendment) (Sheriff Appeal Court) 2015 (SSI 2015/419) r.5 (effective 1 January 2016).

and to such persons and on such occasions as may be prescribed, such particulars as may be so prescribed of any proceedings which—

(a) he knows to be continuing in another jurisdiction; and

(b) are in respect of that civil partnership or capable of affecting its validity.

Mandatory sists

D1.430

33A.81. Where before the beginning of the proof in any action for dissolution of civil partnership it appears to the sheriff on the application of a party to the civil partnership—

(a) that in respect of the same civil partnership proceedings for dissolution or nullity of civil partnership are continuing in a related jurisdiction; and

(b) that the parties to the civil partnership have resided together after the civil partnership was formed or treated as having been formed within the meaning of section 1(1) of the Act of 2004; and

(c) that the place where they resided together when the action was begun or, if they did not then reside together, where they last resided together before the date on which that action was begun is in that jurisdiction; and

(d) that either of the said parties was habitually resident in that jurisdiction throughout the year ending with the date on which they last resided together before the date on which that action was begun;

it shall be the duty of the sheriff, subject to rule 33A.83(2) below, to sist the action before him.

Discretionary sists

D1.431

33A.82.—(1) Where before the beginning of the proof in any action to which this Part applies, it appears to the sheriff—

(a) that any other proceedings in respect of the civil partnership in question or capable of affecting its validity are continuing in another jurisdiction, and

(b) that the balance of fairness (including convenience) as between the parties to the civil partnership is such that it is appropriate for those other proceedings to be disposed of before further steps are taken in the action,

the sheriff may then if he thinks fit sist that action.

(2) In considering the balance of fairness and convenience for the purposes of paragraph (1)(b), the sheriff shall have regard to all factors appearing to be relevant, including the convenience of witnesses and any delay or expense which may result from the proceedings being sisted, or not being sisted.

(3) Paragraph (1) is without prejudice to the duty imposed by rule 33A.81 above.

(4) If, at any time after the beginning of the proof in any action to which this Part applies, the sheriff is satisfied that a person has failed to perform the duty imposed on him in respect of the action and any such other proceedings as aforesaid by rule 33A.80, paragraph (1) shall have effect in relation to that action and to the other proceedings as if the words "before the beginning of the proof" were omitted; but no action in respect of the failure of a person to perform such a duty shall be competent.

Recall of sists

D1.432

33A.83.—(1) Where an action is sisted in pursuance of rule 33A.81 or 33A.82, the sheriff may if he thinks fit, on the application of a party to the action, recall the sist if it appears to him that the other proceedings by reference to which the action was sisted are sisted or concluded or that a party to those other proceedings has delayed unreasonably in prosecuting those other proceedings.

(2) Where an action has been sisted in pursuance of rule 33A.82 by reference to some other proceedings, and the sheriff recalls the sist in pursuance of the preceding paragraph, the sheriff shall not again sist the action in pursuance of the said rule 33A.82.

Orders in sisted actions

33A.84.—(1) The provisions of paragraphs (2) and (3) shall apply where an action to which this Part applies is sisted by reference to proceedings in a related jurisdiction for any of those remedies; and in this rule—

D1.433

> "the other proceedings", in relation to any sisted action, means the proceedings in another jurisdiction by reference to which the action was sisted;
> "relevant order" means an interim order relating to aliment or children; and
> "sisted" means sisted in pursuance of this Part.

(2) Where an action such as is mentioned in paragraph (1) is sisted, then, without prejudice to the effect of the sist apart from this paragraph—

    (a)   the sheriff shall not have power to make a relevant order in connection with the sisted action except in pursuance of sub paragraph (c); and

    (b)   subject to the said sub paragraph (c), any relevant order made in connection with the sisted action shall (unless the sist or the relevant order has been previously recalled) cease to have effect on the expiration of the period of three months beginning with the date on which the sist comes into operation; but

    (c)   if the sheriff considers that as a matter of necessity and urgency it is necessary during or after that period to make a relevant order in connection with the sisted action or to extend or further extend the duration of a relevant order made in connection with the sisted action, the sheriff may do so, and the order shall not cease to have effect by virtue of sub paragraph (b).

(3) Where any action such as is mentioned in paragraph (1) is sisted and at the time when the sist comes into operation, an order is in force, or at a subsequent time an order comes into force, being an order made in connection with the other proceedings and providing for any of the following matters, namely periodical payments for a party to the civil partnership in question, periodical payments for a child, the arrangements to be made as to with whom a child is to live, contact with a child, and any other matter relating to parental responsibilities or parental rights, then, as from the time when the sist comes into operation (in a case where the order is in force at that time) or (in any other case) on the coming into force of the order—

    (a)   any relevant order made in connection with the sisted action shall cease to have effect in so far as it makes for a civil partner or child any provision for any of the said matters as respects which the same or different provision for that civil partner or child is made by the other order; and

    (b)   the sheriff shall not have power in connection with the sisted action to make a relevant order containing for a civil partner or child provision for any of the matters aforesaid as respects which any provision for that civil partner or child is made by the other order.

(4) Nothing in this paragraph affects any power of a sheriff—

    (a)   to vary or recall a relevant order in so far as the order is for the time being in force; or

    (b)   to enforce a relevant order as respects any period when it is or was in force; or

(c) to make a relevant order in connection with an action which was, but is no longer, sisted.

Chapter 33AA[1]

Expeditious Resolution of Certain Causes

Application of Chapter

D1.434   **33AA.1.** This Chapter applies where a cause is proceeding to proof or proof before answer in respect of a crave for an order under section 11 of the Children (Scotland) Act 1995 (court orders relating to parental responsibilities etc.).

Fixing date for Case Management Hearing

D1.435   **33AA.2.**—(1) The sheriff shall fix a date for a case management hearing—

(a) at the Options Hearing in accordance with rule 9.12(3)(f);
(b) at the Procedural Hearing in accordance with rule 10.6(3)(f);
(c) on the motion of any party; or
(d) on the sheriff's own motion.

(2) Except on cause shown, the date and time to be fixed under paragraph (1) shall be not less than 14 days and not more than 28 days after the interlocutor appointing the cause to a proof or proof before answer.

Pre-hearing conference

D1.436   **33AA.3.**—(1) In advance of the case management hearing the parties shall hold a prehearing conference, at which parties must—

(a) discuss settlement of the action;
(b) agree, so far as is possible, the matters which are not in dispute between them;
(c) discuss the information referred to in rule 33AA.4(1).

(2) Prior to the case management hearing the pursuer shall lodge with the court a joint minute of the pre-hearing conference or explain to the sheriff why such a minute has not been lodged.

(3) If a party is not present during the pre-hearing conference, that party's representative must be able to contact the party during the conference, and be in full possession of all relevant facts.

Case Management Hearing

D1.437   **33AA.4.**—(1) At the case management hearing the parties must provide the sheriff with sufficient information to enable the sheriff to ascertain—

(a) the nature of the issues in dispute, including any questions of admissibility of evidence or any other legal issues;
(b) the state of the pleadings and whether amendment will be required;
(c) the state of preparation of the parties;
(d) the scope for agreement of facts, questions of law and matters of evidence;
(e) the scope for use of affidavits and other documents in place of oral evidence;
(f) the scope for joint instruction of a single expert;
(g) the number and availability of witnesses;
(h) the nature of productions;
(i) whether sanction is sought for the employment of counsel;

---

[1] As inserted by the Act of Sederunt (Sheriff Court Rules)(Miscellaneous Amendments) (No.2) 2013 (SI 2013/139) para.2 (effective June 3, 2013).

(j) the reasonable estimate of time needed by each party for examination-in-chief, cross-examination and submissions.

(2) Subject to paragraph (4), at the case management hearing the sheriff will fix—

(a) a diet for proof or a proof before answer;

(b) a pre-proof hearing in accordance with Chapter 28A.

(3) The diet fixed under paragraph (2)(a)—

(a) shall be assigned for the appropriate number of days for resolution of the issues with reference to the information provided under paragraph (1) and subject to paragraph (4);

(b) may only be extended or varied on exceptional cause shown and subject to such orders (including awards of expenses) as the sheriff considers appropriate.

(4) The sheriff may make such orders as thought fit to ensure compliance with this rule and the expeditious resolution of the issues in dispute, including—

(a) restricting the issues for proof;

(b) excluding specified documents, reports and/or witnesses from proof;

(c) fixing other hearings and awarding expenses.

(5) A case management hearing may, on cause shown, be continued to a further case management hearing.

(6) For the purposes of rules 16.2 (decrees where party in default), 33.37 (decree by default in family action) and 33A.37 (decree by default in civil partnership action), a case management hearing shall be a diet in accordance with those rules.

Chapter 33B

Financial Provision For Former Cohabitants

Interpretation of this Chapter

33B. *[Omitted by the Act of Sederunt (Sheriff Court Rules) (Miscellaneous Amendments) 2012 (SSI 2012/188) para.7 (effective August 1, 2012).]*

D1.437.1

Chapter 33C[1]

Referrals to Principal Reporter

Application and interpretation of this Part

33C.1.—(1) In this Chapter—

D1.438

"2011 Act" means the Children's Hearings (Scotland) Act 2011;

"relevant proceedings" means those proceedings referred to in section 62(5)(a) to (j) and (m) of the 2011 Act, ;

"section 62 statement" has the meaning given in section 62(4) of the 2011 Act;

"Principal Reporter" is the person referred to in section 14 of the 2011 Act or any person carrying out the functions of the Principal Reporter by virtue of paragraph 10(1) of schedule 3 to that Act.

(2) This Chapter applies where a sheriff, in relevant proceedings, makes a referral to the Principal Reporter under section 62(2) of the 2011 Act ("a referral").

---

[1] As inserted by the Act of Sederunt (Children's Hearings (Scotland) Act 2011) (Miscellaneous Amendments) 2013 (SI 2013/172) para.5 (effective June 24, 2013).

Intimation to Principal Reporter

D1.439   **33C.2.** Where a referral is made, there shall be attached to the interlocutor a section 62 statement, which shall be intimated forthwith by the sheriff clerk to the Principal Reporter.

Intimation of decision by Principal Reporter

D1.440   **33C.3.**—(1) Where a referral is made and the Principal Reporter considers that it is necessary for a compulsory supervision order to be made in respect of the child and arranges a children's hearing under section 69(2) of the 2011 Act, the Principal Reporter shall intimate to the court which issued the section 62 statement the matters referred to in paragraph (2).

(2) The matters referred to in paragraph (1) are—

    (a) the decision to arrange such a hearing;

    (b) where no appeal is made against the decision of that children's hearing prior to the period for appeal expiring, the outcome of the children's hearing; and

    (c) where such an appeal has been made, that an appeal has been made and, once determined, the outcome of that appeal.

(3) Where a referral has been made and the Principal Reporter determines that—

    (a) none of the section 67 grounds apply in relation to the child; or

    (b) it is not necessary for a compulsory supervision order to be made in respect of the child the Principal Reporter shall intimate that decision to the court which issued the section 62 statement.

Chapter 34

Actions Relating to Heritable Property

Part I – Sequestration for Rent

[Revoked by the Act of Sederunt (Sheriff Court Rules Amendment) (Diligence) 2008 (SSI 2008/121) r.2(1)(a) (effective April 1, 2008).]

Part II – Removing

Action of removing where fixed term of removal

D1.441   **34.5.**—(1) Subject to section 21 of the Agricultural Holdings (Scotland) Act 1991 (notice to quit and notice of intention to quit)—

    (a) where the tenant has bound himself to remove by writing, dated and signed—

        (i) within 12 months after the term of removal; or

        (ii) where there is more than one ish, after the ish first in date to remove;

    an action of removing may be raised at any time; and

    (b) where the tenant has not bound himself, an action of removing may be raised at any time, but—

        (i) in the case of a lease of lands exceeding two acres in extent for three years and upwards, an interval of not less than one year nor more than two years shall elapse between the date of notice of removal and the term of removal first in date;

        (ii) in the case of a lease of lands exceeding two acres in extent, whether written or verbal, held from year to year or under tacit relocation, or for any other period less than three years, an interval of not less than six months shall elapse between the date of notice of removal and the term of removal first in date; and

        (iii) in the case of a house let with or without land attached not exceeding two acres in extent, as also of land not exceeding two acres in extent without houses, as also of mills, fishings, shootings, and all other heritable subjects excepting land exceeding two acres in extent, and let for a year or more, 40 days at least shall elapse between the date of notice of removal and the term of removal first in date.

(2) In any defended action of removing the sheriff may order the defender to find caution for violent profits.

(3) In an action for declarator of irritancy and removing by a superior against a vassal, the pursuer shall call as parties the last entered vassal and such heritable creditors and holders of postponed ground burdens as are disclosed by a search for 20 years before the raising of the action, and the expense of the search shall form part of the pursuer's expenses of process.

Form of notice of removal

34.6.—(1)[1] A notice under the following sections of the Sheriff Courts (Scotland) Act 1907 shall be in Form H2:— **D1.442**

   (a) section 34 (notice in writing to remove where lands exceeding two acres held on probative lease),

   (b) section 35 (letter of removal where tenant in possession of lands exceeding two acres), and

   (c) section 36 (notice of removal where lands exceeding two acres occupied by tenant without written lease).

(2) A letter of removal shall be in Form H3.

Form of notice under section 37 of the Act of 1907

34.7.[2] A notice under section 37 of the Sheriff Courts (Scotland) Act 1907 **D1.443** (notice of termination of tenancy) shall be in Form H4.

Giving notice of removal

34.8—[3](1) A notice under section 34, 35, 36, 37 or 38 of the Sheriff Courts **D1.444** (Scotland) Act 1907 (which relate to notices of removal) may be given by—

   (a) a sheriff officer

   (b) the person entitled to give such notice, or

   (c) the solicitor or factor of such person,

posting the notice by registered post or the first class recorded delivery service at any post office within the United Kingdom in time for it to be delivered at the address on the notice before the last date on which by law such notice must be given, addressed to the person entitled to receive such notice, and bearing the address of that person at the time, if known, or, if not known, to the last known address of that person.

(2) A sheriff officer may also give notice under a section of the Sheriff Courts (Scotland) Act 1907 mentioned in paragraph (1) in any manner in which he may serve an initial writ; and, accordingly, rule 5.4 (service within Scotland by sheriff officer) shall, with the necessary modifications, apply to the giving of notice under this paragraph as it applies to service of an initial writ.

Evidence of notice to remove

34.9.—(1) A certificate of the sending of notice under rule 34.8 dated and **D1.445** endorsed on the lease or an extract of it, or on the letter of removal, signed by the

---

[1] As amended by SI 1996/2445 (effective November 1, 1996).
[2] As amended by SI 1996/2445 (effective November 1, 1996).
[3] As amended by SI 1996/2445 (effective November 1, 1996).

sheriff officer or the person sending the notice, his solicitor or factor, or an acknowledgement of the notice endorsed on the lease or an extract of it, or on the letter of removal, by the party in possession or his agent, shall be sufficient evidence that notice has been given.

(2) Where there is no lease, a certificate of the sending of such notice shall be endorsed on a copy of the notice or letter of removal.

Disposal of applications under Part II of the Conveyancing and Feudal Reform (Scotland) Act 1970 for non-residential purposes

D1.446

34.10.—[1](1) This rule applies to an application or counter-application made by virtue of paragraph 3(2)(a) of the Act of Sederunt (Sheriff Court Rules) (Enforcement of Securities over Heritable Property) 2010.

(2) An interlocutor of the sheriff disposing of an application or counter-application is final and not subject to appeal except as to a question of title or as to any other remedy granted.

Service on unnamed occupiers

D1.447

34.11.—[2](1) Subject to paragraph (2), this rule applies only to a crave for removing in an action of removing against a person or persons in possession of heritable property without right or title to possess the property.

(2) This rule shall not apply with respect to a person who has or had a title or other right to occupy the heritable property and who has been in continuous occupation since that title or right is alleged to have come to an end.

(3) Where this rule applies, the pursuer may apply by motion to shorten or dispense with the period of notice or other period of time in these Rules relating to the conduct of the action or the extracting of any decree.

(4) Where the name of a person in occupation of the heritable property is not known and cannot reasonably be ascertained, the pursuer shall call that person as a defender by naming him as an "occupier".

(5) Where the name of a person in occupation of the heritable property is not known and cannot reasonably be ascertained, the initial writ shall be served (whether or not it is also served on a named person), unless the court otherwise directs, by a sheriff officer—

    (a)   affixing a copy of the initial writ and a citation in Form H5 addressed to "the occupiers" to the main door or other conspicuous part of the premises, and if practicable, depositing a copy of each of those documents in the premises; or

    (b)   in the case of land only, inserting stakes in the ground at conspicuous

---

[1] As substituted by the Act of Sederunt (Sheriff Court Rules) (Enforcement of Securities over Heritable Property) 2010 (SSI 2010/324) para.3 (effective September 30, 2010).

[2] Inserted by the Act of Sederunt (Sheriff Court Ordinary Cause Rules Amendment) (Miscellaneous) 2000 (SSI 2000/239) (effective October 2, 2000).

parts of the occupied land to each of which is attached a sealed transparent envelope containing a copy of the initial writ and a citation in Form H5 addressed to "the occupiers".

Part III[1] – Execution of Deeds

Form of application under section 87 of the Courts Reform (Scotland) Act 2014

34.12. An application for an order for execution under section 87 (power of sheriff to order sheriff clerk to execute deed relating to heritage) of the Courts Reform (Scotland) Act 2014 may be made—

(a) by a crave in the initial writ;

(b) where no such crave has been made, by lodging a minute of amendment to the initial writ; or

(c) where final decree has been pronounced, by lodging a minute in the process of the action to which the application relates.".

D1.448

Chapter 35

Actions of Multiplepoinding

Annotations to Chapter 35 are by Tim Edward, Partner, Maclay Murray and Spens W.S.

GENERAL NOTE

An action of multiplepoinding is used where any number of parties have claims on money or an item of property, whether heritable or moveable, which is held by another party. The purpose of the action is to decide which claimant is entitled to the property or in what proportions it should be divided between claimants. It also enables the holder of the property to part with it in a legally authorised manner. The subject of the action is known as the "fund *in medio*".

Originally, an action of multiplepoinding was competent only where there was double distress, where two or more arrestments of the fund had been lodged in the hands of the holder, but this rule has gradually been relaxed, and multiplepoindings are now competent wherever there are competing claims to one fund.

The court is generally more liberal towards the competency of a claim by the holder of the fund *in medio* than by a claimant, on the principle that the holder cannot raise a direct action, and should not be bound to remain a holder until the day of his death, or until the competing parties settle their claims. A holder has often been held entitled to bring a multiplepoinding even where a claim is obviously bad, since otherwise he would be liable to have to defend an unfounded action by that claimant.

An action of multiplepoinding may involve a succession of separate actions to determine (i) objections to the raising of the action, (ii) the extent and identity of the fund *in medio*, and (iii) the claims of the respective claimants in a competition on that fund.

Jurisdiction

This is regulated by Schedule 8 to the Civil Jurisdiction and Judgments Act 1982 as substituted by SI 2001/3929, Sch.2, para.7. Rule 2(i) of that act, which refers to "proceedings which are brought to assert, declare or determine proprietary or possessory rights, …in or over moveable property, or to obtain authority to dispose of moveable property", is deemed wide enough to include actions of multiplepoinding (Anton and Beaumont, *Civil Jurisdiction in Scotland*, 1995, para.10.42(2)). In such proceedings, the courts where the property is situated have jurisdiction. If the fund *in medio* consists of or includes immoveable property situated in Scotland, rule 5(1)(a) of Sch.8 to the C.J.J.A 1982 confers jurisdiction on the Sheriff Court of the place where it is situated, even if the defender's domicile is outwith the UK (rule 2(h)(ii)). Also, if any one of the defenders in an action of multiplepoinding is domiciled in Scotland, then the Sheriff Court of the place where that defender is domiciled has jurisdiction. (CJJA 1982, Sch.8, rule 2(o)(i)).

Application of this Chapter

35.1.—(1) This Chapter applies to an action of multiplepoinding.

D1.449

---

[1] As inserted by the Act of Sederunt (Rules of the Court of session 1994 and Sheriff Court Rules Amendment) (No.2) (Miscellaneous) 2016 (SSI 2016/229) para.2 (effective 28 November 2016).

Application of Chapters 9 and 10

D1.450   **35.2.** Chapter 10 (additional procedure) and the following rules in Chapter 9 (standard procedure in defended causes) shall not apply to an action of multiplepoinding:—

rule 9.1 (notice of intention to defend),

rule 9.2 (fixing date for Options Hearing),

rule 9.4 (lodging of pleadings before Options Hearing),

rule 9.8 (adjustment of pleadings),

rule 9.9 (effect of sist on adjustment),

rule 9.10 (open record),

rule 9.11 (record for Options Hearing),

rule 9.12 (Options Hearing),

rule 9.15 (applications for time to pay directions).

An action of multiplepoinding has its own procedure, to which many general rules governing ordinary causes do not apply. Rule 35.2 lists these rules; they include the rule on notices of intention to defend and the rules on Options Hearings and related procedure.

Parties

D1.451   **35.3.**—(1) An action of multiplepoinding may be brought by any person holding, or having an interest in, or claim on, the fund *in medio*, in his own name.

(2) The pursuer shall call as defenders to such an action—

(a)   all persons so far as known to him as having an interest in the fund *in medio*; and

(b)   where he is not the holder of the fund, the holder of that fund.

"ANY PERSON HOLDING, OR HAVING AN INTEREST IN, OR CLAIM ON, THE FUND"

The pursuer is the person who raises the action, whether he is the holder of the fund, or someone with an interest in or a claim on the fund. It is raised in his own name. If the holder of the fund raises the action he is known as the "pursuer and real raiser". Any other party raising the action is known as the 'pursuer and nominal raiser'. If the pursuer is not the holder of the fund, he must call the holder as a defender, and must also call as a defender any person whom he knows to have an interest in the fund. If there are heirs and beneficiaries whose identities are not known, the Lord Advocate should be called as representing the Crown as *ultimus haeres*.

The requirement on the pursuer to call as defenders all persons so far as known to him having an interest in the fund *in medio* is not expressly defined or limited and can extend not just to an assertion of ownership but also to the assertion of a right to manage, control or direct the distribution of the fund: *Macallans v W Burrell Homes Ltd*, 2015 S.L.T. (Sh Ct) 243.

Where the pursuer is the holder, the crave will be in the form:

"(1)   To find that the Pursuer is the holder of [specific description of fund *in medio*], which is claimed by the defenders, and that he is only liable in once and single payment thereof, and is entitled on payment, or consignation, to be exonerated thereof, and to obtain payment of his expenses;

(2)   To grant decree in favour of the party or parties who shall be found to have the best right to the fund *in medio*."

"FUND IN MEDIO"

This is the property in dispute in an action of multiplepoinding. There must be a fund *in medio*; an action is incompetent if there is no debt which the holder is obliged to pay to someone. Therefore, it is incompetent to raise an action of multiplepoinding in respect of a right to future rents (*Pentland v Royal Exchange Assce. Co.* (1830) 9 S. 164), or a fund only in expectation (*Provan v Provan* (1840) 2 D. 298), or not yet received (*Anderson v Cameron's Trs* (1844) 17 Sc.Jur. 42). However, the amount or value of the fund need not be definitely ascertained, so long as there is a fund (*Highland Railway Co. v British Linen Co.* (1901) 38 S.L.R. 584).

The fund can consist of heritable property (e.g. *Edinburgh Merchant Maiden's Hospital v Greig's Exrs* (1902) 10 S.L.T. 317; *Boyd's Trs v Boyd* (1906) 13 S.L.T. 878) or moveable property (including right to title deeds: *Baillie v Baillie* (1830) 8 S. 318), or a combination of both heritable and moveable property (*Logan v Byres* (1895) 2 S.L.T. 445).

In the course of a multiplepoinding action the court may have to decide whether the property in dispute falls under the category of heritable or moveable property, for example where rights of succession to that property require to be determined: *Cowan v Cowan* (1887) 14 R. 670.

The fund *in medio* should include only what is in dispute and no other property: *McNab v Waddell* (1894) 21 R. 827; *MacGillvray's Trs v Dallas* (1905) 7 F. 733. If other property is included, then the court may dismiss the action as incompetent (as in *McNab*), or allow the holder to amend the condescendence of the fund (*MacGillvray's Trs*). If, before the conclusion of the action of multiplepoinding, the holder loses title to property in the fund *in medio*, (i.e. by reduction of that title in a separate action), that property to which the holder no longer has title should be excluded from the condescendence of the fund: *Dunn's Trs v Barstow* (1870) 9 M. 281.

"DEFENDERS"

There must be at least two parties called as defenders, otherwise the action must be a direct action and not a multiplepoinding. (See note to rule 35.8.)

"HAVING AN INTEREST IN"

The purpose of an action of multiplepoinding is to dispose of all competing claims to the fund *in medio* and free the holder from any future responsibility towards possible claimants, so all persons who are believed to have some claim on the fund must be called as defenders. Persons not called may be allowed to lodge a claim at a later stage than they would be in most ordinary cause actions: *Morgan v Morris* (1856) 18 D. 797; aff'd. sub. nom. *Young v Morris* (1858) 20 D. (HL)12. Hence the provision for advertisement at rule 35.7.

Condescendence of fund in medio

35.4.—(1) Where the pursuer is the holder of the fund *in medio*, he shall include a detailed statement of the fund in the condescendence in the initial writ.

(2) Where the pursuer is not the holder of the fund *in medio*, the holder shall, before the expiry of the period of notice—

    (a)   lodge in process—

        (i)   a condescendence of the fund *in medio*, stating any claim or lien which he may profess to have on that fund;

        (ii) a list of all persons known to him as having an interest in the fund; and

    (b)   intimate a copy of the condescendence and list to any other party.

"CONDESCENDENCE OF THE FUND IN MEDIO"

There must be a condescendence: *Carmichael v Todd* (1853) 15 D. 473. It is essential that the court be able to establish the extent of the fund *in medio*, otherwise it cannot go on to assess the various claims upon the fund. The condescendence should specify the grounds on which each defender is called, and state the facts which justify the raising of the action.

Where a party's case is founded on a document, that document must be produced and specifically described, either by quoting its critical provisions in the averments, or expressly incorporating the document and holding its provisions as repeated in the averments by reference *brevitatis causa*.

"DETAILED STATEMENT OF THE FUND"

It should be sufficient to identify the property comprising the fund.

"INITIAL WRIT"

This is in Form G1 in Appendix 1 to the Ordinary Cause Rules.

"WHERE THE PURSUER IS NOT THE HOLDER..."

In this case the holder must lodge in process a statement of the property comprising the fund *in medio*, and state any claim or lien which he himself has on the fund as well as a list of all the persons he knows to have an interest in the fund. His failure to state his own claim at this point may not bar the claim, if the claim is stateable by way of retention or compensation, when objections to the condescendence of the fund *in medio* are determined: *Ramsay's JF v British Linen Bank*, 1912 S.C. 206, 208. Trustees holding a fund for administration are obliged to lodge a claim, as trustees, for the whole fund for the purpose of administration: *Hall's Trs v McDonald* (1892)19 R. 567, 577 per Lord Kinnear.

"PERIOD OF NOTICE"

This is determined by reference to rule 3.6.

"INTIMATE"

For methods, see rule 5.3.

Warrant of citation in multiplepoindings

35.5. The warrant of citation of the initial writ in an action of multiplepoinding shall be in Form M1.

"WARRANT OF CITATION"

The writ is served on all defenders, including, where the pursuer is not the holder of the fund in medio, the holder of that fund. The warrant of citation is in the Form M1 in Appendix 1 to the Rules. The defender is ordained to intimate if he or she intends to lodge (a) defences challenging the jurisdiction of the court or the competence of the action; (b) objections to the condescendence of the fund in medio; or (c) a claim on the fund; or any combination of these.

D1.453 **Citation**

35.6.—(1) Subject to rule 5.6 (service where address of person is not known), citation of any person in an action of multiplepoinding shall be in Form M2 which shall be attached to a copy of the initial writ and warrant of citation and shall have appended to it a notice of appearance in Form M4.

(2) The certificate of citation shall be in Form M3 and shall be attached to the initial writ.

"RULE 5.6"

This rule provides for service upon a person whose address is unknown by the publication of an advertisement in a specified newspaper circulating in the area of the last known address of that person, or by displaying on the walls of court a copy of the instance and crave of the initial writ, the warrant of citation, and a notice in Form G4.

"NOTICE OF APPEARANCE"

See rule 35.8.

D1.454 **Advertisement**

35.7. The sheriff may make an order for advertisement of the action in such newspapers as he thinks fit.

"ADVERTISEMENT"

Intimation of the raising of an action of multiplepoinding ensures that all persons entitled to make a claim have an opportunity to do so. Lord Neaves described it as "an essential prerequisite to any judgement in [a] competition": *Connell v Ferguson* (1861) 23 D. 683, at 687.

Further, rule 35.16 states that the sheriff may at any time during the action, either *ex proprio motu* or on the motion of any party, order further service on any person, or advertisement or further advertisement of the action.

D1.455 **Lodging of notice of appearance**

35.8. Where a party intends to lodge—

   (a) defences to challenge the jurisdiction of the court or the competency of the action,

   (b) objections to the condescendence of the fund *in medio*, or

   (c) a claim on the fund,

he shall, before the expiry of the period of notice, lodge a notice of appearance in Form M4.

"DEFENCES TO CHALLENGE THE JURISDICTION... OR THE COMPETENCY..."

N.B. rule 35.12(2): defences must be disposed of before any further procedure in the action, unless the sheriff directs otherwise.

A party may wish to lodge defences on grounds such as lack of jurisdiction (see General Note at rule 35.1), or forum non conveniens (e.g. *Provan v Provan* (1840) 2 D. 298).

Also, an action of multiplepoinding is incompetent in a situation where a direct action is available to the claimant. Greater latitude is allowed, however, where the action is raised by the holder of the fund rather than a claimant. The holder of the fund 'is entitled to be relieved by means of an action of multiplepoinding ... and accordingly it is sufficient justification of the institution of the action, and is the criterion of its competency, that the claims intimated make it impossible for the depositary to pay to one of the parties without running the risk of an action at the instance of the other.': *Winchester v Blakey* (1890) 17 R. 1046, 1050 per Lord MacLaren. Accordingly, it is enough to show that there are competing claims which the holder of the fund is unable to meet. So, for example, actions of multiplepoinding which would otherwise have been dismissed as incompetent, because they raised an issue between two claimants which would have been triable by direct action, were nonetheless allowed when raised by the holders: *Royal Bank of Scotland v Price* (1893) 20 R. 290; *Commercial Bank of Scotland v Muir* (1897) 25 R. 219.

An action of multiplepoinding should not be used by trustees, executors, or those who hold property on behalf of others simply as a means of dealing with disputes over the property, if there is no genuine double distress. For example, an action of multiplepoinding raised by trustees was held to be incompetent where the only dispute was between a beneficiary and a creditor on the estate (*Glen's Trs v Miller*, 1911 S.C. 1178; cf. *Ogilvy's Trs v Chevallier* (1874)1 R. 693 (where a multiplepoinding by testamentary trustees was only reluctantly allowed where the only dispute was between the sole beneficiary and her creditor)) or where a solicitor was called upon to pay over the confirmed estate to the confirmed executor and another party claimed a right to those funds (*Adam Cochran & Co. v Conn*, 1989 S.L.T. (Sh. Ct.) 27).

Executors and trustees should not resort to a multiplepoinding to obtain exoneration and discharge where there is no difficulty obtaining this by the usual means (*Mackenzie's Trs v Gray* (1895) 2 S.L.T. 422); however, it is competent for those holding monies in a fiduciary capacity, such as executors and trustees, to raise an action of multiplepoinding in order to obtain exoneration and discharge if those who have the power to grant this refuse to do so (*Fraser's Exr v Wallace's Trs* (1893) 20 R. 374, 379 per Lord Maclaren), or where they are otherwise unable to grant sufficient exoneration (*Davidson v Ewen* (1895) 3 S.L.T. 162), or where, because of doubts as to the meaning of testamentary bequests it is unclear who is entitled to the fund and able to give valid discharge (*McClement's Trs v Lord Advocate*, 1949 S.L.T. (Notes) 59).

A judicial factor cannot obtain his exoneration and discharge through an action of multiplepoinding; he is appointed by the court in the exercise of its nobile officium and must likewise be discharged through the exercise of those powers: *Campbell v Grant* (1869) 7 M. 227, 233 per Lord Deas.

"OBJECTIONS TO THE CONDESCENDENCE OF THE FUND"

A party may wish to lodge objections to the existence or composition of the fund *in medio*. In *Provan v Provan* (1840) 23 D. 298, the Lord Ordinary himself raised an objection to the competency of the action on the ground that there was no fund *in medio*. A common objection is that there is some property which should be excluded from the condescendence of the fund: e.g. *Walker's Trs v Walker* (1878) 5 R. 678; *Donaldson's Trs v Beattie* 1914 1 S.L.T. 170. However, objections that the fund in medio includes property which is clearly not in dispute, appear to be treated rather as defences challenging the competency of the action itself, and dealt with at the initial stage of disposal of defences under rule 35.12(2): eg *McNab v Waddell* (1894) 21 R. 827. Likewise, an objection that the pursuer is not entitled to the fund is not an objection to the competency of the action, but one which affects the merits: *Greenshields' Trs v Greenshields*, 1915 2 S.L.T. 189.

"CLAIM ON THE FUND"

This is a short sentence in which the claimant claims to be ranked and preferred to the fund *in medio*, or to a particular portion of that fund. A holder's claim may include a right of retention or compensation.

In some circumstances, a claimant has what is known as a "riding claim", where he is ranked on the fund in medio by virtue of his debtor's claim in the multiplepoinding. However, that debtor's claim must be a direct one, and not a riding claim itself: *Gill's Trs v Patrick* (1889) 16 R. 403. A riding claim must be constituted (*Royal Bank of Scotland v Stevenson* (1849) 12 D. 250) and liquid (*Home's Trs v Ralston's Trs.* (1833) 12 S. 727; *Wilson v Young* (1851) 13 D. 1366). The riding claim must be lodged before decree for payment is pronounced in favour of the original claimant (i.e. the debtor): *Anglo-Foreign Banking Co.* (1879) 16 S.L.R. 731. There are no reported decisions to confirm it, but it would appear to be competent for more than one riding claim to be ranked on a principal claim, leading to a separate competition in respect of those riding claims on the principal claimant's share of the fund: Thomson & Middleton, *Manual of Court of Session Practice*, p.124.

"PERIOD OF NOTICE"

This is determined by reference to rule 3.6.

"NOTICE OF APPEARANCE"

The party lodging notice of appearance must specify in the notice the purpose of his intended appearance. The notice, in Form M4, is signed by the party or his solicitor. It is improper for parties with conflicting interests to be represented by the same firm of solicitors: *Dunlop's Trs v Farquharson*, 1956 S.L.T. 16.

If no notice of appearance is lodged, the sheriff may decide to order advertisement, or further advertisement, of the action, in accordance with rule 35.16.

Fixing date for first hearing

D1.456

35.9. Where a notice of appearance, or a condescendence on the fund *in medio* and list under rule 35.4(2)(a) has been lodged, the sheriff clerk shall—

(a) fix a date and time for the first hearing, which date shall be the first suitable court day occurring not sooner than 4 weeks after the expiry of the period of notice;

(b) on fixing the date for the first hearing forthwith intimate that date in Form M5 to each party; and

(c) prepare and sign an interlocutor recording the date of the first hearing.

"INTIMATE"

For methods, see rule 5.3.

"INTERLOCUTOR"

For rules relating to interlocutors, see rule 12.1.

D1.457 **Hearings**

35.10.—(1) The sheriff shall conduct the first, and any subsequent hearing, with a view to securing the expeditious progress of the cause by ascertaining from parties the matters in dispute.

(2)[1] The parties shall provide the sheriff with sufficient information to enable him to—

(a) conduct the hearing as provided for in this Chapter,

(b) consider any child witness notice or vulnerable witness application that has been lodged where no order has been made, or

(c) ascertain whether there is or is likely to be a vulnerable witness within the meaning of section 11(1) of the Act of 2004 who is to give evidence at any proof or hearing and whether any order under section 12(1) of the Act of 2004 requires to be made.

(3) At the first, or any subsequent hearing, the sheriff shall fix a period within which defences, objections or claims shall be lodged, and appoint a date for a second hearing.

(4) Where the list lodged under rule 35.4(2)(a) contains any person who is not a party to the action, the sheriff shall order—

(a) the initial writ to be amended to add that person as a defender;

(b) service of the pleadings so amended to be made on that person, with a citation in Form M6; and

(c) intimation to that person of any condescendence of the fund *in medio* lodged by a holder of the fund who is not the pursuer.

(5) Where a person to whom service has been made under paragraph (4) lodges a notice of appearance under rule 35.8, the sheriff clerk shall intimate to him in Form M5 the date of the next hearing fixed in the action.

GENERAL NOTE

Rule 35.10 focuses on the need for efficiency throughout the course of an action of multiplepoinding, so that the case may be disposed of as quickly and satisfactorily as possible. These provisions are similar to the rules for the conduct of options hearings and procedural hearings in other ordinary causes. (See for example OCR rules 9.12(1), (2) and 10.6(1), (2).)

D1.458 **Lodging defences, objections and claims**

35.11.—(1) Defences, objections and claims by a party shall be lodged with the sheriff clerk in a single document under separate headings.

(2) Each claimant shall lodge with his claim any documents founded on in his claim, so far as they are within his custody or power.

---

[1] As substituted by the Act of Sederunt (Ordinary Cause, Summary Application, Summary Cause and Small Claim Rules) Amendment (Vulnerable Witnesses (Scotland) Act 2004) 2007, r.2(11) (effective November 1, 2007).

This is the equivalent of lodging defences in a normal ordinary cause action. Each party must lodge a single document which, under separate headings, deals with defences, objections and claims. Where a party wishes to state defences to the competency of the action, he lodges defences in the usual form, with any objections or claim by the defender following the pleas-in-law under separate headings.

If a party does not wish to lodge defences to the competency of the action, but wishes to lodge objections, his writ is headed: "OBJECTIONS/for/A.B. [*designed*]/to/Condescendence of the fund *in medio*/in/Action of Multiplepoinding/[*names and designations of parties as in the instance*]." Objections are specifically stated in numbered paragraphs and are followed by appropriate pleas-in-law.

If a party simply wishes to lodge a claim, it is headed: "CONDESCENDENCE AND CLAIM/for/A.B. [*designed*], Claimant/in/Action of Multiplepoinding [etc., *as above*]."

A claim consists of a condescendence, claim, and pleas-in-law. The condescendence is headed "Condescendence" and sets out in numbered paragraphs the facts on which the claimant bases his claim. The claim is headed "Claim" and must set out specifically what is claimed. This is an essential part of the writ: *Connell v Ferguson* (1861) 23 D. 683, per Lord Neaves at 686. In a riding claim, the claimant is described as a riding claimant.

The plea in the pleas-in-law is that the claimant is entitled to be ranked and preferred to the fund *in medio* in terms of his claim.

"DOCUMENTS"

When a document is founded upon or adopted in defences, objections, or claims, it must, so far as in the possession or within the control of the party founding upon it or adopting it, be lodged in process by that party. If the document is not produced, it cannot be considered by the court: *Hayes v Robinson* , 1984 S.L.T. 300, per Lord Ross at 301. Under rule 21.1, the sheriff has power to order the production of any document or grant a commission and diligence for recovery of it.

Disposal of defences

35.12.—(1) Where defences have been lodged, the sheriff may order the initial writ and defences to be adjusted and thereafter close the record and regulate further procedure.

(2) Unless the sheriff otherwise directs, defences shall be disposed of before any further procedure in the action.

The rules set out consecutive procedural stages by which defences, objections and claims are successively disposed of. Unless the sheriff otherwise directs, defences challenging the jurisdiction or competency of an action are dealt with first, before any further procedure. After defences have been lodged, the sheriff may order the initial writ and defences to be adjusted. He then closes the record and regulates further procedure, usually by appointing parties to debate. If the sheriff sustains the objections to jurisdiction or to the competency of the action, the case comes to an end here. If he rejects them, the case will continue to a new hearing at which further procedure will be determined.

Objections to fund in medio

35.13.—(1) Where objections to the fund *in medio* have been lodged, the sheriff may, after disposal of any defences, order the condescendence of the fund and objections to be adjusted, and thereafter close the record and regulate further procedure.

(2) If no objections to the fund *in medio* have been lodged, or if objections have been lodged and disposed of, the sheriff may, on the motion of the holder of the fund, and without ordering intimation to any party approve the condescendence of the fund and find the holder liable only in one single payment.

"objections to the fund in medio"

Objections to the condescendence of the fund are dealt with next, after disposal of defences. The sheriff may order the condescendence and objections to be adjusted, after which he again closes the record and regulates further procedure. He will usually order a debate or proof, and then dispose of objections and fix a further hearing. The interlocutor disposing of the objections may be appealed without leave: *Walker's Trs v Walker* (1878) 5 R. 678; *Harris School Board v Davidson* (1881) 9 R. 371.

D1.459

D1.459.1

"approve the condescendence of the fund"

This is a final interlocutor, which, again, may be appealed without leave: *Harris School Board v Davidson* (1881) 9 R. 371.

The court's approval of the fund is essential, as the interlocutor determines the amount for which the holder is liable to account.

"find the holder liable only in one single payment"

This is a judicial determination that the action is competent.

(The motion in respect of this finding and the approval of the condescendence may be made at an earlier hearing on objections, so that the interlocutor disposing of objections may at the same time approve the condescendence and find the holder liable in one single payment.)

The purpose of this finding, once the objections (if any) are disposed of and the fund is approved, is to enable the holder to make payment (usually by consigning the fund into court) and effectively drop out of the action; that is, unless the holder also wishes to assert a claim on the fund.

D1.460   **Preliminary pleas in multiplepoindings**

35.14.—(1)   A party intending to insist on a preliminary plea shall, not later than 3 days before any hearing to determine further procedure following the lodging of defences, objections or claims, lodge with the sheriff clerk a note of the basis of the plea.

(2)   Where a party fails to comply with the provisions of paragraph (1), he shall be deemed to be no longer insisting on the plea and the plea shall be repelled by the sheriff at the hearing referred to in paragraph (1).

(3)   If satisfied that there is a preliminary matter of law which justifies a debate, the sheriff shall, after having heard parties and considered the note lodged under this rule, appoint the action to debate.

"PRELIMINARY PLEAS"

The provisions relating to preliminary pleas in actions of multiplepoinding are similar to those for other ordinary causes (cf. rule 22.1).

D1.461   **Consignation of the fund and discharge of holder**

35.15.—(1)   At any time after the condescendence of the fund *in medio* has been approved, the sheriff may order the whole or any part of the fund to be sold and the proceeds of the sale consigned into court.

(2)   After such consignation the holder of the fund *in medio* may apply for his exoneration and discharge.

(3)   The sheriff may allow the holder of the fund *in medio*, on his exoneration and discharge, his expenses out of the fund as a first charge on the fund.

"CONSIGNATION OF THE FUND"

The amount consigned is the balance in the hands of the holder after deduction of the holder's taxed expenses (if any).

Unlike the 1983 Ordinary Cause Rules, the current rules make no specific provision for consignation into court where no sale takes place. However, consignation is still probably the appropriate step to take even where there is no sale.

The form of the fund, or part of it, may make consignation difficult. There may be a problem if the fund *in medio* consists of a bulky or valuable object which the parties do not wish to be sold. The only way for the sheriff clerk to keep such an object would be to arrange for it to be commercially stored, incurring costs which may significantly reduce the value of the fund *in medio*. In this situation, therefore, the court may ask the holder to retain it, or ask the parties to agree an arrangement for its safekeeping pending the outcome of the action.

For procedure where the fund *in medio* consists of or includes a heritable security, see *Currie's Trs v. Bothwell* , 1954 S.L.T. (Sh. Ct.) 87.

"EXONERATION AND DISCHARGE"

This allows the holder of the fund *in medio* legally to dispose of the property of which he has been in possession, and free him from the possibility of any future claims by any person: see e.g. *Farquhar v. Farquhar* (1896) 13 R. 596. This will be the end of his involvement in the action.

If the holder of the fund *in medio* is not the pursuer, he will be entitled to the expenses of the condescendence of the fund out of that fund. If the holder is the pursuer and the action was justified, he will usually be entitled to expenses out of the fund. However, if trustees raise an action of multiplepoinding which is subsequently found to be unjustified, they may be found personally liable in expenses: *MacKenzie's Trs v. Sutherland* (1894) 22 R. 233; *Paterson's Trs v. Paterson* (1897) 7 S.L.T. 134; cf. *Gens Trs v. Miller* , 1911 S.C. 1178.

In practice, the steps laid out in rules 35.13(2), and 35.15(2) and (3) are normally combined in a single interlocutor, in which the sheriff: (1) holds the fund *in medio* to be correctly stated in the initial writ or other pleading at the sum therein specified; (2) finds the holder liable in one single payment; (3) finds the holder entitled to payment of his expenses out of the fund *in medio* and allows an account of those expenses to be given in and remits the account, when lodged, to the auditor of court to tax and to report; (4) ordains the holder to lodge the fund *in medio*, with his expenses deducted, in the hands of the sheriff clerk; and (5) upon consignation being made exoners and discharges him of the fund *in medio* and of his whole actings and intromissions therewith. Once this has been done, the holder has no further involvement in the action.

Where the holder is to retain possession of the fund in the circumstances outlined above (in the notes for "*consignation of the fund*"), he cannot yet be exonered and discharged, but he may not wish to be further involved in the litigation. In this situation, the sheriff approves the condescendence of the fund, finds the holder liable only in one single payment, finds him entitled to expenses and has these taxed and approved. Thereafter the holder takes no part in the proceedings. The final interlocutor, as well as ranking and preferring the claimants, ordains delivery on payment of the holder's expenses, and on delivery being made exoners and discharges the holder.

Further service or advertisement

35.16. The sheriff may at any time, of his own motion or on the motion of any party, order further service on any person or advertisement.

See under "*advertisement*" at notes for rule 35.7.

Ranking of claims

35.17.—(1) After disposal of any defences, and approval of the condescendence of the fund *in medio*, the sheriff may, where there is no competition on the fund, rank and prefer the claimants and grant decree in terms of that ranking.

(2) Where there is competition on the fund, the sheriff may order claims to be adjusted and thereafter close the record and regulate further procedure.

If there is no competition, the parties may agree in a joint minute to a ranking of their respective claims, though it is not necessary to do this. The sheriff grants decree, and directs the sheriff clerk to make payment to the claimants out of the consigned fund on the lodging of any necessary clearance certificate, and to require receipts. A decree of ranking and preference may be granted without proof (*Union Bank v. Grade* (1887) 25 S.L.R. 61), although the court may refuse to grant the decree, even where there is no competition, if it appears ex facie of a claimant's claim that he has no right to that part of the fund which he claims: *Clark's Exr v. Clark* , 1953 S.L.T. (Notes) 58.

Once a decree of ranking and preference has been pronounced, it can only be brought under review by a person called as defender in the multiplepoinding, by an action of reduction (*Stodart v. Bell* (1860) 22 D. 1092, 1093 per Lord Cowan); and where payment has been made, the only remedy is an action against the party who has received payment, the holder of the fund being no longer liable (*Geikie v. Morris* (1858) 3 Macq. 353).

The rule that payment must not be made until any necessary clearance certificate has been lodged (see rule 30.2(1)) must be strictly observed: *Simpson's Trs v. Fox* , 1954 S.L.T. (Notes) 12. If any payments are made out of the fund before all government duties have been paid, the court may not grant the holder of the fund exoneration and discharge: *Simpson's Trs v. Fox* , 1954 S.L.T. (Notes) 12. (But note the exception to this rule, at rule 30.2(2), which applies only to multiplepoindings: decree may be granted even though not all of the taxes or duties payable on the estate of a deceased claimant have yet been paid or satisfied.)

It is essential that the interlocutor disposing of an action of multiplepoinding be clearly expressed. Likewise, any joint minute should specify in detail the steps which the court is asked to take when pronouncing decree. In particular, the agreement contained in the joint minute should: (1) ensure that the total fund will be disposed of, and that provision will be made for such matters as the assignation of life policies or the delivery of goods; (2) wherever possible, specify the payments to be made in precise figures or in specific fractions of the total, rather than by reference to any formula; (3) deal clearly with any accrued interest; and (4) deal with expenses.

D1.462

D1.463

"COMPETITION"

A competition arises where the claims amount to more than the value of the fund, or where the claims are competing in respect of a particular part of the fund. The sheriff may order claims to be adjusted and then close the record and regulate further procedure. Here, as at any earlier closings of the record, the case may be heard by debate (provided that a note of the basis of the preliminary plea has been lodged as set out in rule 35.14), or by proof if there is a dispute as to fact. In the interlocutor disposing of the competition, the sheriff will rank and prefer the successful claimant or claimants and repel the claims of the unsuccessful. If the interlocutor deals with expenses it may be appealed without leave by the unsuccessful claimant (*Glasgow Corporation v. General Accident Fire and Life Assurance Corporation Ltd* , 1914 S.C. 835). The sheriff may make an order for payment in the same interlocutor, or he may delay dealing with this, in which case the interlocutor will make findings in fact and in law determining the principles on which division of the fund is to proceed, and grant leave to appeal.

The interlocutor ordering payment or transference of the fund in medio to the successful claimants protects the holder, after payment or transference, from any further claims at the instance of any person (Stair, IV, xvi, 3; Erskine, IV, iii, 23). It constitutes res judicata as against all the parties in the process: *McCaig v. Maitland* (1887) 14 R. 295; *Elder's Trs v. Elder* (1895) 22 R. 505.

D1.464   **Remit to reporter**

35.18.—(1)   Where several claims have been lodged, the sheriff may remit to a reporter to prepare a scheme of division and report.

(2)   The expenses of such remit, when approved by the sheriff, shall be made a charge on the fund, to be deducted before division.

"REPORTER"

In practice, it is rarely necessary for the sheriff to remit to a reporter. If he does, the scheme prepared by the reporter will show the amounts which the decree of ranking and preference determines to be payable to each of the successful claimants.

D1.465

Chapter 36

Actions of Damages

Part AI[1] – Special Procedure for Actions for, or Arising from Personal Injuries

Application and interpretation

Application and interpretation of this Part

D1.466   **36.A1.**—(1)   This Part applies to a personal injuries action.

(2)   In this Part—

"personal injuries action" means an action of damages for, or arising from, personal injuries or death of a person from personal injuries; and
"personal injuries procedure" means the procedure established by rules 36.G1 to 36.L1.

(3)   In the definition of "personal injuries action", "personal injuries" includes any disease or impairment, whether physical or mental.

Raising a personal injuries action

Form of initial writ

D1.467   **36.B1.**—(1)   Subject to rule 36.C1, the initial writ in a personal injuries action shall be in Form P11 and there shall be annexed to it a brief statement containing—

(a)   averments in numbered paragraphs relating only to those facts necessary to establish the claim;

(b)   the names of every medical practitioner from whom, and every hospital or other institution in which, the pursuer or, in an action in respect of the death of a person,

the deceased received treatment for the personal injuries.

---

[1] As inserted by the Act of Sederunt (Ordinary Cause Rules Amendment) (Personal Injuries Actions) 2009 (SSI 2009/285) r.2 (effective November 2, 2009).

(2) An initial writ may include—

(a) warrants for intimation so far as permitted under these Rules, and

(b) a specification of documents in Form PI2.

Actions based on clinical negligence

36.C1.—[1](1) This rule applies to a personal injuries action based on alleged clinical negligence.

D1.468

(2) Where a pursuer intends to make an application under paragraph (3) to have the cause appointed to the procedure in Chapter 36A (case management of certain personal injuries actions), the pursuer must—

(a) present the initial writ for warranting in Form G1 (form of initial writ); and

(b) include in the initial writ a draft interlocutor in Form PI4 (form of interlocutor appointing the cause to the procedure in Chapter 36A).

(3) At the same time as an initial writ which includes a draft interlocutor in Form PI4 is presented for warranting, the pursuer must lodge a written application in the form of a letter addressed to the sheriff clerk to have the cause appointed to the procedure in Chapter 36A.

(4) On the making of an application under paragraph (3), the initial writ will be placed before a sheriff in chambers and in the absence of the parties.

(5) On consideration of the initial writ in accordance with paragraph (4), the sheriff may—

(a) after considering the likely complexity of the action and being satisfied that the efficient determination of the action would be served by doing so, appoint the cause to the procedure in Chapter 36A by signing the draft interlocutor in the initial writ; or

(b) fix a hearing.

(6) The sheriff clerk must notify the parties of the date and time of any hearing under paragraph (5)(b).

(7) At a hearing under paragraph (5)(b), the sheriff may—

(a) refuse the application; or

(b) after considering the likely complexity of the action and being satisfied that the efficient determination of the action would be served by doing so, appoint the cause to the procedure in Chapter 36A by signing the draft interlocutor in the initial writ.

(8) Where the sheriff appoints the cause to the procedure in Chapter 36A under paragraph (5)(a) or (7)(b)—

(a) the sheriff or, as the case may be, the sheriff clerk must sign a warrant in accordance with rule 5.1 (signature of warrants);

(b) the cause will proceed in accordance with Chapter 36A rather than in accordance with personal injuries procedure.

(9) In this rule—

"clinical negligence" means a breach of duty of care by a health care professional in connection with that person's diagnosis or the care and treatment of any person, by act or omission, while the health care professional was acting in a professional capacity;

"health care professional" includes—

(a) a registered medical practitioner;

---

[1] As substituted by the Act of Sederunt (Rules of the Court of Session 1994 and Sheriff Court Rules Amendment) (No. 2) (Personal Injury and Remits) 2015 (SSI 2015/227) para.8 (effective September 22, 2015).

(b)   a registered nurse; or

(c)   any other member of a profession regulated by a body mentioned in section 25(3) (the Professional Standards Authority for Health and Social Care) of the National Health Service Reform and Health Care Professions Act 2002.

Inspection and recovery of documents

D1.469   **36.D1.**—(1)   This rule applies where the initial writ in a personal injuries action contains a specification of documents by virtue of rule 36.B1(2)(b).

(2)   On the granting of a warrant for citation, an order granting commission and diligence for the production and recovery of the documents mentioned in the specification shall be deemed to have been granted and the sheriff clerk shall certify Form PI2 to that effect by attaching thereto a docquet in Form PI3.

(3)   An order which is deemed to have been made under paragraph (2) shall be treated for all purposes as an interlocutor granting commission and diligence signed by the sheriff.

(4)   The pursuer may serve an order under paragraph (2) and the provisions of Chapter 28 (recovery of evidence) shall thereafter apply, subject to any necessary modifications, as if the order were an order obtained on an application under rule 28.2 (applications for commission and diligence for recovery of documents etc.).

(5)   Nothing in this rule shall affect the right of a party to apply under rule 28.2 for a commission and diligence for recovery of documents or for an order under section 1 of the Administration of Justice (Scotland) Act 1972 in respect of any document or other property whether or not mentioned in the specification annexed to the initial writ.

Personal injuries action: application of other rules and withdrawal from personal injuries procedure

Application of other rules

D1.470   **36.E1.**—[1](1)   A defended personal injuries action will, instead of proceeding in accordance with Chapter 9 (standard procedure in defended causes), proceed in accordance with personal injuries procedure.

(2)   But paragraph (1) does not apply to a personal injuries action following its appointment to the procedure in Chapter 36A under rule 36.C1, 36.F1 or 36A.1.

(3)   Paragraphs (4) to (17) apply to a personal injuries action proceeding in accordance with personal injuries procedure but cease to apply when an action is appointed to the procedure in Chapter 36A.

(4)   Despite paragraph (1), the following rules of Chapter 9 apply—

(a)   rule 9.1 (notice of intention to defend);

(b)   rule 9.3 (return of initial writ);

(c)   rule 9.5 (process folder);

(d)   rule 9.6 (defences); and

(e)   rule 9.7 (implied admissions).

(5)   But the defences shall not include a note of pleas-in-law.

(6)   In the application of rule 18.3(1) (applications to amend), a minute of amendment lodged in process must include, where appropriate, confirmation as to whether

---

[1] As substituted by the Act of Sederunt (Rules of the Court of Session 1994 and Sheriff Court Rules Amendment) (No. 2) (Personal Injury and Remits) 2015 (SSI 2015/227) para.8 (effective September 22, 2015).

any warrants are sought under rule 36.B1(2)(a) (warrants for intimation) or whether a specification of documents is sought under rule 36.B1(2)(b) (specification of documents).

(7) In the application of rule 18.5(1)(a) (service of amended pleadings), the sheriff must order any timetable issued in terms of rule 36.G1 to be served together with a copy of the initial writ or record.

(8) Rule 18.5(3) (fixing of hearing following service of amended pleadings and lodging of notice of intention to defend) does not apply.

(9) In the application of rule 19.1 (counterclaims) a counterclaim may also include—

(a) warrants for intimation so far as permitted under these Rules; and

(b) a specification of documents in Form PI2.

(10) In rule 19.4 (disposal of counterclaims), paragraph (b) shall not apply.

(11) In the application of rule 20.4(3) (service on third party), any timetable already issued in terms of rule 36.G1 must also be served with a third party notice.

(12) In the application of rule 20.6 (procedure following answers)—

(a) paragraphs (1) and (2) do not apply; and

(b) where a third party lodges answers, any timetable already issued under rule 36.G1 applies to the third party.

(13) Chapters 22 (preliminary pleas) and 28A (pre-proof hearing) do not apply.

(14) Rule 29.11 does not apply.

(15) References elsewhere in these Rules to the condescendence of an initial writ or to the articles of the condescendence are to be construed as references to the statement required under rule 36.B1(1) and the numbered paragraphs of that statement.

(16) References elsewhere in these Rules to pleas-in-law, an open record, a closed record or a record for an Options Hearing are to be ignored.

(17) References elsewhere in these Rules to any action carried out before or after the closing of the record are to be construed as references to that action being carried out before, or as the case may be, after, the date fixed for completion of adjustment under rule 36.G1(1A)(c).

Disapplication of personal injuries procedure

36.F1.—[1](1) Any party to a personal injuries action proceeding in accordance with personal injuries procedure may, within 28 days of the lodging of defences (or, where there is more than one defender the first lodging of defences), by motion apply to have the action withdrawn from personal injuries procedure and appointed to the procedure in Chapter 36A.

D1.471

(2) No motion under paragraph (1) shall be granted unless the sheriff is satisfied that there are exceptional reasons for not following personal injuries procedure.

(3) In determining whether there are exceptional reasons justifying the granting of a motion made under paragraph (1), the sheriff shall have regard to—

(a) the likely need for detailed pleadings;

(b) the length of time required for preparation of the action; and

(c) any other relevant circumstances.

(4) Where the sheriff appoints the cause to the procedure in Chapter 36A under paragraph (1)—

---

[1] As amended by the Act of Sederunt (Rules of the Court of Session 1994 and Sheriff Court Rules Amendment) (No. 2) (Personal Injury and Remits) 2015 (SSI 2015/227) para.8 (effective September 22, 2015).

(a) the pursuer must within 14 days lodge a revised initial writ in Form G1 (form of initial writ);

(b) the defender must adjust the defences so as to comply with rule 9.6(2) (defences); and

(c) the cause will proceed in accordance with Chapter 36A, rather than in accordance with personal injuries procedure.

Personal injuries procedure

Allocation of diets and timetables

D1.472   **36.G1.**—[1, 2](1) The sheriff clerk shall, on the lodging of defences in the action or, where there is more than one defender, the first lodging of defences—

(a) allocate a diet of proof of the action, which shall be no earlier than 4 months (unless the sheriff on cause shown directs an earlier diet to be fixed) and no later than 9 months from the date of the first lodging of defences; and

(b) issue a timetable stating—

    (i) the date of the diet mentioned in subparagraph (a); and

    (ii) the dates no later than which the procedural steps mentioned in paragraph (1A) are to take place.

(1A) Those procedural steps are—

(a) application for a third party notice under rule 20.1;

(b)[3] the pursuer serving a commission for recovery of documents under rule 36.D1;

(c) the parties adjusting their pleadings;

(d) the pursuer lodging a statement of valuation of claim in process;

(e) the pursuer lodging a record;

(f) the defender (and any third party to the action) lodging a statement of valuation of claim in process;

(g) the parties each lodging in process a list of witnesses together with any productions upon which they wish to rely; and

(h) the pursuer lodging in process the minute of the pre-trial meeting.

(1B) The dates mentioned in paragraph (1)(b)(ii) are to be calculated by reference to periods specified in Appendix 3, which, with the exception of the period specified in rule 36.K1(2), the sheriff principal may vary for his sheriffdom or for any court within his sheriffdom.;

(2) A timetable issued under paragraph (1)(b) shall be in Form PI5 and shall be treated for all purposes as an interlocutor signed by the sheriff; and so far as the timetable is inconsistent with any provision in these Rules which relates to a matter to which the timetable relates, the timetable shall prevail.

(3)[4] Where a party fails to comply with any requirement of a timetable other than that referred to in rule 36.K1(3), the sheriff clerk may fix a date and time for the parties to be heard by the sheriff.

---

[1] As amended by the Act of Sederunt (Sheriff Court Rules) (Miscellaneous Amendments) 2010 (SSI 2010/279) para.4 (effective July 29, 2010).

[2] As amended by the Act of Sederunt (Rules of the Court of Session 1994 and Sheriff Court Rules Amendment) (No. 2) (Personal Injury and Remits) 2015 (SSI 2015/227) para.8 (effective September 22, 2015).

[3] As amended by the Act of Sederunt (Sheriff Court Rules) (Miscellaneous Amendments) (No.3) 2011 (SSI 2011/386) para.4 (effective November 28, 2011).

[4] As amended by the Act of Sederunt (Rules of the Court of Session and Sheriff Court Rules Amendment) (Miscellaneous) 2014 (SSI 2014/201) para.3 (effective July 7, 2014).

(4) The pursuer shall lodge a certified copy of the record, which shall consist of the pleadings of the parties, in process by the date specified in the timetable and shall at the same time send one copy to the defender and any other parties.

(5) The pursuer shall, on lodging the certified copy of the record as required by paragraph (4), apply by motion to the sheriff, craving the court—

    (a)   to allow to parties a preliminary proof on specified matters;

    (b)   to allow a proof; or

   (ba)   to allow a jury trial;

    (c)   to make some other specified order.

(6) The motion lodged under paragraph (5) must specify the anticipated length of the preliminary proof, proof, or jury trial, as the case may be.

(7) In the event that any party proposes to crave the court to make any order other than an order allowing a proof under paragraph (5)(b) or a jury trial under paragraph (5)(ba), that party shall, on making or opposing (as the case may be) the pursuer's motion, specify the order to be sought and give full notice in the motion or the notice of opposition thereto of the grounds thereof.

(8) *[As repealed by Act of Sederunt (Rules of the Court of Session, Ordinary Cause Rules and Summary Cause Rules Amendment) (Miscellaneous) 2014 (SSI 2014/152) para.3 (effective July 7, 2014).]*

(8A) A party who seeks to rely on the evidence of a person not on his or her list lodged in accordance with paragraph (1A)(g) must, if any other party objects to such evidence being admitted, seek leave of the sheriff to admit that evidence whether it is to be given orally or not; and such leave may be granted on such conditions, if any, as the sheriff thinks fit.

(8B) The list of witnesses intimated in accordance with paragraph (1A)(g) must include the name, occupation (where known) and address of each intended witness and indicate whether the witness is considered to be a vulnerable witness within the meaning of section 11(1) of the Act of 2004 and whether any child witness notice or vulnerable witness application has been lodged in respect of that witness.

(9) A production which is not lodged in accordance with paragraph (1A)(g) shall not be used or put in evidence at proof unless—

    (a)   by consent of parties; or

    (b)   with the leave of the sheriff on cause shown and on such conditions, if any, as to expenses or otherwise as the court thinks fit.

(10) In a cause which is one of a number of causes arising out of the same cause of action, the sheriff may—

    (a)   on the motion of a party to that cause; and

    (b)   after hearing parties to all those causes,

appoint that cause or any part of those causes to be the leading cause and to sist the other causes pending the determination of the leading cause.

(11) In this rule, "pursuer" includes additional pursuer or minuter as the case may be.

Applications for sist or for variation of timetable

36.H1.—[1](1) The action may be sisted or the timetable varied by the sheriff on an application by any party to the action by motion.

  (2) An application under paragraph (1)—

    (a)   shall be placed before the sheriff; and

D1.473

---

[1] As amended by the Act of Sederunt (Sheriff Court Rules) (Miscellaneous Amendments) 2010 (SSI 2010/279) para.4 (effective July 29, 2010).

(b)[1]   shall be granted only on cause shown.

(3) Any sist of an action in terms of this rule shall be for a specific period.

(4) Where the timetable issued under rule 36.G1 is varied under this rule, the sheriff clerk shall issue a revised timetable in Form PI5.

(5) A revised timetable issued under paragraph (4) shall have effect as if it were a timetable issued under rule 36.G1 and any reference in this Part to any action being taken in accordance with the timetable shall be construed as a reference to its being taken in accordance with the timetable as varied under this rule.

Statements of valuation of claim

D1.474
36.J1.—(1) Each party to the action shall make a statement of valuation of claim in Form PI6.

(2) A statement of valuation of claim (which shall include a list of supporting documents) shall be lodged in process.

(3) Each party shall, on lodging a statement of valuation of claim—

(a)   intimate the list of documents included in the statement of valuation of claim to every other party; and

(b)   lodge each of those documents.

(4) Nothing in paragraph (3) shall affect—

(a)   the law relating to, or the right of a party to object to, the recovery of a document on the ground of privilege or confidentiality; or

(b)   the right of a party to apply under rule 28.2 for a commission and diligence for recovery of documents or an order under section 1 of the Administration of Justice (Scotland) Act 1972.

(5) Without prejudice to paragraph (2) of rule 36.L1, where a party has failed to lodge a statement of valuation of claim in accordance with a timetable issued under rule 36.G1, the sheriff may, at any hearing under paragraph (3) of that rule—

(a)   where the party in default is the pursuer, dismiss the action; or

(b)   where the party in default is the defender, grant decree against the defender for an amount not exceeding the pursuer's valuation.

Pre-trial meetings

D1.475
36.K1.—[2](1) For the purposes of this rule, a pre-trial meeting is a meeting between the parties to—

(a)   discuss settlement of the action; and

(b)   agree, so far as is possible, the matters which are not in dispute between them.

(2) A pre-trial meeting must—

(a)   be held not later than four weeks before the date assigned for the proof or trial; and

(b)   be attended by parties—

(i)   in person; or

(ii)   by means of video-conference facilities.

(3) Subject to any variation of the timetable in terms of rule 36.H1 (applications for sist or variation of timetable), a joint minute of a pre-trial meeting, made in Form PI7 (minute of pre-trial meeting), must be lodged in process by the pursuer not later than three weeks before the date assigned for proof or trial.

---

[1] As amended by the Act of Sederunt (Rules of the Court of Session and Sheriff Court Rules Amendment) (Miscellaneous) 2014 (SSI 2014/201) para.3 (effective July 7, 2014).
[2] As substituted by the Act of Sederunt (Rules of the Court of Session 1994 and Sheriff Court Rules Amendment) (No. 2) (Personal Injury and Remits) 2015 (SSI 2015/227) para.8 (effective September 22, 2015).

(4)   Where a joint minute in Form PI7 has not been lodged in accordance with paragraph (3) and by the date specified in the timetable the sheriff clerk must fix a date and time for the parties to be heard by the sheriff.

(5)   If a party is not in attendance during the pre-trial meeting, the representative of such party must have access to the party or another person who has authority to commit the party in settlement of the action.

Incidental hearings

36.L1.—(1)[1]   Where the sheriff clerk fixes a date and time for a hearing under paragraph (3) of rule 36.G1 or paragraph (4) of rule 36.K1 he shall—

D1.476

    (a)   fix a date not less than seven days after the date of the notice referred to in subparagraph (b);

    (b)   give notice to the parties to the action—

        (i)   of the date and time of the hearing; and

        (ii)   requiring the party in default to lodge in process a written explanation as to why the timetable has not been complied with and to intimate a copy to all other parties, not less than two clear working days before the date of the hearing.

(2)   At the hearing, the sheriff—

    (a)   shall consider any explanation provided by the party in default;

    (b)   may award expenses against that party; and

    (c)   may make any other appropriate order, including decree of dismissal.

Part I – Intimation to Connected Persons in Certain Actions of Damages

Application and interpretation of this Part

36.1.—[2](1)   This Part applies to an action of damages in which, following the death of any person from personal injuries, damages are claimed—

D1.477

    (a)   in respect of the injuries from which the deceased died; or

    (b)   in respect of the death of the deceased.

(2)   In this Part—

"connected person" means a person, not being a party to the action, who has title to sue the defender in respect of the personal injuries from which the deceased died or in respect of his death;

Averments

36.2.   In an action to which this Part applies, the pursuer shall aver in the condescendence, as the case may be—

D1.478

    (a)   that there are no connected persons;

    (b)   that there are connected persons, being the persons specified in the crave for intimation;

    (c)   that there are connected persons in respect of whom intimation should be dispensed with on the ground that—

        (i)   the names or whereabouts of such persons are not known to, and cannot reasonably be ascertained by, the pursuer; or

        (ii)   such persons are unlikely to be awarded more than £200 each.

---

[1] As amended by the Act of Sederunt (Rules of the Court of Session 1994 and Sheriff Court Rules Amendment) (No. 2) (Miscellaneous) 2016 (SSI 2016/229) para.2 (effective 28 November 2016).
[2] As amended by the Act of Sederunt (Sheriff Court Rules) (Miscellaneous Amendments) (No.2) 2011 (SSI 2011/289) para.2 (effective July 7, 2011).

Warrants for intimation

D1.479   **36.3.**—(1)   Where the pursuer makes averments under rule 36.2(b) (existence of connected persons), he shall include a crave in the initial writ for intimation to any person who is believed to have title to sue the defender in an action in respect of the death of the deceased or the personal injuries from which the deceased died.

(2)   A notice of intimation in Form D1 shall be attached to the copy of the initial writ where intimation is given on a warrant under paragraph (1).

Applications to dispense with intimation

D1.480   **36.4.**—(1)   Where the pursuer makes averments under rule 36.2(c) (dispensing with intimation to connected persons), he shall apply by crave in the initial writ for an order to dispense with intimation.

(2)   In determining an application under paragraph (1), the sheriff shall have regard to—

(a)   the desirability of avoiding a multiplicity of actions; and

(b)   the expense, inconvenience or difficulty likely to be involved in taking steps to ascertain the name or whereabouts of the connected person.

(3)   Where the sheriff is not satisfied that intimation to a connected person should be dispensed with, he may—

(a)   order intimation to a connected person whose name and whereabouts are known;

(b)   order the pursuer to take such further steps as he may specify in the interlocutor to ascertain the name or whereabouts of any connected person; and

(c)   order advertisement in such manner, place and at such times as he may specify in the interlocutor.

Subsequent disclosure of connected persons

D1.481   **36.5.**   Where the name or whereabouts of a person, in respect of whom the sheriff has dispensed with intimation on a ground specified in rule 36.2(c) (dispensing with intimation to connected persons), subsequently becomes known to the pursuer, the pursuer shall apply to the sheriff by motion for a warrant for intimation to such a person; and such intimation shall be made in accordance with rule 36.3(2).

Connected persons entering process

D1.482   **36.6.**—(1)   A connected person may apply by minute craving leave to be sisted as an additional pursuer to the action.

(2)   Such a minute shall also crave leave of the sheriff to adopt the existing grounds of action, and to amend the craves, condescendence and pleas-in-law.

(3)   The period within which answers to a minute under this rule may be lodged shall be 14 days from the date of intimation of the minute.

(4)[1]   Rule 14.13 (procedure following grant of minute) shall not apply to a minute to which this rule applies.

Failure to enter process

D1.483   **36.7.**   Where a connected person to whom intimation is made in accordance with this Part—

(a)   does not apply to be sisted as an additional pursuer to the action,

(b)   subsequently raises a separate action against the same defender in respect of the same personal injuries or death, and

---

[1] As substituted by the Act of Sederunt (Sheriff Court Ordinary Cause Rules Amendment) (Miscellaneous) 1996 (SI 1996/2445) r.3 (effective November 1, 1996).

(c) would, apart from this rule, be awarded the expenses or part of the expenses of that action,

he shall not be awarded those expenses except on cause shown.

Part II – Interim Payments of Damages

Application and interpretation of this Part

36.8.—(1) This Part applies to an action of damages for personal injuries or the death of a person in consequence of personal injuries.

(2) In this Part—

"defender" includes a third party against whom the pursuer has a crave for damages;

"personal injuries" includes any disease or impairment of a physical or mental condition.

Applications for interim payment of damages

36.9.—(1) In an action to which this Part applies, a pursuer may, at any time after defences have been lodged, apply by motion for an order for interim payment of damages to him by the defender or, where there are two or more of them, by any one or more of them.

(2) The pursuer shall intimate a motion under paragraph (1) to every other party on a period of notice of 14 days.

(3) On a motion under paragraph (1), the sheriff may, if satisfied that—

(a) the defender has admitted liability to the pursuer in the action, or

(b) if the action proceeded to proof, the pursuer would succeed in the action on the question of liability without any substantial finding of contributory negligence on his part, or on the part of any person in respect of whose injury or death the claim of the pursuer arises, and would obtain decree for damages against any defender,

ordain that defender to make an interim payment to the pursuer of such amount as the sheriff thinks fit, not exceeding a reasonable proportion of the damages which, in the opinion of the sheriff, are likely to be recovered by the pursuer.

(4) Any such payment may be ordered to be made in one lump sum or otherwise as the sheriff thinks fit.

(5)[1] No order shall be made against a defender under this rule unless it appears to the sheriff that the defender is—

(a) a person who is insured in respect of the claim of the pursuer;

(b) a public authority;

(c) a person whose means and resources are such as to enable him to make the interim payment; or

(d) the person's liability will be met by—

(i) an insurer under section 151 of the Road Traffic Act 1988; or

(ii) an insurer acting under the Motor Insurers Bureau Agreement, or the Motor Insurers Bureau where it is acting itself.

(6) Notwithstanding the grant or refusal of a motion for an interim payment, a subsequent motion may be made where there has been a change of circumstances.

(7) Subject to Part IV (management of damages payable to persons under legal disability) an interim payment shall be paid to the pursuer unless the sheriff otherwise directs.

D1.484

D1.485

---

[1] Amended by the Act of Sederunt (Ordinary Cause, Summary Application and Small Claim Rules) Amendment (Miscellaneous) 2004 (SSI 2004/197) (effective May 21, 2004), para.2(13).

(8) This rule shall, with the necessary modifications, apply to a counterclaim for damages for personal injuries made by a defender as it applies to an action in which the pursuer may apply for an order for interim payment of damages.

Adjustment on final decree

D1.486   **36.10.** Where a defender has made an interim payment under rule 36.9, the sheriff may, when final decree is pronounced, make such order with respect to the interim payment as he thinks fit to give effect to the final liability of that defender to the pursuer; and in particular may order—

(a) repayment by the pursuer of any sum by which the interim payment exceeds the amount which that defender is liable to pay to the pursuer; or

(b) payment by any other defender or a third party, of any part of the interim payment which the defender who made it is entitled to recover from him by way of contribution or indemnity or in respect of any remedy or relief relating to, or connected with, the claim of the pursuer.

Part III – Provisional Damages for Personal Injuries

Application and interpretation of this Part

D1.487   **36.11.**—(1) This Part applies to an action of damages for personal injuries.

(2) In this Part—

"the Act of 1982" means the Administration of Justice Act 1982;
"further damages" means the damages referred to in section 12(4)(b) of the Act of 1982;
"provisional damages" means the damages referred to in section 12(4)(a) of the Act of 1982.

Applications for provisional damages

D1.488   **36.12.** An application under section 12(2)(a) of the Act of 1982 for provisional damages for personal injuries shall be made by including in the initial writ—

(a) a crave for provisional damages;

(b) averments in the condescendence supporting the crave, including averments—

(i) that there is a risk that, at some definite or indefinite time in the future, the pursuer will, as a result of the act or omission which gave rise to the cause of action, develop some serious disease or suffer some serious deterioration of his physical or mental condition; and

(ii) that the defender was, at the time of the act or omission which gave rise to the cause of action, a public authority, public corporation or insured or otherwise indemnified in respect of the claim; and

(c) an appropriate plea-in-law.

Applications for further damages

D1.489   **36.13.**—(1) An application for further damages by a pursuer in respect of whom an order under section 12(2)(b) of the Act of 1982 has been made shall be made by minute in the process of the action to which it relates and shall include—

(a) a crave for further damages;

(b) averments in the statement of facts supporting that crave; and

(c) appropriate pleas-in-law.

(2) On lodging such a minute in process, the pursuer shall apply by motion for warrant to serve the minute on—

(a) every other party; and

(b) where such other party is insured or otherwise indemnified, his insurer or indemnifier, if known to the pursuer.

(3) Any such party, insurer or indemnifier may lodge answers to such a minute in process within 28 days after the date of service on him.

(4) Where answers have been lodged under paragraph (3), the sheriff may, on the motion of any party, make such further order as to procedure as he thinks fit.

Part IV – Management of Damages Payable to Persons under Legal Disability

Orders for payment and management of money

36.14.—(1)[1] In an action of damages in which a sum of money becomes payable, by virtue of a decree or an extra-judicial settlement, to or for the benefit of a person under legal disability (other than a person under the age of 18 years), the sheriff shall make such order regarding the payment and management of that sum for the benefit of that person as he thinks fit.

(2) An order under paragraph (1) shall be made on the granting of decree for payment or of absolvitor.

D1.490

Methods of management

36.15. In making an order under rule 36.14(1), the sheriff may—

(a) appoint a judicial factor to apply, invest or otherwise deal with the money for the benefit of the person under legal disability;

(b) order the money to be paid to—
  (i)   the Accountant of Court, or
  (ii) the guardian of the person under legal disability,

  as trustee, to be applied, invested or otherwise dealt with and administered under the directions of the sheriff for the benefit of the person under legal disability;

(c) order the money to be paid to the sheriff clerk of the sheriff court district in which the person under legal disability resides, to be applied, invested or otherwise dealt with and administered, under the directions of the sheriff of that district, for the benefit of the person under legal disability; or

(d) order the money to be paid directly to the person under legal disability.

D1.491

Subsequent orders

36.16.—(1) Where the sheriff has made an order under rule 36.14(1), any person having an interest may apply for an appointment or order under rule 36.15, or any other order for the payment or management of the money, by minute in the process of the cause to which the application relates.

(2) An application for directions under rule 36.15(b) or (c) may be made by any person having an interest by minute in the process of the cause to which the application relates.

D1.492

Management of money paid to sheriff clerk

36.17.—(1) A receipt in Form D2 by the sheriff clerk shall be a sufficient discharge in respect of the amount paid to him under this Part.

(2) The sheriff clerk shall, at the request of any competent court, accept custody of any sum of money in an action of damages ordered to be paid to, applied, invested or otherwise dealt with by him, for the benefit of a person under legal disability.

D1.493

---

[1] As amended by S.I. 1996 No. 2167 (effective November 1, 1996).

(3)   Any money paid to the sheriff clerk under this Part shall be paid out, applied, invested or otherwise dealt with by the sheriff clerk only after such intimation, service and enquiry as the sheriff may order.

(4)   Any sum of money invested by the sheriff clerk under this Part shall be invested in a manner in which trustees are authorised to invest by virtue of the Trustee Investments Act 1961.

Part IV A[1] – Productions in Certain Actions of Damages

D1.494   **36.17A.–36.17C**   *[Omitted by the Act of Sederunt (Rules of the Court of Session 1994 and Sheriff Court Rules Amendment) (No.2) (Personal Injury and Remits) 2015 (SSI 2015/227) r.8 (effective September 22, 2015).]*

Part V – Sex Discrimination Act 1975

Causes under section 66 of the Act of 1975

D1.495   **36.18.**   *[Omitted by the Act of Sederunt (Ordinary Cause, Summary Application, Summary Cause and Small Claim Rules) Amendment (Equality Act 2006 etc.) 2006 (SSI 2006/509) (effective November 3, 2006).]*

[THE NEXT PARAGRAPH IS D1.497]

Part VI[2] – Mesothelioma Actions: Special Provisions

Mesothelioma actions: special provisions

D1.497   **36.19.**—(1)[3]   This Part applies where liability to a relative of the pursuer may arise under section 5 of the Damages (Scotland) Act 2011 (discharge of liability to pay damages: exception for mesothelioma).

(2)   On settlement of the pursuer's claim, the pursuer may apply by motion for all or any of the following—

(a)   a sist for a specified period;

(b)   discharge of any diet;

(c)   where the action is one to which the personal injuries procedure in Part A1 of this Chapter applies, variation of the timetable issued under rule 36.G1.

(3)   Paragraphs (4) to (7) apply where a motion under paragraph (2) has been granted.

(4)   As soon as reasonably practicable after the death of the pursuer, any agent who immediately prior to the death was instructed in a cause by the deceased pursuer shall notify the court of the death.

(5)   The notification under paragraph (4) shall be by letter to the sheriff clerk and shall be accompanied by a certified copy of the death certificate relative to the deceased pursuer.

(6)   A relative of the deceased may apply by motion for the recall of the sist and for an order for further procedure.

---

[1] As inserted by the Act of Sederunt (Sheriff Court Ordinary Cause Rules Amendment) (Miscellaneous) 2000 (SSI 2000/239) (effective October 2, 2000).

[2] As inserted by the Act of Sederunt (Ordinary Cause Rules Amendment) (Personal Injuries Actions) 2009 (SSI 2009/285) r.2 (effective November 2, 2009).

[3] As amended by the Act of Sederunt (Sheriff Court Rules) (Miscellaneous Amendments) (No.2) 2011 (SSI 2011/289) para.2 (effective July 7, 2011).

(7) On expiration of the period of any sist pronounced on a motion under paragraph (2), the sheriff clerk may fix a date and time for the parties to be heard by the sheriff.

Chapter 36A[1]

Case Management of Certain Personal Injuries Actions

Application and interpretation of this Chapter

36A.1—(1) This Chapter applies to actions appointed to the procedure in this Chapter by virtue of rule 36.C1 (actions based on clinical negligence), rule 36.F1 (disapplication of personal injuries procedure), or under paragraph (2).

D1.497.1

(2) The sheriff may, after considering the likely complexity of an action and being satisfied that the efficient determination of the action would be served by doing so, appoint an action to which Chapter 36 applies (including actions relating to catastrophic injuries) to the procedure in this Chapter, rather than personal injuries procedure.

(3) Any party to an action may apply by motion to have the action withdrawn from the procedure in this Chapter.

(4) No motion under paragraph (3) will be granted unless the court is satisfied that there are exceptional reasons for not following the procedure in this Chapter.

(5) These Rules apply to an action to which this Chapter applies, subject to the following modifications—

(a) Chapters 9, 9A, 10, 22 and 28A do not apply;

(b) despite subparagraph (a), the following rules of Chapter 9 apply—

    (i) rule 9.1 (notice of intention to defend);

    (ii) rule 9.3 (return of initial writ);

    (iii) rule 9.5 (process folder);

    (iv) rule 9.6 (defences);

    (v) rule 9.7 (implied admissions);

(c) in the application of rule 18.3(1) (applications to amend), a minute of amendment lodged in process must include, where appropriate, confirmation as to whether any warrants are sought under rule 36.B1(2)(a) (warrants for intimation) or whether a specification of documents is sought under rule 36.B1(2)(b) (specification of documents);

(d) rule 18.5(3) (fixing of hearing following service of amended pleadings and lodging of notice of intention to defend) does not apply;

(e) in the application of rule 19.1 (counterclaims) a counterclaim may also include—

    (i) warrants for intimation so far as permitted under these Rules; and

    (ii) a specification of documents in Form PI2;

(f) in rule 19.4 (disposal of counterclaims), paragraph (b) does not apply;

(g) in the application of rule 20.6 (procedure following answers)—

    (i) paragraphs (1) and (2) do not apply; and

    (ii) where a third party lodges answers, any timetable already fixed under rule 36A.9(5)(b) will apply to the third party;

(h) rule 29.11 does not apply;

(i) references elsewhere in these Rules to an Options Hearing are to be ignored; and

---

[1] As inserted by the Act of Sederunt (Rules of the Court of Session 1994 and Sheriff Court Rules Amendment) (No.2) (Personal Injury and Remits) 2015 (SSI 2015/227) para.8 (effective September 22, 2015).

(j)   references elsewhere in these Rules to any action carried out before or after the closing of the record will be construed as references to that action being carried out before, or as the case may be, after, the closing of the record under rule 36A.7.

(6) In this Chapter—

"personal injuries", "personal injuries action" and "personal injuries procedure" have the meanings given in rule 36.A1;

"witness statement" means a written statement containing a factual account conveying the evidence of the witness;

"proof" includes jury trial where an action is proceeding in the all Scotland sheriff court, and references to an action being sent to proof are to be construed as including the allowing of a jury trial in the action.

Form of initial writ

D1.497.2   **36A.2** Where the sheriff appoints an action to the procedure in this Chapter under rule 36A.1(2)—

(a)   the pursuer must within 14 days thereof lodge a revised initial writ in Form G1 (form of initial writ); and

(b)   the defender must thereafter adjust the defences so as to comply with rule 9.6(2) (defences).

Averments of medical treatment

D1.497.3   **36A.3.** The condescendence of the initial writ in an action to which this Chapter applies must include averments naming—

(a)   every general medical practitioner or general medical practice from whom; and

(b)   every hospital or other institution in which,

the pursuer or, in an action in respect of the death of a person, the deceased received treatment for the injuries sustained, or disease suffered.

Making up open record

D1.497.4   **36A.4.**—(1) The pursuer must lodge a copy of the pleadings in the form of an open record within the timescale in paragraph (2), (3) or (4), as the case may be.

(2) As regards an action appointed to this Chapter under rule 36.C1 (actions based on clinical negligence), the open record must be lodged within 14 days after the date on which defences are lodged under rule 9.6.

(3) As regards an action appointed to this Chapter under rule 36.F1 (disapplication of personal injuries procedure), the open record must be lodged within 14 days after the date on which defences are adjusted in accordance with rule 36.F1(4)(b).

(4) As regards an action appointed to this Chapter under rule 36A.1 (actions withdrawn from Chapter 36 by sheriff), the open record must be lodged—

(a)   where the action is appointed to this Chapter before the lodging of defences, within 14 days after the date on which defences are lodged under rule 9.6; or

(b)   where the action is appointed to this Chapter following the lodging of defences, within 14 days after the date on which defences are adjusted in accordance with rule 36A.2(b).

Period for adjustment

D1.497.5   **36A.5.**—(1) Where, under rule 36.C1 (actions based on clinical negligence), 36.F1 (disapplication of personal injuries procedure), or 36A.1 (actions withdrawn from Chapter 36 by sheriff), the sheriff orders that a cause will proceed in accordance with this Chapter, the sheriff must continue the cause for adjustment for a period of 8 weeks, which will commence the day after the lodging of the open record under rule 36A.4.

(2) Paragraphs (2) and (3) of rule 9.8 (exchange and record of adjustments) apply to a cause in which a period for adjustment under paragraph (1) of this rule has been allowed as they apply to the period for adjustment under that rule.

Variation of adjustment period

36A.6.—(1) At any time before the expiry of the period for adjustment the sheriff may close the record if parties, of consent or jointly, lodge a motion seeking such an order.

D1.497.6

(2) The sheriff may, if satisfied that there is sufficient reason for doing so, extend the period for adjustment for such period as the sheriff thinks fit, if any party—

(a) lodges a motion seeking such an order; and

(b) lodges a copy of the record adjusted to the date of lodging of the motion.

(3) A motion lodged under paragraph (2) must set out—

(a) the reasons for seeking an extension of the period for adjustment; and

(b) the period for adjustment sought.

Closing record

36A.7.—(1) On the expiry of the period for adjustment, the record closes.

D1.497.7

(2) Following the closing of the record, the sheriff clerk must, without the attendance of parties—

(a) prepare and sign an interlocutor recording the closing of the record and fixing the date of the Procedural Hearing under rule 36A.9, which date must be on the first suitable court day occurring not sooner than 21 days after the closing of the record; and

(b) intimate the date of the hearing to each party.

(3) The pursuer must, no later than 7 days before the Procedural Hearing fixed under paragraph (2)—

(a) send a copy of the closed record to the defender and to every other party; and

(b) lodge a certified copy of the closed record in process.

(4) The closed record is to consist only of the pleadings of the parties and any adjustments and amendments to them.

Lodging of written statements

36A.8. Each party must, no later than 7 days before the Procedural Hearing fixed under rule 36A.7(2) lodge in process and send to every other party a written statement containing proposals for further procedure which must state—

D1.497.8

(a) whether the party is seeking to have the action appointed to debate or to have the action sent to proof;

(b) where it is sought to have the action appointed to debate—

(i) the legal argument on which any preliminary plea should be sustained or repelled; and

(ii) the principal authorities (including statutory provisions) on which the argument is founded;

(c) where it is sought to have the action appointed to proof—

(i) the issues for proof;

(ii) the names, occupations (where known) and addresses of the witnesses who are intended to be called to give evidence, including the matters to which each witness is expected to speak and the time estimated for each witness;

(iii) whether any such witness is considered to be a vulnerable witness within the meaning of section 11(1) of the Act of 2004 and whether any child witness notice under section 12(2) of that Act or vulnerable witness application under section 12(6) of that Act has been, or is to be, lodged in respect of that witness;

(iv) the progress made in preparing and exchanging the reports of any skilled persons;

(v) the progress made in obtaining and exchanging records, particularly medical records;

(vi) the progress made in taking and exchanging witness statements;

(vii) the time estimated for proof and how that estimate was arrived at;

(viii) any other progress that has been made, is to be made, or could be made in advance of the proof;

(ix) whether an application has been or is to be made under rule 36B.2 (applications for jury trial).

Procedural Hearing

D1.497.9 **36A.9.**—(1) At the Procedural Hearing, the sheriff, after considering the written statements lodged by the parties under rule 36A.8 and hearing from the parties, is to determine whether the action should be appointed to debate or sent to proof on the whole or any part of the action.

(2) Before determining whether the action should be appointed to debate the sheriff is to hear from the parties with a view to ascertaining whether agreement can be reached on the points of law in contention.

(3) Where the action is appointed to debate, the sheriff may order that written arguments on any question of law are to be submitted.

(4) Before determining whether the action should be sent to proof, the sheriff is to hear from parties with a view to ascertaining—

(a) the matters in dispute between the parties;

(b) the readiness of parties to proceed to proof; and

(c) without prejudice to the generality of subparagraphs (a) and (b)—

(i) whether reports of skilled persons have been exchanged;

(ii) the nature and extent of the dispute between skilled persons;

(iii) whether there are facts that can be agreed between parties, upon which skilled persons can comment;

(iv)[1] the extent to which agreement can be reached between the parties on the relevant literature upon which skilled persons intend to rely;

(v) whether there has been a meeting between skilled persons, or whether such a meeting would be useful;

(vi) whether a proof on a particular issue would allow scope for the matter to be resolved;

(vii) whether witness statements have been exchanged;

(viii) whether any party is experiencing difficulties in obtaining precognition facilities;

(ix) whether all relevant records have been recovered and whether there is an agreed bundle of medical records;

---

[1] As amended by the Act of Sederunt (Rules of the Court of Session 1994 and Sheriff Court Rules Amendment) (No.2) (Personal Injury and Remits) 2015 (SI 2015/227) r.8, as amended by the Act of Sederunt (Ordinary Cause Rules 1993 Amendment and Miscellaneous Amendments) 2015 (SSI 2015/296) r.4(3) (effective 1 January 2016).

    (x)   whether there is a relevant case that is supported by evidence of skilled persons;

    (xi)   if there is no evidence of skilled persons to support a relevant case, whether such evidence is necessary;

    (xii)   whether there is a relevant defence to any or all of the cases supported by evidence of skilled persons;

    (xiii)   if there is no evidence of skilled persons to support a relevant defence, whether such evidence is necessary;

    (xiv)   whether causation of some or all of the injuries is the main area of dispute and, if so, what the position of the respective skilled person is;

    (xv)   whether valuations have been, or could be, exchanged;

    (xvi)   if valuations have been exchanged showing a significant disparity, whether parties should be asked to provide an explanation for such disparity;

    (xvii)   whether a joint minute has been considered;

    (xviii)   whether any of the heads of damage can be agreed;

    (ixx)   whether any orders would facilitate the resolution of the case or the narrowing of the scope of the dispute;

    (xx)   whether a pre-trial meeting should be fixed;

    (xxi)   whether amendment, other than updating, is anticipated; and

    (xxii)   the time required for proof.

(5) Where the action is sent to proof the sheriff must—

    (a)   fix a date for the hearing of the proof;

    (b)   fix a pre-proof timetable in accordance with rule 36A.10.

(6) The sheriff may fix a further Procedural Hearing—

    (a)   on the motion of any party;

    (b)   on the sheriff's own initiative.

(7) A further hearing under paragraph (6) may be fixed—

    (a)   at the Procedural Hearing or at any time thereafter;

    (b)   whether or not the action has been appointed to debate or sent to proof.

Pre-proof timetable

36A.10.—(1) The pre-proof timetable mentioned in rule 36A.9(5)(b) must **D1.497.10** contain provision for the following—

    (a)   no later than 24 weeks before the proof—

        (i)   a date for a pre-proof hearing;

        (ii)   the last date for the lodging of a draft valuation and vouchings by the pursuer;

    (b)   no later than 20 weeks before the proof, the last date for the lodging of a draft valuation and vouchings by the defender;

    (c)[1]   no later than 16 weeks before the proof, the last date for the lodging of witness lists and productions, including a paginated joint bundle of medical records, by the parties;

    (d)   no later than 12 weeks before the proof, the last date for a pre-trial meeting;

    (e)   no later than 8 weeks before the proof, a date for a further pre-proof hearing.

---

[1] As amended by the Act of Sederunt (Sheriff Court Rules Amendment) (Miscellaneous) 2016 (SSI 2016/367) para.2 (effective 28 November 2016).

(2) Rule 36.K1(1), (2)(b) and (5) applies to a pre-trial meeting held under this Chapter as it applies to a pre-trial meeting held under Chapter 36.

(3) Prior to the pre-proof hearing mentioned in subparagraph (1)(e)—

    (a) the pursuer must lodge in process a joint minute of the pre-trial meeting in Form PI7 (minute of pre-trial meeting);

    (b) the parties must lodge in process any other joint minutes.

(4) At any time the sheriff may, at the sheriff's own instance or on the motion of a party—

    (a) fix a pre-proof hearing;

    (b) vary the pre-proof timetable,

where the sheriff considers that the efficient determination of the action would be served by doing so.

Power of sheriff to make orders

D1.497.11 **36A.11.**—(1) Following the fixing of a hearing under rule 36A.9(6) or 36A.10(4)(a), or the variation of the pre-proof timetable under rule 36A.10(4)(b), the sheriff may make such orders as the sheriff thinks necessary to secure the efficient determination of the action

(2) In particular, the sheriff may make orders to resolve any matters arising or outstanding from the written statements lodged by the parties under rule 36A.8 or the pre-proof timetable fixed under rule 36A.9(5)(b).

Chapter 36B[1]

Jury Trials

Application and interpretation of this Chapter

D1.497.12 **36B.1.**—(1) This Chapter applies where a personal injuries action is—

    (a) proceeding in the all-Scotland sheriff court; and

    (b) an interlocutor has been issued allowing a jury trial—

        (i) following an application under rule 36.G1 (allocation of diets and timetables); or

        (ii) under rule 36A.9 (procedural hearing).

(2) For the purposes of this Chapter, references in other provisions of these Rules to proof are to be construed as including jury trial.

(3) In this Chapter—

    (a) the "issue" or "issues" for jury trial means the question or questions to be put to the jury within the meaning of section 63 of the 2014 Act;

    (b) "personal injuries action" has the meaning given in rule 36.A1.

Applications for jury trial

D1.497.13 **36B.2.**—(1) Within 14 days after the date of an interlocutor allowing a jury trial, the pursuer must lodge in process the proposed issue for jury trial and a copy of it for the use of the court.

(2) Where the pursuer fails to lodge a proposed issue—

    (a) the pursuer is held to have departed from the right to jury trial unless—

        (i) the court, on cause shown, otherwise orders; or

        (ii) another party lodges a proposed issue under paragraph (3);

    (b) any other party may apply by motion for a proof.

---

[1] As inserted by the Act of Sederunt (Rules of the Court of Session 1994 and Sheriff Court Rules Amendment) (No.2) (Personal Injury and Remits) 2015 (SSI 2015/227) para.8 (effective September 22, 2015).

(3)   Where a pursuer fails to lodge a proposed issue, any other party may, within 7 days after the expiry of the period specified in paragraph (1), lodge in process a proposed issue for jury trial and a copy of it.

(4)   Where a proposed issue has been lodged under paragraph (1) or (3), any other party may, within 7 days after the date on which the proposed issue has been lodged, lodge in process a proposed counter-issue and a copy of it for the use of the court.

(5)   A proposed counter-issue may include any question of fact which is made the subject of a specific averment on record or is relevant to the party's pleas-in-law notwithstanding that it does not in terms meet the proposed issue.

(6)   The party lodging a proposed issue must, on the day after the date on which the period for lodging a proposed counter-issue expires, apply by motion for approval of the proposed issue.

(7)   Any party who has lodged a proposed counter-issue under paragraph (4) must, within 7 days after the lodging of a motion for approval of a proposed issue under paragraph (6), apply by motion for approval of the proposed counter-issue.

(8)   Where a motion for approval of a proposed counter-issue has been lodged, the motion for approval of a proposed issue will be heard at the same time as that motion.

(9)   The sheriff, on granting a motion for approval of a proposed issue or proposed counter-issue, must specify in an interlocutor the approved issues to be put to the jury.

Citation of jurors

36B.3.—(1)   The interlocutor of a sheriff issued under rule 36B.2(9) is sufficient   **D1.497.14**
authority for the sheriff clerk to summon persons to attend as jurors at the diet for jury trial in accordance with this rule.

(2)   Where an interlocutor is issued under rule 36B.2(9)—

   (a)   a list of not less than 36 jurors is to be prepared of an equal number of men and women from the lists of potential jurors maintained for the sheriff court district of Edinburgh in accordance with section 3 of the Jurors (Scotland) Act 1825; and

   (b)   the sheriff clerk is to summon those persons to attend as jurors at the diet for jury trial.

(3)   A citation of a person to attend as a juror is to be in Form G13A (form of citation of juror) and is to be executed by post.

Ineligibility for, and excusal from, jury service

36B.4.—(1)   A person summoned to serve on a jury may, as soon as possible   **D1.497.15**
after receipt of Form G13A, apply to the sheriff clerk to be released from the citation by completing and returning that Form.

(2)   The sheriff clerk may, if satisfied that—

   (a)   there are good and sufficient grounds for excusal; or

   (b)   the person is ineligible for jury service,

grant the application.

(3)   The sheriff to preside at the jury trial may, at any time before the jury is empanelled, excuse any person summoned to attend as a juror from attendance if satisfied that there are good and sufficient grounds for doing so.

Application of certain rules relating to proofs

36B.5.—(1)   Chapter 29 of these Rules applies to an action in which issues have   **D1.497.16**
been approved for jury trial as they apply to an action in which a proof has been allowed.

(2) Despite paragraph (1), the following rules of Chapter 29 do not apply—

    (a) rule 29.4 (renouncing probation);

    (b) rule 29.5 (orders for proof);

    (c) rule 29.6 (hearing parts of proof separately);

    (d) rule 29.11 (lodging productions);

    (e) rule 29.15 (instruction of shorthand writer).

Failure of party to appear at jury trial

D1.497.17 **36B.6.** Where a party does not appear at the diet for jury trial, then—

    (a) if the party appearing is the pursuer or the party on whom the burden of proof lies, that party will be entitled to lead evidence, and go to the jury for a verdict;

    (b) if the party appearing is the defender or the party on whom the burden of proof does not lie, that party will be entitled to obtain a verdict in that party's favour without leading evidence.

Administration of oath or affirmation to jurors

D1.497.18 **36B.7.**—(1) Subject to paragraph (2), the sheriff clerk must administer the oath collectively to the jury in Form PI8 (form of oath for jurors).

(2) Where a juror elects to affirm, the sheriff clerk will administer the affirmation to that juror in Form PI9 (form of affirmation for jurors).

Exceptions to sheriff's charge

D1.497.19 **36B.8.**—(1) Where a party seeks to take exception to a direction on a point of law given by the sheriff in the sheriff's charge to the jury or to request the sheriff to give a direction differing from or supplementary to the directions in the charge, that party must, immediately on the conclusion of the charge, so intimate to the sheriff, who will hear the parties in the absence of the jury.

(2) The party dissatisfied with the charge to the jury must formulate in writing the exception taken or the direction sought; and the exception or direction, as the case may be, and the sheriff's decision on it, must be recorded in a note of exception under the direction of the sheriff and is to be certified by the sheriff.

(3) After the note of exception has been certified, the sheriff may give such further or other directions to the jury in open court as the sheriff thinks fit before the jury considers its verdict.

Further questions for jury

D1.497.20 **36B.9.**—(1) The sheriff may, after the evidence has been led, submit to the jury such further questions as the sheriff thinks fit.

(2) Any such questions must be specified by the sheriff in an interlocutor and submitted to the jury in writing along with the issue and any counter-issue.

Application of verdicts

D1.497.21 **36B.10.** Any party may, after the expiry of 7 days after the date on which the verdict was returned in accordance with section 68 of the 2014 Act, apply by motion to apply the verdict, grant decree in accordance with it and make any award in relation to expenses.

Recording of proceedings at jury trial

D1.497.22 **36B.11.**—(1) Subject to any other provisions in these Rules, proceedings at a jury trial must be recorded by—

    (a) a shorthand writer to whom the oath *de fideli administratione* in connection with the sheriff court service generally has been administered; or

    (b) tape recording or other mechanical means approved by the court.

(2)   In paragraph (1), "the proceedings" means the whole proceedings including, without prejudice to that generality—

    (a)   discussions—

        (i)   with respect to any challenge of a juror; and

        (ii) on any question arising in the course of the trial;

    (b)   the decision of the sheriff on any matter referred to in subparagraph (a);

    (c)   the evidence led at the trial;

    (d)   the sheriff's charge to the jury;

    (e)   the speeches of counsel or solicitors;

    (f)   the verdict of the jury; and

    (g)   any request for a direction to be given under rule 36B.8, any hearing in relation to such a request and any direction so given.

(3)   A transcript of the record of proceedings will be made only on the direction of the court and the cost must, in the first instance, be borne by the solicitors for the parties in equal proportions.

(4)   Any transcript so made must be certified as a faithful record of proceedings—

    (a)   where the recording was under paragraph (1)(a), by whoever recorded the proceedings; and

    (b)   where it was under paragraph (1)(b), by whoever transcribed the record.

(5)   The sheriff may make such alterations to the transcript as appear to the sheriff to be necessary after hearing the parties and, where such alterations are made, the sheriff must authenticate the alterations.

(6)   Where a transcript has been so made for the use of the court, copies of it may be obtained by any party from the transcriber on payment of the transcriber's fee.

(7)   Except with leave of the court, the transcript may be borrowed from process only for the purpose of enabling a party to consider whether to appeal against the interlocutor of the sheriff applying the verdict of the jury or whether to apply for a new trial.

(8)   Where a transcript is required for a purpose mentioned in paragraph (7) but has not been directed to be transcribed under paragraph (3), a party—

    (a)   may request such a transcript from the shorthand writer, or as the case may be, from a person who might have transcribed the recording had there been such a direction, the cost of the requested transcript being borne by the solicitor for the requester in the first instance; and

    (b)   must lodge the transcript in process;

and copies of it may be obtained by any party from the transcriber on payment of the transcriber's fee.

[THE NEXT PARAGRAPH IS D1.498]

Chapter 37

Causes under the Presumption of Death (Scotland) Act 1977

Interpretation of this Chapter

37.1.   In this Chapter—   **D1.498**

"the Act of 1977" means the Presumption of Death (Scotland) Act 1977;

"action of declarator" means an action under section 1(1) of the Act of 1977;

"missing person" has the meaning assigned in section 1(1) of the Act of 1977.

Parties to, and service and intimation of, actions of declarator

D1.499   **37.2.**—(1)[1,2] In an action of declarator—

   (a)   the missing person shall be named as the defender;

   (b)   subject to paragraph (2), service on that person shall be executed by advertisement in such newspaper or other publication as the sheriff thinks fit of such facts relating to the missing person and set out in the initial writ as the sheriff may specify; and

   (c)   the period of notice shall be 21 days from the date of publication of the advertisement unless the sheriff otherwise directs.

   (2)[3] The advertisement mentioned in paragraph (1) shall be in Form P1.

   (3)   Subject to paragraph (5), in an action of declarator, the pursuer shall include a crave for a warrant for intimation to—

   (a)   the missing person's—

      (i)   spouse, and

      (ii)   children, or, if he has no children, his nearest relative known to the pursuer,

   (b)   any person, including any insurance company, who so far as known to the pursuer has an interest in the action, and

   (c)   the Lord Advocate,

in the following terms:— "For intimation to (*name and address*) as [husband or wife, child *or* nearest relative] [a person having an interest in the presumed death] of (*name and last known address of the missing person*) and to the Lord Advocate.".

   (4)[4] A notice of intimation in Form P2 shall be attached to the copy of the initial writ where intimation is given on a warrant under paragraph (3).

   (5)   The sheriff may, on the motion of the pursuer, dispense with intimation on a person mentioned in paragraph (3)(a) or (b).

   (6)   An application by minute under section 1(5) of the Act of 1977 (person interested in seeking determination or appointment not sought by pursuer) shall contain a crave for the determination or appointment sought, averments in the answers to the condescendence in support of that crave and an appropriate plea-in-law.

   (7)   On lodging a minute under paragraph (6), the minuter shall—

   (a)   send a copy of the minute by registered post or the first class recorded delivery service to each person to whom intimation of the action has been made under paragraph (2); and

   (b)   lodge in process the Post Office receipt or certificate of posting of that minute.

Further advertisement

D1.500   **37.3.** Where no minute has been lodged indicating knowledge of the present whereabouts of the missing person, at any time before the determination of the action, the sheriff may, of his own motion or on the motion of a party, make such order for further advertisement as he thinks fit.

---

[1] As amended by the Act of Sederunt (Sheriff Court Ordinary Cause Rules Amendment) (Miscellaneous) 1996 (SI 1996/2445) (effective November 1, 1996) (clerical error).

[2] Substituted by the Act of Sederunt (Sheriff Court Ordinary Cause Rules Amendment) (Miscellaneous) 2000 (SSI 2000/239) (effective October 2, 2000).

[3] Substituted by the Act of Sederunt (Sheriff Court Ordinary Cause Rules Amendment) (Miscellaneous) 2000 (SSI 2000/239) (effective October 2, 2000).

[4] As amended by the Act of Sederunt (Sheriff Court Ordinary Cause Rules Amendment) (Miscellaneous) 2000 (SSI 2000/239) (effective 2 October 2000).

Applications for proof

37.4.—(1) In an action of declarator where no minute has been lodged, the pursuer shall, after such further advertisement as may be ordered under rule 37.3, apply to the sheriff by motion for an order for proof.

(2) A proof ordered under paragraph (1) shall be by affidavit evidence unless the sheriff otherwise directs.

D1.501

Applications for variation or recall of decree

37.5.—(1) An application under section 4(1) of the Act of 1977 (variation or recall of decree) shall be made by minute in the process of the action to which it relates.

D1.502

(2) On the lodging of such a minute, the sheriff shall make an order—

    (a) for service on the missing person, where his whereabouts have become known;

    (b) for intimation to those persons mentioned in rule 37.2(3) or to dispense with intimation to a person mentioned in rule 37.2(3)(a) or (b); and

    (c) for any answers to the minute to be lodged in process within such period as the sheriff thinks fit.

(3) An application under section 4(3) of the Act of 1977 (person interested seeking determination or appointment not sought by applicant for variation order) shall be made by lodging answers containing a crave for the determination or appointment sought.

(4) A person lodging answers containing a crave under paragraph (3) shall, as well as sending a copy of the answers to the minuter—

    (a) send a copy of the answers by registered post or the first class recorded delivery service to each person on whom service or intimation of the minute was ordered; and

    (b) lodge in process the Post Office receipt or certificate of posting of those answers.

Appointment of judicial factors

37.6.—(1) The Act of Sederunt (Judicial Factors Rules) 1992 shall apply to an application for the appointment of a judicial factor under section 2(2)(c) or section 4(2) of the Act of 1977 as it applies to a petition for the appointment of a judicial factor.

D1.503

(2) In the application of rule 37.5 (applications for variation or recall of decree) to an application under section 4(1) of the Act of 1977 in a cause in which variation or recall of the appointment of a judicial factor is sought, for reference to a minute there shall be substituted references to a note.

Chapter 38

European Court

Interpretation of this Chapter

38.1.—(1) In this Chapter—

D1.504

    "appeal" includes an application for leave to appeal;

    "the European Court" means the Court of Justice of the European Communities;

    "reference" means a reference to the European Court for

        (a)[1,2] a preliminary ruling under Article 267 of the Treaty on the

---

[1] As amended by the Act of Sederunt (Sheriff Court Ordinary Cause Rules Amendment) (Miscellaneous) 2000 (SSI 2000/239) (effective October 2, 2000).

Functioning of the European Union, Article 150 of the Euratom Treaty or Article 41 of the E.C.S.C. Treaty; or

(b) a ruling on the interpretation of the Conventions, as defined in section 1(1) of the Civil Jurisdiction and Judgments Act 1982, under Article 3 of Schedule 2 to that Act.

(2)[1] The expressions "Euratom Treaty" and "E.C.S.C. Treaty" have the meanings assigned respectively in Schedule 1 to the European Communities Act 1972.

(3)[2] In paragraph (1), "the Treaty on the Functioning of the European Union" means the treaty referred to in section 1(2)(s) of the European Communities Act 1972.

Applications for reference

D1.505

38.2.—(1) A reference may be made by the sheriff of his own motion or on the motion of a party.

(2) *[Repealed by SSI 2000/239 (effective October 2, 2000).]*

Preparation of case for reference

D1.506

38.3.—(1) Where the sheriff decides that a reference shall be made, he shall continue the cause for that purpose and, within 4 weeks after the date of that continuation, draft a reference.

(1A)[3] Except in so far as the sheriff may otherwise direct, a reference shall be prepared in accordance with Form E1, having regard to the guidance set out in the Notes for Guidance issued by the Court of Justice of the European Communities.

(2) On the reference being drafted, the sheriff clerk shall send a copy to each party.

(3) Within 4 weeks after the date on which copies of the draft have been sent to parties, each party may—

(a) lodge with the sheriff clerk, and

(b) send to every other party,

a note of any adjustments he seeks to have made in the draft reference.

(4) Within 14 days after the date on which any such note of adjustments may be lodged, the sheriff, after considering any such adjustments, shall make and sign the reference.

(5) The sheriff clerk shall forthwith intimate the making of the reference to each party.

Sist of cause

D1.507

38.4.—(1) Subject to paragraph (2), on a reference being made, the cause shall, unless the sheriff when making such a reference otherwise orders, be sisted until the European Court has given a preliminary ruling on the question referred to it.

(2) The sheriff may recall a sist made under paragraph (1) for the purpose of making an interim order which a due regard to the interests of the parties may require.

---

[2] As amended by the Act of Sederunt (Sheriff Court Rules) (Miscellaneous Amendments) (No.3) 2012 (SSI 2012/271) para.6 (effective November 1, 2012).

[1] As amended by the Act of Sederunt (Sheriff Court Rules) (Miscellaneous Amendments) (No.3) 2012 (SSI 2012/271) para.6 (effective November 1, 2012).

[2] As inserted by the Act of Sederunt (Sheriff Court Rules) (Miscellaneous Amendments) (No.3) 2012 (SSI 2012/271) para.6 (effective November 1, 2012).

[3] Inserted by the Act of Sederunt (Sheriff Court Ordinary Cause Rules Amendment) (Miscellaneous) 2000 (S.S.I 2000 No. 239) (effective October 2, 2000).

Transmission of reference

38.5.—(1)   Subject to paragraph (2), a copy of the reference, certified by the   **D1.508**
sheriff clerk, shall be transmitted by the sheriff clerk to the Registrar of the European
Court.

(2)   Unless the sheriff otherwise directs, a copy of the reference shall not be sent
to the Registrar of the European Court where an appeal against the making of the
reference is pending.

(3)   For the purpose of paragraph (2), an appeal shall be treated as pending—

(a)   until the expiry of the time for making that appeal; or

(b)   where an appeal has been made, until that appeal has been determined.

Chapter 39[1]

Provisions in Relation to Curators Ad Litem

Fees and outlays of curators ad litem in respect of children

39.1.—(1)   This rule applies to any civil proceedings whether or not the child is   **D1.509**
a party to the action.

(2)   In an action where the sheriff appoints a curator ad litem to a child, the
pursuer shall in the first instance, unless the court otherwise directs, be responsible
for the fees and outlays of the curator ad litem incurred during the period from his
appointment until the occurrence of any of the following events:

(a)   he lodges a minute stating that he does not intend to lodge defences or to
enter the process;

(b)   he decides to instruct the lodging of defences or a minute adopting
defences already lodged; or(c) the discharge, before the occurrence of the
events mentioned in sub paragraphs (a) and (b), of the curator.

Chapter 40[2]

Commercial Actions

Annotations by Sheriff James Taylor

GENERAL NOTE

In 1994 new rules were introduced to the Court of Session governing commercial actions (RCS,   **D1.510**
Chapter 47). These were deemed to be a success and provided litigants with a more efficient means of
resolving commercial disputes. It was sometimes referred to as a "fast track" procedure but this could be
misleading. Undoubtedly some actions can be decided with a minimum of procedure, such as a dispute
which turns on the interpretation of a contract, thus rendering the description appropriate. However, it
was accepted that there are some actions which require a reasonable amount of time for the appropriate
experts to be instructed and report and notice be given to the opponent. The advantage of using Chapter
47 procedure was that there was case management from the bench. This resulted in an efficient procedure.

Sheriff Principal Bowen, Q.C., the sheriff principal of Glasgow and Strathkelvin, decided in 1999 to
introduce a similar procedure to Glasgow Sheriff Court. Four sheriffs were designated as commercial
sheriffs. There were however no rules equivalent to Chapter 47. One of the essential features of Chapter
47 is the preliminary hearing which must take place before the assigned judge within 14 days of defences
being lodged. Under the Ordinary Cause Rules of the sheriff court a case would not come before a sheriff
until the options hearing. The options hearing requires to be fixed not sooner than 10 weeks after the
expiry of the period of notice (OCR, r.9.2). If the advantages of Chapter 47 procedure were to be
replicated, the case would need to call before then. To overcome this difficulty the Civil Department of
the Sheriff Clerk's Office identified cases which appeared to fit the description of a commercial action using the same definition as in the Practice Note for Commercial Actions in the Court of Session (No. 12 of
1994). After defences had been lodged the solicitors in the case were invited to attend a preliminary
hearing. At this hearing the issues in the case were identified and a procedure agreed for resolving the
issues. At first, approximately 50 per cent of the cases in which invitations were extended had preliminary

---

[1]   Inserted by the Act of Sederunt (Sheriff Court Ordinary Cause Rules Amendment) (Miscellaneous)
2000 (SSI 2000/239) (effective October 2, 2000).

[2]   Inserted by the Act of Sederunt (Ordinary Cause Rules) Amendment (Commercial Actions) 2001
(SSI 2001/8).

hearings, but as the procedure became more familiar that rose to over 90 per cent. Due to the lack of rules the procedure required to be agreed. There was no sanction if one of the parties did not comply. This problem was resolved with the introduction of Chapter 40 to the Ordinary Cause Rules (Act of Sederunt (Ordinary Cause Rules) Amendment (Commercial Actions) 2001 (SSI 2001/8)).

D1.511   **Application and interpretation of this Chapter**

     40.1.—(1)   This Chapter applies to a commercial action.

     (2)   In this Chapter—

       (a)   "commercial action" means—an action arising out of, or concerned with, any transaction or dispute of a commercial or business nature including, but not limited to, actions relating to—

         (i)   the construction of a commercial document;

         (ii)   the sale or hire purchase of goods;

         (iii)   the export or import of merchandise;

         (iv)   the carriage of goods by land, air or sea;

         (v)   insurance;

         (vi)   banking;

         (vii)   the provision of services;

         (viii)   a building, engineering or construction contract; or

         (ix)   a commercial lease; and

       (b)   "commercial action" does not include an action in relation to consumer credit transactions.

     (3)   A commercial action may be raised only in a sheriff court where the Sheriff Principal for the sheriffdom has directed that the procedure should be available.

GENERAL NOTE

Before advantage can be taken of this chapter the sheriff principal must direct that these rules will apply to the particular court in the sheriffdom in which the action is raised. The only courts in which there is such a direction are Glasgow, Jedburgh, Selkirk and Duns Sheriff Courts. Jedburgh, Selkirk and Duns are included because the sheriff presently appointed to these courts was one of the original commercial sheriffs in Glasgow.

The definition of a commercial action closely follows the definition under Chapter 47 procedure in the Court of Session.

"The provision of services"

The minor differences between the two definitions are that where the Court of Session definition refers to "the provision of financial services", the equivalent description in Chapter 40 is "the provision of services". The sheriff court definition can thus be seen to be broader. The Court of Session definition also refers specifically to actions relating to "mercantile agency" and "mercantile usage or a custom of trade". There is no equivalent in Chapter 40.

"Arising out of, or concerned with, any transaction or dispute of a commercial or business nature"

The differences between the Court of Session and Ordinary Cause Rules are of no significance since the examples in both sets of rules are not limiting and the overarching criteria is the same in both, namely that the action should arise out of, or be concerned with, a commercial or business dispute. This phrase is intended to be of broad scope and is habile to include an action by a trustee in sequestration for declarator of vesting of acquirenda, where the issue was one of insolvency and not of succession: *Rankin's Trs v HC Somerville & Russell*, 1999 S.C. 166.

"Does not include an action in relation to consumer credit transactions"

This exclusion is self-explanatory.

D1.512   **Proceedings before a nominated sheriff**

     40.2.   All proceedings in a commercial action shall be brought before—

       (a)   a sheriff of the sheriffdom nominated by the Sheriff Principal; or

       (b)   where a nominated sheriff is not available, any other sheriff of the sheriffdom.

GENERAL NOTE

The working party, which consulted before the introduction of Chapter 47 procedures to the Court of Session, recognised a demand for a forum where commercial disputes could be resolved before a judge who had commercial experience. To reflect this expression, there requires to be in the sheriff court where the procedures are available, a sheriff or sheriffs designated by the sheriff principal to deal with commercial business. As a backstop, where a designated commercial sheriff is unavailable another sheriff can deal with proceedings in a commercial action. There are currently three designated commercial sheriffs in Glasgow and one in Jedburgh, Selkirk and Duns.

Procedure in commercial actions

40.3.—(1) In a commercial action the sheriff may make such order as he thinks fit for the progress of the case in so far as not inconsistent with the provisions in this Chapter.

(2) Where any hearing is continued, the reason for such continuation shall be recorded in the interlocutor.

D1.513

GENERAL NOTE

"May make such order as he thinks fit"

The intent of the rules is that the sheriff, counsel and solicitors who may be involved in the action should not be constrained by rules of procedure in dealing efficiently with a case. Thus it is deemed that an order is competent unless it is inconsistent with the commercial rules. A specific enabling power is not necessary.

Election of procedure for commercial actions

40.4. The pursuer may elect to adopt the procedure in this Chapter by bringing an action in Form G1A.

D1.514

GENERAL NOTE

In order to distinguish a commercial action from an ordinary action, all that is required is for the pursuer's solicitor to type the words "Commercial Action" above the words "Initial Writ" in the instance of the initial writ. Thus the pursuer has the right to elect for Chapter 40 procedure. The defender is protected, should the election be inappropriate, by the terms of rule 40.6(1). To facilitate communication, Glasgow Sheriff Court request that the initial writ, notice of intention to defend and defences should have marked on them the name of the individual solicitor dealing with the case and that individual's telephone number and e-mail address.

Transfer of action to be a commercial action

40.5.—(1) In an action within the meaning of rule 40.1(2) in which the pursuer has not made an election under rule 40.4, any party may apply by motion at any time to have the action appointed to be a commercial action.

(2) An interlocutor granted under paragraph (1) shall include a direction as to further procedure.

D1.515

GENERAL NOTE

If the pursuer does not elect for the action to be dealt with as a commercial action at the time when the action is raised, it is still open to the pursuer, or any other party, once the action has been warranted, to move that these rules should apply.

Since these rules are applicable in Glasgow, Jedburgh, Selkirk and Duns Sheriff Courts only, there have been motions made in other courts, where the rules are not available, for particular cases to be remitted to one of the four courts. These have usually involved the defender prorogating the jurisdiction of one of the four courts. Glasgow is prepared to accept such remits, but the Borders Courts are not.

Appointment of a commercial action as an ordinary cause

40.6.—(1) At any time before, or at the Case Management Conference, the sheriff shall appoint a commercial action to proceed as an ordinary cause—

    (a) on the motion of a party where—

        (i) detailed pleadings are required to enable justice to be done between the parties; or

        (ii) any other circumstances warrant such an order being made; or

    (b) on the joint motion of parties.

D1.516

(2) If a motion to appoint a commercial action to proceed as an ordinary action is refused, no subsequent motion to appoint the action to proceed as an ordinary cause shall be considered except on a material change of circumstances.

(3) Where the sheriff orders that a commercial action shall proceed as an ordinary cause the interlocutor granting such shall prescribe—

(a) a period of adjustment, if appropriate; and

(b) the date, time and place for any options hearing fixed.

(4) In determining what order to make in deciding that a commercial action proceed as an ordinary cause the sheriff shall have regard to the periods prescribed in rule 9.2.

GENERAL NOTE

This rule provides for an action being remitted from the commercial roll to the ordinary roll on the motion of any party or on joint motion.

"Detailed pleadings are required"

The only guidance as to when such a motion should be considered, apart from the generality that "circumstances warrant such", is if detailed pleadings are required. It is submitted that this is a strange provision. Several of the commercial actions raised under these rules have involved detailed pleading. There is nothing in the rules which makes the rules unsuitable to regulate actions where detailed pleading is required. No motion to have the case remitted to the ordinary roll has succeeded when reliance has been placed on this specific provision only.

The rule does not give the sheriff power *ex proprio motu* to remit the case to the ordinary role. This was originally the case under Chapter 47 procedure in the Court of Session. That was remedied in the Court of Session by para.2(7) of SSI 2000/66, which gives the commercial judge power, *ex proprio motu*, to remit the case to the ordinary roll.

In the event that a motion to remit to the ordinary roll is successful, the interlocutor shall allow a period of adjustment, if appropriate. If the reason for the motion succeeding is that detailed pleadings are required, it would be consistent for there to be a further period allowed for adjustment. One might expect a subsequent motion to seek that the action be dealt with in terms of Chapter 10.

D1.517 **Special requirements for initial writ in a commercial action**

40.7.—(1) Where the construction of a document is the only matter in dispute no pleadings or pleas-in-law require to be included in the initial writ.

(2) There shall be appended to an initial writ in Form G1A a list of the documents founded on or adopted as incorporated in the initial writ.

GENERAL NOTE

This provision enables a pursuer who considers that the construction of a document will resolve a dispute to put that clearly in focus in the initial writ. There will still require to be a crave in which it would be open to a pursuer to seek declarator that the provisions of the document in question, properly understood, have a particular meaning. There could still be a secondary crave dealing with the consequences in the event of declarator being granted, e.g. a crave for payment or specific implement. Averments will still be required to establish jurisdiction. It would be appropriate, although not necessary, in such circumstances to set out in outline in the condescendence, the argument to be deployed by the pursuer in submitting that the document should be said to have the construction for which he contends. It might even be thought appropriate to cite any authorities said to support the desired construction.

"List of the documents founded on"

Rule 40.7(2) reflects the provisions of rule 47.3(3) of the Court of Session Rules. It would be good practice to send to the defender's solicitor a copy of the documents founded upon as soon as a notice of intention to defend the action is intimated if these have not been served with the initial writ. This will enable the issues to be more easily identified at the case management conference. Absent any specific order of the Court in terms of rule 40.12, all productions will require to be lodged not later than 14 days before the diet of proof (rule 29.11(1)).

D1.518 **Notice of Intention to Defend**

40.8.—(1) Where the defender intends to—

(a) challenge the jurisdiction of the court;

(b) state a defence; or

(c) make a counterclaim,

he shall, before the expiry of the period of notice lodge with the sheriff clerk a notice of intention to defend in Form O7 and shall, at the same time, send a copy to the pursuer.

(2) The lodging of a notice of intention to defend shall not imply acceptance of the jurisdiction of the court.

GENERAL NOTE

A defender who wishes to defend a commercial action requires to lodge a notice of intention to defend in the same way and within the same period of notice as he would were the action an ordinary action. As for ordinary actions, the rules specifically provide that the defender can lodge a notice of intention to defend and still challenge the jurisdiction of the court to hear the case.

Defences   D1.519

40.9.—(1) Where a notice of intention to defend has been lodged, the defender shall lodge defences within 7 days after the expiry of the period of notice.

(2) There shall be appended to the defences a list of the documents founded on or adopted as incorporated in the defences.

(3) Subject to the requirement that each article of condescendence in the initial writ need not be admitted or denied, defences shall be in the form of answers that allow the extent of the dispute to be identified and shall have appended a note of the pleas in law of the defender.

GENERAL NOTE

In a commercial action the defender has only seven days from the expiry of the period of notice in which to lodge defences as opposed to 14 days in an ordinary action (rule 9.6(1)). Unlike an ordinary action there will be no intimation from the sheriff clerk specifying the date by which defences require to be lodged. As a pursuer has to append a list of documents to the initial writ, so a defender has to append a list of the documents upon which he founds, or which have been incorporated into the pleadings, to the defences. It is considered good practice for the documents to be lodged in process before the first case management conference. The defences should contain the name of the solicitor dealing with the case together with the telephone number and e-mail address.

"Each article of condescendence in the initial writ need not be admitted or denied"

The defences do not require to be in traditional form where the defender repeats *ad longum* which of the pursuer's averments are admitted. It has never been good practice to adopt such an approach with regard to denials. It would appear therefore that the reference to each article of condescendence not requiring to be denied is meant to convey that a defender will no longer be deemed to have admitted a fact which is subject to an averment by the pursuer and which is within the defender's knowledge but which is not covered by a general denial.

"Answers that allow the extent of the dispute to be identified"

The guiding principle is always whether fair notice is given to the other side to enable them to know the case which they require to meet and to be able to properly prepare for proof. The means of achieving that can take a number of forms. Lengthy narrative is discouraged. Parties regularly use spreadsheets or schedules to set out their position with regard to particular issues. The sheriffs welcome this. It is a cardinal feature of commercial actions that parties make full and frank disclosure. Some guidance as to the degree of specification required can be found in *Kaur v Singh* , 1998 S.C. 233 at 237C, per Lord Hamilton, and *Johnston v WH Brown Construction (Dundee) Ltd* , 2000 S.L.T. 223.

"Shall have appended a note of the pleas-in-law"

It is worth noting that the defences require that there be pleas-in-law appended to them. There is no dispensation for defences as there is with an initial writ when the only matter in dispute is the construction of a document as one finds in rule 40.7(1).

Fixing date for Case Management Conference   D1.520

40.10.—(1) On the lodging of defences, the sheriff clerk shall fix a date and time for a Case Management Conference, which date shall be on the first suitable court day occurring not sooner than 14 days, nor later than 28 days after the date of expiry of the period of notice.

(2) On fixing the date for the Case Management Conference, the sheriff clerk shall—

(a) forthwith intimate to the parties the date and time of the Case Management Conference; and

(b) prepare and sign an interlocutor recording that information.

(3) The fixing of the date of the Case Management Conference shall not affect the right of a party to make application by motion, to the court.

GENERAL NOTE

On defences being lodged the process is normally placed before one of the commercial sheriffs who will decide whether the first case management conference will be conducted in court, chambers, or, in Glasgow, by conference call. The majority of case management conferences in Glasgow Sheriff Court are now dealt with by conference call which the sheriff initiates. The introduction of conference call facilities was in response to the profession and litigants being concerned by the inefficiency of having to travel to court and wait for their case to call. If a solicitor does not wish to make use of the conference call facility, he or she is entitled to request a traditional hearing. The date of the case management conference, which must not be sooner than 14 days after the period of notice nor later than 28 days after its expiry, is then intimated to the parties. In Glasgow Sheriff Court this intimation informs the parties of the date and time for the case management conference, whether it will be in court or chambers or whether it can proceed by conference call, the identity of the commercial sheriff allocated to the case and the e-mail address for that particular sheriff. Wherever possible that sheriff will deal with all hearings in the case.

It is important that the solicitor with responsibility for the case is available for the case management conference and it is not uncommon for the initial date and time to be altered to suit solicitors' diaries.

The rules make it clear that the fixing of a case management conference will not preclude a party from enrolling a motion. Very often the motion will be dealt with at the case management conference but where there is a degree of urgency the motion can usually be accommodated in advance of that date.

D1.521   **Applications for summary decree in a commercial action**

40.11. *[Repealed by the Act of Sederunt (Sheriff Court Rules) (Miscellaneous Amendments) 2012 (SSI 2012/188) r.3(3) (effective August 1, 2012: repeal has effect subject to savings specified in SSI 2012/188 r.15).]*

GENERAL NOTE

In an ordinary action should a pursuer, or counterclaiming defender, enrol a motion for summary decree, notice of opposition must be given within seven days (rule 15.3(1)(c)). That period is shortened to 48 hours in a commercial action.

D1.522   **Case Management Conference**

40.12.—(1) At the Case Management Conference in a commercial action the sheriff shall seek to secure the expeditious resolution of the action.

(2) Parties shall be prepared to provide such information as the sheriff may require to determine—

(a) whether, and to what extent, further specification of the claim and defences is required; and

(b) the orders to make to ensure the expeditious resolution of the action; and

(c)[1] whether there is or is likely to be a vulnerable witness within the meaning of section 11(1) of the Act of 2004 who is to give evidence at any proof or hearing, consider any child witness notice or vulnerable witness application that has been lodged where no order has been made and consider whether any order under section 12(1) of the Act of 2004 requires to be made.

(3) The orders the sheriff may make in terms of paragraph 2(b) may include but shall not be limited to—

(a) the lodging of written pleadings by any party to the action which may be restricted to particular issues;

---

[1] As inserted by the Act of Sederunt (Ordinary Cause, Summary Application, Summary Cause and Small Claim Rules) Amendment (Vulnerable Witnesses (Scotland) Act 2004) 2007, r.2(12) (effective November 1, 2007).

(b)   the lodging of a statement of facts by any party which may be restricted to particular issues;

(c)   allowing an amendment by a party to his pleadings;

(d)   disclosure of the identity of witnesses and the existence and nature of documents relating to the action or authority to recover documents either generally or specifically;

(e)   the lodging of documents constituting, evidencing or relating to the subject matter of the action or any invoices, correspondence or similar documents;

(f)   the exchanging of lists of witnesses;

(g)   the lodging of reports of skilled persons or witness statements;

(h)   the lodging of affidavits concerned with any of the issues in the action;

(i)   the lodging of notes of arguments setting out the basis of any preliminary plea;

(j)   fixing a debate or proof, with or without any further preliminary procedure, to determine the action or any particular aspect thereof;

(k)   the lodging of joint minutes of admission or agreement;

(l)   recording admissions made on the basis of information produced; or

(m)   any order which the sheriff thinks will result in the speedy resolution of the action (including the use of alternative dispute resolution), or requiring the attendance of parties in person at any subsequent hearing.

(4)   In making any order in terms of paragraph (3) the sheriff may fix a period within which such order shall be complied with.

(5)   The sheriff may continue the Case Management Conference to a specified date where he considers it necessary to do so—

(a)   to allow any order made in terms of paragraph (3) to be complied with; or

(b)   to advance the possibility of resolution of the action.

(6)   Where the sheriff makes an order in terms of paragraph (3) he may ordain the pursuer to—

(a)   make up a record; and

(b)   lodge that record in process,

within such period as he thinks fit.

GENERAL NOTE

The Ordinary Cause Rules did not follow the Court of Session model and avoided having both a preliminary and procedural hearing. Instead there is a case management conference which serves the purpose of both. If the action involves the interpretation of a contract it can be sent straight to a debate. The only further procedure in such a case might be the preparation of notes of argument and lists of authorities. Otherwise the purpose of the case management conference is to identify the issues and agree upon a framework for their resolution. For example, it is quite common to restrict the first stage to identifying the contractual terms regulating the relationship between the parties, should these be in issue. Sometimes liability is determined first leaving quantum for a later stage. Further factual information may well be required to properly identify the issues. The case management conference can be continued for this purpose. There is often a time frame agreed within which the information is to be obtained and exchanged.

Form of the case management conference

In Glasgow Sheriff Court the case management conference will often be conducted by telephone conference call which is initiated by the sheriff. If there is a hearing, wigs and gowns are not worn and parties remain seated. It is intended that the hearing be conducted as a business meeting. One of the advantages of conference calls is that the principal solicitor is able to conduct the hearing regardless of where his office is located. Conference call facilities are not presently available in the Borders Courts. If the principal solicitor is unable to appear at the case management conference, it is vital that the solicitor instructed to appear is properly briefed and able to contribute fully to the discussion.

Written pleadings

Although written pleadings remain the most common vehicle for focusing issues, spreadsheets, schedules and similar forms are increasingly used. Intimation of pleadings, etc. is usually given in electronic form both between solicitors and to the sheriff. If there are issues with regard to a lack of specification, these are normally discussed and resolved at a case management conference and should not thereafter be the focus for a debate. Any adjustment to the initial writ and defences should be achieved by red lining, striking out or similar. The court will not welcome receipt of a traditional "note of adjustment".

Recovery and disclosure of documents

The procedures in Chapter 28 for recovery of evidence are still available to the parties. However, recourse to this provision is not usually required when the documents, the production of which is sought, are in the hands of the parties to the litigation. It is normally agreed that such documents should be produced and the timescale for achieving this.

Exchange of lists of witnesses

Unlike Chapter 47 procedure in the Court of Session, lists of witnesses are not normally required in advance of proof being allowed. However, parties are required to know how many witnesses they will be leading in evidence in order that the appropriate number of days can be allowed for the proof. A list of witnesses is normally required at least 28 days before the diet of proof.

Reports of skilled persons and witness statements

If parties have retained expert witnesses it is customary for their reports to be lodged and exchanged before proof is allowed. If this is not done voluntarily it is unlikely that a party will be able to resist a motion that their expert's report should be lodged as a production. Little recourse is made to the production of witness statements.

Affidavits

As for witness statements, parties are not usually put to the expense of preparing affidavits. The exception to this is when there is a motion for summary decree. On such occasions the commercial sheriff may require that an affidavit be produced, usually by the defender, covering a particularly critical averment.

Notes of argument

If there has been a full discussion of the basis of a preliminary plea at a case management conference, the lodging of a note of argument might be dispensed with. However, it is more than likely that the commercial sheriff will require a note of argument in advance of the debate being allowed. Although there is no specific provision in the rules for producing a note on further procedure, this is sometimes ordered at the same time as is the note of argument. The two documents then assist the sheriff in deciding whether there should be some form of enquiry into the facts or whether the case should go to debate. In advance of any debate the commercial sheriff will normally require that lists of authorities be exchanged. The commercial sheriff is not obliged to send a case to debate only because one of the parties has tabled a preliminary plea.

"Speedy resolution"

Perhaps this is an unfortunate expression as it might give the impression that thoroughness and fairness will be sacrificed at the altar of speed. A more balanced expression might be "efficient resolution".

Record

It should be noted that unless ordained so to do the pursuer does not require to lodge a record. The initial writ and defences, as these have been adjusted, are often sufficient for the purposes of the commercial sheriff and the parties.

D1.523   **Lodging of productions**

40.13 Prior to any proof or other hearing at which the documents listed in terms of rules 40.7(2) and 40.9(2) are to be referred to parties shall, in addition to lodging the productions in terms of rule 21.1, prepare, for the use of the sheriff, a working bundle in which the documents are arranged chronologically or in another appropriate order.

This rule reflects the terms of para.14 of Court of Session Practice Note No. 12 of 1994. In practice it is not always insisted upon by the commercial sheriff. In advance of the hearing solicitors should ascertain from the sheriff if the terms of this rule can be dispensed with.

Hearing for further procedure

40.14. At any time before final judgement, the sheriff may—

    (a)   of his own motion or on the motion of any party, fix a hearing for further procedure; and

    (b)   make such other order as he thinks fit.

GENERAL NOTE

The main thrust of Chapter 40 rules is that the commercial sheriff should be involved in managing all procedural aspects of the case. This rule enables the sheriff to put a case out for a by order hearing at any time before final judgment when the sheriff would, in any event, be functus. It is sometimes used by the sheriff to convene a pre-proof hearing to ascertain how preparations for the proof are proceeding and if there is likely to be a settlement. It is also used after there has been a debate or preliminary proof to discuss what further procedure there should be once the decision on the debate or preliminary point is known.

Failure to comply with rule or order of sheriff

40.15 Any failure by a party to comply timeously with a provision in this Chapter or any order made by the sheriff in a commercial action shall entitle the sheriff, of his own motion—

    (a)   to refuse to extend any period for compliance with a provision in these Rules or an order of the court;

    (b)   to dismiss the action or counterclaim, as the case may be, in whole or in part;

    (c)   to grant decree in respect of all or any of the craves of the initial writ or counterclaim, as the case may be; or

    (d)   to make an award of expenses,

as he thinks fit.

GENERAL NOTE

This rule provides the commercial sheriff with the necessary sanctions to attain the aim of achieving an efficient determination of commercial actions.

Determination of action

40.16. It shall be open to the sheriff, at the end of any hearing, to restrict any interlocutor to a finding.

GENERAL NOTE

This provision may be thought to dispense with the requirement to make findings in fact at the conclusion of a diet of proof or proof before answer. Such dispensation would be consistent with the stated desire to achieve a speedy decision.

Parts of Process

40.17. All parts of process lodged in a commercial action shall be clearly marked "Commercial Action".

D1.524

D1.525

D1.526

D1.527

Not only should the initial writ bear the expression "Commercial Action" but all steps in the process should also be so distinguished.

D1.528

Chapter 41[1]

Protection from Abuse (Scotland) Act 2001

Interpretation

41.1.—(1) In this Chapter a section referred to by number means the section so numbered in the Protection from Abuse (Scotland) Act 2001.

(2) Words and expressions used in this Chapter which are also used in the Protection from Abuse (Scotland) Act 2001 have the same meaning as in that Act.

Attachment of power of arrest to interdict

D1.529

41.2.—[2](1) An application under section 1(1) (application for attachment of power of arrest to interdict)—

    (a)   shall be made in the crave in the initial writ, defences or counterclaim in which the interdict to which it relates is applied for, or, if made after the application for interdict, by motion in the process of the action in which the interdict was sought, or by minute, with answers if appropriate, should the sheriff so order; and

    (b)   shall be intimated to the person against whom the interdict is sought or was obtained.

(2)[3] Where the sheriff attaches a power of arrest under section 1(2) or (1A) (order attaching power of arrest) the following documents shall be served along with the power of arrest in accordance with section 2(1) (documents to be served along with power of arrest)—

    (a)   a copy of the application for interdict;

    (b)   a copy of the interlocutor granting interdict; and

    (c)   where the application to attach the power of arrest was made after the interdict was granted, a copy of the certificate of service of the interdict.

(3) After the power of arrest has been served, the following documents shall be delivered by the person who obtained the power to the chief constable in accordance with section 3(1) (notification to police)—

    (a)   a copy of the application for interdict;

    (b)   a copy of the interlocutor granting interdict;

    (c)   a copy of the certificate of service of the interdict; and

    (d)   where the application to attach the power of arrest was made after the interdict was granted—

        (i)   a copy of the application for the power of arrest;

        (ii)   a copy of the interlocutor granting it; and

        (iii)   a copy of the certificate of service of the power of arrest and the documents that required to be served along with it in accordance with section 2(1).

---

[1] Inserted by the Act of Sederunt (Ordinary Cause Rules) Amendment (Applications under the Protection from Abuse (Scotland) Act 2001) 2002 (SSI 2002/128), para.2.

[2] As amended by the Act of Sederunt (Ordinary Cause, Summary Application, Summary Cause and Small Claim Rules) Amendment (Miscellaneous) 2003 (SSI 2003/26), para.2(13) (effective January 24, 2003).

[3] As amended by Act of Sederunt (Ordinary Cause Rules) Amendment (Family Law (Scotland) Act 2006 etc.) 2006, para.2 (SSI 2006/207) (effective 4 May 2006).

(e)[1]   where a determination has previously been made in respect of such interdict under section 3(1) of the Domestic Abuse (Scotland) Act 2011, a copy of the interlocutor in Form DA1.

Extension or recall of power of arrest
41.3.—(1)   An application under either of the following provisions shall be made by minute in the process of the action in which the power of arrest was attached—   **D1.530**
(a)   section 2(3) (extension of duration of power of arrest);
(b)   section 2(7) (recall of power of arrest).
(2)   Where the sheriff extends the duration of, or recalls, a power of arrest, the person who obtained the extension or recall must deliver a copy of the interlocutor granting the extension or recall in accordance with section 3(1).

Documents to be delivered to chief constable in relation to recall or variation of interdict
41.4.   Where an interdict to which a power of arrest has been attached under section 1(2) is varied or recalled, the person who obtained the variation or recall must deliver a copy of the interlocutor varying or recalling the interdict in accordance with section 3(1).   **D1.531**

Certificate of delivery of documents to chief constable
41.5.   Where a person is in any circumstances required to comply with section 3(1) he shall, after such compliance, lodge in process a certificate of delivery in Form PA1.   **D1.532**

Chapter 41A[2]

Domestic Abuse (Scotland) Act 2011

Interpretation and application of this Chapter
41A.1.—(1)   In this Chapter—   **D1.533**

"the 2011 Act" means the Domestic Abuse (Scotland) Act 2011;
"interdict" includes interim interdict.
(2)   This Chapter applies to an application for a determination under section 3(1) of the 2011 Act that an interdict is a domestic abuse interdict.

Applications for a determination that an interdict is a domestic abuse interdict
41A.2.—(1)   An application made before the interdict is obtained must be made by crave in the initial writ, defences or counterclaim in which the interdict is sought.   **D1.534**
(2)   An application made after the interdict is obtained must be made by minute.
(3)   Where a determination is made under section 3(1) of the 2011 Act, the interlocutor shall be in Form DA1.
(4)   In pursuance of section 3(4) of the 2011 Act, the applicant must serve a copy of the interlocutor in Form DA1 on the person against whom the interdict has been granted and lodge in process a certificate of service in Form DA2.
(5)   Where a determination is recalled under section 3(5)(b) of the 2011 Act, the interlocutor shall be in Form DA3.
(6)   Paragraph (7) applies where, in respect of the same interdict—
(a)   a power of arrest under section 1 of the Protection from Abuse (Scotland) Act 2001 is in effect; and

---

[1] As inserted by the Act of Sederunt (Sheriff Court Rules) (Miscellaneous Amendments) (No.2) 2011 (SSI 2011/289) para.2 (effective July 20, 2011).
[2] As inserted by the Act of Sederunt (Sheriff Court Rules) (Miscellaneous Amendments) (No.2) 2011 (SSI 2011/289) para.5 (effective July 20, 2011).

(b)   a determination under section 3(1) of the 2011 Act is made.

(7)[1]   Where a determination is made or where such determination is recalled, the sheriff must appoint a person to send forthwith to the chief constable of the Police Service of Scotland a copy of—

(a)   the interlocutor in Form DA1 and the certificate of service in Form DA2; or

(b)   the interlocutor in Form DA3,

as the case may be.

(8)[2]   Where a person is required by virtue of this Chapter to send documents to the chief constable, such person must, after each such compliance, lodge in process a certificate of sending in Form DA4.

Chapter 42[3]

Competition Appeal Tribunal

Interpretation

D1.535   **42.1.** In this Chapter—

"the 1998 Act" means the Competition Act 1998; and
"the Tribunal" means the Competition Appeal Tribunal established by section 12 of the Enterprise Act 2002.

Transfer of proceedings to the Tribunal

D1.536   **42.2.**—(1)[4] Where proceedings (or any part of them) relate to an infringement issue, within the meaning of section 16(6) of the Enterprise Act 2002, the sheriff may make an order transferring those proceedings (or that part of them) to the Tribunal—

(a)   of the sheriff's own accord, or

(b)   on the motion of a party.

(1A)[5] Where the sheriff orders that such proceedings (or any part of them) are transferred to the Tribunal, the sheriff may make such orders as the sheriff thinks fit to allow the Tribunal to determine the issue.

(2)   Where the sheriff orders that such proceedings (or any part of them) are transferred to the Tribunal, the sheriff clerk shall, within 7 days from the date of such order—

(a)   transmit the process (or the appropriate part) to the clerk of the Tribunal;

(b)   notify each party to the proceedings in writing of the transmission under sub paragraph (a); and

(c)   certify, by making an appropriate entry on the interlocutor sheet, that he has made all notifications required under sub paragraph (b).

---

[1] As amended by the Act of Sederunt (Sheriff Court Rules)(Miscellaneous Amendments) 2013 (SSI 2013/135) para.4 (effective May 27, 2013).
[2] As amended by the Act of Sederunt (Sheriff Court Rules)(Miscellaneous Amendments) 2013 (SSI 2013/135) para.4 (effective May 27, 2013).
[3] Inserted by the Act of Sederunt (Ordinary Cause Rules) Amendment (Competition Appeal Tribunal) 2004 (SSI 2004/350), para.2 (effective August 20, 2004).
[4] As substituted by the Act of Sederunt (Sheriff Court Rules Amendment) (Miscellaneous) 2015 (SSI 2015/424) para.2 (effective 1 February 2016).
[5] As inserted by the Act of Sederunt (Sheriff Court Rules Amendment) (Miscellaneous) 2015 (SSI 2015/424) para.2 (effective 1 February 2016).

(3) Transmission of the process under paragraph (2)(a) shall be valid notwithstanding any failure by the sheriff clerk to comply with paragraph (2)(b) and (c).

CHAPTER 42A

APPLICATIONS IN COMPETITION PROCEEDINGS

Interpretation of this Chapter

42A.1.[1] In this Chapter—   D1.536.1

"the 1998 Act" means the Competition Act 1998;
"competition authority" has the meaning given by paragraph 3(1) of schedule 8A of the 1998 Act;
"competition proceedings" has the meaning given by paragraph 2(4) of schedule 8A of the 1998 Act; and
"the Directive" means Directive 2014/104/EU of the European Parliament and of the Council of 26 November 2014 on certain rules governing actions for damages under national law for infringements of the competition law provisions of the Member States and of the European Union as amended from time to time; and
"investigation materials" has the meaning given by paragraph 3(3) of schedule 8A of the 1998 Act.

Recovery of evidence

42A.2—[2](1) This rule applies where a party in competition proceedings makes   D1.536.2
an application under rule 28.2(1) for—

(a) a commission and diligence for the recovery of a document; or

(b) an order under section 1 of the Administration of Justice (Scotland) Act 1972.

(2) The applicant must intimate a copy of the motion made under rule 28.2(1) and the specification lodged under rule 28.2(2) to the Advocate General for Scotland.

(3) An application in relation to a document or other evidence that is in the possession of a competition authority must contain a statement that there is no person, other than the competition authority, reasonably able to provide the document or evidence sought.

(4) An application in relation to the investigation materials of a competition authority must contain a statement that the investigation to which those materials relate has closed.

(5) In deciding whether to grant an application made under this rule, the court must take into account Article 5(3), and, where the document or other evidence sought is in the possession of a competition authority, Article 6(4), of the Directive.

Applications in relation to alleged cartel leniency statement or settlement submission

42A.3—[3](1) An application by a party under—   D1.536.3

(a) paragraph 4(7) of schedule 8A of the 1998 Act for a determination by the court as to whether information is a cartel leniency statement; or

---

[1] As inserted by the Act of Sederunt (Rules of the Court of Session 1994 and Ordinary Cause Rules 1993 Amendment) (Competition Proceedings) 2017 (SSI 2017/130) para.3 (effective 26 May 2017).
[2] As inserted by the Act of Sederunt (Rules of the Court of Session 1994 and Ordinary Cause Rules 1993 Amendment) (Competition Proceedings) 2017 (SSI 2017/130) para.3 (effective 26 May 2017).
[3] As inserted by the Act of Sederunt (Rules of the Court of Session 1994 and Ordinary Cause Rules 1993 Amendment) (Competition Proceedings) 2017 (SSI 2017/130) para.3 (effective 26 May 2017).

(b) paragraph 5(3) of schedule 8A of the 1998 Act for a determination by the court as to whether a document is a settlement submission,

must be made by motion.

(2) A party enrolling a motion under paragraph (1) must intimate that motion to—

(a) the Advocate General for Scotland; and

(b) the author (where known) of the document or information in question.

(3) The hearing of a motion enrolled under paragraph (1) must be held in private and only the persons mentioned in paragraph (2)(a) and (b) may appear at that hearing.

[THE NEXT PARAGRAPH IS D1.537]

Chapter 43[1]

Causes Relating to Articles 101 and 102 of the Treaty Establishing the European Community

Intimation of actions to the Office of Fair Trading

D1.537   43.1—(1) In this rule—

"the Treaty" means Treaty on the Functioning of the European Union, as referred to in section 1(2)(s) of the European Communities Act 1972; and

"the OFT" means the Office of Fair Trading.

(2) In an action where an issue under Article 101 or 102 of the Treaty is raised—

(a) by the pursuer in the initial writ;

(b) by the defender in the defences;

(c) by any party in the pleadings;

intimation of the action shall be given to the OFT by the party raising the issue by a notice of intimation in Form OFT1.

(3) The initial writ, defences or pleadings in which the issue under Article 81 or 82 of the Treaty is raised shall include a crave for warrant for intimation to the OFT.

(4) A certified copy of an interlocutor granting a warrant under paragraph (3) shall be sufficient authority for the party to intimate by notice in Form OFT1.

(5) A notice of intimation under paragraph (2) shall be on a period of notice of 21 days unless the sheriff otherwise orders; but the sheriff shall not order a period of notice of less than 2 days.

(6) There shall be attached to the notice of intimation—

(a) a copy of the initial writ, defences or pleadings (including any adjustments and amendments), as the case may be;

(b) a copy of the interlocutor allowing intimation of the notice; and

(c) where the pleadings have not been amended in accordance with any minute of amendment, a copy of that minute.

Chapter 44[2]

The Equality Act 2010

Interpretation and application

D1.538   44.1.—[3](1) In this Chapter—

"the Commission" means the Commission for Equality and Human Rights; and

---

[1] Inserted by Act of Sederunt (Ordinary Cause Rules) Amendment (Causes Relating to Articles 81 and 82 of the Treaty Establishing the European Community) 2006 (SSI 2006/293) (effective June 16,

"the 2010 Act" means the Equality Act 2010.

(2) This Chapter applies to claims made by virtue of section 114(1) of the 2010 Act including a claim for damages.

Intimation to Commission

44.2.[1] The pursuer shall send a copy of the initial writ to the Commission by registered or recorded delivery post.

D1.539

Assessor

44.3.—(1) The sheriff may, of his own motion or on the motion of any party, appoint an assessor.

D1.540

(2) The assessor shall be a person who the sheriff considers has special qualifications to be of assistance in determining the cause.

Taxation of Commission expenses

44.4. *[Omitted by the Act of Sederunt (Sheriff Court Rules) (Miscellaneous Amendments) 2008 (SSI 2008/223) para.4(3)(c) (effective July 1, 2008).]*

National security

44.5.—[2](1) Where, on a motion under paragraph (3) or of the sheriff's own motion, the sheriff considers it expedient in the interests of national security, the sheriff may—

D1.541

    (a) exclude from all or part of the proceedings—
        (i) the pursuer;
        (ii) the pursuer's representatives;
        (iii) any assessors;
    (b) permit a pursuer or representative who has been excluded to make a statement to the court before the commencement of the proceedings or the part of the proceedings, from which he or she is excluded;
    (c) take steps to keep secret all or part of the reasons for his or her decision in the proceedings.

(2) The sheriff clerk shall, on the making of an order under paragraph (1) excluding the pursuer or the pursuer's representatives, notify the Advocate General for Scotland of that order.

(3) A party may apply by motion for an order under paragraph (1).

(4) The steps referred to in paragraph (1)(c) may include the following—

    (a) directions to the sheriff clerk; and
    (b) orders requiring any person appointed to represent the interests of the pursuer in proceedings from which the pursuer or the pursuer's representatives are excluded not to communicate (directly or indirectly) with any persons (including the excluded pursuer)—
        (i) on any matter discussed or referred to;

2006) and amended by the Act of Sederunt (Sheriff Court Rules) (Miscellaneous Amendments) (No.3) 2012 (SSI 2012/271) para.6 (effective November 1, 2012).

[2] As inserted by the Act of Sederunt (Ordinary Cause, Summary Application, Summary Cause and Small Claim Rules) Amendment (Equality Act 2006 etc.) 2006 (SSI 2006/509), (effective November 3, 2006). Chapter title amended by the Act of Sederunt (Sheriff Court Rules) (Equality Act 2010) 2010 (SSI 2010/340) para.2 (effective October 1, 2010).

[3] As substituted by the Act of Sederunt (Sheriff Court Rules) (Equality Act 2010) 2010 (SSI 2010/340) para.2 (effective October 1, 2010).

[1] As inserted by the Act of Sederunt (Sheriff Court Rules) (Miscellaneous Amendments) 2008 (SSI 2008/223) para.4(3)(b) (effective July 1, 2008).

[2] As substituted by the Act of Sederunt (Sheriff Court Rules) (Equality Act 2010) 2010 (SSI 2010/340) para.2 (effective October 1, 2010).

(ii)   with regard to any material disclosed,

during or with reference to any part of the proceedings from which the pursuer or the pursuer's representatives are excluded.

(5)   Where the sheriff has made an order under paragraph (4)(b), the person appointed to represent the interests of the pursuer may apply by motion for authority to seek instructions from or otherwise communicate with an excluded person.

Transfer to Employment Tribunal

D1.542   **44.6.**—[1](1)   On transferring proceedings to an employment tribunal under section 140(2) of the 2010 Act, the sheriff—

(a)   shall state his or her reasons for doing so in the interlocutor; and

(b)   may make the order on such conditions as to expenses or otherwise as he or she thinks fit.

(2)   The sheriff clerk must, within 7 days from the date of such order—

(a)   transmit the process to the Secretary of the Employment Tribunals (Scotland);

(b)   notify each party to the proceedings in writing of the transmission under subparagraph (a); and

(c)   certify, by making an appropriate entry on the interlocutor sheet, that he or she has made all notifications required under subparagraph (b).

(3)   Transmission of the process under paragraph (2)(a) will be valid notwithstanding any failure by the sheriff clerk to comply with paragraph (2)(b) and (c).

Transfer from Employment Tribunal

D1.543   **44.7.**—[2](1)   On receipt of the documentation in proceedings which have been remitted from an employment tribunal under section 140(3) of the 2010 Act, the sheriff clerk must—

(a)   record the date of receipt on the first page of the documentation;

(b)   fix a hearing to determine further procedure not less than 14 days after the date of receipt of the process; and

(c)   forthwith send written notice of the date of the hearing fixed under subparagraph (b) to each party.

(2)   At the hearing fixed under paragraph (1)(b) the sheriff may make such order as he or she thinks fit to secure so far as practicable that the cause thereafter proceeds in accordance with these Rules.

Chapter 45[3]

Vulnerable Witnesses (Scotland) Act 2004

Interpretation

D1.544   **45.1.**   In this Chapter—

"child witness notice" has the meaning given in section 12(2) of the Act of 2004;

"review application" means an application for review of arrangements for vulnerable witnesses pursuant to section 13 of the Act of 2004;

---

[1] As inserted by the Act of Sederunt (Sheriff Court Rules) (Equality Act 2010) 2010 (SSI 2010/340) para.2 (effective October 1, 2010).

[2] As inserted by the Act of Sederunt (Sheriff Court Rules) (Equality Act 2010) 2010 (SSI 2010/340) para.2 (effective October 1, 2010).

[3] As inserted by the Act of Sederunt (Ordinary Cause, Summary Application, Summary Cause and Small Claim Rules) Amendment (Vulnerable Witnesses (Scotland) Act 2004) 2007, r.2(13) (effective November 1, 2007).

"vulnerable witness application" has the meaning given in section 12(6) of the Act of 2004.

Child Witness Notice

45.2. A child witness notice lodged in accordance with section 12(2) of the Act of 2004 shall be in Form G19.

D1.545

Vulnerable Witness Application

45.3. A vulnerable witness application lodged in accordance with section 12(6) of the Act of 2004 shall be in Form G20.

D1.546

Intimation

45.4.—(1) The party lodging a child witness notice or vulnerable witness application shall intimate a copy of the child witness notice or vulnerable witness application to all the other parties to the proceedings and complete a certificate of intimation.

D1.547

(2) A certificate of intimation referred to in paragraph (1) shall be in Form G21 and shall be lodged with the child witness notice or vulnerable witness application.

Procedure on lodging child witness notice or vulnerable witness application

45.5.—(1) On receipt of a child witness notice or vulnerable witness application, the sheriff may—

D1.548

(a) make an order under section 12(1) or (6) of the Act of 2004 without holding a hearing;

(b) require further information from any of the parties before making any further order;

(c) fix a date for a hearing of the child witness notice or vulnerable witness application.

(2) The sheriff may, subject to any statutory time limits, make an order altering the date of the proof or other hearing at which the child or vulnerable witness is to give evidence and make such provision for intimation of such alteration to all parties concerned as he deems appropriate.

(3) An order fixing a hearing for a child witness notice or vulnerable witness application shall be intimated by the sheriff clerk—

(a) on the day the order is made; and

(b) in such manner as may be prescribed by the sheriff,

to all parties to the proceedings and such other persons as are named in the order where such parties or persons are not present at the time the order is made.

Review of arrangements for vulnerable witnesses

45.6.—(1) A review application shall be in Form G22.

D1.549

(2) Where the review application is made orally, the sheriff may dispense with the requirements of paragraph (1).

Intimation of review application

45.7.—(1) Where a review application is lodged, the applicant shall intimate a copy of the review application to all other parties to the proceedings and complete a certificate of intimation.

D1.550

(2) A certificate of intimation referred to in paragraph (1) shall be in Form G23 and shall be lodged together with the review application.

Procedure on lodging a review application

45.8.—(1) On receipt of a review application, the sheriff may—

D1.551

(a) if he is satisfied that he may properly do so, make an order under section

13(2) of the Act of 2004 without holding a hearing or, if he is not so satisfied, make such an order after giving the parties an opportunity to be heard;

    (b)   require of any of the parties further information before making any further order;

    (c)   fix a date for a hearing of the review application.

(2) The sheriff may, subject to any statutory time limits, make an order altering the date of the proof or other hearing at which the child or vulnerable witness is to give evidence and make such provision for intimation of such alteration to all parties concerned as he deems appropriate.

(3) An order fixing a hearing for a review application shall be intimated by the sheriff clerk—

    (a)   on the day the order is made; and

    (b)   in such manner as may be prescribed by the sheriff,

to all parties to the proceedings and such other persons as are named in the order where such parties or persons are not present at the time the order is made.

Determination of special measures

D1.552   **45.9.** When making an order under section 12(1) or (6) or 13(2) of the Act of 2004 the sheriff may, in light thereof, make such further orders as he deems appropriate in all the circumstances.

Intimation of an order under section 12(1) or (6) or 13(2)

D1.553   **45.10.** An order under section 12(1) or (6) or 13(2) of the Act of 2004 shall be intimated by the sheriff clerk—

    (a)   on the day the order is made; and

    (b)   in such manner as may be prescribed by the sheriff,

to all parties to the proceedings and such other persons as are named in the order where such parties or persons are not present at the time the order is made.

Taking of evidence by commissioner

D1.554   **45.11.**—(1) An interlocutor authorising the special measure of taking evidence by a commissioner shall be sufficient authority for the citing the witness to appear before the commissioner.

(2) At the commission the commissioner shall—

    (a)   administer the oath *de fideli administratione* to any clerk appointed for the commission; and

    (b)   administer to the witness the oath in Form G14, or where the witness elects to affirm, the affirmation in Form G15.

(3) The commission shall proceed without interrogatories unless, on cause shown, the sheriff otherwise directs.

Commission on interrogatories

D1.555   **45.12.**—(1) Where interrogatories have not been dispensed with, the party citing or intending to cite the vulnerable witness shall lodge draft interrogatories in process.

(2) Any other party may lodge cross-interrogatories.

(3) The interrogatories and cross-interrogatories, when adjusted, shall be extended and returned to the sheriff clerk for approval and the settlement of any dispute as to their contents by the sheriff.

(4) The party who cited the vulnerable witness shall—

    (a)   provide the commissioner with a copy of the pleadings (including any adjustments and amendments), the approved interrogatories and any cross-interrogatories and a certified copy of the interlocutor of his appointment;

(b)   instruct the clerk; and

(c)   be responsible in the first instance for the fee of the commissioner and his clerk.

(5)   The commissioner shall, in consultation with the parties, fix a diet for the execution of the commission to examine the witness.

Commission without interrogatories

45.13.   Where interrogatories have been dispensed with, the party citing or intending to cite the vulnerable witness shall—   **D1.556**

(a)   provide the commissioner with a copy of the pleadings (including any adjustments and amendments) and a certified copy of the interlocutor of his appointment;

(b)   fix a diet for the execution of the commission in consultation with the commissioner and every other party;

(c)   instruct the clerk; and

(d)   be responsible in the first instance for the fees of the commissioner and his clerk.

Lodging of video record and documents

45.14.—(1)   Where evidence is taken on commission pursuant to an order made under section 12(1) or (6) or 13(2) of the Act of 2004 the commissioner shall lodge the video record of the commission and relevant documents with the sheriff clerk.   **D1.557**

(2)   On the video record and any documents being lodged the sheriff clerk shall—

(a)   note—

(i)   the documents lodged;

(ii)   by whom they were lodged; and

(iii)   the date on which they were lodged, and

(b)   intimate what he has noted to all parties concerned.

Custody of video record and documents

45.15.—(1)   The video record and documents referred to in rule 45.14 shall, subject to paragraph (2), be kept in the custody of the sheriff clerk.   **D1.558**

(2)   Where the video record of the evidence of a witness is in the custody of the sheriff clerk under this rule and where intimation has been given to that effect under rule 45.14(2), the name and address of that witness and the record of his evidence shall be treated as being in the knowledge of the parties; and no party shall be required, notwithstanding any enactment to the contrary—

(a)   to include the name of that witness in any list of witnesses; or

(b)   to include the record of his evidence in any list of productions.

Application for leave for party to be present at the commission

45.16.   An application for leave for a party to be present in the room where the commission proceedings are taking place shall be by motion..   **D1.559**

(1)   In Appendix 1—

(a)   for Form G13 there shall be substituted the form set out in Part 1 of Schedule 1 to this Act of Sederunt; and

(b)   after Form G18 there shall be inserted the forms set out in Part 2 of Schedule 1 to this Act of Sederunt.

Chapter 46[1]

Companies Act 2006

Leave to raise derivative proceedings

D1.560 **46.1.**—(1)   Where leave of the court is required under section 266(1) (derivative proceedings: requirement for leave and notice) of the Companies Act 2006 (the "2006 Act"), the applicant must lodge, along with the initial writ, a written application in the form of a letter addressed to the sheriff clerk stating the grounds on which leave is sought.

(2)   Subject to paragraph (4), an application under paragraph (1) is not to be served on, or intimated to, any party.

(3)   The application is to be placed before the sheriff, who shall consider it for the purposes of section 266(3) of the 2006 Act without hearing the applicant.

(4)   Service under section 266(4)(a) of the 2006 Act may be given by any of the methods provided for in Chapter 5 (citation, service and intimation) and a certificate of service must be lodged.

(5)   If the company wishes to be heard it must, within 21 days after the date of service of the application, lodge written submissions setting out its position in relation to the application.

(6)   Subject to section 266(4)(b) of the 2006 Act, the next stage in the proceedings is a hearing at which the applicant and the company may be heard.

(7)   The sheriff clerk is to fix the hearing and intimate its date to the applicant and the company.

(8)   Where an application under paragraph (1) is granted, a copy of the sheriff's interlocutor must be served on the defender along with the warrant of citation.

Application to continue proceedings as derivative proceedings

D1.561 **46.2.**   An application under section 267(2) (application to continue proceedings as derivative proceedings) of the 2006 Act is to be in the form of a minute and Chapter 14 (applications by minute) applies with the necessary modifications.

Chapter 47[2]

Actions of Division and Sale and Orders for Division and/or Sale of Property

Remit to reporter to examine heritable property

D1.562 **47.1.**—(1)   In an action of division and sale of heritable property, the sheriff may, in accordance with paragraph (2), remit to a reporter to examine the property and to report to the sheriff—

(a)   whether the property is capable of division in a manner equitable to the interests of the *pro indiviso* proprietors and, if so, how such division may be effected; and

(b)   in the event that the property is to be sold—
   (i)   whether the property should be sold as a whole or in lots and, if in lots, what those lots should be;
   (ii)   whether the property should be exposed for sale by public roup or private bargain;

---

[1] As inserted by the Act of Sederunt (Sheriff Court Rules) (Miscellaneous Amendments) 2010 (SSI 2010/279) r.5 (effective July 29, 2010).
[2] As inserted by the Act of Sederunt (Sheriff Court Rules) (Miscellaneous Amendments) (No.3) 2011 (SSI 2011/386) para.2 (effective 28 November 2011).

  (iii) whether the sale should be subject to any upset or minimum price and, if so, the amount;

  (iv) the manner and extent to which the property should be advertised for sale; and

  (v) any other matter which the reporter considers pertinent to a sale of the property.

(2) A remit under paragraph (1) shall be made—

  (a) where the action is undefended, on the motion of the pursuer at any time after the expiry of the period of notice;

  (b) where the action is defended—

    (i) at the options hearing, on the motion of any party to the action;

    (ii) on the sheriff finding, after a debate or proof, that the pursuer is entitled to bring and insist in the action of division and sale; or

    (iii) at such other time as the sheriff thinks fit.

(3) On completion of a report made under paragraph (1), the reporter shall send the report, with a copy for each party, to the sheriff clerk.

(4) On receipt of such report, the sheriff clerk must—

  (a) lodge the report in process; and

  (b) give written intimation to each party that this has been done and that parties may uplift a copy of the report from the process.

(5) After the lodging of such a report, any party may apply by motion for further procedure or for approval of the report.

(6) At the hearing of a motion under paragraph (5), the sheriff may—

  (a) in the event of a challenge to any part of the report, order parties to state their objections to the report and answers to such objections and lodge them within such period as the sheriff thinks fit; or

  (b) in the absence of such challenge, order that the property be divided or sold, as the case may be, in accordance with the recommendations of the reporter, subject to such modification, if any, as the sheriff thinks fit.

(7) Where, in accordance with paragraph (6)(a), the lodging of objections and answers has been ordered, the sheriff clerk will fix a date and time for the parties to be heard by the sheriff; and the sheriff may make such order for further procedure as he or she thinks fit.

Division and/or sale of property

47.2.—(1) Where the sheriff orders the division and/or sale of property, heritable or otherwise, the sheriff shall direct that the division and/or sale, as the case may be, shall be conducted under the oversight and direction of the sheriff clerk or any other fit person whom the sheriff may appoint for that purpose. **D1.563**

(2) The sheriff clerk or person appointed under paragraph (1), as the case may be, may report any matter of difficulty arising in the course of the division and/or sale to the sheriff.

(3) At a hearing on a report made under paragraph (2), the sheriff may give such directions as the sheriff thinks fit, including authority to the sheriff clerk to sign, on behalf of any proprietor, a disposition of his or her interest in the property.

(4) On the conclusion of a sale of property—

  (a) the proceeds of the sale, under deduction of the expenses of the sale, shall be consigned into court; and

  (b) the sheriff clerk or the person appointed under paragraph (1), as the case may be, shall lodge in process a report of the sale and a proposed scheme of division of the proceeds of sale.

(5) At the hearing of a motion for approval of a report of the sale of property lodged under paragraph (4) and the proposed scheme of division, the sheriff may—

(a) approve the report and scheme of division, and direct that payment of the proceeds of sale be made in terms of the report;

(b) deal with any question as to the expenses of process or of sale; and

(c) make such other order as the sheriff thinks fit.

Chapter 48[1, 2]

Reporting Restrictions

Interpretation and application of this Chapter

D1.564

48.1.—(1) This Chapter applies to orders which restrict the reporting of proceedings.

(2) In this Chapter, *"interested person"* means a person—

(a) who has asked to see any order made by the sheriff which restricts the reporting of proceedings, including an interim order; and

(b) whose name is included on a list kept by the Lord President for the purposes of this Chapter.

Application for an order

48.1A.—[3](1) A party to the proceedings may apply to the court for an order under this Chapter to restrict the reporting of the proceedings.

(2) An application for an order under this Chapter must be made by motion and be accompanied by Form 48.1A.

Interim orders

D1.565

48.2.—[4](1) Where the sheriff is considering making an order, the sheriff must first make an interim order.

(2) The sheriff clerk shall immediately send a copy of the interim order to any interested person.

(3) The sheriff shall specify in the interim order why the sheriff is considering making an order.

Representations

D1.566

48.3.—[5](1) *[Repealed by the Act of Sederunt (Rules of the Court of Session 1994, Sheriff Appeal Court Rules and Sheriff Court Rules Amendment) (Reporting Restrictions) 2020 (SSI 2020/28) r.4(2) (effective 2 March 2020).]*

(2) An interested person who would be directly affected by the making of an order shall have an opportunity to make representations to the sheriff before an order is made.

(3) Representations shall—

(a) be made by letter addressed to the sheriff clerk;

---

[1] As inserted by the Act of Sederunt (Sheriff Court Rules) (Miscellaneous Amendments) (No.3) 2011 (SSI 2011/386) para.3 (effective 28 November 2011).

[2] As substituted by the Act of Sederunt (Rules of the Court of Session and Sheriff Court Rules Amendment No. 3) (Reporting Restrictions) 2015 (SSI 2015/85) para.3 (effective 1 April 2015).

[3] As inserted by the Act of Sederunt (Rules of the Court of Session 1994, Sheriff Appeal Court Rules and Sheriff Court Rules Amendment) (Miscellaneous) 2023 (SSI 2023/196) r.5(2) (effective 2 October 2023).

[4] As amended by the Act of Sederunt (Rules of the Court of Session 1994, Sheriff Appeal Court Rules and Sheriff Court Rules Amendment) (Reporting Restrictions) 2020 (SSI 2020/28) r.4(2) (effective 2 March 2020).

[5] As amended by the Act of Sederunt (Rules of the Court of Session 1994, Sheriff Appeal Court Rules and Sheriff Court Rules Amendment) (Reporting Restrictions) 2020 (SSI 2020/28) r.4(2) (effective 2 March 2020).

(b) where an urgent hearing is sought, include reasons explaining why an urgent hearing is necessary;

(c) be lodged no later than 2 days after the interim order is sent to interested persons in accordance with rule 48.2(2).

(4) Where the period for lodging representations expires on a Saturday, Sunday, or public or court holiday, it shall be deemed to expire on the next day on which the sheriff clerk's office is open for civil court business.

(5) On representations being made—

  (a) the sheriff shall appoint a date and time for a hearing—

    (i) on the first suitable court day thereafter; or

    (ii) where the sheriff is satisfied that an urgent hearing is necessary, at such earlier date and time as the sheriff may determine;

  (b) the sheriff clerk shall—

    (i) notify the date and time of the hearing to the parties to the proceedings and the person who has made representations; and

    (ii) send a copy of the representations to the parties to the proceedings.

(6) Where no interested person makes representations in accordance with rule 48.3(2), the sheriff clerk shall put the interim order before the sheriff in chambers in order that the sheriff may resume consideration as to whether to make an order.

(7) Where the sheriff, having resumed consideration under rule 48.3(6), makes no order, the sheriff shall recall the interim order.

(8) Where the sheriff recalls an interim order, the sheriff clerk shall immediately notify any interested person.

Notification of reporting restrictions

48.4.—(1) Where the court makes an order, the sheriff clerk shall immediately— **D1.566.1**

  (a) send a copy of the order to any interested person;

  (b) arrange for the publication of the making of the order on the Scottish Court Service website.

Applications for variation or revocation

48.5.—(1) A person aggrieved by an order may apply to the sheriff for its varia- **D1.566.2** tion or revocation.

(2) An application shall be made by letter addressed to the sheriff clerk.

(3) On an application being made—

  (a) the sheriff shall appoint the application for a hearing;

  (b) the sheriff clerk shall—

    (i) notify the date and time of the hearing to the parties to the proceedings and the applicant;

    (ii) send a copy of the application to the parties to the proceedings.

(4) The hearing shall, so far as reasonably practicable, be before the sheriff who made the order.

[THE NEXT PARAGRAPH IS D1.567]

Chapter 49[1]

Admiralty Actions

Interpretation of this Chapter

49.1. In this Chapter— **D1.567**

[1] As inserted by the Act of Sederunt (Sheriff Court Rules) (Miscellaneous Amendments) 2012 (SSI 2012/188) para.10 (effective 1 August 2012).

"Admiralty action" means an action having a crave appropriate for the enforcement of a claim to which section 47(2) of the Administration of Justice Act 1956 applies;

"ship" has the meaning assigned in section 48(f) of that Act.

Forms of action

D1.568   **49.2.**—(1) An Admiralty action against the owners or demise charterers of, or other parties interested in, a ship or the owners of the cargo may be brought—

    (a)   in rem, where the crave of the initial writ is directed to recovery in respect of a maritime lien against the ship or cargo or the proceeds of it as sold under order of the sheriff or where arrestment in rem may be made under section 47(3) of the Administration of Justice Act 1956;

    (b)   in personam, where the crave of the initial writ is directed to a decree against the defender; or

    (c)   both in rem and in personam, where sub-paragraphs (a) and (b) apply.

(2) When bringing an Admiralty action, the pursuer shall use Form G1 (initial writ) and insert the words "Admiralty Action in rem", "Admiralty Action in personam" or "Admiralty Action in rem and in personam", as the case may be, immediately below where the Sheriffdom and court are designed, above the instance.

Actions in rem

D1.569   **49.3.**—(1) In an Admiralty action in rem—

    (a)   where the owners or demise charterers of, or other parties interested in, the ship or the owners of the cargo against which the action is directed are known to the pursuer, they shall be called as defenders by name;

    (b)   where such owners or demise charterers or other parties are unknown to the pursuer—

        (i)   the pursuer may call them as defenders as "the owners of or parties interested in the ship (*name and identify by its port of registry*) or the owners of the cargo"; and

        (ii)   the master, if known, shall also be called as a defender representing the owners or demise charterers.

(2) In an Admiralty action in rem, the ship or cargo shall be arrested in rem and a warrant for such arrestment may include warrant to dismantle where craved in the initial writ.

Actions in personam

D1.570   **49.4.**—(1) In an Admiralty action in personam directed against the owners or demise charterers, or other parties, interested in a ship, or the owners of cargo, the defenders shall, if known to the pursuer, be called as defenders by name.

(2) In such an action, where—

    (a)   the vessel is not a British ship, and

    (b)   the names of the owners or demise charterers are not known to the pursuer,

the master of the ship may be called as the defender representing the owners or demise charterers.

(3) In an action to which paragraph (2) applies, any warrant to arrest to found jurisdiction shall be executed against the master of the ship in his or her representative capacity.

(4) In an action to which paragraph (2) applies, any decree shall be pronounced against the master in his or her representative capacity.

(5) A decree in an Admiralty action in personam may be pronounced against an owner or demise charterer of, or other party interested in, the ship or the owner of

the cargo only where that owner or demise charterer or other party interested, as the case may be, has been called or added as a defender.

Sale of ship or cargo

49.5.—(1) This rule shall not apply to the sale of a cargo arrested on the dependence of an Admiralty action in personam.   **D1.571**

(2) Where, in an Admiralty action or an action of declarator and sale of a ship—

(a) the sheriff makes a finding that the pursuer has a claim which falls to be satisfied out of an arrested ship or cargo, or

(b) a decree for a sum of money has been granted in an action in which a ship has been arrested on the dependence,

the pursuer may apply by motion for an order for the sale of that ship or a share in it, or the cargo, as the case may be, by public auction or private bargain.

(3) Before making such an order, the sheriff shall remit to a reporter for the purpose of obtaining—

(a) an inventory of,

(b) a valuation and recommendation upset price for, and

(c) any recommendation as to the appropriate advertisement for the sale of, the ship, share or cargo.

(4) Where a remit is made under paragraph (3), the pursuer shall instruct the reporter within 14 days after the date of the interlocutor making the remit and be responsible, in the first instance, for payment of his or her fee.

(5) On completion of a report following a remit under paragraph (3), the reporter shall send the report and a copy for each party to the sheriff clerk.

(6) On receipt of such a report, the sheriff clerk shall—

(a) give written intimation to each party of receipt of the report;

(b) request the pursuer to show to him or her a discharge in respect of the fee for which the pursuer is responsible under paragraph (4); and

(c) after sight of such a discharge—

(i) lodge the report in process;

(ii) give written intimation to each party that this has been done and that he or she may uplift a copy of the report from process; and

(iii) cause the action to call for a procedural hearing.

(7) Where the sheriff orders the sale of a ship, share or cargo, the conduct of the sale, including any advertisement of it, shall be under the direction of the sheriff clerk.

(8) Where such a sale is the sale of a ship or a share in it, the interlocutor ordering the sale shall include a declaration that the right to transfer the ship or share to the purchaser is vested in the sheriff clerk.

(9) Where, in such a sale, no offer to purchase the ship, share or cargo, as the case may be, has reached the upset price, the pursuer may apply by motion for authority to expose such ship, share or cargo for sale at a reduced upset price.

(10) The proceeds of such a sale shall be consigned into court, under deduction of all dues to the date the sheriff adjudges the ship, share or cargo to belong to the purchaser under paragraph (11)(a), payable to Her Majesty's Revenue and Customs or to the port or harbour authority within the jurisdiction of which the ship or cargo lies and in respect of which such port or harbour authority has statutory power to detain the ship or cargo.

(11) On consignation being made under paragraph (10), the sheriff shall—

(a) adjudge the ship, share or cargo, as the case may be, declaring the same to belong to the purchaser, freed and disburdened of all bonds, mortgages, liens, rights of retention and other incumbrances affecting it and ordering such ship, share or cargo to be delivered to the purchaser on production of a certified copy of the interlocutor pronounced under this subparagraph; and

(b) order such intimation and advertisement, if any, for claims on the consigned fund as the sheriff thinks fit.

(12) The sheriff shall, after such hearing or inquiry as the sheriff thinks fit—

(a) determine all questions of expenses;

(b) rank and prefer any claimants in order of preference; and

(c) make such other order, if any, as the sheriff thinks fit.

Ship collisions and preliminary acts

D1.572

49.6.—(1) Subject to rule 49.7 (applications to dispense with preliminary acts), this rule applies to an Admiralty action of damages arising out of a collision between ships at sea.

(2) An action to which this rule applies may be brought in rem, in personam or in rem and in personam.

(3) An initial writ in such an action shall not contain a condescendence or pleas-in-law.

(4) Where such an action is brought in personam, the crave of the initial writ shall contain sufficient detail to enable the defender to identify the date and place of and the ships involved in the collision.

(5) Where a notice of intention to defend has been lodged Rule 9.2 shall, subject to paragraph 11 of this rule, not apply.

(6) Within 7 days after the expiry of the period of notice, the pursuer shall lodge in process a sealed envelope containing—

(a) a preliminary act in Form 49.6; and

(b) a brief condescendence and appropriate pleas-in-law.

(7) Within 28 days after the preliminary act for the pursuer has been lodged under paragraph (6), the defender shall lodge in process a sealed envelope containing a preliminary act in Form 49.6.

(8) A party who lodges a preliminary act under paragraph (6) or (7) shall not send a copy of it to any other party.

(9) On the lodging of a preliminary act by the defender under paragraph (7) the sheriff clerk shall—

(a) open both sealed envelopes;

(b) mark the contents of those envelopes with appropriate numbers of process; and

(c) give written intimation to each party that subparagraphs (a) and (b) have been complied with.

(10) On receipt of the written intimation under paragraph (9)(c), the pursuer and defender shall exchange copies of the contents of their respective envelopes.

(11) Within 7 days after the sealed envelopes have been opened up under paragraph (9), the sheriff clerk shall fix a date and time for an Options Hearing and send parties Form G5 in terms of Rule 9.2.

(12) When the pursuer lodges a record in terms of Rule 9.11 he or she shall do so with a copy of each of the preliminary acts appended to it.

(13) No amendment, adjustment or alteration may be made to a preliminary act except by order of the sheriff.

Applications to dispense with preliminary acts

D1.573

49.7.—(1) Within 7 days after the expiry of the period of notice, any party may apply for an order to dispense with preliminary acts in an action to which rule 49.6 applies.

(2) An application under paragraph (1) shall be made by minute craving the sheriff to dispense with preliminary acts and setting out the grounds on which the application is made.

(3) Before lodging such a minute in process, the party making the application shall intimate a copy of the minute, and the date on which it will be lodged, to every other party.

(4) Any other party may lodge in process answers to such a minute within 14 days after such a minute has been lodged.

(5) After the expiry of the period mentioned in paragraph (4), the sheriff may, on the motion of any party, after such further procedure, if any, as the sheriff thinks fit, dispense with preliminary acts.

(6) Where the sheriff dispenses with preliminary acts, the pursuer shall lodge a condescendence with appropriate pleas-in-law within such period as the sheriff thinks fit; and the action shall thereafter proceed in the same way as an ordinary action.

(7) Where the sheriff refuses to dispense with preliminary acts, the sheriff shall ordain a party or parties, as the case may be, to lodge preliminary acts under rule 49.6 within such period as the sheriff thinks fit.

(8) An interlocutor dispensing or refusing to dispense with preliminary acts shall be final and not subject to review.

Ship collision and salvage actions

49.8.—(1) Without prejudice to rule 29.11 (lodging productions), in an Admiralty action arising out of a collision between ships at sea or salvage, the parties shall—   **D1.574**

    (a) within 4 days after the interlocutor allowing proof,

    (b) within 4 days before the taking of evidence on commission, or

    (c) on or before such other date as the sheriff, on special cause shown, shall determine,

lodge in process the documents, if any, mentioned in paragraph (2).

(2) The documents to be lodged under paragraph (1) are—

    (a) the log books, including scrap log books, of the ships concerned;

    (b) all *de recenti* written reports in connection with the collision or salvage, as the case may be, by the masters or mates of the vessels concerned to their respective owners; and

    (c) reports of any surveys of the ship in respect of which damage or salvage is claimed.

Arrestment of ships and arrestment in rem of cargo on board ship

49.9.—(1) An arrestment of a ship in rem or on the dependence, or an arrestment in rem of cargo on board ship, may be executed on any day by a sheriff officer who shall affix the schedule of arrestment—   **D1.575**

    (a) to the mainmast of the ship;

    (b) to the single mast of the ship; or

    (c) where there is no mast, to some prominent part of the ship.

(2) In the execution of an arrestment of a ship on the dependence, the sheriff officer shall, in addition to complying with paragraph (1), mark the initials "ER" above the place where the schedule of arrestment is fixed.

(3) On executing an arrestment under paragraph (1), the sheriff officer shall deliver a copy of the schedule of arrestment and a copy of the certificate of execution of it to the master of the ship, or other person on board in charge of the ship or cargo, as the case may be, as representing the owners or demise charterers of, or parties interested in, the ship or the owners of the cargo, as the case may be.

(4) Where the schedule of arrestment and the copy of the certificate of execution of it cannot be delivered as required under paragraph (3)—

    (a) the certificate of execution shall state that fact; and

    (b) either—

        (i) the arrestment shall be executed by serving it on the harbour master of the port where the ship lies; or

        (ii) where there is no harbour master, or the ship is not in a harbour, the pursuer shall enrol a motion for such further order as to intimation and advertisement, if any, as may be necessary.

(5) A copy of the schedule of arrestment and a copy of the certificate of execution of it shall be delivered by the sheriff officer to the harbour master, if any, of any port where the ship lies.

Arrestment of cargo

D1.576   **49.10.**—(1) An arrestment of cargo on board a ship shall be executed by a sheriff officer who shall serve the schedule of arrestment on—

    (a) the master of the ship;

    (b) any other person in charge of the ship or cargo; or

    (c) other proper arrestee.

(2) Where the schedule of arrestment cannot be executed in accordance with paragraph (1), the arrestment may be executed as provided for in rule 49.9(4) and (5).

Forms for diligence in admiralty actions

D1.577   **49.11.**—(1) In the execution of diligence in an Admiralty action, the following forms shall be used—

    (a) in the case of—

        (i) an arrestment to found jurisdiction (other than the arrestment of a ship), a schedule in Form 49.11-A and a certificate of execution in Form 49.11-E;

        (ii) an arrestment of a ship to found jurisdiction, a schedule in Form 49.11-AA and a certificate of execution in Form 49.11-F;

    (b) subject to subparagraph (e), in the case of an arrestment on the dependence, a schedule in Form G4B and a certificate of execution in Form 49.11-E;

    (c) in the case of an arrestment in rem of a ship, cargo or other maritime *res* to enforce a maritime hypothec or lien, a schedule in Form 49.11-B and a certificate of execution in Form 49.11-G;

    (d) in the case of an arrestment in rem of a ship to enforce a non-pecuniary claim, a schedule in Form 49.11-C and a certificate of execution in Form 49.11-G;

    (e) in the case of an arrestment on the dependence of—

        (i) a cargo on board a ship, a schedule in Form G4B;

        (ii) a ship, a schedule in Form 49.11-D,

and a certificate of execution in Form 49.11-H.

(2) Where two or more of the arrestments mentioned in paragraph (1)(a), (b) and (c) are to be executed, they may be combined in one schedule of arrestment.

Movement of arrested property

D1.578   **49.12.**—(1) Any person who has an interest in a ship or cargo which is the subject of an arrestment under this Chapter may apply by motion for a warrant authorising the movement of the ship or cargo.

(2)   Where the sheriff grants a warrant sought under paragraph (1), the sheriff may make such further order as the sheriff thinks fit to give effect to that warrant.

Arrestment before service
49.13.   Before the service of an Admiralty action, where it is craved in the initial writ, the pursuer may apply by motion for warrant for arrestment of any of the types of arrestment mentioned in this Chapter.

D1.579

Chapter 50[1]

Lodging Audio or Audio-visual Recordings of Children

Interpretation
50.1.   In this Chapter "child" is a person under the age of 16 on the date of commencement of the proceedings and "children" shall be construed accordingly.

D1.580

Lodging an audio or audio-visual recording of a child
50.2.—(1)   Where a party seeks to lodge an audio or audio-visual recording of a child as a production, such party must—

D1.581

   (a)   ensure that the recording is in a format that can be heard or viewed by means of equipment available in court;

   (b)   place the recording together with a copy of the relevant inventory of productions in a sealed envelope marked with—

     (i)   the names of the parties to the court action;

     (ii)   the case reference number;

     (iii)   (where available) the date and time of commencement and of termination of the recording; and

     (iv)   "recording of a child - confidential".

(2)   The sealed envelope must be lodged with the sheriff clerk.

(3)   In the remainder of this Chapter a "recording of a child" means any such recording lodged under this rule.

Separate inventory of productions
50.3.—(1)   On each occasion that a recording of a child is lodged, a separate inventory of productions shall be lodged in process.

D1.582

(2)   The sheriff clerk will mark the date of receipt and the number of process on the sealed envelope containing a recording of a child.

Custody of a recording of a child
50.4.—(1)   A recording of a child—

D1.583

   (a)   must be kept in the safe custody of the sheriff clerk;

   (b)   subject to rule 50.5, will not form a borrowable part of the process.

(2)   The seal of the envelope containing a recording of a child shall be broken only with the authority of the sheriff and on such conditions as the sheriff thinks fit (which conditions may relate to listening to or viewing the recording).

Access to a recording of a child
50.5.—(1)   A party may lodge a written motion to gain access to and listen to or view a recording of a child.

D1.584

(2)   The sheriff may refuse a motion or grant it on such conditions as the sheriff thinks fit, including—

---

[1] As inserted by the Act of Sederunt (Sheriff Court Rules) (Miscellaneous Amendments) (No.3) 2012 (SSI 2012/271) para.2 (effective November 1, 2012).

(a)   allowing only such persons as the sheriff may specify to listen to or view the recording;

(b)   specifying the location where such listening or viewing is to take place;

(c)   specifying the date and time when such listening or viewing is to take place;

(d)   allowing a copy of the recording to be made (in the same or different format) and arrangements for the safe-keeping and disposal of such copy;

(e)   arrangements for the return of the recording and re-sealing the envelope.

(3)[1]   An application for leave to appeal against the decision of the sheriff on that motion must be made immediately.

Incidental appeal against rulings on access to a recording of a child

D1.585

50.6.   *[Repealed by the Act of Sederunt (Rules of the Court of Session, Sheriff Appeal Court Rules and Sheriff Court Rules Amendment) (Sheriff Appeal Court) 2015 (SSI 2015/419) r.5 (effective 1 January 2016).]*

Exceptions

D1.586

50.7.—(1)   The sheriff may, on the application of a party and on cause shown, disapply the provisions of this Chapter.

(2)   An application under paragraph (1) shall be made—

(a)   at the time of presenting the recording for lodging;

(b)   by letter addressed to the sheriff clerk stating the grounds on which the application is made.

Application of other rules

D1.587

50.8.—(1)   The following rules do not apply to a recording of a child—

(a)   rule 9A.2(2) (inspection of documents);

(b)   rule 11.6(1) (intimation of parts of process and adjustments), in so far as it would otherwise require a party to deliver a copy of a recording of a child to every other party;

(c)   rule 29.12(1) (copy productions).

Chapter 51[2]

Land Registration Etc.

Interpretation of this Chapter

D1.587.1

51.1.   In this Chapter—

"the 2012 Act" means the Land Registration etc. (Scotland) Act 2012;

"plot of land" has the meaning given by section 3(4) and (5) of the 2012 Act;

"proprietor" has the meaning given by section 113(1) of the 2012 Act.

Applications under Part 6 of the 2012 Act

D1.587.2

51.2.—(1)   An application under section 67(2) (warrant to place a caveat) of the 2012 Act shall be made by motion.

(2)   The motion shall—

(a)   identify, by reference to section 67(1) of the 2012 Act, the type of civil proceedings constituted by the action;

---

[1]   As inserted by the Act of Sederunt (Rules of the Court of Session, Sheriff Appeal Court Rules and Sheriff Court Rules Amendment) (Sheriff Appeal Court) 2015 (SSI 2015/419) r.5 (effective 1 January 2016).

[2]   As inserted by the Act of Sederunt (Rules of the Court of Session and Sheriff Court Rules Amendment No.2) (Miscellaneous) 2014 (SSI 2014/291) r.3 (effective December 8, 2014).

    (b)   in respect of each plot of land, contain—
        (i)   a description of the registered plot of land;
        (ii)   the title number; and
        (iii)   the name and address of the proprietor;
    (c)   where the caveat is to apply only to part of a plot of land, be accompanied by a plan indicating the part so affected.

(3) An application under the following provisions of the 2012 Act shall be made by motion—

    (a)   section 69(1) (renewal of caveat);
    (b)   section 70(1) (restriction of caveat);
    (c)   section 71(1) (recall of caveat).

Form of orders under Part 6 of the 2012 Act

51.3.—(1) An order under section 67(3) or 69(2) of the 2012 Act shall be in Form 51.3-A.   **D1.587.3**

(2) An order under section 70(2) of the 2012 Act shall be in Form 51.3-B.

(3) An order under section 71(2) of the 2012 Act shall be in Form 51.3-C.

Effect of warrant to place or renew caveat

51.4. A certified copy of an order in Form 51.3-A may be registered in the Register of Inhibitions and Adjudications.   **D1.587.4**

Form of order for rectification of a document

51.5. An order for rectification under section 8 of the Law Reform (Miscellaneous Provisions) (Scotland) Act 1985 in respect of a document which has been registered in the Land Register of Scotland shall be in Form 51.5.   **D1.587.5**

Chapter 52[1]

Mutual Recognition of Protection Measures in Civil Matters

[Revoked by Act of Sederunt (Rules of the Court of Session 1994 and Sheriff Court Rules Amendment) (Civil Protection Measures (EU Exit)) 2022 (SSI 2022/329) para.3 (effective 1 December 2022).]   **D1.587.6**

Chapter 53[2]

Proving the Tenor

Application of this Chapter

53.1. This Chapter applies to an action of proving the tenor.   **D1.587.14**

Parties

53.2.—(1) The pursuer must call as a defender every person who (so far as known to the pursuer) has an interest in the document to be proved.   **D1.587.15**

(2) Where only the pursuer has such an interest, the pursuer must call the Lord Advocate as a defender, as representing the public interest.

Supporting evidence

53.3. When lodging an initial writ, the pursuer must lodge in process supporting documentary evidence of the tenor of the document to be proved, so far as in the possession or control of the pursuer.   **D1.587.16**

---

[1] As inserted by the Act of Sederunt (Rules of the Court of Session and Sheriff Court Rules Amendment No.3) (Mutual Recognition of Protection Measures) 2014 (SSI 2014/371) para.3 (effective 11 January 2015).

[2] As inserted by the Act of Sederunt (Ordinary Cause Rules Amendment) (Proving the Tenor and Reduction) 2015 (SSI 2015/176) para.2 (effective 25 May 2015).

Undefended actions

D1.587.17   **53.4.**—(1) This rule applies where no notice of intention to defend has been lodged.

(2) Evidence is to be given by affidavit unless the sheriff otherwise directs.

(3) The pursuer may apply for decree by minute in Form 53.4.

(4) The sheriff may, on consideration of that minute, supporting documentary evidence and affidavits, without requiring appearance—

(a) grant decree in terms of the minute; or

(b) remit the cause for further procedure (including proof by parole evidence).

Chapter 54[1]

Reduction

Application of this Chapter

D1.587.18   **54.1.** This Chapter applies to an action of reduction.

Craves for suspension and interdict

D1.587.19   **54.2.**—(1) This rule applies to an action that seeks to reduce a document upon which real or personal diligence may proceed.

(2) The pursuer may include in the initial writ, in relation to that diligence, craves for suspension and interdict.

Production: objection by defender

D1.587.20   **54.3.**—(1) This rule applies where a defender objects to satisfying a crave for production of a document sought to be reduced.

(2) The defender must state in the defences—

(a) the grounds of objection; and

(b) any defence on the merits of the action.

(3) The defender is not required to satisfy a crave for production at the time of lodging defences.

(4) Where the sheriff repels or reserves an objection to satisfying a crave for production, the defender must be ordered to satisfy that crave within such period as the sheriff thinks fit.

(5) Where the defender, following that order, lodges in process any document, a motion to hold production satisfied (or satisfied in respect of the document lodged) must also be made.

(6) Where the defender does not comply with that order, the pursuer may make a motion for decree by default.

Production: no objection by defender

D1.587.21   **54.4.**—(1) This rule applies where a defender does not state an objection to satisfying a crave for production of a document sought to be reduced.

(2) The defender must, when lodging defences—

(a) lodge in process any such document in the defender's possession or control; and

(b) make a motion to hold production satisfied (or satisfied in respect of the document lodged).

(3) If the defender does not do so, the pursuer may make a motion for decree by default.

---

[1] As inserted by the Act of Sederunt (Ordinary Cause Rules Amendment) (Proving the Tenor and Reduction) 2015 (SSI 2015/176) para.2 (effective 25 May 2015).

Production: no objection by defender

54.5.—(1) This rule applies where the pursuer has possession or control of a **D1.587.22** document in respect of which reduction is craved.

(2) The pursuer must lodge that document in process with the initial writ.

(3) The sheriff may, at any stage, order the pursuer to satisfy a crave for production of a document sought to be reduced.

(4) Where the pursuer does not comply with that order, the defender may make a motion for dismissal.

(5) When lodging a document under subparagraph (2) or (3), the pursuer must make a motion to hold production satisfied (or satisfied in respect of the document lodged).

Production: joint minute for reduction

54.6.—(1) This rule applies where—   **D1.587.23**

  (a) a crave for production has not been satisfied, and

  (b) parties enter into a joint minute in terms of which the decree of reduction is to be pronounced.

(2) The document to be reduced must be lodged in process with the joint minute.

(3) The terms of the joint minute must be sufficient to enable the sheriff to hold the crave for production satisfied.

Production: satisfaction by a copy

54.7.— The sheriff may, with the consent of the parties, hold production to be **D1.587.24** satisfied by a copy of the document sought to be reduced.

[THE NEXT PARAGRAPH IS D1.588]
FORMS

Appendix 1
  Rule 1.4

FORM 1A.2[1, 2]   **D1.588**

Rule 1A.2(2)(b)

Statement by prospective lay representative for Pursuer/Defender*

Case Ref. No.:

in the cause
SHERIFFDOM OF (*insert name of sheriffdom*)
AT (*insert place of sheriff court*)
[A.B.], (*insert designation and address*), Pursuer
against
[C.D.], (*insert designation and address*), Defender
Court ref. no:

Name and address of prospective lay representative who requests permission to represent party litigant:
Identify hearing(s) in respect of which permission for lay representation is sought:
The prospective lay representative declares that:

---

[1] As inserted by the Act of Sederunt (Sheriff Court Rules) (Lay Representation) 2013 (SSI 2013/91) r.2 (effective 4 April 2013).

[2] As amended by the Act of Sederunt (Rules of the Court of Session, Sheriff Appeal Court Rules and Sheriff Court Rules Amendment) (Lay Representation) 2017 (SSI 2017/186) r.4(3) (effective 3 July 2017).

(a)	I have no financial interest in the outcome of the case or I have the following financial interest in it:*
(b)	I am not receiving remuneration or other reward directly or indirectly from the litigant for my assistance and will not receive directly or indirectly such remuneration or other reward from the litigant.
(c)	I accept that documents and information are provided to me by the litigant on a confidential basis and I undertake to keep them confidential.
(d)	I have no previous convictions *or* I have the following convictions: (list convictions)*
(e)	I have not been declared a vexatious litigant under the Vexatious Actions (Scotland) Act 1898 *or* I was declared a vexatious litigant under the Vexatious Actions (Scotland) Act 1898 on [insert date].*

(Signed)
[Name of prospective lay representative]
[Date]

(Insert Place/Date)
The Sheriff grants/refuses* the application.

[Signed]
Sheriff Clerk
[Date]

(*delete as appropriate)

FORM G1
Form of initial writ

Rule 3.1(1)(a)

INITIAL WRIT

SHERIFFDOM OF *(insert name of sheriffdom)*
AT *(insert place of sheriff court)*
[A.B.] *(design and state any special capacity in which the pursuer is suing)*. Pursuer.

Against

[C.D.] *(design and state any special capacity in which the defender is being sued)*. Defender.

The Pursuer craves the court *(here state the specific decree, warrant or order sought)*.

CONDESCENDENCE
(State in numbered paragraphs the facts which form the ground of action)
PLEAS-IN-LAW
(State in numbered sentences)

Signed
[A.B.], Pursuer.

or [X.Y.], Solicitor for the pursuer *(state designation and business address)*[1]

FORM G1A
Form of initial writ in a commercial action

Rule 3.1(1)(b) and 40.4

---

[1] Inserted by the Act of Sederunt (Ordinary Cause Rules) Amendment (Commercial Actions) Rules 2001 (SSI 2001/8) (effective March 1, 2001).

SHERIFFDOM OF (*insert name of sheriffdom*)

AT (*insert place of sheriff court*)

COMMERCIAL ACTION

[A.B.] (*design and state any special capacity in which the pursuer is being sued*). Pursuer.

Against

[C.D.] (*design and state any special capacity in which the defender is being sued*). Defender.

[A.B.] for the Pursuer craves the court (*specify the orders sought*)

CONDESCENDENCE

(*provide the following, in numbered paragraphs—*

information sufficient to identify the transaction or dispute from which the action arises; a summary of the circumstances which have resulted in the action being raised; and details setting out the grounds on which the action proceeds.)

Note: Where damages are sought, the claim may be summarised in the pleadings— in the form of a statement of damages; or

by lodging with the initial writ a schedule detailing the claim.

PLEAS-IN-LAW

(*state in numbered sentences*)

Signed

[A.B.], Pursuer

or [X.Y.], Solicitor for the Pursuer (*state designation and business address*)

FORM G2

Rule 4.2(1)

[*Omitted by* Act of Sederunt (Sheriff Court Caveat Rules) 2006 (SI 2006/198), *effective April 28, 2006*]

FORM G3

Form of advertisement

Rule 5.6(1)(a)

NOTICE TO [C.D.].............. Court ref. no...........

An action has been raised in..........Sheriff Court by [A.B.], Pursuer, calling as a Defender [C.D.] whose last known address was (*insert last known address of defender*). If [C.D.] wishes to defend the action [*where notice is given in a family action add*: or make any claim or seek any order] he [*or* she] should immediately contact the sheriff clerk at (*insert address*) from whom the service copy initial writ may be obtained. If he [*or* she] fails to do so decree may be granted against him [*or* her].

Signed

[X.Y.], (*add designation and business address*)

Solicitor for the pursuer *or* [P.Q.], (*add business address*)

Sheriff officer

FORM G4

Form of notice for walls of court

Rule 5.6(1)(b)

NOTICE TO [C.D.].............. Court ref. no...........

An action has been raised in..........Sheriff Court by [A.B.], Pursuer, calling as a Defender [C.D.] whose last known address was (*insert last known address of defender*). If [C.D.] wishes to defend the action [*where notice is to be given in a family action add*: or make any claim or seek any order] he [*or* she] should immediately contact the sheriff clerk at (*insert address*) from whom the service copy initial writ may be obtained. If he [*or* she] fails to do so decree may be granted against him [*or* her].

Date (*insert date*)...............(*Signed*)

Sheriff clerk (depute)

Telephone no. (*insert telephone number of sheriff clerk's office*)[1]

FORM G4A

Rule 6.A2(2)

Statement to accompany application for interim diligence

DEBTORS (SCOTLAND) ACT 1987 Section 15D [or DEBT ARRANGEMENT
AND ATTACHMENT (SCOTLAND) ACT 2002 Section 9C]

Sheriff Court..........

In the Cause (Cause Reference No.)

[A.B.] (*designation and address*)

Pursuer

against

[C.D.] (*designation and address*)

Defender

Statement

1. The applicant is the pursuer [*or* defender] in the action by [A.B] (*design*)
against [C.D.] (*design*).
2. [The following persons have an interest (*specify names and addresses*)].
3. The applicant is [*or* is not] seeking the grant under section 15E(1) of the
1987 Act of warrant for diligence [*or* section 9D(1) of the 2002 Act of interim
attachment] in advance of a hearing on the application.
4. [*Here provide such other information as may he prescribed by regulations
made by the Scottish Ministers under* section 15D(2)(d) of the 1987 Act or
9C(2)(d) of the 2002 Act]

(*Signed*)

Solicitor [*or* Agent] for A.B. [*or* C.D.]

(include full designation)[2]

FORM G4B

Rule 6.A8

Form of schedule of arrestment on the dependence

Schedule of Arrestment On the Dependence

Date: (*date of execution*)

Time: (*time arrestment executed*)

To: (*name and address of arrestee*)

IN HER MAJESTY'S NAME AND AUTHORITY AND IN NAME AND
AUTHORITY OF THE SHERIFF, I, (*name*), Sheriff Officer, by virtue of:

- an initial writ containing warrant which has been granted for arrestment on
the dependence of the action at the instance of (*name and address of pursuer*)
against (*name and address of defender*) and dated (*date*);
- a counterclaim containing a warrant which has been granted for arrestment
on the dependence of the claim by (*name and address of creditor*) against
(*name and address of debtor*) and dated (*date of warrant*);
- an order of the Sheriff at (*place*) dated (*date of order*) granting warrant [for
arrestment on the dependence of the action raised at the instance of (*name
and address of pursuer*) against (*name and address of defender*)] [*or* for ar-

---

[1] As inserted by the Act of Sederunt (Sheriff Court Rules Amendment) (Diligence) (SSI 2008/121)
r.5(7) (effective April 1, 2008).

[2] As inserted by the Act of Sederunt (Sheriff Court Rules Amendment) (Diligence) 2008 (SSI 2008/
121) r.5(7) (effective April 1, 2008) and substituted by the Act of Sederunt (Sheriff Court Rules
Amendment) (Diligence) 2009 (SSI 2009/107) (effective April 22, 2009).

restment on the dependence of the claim in the counterclaim [*or* third party notice] by (*name and address of creditor*) against (*name and address or debtor*)],

arrest in your hands (i) the sum of (*amount*), in excess of the Protected Minimum Balance, where applicable (*see Note 1*), more or less, due by you to (*defender's name*) [*or name and address of common debtor if common debtor is not the defender*] or to any other person on his [*or* her] [*or* its] [*or* their] behalf; and (ii) all moveable things in your hands belonging or pertaining to the said (*name of common debtor*), to remain in your hands under arrestment until they are made forthcoming to (*name of pursuer*) [*or name and address of creditor if he is not the pursuer*] or until further order of the court.

This I do in the presence of (*name, occupation and address of witness*).

(*Signed*)
Sheriff Officer
(*Address*)

NOTE

1. This Schedule arrests in your hands (i) funds due by you to (*name of common debtor*) and (ii) goods or other moveables held by you for him. **You should not pay any funds to him or hand over any goods or other moveables to him without taking legal advice.**
2. This Schedule may be used to arrest a ship or cargo. If it is, you should consult your legal adviser about the effect of it.
3. The Protected Minimum Balance is the sum referred to in section 73F(4) of the Debtors (Scotland) Act 1987. This sum is currently set at [*insert current sum*]. The Protected Minimum Balance applies where the arrestment attaches funds standing to the credit of a debtor in an account held by a bank or other financial institution and the debtor is an individual. The Protected Minimum Balance does not apply where the account is held in the name of a company, a limited liability partnership, a partnership or an unincorporated association or where the account is operated by the debtor as a trading account.
4. Under section 73G of the Debtors (Scotland) Act 1987 you must also, within the period of 3 weeks beginning with the day on which the arrestment is executed, disclose to the creditor the nature and value of the funds and/or moveable property which have been attached. This disclosure must be in the form set out in Schedule 8 to the Diligence (Scotland) Regulations 2009. Failure to comply may lead to a financial penalty under section 73G of the Debtors (Scotland) Act 1987 and may also be dealt with as a contempt of court. You must, at the same time, send a copy of the disclosure to the debtor and to any person known to you who owns (or claims to own) attached property and to any person to whom attached funds are (or are claimed to be due), solely or in common with the debtor.

IF YOU WISH FURTHER ADVICE CONTACT ANY CITIZENS ADVICE BUREAU/LOCAL ADVICE CENTRE/SHERIFF CLERK OR SOLICITOR

FORM G4C[1]

Form of certificate of execution of arrestment on the dependence

Rule 6.A8

CERTIFICATE OF EXECUTION

---

[1] As inserted by the Act of Sederunt (Sheriff Court Rules Amendment) (Diligence) 2008 (SSI 2008/121) r.5(7) (effective 1 April 2008) and substituted by the Act of Sederunt (Sheriff Court Rules Amendment) (Diligence) 2009 (SSI 2009/107) (effective 22 April 2009).

I, (*name*), Sheriff Officer, certify that I executed an arrest on the dependence, by virtue of an interlocutor of the Sheriff at (*place*) on (*date*) obtained at the instance of (*name and address of party arresting*) against (*name and address of defender*) on (name of arrestee)—

* by delivering the schedule of arrestment to (*name of arrestee or other person*) at (*place*) personally on (*date*).

* by leaving the schedule of arrestment with (*name and occupation of person with whom left*) at (*place*) on (*date*) [and by posting a copy of the schedule to the arrestee by registered post or first class recorded delivery to the address specified on the receipt annexed to this certificate].

* by depositing the schedule of arrestment in (*place*) on (*date*). (*Specify that enquiry made and reasonable grounds exist for believing that the person on whom service is to be made resides at the place but is not available*) [and by posting a copy of the schedule to the arrestee by registered post or first class recorded delivery to the address specified on the receipt annexed to this certificate].

* by affixing the schedule of arrestment to the door at (*place*) on (*date*). (*Specify that enquiry-made and that reasonable grounds exist for believing that the person on whom service is to be made resides at the place but is not available*) [and by posting a copy of the schedule to the arrestee by registered post or first class recorded delivery to the address specified on the receipt annexed to this certificate].

* by leaving the schedule of arrestment with (*name and occupation of person with whom left*) at (*place of business*) on (*date*) [and by posting a copy of the schedule to the arrestee by registered post or first class recorded delivery to the address specified on the receipt annexed to this certificate].

* by depositing the schedule of arrestment at (*place of business*) on (*date*). (*Specify that enquiry made and that reasonable grounds exist for believing that the person on whom service is to be made carries on business at that place*) [and by posting a copy of the schedule to the arrestee by registered post or first class recorded delivery to the address specified on the receipt annexed to this certificate].

* by affixing the schedule of arrestment to the door at (*place of business*) on (*date*). (*Specify that enquiry made and that reasonable grounds exist for believing that the person on whom service is to be made carries on business at that place.*) [and by posting a copy of the schedule to the arrestee by registered post or first class recorded delivery to the address specified on the receipt annexed to this certificate].

* by leaving the schedule of arrestment at (*registered office*) on (*date*), in the hands of (*name of person*) [and by posting a copy of the schedule to the arrestee by registered post or first class recorded delivery to the address specified on the receipt annexed to this certificate].

* by depositing the schedule of arrestment at (*registered office*) on (*date*) [and by posting a copy of the schedule to the arrestee by registered post or first class recorded delivery to the address specified on the receipt annexed to this certificate].

* by affixing the schedule of arrestment to the door at (*registered office*) on (*date*) [and by posting a copy of the schedule to the arrestee by registered post or first class recorded delivery to the address specified on the receipt annexed to this certificate].

I did this in the presence of (*name, occupation and address of witness*).

(*Signed*)

Sheriff Officer
(*Address*)
(*Signed*)
(*Witness*)

*Delete where not applicable

NOTE

A copy of the Schedule of arrestment on the dependence is to be attached to this certificate.[1]

FORM G5

Form of intimation of Options Hearing

Rules 9.2(2)(a) and 33.16(3)(b)

Sheriff Court (insert address and telephone number)............... Court ref. no...........

[A.B.] (design) Pursuer against [C.D.] (*design*) Defender

You are given notice that in this action:—

(insert date)	is the last day for lodging defences;
(insert date)	is the last day for making adjustments to the writ or defences;
(insert date, time and place)	is the date, time and place for the Options Hearing.

Date (insert date).............. (Signed)..........

Sheriff clerk (depute)

NOTE:

If you fail to comply with the terms of this notice or with any of the rules 9.3, 9.4, 9.6, 9.10 and 9.11 of the Standard Procedure of the Ordinary Cause Rules of the Sheriff Court or, where applicable, rule 33.37 (decree by default in a family action), decree by default may be granted in terms of rule 16.2(2) of those Rules.

NOTE TO BE ADDED WHERE PARTY UNREPRESENTED

Note

IF YOU ARE UNCERTAIN WHAT ACTION TO TAKE you should consult a solicitor. You may be eligible for legal aid depending on your income, and you can get information from any Citizens Advice Bureau or other advice agency.

FORM G5A[2]

Rule 33.16(3)(b), 33.22A(2)(a), 33.36A(3)(a), 33A.I6(3)(b)
33A.23(2)(a) and 33A.36A(3)(a)

Form of intimation of Initial Case Management Hearing in defended family and civil actions

Sheriff Court (*insert address and telephone number*)

Court ref. no. (*insert*)

[A.B.] (*design*)

Pursuer

against

[C.D.] (*design*)

---

[1] As amended by SI 1996/2445 (effective 1 November 1996)

[2] Inserted by the Act of Sederunt (Ordinary Cause Rules 1993 Amendment) (Case Management of Defended Family and Civil Partnership Actions) 2022 (SSI 2022/289) Sch.(effective 25 September 2023 subject to transitional provision specified in SSI 2022/289 r.3).

Defender

You are given notice that in this action:-

(insert date)	is the last day for lodging defences;
(insert date)	is the last day for the return of the initial writ;
(insert date, time and place)	is the date, time and place for the Initial Case Management Hearing;
(insert date, time and place)	is the date, time and place for the Child Welfare Hearing

Parties are required to attend Initial Case Management Hearings unless they are excused by the sheriff.

Date *(insert date)*

(Signed)

Sheriff clerk (depute)

NOTE: If you fail to comply with the terms of this notice or with any of rules 33.36C, 33.36D, 33.36F, 33.36I, 33.36N and 33A.36C, 33A.36D, 33A.36F, 33A.36I and 33A.36N of the Ordinary Cause Rules of the Sheriff Court or, where applicable, rule 33.37 (decree by default in a family action) or rule 33A.37 (decree by default in a civil partnership action), decree by default may be granted in terms of rule 16.2(2) of those Rules.

[NOTE TO BE ADDED WHERE PARTY UNREPRESENTED]

NOTE:

IF YOU ARE UNCERTAIN WHAT ACTION TO TAKE you should consult a solicitor. You may be eligible for legal aid and you can get information from any Citizens Advice Bureau or other advice agency.

FORM G6

Form of motion

Rule 15.1(1)(b)

SHERIFFDOM OF *(insert name of sheriffdom)*............... Court ref. no...........

AT *(insert place of sheriff court)*

MOTION FOR THE PURSUER [or DEFENDER]

in the cause

[A.B.] *(insert designation and address)*

Pursuer

against

[C.D.] *(insert designation and address)*

Defender

The *(insert description of party)* moves the court to *(insert details of motion and, where appropriate, the reason (s) for seeking the order)*.

List the documents or parts of process lodged with the motion:—

(Insert description of document or name part of process)

Date (insert date)............... (Signed)..........

Party (insert name and description of party)

or Solicitor for party (insert designation and business address)

FORM G6A[1]

Form of motion by email

Rule 15A.4(1)

---

[1] As inserted by the Act of Sederunt (Rules of the Court of Session 1994 and Sheriff Court Rules Amendment) (No.2) (Personal Injury and Remits) 2015 (SSI 2015/227) para.8 (effective 22 September 2015).

SHERIFFDOM OF LOTHIAN AND BORDERS
AT EDINBURGH
IN THE ALL-SCOTLAND SHERIFF COURT
Unopposed [*or* Opposed] motion

To: (email address of the court)

1. Case name:..........
2. Court ref number:..........
3. Is the case in court in the next 7 days?..........
4. Solicitors or party lodging motion:..........
(a) Reference:..........
(b) Telephone number:..........
(c) Email address:..........
5. Lodging motion on behalf of:..........
6. Motion (in brief terms):..........
7. Submissions in support of motion (if required):..........
8. Date of lodging of motion:..........
9. Intimation made to:..........
(a) Provided email address(es):..........
(b) Additional email address(es) of fee-earner or other person(s) dealing with the case on behalf of a receiving party (if applicable):..........
10. Date intimations sent:..........
11. Opposition must be intimated to opponent not later than 5 p.m. on:..........
12. Is motion opposed or unopposed?..........
13. Has consent to the motion been provided?..........
14. Document(s) intimated and lodged with motion:..........

EXPLANATORY NOTE TO BE ADDED WHERE RECEIVING PARTY IS NOT

LEGALLY REPRESENTED OPPOSITION TO THE MOTION MAY BE MADE by completing Form G9A (Form of opposition to motion by email) and intimating it to the party intending to lodge the motion (insert email address) on or before the last date for intimating opposition (see paragraph 11 above).

IN THE EVENT OF A FORM OF OPPOSITION BEING INTIMATED, the party intending to lodge the motion will lodge an opposed motion and the sheriff clerk will assign a date, time and place for hearing parties on the motion. Intimation of this hearing will be sent to parties by the sheriff clerk.

IF NO NOTICE OF OPPOSITION IS LODGED, OR IF CONSENT TO THE MOTION IS INTIMATED TO THE PARTY INTENDING TO LODGE THE MOTION, the motion will be considered without the attendance of parties.

IF YOU ARE UNCERTAIN WHAT ACTION TO TAKE you should consult a solicitor. You may also obtain advice from a Citizens Advice Bureau or other advice agency.

FORM G6B[1]
Rule 33.36J(5) and 33A.36J(5)
Form of intimation of Full Case Management Hearing in defended family and civil partnership actions

Sheriff Court (*insert address and telephone number*)

Court ref. no. (*insert*)

[A.B.] (*design*)

---

[1] Inserted by the Act of Sederunt (Ordinary Cause Rules 1993 Amendment) (Case Management of Defended Family and Civil Partnership Actions) 2022 (SSI 2022/289) Sch. (effective 25 September 2023 subject to transitional provision specified in SSI 2022/289 r.3).

Pursuer

against
[C.D.] (*design*)

Defender

You are given notice that in this action:-

(*insert date*)	is the last day for lodging a note of the basis for any preliminary pleas:
(*insert date*)	is the last day for making adjustments to the writ or defences:
(*insert date, time and place*)	is the last day for lodging a copy of the record:
(*insert date, time and place*)	is the date, time and place for the Full Case Management Hearing.

Parties are required to attend Full Case Management Hearings unless they are excused by the sheriff.

Date (*insert date*)

(*Signed*)

Sheriff clerk (depute)

NOTE: If you fail to comply with the terms of this notice or with any of rules 33.36C, 33.36D, 33.36F, 33.36I, 33.36N and 33A.36C, 33A.36D, 33A.36F, 33A.36I and 33A.36N of the Ordinary Cause Rules of the Sheriff Court or, where applicable, rule 33.37 (decree by default in a family action) or rule 33A.37 (decree by default in a civil partnership action), decree by default may be granted in terms of rule 16.2(2) of those Rules.

[NOTE TO BE ADDED WHERE PARTY UNREPRESENTED]

NOTE:

IF YOU ARE UNCERTAIN WHAT ACTION TO TAKE you should consult a solicitor. You may be eligible for legal aid and you can get information from any Citizens Advice Bureau or other advice agency.[1]

FORM G7

Form of intimation of motion

Rule 15.2(1) Cause Rules 1993

SHERIFFDOM OF (insert name of sheriffdom)............... Court ref. no...........

AT (insert place of sheriff court)

in the cause

[A.B.] (insert name and address)

Pursuer

against
[C.D.] (insert name and address)

Defender

LAST DATE FOR LODGING NOTICE OF OPPOSITION:

APPLICATION IS MADE BY MOTION FOR THE ORDER(S) SOUGHT IN THE ATTACHED FORM (attach a copy of the motion in Form G6)

* A copy of the document(s) or part(s) of process referred to in Form G6 is/are attached.

---

[1] Substituted by SI 1996/2445 (effective 1 November 1996).

OPPOSITION TO THE MOTION MAY BE MADE by completing Form G9 (notice of opposition to motion) and lodging it with the sheriff clerk at (insert address) on or before the last date for lodging notice of opposition. A copy of the notice of opposition must be sent immediately to any other party in the action.

IN THE EVENT OF A NOTICE OF OPPOSITION BEING LODGED the sheriff clerk will assign a date, time and place for hearing parties on the motion. Intimation of this hearing will be sent to parties by the sheriff clerk.

IF NO NOTICE OF OPPOSITION IS LODGED, the motion may be considered by the sheriff without the attendance of parties.

Date (*insert date*)................... (*Signed*)

Pursuer (*or as the case may be*)

[*or* Solicitor for pursuer [*or as the case may be*]

(*insert name and business address*)]

Explanatory Note to Be Added Where Party to Whom Intimation is Made is Not Legally Represented

---

IF YOU ARE UNCERTAIN WHAT ACTION TO TAKE you should consult a solicitor. You may also obtain advice from a Citizens Advice Bureau or other advice agency.

NOTE: If YOU intend to oppose the motion you must appear or be represented on the date of the hearing. If you return Form G9 (notice of opposition to motion) and then fail to attend or be represented at the court hearing, the court may consider the motion in your absence and may grant the order(s) sought.

* Delete if not applicable

FORM G7A[1]

Form of intimation of minute (answers lodged)

Rule 14.4(1)(a)

SHERIFFDOM OF (insert name of sheriffdom).............. Court ref. no.

AT (*insert place of sheriff court*)

in the cause

[A.B.] (*insert name and address*)

Pursuer

against

[C.D.] (insert name and address)

Defender

LAST DATE FOR LODGING ANSWERS:

APPLICATION IS MADE BY MOTION FOR THE ORDER(S) SOUGHT IN THE MINUTE ATTACHED (attach a copy of minute and interlocutor)

* A copy of the document(s) or part(s) of process referred to in the minute is/are attached.

IN THE EVENT OF ANSWERS BEING LODGED the sheriff clerk will assign a date, time and place for hearing parties on the minute and answers. Intimation of this hearing will be sent to parties by the sheriff clerk.

IF NO ANSWERS ARE LODGED, the motion may be considered by the sheriff without the attendance of parties.

Date (insert date).............. (Signed)

---

[1] Inserted by SI 1996/2445 (effective 1 November 1996).

Pursuer (or as the case may be)

[or Solicitor for pursuer [or as the case may he]

(Add name and business address)]

Explanatory Note to Be Added Where Party to Whom Intimation is Made is Not Legally Represented

IF YOU ARE UNCERTAIN WHAT ACTION TO TAKE you should consult a solicitor. You may also obtain advice from a Citizens Advice Bureau or other advice agency.

NOTE: If you intend to oppose the minute you must appear or be represented on the date of the hearing. If you return Form G9 (notice of opposition to minute) and then fail to attend or be represented at the court hearing, the court may consider the minute in your absence and may grant the order(s) sought.

* Delete if not applicable

FORM G7B[1]

Form of intimation of minute (no order for answers or no hearing fixed)

Rule 14.4(1)(a)

SHERIFFDOM OF (insert name of sheriffdom)............... Court ref. no.

AT (insert place of sheriff court)

in the cause

[A.B.] (insert name and address)

Pursuer

against

[C.D.] (insert name and address)

Defender

LAST DATE FOR LODGING NOTICE OF OPPOSITION:

APPLICATION IS MADE BY MINUTE FOR THE ORDER(S) SOUGHT IN THE MINUTE ATTACHED (*attach a copy of minute and interlocutor*)

* A copy of the document(s) or part(s) of process referred to in the minute is/are attached.

OPPOSITION TO THE MOTION MAY BE MADE by completing Form G9 (notice of opposition to motion) and lodging it with the sheriff clerk at (*insert address*) on or before the last date for lodging notice of opposition. A copy of the notice of opposition must be sent immediately to any other party in the action.

IN THE EVENT OF A NOTICE OF OPPOSITION BEING LODGED the sheriff clerk will

assign a date, time and place for hearing parties on the minute. Intimation of this hearing will be sent to parties by the sheriff clerk.

IF NO NOTICE OF OPPOSITION IS LODGED, the minute may be considered by the sheriff without the attendance of parties.

Date (*insert date*)...............(*Signed*)

Pursuer (or as the case may be)

[or Solicitor for pursuer [or as the case may be]

(Add name and business address)]

Explanatory Note to Be Added Where Party to Whom Intimation is Made is Not Legally Represented

---

[1] Inserted by SI 1996/2445 (effective 1 November 1996).

IF YOU ARE UNCERTAIN WHAT ACTION TO TAKE you should consult a solicitor. You may also obtain advice from a Citizens Advice Bureau or other advice agency.

NOTE: If YOU intend to oppose the minute you must appear or be represented on the date of the hearing. If you return Form G9 (notice of opposition to minute) and then fail to attend or be represented at the court hearing, the court may consider the motion in your absence and may grant the order(s) sought.

* Delete if not applicable

FORM G7C[1]
Form of intimation of minute (hearing fixed)

Rule 14.4(1)(a)

SHERIFFDOM OF (*insert name of sheriffdom*)............... Court ref. no.

AT (*insert place of sheriff court*)

in the cause

[A.B.] (*insert name and address*)

Pursuer

against
[C.D.] (*insert name and address*)

Defender

DATE AND TIME FOR HEARING MINUTE:

*DATE FOR LODGING ANSWERS OR AFFIDAVIT EVIDENCE:

APPLICATION IS MADE FOR THE ORDER(S) SOUGHT IN THE MINUTE ATTACHED (*attach a copy of minute and interlocutor*)

* A copy of the document(s) or part(s) of process referred to in the minute is/are attached.

IF YOU WISH TO OPPOSE THE MINUTE OR MAKE ANY REPRESENTATIONS you must attend or be represented at (insert name and address of court) on the date and time referred to above.

* If an order has been made for you to lodge answers or affidavit evidence these must be lodged with the sheriff clerk (insert address) on or before the above date.

IF YOU FAIL TO ATTEND OR BE REPRESENTED the minute may be determined in your absence.

Date (*insert date*).............. (*Signed*)

Pursuer (or as the case may be)
[or Solicitor for pursuer [or as the case may be]
(Add name and business address)]

Explanatory Note to Be Added Where Party to Whom Intimation is Made is Not Legally Represented

IF YOU ARE UNCERTAIN WHAT ACTION TO TAKE you should consult a solicitor. You may also obtain advice from a Citizens Advice Bureau or other advice agency.

NOTE: If you intend to oppose the minute you must appear or be represented on the date of the hearing. If you return Form G9 (notice of opposition to minute) and

---

[1] Inserted by SI 1996/2445 (effective 1 November 1996).

then fail to attend or be represented at the court hearing, the court may consider the minute in your absence and may grant the order(s) sought.

* Delete if not applicable

Rules 14.6 and 15.1(2)[1]

FORM G8

Form of certificate of intimation of motion or minute

CERTIFICATE OF INTIMATION OF MOTION [*or* MINUTE]

I certify that intimation of the motion [*or* minute] was made to (*insert names of parties or solicitors for the parties, as appropriate*) by (*insert method of intimation; where intimation is by facsimile transmission, insert fax number to which Intimation sent*) on (*insert date of intimation*).

Date (*insert date*)

(*Signed*)

Solicitor [*or* Sheriff Officer]

(*Add name and business address*)

Rules 14.7(1)(a) and 15.3(1)(a)[2]

FORM G9

Form of notice of opposition to motion or minute

NOTICE OF OPPOSITION TO MOTION [*or* MINUTE]

SHERIFFDOM OF (*insert name of sheriffdom*)

Court ref. no.:

AT (*insert place of sheriff court*)

in the cause

[A.B.] (*insert name and address*)

Pursuer

against

[C.D.] (*insert name and address*)

Defender

Notice of opposition to motion [*or* minute] given by (*insert name of party opposing motion*) to (*insert names of all other parties, or solicitors for the parties, to the action*) by (*insert method of intimation; where intimation is made by facsimile transmission, Insert fax number to which notice of opposition sent*) on (*insert date of intimation*).

Date (*insert date*)

(*Signed*)

Pursuer (*or as the case may be*)

(*insert name and address of party*)
[*or* Solicitor for Pursuer [*or as the case may be*]
(*Add name and business address*)]

Rule 24.2(3)

FORM G9A[3]
Form of opposition to motion by email

Rule 15A.5(1)

SHERIFFDOM OF LOTHIAN AND BORDERS
AT EDINBURGH
IN THE ALL-SCOTLAND SHERIFF COURT

---

[1] Substituted by SI 1996/2445 (effective November 1, 1996).
[2] Substituted by SI 1996/2445 (effective November 1, 1996).
[3] As inserted by the Act of Sederunt (Rules of the Court of Session 1994 and Sheriff Court Rules Amendment) (No.2) (Personal Injury and Remits) 2015 (SSI 2015/227) para.8 (effective September 22, 2015).

TO BE INTIMATED TO THE PARTY INTENDING TO LODGE THE MOTION

1. Case name:..........
2. Court ref number:..........
3. Date of intimation of motion:..........
4. Date of intimation of opposition to motion:..........
5. Solicitors or party opposing motion:..........
(a) Reference:..........
(b) Telephone number:..........
(c) Email address:..........
6. Opposing motion on behalf of:..........
7. Grounds of opposition:..........
8. Estimated duration of hearing:..........[1]

FORM G10

Form of intimation to a party whose solicitor has withdrawn

SHERIFFDOM OF (*insert name of sheriffdom*) AT (*insert place of sheriff court*)

in the cause

[A.B.] (*insert designation*)

Pursuer

against

[C.D.] (*insert designation*)

Defender

Court ref. no.

The court has been informed that your solicitors have ceased to act for you.

As a result the sheriff has ordered that you appear or be represented on (insert date and time) within the Sheriff Court at the above address. A copy of the order is attached.

When you appear you will be asked by the sheriff to state whether you intend to proceed with your action [or defences or answers].

NOTE:

IF YOU ARE UNCERTAIN WHAT ACTION TO TAKE you should consult a solicitor. You may also obtain advice from a Citizens Advice Bureau or other advice agency.

Rule 28.3(1)

FORM G11[2]

Rule 28.3(2)

Form of notice in optional procedure for commission and diligence

Court ref. no: (*insert court reference number*)

SHERIFFDOM OF (*insert name of sheriffdom*)

AT (*insert place of sheriff court*)

in the cause

[A.B.], (*insert name and address*), Pursuer

against

[C.D.], (*insert name and address*), Defender

To: (*insert name and address of party or parties or named third party haver, from whom the documents are sought to be recovered*).

---

[1] As amended by SI 1996/2445 (effective November 1, 1996).

[2] As substituted by the Act of Sederunt (Rules of the Court of Session, Ordinary Cause Rules and Summary Cause Rules Amendment) (Miscellaneous) 2014 (SSI 2014/152) Sch.1 para.1 (effective July 7, 2014).

1. You are hereby required to produce to the agent for the Pursuer or as the case may be, (*insert name and address of agents*) within seven days of the service on you of this Order—

  (a) this Order which must be produced intact;

  (b) the certificate below duly dated and signed by you; and

  (c) all documents in your possession falling within the enclosed specification and a list or inventory of such documents signed by you relating to this Order and your certificate.

2. Subject to note (1) below, you may produce these documents either by sending them by registered post or by the first class recorded delivery, or by hand to the address above.

Date: (*insert date on which service was executed. N.B. Rule 5.3(2) relating to postal service or intimation.*) (*Signed*) ....

Solicitor for party (*add designation and business address of the solicitor for the party in whose favour commission and diligence has been granted*)

NOTES

1. If you claim that any of the documents produced by you are **confidential**, you must still produce such documents but may place them in a separate sealed packet by themselves, marked "confidential". In that event, they should NOT be sent to the address above. They must be hand delivered or sent by registered post or by the first class recorded delivery service or registered postal packet to the sheriff clerk at (*insert name and address of sheriff court*).

2. The document will be considered by the parties to the action and they may or may not be lodged in the court process. A written receipt will be given or sent to you by the party recovering the documents, who may thereafter allow them to be inspected by the other parties. The party in whose possession the documents are will be responsible for their safekeeping.

3. Parties are obliged by rules of court to return the documents to you when their purpose with the documents is finished. If they do not do so, you will be entitled to apply to the court, under rule 28.3(9) of the Ordinary Cause Rules, for an order to have this done and you may apply for an award of the expenses incurred in doing so. Further information about this can be obtained from the sheriff clerk's office at (*insert name and address of sheriff court*).

Certificate

I hereby certify with reference to the above order of the sheriff at (*insert name of sheriff court*) in the cause (*insert court reference number*) and the enclosed specification of documents, served on me and marked respectively X and Y:—

1. That the documents which are produced and which are listed in the enclosed inventory signed by me and marked Z, are all documents in my possession falling within the specification.

or

That I have no documents in my possession falling within the specification.

2. That, to the best of my knowledge and belief, there are in existence other documents falling within the specification, but not in my possession. These documents are as follows:—

(*describe them by reference to the descriptions of documents in the specification*).

They were last seen by me on or about (*date*), at (*place*), in the hands of (*insert name and address of the person*).

or

That I know of the existence of no documents in the possession of any person, other than myself, which fall within the specification.

(*Insert date*) ....

(*Signed*) ....

(*Name and address*) ....

FORM G11A[1]

Rule 28.3(4)(a)

Form of intimation to the sheriff clerk and other parties of documents recovered under optional procedure

Court ref. no: (*insert court reference number*)

SHERIFFDOM OF (*insert name of sheriffdom*)

AT (*insert place of sheriff court*)

in the cause

[A.B.], (*insert name and address*), Pursuer

against

[C.D.], (*insert name and address*), Defender

The undernoted document[s] was [were] recovered from (*insert name and address of haver*) on (*insert date of receipt*) under order of the sheriff at (*insert name of sheriff court*) dated (*insert date of interlocutor authorising commission and diligence*) in so far as it relates to the specification of documents No. .... of Process.

Document[s] received:— (*identify each document*).

Date: ....

(*Signed*) ....

Solicitor for party (*add designation and business address of the solicitor for the party in whose favour commission and diligence has been granted*)

FORM G11B[2]

Rule 28.3(4)(b)

Form of receipt to haver for documents recovered under optional procedure

Court ref. no: (*insert court reference number*)

SHERIFFDOM OF (*insert name of sheriffdom*)

AT (*insert place of sheriff court*)

in the cause

[A.B.], (*insert name and address*), Pursuer

against

[C.D.], (*insert name and address*), Defender

The document[s] noted below, being recovered by order of the sheriff at (*insert name of sheriff court*) dated (*insert date of interlocutor authorising commission and diligence*) in so far as it relates to the specification of documents No .... of Process, have been recovered from (*insert name and address of haver*).

Document[s] received:— (*identify each document*)

---

[1] As inserted by the Act of Sederunt (Rules of the Court of Session, Ordinary Cause Rules and Summary Cause Rules Amendment) (Miscellaneous) 2014 (SSI 2014/152) Sch.1 para.1 (effective July 7, 2014).

[2] As inserted by the Act of Sederunt (Rules of the Court of Session, Ordinary Cause Rules and Summary Cause Rules Amendment) (Miscellaneous) 2014 (SSI 2014/152) Sch.1 para.1 (effective July 7, 2014).

Date: ....   (*Signed*) ....
                                   Solicitor for party (*add designation and
                                   business address of the solicitor for the
                                   party in whose favour commission and
                                   diligence has been granted*)

FORM G11C[1]

Rule 28.3(6)(b)

Form of receipt from party other than party who originally recovered documents under optional procedure

Court ref. no: (*insert court reference number*)

SHERIFFDOM OF (*insert name of sheriffdom*)

AT (*insert place of sheriff court*)

in the cause

[A.B.], (*insert name and address*), Pursuer

against

[C.D.], (*insert name and address*), Defender

I acknowledge receipt of the undernoted document[s] received from you and recovered under order of the sheriff at (*insert name of sheriff court*) dated (*insert date of interlocutor authorising commission and diligence*).

Document[s] received:— (*identify each document*)

Date: ....   (*Signed*) ....
                                   Solicitor for party (*add designation and
                                   business address of the solicitor for the
                                   party receiving documents*)

FORM G11D[2]

Rule 28.3A(2)

Form of notice in optional procedure for commission and diligence in party litigant cases

Court ref. no: (*insert court reference number*)

SHERIFFDOM OF (*insert name of sheriffdom*)

AT (*insert place of sheriff court*)

in the cause

[A.B.], (*insert name and address*), Pursuer

against

[C.D.], (*insert name and address*), Defender

To: (*insert name and address of party or parties or named third party haver, from whom the documents are sought to be recovered*).

1. You are hereby required to produce to the sheriff clerk at (*insert name and address of sheriff court*) within seven days of the date of service on you of this Order—

(a)   this Order which must be produced intact;

(b)   the certificate below duly dated and signed by you; and

(c)   all documents in your possession falling within the enclosed specification

---

[1] As inserted by the Act of Sederunt (Rules of the Court of Session, Ordinary Cause Rules and Summary Cause Rules Amendment) (Miscellaneous) 2014 (SSI 2014/152) Sch.1 para.1 (effective July 7, 2014).

[2] As inserted by the Act of Sederunt (Rules of the Court of Session, Ordinary Cause Rules and Summary Cause Rules Amendment) (Miscellaneous) 2014 (SSI 2014/152) Sch.1 para.1 (effective July 7, 2014).

and a list or inventory of such documents signed by you relating to this Order and your certificate.

2. You may produce these documents either by lodging them at the sheriff clerk's office at (*insert name and address of sheriff court*) or by sending them by registered post or by the first class recorded delivery service, addressed to the sheriff clerk at (*insert name and address of sheriff court*).

Date: (*insert date on which service was executed. N.B.* Rule 5.3(2) *relating to postal service or intimation.*)   (*Signature, name and address of party in whose favour commission and diligence has been granted*)

NOTES

1. If you claim that any of the documents produced by you are **confidential**, you must still produce such documents but may place them in a separate sealed packet by themselves, marked "confidential".

2. The documents will be considered by the parties to the action and they may or may not be lodged in the court process. If they are not so lodged they will be returned to you by the sheriff clerk. The party in whose possession the documents are will be responsible for their safekeeping.

3. Parties are obliged by rules of court to return the documents to you when their purpose with the documents is finished. If they do not do so, you will be entitled to apply to the court, under rule 28.3A(10) of the Ordinary Cause Rules, for an order to have this done and you may apply for an award of the expenses incurred in doing so. Further information about this can be obtained from the sheriff clerk's office at (*insert name and address of sheriff court*).

Certificate

I hereby certify with reference to the above order of the sheriff at (*insert name of sheriff court*) in the cause (*insert court reference number*) and the enclosed specification of documents, served on me and marked respectively X and Y:—

1. That the documents which are produced and which are listed in the enclosed inventory signed by me and marked Z, are all documents in my possession falling within the specification.

or

That I have no documents in my possession falling within the specification.

2. That, to the best of my knowledge and belief, there are in existence other documents falling within the specification, but not in my possession. These documents are as follows:—

(*describe them by reference to the descriptions of documents in the specification*).

They were last seen by me on or about (*date*), at (*place*), in the hands of (*insert name and address of the person*).

or

That I know of the existence of no documents in the possession of any person, other than myself, which fall within the specification.

(*Insert date*) ....   (*Signed*) ....
(*Name and address*) ....

NOTES

1. If you claim that any of the documents produced by you are **confidential**, you must still produce such documents but may place them in a separate sealed packet by themselves, marked "confidential".

2. The documents will be considered by the parties to the action and they may or may not be lodged in the court process. If they are not so lodged they will be returned to you by the sheriff clerk. The party in whose possession the documents are will be responsible for their safekeeping.

3. Parties are obliged by rules of court to return the documents to you when their purpose with the documents is finished. If they do not do so, you will be entitled to apply to the court, under rule 28.3A(10) of the Ordinary Cause Rules, for an order to have this done and you may apply for an award of the expenses incurred in doing so. Further information about this can be obtained from the sheriff clerk's office at (*insert name and address of sheriff court*).

Certificate

I hereby certify with reference to the above order of the sheriff at (*insert name of sheriff court*) in the cause (*insert court reference number*) and the enclosed specification of documents, served on me and marked respectively X and Y:—

1. That the documents which are produced and which are listed in the enclosed inventory signed by me and marked Z, are all documents in my possession falling within the specification.

or

That I have no documents in my possession falling within the specification.

2. That, to the best of my knowledge and belief, there are in existence other documents falling within the specification, but not in my possession. These documents are as follows:—

(*describe them by reference to the descriptions of documents in the specification*).

They were last seen by me on or about (*date*), at (*place*), in the hands of (*insert name and address of the person*).

or

That I know of the existence of no documents in the possession of any person, other than myself, which fall within the specification.

(*Insert date*) ....   (*Signed*) ....

                                       (*Name and address*) ....

Rules 28.4(4) and 29.7(4)

FORM G12
Form of certificate of citation of witness or haver

I certify that on (*insert date of citation*).......... I duly cited [K.L.], (*design*) to attend at (*insert name of sheriff court*) Sheriff Court on (*insert date*) at (*insert time*) as a witness for the pursuer [*or* defender] in the action at the instance of [A.B.] (*design*), Pursuer, against [C.D.] (*design*), Defender, [and I required him [*or* her] to bring with him [*or* her] (*specify documents*)]. This I did by (*state mode of citation*).

Date (insert date)

                                           (*Signed*)

                           [P.Q.], Sheriff officer;

            or [X.Y.], (*add designation and business address*)

                         Solicitor for the pursuer [*or*

defender][1]

FORM G13
Form of citation of witness or haver

Rule 28.4(4) and 29.7(4)

---

[1] As substituted by SSI 2007/463 (effective November 1, 2007).

(date)

Citation

SHERIFFDOM OF *(insert name of sheriffdom)*

AT *(insert place of sheriff court)*

To [A.B.] *(design)*

(Name) who is pursuing/defending a case against *(name)* [or is a *(specify)* in the case of *(name)* against *(name)* has asked you to be a witness. You must attend the above sheriff court on *(insert date)* at *(insert time)* for that purpose, [and to bring with you *(specify documents)*].

If you would like to know more about being a witness

are a child under the age of 16

think you may be a vulnerable witness within the meaning of section 11(1) of the Vulnerable Witnesses (Scotland) Act 2004 (that is someone the court considers may be less able to give their evidence due to mental disorder or fear or distress connected to giving your evidence at the court hearings)

you should contact *(specify the solicitor acting for the party or the litigant citing the witness)* for further information.

If you are a vulnerable witness (including a child under the age of 16), then you should be able to use a special measure (such measures include the use of a screen, a live TV link or a supporter, or a commissioner) to help you give evidence.

Expenses

You may claim back money which you have to spend and any earnings you have lost within certain specified limits, because you have to come to court on the above date. These may be paid to you if you claim within specified time limits. Claims should be made to the person who has asked you to attend court. Proof of any loss of earnings should be given to that person.

If you wish your travelling expenses to be paid before you go to court, you should apply for payment to the person who has asked you to attend court.

Failure to attend

It is very important that you attend court and you should note that failure to do so may result in a warrant being granted for your arrest. In addition, if you fail to attend without any good reason, having requested and been paid your travelling expenses, you may be ordered to pay a penalty not exceeding £250.

If you have any questions about anything in this citation, please contact *(specify the solicitor acting for the party or the party litigant citing the witness)* for further information.

Signed

[P.Q.], Sheriff Officer,

or [X.Y.], *(add designation and business address)*

Solicitor for the pursuer [*or defender*] [*or specify*]

Rules 28.4(6)(b), 28.10(4)(b) and 29.16

FORM G13A[1]

Form of citation of juror

Rule 36B.3

SHERIFFDOM OF LOTHIAN AND BORDERS
AT EDINBURGH
IN THE ALL-SCOTLAND SHERIFF COURT
JUROR'S CITATION

---

[1] As inserted by the Act of Sederunt (Rules of the Court of Session 1994 and Sheriff Court Rules Amendment) (No.2) (Personal Injury and Remits) 2015 (SSI 2015/227) para.8 (effective September 22, 2015).

Citation Number:..........

To:..........

Date:..........

Time:..........

Place:..........

Name of case:..........

You are cited to attend personally on the date and at the time and place stated above, and on such succeeding days as may be necessary to serve, if required, as a juror. If you fail to attend, you will be liable to the penalty prescribed by law.

Sheriff Clerk Depute

Please read the enclosed leaflets carefully BEFORE attending court for selection.

Expenses: Claims for loss of earnings and/or expenses should be made at the end of your jury service. You will be provided with an envelope for return of the completed form, and payment will be made by cheque to your home address, seven to ten days from receipt of the claim.

YOU MUST BRING THIS CITATION WITH YOU TO COURT

If you wish to apply for exemption or excusal from jury service, please complete this form and return it as soon as possible to: **Sheriff Clerk, Edinburgh Sheriff Court, 27 Chambers Street, Edinburgh EH1 1LB.**

DECLARATION: *Please state why you are applying for exemption or excusal from jury service:*

[ ] **Age:**   I am .... years of age. My date of birth is ....

[ ] **Occupation:**   I am employed as .... and therefore statutorily exempt from service.

[ ] **Medical Condition:**   I am medically unfit for jury service and enclose a medical certificate from my doctor.

[ ] **Special Reason:**   ....

N.B. *Should you be **excused** from jury service on this occasion, a further juror's citation may be sent out to you within twelve months.*

I declare that the foregoing information is correct and acknowledge that I may be asked for proof of any statement made above.

Signature ....   Date ....

If you have any queries telephone **0131 225 2525.** *Please quote citation number and date of attendance.*

Unfortunately there are no facilities for car parking at or near the court.

CLAIMING FOR TRAVELLING/FINANCIAL LOSS

If you wish to claim for travelling/financial loss, you must read the guidance sheet enclosed and complete this form carefully and accurately. If you are claiming loss of earnings/benefit or childminding/adult dependant carer allowance you must get your employer/the carer to complete the certificate that is enclosed and return it with this claim form. If it is not enclosed then payment cannot be made. Please note: the allowances are meant to compensate you for your out-of-pocket expenses and loss of earnings or benefit. They are not meant to compensate your partner or spouse. There is a maximum amount which can be claimed. The rate is fixed by Scottish Ministers, and is reviewed every year.

There is no scope for any juror to be paid more than these maximum amounts. Receipts or tickets must be attached, otherwise we will be unable to pay your claim.

	OFFICIAL USE ONLY *(delete as applicable)		
	Allowed	No. of days	Total

TRAVELLING
By public transport
  (a) Say whether rail, bus &c
      ....
      ....
  (b) Daily return fare £
      ....
      ....
      ....
In own car, &c
  (a) Car, m/cycle &c ....
      Engine capacity .... c.c.
  (b) Daily mileage (round trip)
      ....
      ....
  (c) Could you have travelled by public transport? *YES/NO
If YES, indicate how much time was saved by using your own vehicle.
SUBSISTENCE
On the days on which the court has NOT provided meals for you, have you necessarily incurred expenses on subsistence?
*YES/NO
If YES, give number of hours, including travelling time you were away from your home or place of business.
	£ .... p		£ .... p

	OFFICIAL USE ONLY *(delete as applicable)		
	Allowed	**No. of days**	**Total**
(If you attended Court on more than one day, show the number of hours for each day) .... LOSS OF EARNINGS (only refundable if certified above) Will you suffer any loss of earnings as a result of your attendance for jury service? *YES/NO If YES, please state (a) your occupation .... (b) daily or hourly rate (or equivalent) £ .... (c) number of days and half-days lost .... Have you paid any person to act as a substitute for you during your attendance for jury service (*e.g.* at your place of employment, or to look after your children or a dependent adult &c)? *YES/NO If YES, please state (a) capacity in which paid substitute			

	OFFICIAL USE ONLY *(delete as applicable)		
	Allowed	**No. of days**	**Total**
employed .... (b) his/her daily or hourly rate £ .... (c) number of days and half-days paid substitute employed .... I DECLARE that to the best of my knowledge and belief the particulars in the foregoing claim are correct			
TOTALS			
.... Signature of Claimant			

FORM G14

Form of oath for witness

The witness to raise his right hand and repeat after the sheriff [*or* commissioner]: "I swear by Almighty God that I will tell the truth, the whole truth and nothing but the truth".

Rules 28.4(6)(b), 28.10(4)(b) and 29.16

FORM G15

Form of affirmation for witness

The witness to repeat after the sheriff [*or* commissioner]: "I solemnly, sincerely and truly declare and affirm that I will tell the truth, the whole truth and nothing but the truth".[1]

FORM G16

Rules 28.14(3) and 28.14A(2)

Form of minute for [letter of request] [taking of evidence in the European Community]*

SHERIFFDOM OF (*insert name of sheriffdom*)

---

[1] As substituted by the Act of Sederunt (Taking of Evidence in the European Community) 2003 (SSI 2003/601).

AT (*insert place of sheriff court*)
MINUTE FOR PURSUER [DEFENDER]*
in the cause
[A.B.] (*insert designation and address*)

Pursuer

against
[C.D.] (*insert designation and addres*)

Defender

Court ref. no.

The Minuter states that the evidence specified in the attached [letter of request] [Form A] [Form I]* is required for the purpose of these proceedings and craves the court to issue [a letter of request] [that Form]* to (*specify in the case of a letter of request the central or other appropriate authority of the country or territory in which the evidence is to he obtained, and in the case of Form A or I the applicable court, tribunal, central body or competent authority*) to obtain the evidence specified.

Date (*insert date*)

Signed

(*insert designation and address*)

* *delete as applicable*

FORM G17

Rule 28.14(3)

Form of letter of request

Letter of Request

1. Sender	(insert name and address)
2. Central authority of the requested state	(insert name and address)
3. Person to whom the executed request is to be returned	(insert name and address)

4. The undersigned applicant has the honour to submit the following request:

5. a. Requesting judicial authority	(insert name and address)
b. To the competent authority	(insert name of requested state)

6. Names and addresses of the parties and their representatives

a. Pursuer

b. Defender

c. Other parties

7. Nature and purpose of the proceedings and summary of facts

8. Evidence to be obtained or other judicial act to be performed

(Items to be completed where applicable)

9. Identity and address of any person to be examined

10. Questions to be put to the persons to be examined or statement of the subject-matter about which they are to be examined	(or see attached list)

Letter of Request

11. Documents or other property to be inspected

(specify whether it is to he produced, copied, valued, etc.)

12. Any requirement that the evidence be given on oath or affirmation and any special form to be used

(in the event that the evidence cannot be taken in the manner requested, specify whether it is to be taken in such manner as provided by local law for the formal taking of evidence)

13. Special methods or procedure to be followed

14. Request for notification of the time and place for the execution of the request and identity and address of any person to be notified

15. Request for attendance or participation of judicial personnel of the requesting authority at the execution of the letter of request

16. Specification of privilege or duty to refuse to give evidence under the law of the state of origin

17. The fees and expenses (costs) incurred will be borne by

(insert name and address)

(Items to be included in all letters of request)

18. Date of request

19. Signature and seal of the requesting authority

FORM G18

Rule 30.3(2)

Form of certificate of rate of exchange

Certificate of Rate of Exchange

I (insert designation and address) certify that the rates current in London for the purchase of (state the unit of currency in which the decree is expressed) on (insert date) was (state rate of exchange) to the £ sterling and at this rate the sum of (state the amount of the sum in the decree) amounts to (insert sterling equivalent).

Date (Insert date)

Signed

For and on behalf of the bank manager or other official

FORM G19[1]

Form of child witness notice

Rule 45.2

VULNERABLE WITNESSES (SCOTLAND) ACT 2004 Section 12

Received the day of 20

---

[1] As inserted by the Act of Sederunt (Ordinary Cause, Summary Application, Summary Cause and Small Claim Rules) Amendment (Vulnerable Witnesses (Scotland) Act 2004) 2007 (SSI 2007/463) (effective 1 November 2007).

(Date of receipt of this notice)

..........(signed)
Sheriff Clerk

Child Witness Notice

Sheriff Court..........

..........20..........
Court Ref. No.

1. The applicant is the pursuer [or defender] in the action by [A.B.] (design) against [C.D.] (design).

2. The applicant has cited [or intends to cite] [E.F.] (date of birth) as a witness.

3. [E.F.] is a child witnesses under section 11 of the Vulnerable Witnesses (Scotland) Act 2004 [and was under the age of sixteen on the date of the commencement of proceedings].

4. The applicant considers that the following special measure[s] is [are] the most appropriate for the purpose of taking the evidence of [E.F.][or that [E.F.] should give evidence without the benefit of any special measure]:—

(delete as appropriate and specify any special measure(s) sought).

5. [(a) The reason[s] this [these] special measure[s] is [are] considered the most appropriate is [are] as follows:—

(here specify the reason(s) for the special measure(s) sought)].

OR

[(b) The reason[s] it is considered that [E.F.] should give evidence without the benefit of any special measure is [are]:—

(here explain why it is felt that no special measures are required)].

6. [E.F.] and the parent[s] of [or person[s] with parental responsibility for] [E.F.] has [have] expressed the following view[s] on the special measure[s] that is [are] considered most appropriate [or [the appropriateness of [E.F.] giving evidence without the benefit of any special measure]:—

(delete as appropriate and set out the views(s) expressed and how they were obtained)

7. Other information considered relevant to this application is as follows:—

(here set out any other information relevant to the child witness notice).

8. The applicant asks the court to —

(a)   consider this child witness notice;

(b)   make an order authorising the special measure[s] sought; or

(c)   make an order authorising the giving of evidence by [E.F.] without the benefit of special measures.

(delete as appropriate)

(Signed)
[A.B. or CD]
[or Legal representative of A.B. [or C.D.]] (include full designation)

NOTE: This form should be suitably adapted where section 16 of the Act of 2004 applies.

FORM G20[1]

Form of vulnerable witness application

Rule 45.3

VULNERABLE WITNESSES (SCOTLAND) ACT 2004 Section 12

Received the..........day of..........20..........

---

[1] As inserted by the Act of Sederunt (Ordinary Cause, Summary Application, Summary Cause and Small Claim Rules) Amendment (Vulnerable Witnesses (Scotland) Act 2004) 2007 (SSI 2007/463) (effective 1 November 2007).

(Date of receipt of this notice)
..........*(signed)*
Sheriff Clerk

VULNERABLE WITNESS APPLICATION

Sheriff Court....................

..........20.........

Court Ref. No.

1. The applicant is the pursuer [*or* defender] in the action by [A.B] *(design)* against [C.D.] *(design)*.

2. The applicant has cited [*or* intends to cite] [E.F.] *(date of birth)* as a witness.

3. The applicant considers that [E.F.] is a vulnerable witness under section 11(1)(b) of the Vulnerable Witnesses (Scotland) Act 2004 for the following reasons:—

(here specify reasons witness is considered to be a vulnerable witness).

4. The applicant considers that the following special measure[s] is [are] the most appropriate for the purpose of taking the evidence of [E.F.]:—

(specify any special measure(s) sought).

5. The reason[s] this [these] special measure[s] is [are] considered the most appropriate is [are] as follows:—

(here specify the reason(s) for the special measures(s) sought).

6. [E.F.] has expressed the following view[s] on the special rneasure[s] that is [are] considered most appropriate:—

(set out the views expressed and how they were obtained).

7. Other information considered relevant to this application is as follows:—

(here set out any other information relevant to the vulnerable witness application).

8. The applicant asks the court to—

(a)   consider this vulnerable witness application;

(b)   make an order authorising the special measure[s] sought.

...............*(Signed)*

[A.B. *or* C.D.]
[*or* Legal representative of A.B. [*or* C.D.]] *(include full designation)*
NOTE: This form should be suitably adapted where section 16 of the Act of 2004
applies.

FORM G21[1]
Form of certificate of intimation

Rule 45.4(1)

VULNERABLE WITNESSES (SCOTLAND) ACT 2004 Section 12
CERTIFICATE OF INTIMATION

Sheriff Court..........

..........20.........
Court Ref. No.

I certify that intimation of the child witness notice [*or* vulnerable witness application] relating to *(insert name of witness)* was made to *(insert names of parties or solicitors for parties, as appropriate)* by *(insert method of intimation; where intimation is by facsimile transmission, insert fax number to which intimation sent)* on *(insert dale of intimation).*

Date:..........

..........*(Signed)*

---

[1] As inserted by the Act of Sederunt (Ordinary Cause, Summary Application, Summary Cause and Small Claim Rules) Amendment (Vulnerable Witnesses (Scotland) Act 2004) 2007 (SSI 2007/463) (effective 1 November 2007).

Solicitor [*or* Sheriff Officer]
(*include full business designation*)

FORM G22[1]
Form of application for review

Rule 45.6

VULNERABLE WITNESSES (SCOTLAND) ACT 2004 Section 13

Received the..........day of..........20..........

(date of receipt of this notice)

..............(*signed*)

Sheriff Clerk

APPLICATION FOR REVIEW OF ARRANGEMENTS FOR VULNERABLE WITNESS

Sheriff Court...............

..........20..........

Court Ref. No.

1. The applicant is the pursuer [*or* defender] in the action by [A.B.] *(design)* against [C.D.] *(design)*.

2. A proof [*or* hearing] is fixed for *(date)* at *(time)*.

3. [E.F.] is a witness who is to give evidence at, or for the purposes of, the proof [*or* hearing]. [E.F.] is a child witness [*or* vulnerable witness] under section 11 of the Vulnerable Witnesses (Scotland) Act 2004.

4. The current arrangements for taking the evidence of [E.F.] are *(here specify current arrangements)*.

5. The current arrangements should be reviewed as *(here specify reasons for review)*.

6. [E.F.] [and the parent[s] of [*or* person[s] with parental responsibility for] [E.F.]] has [have] expressed the following view[s] on [the special measure[s] that is [are] considered most appropriate] [*or* the appropriateness of [E.F.] giving evidence without the benefit of any special measure]:—

(delete as appropriate and set out the view(s) expressed and how they were obtained).

7. The applicant seeks (here specify the order sought).

(Signed)

[A.B. *or* C.D.]

[*or* Legal representative of A.B. [*or* C.D.]] *(include full designation)*

NOTE: This form should be suitably adapted where section 16 of the Act of 2004 *applies.*

FORM G23[2]
Form of certificate of intimation

Rule 45.7(2)

VULNERABLE WITNESSES (SCOTLAND) ACT 2004 Section 13
CERTIFICATE OF INTIMATION

Sheriff Court..........

..........20..........

Court Ref. No.

---

[1] As inserted by the Act of Sederunt (Ordinary Cause, Summary Application, Summary Cause and Small Claim Rules) Amendment (Vulnerable Witnesses (Scotland) Act 2004) 2007 (SSI 2007/463) (effective 1 November 2007).

[2] As inserted by the Act of Sederunt (Ordinary Cause, Summary Application, Summary Cause and Small Claim Rules) Amendment (Vulnerable Witnesses (Scotland) Act 2004) 2007 (SSI 2007/463) (effective 1 November 2007).

I certify that intimation of the review application relating to (*insert name of witness*) was made to (*insert names of parties or solicitors for parties, as appropriate*) by (*insert method of intimation; where intimation is by facsimile transmission, insert fax number to which intimation sent*) on (*insert date of intimation*).

Date:..........
(*Signed*)
Solicitor [*or* Sheriff Officer]
(*include full business designation*)

FORM O1
Form of warrant of citation
Rule 3.3(1)

(*Insert place and date*) Grants warrant to cite the defender (*insert name and address*) by serving upon him [*or* her] a copy of the writ and warrant on a period of notice of (*insert period of notice*) days, and ordains him [*or* her], if he [*or* she] intends to defend the action or make any claim, to lodge a notice of intention to defend with the sheriff clerk at (*insert place of sheriff court*) within the said period of notice after such service [and grants warrant to arrest on the dependence].

[Meantime grants interim interdict; *or* grants warrant to arrest to found jurisdiction; *or* sequestrates and grants warrant to inventory; *or otherwise, as the case may be*.]

Signed
Sheriff [*or* sheriff clerk]

FORM O2[1]
Form of warrant of citation where time to pay direction or time order may be applied for
Rule 3.3(2)

(*Insert place and date*) Grants warrant to cite the defender (*insert name and address*) by serving a copy of the writ and warrant, with Form O3, on a period of notice of (*insert period of notice*) days and ordains him [*or* her] if he [*or* she]—
  (a) intends to defend the action or make any claim, to lodge a notice of intention to defend; or
  (b) admits the claim and intends to apply for a time to pay direction [*or* time order] [and apply for recall or restriction of an arrestment] to lodge the appropriate part of Form O3 duly completed;
with the sheriff clerk at (*insert place of sheriff court*) within the said period of notice after such service [and grants warrant to arrest on the dependence].

[Meantime grants interim interdict, *or* grants warrant to arrest to found jurisdiction; *or* sequestrates and grants warrant to inventory; *or otherwise, as the case may be*.]

Signed
Sheriff [*or* sheriff clerk]

FORM O2A
Form of warrant in an action to which rule 3.2(3) applies
[*Repealed by the* Act of Sederunt (Sheriff Court Rules) (Enforcement of Securities over Heritable Property) 2010 (SSI 2010/324) para.2 (*effective September 30, 2010*).][2, 3]

---

[1] As amended by the Act of Sederunt (Ordinary Cause, Summary Application, Summary Cause and Small Claim Rules) Amendment (Miscellaneous) 2007 (SSI 2007/6) para.2(16) (effective 29 January 2007).

[2] As amended by SSI 2007/6 (effective 29 January 2007) and substituted by the Act of Sederunt (Sheriff Court Rules) (Miscellaneous Amendments) 2009 (SSI 2009/294) r.2 (effective 1 December 2009).

[3] As amended by the Act of Sederunt (Sheriff Court Rules) (Miscellaneous Amendments) 2011 (SSI 2011/193) r.9 (effective 4 April 2011).

FORM O3

Form of notice to be served on defender in ordinary action where time to pay direction or time order may be applied for

Rule 3.3(3), 7.3(2) and 18.5(1)(a)

ACTION RAISED BY

..........PURSUER..........DEFENDER

AT...............SHERIFF COURT

(Including address)

COURT REF. NO.

DATE OF EXPIRY OF

PERIOD OF NOTICE

THIS SECTION MUST BE COMPLETED BY THE PURSUER BEFORE SERVICE

(1) Time to pay directions

The Debtors (Scotland) Act 1987 gives you the right to apply to the court for a "time to pay direction" which is an order permitting you to pay any sum of money you are ordered to pay to the pursuer (which may include interest and court expenses) either by way of instalments or deferred lump sum. A deferred lump sum means that you must pay all the amount at one time within a period specified by the court.

When making a time to pay direction the court may recall or restrict an arrestment made on your property by the pursuer in connection with the action or debt (for example, your bank account may have been frozen).

(2) Time Orders

The Consumer Credit Act 1974 allows you to apply to the court for a "time order" during a court action, to ask the court to give you more time to pay a loan agreement. **A time order is similar to a time to pay direction, but can only be applied for where the court action is about a credit agreement regulated by the Consumer Credit Act**. The court has power to grant a time order in respect of a regulated agreement to reschedule payment of the sum owed. This means that a time order can change:

- the amount you have to pay each month
- how long the loan will last
- in some cases, the interest rate payable

A time order can also stop the creditor taking away any item bought by you on hire purchase or conditional sale under the regulated agreement, so long as you continue to pay the instalments agreed.

HOW TO APPLY FOR A TIME TO PAY DIRECTION OR TIME ORDER WHERE YOU ADMIT THE CLAIM AND YOU DO NOT WANT TO DEFEND THE ACTION

1. The appropriate application forms are attached to this notice. If you want to make an application you should lodge the completed application with the sheriff clerk at the above address before the expiry of the period of notice, the date of which is given above. No court fee is payable when lodging the application.

2. Before completing the application please read carefully the notes on how to complete the application. In the event of difficulty you may contact the court's civil department at the address above or any sheriff clerk's office, solicitor, Citizens Advice Bureau or other advice agency. Written guidance can also be obtained from the Scottish Court Service website (www.scotcourts.gov.uk).

NOTE

Where this form is being served on a defender along with Form O9 (notice to additional defender) the reference to "date of expiry of period of notice" should be amended to "date for lodging of defences or an application for a time to pay direction or time order" and the reference to "before the expiry of the period of notice" should be amended to "on or before the date for lodging of defences or an application for a time to pay direction or time order".

WHAT WILL HAPPEN NEXT

If the pursuer objects to your application, a hearing will be fixed and the court will advise you in writing of the date and time.

If the pursuer does not object to your application, a copy of the court order for payment (called an extract decree) will be served on you by the pursuer's solicitor advising when instalment payments should commence or deferred payment be made.

Court ref. no.

APPLICATION FOR A TIME TO PAY DIRECTION UNDER THE
DEBTORS (SCOTLAND) ACT 1987

*PART A

By

*(This section must be completed by pursuer before service)

DEFENDER
In an action raised by
PURSUER

HOW TO COMPLETE THE APPLICATION
PLEASE WRITE IN INK USING BLOCK CAPITALS

PART A of the application will have been completed in advance by the pursuer and gives details of the pursuer and you as the defender.

PART B If you wish to apply to pay by instalments enter the amount and tick the appropriate box at B3(1). If you wish to apply to pay the full sum due in one deferred payment enter the period of deferment you propose at B3(2).

PART C Give full details of your financial position in the space provided.

PART D If you wish the court, when making the time to pay direction, to recall or restrict an arrestment made in connection with the action, enter the appropriate details about what has been arrested and the place and date of the arrestment at D5, and attach the schedule of arrestment or copy.

Sign the application where indicated. Retain the copy initial writ and the form of notice which accompanied this application form as you may need them at a later stage. You should ensure that your application arrives at the court before the expiry of the period of notice.

Part B
1. The applicant is a defender in the action brought by the above named pursuer.
2. The defender admits the claim and applies to the court for a time to pay direction.
3. The defender applies
(1) To pay by instalments of £
(Tick one box only)

EACH WEEK　　　　FORTNIGHT　　　　MONTH

OR

(2) To pay the sum ordered in one payment within
WEEKS/MONTHS
Please state in this box why you say a time to pay direction should be made. In doing so, please consider the Note below.

NOTE

Under the 1987 Act **, the court is required to make a time to pay direction if satisfied that it is reasonable in the circumstances to do so, and having regard in particular to the following matters—**

The nature of and reasons for the debt in relation to which decree is granted or the order is sought

Any action taken by the creditor to assist the debtor in paying the debt

The debtor's financial position

The reasonableness of any proposal by the debtor to pay that debt

The reasonableness of any refusal or objection by the creditor to any proposal or offer by the debtor to pay the debt.

PART C

4. **Defender's financial position**

I am employed /self employed / unemployed

My net income is:	weekly, fortnightly or monthly	My outgoings are:	weekly, fortnightly or monthly
Wages	£	Mortgage/rent	£
State benefits	£	Council tax	£
Tax credits	£	Gas/electricity etc	£
Other	£	Food	£
		Credit and loans	£
		Phone	£
		Other	£
Total	£	Total	£

People who rely on your income (e.g. spouse/civil partner/partner/children) — how many

Here list all assets (if any) e.g. value of house; amounts in bank or building society accounts; shares or other investments:

Here list any outstanding debts:

Part D

5. The defender seeks to recall or restrict an arrestment of which the details are as follows (*please state, and attach the schedule of arrestment or copy*).

6. This application is made under sections 1(1) and 2(3) of the Debtors (Scotland) Act 1987.

Therefore the defender asks the court
*to make a time to pay direction
*to recall the above arrestment
*to restrict the above arrestment (*in which case state restriction wanted*)

Date (*insert date*)
Signed
Defender
Court ref. no.

APPLICATION FOR A TIME ORDER UNDER THE CONSUMER CREDIT ACT 1974

*PART A

By

*(This section must be completed by pursuer before service)

DEFENDER

In an action raised by

PURSUER

HOW TO COMPLETE THE APPLICATION
PLEASE WRITE IN INK USING BLOCK CAPITALS

PART A of the application will have been completed in advance by the pursuer and gives details of the pursuer and you as the defender.

PART B If you wish to apply to pay by instalments enter the amount and tick the appropriate box at B3. If you wish the court to make any additional orders, please give details at B4. Please give details of the regulated agreement at B5.

PART C Give full details of your financial position in the space provided.

Sign the application where indicated. Retain the copy initial writ and the form of notice which accompanied this application form as you may need them at a later stage. You should ensure that your application arrives at the court before the expiry of the period of notice.

Part B

1. The Applicant is a defender in the action brought by the above named pursuer.

I/WE WISH TO APPLY FOR A TIME ORDER under the Consumer Credit Act 1974

2. **Details of order(s) sought**

The defender wishes to apply for a time order under section 129 of the Consumer Credit Act 1974

The defender wishes to apply for an order in terms of section..........of the Consumer Credit Act 1974

3. **Proposals for payment**

I admit the claim and apply to pay the arrears and future instalments as follows:

By instalments of £.......... per *week/fortnight/month

No time to pay direction or time to pay order has been made in relation to this debt.

4. **Additional orders sought**

The following additional order(s) is (are) sought: (*specify*)

The order(s) sought in addition to the time order is (are) sought for the following reasons:

5. **Details of regulated agreement**

(*Please attach a copy of the agreement if you have retained it and insert details of the agreement where known*)

(a) Date of agreement

(b) Reference number of agreement

(c) Names and addresses of other parties to agreement

(d) Name and address of person (if any) who acted as surety (guarantor) to the agreement

(e) Place where agreement signed (e.g. the shop where agreement signed, including name and address)

(f) Details of payment arrangements

    i. The agreement is to pay instalments of £..........per week/month

    ii. The unpaid balance is £........../ I do not know the amount of arrears

    iii. I am £..........in arrears / I do not know the amount of arrears

Part C

4. Defender's financial position

I am employed /self employed / unemployed

My net income is:	weekly, fortnightly or monthly	My outgoings are:	weekly, fortnightly or monthly
Wages	£	Mortgage/rent	£
State benefits	£	Council tax	£
Tax credits	£	Gas/electricity etc	£
Other	£	Food	£
Credit and loans	£	Phone	£
		Other	£
Total	£	Total	£

People who rely on your income (e.g. spouse/civil partner/partner/children) — how many

Here list all assets (if any) e.g. value of house; amounts in bank or building society accounts; shares or other investments:

Here list any outstanding debts:

Therefore the defender asks the court to make a time order

Date...............Signed..........

...............Defender..........

Rule 7.3(4)

[1]

FORM O3A

Form of pursuer's response objecting to application for time to pay direction or time order

Court ref no:

SHERIFFDOM OF (*insert name of sheriffdom*)

AT (*insert place of sheriff court*)

PURSUER'S RESPONSE OBJECTING TO APPLICATION FOR TIME TO PAY DIRECTION OR TIME ORDER

in the cause

[A.B.], (*insert designation and address*), Pursuer

against

[C.D.], (*insert designation and address*), Defender

1. The pursuer received a copy application for a time to pay direction or time order lodged by the defender on (*date*).

2. The pursuer does not accept the offer.

3. The debt is (*please specify the nature of the debt*).

4. The debt was incurred on (*specify date*) and the pursuer has contacted the defender in relation to the debt on (*specify date(s)*).

*5. The contractual payments were (*specify amount*).

*6. (*Specify any action taken by the pursuer to assist the defender to pay the debt*).

*7. The defender has made payment(s) towards the debt of (*specify amount(s)*) on (*specify date(s)*).

---

[1] As inserted by Act of Sederunt (Sheriff Court Rules) (Miscellaneous Amendments) 2009 (SSI 2009/294) r.2 (effective December 1, 2009).

*8. The debtor has made offers to pay (*specify amount(s)*) on (*specify date(s)*) which offer(s) was [were] accepted [*or* rejected] and (*specify amount*) was paid on (*specify date(s)*).

9. (*Here set out any information you consider relevant to the court's determination of the application*).

* delete as appropriate

Minute for decree

(*Signed*)

Pursuer *or* Solicitor for pursuer

(*Date*)

Rule 5.2(1) [1, 2]

FORM O4

Form of Citation

CITATION

SHERIFFDOM OF (*insert name of Sheriffdom*)

AT (*insert place of sheriff court*)

[A.B.], (*insert designation and address*), Pursuer, against [C.D.], (*insert designation and address*), Defender

Court Ref No:

(*Insert place and date*). You [C.D.], are hereby served with this copy writ and warrant, with Form O7 (notice of intention to defend).

Form O7 is served on you for use should you wish to intimate an intention to defend this action.

IF YOU WISH TO DEFEND THIS ACTION you should consult a solicitor with a view to lodging a notice of intention to defend (Form O7). The notice of intention to defend, together with the court fee of £ (*insert amount*) must be lodged with the Sheriff Clerk at the above address within 21 days (*or insert the appropriate period of notice*) of (*insert the date on which service was executed NB*. Rule 5.3(2) *relating to postal service*).

A copy of any notice of intention to defend should be sent to the Solicitor for the pursuer at the same time as your notice of intention to defend is lodged with the Sheriff Clerk.

IF THE WORDS "COMMERCIAL ACTION" APPEAR AT THE HEAD OF THIS INITIAL WRIT then you should note that this action is a commercial action governed by Chapter 40 of the Ordinary Cause Rules 1993. You should also note in particular that if you lodge a notice of intention to defend you must then lodge defences within 7 days of the expiry of the period of notice. You will receive no further notification of this requirement from the court.

IF YOU ARE UNCERTAIN WHAT ACTION TO TAKE you should consult a solicitor. You may be eligible for legal aid depending on your income, and you can get information about legal aid from a solicitor. You may also obtain advice from any Citizens' Advice Bureau or other advice agency.

---

[1] As substituted by the Act of Sederunt (Sheriff Court Ordinary Cause Rules Amendment) (Miscellaneous) 2000 (SSI 2000/239) (effective October 2, 2000).

[2] As amended by the Act of Sederunt (Sheriff Court Rules) (Miscellaneous Amendments) (No.2) 2008 (SSI 2008/365) para.2 (effective December 1, 2008).

> **PLEASE NOTE THAT IF YOU DO NOTHING IN ANSWER TO THIS DOCUMENT** the court may regard you as admitting the claim made against you and the pursuer may obtain decree against you in your absence.

Signed

[P.Q.], Sheriff Officer

or [X.Y.] (*add designation and business address*)

Solicitor for the Pursuer

Rule 5.2(2)

[1, 2]

FORM O5

Form of citation where time to pay direction or time order may be applied for

CITATION

SHERIFFDOM OF (*insert name of Sheriffdom*)

AT (*insert place of Sheriff Court*)

[A.B.], (*insert designation and address*) Pursuer against [C.D.], (*insert designation and address*) Defender

Court Ref No:

(*insert place and date*). You [C.D.], are hereby served with this copy writ and warrant, together with the following forms—

Form 03 (application for time to pay direction or time order); and

Form 07 (notice of intention to defend).

> **Form 03** is served on you because it is considered that you may be entitled to apply for a time to pay direction or time order [and for the recall or restriction of an arrestment used on the dependence of the action or in security of the debt referred to in the copy writ]. See Form 03 for further details.
>
> **IF YOU ADMIT THE CLAIM AND WISH TO APPLY FOR A TIME TO PAY DIRECTION OR TIME ORDER**, you must complete Form 03 and return it to the Sheriff Clerk at (*insert address*) within 21 days (*or insert the appropriate period of notice*) of (*insert the date on which service was executed. NB Rule 5.3 (2) relating to postal service*).

> **IF YOU ADMIT THE CLAIM AND WISH TO AVOID A COURT ORDER BEING MADE AGAINST YOU**, the whole sum claimed including interest and any expense due should be paid to the pursuer or his solicitor in good time before the expiry of the period of notice.

> **Form 07** is served on you for use should you wish to intimate an intention to defend the action.
>
> **IF YOU WISH TO DEFEND THIS ACTION** you should consult a solicitor with a view to lodging a notice of intention to defend (Form 07). The notice of intention to defend, together with the court fee of £ (*insert amount*) must be lodged with the Sheriff Clerk at the above address within 21 days (*or insert the*

---

[1] As substituted by the Act of Sederunt (Sheriff Court Ordinary Cause Rules Amendment) (Miscellaneous) 2000 (SSI 2000/239) (effective October 2, 2000) and amended by the Act of Sederunt (Ordinary Cause, Summary Application, Summary Cause and Small Claim Rules) Amendment (Miscellaneous) 2007 (SSI 2007/6), para.2(16) (effective January 29, 2007).

[2] As amended by the Act of Sederunt (Sheriff Court Rules) (Miscellaneous Amendments) (No.2) 2008 (SSI 2008/365) para.2 (effective December 1, 2008).

appropriate period of notice) of (*insert the date on which service was executed. NB Rule 5.3(2) relating to postal service*).

A copy of any notice of intention to defend should be sent to the Solicitor for the pursuer at the same time as your notice of intention to defend is lodged with the Sheriff Clerk.

IF THE WORDS "COMMERCIAL ACTION" APPEAR AT THE HEAD OF THIS INITIAL WRIT then you should note that this action is a commercial action governed by Chapter 40 of the Ordinary Cause Rules 1993. You should also note in particular that if you lodge a notice of intention to defend you must then lodge defences within 7 days of the expiry of the period of notice. You will receive no further notification of this requirement from the court.

IF YOU ARE UNCERTAIN WHAT ACTION TO TAKE you should consult a solicitor. You may be eligible for legal aid depending on your income, and you can get information about legal aid from a solicitor. You may also obtain advice from any Citizens' Advice Bureau or other advice agency.

PLEASE NOTE THAT IF YOU DO NOTHING IN ANSWER TO THIS DOCUMENT the court may regard you as admitting the claim made against you and the pursuer may obtain decree against you in your absence.

Signed

[P.Q.], Sheriff Officer

or [X.Y.] (*add designation and business address*)

Solicitor for the Pursuer

FORM O5A

Form of citation in an action to which rule 3.2(3) applies

[*Repealed by the* Act of Sederunt (Sheriff Court Rules) (Enforcement of Securities over Heritable Property) 2010 (SSI 2010/324) para.2 (*effective September 30, 2010*).]

Rule 5.2(3)

FORM O6

Form of certificate of citation

CERTIFICATE OF CITATION

(*Insert place and date*) I, hereby certify that upon the day of I duly cited [C.D.], Defender, to answer to the foregoing writ. This I did by (*state method of service; if by officer and not by post, add*: in presence of [L.M.], (*insert designation*), witness hereto with me subscribing; *and where service executed by post state whether by registered post or the first class recorded delivery service*).

(*In actions in which a time to pay direction may be applied for, state whether Form O2 and Form O3 were sent in accordance with* rule 3.3).

Signed

[P.Q.], Sheriff officer

[L.M.], witness

---

[1] As substituted by the Act of Sederunt (Amendment of Ordinary Cause Rules and Summary Applications, Statutory Applications and Appeals etc. Rules) (Applications under the Mortgage Rights (Scotland) Act 2001) 2002 (SSI 2002 No.7), para.2(6) and amended by the Act of Sederunt (Sheriff Court Rules) (Enforcement of Securities over Heritable Property) 2010 (SSI 2010/324) para.2 (effective September 30, 2010).

or [X.Y.]. (*add designation and business address*)
Solicitor for the pursuer

Rules 5.2(1) and 9.1(1)¹

FORM O7
Form of notice of intention to defend
NOTICE OF INTENTION TO DEFEND

*PART A   in an action raised at   Sheriff Court

Court Ref No

(Insert name and business address of solicitor for the Pursuer)

_____

Pursuer

Solicitor for the
pursuer

_____

Defender

*(This section to be completed by the
Pursuer before service)**

DATE OF   DATE OF EXPIRY OF PERIOD OF NOTICE:
SERVICE:

Part B
**(This section to be completed by the defender or defender's solicitors, and
both parts of this form to be returned to the Sheriff Clerk (insert address of
Sheriff Clerk) on or before the date of expiry of the period of notice referred to
in PART A above. At the same time a copy of the form should be sent to the
Solicitor for the Pursuer).**

(*Insert place and date*)

[C.D.], (*insert designation and address*), Defender, intends to defend the action
raised by [A.B.], (*insert designation and address*), Pursuer, against him (and others).

Signed
[C.D.], Defender
or [X.Y.], (*add designation and business address*)
Solicitor for the defender

Paragraph 4(4)²
FORM O7A

Rule 13A.3(1)

Form of minute of intervention by the Commission for Equality and Human Rights
SHERIFFDOM OF (*insert name of sheriffdom*)

Court ref. no.

AT (*insert place of sheriff court*)

---

¹ As substituted by the Act of Sederunt (Sheriff Court Ordinary Cause Rules Amendment) (Miscellaneous) 2000 (SSI 2000/239) (effective October 2, 2000).
² As inserted by the Act of Sederunt (Sheriff Court Rules) (Miscellaneous Amendments) 2008 (SSI 2008/223) para.4(4) (effective July 1, 2008).

Application for Leave to Intervene by the Commission for Equality And Human
Rights
in the cause
[A.B.] *(designation and address)*, Pursuer
against
[C.D.] *(designation and address)*, Defender
[Here set out briefly:
(a) *the Commission's reasons for believing that the proceedings are relevant to*
a matter in connection with which the Commission has a function;
(b) *the issue in the proceedings which the Commission wishes to address; and*
(c) *the propositions to be advanced by the Commission and the Commission's*
reasons for believing that they are relevant to the proceedings and that they
will assist the court.]

FORM O7B

Rule 13B.2(1)
Form of minute of intervention by the Scottish Commission for Human Rights
SHERIFFDOM OF *(insert name of sheriffdom)*

Court ref. no.

AT *(insert place of sheriff court)*
APPLICATION FOR LEAVE TO INTERVENE BY THE SCOTTISH COMMIS-
SION FOR HUMAN RIGHTS
in the cause
[A.B.] *(designation and address)*, Pursuer
against
[C.D.] *(designation and address)*, Defender
[Here set out briefly:
(a) *the issue in the proceedings which the Commission intends to address;*
(b) *a summary of the submission the Commission intends to make.]*

FORM O7C

Rule 13B.3(1)
Invitation to the Scottish Commission for Human Rights to intervene
SHERIFFDOM OF *(insert name of sheriffdom)*

Court ref. no.

AT *(insert place of sheriff court)*
INVITATION TO THE SCOTTISH COMMISSION FOR HUMAN RIGHTS TO
INTERVENE
in the cause
[A.B.] *(designation and address)*, Pursuer
against
[C.D.] *(designation and address)*, Defender
[Here set out briefly:
(a) *the facts, procedural history and issues in the proceedings;*
(b) *the issue in the proceedings on which the court seeks a submission.]*

---

[1] As inserted by the Act of Sederunt (Sheriff Court Rules) (Miscellaneous Amendments) 2008 (SSI
2008/223) para.4(4) (effective July 1, 2008).
[2] As inserted by the Act of Sederunt (Sheriff Court Rules) (Miscellaneous Amendments) 2008 (SSI
2008/223) para.4(4) (effective July 1, 2008).

FORM O8

Rule 18.5(1)(a)(i)

Form of notice to additional or substitute defender where time to pay direction or time order may be applied for

SHERIFFDOM OF (*insert name of sheriffdom*)

AT (*insert place of sheriff court*)

To [E.F.] (*insert designation and address of additional* [*or substitute*] *defender*) Court ref. no.

You [E.F.] are given notice that in this action in which [A.B.] is the pursuer and [C.D.] is the defender, your name has, by order of the court dated (*insert date of court order*) been added [*or* substituted] as a defender to the said action; and the action, originally against [C.D.] is now [*or* also] directed against you.

Enclosed with this notice are the following documents—

Copies of the [*insert as appropriate*, pleadings as adjusted *or* closed record];

Form O3 (application for a time to pay direction or time order); and

Form O7 (notice of intention to defend).

Form O3 is served on you because it is considered that you may be entitled to apply for a time to pay direction or time order [and for the recall or restriction of an arrestment used on the dependence of the action or in security of the debt referred to in the copy writ]. See Form O3 for further details.

IF YOU ADMIT THE CLAIM AND WISH TO APPLY FOR A TIME TO PAY DIRECTION OR TIME ORDER, you must complete Form O3 and return it to the sheriff clerk at (*insert address*) within 21 days (*or insert the appropriate period of notice*) of (*Insert the date on which service was executed. N.B. Rule 5.3(2) relating to postal citation*).

IF YOU ADMIT THE CLAIM AND WISH TO AVOID A COURT ORDER BEING MADE AGAINST YOU, the whole sum claimed including interest and any expenses due should be paid to the pursuer or his solicitor in good time before the expiry of the period of notice.

Form O7 is served on you for use should you wish to intimate an intention to defend the action.

IF YOU WISH TO DEFEND THIS ACTION you should consult a solicitor with a view to lodging a notice of intention to defend (Form O7). The notice of intention to defend, together with the court fee of £ (*insert amount*) must be lodged with the sheriff clerk at the above address within 21 days (*or insert the appropriate period of notice*) of (*insert the date on which service was executed. N.B. See Rule 5.3(2) relating to postal service*).

IF YOU ARE UNCERTAIN WHAT ACTION TO TAKE you should consult a solicitor. You may be eligible for legal aid depending on your income, and you can get information about legal aid from a solicitor. You may also obtain advice from any Citizens Advice Bureau or other advice agency.

PLEASE NOTE THAT IF YOU DO NOTHING IN ANSWER TO THIS DOCUMENT the court may regard you as admitting the claim made against you and the pursuer may obtain decree against you in your absence.

Signed

[P.Q.], Sheriff officer

or [X.Y.] (*add designation and business address*)

---

[1] As amended by the Act of Sederunt (Ordinary Cause, Summary Application, Summary Cause and Small Claim Rules) Amendment (Miscellaneous) 2007 (SSI 2007/6) para.2(16) (effective January 29, 2007).

Solicitor for the pursuer [or defender]
FORM O9
Rule 18.5(1)(a)(ii)

Form of notice to additional or substitute defender

SHERIFFDOM OF (*insert name of sheriffdom*)

AT (*insert place of sheriff court*)

To [E.F.] (*insert designation and address of additional* [or *substitute*] defender)
Court ref. no.

You [E.F.] are given notice that in this action in which [A.B.] is the pursuer and [C.D.] is the defender, your name has, by order of the court dated (*insert date of court order*) been added [or substituted] as a defender to the said action; and the action, originally against the said [C.D.] is now [or also] directed against you.

Enclosed with this notice are the following documents—

Copies of the [*insert as appropriate* pleadings as adjusted *or* closed record]; and Form O7 (notice of intention to defend).

Form O7 is served on you for use should you wish to intimate an intention to defend the action.

IF YOU WISH TO DEFEND THIS ACTION you should consult a solicitor with a view to lodging a notice of intention to defend (Form O7). The notice of intention to defend, together with the court fee of £ (insert amount) must be lodged with the sheriff clerk at the above address with 28 days (*or insert the appropriate period of notice*) of (*insert the date on which service was executed. N.B.* Rule 5.3(2) *relating to postal service*).

IF YOU ARE UNDERTAIN WHAT ACTION TO TAKE you should consult a solicitor. You may be eligible for legal aid depending on your income, and you can get information about legal aid from a solicitor. You may also obtain advice from any Citizens Advice Bureau or other advice agency.

PLEASE NOTE THAT IF YOU DO NOTHING IN ANSWER TO THIS DOCUMENT the court may regard you as admitting the claim made against you and the pursuer may obtain decree against you in your absence.

Signed

[P.Q.], Sheriff officer

or [X.Y.] (*add designation and business address*)

Solicitor for the pursuer [*or* defender][1]
FORM O10
Rule 20.1

Form of third party notice

SHERIFFDOM OF (*insert name of sheriffdom*)

Court ref. no.

AT (*insert place of sheriff court*)...............

THIRD PARTY NOTICE

in the cause

[A.B.], (*insert designation and address*), Pursuer

against

[C.D.], (*insert designation and address*), Defender

To [E.F.]

You are given notice by [C.D.] of an order granted by Sheriff (*insert name of sheriff*) in this action in which [A.B.] is the pursuer and [C.D.] the defender. In the action the pursuer claims against the defender the sum of £ as damages in respect of

---

[1] As amended by SI 1996/2445 (effective November 1,1996) (clerical error).

(*insert brief account of the circumstances of the claim*) as more fully appears in the [*insert as appropriate*, pleadings as adjusted *or* amended *or* closed record] enclosed.

*The defender admits [*or* denies] liability to the pursuer but claims that, if he [*or* she] is liable to the pursuer, you are liable to relieve him [*or* her] wholly [*or* partially] of his [*or* her] liability because (*set forth contract or other right of contribution, relief, or indemnity*) as more fully appears from the defences lodged by him [*or* her] in the action,

or

*Delete as appropriate.

*The defender denies liability for the injury claimed to have been suffered by the pursuer and maintains that liability, if any, to the pursuer rests solely on you [along with (*insert names of any other person whom defender maintains is liable to him [or her] by way of contribution, relief or indemnity*)] as more fully appears from the defences lodged by him [*or* her] in the action.

or

*The defender denies liability for the injury said to have been suffered by the pursuer but maintains that if there is any liability he [*or* she] shares that with you, as more fully appears from the defences lodged by him [*or* her] in the action.

or

*The defender admits liability in part for the injury suffered by the pursuer but disputes the amount of damages and maintains that liability falls to be shared by you, as more fully appears from the defences lodged by him [*or* her] in the action.

or

*The defender admits liability in part for the injury suffered by the pursuer and for the damages claimed but maintains that liability falls to be shared by you, as more fully appears from the defences lodged by him [*or* her] in the action.

or

*(*Otherwise as the case may be*)

IF YOU WISH TO resist either the claim of the pursuer against the defender, or the claim of the defender against you, you must lodge answers with the sheriff clerk at the above address within 28 days of (*insert the date on which service was executed. N.B.* Rule 5.3(2) *relating to postal service*). You must also pay the court fee of £ (*insert amount*).

Date (*insert date*)...............(*Signed*)

Solicitor for the defender.

Rule 31.4(1)

FORM A1

[Repealed by the Act of Sederunt (Rules of the Court of Session, Sheriff Appeal Court Rules and Sheriff Court Rules Amendment) (Sheriff Appeal Court) 2015 (SSI 2015/419) r.5 (effective 1 January 2016).]

Rule 33.7(1)(a)

FORM F1

Form of intimation to children and next-of-kin in an action of divorce or separation where the defender's address is not known

Court ref. no.

To (*insert name and address as in warrant*)

You are given NOTICE that an action of divorce [*or* separation] has been raised against (*insert name*) your (*insert relationship, e.g. father, mother, brother or other relative as the case may be*). If you know of his [*or* her] present address, you are requested to inform the sheriff clerk (*insert address of sheriff clerk*) in writing immediately. If you wish to appear as a party you must lodge a minute with the sheriff clerk for leave to do so. Your minute must be lodged within 21 days of (*insert date on which intimation was given. N.B.* Rule 5.3(2) *relating to postal service or intimation*).

Date (*insert date*)

(*Signed*)

Solicitor for the pursuer (*add designation and business address*)

NOTE

If you decide to lodge a minute it may be in your best interest to consult a solicitor. The minute should be lodged with the sheriff clerk together with the appropriate fee of (*insert amount*) and a copy of this intimation.

IF YOU ARE UNCERTAIN WHAT ACTION TO TAKE you should consult a solicitor. You may be entitled to legal aid depending on your financial circumstances, and you can get information about legal aid from a solicitor. You may also obtain advice from any Citizens Advice Bureau or other advice agency.

Rule 33.7(1)(b)

FORM F2

Form of intimation to alleged adulterer in action of divorce or separation

To (*insert name and address as in warrant*)

Court ref. no.

You are given NOTICE that in this action, you are alleged to have committed adultery. A copy of the initial writ is attached. If you wish to dispute the truth of the allegation made against you, you must lodge a minute with the sheriff clerk (*insert address of sheriff clerk*) for leave to appear as a party. Your minute must be lodged within 21 days of (*insert date on which intimation was given. N.B.* Rule 5.3(2) *relating to postal service or intimation*).

Date (*insert date*)

(*Signed*)

Solicitor for the pursuer

NOTE

If you decide to lodge a minute it may be in your best interest to consult a solicitor. The minute should be lodged with the sheriff clerk together with the appropriate fee of (*insert amount*) and a copy of this intimation.

IF YOU ARE UNCERTAIN WHAT ACTION TO TAKE you should consult a solicitor. You may be entitled to legal aid depending on your financial circumstances, and you can get information about legal aid from a solicitor. You may also obtain advice from any Citizens Advice Bureau or other advice agency.

Rule 33.7(1)(c)

FORM F3

Form of intimation to children, next-of-kin and *curator bonis* in an action of divorce or separation where the defender suffers from a mental disorder

To (*insert name and address as in warrant*)

Court ref. no.

You are given NOTICE that an action of divorce [*or* separation] has been raised against (*insert name and designation*) your (*insert relationship, e.g. father, mother, brother or other relative, or ward, as the case may be*). A copy of the initial writ is enclosed. If you wish to appear as a party, you must lodge a minute with the sheriff clerk (*insert address of sheriff clerk*), for leave to do so. Your minute must be lodged within 21 days of (*insert date on which intimation was given. N.B.* Rule 5.3(2) *relating to postal service or intimation*).

Date (*insert date*)

(*Signed*)

Solicitor for the pursuer (*insert designation and business address*)

NOTE

If you decide to lodge a minute it may be in your best interest to consult a solicitor. The minute should be lodged with the sheriff clerk together with the appropriate fee of (*insert amount*) and a copy of this intimation.

IF YOU ARE UNCERTAIN WHAT ACTION TO TAKE you should consult a solicitor. You may be entitled to legal aid depending on your financial circumstances, and you can get information about legal aid from a solicitor. You may also obtain advice from any Citizens Advice Bureau or other advice agency.

IF YOU ARE UNCERTAIN WHAT ACTION TO TAKE you should consult a solicitor. You may be entitled to legal aid depending on your financial circumstances, and you can get information about legal aid from a solicitor. You may also obtain advice from any Citizens Advice Bureau or other advice agency.

Rule 33.7(1)(d)

FORM F4

Form of intimation to additional spouse of either party in proceedings relating to a polygamous marriage

To (*name and address as in warrant*)

Court ref. no.

You are given NOTICE that this action for divorce [*or* separation], involves (*insert name and designation*) your spouse. A copy of the initial writ is attached. If you wish to appear as a party, you must lodge a minute with the sheriff clerk (*insert address of sheriff clerk*) for leave to do so. Your minute must be lodged within 21 days of (*insert date on which intimation was given. N.B.* Rule 5.3(2) *relating to postal service or intimation*).

Date (*insert date*)

(*Signed*)

Solicitor for the pursuer

NOTE

If you decide to lodge a minute it may be in your best interest to consult a solicitor. The minute should be lodged with the sheriff clerk together with the appropriate fee of (*insert amount*) and a copy of this intimation.

IF YOU ARE UNCERTAIN WHAT ACTION TO TAKE you should consult a solicitor. You may be entitled to legal aid depending on your financial circumstances, and you can get information about legal aid from a solicitor. You may also obtain advice from any Citizens Advice Bureau or other advice agency.

Rule 33.7(1)(e)(i) and (ii)[1]

---

[1] Substituted by SI 1996/216 (effective November 1, 1996).

FORM F5

Form of intimation to a local authority or third party who may be liable to maintain a child

To (*insert name and address as in warrant*)

Court ref. no.

YOU ARE GIVEN NOTICE that in this action, the court may make an order under section 11 of the Children (Scotland) Act 1995 in respect of (*insert name and address*), a child in your care [or liable to be maintained by you]. A copy of the initial writ is attached. If you wish to appear as a party, you must lodge a minute with the sheriff clerk (*insert address of sheriff clerk*) for leave to do so. Your minute must be lodged within 21 days of (*insert date on which intimation was given. N.B. Rule 5.3(2) relating to postal service or intimation*).

Date (*insert date*)

(*Signed*)

Solicitor for the pursuer

NOTE

If you decide to lodge a minute it may be in your best interests to consult a solicitor. The minute should be lodged with the sheriff clerk together with the appropriate fee of (*insert amount*) and a copy of this intimation.

IF YOU ARE UNCERTAIN WHAT ACTION TO TAKE you should consult a solicitor. You may be entitled to legal aid depending on your financial circumstances, and you can get information about legal aid from a solicitor. You may also obtain advice from any Citizens Advice Bureau or other advice agency.

Rule 33.7(1)(e)(iii)[1]

FORM F6

Form of intimation to person who in fact exercises care or control of a child

To (*insert name and address as in warrant*)

Court ref. no.

YOU ARE GIVEN NOTICE that in this action, the court may make an order under section 11 of the Children (Scotland) Act 1995 in respect of (*insert name and address*) a child at present in your care or control. A copy of the initial writ is attached. If you wish to appear as a party, you must lodge a minute with the sheriff clerk (*insert address of sheriff clerk*) for leave to do so. Your minute must be lodged within 21 days of (*insert date on which intimation was given. N.B. Rule 5.3(2) relating to postal service or intimation*).

Date (*insert date*)...............(*Signed*)

Solicitor for the pursuer

NOTE

If you decide to lodge a minute it may be in your best interests to consult a solicitor. The minute should be lodged with the sheriff clerk together with the appropriate fee of (*insert amount*) and a copy of this intimation.

IF YOU ARE UNCERTAIN WHAT ACTION TO TAKE you should consult a solicitor. You may be entitled to legal aid depending on your financial circumstances, and you can get information about legal aid from a solicitor. You may also obtain advice from any Citizens Advice Bureau or other advice agency.

---

[1] Substituted by SI 1996/2167 (effective November 1, 1996).

FORM F7[1]

Form of notice to parent or guardian in action for a section 11 order in respect of a child

Rule 33.7(1)(f)

1. YOU ARE GIVEN NOTICE that in this action, the pursuer is applying for an order under section 11 of the Children (Scotland) Act 1995 in respect of the child (*insert name of child*). A copy of the initial writ is served on you and is attached to this notice.

2. If you wish to oppose this action, or oppose the granting of any order applied for by the pursuer in respect of the child, you must lodge a notice of intention to defend (Form F26). See Form F26 attached for further details.

Date (*insert date*)

(*Signed*)

Pursuer

or Solicitor for the pursuer (*add designation and business address*)

NOTE: IF YOU ARE UNCERTAIN WHAT ACTION TO TAKE you should consult a solicitor. You may be entitled to legal aid depending on your financial circumstances, and you can get information about legal aid from a solicitor. You may also obtain advice from any Citizens Advice Bureau or other advice agency.[2]

FORM F8

Form of notice to local authority

Rules 33.7(1)(g), 33.7(4) and 33.12(2) and (3)

To (insert name and address)

Court ref. no.

1. YOU ARE GIVEN NOTICE that in an action in the Sheriff Court at (*insert address*) the pursuer has applied for a residence order in respect of the child (*insert name of child*). A copy of the initial writ is enclosed.

2. If you wish to oppose this action, or oppose the granting of any order applied for by the pursuer in respect of the child, you must lodge a notice of intention to defend (Form F26). See Form F26 attached for further details.

Date (*insert date*)

(*Signed*)

Solicitor for the pursuer (*add designation and business address*)

---

[1] Substituted by SI 1996/2167 (effective 1 November 1996).

[2] Substituted by SI 1996/2167 (effective 1 November 1996) and SSI 2010/416 (effective 1 January 2011).

FORM F9[1]

[Insert court] Sheriff Court | Ref: [insert case reference] | Form F9

Name
Address Line1
Address Line 2
City
Postcode

Dear [insert child's first name]

You have been sent this letter because the sheriff will need to make a decision about you. The sheriff (sometimes called a judge) is a person who makes important decisions for children and families. [Insert short summary of the section 11 order(s) sought, using child-friendly language.] The sheriff has to decide about that.

The sheriff wants to know what you think about that. You have a right to tell the sheriff what you think, but you do not have to tell the sheriff what you think if you do not want to. What you think is very important, and it will help the sheriff to make a decision about what is best for you. Sometimes this might be different from what you would like to happen.

If you want to tell the sheriff what you think, you can use the **What I Think** form sent with this letter. You can write or draw anything you like. There is no right or wrong answer. Please send the form back to the sheriff when you have filled it in. We have sent you an envelope, which should already have a stamp on it. Just put the form in the envelope and put the envelope in a post box **within 2 weeks, or as soon as you can.**

The sheriff might not tell anyone exactly what you have written or said, but the sheriff has to think about this and say in court what you would like to happen.

If you are not sure what to do, you can show this letter to someone you trust. If you want to know more about what will happen next, you might get free help from a lawyer or from these places that can help children:

The Scottish Child Law Centre – the free phone number is 0800 328 8970 or 0300 330 1421 (from a mobile) and the website is www.sclc.org.uk

Clan Childlaw – the free phone number is 0808 129 0522 and the website is www.clanchildlaw.org

If there's anything you are worried or upset about and you don't know what to do, you can speak to someone at ChildLine who will listen and help you. You can phone ChildLine free on 0800 1111.

If what you think changes, you can contact a lawyer or call the phone numbers for the Scottish Child Law Centre or Clan Childlaw.

From
the Sheriff Clerk (the person who helps the sheriff)

---

[1] As amended by the Act of Sederunt (Rules of the Court of Session 1994 and Ordinary Cause Rules 1993 Amendment) (Views of the Child) 2019 (SSI 2019/123) r.3 (effective 24 June 2019).

What I Think Form

Name:

How do you feel just now about [insert short summary of the section 11 order(s) sought, using child-friendly language]?

Good

In the middle

Not good

☐ Good ☐ In the middle ☐ Not good

If you would like to tell the sheriff why you feel like this, use the space below or another piece of paper.

Use another piece of paper if you need more space.

[Insert court] Sheriff Court | Ref: *[insert case reference]* | Form F9

Is there anything else you would like to happen?

_____
_____
_____
_____
_____

Would you like to say what you think in a different way?

Yes **No**

☐ Yes ☐ No

What different way would you like to say what you think?

_____
_____
_____
_____
_____

[*Insert court*] **Sheriff Court | Ref:** [*insert case reference*] | **Form F9**

In the letter with this form, there are Freephone numbers for the Scottish Child Law Centre and Clan Childlaw, if you want some other ideas.

If someone has helped you with this **What I Think** form, please write their name and how you know them here:

The sheriff will think about what you have said. It will help the sheriff to decide what happens next.

You can put this **What I Think** form in the envelope and send it back to the sheriff **within 2 weeks, or as soon as you can.** The envelope should already have a stamp on it.

Thank you.

FORM F9A[1]

Rules 33.19(2)(b), 33.19A(2)(b), 33.19B(2)(b), 33.19C(2)(b)(i), 33.44B(2)(b), 33.44C(2)(b), 33.44D(2)(b)(i), 33A.19(2)(b), 33A.19A(2)(b), 33A.19B(2)(b), 33A.19C(2)(b)(i), 33A.41B(2)(b), 33A.41C(2)(b) and 33A.41D(2)(b)(i)

Form of certificate of intimation of Form F9

CERTIFICATE OF INTIMATION OF FORM F9

(*Insert court*) Sheriff Court

---

[1] As amended by the Act of Sederunt (Rules of the Court of Session 1994 and Ordinary Cause Rules 1993 Amendment) (Views of the Child) 2019 (SSI 2019/123) r.3 (effective 24 June 2019).

Court Ref. No. (*insert*)

I certify that intimation of the Form F9 that was submitted to the sheriff clerk under (*rule 33.7A(1)(b), rule 33.34(4A)(b), rule 33.44A(1)(b), rule 33A.7A(1)(b), rule 33A.34(4A)(b) or rule 33A.41A(1)(b)*) was made to (*insert name(s) of child(ren)*) by (*specify whether first class, second class, recorded delivery service, etc.*) post to (*insert address*) on (*insert date*).

[*Where, in approving the draft Form F9 as provided for in rule 33.7A(3), 33.34(4C), 33.44A(3), 33A.7A(3), 33A.34(4C) or 33A.41A(3), the sheriff has requested an amendment to the draft Form F9 that was submitted,* The Form F9 was amended in accordance with the sheriff's request.]

[*Where the pursuer or minuter has amended the draft Form F9 so as to narrate the section 11 order sought by the defender or respondent,* The Form F9 was (*further*) amended as appropriate so as also to narrate the section 11 order sought by the (*defender or respondent*).]

Date (*insert date*)

(*Signed*)

Solicitor for the (*pursuer/defender/minuter/respondent*)

(*add designation and business address*)

or

(*Pursuer/Defender/Minuter/Respondent*)

FORM F9B[1]

Rule 33.19D(5)(b)(ii) and 33A.19D(5)(b)(ii)

Form of certificate of intimation of Form F9 (where ordered under rule 33.19D or 33A.19D)

CERTIFICATE OF INTIMATION OF FORM F9

(*Insert court*) Sheriff Court

Court Ref. No. (*insert*)

I certify that intimation of the Form F9, a copy of which is attached to this certificate in accordance with rule (*33.19D(5)(b)(i) or 33A.19D(5)(b)(i)*) was made to (*insert name(s) of child(ren)*) by (*specify whether first class, second class, recorded delivery service, etc.*) post to (*insert address*) on (*insert date*).

Date (*insert date*)

(*Signed*)

Solicitor for the (*pursuer/defender/minuter/respondent*)

(*add designation and business address*)

or

(*Pursuer/Defender/Minuter/Respondent*)

FORM F10

Form of intimation to creditor in application for order for the transfer of property under section 8 of the Family Law (Scotland) Act 1985

To (*insert name and address as in warrant*)

Court ref. no.

You are given NOTICE that in this action an order is sought for the transfer of property (*specify the order*), over which you hold a security. A copy of the initial writ is attached. If you wish to appear as a party, you must lodge a minute with the sheriff clerk (*insert address of sheriff clerk*) for leave to do so. Your minute must be lodged within 21 days of (*insert date on which intimation was given. N.B. Rule 5.3(2) relating to postal service or intimation*).

---

[1] As inserted by the Act of Sederunt (Rules of the Court of Session 1994 and Ordinary Cause Rules 1993 Amendment) (Views of the Child) 2019 (SSI 2019/123) r.3 (effective 24 June 2019).

Date (*insert date*)

(*Signed*)

Solicitor for the pursuer

NOTE

If you decide to lodge a minute it may be in your best interests to consult a solicitor. The minute should be lodged with the sheriff clerk together with the appropriate fee of (*insert amount*) and a copy of this intimation.

IF YOU ARE UNCERTAIN WHAT ACTION TO TAKE you should consult a solicitor. You may be entitled to legal aid depending on your financial circumstances, and you can get information about legal aid from a solicitor. You may also obtain advice from any Citizens Advice Bureau or other advice agency.

FORM F11

Form of intimation in an action where the pursuer makes an application for an order under section 18 of the Family Law (Scotland) Act 1985

Rule 33.7(1)(j)

To (*insert name and address as in warrant*)

Court ref. no.

You are given NOTICE that in this action, the pursuer craves the court to make an order under section 18 of the Family Law (Scotland) Act 1985. A copy of the initial writ is attached. If you wish to appear as a party, you must lodge a minute with the sheriff clerk (*insert address of sheriff clerk*) for leave to do so. Your minute must be lodged within 21 days of (*insert date on which intimation was given. N.B. Rule 5.3(2) relating to postal service or intimation*).

Date (a*insert date*)

(*Signed*)

Solicitor for the pursuer

NOTE

If you decide to lodge a minute it may be in your best interests to consult a solicitor. The minute should be lodged with the sheriff clerk together with the appropriate fee of (*insert amount*) and a copy of this intimation.

IF YOU ARE UNCERTAIN WHAT ACTION TO TAKE you should consult a solicitor. You may be entitled to legal aid depending on your financial circumstances, and you can get information about legal aid from a solicitor. You may also obtain advice from any Citizens Advice Bureau or other advice agency.

FORM F12

Form of intimation in an action where a non-entitled pursuer makes an application for an order under the Matrimonial Homes (Family Protection) (Scotland) Act 1981

Rule 33.7(1)(k)

To (*insert name and address as in warrant*)

Court ref. no.

You are given NOTICE that in this action, the pursuer craves the court to make an order under section (*insert the section under which the order(s) is sought*) of the Matrimonial Homes (Family Protection) (Scotland) Act 1981. A copy of the initial writ is attached. If you wish to appear as a party, you must may lodge a minute with the sheriff clerk (*insert address of sheriff clerk*) for leave to do so. Your minute must be lodged within 21 days of (*insert date on which intimation was given. N.B. Rule 5.3(2) relating to postal service or intimation*).

Date (*insert date*)

(*Signed*)

Solicitor for the pursuer

NOTE

If you decide to lodge a minute it may be in your best interests to consult a solicitor. The minute should be lodged with the sheriff clerk together with the appropriate fee of (*insert amount*) and a copy of this intimation.

IF YOU ARE UNCERTAIN WHAT ACTION TO TAKE you should consult a solicitor. You may be entitled to legal aid depending on your financial circumstances, and you can get information about legal aid from a solicitor. You may also obtain advice from any Citizens Advice Bureau or other advice agency.

Rule 33.7(1)(l)

<h3 style="text-align:center">FORM F12A[1]</h3>

Form of intimation to person responsible for pension arrangement in relation to order for payment in respect of pension lump sum under section 12A of the Family Law (Scotland) Act 1985

To (*insert name and address as in warrant*)

Court ref. no.

You are given NOTICE that in this action the pursuer has applied for an order under section 8 of the Family Law (Scotland) Act 1985 for a capital sum in circumstances where the matrimonial property includes rights in a pension scheme under which a lump sum is payable. The relevant pension scheme is (*give brief details, including number, if known*). If you wish to apply to appear as a party, you must lodge a minute with the sheriff clerk (*insert address of sheriff clerk*) for leave to do so. Your minute must be lodged within 21 days of (*insert date on which intimation was given. N.B.* rule 5.3(2) *relating to postal service or intimation.*)

Date (*insert date*)

(Signed)
Solicitor for the pursuer
(add designation and business address)

NOTE

If you decide to lodge a minute it may be in your best interests to consult a solicitor. The minute should be lodged with the sheriff clerk together with the appropriate fee of (*insert amount*) and a copy of this intimation.

IF YOU ARE UNCERTAIN WHAT ACTION TO TAKE you should consult a solicitor. You may be entitled to legal aid depending on your financial circumstances, and you can get information about legal aid from a solicitor. You may also obtain advice from any Citizens Advice Bureau or other advice agency.

Rule 33.7(1)(m)

<h3 style="text-align:center">FORM F12B[2]</h3>

Form of intimation to person responsible for the pension arrangement in relation to pension sharing order under section 8(1)(baa) of the Family Law (Scotland) Act 1985.

Court ref. no.

To (*insert name and address as in warrant*)

You are given NOTICE that in this action the pursuer has applied under section 8 of the Family Law (Scotland) Act 1985 for a pension sharing order in circumstances where the matrimonial property includes rights in a pension scheme. The relevant pension scheme is (give brief details, including number, if known). If you wish to apply to appear as a party, you must lodge a minute with the sheriff clerk (insert ad-

---

[1] Inserted by SI 1996/2445 (effective 1 November 1996) and amended by the Act of Sederunt (Ordinary Cause Rules) Amendment (No.2) (Pension Sharing on Divorce etc.) 2000 (SSI 2000/408) para.2(3)(a).
[2] Inserted by the Act of Sederunt (Ordinary Cause Rules) Amendment (No.2) (Pension Sharing on Divorce etc.) 2000 (SSI 2000/408) para.2(3)(b).

dress of sheriff clerk) for leave to do so. Your minute must be lodged within 21 days of (*insert date on which intimation was given, N.B.* rule 5.3(2) *relating to postal service or intimation.*)

Date (*insert date*)

(*Signed*)
Solicitor for the pursuer
(*add designation and business address*)

NOTE

If you decide to lodge a minute it may be in your best interests to consult a solicitor. The minute should be lodged with the sheriff clerk together with the appropriate fee of (insert amount) and a copy of this intimation.

IF YOU ARE UNCERTAIN WHAT ACTION TO TAKE you should consult a solicitor. You may be entitled to legal aid depending on your financial circumstances, and you can get information about legal aid from a solicitor. You may also obtain advice from any Citizens Advice Bureau or other advice agency.

Rule 33.7(1)(n)

FORM F12C[1]

Form of intimation to Board of the Pension Protection Fund in relation to pension compensation sharing order under section 8(1)(bab) of the Family Law (Scotland) Act 1985

Court ref. no.

To (*insert name and address as in warrant*)

You are given NOTICE that in this action the pursuer has applied under section 8(1)(bab) of the Family Law (Scotland) Act 1985 for a pension compensation sharing order in circumstances where the matrimonial property includes rights to Pension Protection Fund compensation. The relevant pension arrangement is (*give brief details, including number, if known*). If you wish to appear as a party, you must lodge a minute with the sheriff clerk (*insert address of sheriff clerk*), for leave to do so. Your minute must be lodged within 21 days of (*insert date on which intimation was given. N.B.* Rule 5.3(2) *relating to postal service or intimation*).

Date (*insert date*)

(*Signed*)
Solicitor for the pursuer
(*insert designation and business address*)

Rule 33.7(1)(o)

FORM F12D[2]

Form of intimation to Board of the Pension Protection Fund in relation to an order under section 12B(2) of the Family Law (Scotland) Act 1985

Court ref. no.

To (*insert name and address as in warrant*)

You are given NOTICE that in this action the pursuer has applied under section 8(1)(bb) of the Family Law (Scotland) Act 1985 for an order under section 12B(2) of the Act in circumstances where the matrimonial properly includes rights to Pension Protection Fund compensation. The relevant pension arrangement is (*give brief details, including number, if known*). If you wish to appear as a party, you must lodge a minute with the sheriff clerk (*insert address of sheriff clerk*), for leave to do

---

[1] As inserted by the Act of Sederunt (Sheriff Court Rules) (Miscellaneous Amendments) 2011 (SSI 2011/193) r.15 (effective 6 April 2011).

[2] As inserted by the Act of Sederunt (Sheriff Court Rules) (Miscellaneous Amendments) 2011 (SSI 2011/193) r.15 (effective 6 April 2011).

so. Your minute must be lodged within 21 days of (*insert date on which intimation was given. N.B.* Rule 5.3(2) *relating to postal service or intimation*).

Date (*insert date*)

(*Signed*)
Solicitor for the pursuer
(*insert designation and business address*)

Rule 33.7(1)(p)

FORM F12E[1,2]

Form of intimation of application for financial provision on intestacy under section 29(2) of the Family Law (Scotland) Act 2006

To: (insert name and address as in war-   Court ref no.
rant)

You are given NOTICE that the pursuer has applied for an order for financial provision on intestacy under section 29(2) of the Family Law (Scotland) Act 2006. A copy of the initial writ is attached. If you wish to appear as a party, you must lodge a minute with the sheriff clerk (*insert address of sheriff clerk*) for leave to do so. Your minute must be lodged within 21 days of (*insert date on which intimation is given. N.B.* rule 5.3(2) *relating to postal service or intimation*).

Date (insert date)   (signed)
                                        Solicitor for the pursuer

---

NOTE

If you decide to lodge a minute it may be in your best interests to consult a solicitor. The minute should be lodged with the sheriff clerk together with the appropriate fee of (*insert amount*) and a copy of this intimation.

IF YOU ARE UNCERTAIN WHAT ACTION TO TAKE you should consult a solicitor.
You may be entitled to legal aid depending on your financial circumstances, and you can get information about legal aid from a solicitor. You may also obtain advice from any Citizens Advice Bureau or other advice agency.

Rule 33.8(3)

FORM F13

Form of intimation to person with whom an improper association is alleged to have occurred

To (*insert name and address as in war-   Court ref. no.
rant*)

You are given NOTICE that in this action, the defender is alleged to have had an improper association with you. A copy of the initial writ is attached. If you wish to dispute the truth of the allegation made against you, you must lodge a minute with the sheriff clerk (*insert address of sheriff clerk*) for leave to appear as a party. Your

---

[1] Inserted by Act of Sederunt (Ordinary Cause Rules) Amendment (Family Law (Scotland) Act 2006 etc.) 2006 (SSI 2006/207) para.2 (effective 4 May 2006).
[2] As amended and renumbered by the Act of Sederunt (Sheriff Court Rules) (Miscellaneous Amendments) 2012 (SSI 2012/188) para.8 (effective 1 August 2012).

363

minute must be lodged within 21 days of (*insert date on which intimation was given. N.B.* Rule 5.3(2) *relating to postal service or intimation*).

Date (*insert date*)   (*Signed*)
                                                            Solicitor for the pursuer

---

NOTE

If you decide to lodge a minute it may be in your best interests to consult a solicitor. The minute should be lodged with the sheriff clerk together with the appropriate fee of (*insert amount*) and a copy of this intimation.

IF YOU ARE UNCERTAIN WHAT ACTION TO TAKE you should consult a solicitor.
You may be entitled to legal aid depending on your financial circumstances, and you can get information about legal aid from a solicitor. You may also obtain advice from any Citizens Advice Bureau or other advice agency.

Rules 33.9(c) and 33.34(4)

FORM F13A[1]

Form of statement of matrimonial property in the cause
SHERIFFDOM OF (*insert name of sheriffdom*)
AT (*insert place of sheriff court*)
[A.B.], (*insert designation and address*, Pursuer against
[C.D..], (*insert designation and address*, Defender
Court ref. no:

The [Pursuer] [Defender]'s* financial position at (*insert date*), being the relevant date as defined in section 10(3) of the Family Law (Scotland) Act 1985
Here list all assets owned by you, including assets which are jointly owned (if any) e.g. bank or building society accounts; shares or other investments; houses; land; pension entitlement; and life policies:
Here list your outstanding debts including joint debts with the other party:
Date (*insert date*)
I certify that this information is correct to the best of my knowledge and belief.
(*Signed*)
[Pursuer][Defender]*

(*delete as applicable)

FORM F14[2]

Rule 33.10

Form of warrant of citation in family action
                                                    Court Ref. No. (*insert*)

(*Insert place and date*)

Grants warrant to cite the defender (*insert name and address of defender*) by serving upon him *[or* her] a copy of the writ and warrant upon a period of notice of

---

[1] As inserted by the Act of Sederunt (Sheriff Court Rules) (Miscellaneous Amendments) 2012 (SSI 2012/188) para.4 (effective 1 August 2012).
[2] As amended by the Act of Sederunt (Rules of the Court of Session 1994 and Ordinary Cause Rules 1993 Amendment) (Views of the Child) 2019 (SSI 2019/123) r.3 (effective 24 June 2019).

(*insert period of notice*) days, and ordains the defender to lodge a notice of intention to defend with the sheriff clerk at (*insert address of sheriff court*) if he [*or* she] wishes to:

(a)   challenge the jurisdiction of the court;
(b)   oppose any claim made or order sought;
(c)   make any claim or seek any order.

[Meantime grants interim interdict, *or* warrant to arrest on the dependence.]

[*Where a crave for a section 11 order is sought, one of the following must also be included:*

*Subject to the requirements of rule 33.7A(6), grants warrant for intimation and the seeking of views in Form F9 to (*insert child(ren)'s name(s) and address(es)*).

*Dispenses with intimation and the seeking of views in Form F9 to (*insert child(ren)'s name(s) and address(es)*) for the following reason(s): (*insert summary of reasons*).

Delete as appropriate.]

(*Signed*)
Sheriff

Rules 33.11(1) and 33.13(1)(a)   **FORM F15**

Form of citation in family action

CITATION
SHERIFFDOM OF (*insert name of sheriffdom*)
AT (*insert place of sheriff court*)
[A.B.], (*insert designation and address*), Pursuer, against [C.D.], (*insert designation and address*), Defender.

(*Insert place and date*)   Court ref. no.

You [C.D.], are hereby served with this copy writ and warrant, with Form F26 (notice of intention to defend) [and (*insert details of any other form of notice served, e.g. any of the forms served in accordance with* rule 33.14.)].

FORM F26 is served on you for use should you wish to intimate an intention to defend the action.

IF YOU WISH TO—
(a)   challenge the jurisdiction of the court;
(b)   oppose any claim made or order sought;
(c)   make any claim or seek any order; or
(d)   seek any order;

you should consult a solicitor with a view to lodging a notice of intention to defend (Form F26). The notice of intention to defend, together with the court fee of £ (*insert amount*) must be lodged with the sheriff clerk at the above address within 21 days (*or insert appropriate period of notice*) of (*insert the date on which service was executed. N.B.* Rule 5.3(2) *relating to postal service or intimation*).

IF YOU ARE UNCERTAIN WHAT ACTION TO TAKE you should consult a solicitor. You may be entitled to legal aid depending on your financial circumstances, and you can get information about legal aid from a solicitor. You may also obtain advice from any Citizens Advice Bureau or other advice agency.

> **PLEASE NOTE THAT IF YOU DO NOTHING IN ANSWER TO THIS DOCUMENT** the court may regard you as admitting the claim made against you and the pursuer may obtain decree against you in your absence.

Signed

[P.Q.], Sheriff officer

or

[X.Y.], (*add designation and business address*)

Solicitor for the pursuer

Rule 33.11(2)   **FORM F16**

Form of certificate of citation in family action

CERTIFICATE OF CITATION

(*Insert place and date*) I, ... hereby certify that upon the .... day of .... I duly cited [C.D.], Defender, to answer to the foregoing writ. This I did by (*state method of service; if by officer and not by post, add*: in presence of [L.M.], (*insert designation*), witness hereto with me subscribing; *and (insert details of any forms of intimation or notice sent including details of the person to whom intimation sent and the method of service*).

Signed

[P.Q.], Sheriff officer

[L.M.], witness

or

[X.Y.] (*add designation and business address*)

Solicitor for the pursuer

FORM F17

Rule 33.13(1)(c)

Form of request to medical officer of hospital or similar institution

To (*insert name and address of medical officer*)

In terms of rule 33.13(1)(c) of the Ordinary Cause Rules of the Sheriff Court a copy of the initial writ at the instance of (*insert name and address of pursuer*), Pursuer, against (*insert name and address of defender*), Defender, is enclosed and you are requested to

    (a)   deliver it personally to (*insert name of defender*), and

    (b)   explain the contents to him or her,

unless you are satisfied that such delivery or explanation would be dangerous to his or her health or mental condition. You are further requested to complete and return to me in the enclosed stamped addressed envelope the certificate appended hereto, making necessary deletions.

    Date (*insert date*)

(*Signed*)

Solicitor for the pursuer (*add designation and business address*)

FORM F18

Rules 33.13(1)(d) and 33.13(2)

Form of certificate by medical officer of hospital or similar institution

Court ref. no.

I (*insert name and designation*) certify that I have received a copy initial writ in an action of (*type of family action to be inserted by the party requesting service*) at the instance of (*insert name and designation*), Pursuer, against (*insert name and designation*), Defender, and that

366

* I have on the.......... day of.......... personally delivered a copy thereof to the said defender who is under my care at (*insert address*) and I have explained the contents or purport thereof to him or her, *or*

* I have not delivered a copy thereof to the said defender who is under my care at (*insert address*) and I have not explained the contents or purport thereof to him or her because (*state reasons*).

Date (*insert date*)

(*Signed*)

Medical officer (*add designation and address*)

* Delete as appropriate.[1]

FORM F19

Rule 33.14(1)(a)(i)

Form of notice to defender where it is stated that defender consents to the granting of decree of divorce

YOU ARE GIVEN NOTICE that the copy initial writ served on you with this notice states that you consent to the grant of decree of divorce.

1. If you do so consent the consequences for you are that:—

[2](a)   provided the pursuer establishes the fact that he [or she] has not cohabited with you at any time during a continuous period of one year after the date of your marriage and immediately preceding the bringing of this action and that you consent, a decree of divorce will be granted;

(b)   on the grant of a decree of divorce you may lose your rights of succession to the pursuer's estate; and

(c)   decree of divorce will end the marriage thereby affecting any right to such pension as may depend on the marriage continuing, or, on your being left a widow the state widow's pension will not be payable to you when the pursuer dies.

Apart from these, there may be other consequences for you depending upon your particular circumstances.

2. You are entitled, whether or not you consent to the grant of decree of divorce in this action, to apply to the sheriff in this action—

(a)   to make financial or other provision for you under the Family Law (Scotland) Act 1985;

(b)   for an order under section 11 of the Children (Scotland) Act 1995 in respect of any child of the marriage, or any child accepted as such, who is under 16 years of age; or

(c)   for any other competent order.

3. IF YOU WISH TO APPLY FOR ANY OF THE ABOVE ORDERS you should consult a solicitor with a view to lodging a notice of intention to defend (Form F26).

4. If, after consideration, you wish to consent to the grant of decree of divorce in this action, you should complete and sign the attached notice of consent (Form F20) and send it to the sheriff clerk at the sheriff court referred to in the initial writ within 21 days of (*insert the date on which service was executed. N.B. Rule 5.3(2) relating to postal service*).

5. If at a later stage, you wish to withdraw your consent to decree being granted against you in this action, you must inform the sheriff clerk immediately in writing.

Date (*insert date*)

(*Signed*)

---

[1] Substituted by SI 1996/2167 (effective November 1, 1996).

[2] As amended by Act of Sederunt (Ordinary Cause Rules) Amendment (Family Law (Scotland) Act 2006 etc.) 2006 (SSI 2006/207) r.2 (effective 4 May 2006).

Solicitor for the pursuer (*add designation and business address*)
FORM F20
Rules 33.14(1)(a)(i) and 33.18(1)
Form of notice of consent in actions of divorce under section 1(2)(d) of the Divorce (Scotland) Act 1976

Court ref. no.

[A.B.], (*insert designation and address*), Pursuer, against [C.D.], (*insert designation and address*), Defender.

I (*full name and address of the defender to be inserted by pursuer or pursuer's solicitor before sending notice*) have received a copy of the initial writ in the action against me at the instance of (*full name and address of pursuer to be inserted by pursuer or pursuer's solicitor before sending notice*). I understand that it states that I consent to the grant of decree of divorce in this action. I have considered the consequences for me mentioned in the notice (Form F19) sent to me with this notice. I consent to the grant of decree of divorce in this action.

Date (*insert date*)

(*Signed*)

Defender[1, 2]
FORM F21
Rule 33.14(1)(a)(ii)
Form of notice to defender where it is stated that defender consents to the granting of decree of separation

YOU ARE GIVEN NOTICE that the copy initial writ served on you with this notice states that you consent to the grant of decree of separation.

1. If you do so consent the consequences for you are that—

   [3](a)   provided the pursuer establishes the fact that he [or she] has not cohabited with you at any time during a continuous period of one year after the date of your marriage and immediately preceding the bringing of this action and that you consent, a decree of separation will be granted;

   (b)   on the grant of a decree of separation you will be obliged to live apart from the pursuer but the marriage will continue to subsist; you will continue to have a legal obligation to support your spouse and children;

Apart from these, there may be other consequences for you depending upon your particular circumstances.

2. You are entitled, whether or not you consent to the grant of decree of separation in this action, to apply to the sheriff in this action—

   (a)   to make financial or other provision for you under the Family Law (Scotland) Act 1985;

   (b)   for an order under Section 11 of the Children (Scotland) Act 1995 in respect of any child of the marriage, or any child accepted as such, who is under 16 years of age; or

   (c)   for any other competent order.

3. IF YOU WISH TO APPLY FOR ANY OF THE ABOVE ORDERS you

---

[1] Substituted by SI 1996/2167 (effective November 1, 1996).

[2] As amended by Act of Sederunt (Rules of the Court of Session and Sheriff Court Rules Amendment No. 2) (Marriage and Civil Partnership (Scotland) Act 2014) 2014 (SSI 2014/302) r.6 (effective December 16, 2014).

[3] As amended by Act of Sederunt (Ordinary Cause Rules) Amendment (Family Law (Scotland) Act 2006 etc.) 2006, para.2 (SSI 2006/207) (effective May 4, 2006).

should consult a solicitor with a view to lodging a notice of intention to defend (Form F26).

4. If, after consideration, you wish to consent to the grant of decree of separation in this action, you should complete and sign the attached notice of consent (Form F22) and send it to the sheriff clerk at the sheriff court referred to in the initial writ and other papers within 21 days of (*insert the date on which service was executed. N.B.* Rule 5.3(2) *relating to postal service or intimation*).

5. If at a later stage you wish to withdraw your consent to decree being granted against you in this action, you must inform the sheriff clerk immediately in writing.

Date (*insert date*)

(*Signed*)

Solicitor for the pursuer (*add designation and business address*)

FORM F22

Rules 33.14(1)(a)(ii) and 33.18(1)

Form of notice of consent in actions of separation under section 1 (2)(d) of the Divorce (Scotland) Act 1976

Court ref. no.

[A.B.], (*insert designation and address*), Pursuer against [C.D.], (*insert designation and address*), Defender.

I (*full name and address of the defender to be inserted by pursuer or pursuer's solicitor before sending notice*) confirm that I have received a copy of the initial writ in the action against me at the instance of (*full name and address of pursuer to be Inserted by pursuer or pursuer's solicitor before sending notice*). I understand that it states that I consent to the grant of decree of separation in this action. I have considered the consequences for me mentioned in the notice (Form F21) sent together with this notice. I consent to the grant of decree of separation in this action.

Date (*insert date*)

(*Signed*)

Defender[1]

FORM F23

Rule 33.14(1)(b)(i)[2]Form of notice to defender in an action of divorce where it is stated there has been two years' non-cohabitation

YOU ARE GIVEN NOTICE that—

[3]1. The copy initial writ served on you with this notice states that there has been no cohabitation between you and the pursuer at any time during a continuous period of two years after the date of the marriage and immediately preceding the commencement of this action. If the pursuer establishes this as a fact and the sheriff is satisfied that the marriage has broken down irretrievably, a decree will be granted.

2. Decree of divorce will end the marriage thereby affecting any right to such pension as may depend on the marriage continuing, or, on your being left a widow the state widow's pension will not be payable to you when the pursuer dies. You may also lose your rights of succession to the pursuer's estate.

---

[1] Substituted by SI 1996/2167 (effective November 1, 1996).

[2] As amended by Act of Sederunt (Ordinary Cause Rules) Amendment (Family Law (Scotland) Act 2006 etc.) 2006 (SSI 2006/207) r.2 (effective 4 May 2006).

[3] As amended by Act of Sederunt (Ordinary Cause Rules) Amendment (Family Law (Scotland) Act 2006 etc.) 2006 (SSI 2006/207) r.2 (effective 4 May 2006).

[1]3. You are entitled, whether or not you dispute that there has been no such cohabitation during that two year period, to apply to the sheriff in this action—

    (a) to make financial or other provision for you under the Family Law (Scotland) Act 1985;

    (b) for an order under section 11 of the Children (Scotland) Act 1995 in respect of any child of the marriage, or any child accepted as such, who is under 16 years of age; or

    (c) for any other competent order.

4. IF YOU WISH TO APPLY FOR ANY OF THE ABOVE ORDERS you should consult a solicitor with a view to lodging a notice of intention to defend (Form F26).

Date (*insert date*)

                                                    (*Signed*)

Solicitor for the pursuer (*add designation and business address*)

NOTE[2, 3]
FORM F24

Rule 33.14(1)(b)(ii)[4]Form of notice to defender in an action of separation where it is stated there has been two years' non-cohabitation

YOU ARE GIVEN NOTICE that—

[5]1. The copy initial writ served on you together with this notice states that there has been no cohabitation between you and the pursuer at any time during a continuous period of two years after the date of the marriage and immediately preceding the commencement of this action and that if the pursuer establishes this as a fact, and the sheriff is satisfied that there are grounds justifying decree of separation, a decree will be granted.

2. On the granting of decree of separation you will be obliged to live apart from the pursuer but the marriage will continue to subsist. You will continue to have a legal obligation to support your spouse and children.

[6]3. You are entitled, whether or not you dispute that there has been no such cohabitation during that two year period, to apply to the sheriff in this action—

    (a) to make provision under the Family Law (Scotland) Act 1985;

    (b) for an order under section 11 of the Children (Scotland) Act 1995 in respect of any child of the marriage, or any child accepted as such, who is under 16 years of age; or

    (c) for any other competent order.

4. **IF YOU WISH TO APPLY FOR ANY OF THE ABOVE ORDERS** you should consult a solicitor with a view to lodging a notice of intention to defend (Form F26).

---

[1] As amended by Act of Sederunt (Ordinary Cause Rules) Amendment (Family Law (Scotland) Act 2006 etc.) 2006 (SSI 2006/207) r.2 (effective 4 May 2006).

[2] Substituted by SI 1996/2167 (effective November 1, 1996).

[3] As amended by Act of Sederunt (Rules of the Court of Session and Sheriff Court Rules Amendment No.2) (Marriage and Civil Partnership (Scotland) Act 2014) 2014 (SSI 2014/302) para.6 (effective December 16, 2014).

[4] As amended by Act of Sederunt (Ordinary Cause Rules) Amendment (Family Law (Scotland) Act 2006 etc.) 2006, para.2 (SSI 2006/207) (effective May 4, 2006).

[5] As amended by Act of Sederunt (Ordinary Cause Rules) Amendment (Family Law (Scotland) Act 2006 etc.) 2006, para.2 (SSI 2006/207) (effective May 4, 2006).

[6] As amended by Act of Sederunt (Ordinary Cause Rules) Amendment (Family Law (Scotland) Act 2006 etc.) 2006, para.2 (SSI 2006/207) (effective May 4, 2006).

Date (*insert date*)

(*Signed*)

Solicitor for the pursuer (*add designation and business address*)[1, 2]

FORM F24A

Rule 33.14(1)(c)

Form of notice to defender in action of divorce where an interim gender recognition certificate has been issued

YOU ARE GIVEN NOTICE that—

1. The copy initial writ served on you together with this notice states that an interim gender recognition certificate has been issued to you [or the pursuer]. If the pursuer establishes this as a matter of fact, and that the Gender Recognition Panel has not issued a full gender recognition certificate, decree will be granted.

2. Decree of divorce will end the marriage thereby affecting any right to such pension as may depend on the marriage continuing, or, on your being left a widow the state widow's pension will not be payable to you when the pursuer dies. You may also lose your rights of succession to the pursuer's estate.

3. If the pursuer is entitled to a decree of divorce, you are nevertheless entitled to apply to the sheriff in this action—

    (a) to make financial or other provision for you under the Family Law (Scotland) Act 1985;

    (b) for an order under section 11 of the Children (Scotland) Act 1995 in respect of any child of the marriage, or any child accepted as such, who is under 16 years of age; or

    (c) for any competent order.

4. IF YOU WISH TO APPLY FOR ANY OF THE ABOVE ORDERS you should consult a solicitor with a view to lodging a notice of intention to defend (Form F26).

Date (*insert date*)

(*Signed*)

Solicitor for the pursuer (*add designation and business address*)

FORM F25

[Removed by SI 1996/2167 (effective November 1, 1996).][3]

FORM F26

Rules 33.11(1) and 33.34(2)(a)

Form of notice of intention to defend in family action

NOTICE OF INTENTION TO DEFEND

PART A

---

[1] Inserted by Act of Sederunt (Ordinary Cause Rules) Amendment (Family Law (Scotland) Act 2006 etc.) 2006, para.2 (SSI 2006/207) (effective May 4, 2006).

[2] As amended by Act of Sederunt (Rules of the Court of Session and Sheriff Court Rules Amendment No. 2) (Marriage and Civil Partnership (Scotland) Act 2014) 2014 (SSI 2014/302) r.6 (effective December 16, 2014).

[3] Substituted by Act of Sederunt (Ordinary Cause, Summary Application, Summary Cause and Small Claim Rules) Amendment (Miscellaneous) 2005 (SSI 2005/648), para.2 (effective January 2, 2006). As amended by the Act of Sederunt (Rules of the Court of Session 1994 and Ordinary Cause Rules 1993 Amendment) (Views of the Child) 2019 (SSI 2019/123) r.3 (effective 24 June 2019).

PART A (This section to be completed by the pursuer's solicitor before service.) [Insert name and business address of solicitor for the pursuer]	Court ref. No. In an action brought in Sheriff Court	Date of expiry of period of notice
	Pursuer	
	Defender Date of service:	

PART B

(This section to be completed by the defender or defender's solicitor, and both parts of the form to be returned to the Sheriff Clerk at the above Sheriff Court on or before the date of expiry of the period of notice referred to in Part A above.)

(Insert place and date)

[C.D.] (Insert designation and address), Defender, intends to

(a) challenge the jurisdiction of the court;

(b) oppose a crave in the initial writ;

(c) make a claim;

(d) seek an order;

in the action against him [or her] raised by [A.B.], (insert designation and address), Pursuer.

PART C

(This section to be completed by the defender or the defender's solicitor where an order under section 11 of the Children (Scotland) Act 1995 in respect of a child is opposed by the defender).

DO YOU WISH TO OPPOSE THE MAKING OF ANY ORDER CRAVED BY THE PURSUER IN RESPECT OF A CHILD?

YES/NO*

*delete as appropriate

If you answered YES to the above question, please state here the order(s) which you wish to oppose and the reasons why the court should not make such order(s).

PART D

(This section to be completed by the defender or the defender's solicitor where an order under section 11 of the Children (Scotland) Act 1995 in respect of a child is sought by the defender).

DO YOU WISH THE COURT TO MAKE ANY ORDER UNDER SECTION 11 OF THE CHILDREN (SCOTLAND) ACT 1995 IN RESPECT OF A CHILD?

YES/NO*

*delete as appropriate

If you answered YES to the above question, please state here the order(s) which you wish the court to make and the reasons why the court should make such order(s).

PART E

IF YOU HAVE ANSWERED YES AT PART D OF THIS FORM AND THE INITIAL WRIT DOES NOT INCLUDE A CRAVE FOR A SECTION 11 ORDER, YOU MUST INCLUDE EITHER CRAVE (1) OR (2) BELOW (*delete as appropriate)

(1) * Warrant for intimation to the child(ren) (insert full name(s) and date(s) of birth) is sought, by way of Form F9, which also seeks the child(ren)'s views.

(2) * I seek to dispense with intimation to the child(ren) (insert full name(s) and

date(s) of birth) and seeking the child(ren)'s views in Form F9 for the following reasons:—

Signed

[C.D.] Defender [or [X.Y.] (add designation and business address) Solicitor for Defender]

FORM F27

Rule 33.29(1)(b)

Form of minute for decree in family action to which rule 33.28 applies

(*Insert name of solicitor for the pursuer*) having considered the evidence contained in the affidavits and the other documents all as specified in the schedule hereto, and being satisfied that upon the evidence a motion for decree (in terms of the crave of the initial writ) [*or in such restricted terms as may be appropriate*] may properly be made, moves the court accordingly.

In respect whereof

Signed

Solicitor for the Pursuer (*add designation and business address*)

Schedule

(*Number and specify documents considered*)

FORM F28

Rules 33.40(c) and 33.64(1)(c)

Form of notice of intimation to local authority or third party to whom care of a child is to be given

To (*name and address as in warrant*)

Court ref. no.

You are given NOTICE that in this action, the sheriff proposes to commit to your care the child (*insert name and address*). A copy of the initial writ is attached. If you wish to appear as a party, you must lodge a minute with the sheriff clerk (*insert address of sheriff clerk*) for leave to do so. Your minute must be lodged within 21 days of (*insert date on which intimation was given. N.B.* Rule 53(2) *relating to postal service or intimation*).

Date (*insert date*)

(*Signed*)

Solicitor for the pursuer

NOTE

If you decide to lodge a minute it may be in your best interest to consult a solicitor. The minute should be lodged with the sheriff clerk together with the appropriate fee of (*insert amount*) and a copy of this intimation.

IF YOU ARE UNCERTAIN WHAT ACTION TO TAKE you should consult a solicitor. You may be entitled to legal aid depending on your financial circumstances, and you can get information about legal aid from a solicitor. You may also obtain advice from any Citizens Advice Bureau or other advice agency.

FORM F29

Rules 33.41 and 33.64(2)

Form of notice of intimation to local authority of supervision order

[A.B.], (*insert designation and address*), Pursuer, against [C.D.], (*Insert designation and address*), Defender.

To (*insert name and address of local authority*)

Court ref. no.

You are given NOTICE that on (*insert date*) in the Sheriff Court at (*insert place*) the sheriff made a supervision order under section 12 of the Matrimonial Proceedings (Children) Act 1958 [*or* section 1 1(1)(b) of the Guardianship Act 1973] placing the child (*insert name and address of child*) under your supervision. A certified copy of the sheriffs interlocutor is attached.

Date (*Insert date*)

(*Signed*)
Sheriff clerk (depute)

FORM F30
Rules 33.72(1) and 33.72(2)
[*Omitted by Act of Sederunt (Ordinary Cause Rules) Amendment (Family Law (Scotland) Act 2006 etc.) 2006, para.2 (SSI 2006/207) (effective 4 May 2006).*][1, 2, 3, 4, 5]

FORM F31[6]
Rule 33.74(1)
Form of simplified divorce application under section 1(2)(d) of the Divorce (Scotland) Act 1976

Sheriff Clerk
Sheriff Court House

....

....

(Telephone) ....

APPLICATION FOR DIVORCE WITH CONSENT OF OTHER PARTY TO THE MARRIAGE (SPOUSES HAVING LIVED APART FOR AT LEAST ONE YEAR)

Before completing this form, you should have read the leaflet entitled "Do it yourself Divorce", which explains the circumstances in which a divorce may be sought by this method. If simplified procedure appears to suit your circumstances, you may use this form to apply for divorce. Below you will find directions designed to assist you with your application. Please follow them carefully. In the event of difficulty, you may contact any sheriff clerk's office or Citizens Advice Bureau.

Directions for making application
WRITE IN INK, USING BLOCK CAPITALS

Application (Part 1)	1. Complete and sign Part 1 of the form (pages 3–7), paying particular attention to the notes opposite each section.
Consent of husband/wife (Part 2)	2. When you have completed Part 1 of the form, attach the (blue) instruction sheet SP3 to it and send both documents to your spouse for completion of the consent at Part 2 (page 9).

[1] As amended by SI 1996/2445 (effective 1 November 1996) and the Act of Sederunt (Ordinary Cause Rules) Amendment (Form of Simplified Divorce Application) 2003 (SSI 2003/ 25), para.2(2)(a) (effective 31 January 2003).
[2] As amended by Act of Sederunt (Ordinary Cause Rules) Amendment (Family Law (Scotland) Act 2006 etc.) 2006, para.2 (SSI 2006/207) (effective 4 May 2006).
[3] As amended by the Act of Sederunt (Ordinary Cause, Summary Application, Summary Cause and Small Claim Rules) Amendment (Miscellaneous) 2007 (SSI 2007/6), para.2(16)(f) (effective 26 February 2007).
[4] As amended by Act of Sederunt (Rules of the Court of Session and Sheriff Court Rules Amendment No.2) (Marriage and Civil Partnership (Scotland) Act 2014) 2014 (SSI 2014/302) r.6 (effective 16 December 2014).
[5] As amended by the Act of Sederunt (Rules of the Court of Session 1994 and Sheriff Court Rules Amendment) (Curators ad litem) 2017 (SSI 2017/132) r.2(6)(a) (effective 1 June 2017 subject to saving specified in SSI 2017/132 r.4).
[6] As amended by the Act of Sederunt (Rules of the Court of Session 1994 and Sheriff Court Rules Amendment) (Miscellaneous) 2021 (SSI 2021/75) r.3(4)(a) (effective 1 March 2021).

NOTE: If your spouse does NOT complete and sign the form of consent, your application cannot proceed further under the simplified procedure. In that event, if you still wish to obtain a divorce, you should consult a solicitor.

Affidavit (Part 3)

3. When the application has been returned to you with the consent (Part 2) duly completed and signed, you should take the form to a Justice of the Peace, Notary Public, Commissioner for Oaths or other duly authorised person so that your affidavit at Part 3 (page 10) may be completed and sworn.

Returning completed application form to court

4. When directions 1–3 above have been complied with, your application is now ready to be sent to the sheriff clerk at the above address. With it you must enclose:

(i) your marriage certificate (the document headed "Extract of an entry in a Register of Marriages", which will be returned to you in due course), and

(ii) either a cheque or postal order in respect of the court fee, crossed and made payable to "the Scottish Courts and Tribunals Service" or a completed fee exemption form,

or a completed form SP15, claiming exemption from the court fee.

5. Receipt of your application will be promptly acknowledged. Should you wish to withdraw the application for any reason, please contact the sheriff clerk immediately.

PART 1
WRITE IN INK, USING BLOCK CAPITALS
1. NAME AND ADDRESS OF APPLICANT

Surname ....

Other name(s) in full ....

....

Present address ....

....

Daytime telephone number (if any)

....

2. NAME AND ADDRESS OF SPOUSE

Surname ....

Other name(s) in full ....

....

Present address ....

....

Daytime telephone number (if any) ....

3. JURISDICTION

Please indicate with a tick (✔) in the appropriate box or boxes which of the following apply:

Please complete both Part A and Part B

PART A

(i)   I am domiciled in Scotland on the date I signed this application   ☐

(ii)   My spouse is domiciled in Scotland on the date I signed ☐
this application

(iii)   I was habitually resident in Scotland throughout the period ☐
of one year ending with the date I signed this application

(iv)   My spouse was habitually resident in Scotland throughout ☐
the period of one year ending with the date I signed this
application

PART B

(i)   I have lived at the address shown above for at least 40 days ☐
immediately before the date I signed this application

(ii)   My spouse has lived at the address shown above for at ☐
least 40 days immediately before the date I signed this application

(iii)   I lived at the address shown above for a period of at least ☐
40 days ending not more than 40 days before the date I
signed this application and have no known residence in
Scotland at that date

(iv)   My spouse lived at the address shown above for a period ☐
of at least 40 days ending not more than 40 days before the
date I signed this application and has no known residence
in Scotland at that date

4. DETAILS OF PRESENT MARRIAGE

Place of Marriage............... (Registration District)
Date of Marriage: Day .... month .... year ....

5. Period of Separation

(i)   Please the date on which you ceased to live with your
spouse. (If more than 1 year, just give the month and
year)

Day .... Month .... Year ....

(ii)   Have you lived with your spouse since that date?   *[YES/NO]

(iii)   If yes, for how long in total did you live together
before finally separating again?

.... months

6. RECONCILIATION

Is there any reasonable prospect of reconciliation with your   *[YES/NO]
spouse?

Do you consider that the marriage has broken down ir-   *[YES/NO]
retrievably?

7. CONSENT

Does your spouse consent to a divorce being granted?   *[YES/NO]

8. MENTAL DISORDER

As far as you are aware, does your spouse have any mental   *[YES/NO]
disorder (whether mental illness, personality disorder or
learning disability)?..........(if yes, give details)

9. CHILDREN

Are there any children of the marriage under the age of 16?   *[YES/NO]

10. OTHER COURT ACTIONS

Are you aware of any court actions currently proceeding in   *[YES/NO]
any

country (including Scotland) which may affect your
marriage?..........(If yes, give details)   *Delete as appropriate

11. DECLARATION AND REQUEST FOR DIVORCE

I confirm that the facts stated in paragraphs 1–10 above apply to my marriage.

I do NOT ask the sheriff to make any financial provision in connection with this application.

I do NOT ask the court to postpone the grant of decree under section 3A of the Divorce (Scotland) Act 1976.

I request the sheriff to grant decree of divorce from my spouse.

Date .... Signature of applicant's spouse ....

IMPORTANT

Part 1 MUST be completed, signed and dated before sending the application form to your spouse.

PART 2

NOTICE TO CONSENTING SPOUSE

(Insert name and address of consenting spouse)

CONSENT TO APPLICATION FOR DIVORCE (SPOUSES HAVING LIVED
APART FOR AT LEAST ONE YEAR)

In Part 1 of the enclosed application form your spouse is applying for divorce on the ground that the marriage has broken down irretrievably because you and he [*or* she] have lived apart for at least one year and you consent to the divorce being granted.

Such consent must be given formally in writing at Part 2 of the application form. BEFORE completing that part, you are requested to read it over carefully so that you understand the effect of consenting to divorce. Thereafter if you wish to consent—

(a)   check the details given by the Applicant at Part 1 of the form to ensure that they are correct to the best of your knowledge;

(b)   complete Part 2 (Consent by Applicant's spouse to divorce) by entering your name and address at the appropriate place and adding your signature and the date; and

(c)   return the whole application form to your spouse at the address given in Part 1.

Once your husband or wife has completed the remainder of the form and has submitted it to the court, a copy of the whole application (including your consent) will later be served upon you formally by the sheriff clerk.

In the event of the divorce being granted, you will automatically be sent a copy of the extract decree. (Should you change your address before receiving the copy extract decree, please notify the sheriff clerk immediately.)

If you do NOT wish to consent please return the application form, with Part 2 uncompleted, to your spouse and advise him or her of your decision.

The sheriff will NOT grant a divorce on this application if Part 2 of the form is not completed by you.

Sheriff clerk (depute)

Sheriff Court (*insert address*)

CONSENT BY APPLICANT'S SPOUSE TO DIVORCE

NOTE: Before completing this part of the form, please read the notes opposite (page 8)

I, ...

(*Insert full name, in BLOCK letters, of Applicant's spouse*)

residing at

....

(*Insert address, also in BLOCK letters*)

....

....

HEREBY STATE THAT

(a)   I have read Part 1 of this application;

(b)   the Applicant has lived apart from me for a continuous period of one year immediately preceding the date of the application (paragraph 11 of Part 1);

(c)   I do not ask the sheriff to make any financial provision for me including—

    (i)   the payment by the Applicant of a periodical allowance (i.e. a regular payment of money weekly or monthly, etc. for maintenance);

    (ii)   the payment by the Applicant of a capital sum (i.e. a lump sum payment);

(d)   I understand that divorce may result in the loss to me of property rights;

(e)   I do not ask the court to postpone the grant of decree under section 3A of the Divorce (Scotland) Act 1976; and

(f)   I CONSENT TO DECREE OF DIVORCE BEING GRANTED IN RE-SPECT OF THIS APPLICATION.

Date .... Signature ....

NOTE: You may withdraw your consent, even after giving it, at any time before divorce is granted by the sheriff. Should you wish to do so, please contact the sheriff clerk immediately.

PART 3

APPLICANT'S AFFIDAVIT

To be completed by the Applicant only after Parts 1 and 2 have been signed and dated.

I, (*insert Applicant's full name*) ....

residing at (*insert Applicant's present home address*) ....

....

....

SWEAR that to the best of my knowledge and belief:

(1)   the facts stated in Part 1 of this Application are true; and

(2)   the signature in Part 2 of this Application is that of my spouse.

Signature of Applicant..............

To be completed by Justice of the Peace, Notary Public or Commissioner for Oaths	SWORN at (insert place) .... this .... day of ....19.......... before me (*insert full name*) .... (*insert full address*).............. ....

....

Signature ....

*Justice of the Peace/Notary Public/Commissioner for Oaths

*Delete as appropriate

I

FORM F32[2, 3, 4, 5, 6]

FORM F33[7]

Rule 33.74(2)

Form of simplified divorce application under section 1(2)(e) of the Divorce (Scotland) Act 1976

Sheriff Clerk

Sheriff Court House

....

....

(Telephone)...............

APPLICATION FOR DIVORCE (SPOUSES HAVING LIVED APART FOR AT LEAST TWO YEARS)

Before completing this form, you should have read the leaflet entitled "Do it yourself Divorce", which explains the circumstances in which a divorce may be sought by this method. If the simplified procedure appears to suit your circumstances, you may use this form to apply for divorce.

Below you will find directions to assist you with your application. Please follow them carefully. In the event of difficulty, you may contact any sheriff clerk's office or Citizens Advice Bureau.

Directions for making application

WRITE IN INK, USING BLOCK CAPITALS

Application (Part 1)	1. Complete and sign Part 1 of the form (pages 3-7), paying particular attention to the notes opposite each section.
Affidavits (Part 2)	2. When you have completed Part 1, you should take the form to a Justice of the Peace, Notary Public, Commissioner for Oaths or other duly authorised person in order that your affidavit in Part 2 (page 8) may be completed and sworn.

---

[1] Repealed by SI 1996/2445 (effective 1 November 1996).

[2] As amended by SI 1996/2445 (effective 1 November 1996) and the Act of Sederunt (Ordinary Cause Rules) Amendment (Form of Simplified Divorce Application) 2003 (SSI 2003/ 25), para.2(2)(b) (effective 31 January 2003).

[3] As amended by Act of Sederunt (Ordinary Cause Rules) Amendment (Family Law (Scotland) Act 2006 etc.) 2006, para.2 (SSI 2006/207) (effective 4 May 2006).

[4] As amended by the Act of Sederunt (Ordinary Cause, Summary Application, Summary Cause and Small Claim Rules) Amendment (Miscellaneous) 2007 (SSI 2007/6), para.2(16)(g) (effective 26 February 2007).

[5] As amended by Act of Sederunt (Rules of the Court of Session and Sheriff Court Rules Amendment No. 2) (Marriage and Civil Partnership (Scotland) Act 2014) 2014 (SSI 2014/302) para.6 (effective 16 December 2014).

[6] As amended by the Act of Sederunt (Rules of the Court of Session 1994 and Sheriff Court Rules Amendment) (Curators ad litem) 2017 (SSI 2017/132) r.2(6)(b) (effective 1 June 2017 subject to saving specified in SSI 2017/132 r.4).

[7] As amended by the Act of Sederunt (Rules of the Court of Session 1994 and Sheriff Court Rules Amendment) (Miscellaneous) 2021 (SSI 2021/75) r.3(4)(b) (effective 1 March 2021).

Returning
completed
application
form to
court

3. When directions 1 and 2 above have been complied with, your is now ready to be sent to the sheriff clerk at the above address. With it you application must enclose:

(i) your marriage certificate (the document headed "Extract of an entry in a Register of Marriages", which will be returned to you in due course). Check the notes on page 2 to see if you need to obtain a letter from the National Records of Scotland stating that there is no record of your spouse having divorced you, and

(ii) either a cheque or postal order in respect of the court fee, crossed and made out to "the Scottish Court Service" or a completed fee exemption form.

4. Receipt of your application will be promptly acknowledged. Should you wish to withdraw the application for any reason, please contact the sheriff clerk immediately.

PART 1

WRITE IN INK, USING BLOCK CAPITALS

1. NAME AND ADDRESS OF APPLICANT

Surname ....

Other name(s) in full ....

Present address ....

    ....

    ....

Daytime telephone number (if any) ....

2. NAME OF SPOUSE

Surname ....

Other name(s) in full ....

3. ADDRESS OF SPOUSE (if the address of your spouse is not known, please enter "not known" in this paragraph and proceed to paragraph 4)

Present address ....

    ....

    ....

Daytime telephone (if any) ....

4. Only complete this paragraph if you do not know the present address of your spouse

NEXT-OF-KIN

Name ....

Address ....

    ....

    ....

Relationship to your spouse ....

CHILDREN OF THE MARRIAGE

Names and dates of birth	Addresses
....	....
	....
....	....

....

....

....

If insufficient space is available to list all the children of the marriage, please continue on a separate sheet and attach to this form.

5. JURISDICTION

Please indicate with a tick (✔) in the appropriate box or boxes which of the following apply:

Please complete both Part A and Part B

PART A

(i)   I am domiciled in Scotland on the date I signed this application   ☐

(ii) My spouse is domiciled in Scotland on the date I signed this application   ☐

(iii) I was habitually resident in Scotland throughout the period of one year ending with the date I signed this application   ☐

(iv) My spouse was habitually resident in Scotland throughout the period of one year ending with the date I signed this application   ☐

PART B

(i)   I have lived at the address shown above for at least 40 days immediately before the date I signed this application   ☐

(ii) My spouse has lived at the address shown above for at least 40 days immediately before the date I signed this application   ☐

(iii) I lived at the address shown above for a period of at least 40 days ending not more than 40 days before the date I signed this application and have no known residence in Scotland at that date   ☐

(iv) My spouse lived at the address shown above for a period of at least 40 days ending not more than 40 days before the date I signed this application and has no known residence in Scotland at that date   ☐

6. DETAILS OF PRESENT MARRIAGE

Place of Marriage .... (Registration District)

Date of Marriage: Day .... month .... year ....

7. PERIOD OF SEPARATION

(i)   Please state the date on which you ceased to live with your spouse. (If more than 2 years, just give the month and year) Day .... Month .... Year ....

(ii) Have you lived with your spouse since that date?   *[YES/NO]

(iii) If yes, for how long in total did you live together before finally separating again?

.... months

8. RECONCILIATION

Is there any reasonable prospect of reconciliation with your spouse?   *[YES/NO]

Do you consider that the marriage has broken down irretriev- ably?   *[YES/NO]

9. MENTAL DISORDER

As far as you are aware, does your spouse have any mental disorder (whether mental illness, personality disorder or learn- ing diability)?..........(If yes, give details)   *[YES/NO]

10. CHILDREN

Are there any children of the marriage under the age of 16?   *[YES/NO]

11. Other Court Actions

Are you aware of any court actions currently proceeding in any country (including Scotland) which may affect your marriage?   *[YES/NO]

(If yes, give details)   *Delete as appropriate

12. DECLARATION AND REQUEST FOR DIVORCE

I confirm that the facts stated in paragraphs 1–12 above apply to my marriage.

I do NOT ask the sheriff to make any financial provision in connection with this application.

I do NOT ask the court to postpone the grant of decree under section 3A of the Divorce (Scotland) Act 1976.

I request the sheriff to grant decree of divorce from my spouse.

Date ....

Signature of Applicant ....

PART 2

APPLICANT'S AFFIDAVIT

(To be completed by the Applicant only after Part 1 has been signed and dated.)

I, (*insert full name*) ....

residing at (*insert present home address*) ....

....

SWEAR that to the best of my knowledge and belief the facts stated in Part 1 of this Application are true.

Signature of Applicant ....

SWORN at (*insert place*)

To be completed by Justice of the Peace, Notary Public or Commissioner for Oaths

this .... day of .... 19.......... before me (*insert full name*) .... of (insert full address) ....

....

....

Signature ....

*Justice of the Peace/Notary Public/Commissioner for Oaths

*Delete as appropriate

1, 2, 3, 4

FORM F33A[5]

Rule 33.74(1)(3)

Form of simplified divorce application under section 1(1)(b) of the Divorce (Scotland) Act 1976

Sheriff Clerk
Sheriff Court House

....

....

(Telephone) ....

APPLICATION FOR DIVORCE (INTERIM GENDER RECOGNITION CERTIFICATE ISSUED TO ONE OF THE PARTIES AFTER THE MARRIAGE

Before completing this form, you should have read the leaflet entitled "Do it yourself Divorce", which explains the circumstances in which a divorce may be sought by this method. If the simplified procedure appears to suit your circumstances, you may use this form to apply for divorce. Below you will find directions designed to assist you with your application. Please follow them carefully. In the event of difficulty, you may contact any sheriff clerk's office or Citizen's Advice Bureau.

Directions for making application

WRITE IN INK, USING BLOCK CAPITALS

Application (Part 1)	1. Complete and sign Part 1 of the form (pages 3-7), paying particular attention to the notes opposite each section.
Affidavits (Part 2)	2. When you have completed Part 1, you should take the form to a Justice of the Peace, Notary Public, Commissioner for Oaths or other duly authorised person so that your affidavit at Part 2 (page 8) may be completed and sworn.
Returning completed application form to court	3. When directions 1 and 2 above have been complied with, your application is now ready to be sent to the sheriff clerk at the above address. With it you must enclose:

    (i)   your marriage certificate (the document headed "Extract of an entry in a Register of Marriages", which will be returned to you in due course). Check the notes on page 2 to see if you also need to obtain a letter from the National Records of Scotland stating that there is no record that your spouse has divorced you,

    (ii) either a cheque or postal order in respect of the court fee, crossed and made payable to "the Scottish Courts and

---

[1] Inserted by Act of Sederunt (Ordinary Cause Rules) Amendment (Family Law (Scotland) Act 2006 etc.) 2006, para.2 (SSI 2006/207) (effective May 4, 2006).

[2] As amended by the Act of Sederunt (Ordinary Cause, Summary Application, Summary Cause and Small Claim Rules) Amendment (Miscellaneous) 2007 (SSI 2007/6), para.2(16)(h) (effective February 26, 2007).

[3] As amended by Act of Sederunt (Rules of the Court of Session and Sheriff Court Rules Amendment No. 2) (Marriage and Civil Partnership (Scotland) Act 2014) 2014 (SSI 2014/302) para.6 (effective December 16, 2014).

[4] As amended by the Act of Sederunt (Rules of the Court of Session 1994 and Sheriff Court Rules Amendment) (Curators ad litem) 2017 (SSI 2017/132) r.2(6)(c) (effective 1 June 2017 subject to saving specified in SSI 2017/132 r.4).

[5] As amended by the Act of Sederunt (Rules of the Court of Session 1994 and Sheriff Court Rules Amendment) (Miscellaneous) 2021 (SSI 2021/75) r.3(4)(c) (effective 1 March 2021).

Tribunals Service", or a completed fee exemption form, and

(iii)   the interim gender recognition certificate or a copy sealed with the seal of the Gender Recognition Panels and certified to be a true copy by an officer authorised by the President of Gender Recognition Panels.

4. Receipt of your application will be promptly acknowledged. Should you wish to withdraw the application for any reason, please contact the sheriff clerk immediately.

Part 1
WRITE IN INK, USING BLOCK CAPITALS
1. NAME AND ADDRESS OF APPLICANT
Surname...............
Other name(s) in full...............

....
Present address...............

....
Daytime telephone number (if any)...............
2. NAME OF SPOUSE
Surname...............
Other name(s) in full...............
3. ADDRESS OF SPOUSE (if the address of your spouse is not known, please enter "not known" in this paragraph and proceed to paragraph 4)
Present address...............

....
....
Daytime telephone (if any)...............
4. Only complete this paragraph if you do not know the present address of your spouse
NEXT-OF-KIN
Name...............
Address...............

....
....
Relationship to your spouse...............
CHILDREN OF THE MARRIAGE

Names and dates of birth	Addresses
....	....
	....
....	....
	....
....	....
	....

If insufficient space is available to list all the children of the marriage, please continue on a separate sheet and attach to this form.
5. JURISDICTION
Please complete both Part A and Part B
PART A

(i)	I am domiciled in Scotland on the date I signed this application	☐
(ii)	My spouse is domiciled in Scotland on the date I signed this application	☐
(iii)	I was habitually resident in Scotland throughout the period of one year ending with the date I signed this application	☐
(iv)	My spouse was habitually resident in Scotland throughout the period of one year ending with the date I signed this application	☐

PART B

(i)	I have lived at the address shown above for at least 40 days immediately before the date I signed this application	☐
(ii)	My spouse has lived at the address shown above for at least 40 days immediately before the date I signed this application	☐
(iii)	I lived at the address shown above for a period of at least 40 days ending not more than 40 days before the date I signed this application and have no known residence in Scotland at that date	☐
(iv)	My spouse lived at the address shown above for a period of at least 40 days ending not more than 40 days before the date I signed this application and has no known residence in Scotland at that date	☐

6. DETAILS OF PRESENT MARRIAGE

Place of Marriage.......... (Registration District)

Date of Marriage: Day.......... month.......... year..........

7. DETAILS OF ISSUE OF INTERIM GENDER RECOGNITION CERTIFICATE

(i) Please state whether the interim gender recognition certificate has been issued to you or your spouse

(ii) Please state the date the interim gender recognition certificate was issued Day.......... Month.......... Year..........

Please answer the following question only if the interim gender recognition certificate was issued to you—

(iii) Has the Gender Recognition Panel issued you with a full   *[YES/NO]
gender recognition certificate?

Please answer the following question only if the interim gender recognition certificate was issued to your spouse—

(iv) Since the date referred to in question (ii), have you made a   *[YES/NO]
statutory declaration consenting to the marriage continuing?

8. MENTAL DISORDER

As far as you are aware, does your spouse have any mental   *[YES/NO]
disorder (whether mental illness, personality disorder or learning disability)? (If yes, give details)

9. CHILDREN

Are there any children of the marriage under the age of 16?   *[YES/NO]

10. OTHER COURT ACTIONS

Are you aware of any court actions currently proceeding in any   *[YES/NO]
country (including Scotland) which may affect your marriage?
(If yes, give details)

* Delete as appropriate

11. DECLARATION AND REQUEST FOR DIVORCE

I confirm that the facts stated in paragraphs 1–10 above apply to my marriage.

I do NOT ask the sheriff to make any financial provision in connection with this application.

I do NOT ask the court to postpone the grant of decree under section 3A of the Divorce (Scotland) Act 1976.

I request the sheriff to grant decree of divorce from my spouse.

Date.............. Signature of Applicant..............

PART 2

APPLICANT'S AFFIDAVIT

To be completed by the Applicant only after Part 1 has been signed and dated.

I, (*Insert Applicant's full name*)..............
residing at (insert Applicant's present home address)..............
....
....

SWEAR that to the best of my knowledge and belief the facts stated in Part 1 of this Application are true.

Signature of Applicant....................

To be completed by   SWORN at (*insert place*).............. this.......... day
Justice of the Peace,   of.......... 20.......... before me (*insert full*
Notary Public or Com-   *name*)..............of (*insert full address*)....................
missioner for Oaths

Signature..............
*Justice of the Peace/Notary Public/Commissioner for Oaths
*Delete as appropriate

1, 2, 3

FORM F34

Rule 33.76(3)(a)

Form of citation in application relying on the facts in section 1(2)(d) of the Divorce (Scotland) Act 1976

(*Insert name and address of non-applicant spouse*)

APPLICATION FOR DIVORCE (SPOUSES HAVING LIVED APART FOR AT LEAST ONE YEAR WITH CONSENT OF OTHER PARTY)

---

[1] As amended by Act of Sederunt (Ordinary Cause Rules) Amendment (Family Law (Scotland) Act 2006 etc.) 2006, para.2 (SSI 2006/207) (effective May 4, 2006).

[2] As amended by the Act of Sederunt (Ordinary Cause, Summary Application, Summary Cause and Small Claim Rules) Amendment (Miscellaneous) 2007 (SSI 2007/6), para.2(16)(i) (effective February 26, 2007).

[3] As amended by Act of Sederunt (Rules of the Court of Session and Sheriff Court Rules Amendment No. 2) (Marriage and Civil Partnership (Scotland) Act 2014) 2014 (SSI 2014/302) para.6 (effective December 16, 2014).

Your spouse has applied to the sheriff for divorce on the ground that the marriage has broken down irretrievably because you and he or she have lived apart for a period of at least one year and you consent to divorce being granted.

A copy of the application is hereby served upon you.

1. Please note:

(a)   that the sheriff may not make financial provision under this procedure and that your spouse is making no claim for—

    (i)   the payment by you of a periodical allowance (i.e. a regular payment of money weekly or monthly, etc. for maintenance);

    (ii)   the payment by you of a capital sum (i.e. a lump sum payment);

(b)   that no application may be made under this procedure for postponement of decree under section 3A of the Divorce (Scotland) Act 1976 (postponement of decree where impediment to religious marriage exists).

2. Divorce may result in the loss to you of property rights (e.g. the right to succeed to the Applicant's estate on his or her death) or the right, where appropriate, to a widow's pension.

3. If you wish to oppose the granting of a divorce, you should put your reasons in writing and send your letter to the address shown below. Your letter must reach the sheriff clerk before (insert date).

4. In the event of the divorce being granted, you will be sent a copy of the extract decree. Should you change your address before receiving the copy extract decree, please notify the sheriff clerk immediately.

Signed
Sheriff clerk (depute)

(insert address and telephone number of the sheriff clerk) or Sheriff officer

NOTE: If you wish to exercise your right to make a claim for financial provision, or if you wish to apply for postponement of decree under section 3A of the Divorce (Scotland) Act 1976 (postponement of decree where impediment to religious marriage exists), you should immediately advise the sheriff clerk that you oppose the application for that reason, and thereafter consult a solicitor.[1, 2, 3]

FORM F35

Rule 33.76(3)(b)

Form of citation in application relying on the facts in section 1 (2)(e) of the
Divorce (Scotland) Act 1976

(Insert name and address of non-applicant spouse)

APPLICATION FOR DIVORCE (SPOUSES HAVING LIVED APART FOR AT LEAST TWO YEARS)

Your spouse has applied to the sheriff for divorce on the ground that the marriage has broken down irretrievably because you and he or she have lived apart for a period of at least two years.

A copy of the application is hereby served upon you.

1. Please note:

(a)   that the sheriff may not make financial provision under this procedure and

---

[1] As amended by Act of Sederunt (Ordinary Cause Rules) Amendment (Family Law (Scotland) Act 2006 etc.) 2006, para.2 (SSI 2006/207) (effective May 4, 2006).

[2] As amended by the Act of Sederunt (Ordinary Cause, Summary Application, Summary Cause and Small Claim Rules) Amendment (Miscellaneous) 2007 (SSI 2007/6), para.2(16)G) (effective February 26, 2007).

[3] As amended by Act of Sederunt (Rules of the Court of Session and Sheriff Court Rules Amendment No. 2) (Marriage and Civil Partnership (Scotland) Act 2014) 2014 (SSI 2014/302) para.6 (effective December 16, 2014).

that your spouse is making no claim for—
- (i) the payment by you of a periodical allowance (i.e. a regular payment of money weekly or monthly, etc., for maintenance);
- (ii) the payment by you of a capital sum (i.e. a lump sum payment);
- (b) that no application may be made under this procedure for postponement of decree under section 3A of the Divorce (Scotland) Act 1976 (postponement of decree where impediment to religious marriage exists).

2. Divorce may result in the loss to you of property rights (e.g. the right to succeed to the Applicant's estate on his or her death) or the right, where appropriate, to a widow's pension.

3. If you wish to oppose the granting of a divorce, you should put your reasons in writing and send your letter to the address shown below. Your letter must reach the sheriff clerk before (*insert date*).

4. In the event of the divorce being granted, you will be sent a copy of the extract decree. Should you change your address before receiving the copy extract decree, please notify the sheriff clerk immediately.

Signed..........
Sheriff clerk (depute)

(*insert the address and telephone number of the sheriff court*)
or Sheriff officer

NOTE: If you wish to exercise your right to make a claim for financial provision, or if you wish to apply for postponement of decree under section 3A of the Divorce (Scotland) Act 1976 (postponement of decree where impediment to religious marriage exists), you should immediately advise the sheriff clerk that you oppose the application for that reason, and thereafter consult a solicitor.[1,2]

FORM 35A

Rule 33.76(3)(c)

Form of citation in application on grounds under section 1(1)(b) of the Divorce (Scotland) Act 1976

(*Insert name and address of non-applicant spouse*)

APPLICATION FOR DIVORCE (INTERIM GENDER RECOGNITION CERTIFICATE ISSUED TO ONE OF THE PARTIES AFTER THE MARRIAGE)

Your spouse has applied to the sheriff for divorce on the ground that an interim gender recognition certificate has been issued to you or your spouse after your marriage.

A copy of the application is hereby served upon you.

1. Please note that the sheriff may not make financial provision under this procedure and that your spouse is making no claim for—
- (a) the payment by you of a periodical allowance (i.e. a regular payment of money weekly or monthly, etc. for maintenance);
- (b) the payment by you of a capital sum (i.e. a lump sum payment).

2. Divorce may result in the loss to you of property rights (e.g. the right to succeed to the Applicant's estate on his or her death) or the right, where appropriate, to a pension.

---

[1] As inserted by Act of Sederunt (Ordinary Cause Rules) Amendment (Family Law (Scotland) Act 2006 etc.) 2006, para.2 (SSI 2006/207) (effective May 4, 2006).

[2] As amended by the Act of Sederunt (Ordinary Cause, Summary Application, Summary Cause and Small Claim Rules) Amendment (Miscellaneous) 2007 (SSI 2007/6), para.2(16)(k) (effective February 26, 2007).

2A. Please note that no application may be made under this procedure for postponement of decree under section 3A of the Divorce (Scotland) Act 1976 (postponement of decree where impediment to religious marriage exists).

3. If you wish to oppose the granting of a decree of divorce, you should put your reasons in writing and send your letter to the address shown below. Your letter must reach the sheriff clerk before (*insert date*).

4. In the event of the decree of divorce being granted, you will be sent a copy of the extract decree. Should you change your address before receiving the copy extract decree, please notify the sheriff clerk immediately.

(Signed)

Sheriff clerk (depute) (*insert address and telephone number of the sheriff clerk*) [*or* Sheriff officer]

NOTE: If you wish to exercise your right to make a claim for financial provision, or if you wish to apply for postponement of decree under section 3A of the Divorce (Scotland) Act 1976 (postponement of decree where impediment to religious marriage exists), you should immediately advise the sheriff clerk that you oppose the application for that reason, and thereafter consult a solicitor.

FORM F36

Rule 33.77(1)(a)

Form of intimation of simplified divorce application for display on the walls of court

Court ref. no.

An application for divorce has been made in this sheriff court by [A.B.], (*insert designation and address*), Applicant, naming [C.D.], (*insert designation and address*) as Respondent.

If [C.D.] wishes to oppose the granting of decree of divorce he [*or* she] should immediately contact the sheriff clerk from whom he [*or* she] may obtain a copy of the application.

Date (*insert date*)

Signed
Sheriff clerk (depute)

FORM F37

Rule 33.77(2)

Form of intimation to children and next-of-kin in simplified divorce application
To (*insert name and address*)

Court ref. no.

You are hereby given NOTICE that an application for divorce has been made against (*insert name of respondent*) your (*insert relationship e.g. father, mother, brother or other relative as the case may be*). A copy of this application is attached.

If you know of his or her present address, you are requested to inform the sheriff clerk (*insert address of sheriff clerk*) in writing immediately. You may also, if you wish, oppose the granting of decree of divorce by sending a letter to the court giving your reasons for your opposition to the application. Your letter must be sent to the sheriff clerk within 21 days of (*insert date on which intimation was given. N.B.* Rule 53(2) *relating to postal service or intimation*).

Date (*insert date*)

Signed
Sheriff clerk (depute)

NOTE

IF YOU ARE UNCERTAIN WHAT ACTION TO TAKE you should consult a solicitor. You may be entitled to legal aid depending on your financial circumstances, and you can get information about legal aid from a solicitor. You may also obtain advice from any Citizens Advice Bureau or other advice agency.

Rule 33.80(2)

FORM F38

Form of extract decree of divorce in simplified divorce application

At (*insert place and date*)

in an action in the Sheriff Court of the Sheriffdom of (*insert name of sheriffdom*) at (*insert place of sheriff court*)

at the instance of [A.B.], (*insert full name of applicant*), Applicant,

against (*insert full name of respondent*), Respondent,

who were married at (*insert place*) on (*insert date*),

the sheriff pronounced decree divorcing the Respondent from the Applicant. Extracted at (*insert place and date*)

by me, sheriff clerk of the Sheriffdom of (*insert name of sheriffdom*).

Signed
Sheriff clerk (depute)

Rule 33.90

FORM F39

Form of certificate relating to the making of a maintenance assessment under the Child Support Act 1991

Sheriff Court (*insert address*)

Date (*insert date*)

I certify that notification has been received from the Secretary of State under section 10 of the Child Support Act 1991 of the making of a maintenance assessment under that Act which supersedes the decree or order granted on (*insert date*) in relation to aliment for (*insert the name(s) of child(ren)*) with effect from (*insert date*).

Signed
Sheriff clerk (depute)

Rule 33.90

FORM F40

Form of certificate relating to the cancellation or ceasing to have effect of a maintenance assessment under the Child Support Act 1991

Sheriff Court (*insert address*) Date (*insert date*)

I certify that notification has been received from the Secretary of State under section 10 of the Child Support Act 1991 that the maintenance assessment made on (*insert date*) has been cancelled [*or* ceased to have effect] on (*insert date*).

Signed
Sheriff clerk (depute)

Rule 33.22A(2)[1]

FORM F41

Form of intimation to parties of a Child Welfare Hearing

Sheriff Court (*insert address and telephone number*)

Court Ref No:

In the action [A.B.], (*design*), Pursuer against [C.D.], (*design*), Defender

YOU ARE GIVEN NOTICE that a Child Welfare Hearing has been fixed for (*insert time*) on (*insert date*) at (*insert place*).

Date (*insert date*)

Signed..............
Sheriff Clerk (Depute)

---

[1] Substituted by SSI 2000/239 (effective October 2, 2000).

NOTE

Please note that in terms of Rule 33.22A(5) **parties to the action must attend personally**

* *IF YOU ARE UNCERTAIN WHAT ACTION TO TAKE* you should consult a solicitor. You may be eligible for legal aid depending on your financial circumstances, and you can get information about legal aid from a solicitor. You may also obtain information from any Citizens' Advice Bureau or other advice agency.

* This section to be deleted where service is to be made on a solicitor.

Rule 33.27A(1)

FORM F42[1]

FORM F43[2]

FORM F44[3, 4]

Rule 33.21(4)

Form of annex to interlocutor appointing a child welfare reporter

☐ Appointment of Child Welfare Reporter under rule 33.21(1)(a).

Where this box is ticked the Child Welfare Reporter is required to seek the views of the child [or children] on the issue(s) specified in Part 1 below.

☐ Appointment of Child Welfare Reporter under rule 33.21(1)(b).

Where this box is ticked the Child Welfare Reporter is required to carry out the enquiries specified in Part 2 below, and to address the issue(s) specified in Part 3 below.

PART 1

Issue(s) in respect of which views of the child [or children] are to be sought *[specify]*

Is a copy of the report to be provided to the parties under rule 33.21(9)(d)?

☐ Yes
☐ No

PART 2

Enquiries to be undertaken—

☐ Seek views of child

---

[1] Omitted by the Act of Sederunt (Rules of the Court of Session 1994 and Ordinary Cause Rules 1993 Amendment) (Child Welfare Reporters) 2015 (SSI 2015/312) para.4 (effective 26 October 2015).
[2] Omitted by the Act of Sederunt (Rules of the Court of Session 1994 and Ordinary Cause Rules 1993 Amendment) (Child Welfare Reporters) 2015 (SSI 2015/312) para.4 (effective 26 October 2015).
[3] As inserted by the Act of Sederunt (Rules of the Court of Session 1994 and Ordinary Cause Rules 1993 Amendment) (Child Welfare Reporters) 2015 (SSI 2015/312) para.4 (effective 26 October 2015).
[4] As amended by the Act of Sederunt (Rules of the Court of Session 1994 and Ordinary Cause Rules 1993 Amendment) (Views of the Child) 2019 (SSI 2019/123) r.3 (effective 24 June 2019).

☐   Visit home of *[specify]*
☐   Visit nursery / school / child minder / other *[specify]*
☐   Interview mother / father
☐   Interview other family members *[specify]*
☐   Interview child minder / nanny
☐   Interview teacher / head teacher
☐   Interview child's health visitor / GP / other health professional *[specify]*
☐   Interview a party's GP / other health professional *[specify]*
☐   Interview social worker *[specify]*
☐   Interview domestic abuse case worker *[specify]*
☐   Interview other persons *[specify]*
☐   Obtain criminal conviction certificate under section 112 of the Police Act 1997 in respect of *[specify party]*
☐   Observe contact *[specify]*
☐   Observe child in home environment pre/post contact *[specify]*
☐   Obtain record of parties' attendance from contact centre
☐   Other *[specify]*

PART 3

Issues to be addressed in report *[specify]*

Where the views of the child form part of the enquiries to be undertaken, should the views of the child be recorded in a separate report?

☐   Yes
☐   No

If yes, is a copy of that report to be provided to the parties under rule 33.21(9)(d)?

☐   Yes
☐   No

FORM CP1[1]

Rule 33A.7(1)(a)
Form of intimation to children and next-of-kin in an action of dissolution of civil partnership or separation of civil partners where defender's address is not known

Court ref. no.

To (*insert name and address as in warrant*)

You are given NOTICE that an action of dissolution of a civil partnership [or separation of civil partners] has been raised against (*insert name*) your (*insert relationship, e.g. father, mother, brother or other relative as the case may be*). If you know of his [or her] present address, you are requested to inform the sheriff clerk

---

[1] Inserted by Act of Sederunt (Ordinary Cause Rules) Amendment (Civil Partnership Act 2004) 2005 (SSI 2005/638), para.3 (effective December 8, 2005).

(*insert address of sheriff clerk*) in writing immediately. If you wish to appear as a party you must lodge a minute with the sheriff clerk for leave to do so. Your minute must be lodged within 21 days of (*insert date on which intimation was given. N.B. Rule 5.3(2) relating to postal service or intimation*).

Date (*insert date*)

(*Signed*)
Solicitor for the pursuer
(*insert designation and business address*)

NOTE

If you decide to lodge a minute it may be in your best interests to consult a solicitor. The minute should be lodged with the sheriff clerk together with the appropriate fee of (*insert amount*) and a copy of this intimation.

IF YOU ARE UNCERTAIN WHAT ACTION TO TAKE you should consult a solicitor. You may be entitled to legal aid depending on your financial circumstances, and you can get information about legal aid from a solicitor. You may also obtain advice from any Citizens Advice Bureau or other advice agency.

FORM CP2[1]

Rule 33A.7(1)(b)

Form of intimation to children, next-of-kin, guardian and attorney in action of dissolution of civil partnership or separation of civil partners where defender suffers from a mental disorder

Court ref. no.

To (*insert name and address as in warrant*)

You are given NOTICE that an action of dissolution of a civil partnership [*or* separation of civil partners] has been raised against (*insert name*) your (*insert relationship, e.g. father, mother, brother or other relative, ward or granter of a power of attorney as the case may be*). A copy of the initial writ is enclosed. If you wish to appear as a party, you must lodge a minute with the sheriff clerk (*insert address of sheriff clerk*), for leave to do so. Your minute must be lodged within 21 days of (*insert date on which intimation was given. N.B. Rule 5.3(2) relating to postal service or intimation*).

Date (*insert date*)

(*Signed*)
Solicitor for the pursuer
(*insert designation and business address*)

NOTE

If you decide to lodge a minute it may be in your best interests to consult a solicitor. The minute should be lodged with the sheriff clerk together with the appropriate fee of (*insert amount*) and a copy of this intimation.

IF YOU ARE UNCERTAIN WHAT ACTION TO TAKE you should consult a solicitor. You may be entitled to legal aid depending on your financial circumstances, and you can get information about legal aid from a solicitor. You may also obtain advice from any Citizens Advice Bureau or other advice agency.

FORM CP3[2]

Rule 33A.7(1)(c)(i) and (ii)

Form of intimation to a local authority or third party who may be liable to maintain a child in a civil partnership action

---

[1] Inserted by Act of Sederunt (Ordinary Cause Rules) Amendment (Civil Partnership Act 2004) 2005 (SSI 2005/638), para.3 (effective December 8, 2005).
[2] Inserted by Act of Sederunt (Ordinary Cause Rules) Amendment (Civil Partnership Act 2004) 2005 (SSI 2005/638), para.3 (effective December 8, 2005).

Court ref. no.

To (*insert name and address as in warrant*)

YOU ARE GIVEN NOTICE that in this action, the court may make an order under section 11 of the Children (Scotland) Act 1995 in respect of (*insert name and address*), a child in your care *[or liable to be maintained by you]*. A copy of the initial writ is attached. If you wish to appear as a party, you must lodge a minute with the sheriff clerk (*insert address of sheriff clerk*), for leave to do so. Your minute must be lodged within 21 days of (*insert date on which intimation was given.* N.B. Rule 5.3(2) *relating to postal service or intimation*).

Date (*insert date*)

(*Signed*)
Solicitor for the pursuer
(*insert designation and business address*)

NOTE

If you decide to lodge a minute it may be in your best interests to consult a solicitor. The minute should be lodged with the sheriff clerk together with the appropriate fee of (*insert amount*) and a copy of this intimation.

IF YOU ARE UNCERTAIN WHAT ACTION TO TAKE you should consult a solicitor. You may be entitled to legal aid depending on your financial circumstances, and you can get information about legal aid from a solicitor. You may also obtain advice from any Citizens

FORM CP4[1]

Rule 33A.7(1)(c)(iii)

Form of intimation to person who in fact exercises care or control of a child in a civil partnership action

Court ref. no.

To (*insert name and address as in warrant*)

YOU ARE GIVEN NOTICE that in this action, the court may make an order under section 11 of the Children (Scotland) Act 1995 in respect of (*insert name and address*), a child at present in your care or control. A copy of the initial writ is attached. If you wish to appear as a party, you must lodge a minute with the sheriff clerk (*insert address of sheriff clerk*), for leave to do so. Your minute must be lodged within 21 days of (*insert date on which Intimation was given.* N.B. Rule 5.3(2) *relating to postal service or intimation*).

Date (*insert date*)

(*Signed*)
Solicitor for the pursuer
(*insert designation and business address*)

NOTE

If you decide to lodge a minute it may be in your best interests to consult a solicitor. The minute should be lodged with the sheriff clerk together with the appropriate fee of (*insert amount*) and a copy of this intimation.

IF YOU ARE UNCERTAIN WHAT ACTION TO TAKE you should consult a solicitor. You may be entitled to legal aid depending on your financial circumstances, and you can get information about legal aid from a solicitor. You may also obtain advice from any Citizens Advice Bureau or other advice agency.

---

[1] Inserted by Act of Sederunt (Ordinary Cause Rules) Amendment (Civil Partnership Act 2004) 2005 (SSI 2005/638), para.3 (effective December 8, 2005).

FORM CP5[1]

Rule 33A.7(1)(d)

Form of notice to parent or guardian in a civil partnership action which includes a crave for a section 11 order in respect of a child

Court ref. no.

1. YOU ARE GIVEN NOTICE that in this action, the pursuer is applying for an order under section 11 of the Children (Scotland) Act 1995 in respect of the child (*insert name of child*). A copy of the initial writ is served on you and is attached to this notice.

2. If you wish to oppose this action, or oppose the granting of any order applied for by the pursuer in respect of the child, you must lodge a notice of intention to defend (Form CP16). See Form CP16 attached for further details.

Date (*insert date*)

(*Signed*)
Pursuer
[*or* Solicitor for the pursuer]
(*insert designation and business address*)

NOTE: IF YOU ARE UNCERTAIN WHAT ACTION TO TAKE you should consult a solicitor. You may be entitled to legal aid depending on your financial circumstances, and you can get information about legal aid from a solicitor. You may also obtain advice from any Citizens Advice Bureau or other advice agency.

FORM CP6[2]

Rule 33A.7(1)(e), 33A.7(4) and 33A.12(2) and (3)

Form of notice to local authority

Court ref. no.

To (*insert name and address*)

1. YOU ARE GIVEN NOTICE that in an action in the Sheriff Court at (*insert address*) the pursuer has applied for a residence order in respect of the child (*insert name of child*). A copy of the initial writ is enclosed.

2. If you wish to oppose this action, or oppose the granting of any order applied for by the pursuer in respect of the child, you must lodge a notice of intention to defend (Form CP16). See Form CP16 attached for further details.

Date (*insert date*)

(*Signed*)
Solicitor for the pursuer
(*insert designation and business address*)

FORM CP8[3]

Rule 33A.7(1)(g)

Form of intimation to creditor in application for order for the transfer of property under section 8 of the Family Law (Scotland) Act 1985 in a civil partnership action

Court ref. no.

To (*insert name and address as in warrant*)

You are given NOTICE that in this action, an order is sought for the transfer of property (*specify the order*), over which you hold a security. A copy of the initial

---

[1] Inserted by Act of Sederunt (Ordinary Cause Rules) Amendment (Civil Partnership Act 2004) 2005 (SSI 2005/638), para.3 (effective December 8, 2005).

[2] Inserted by Act of Sederunt (Ordinary Cause Rules) Amendment (Civil Partnership Act 2004) 2005 (SSI 2005/638), para.3 (effective December 8, 2005) and substituted by the Act of Sederunt (Sheriff Court Rules) (Miscellaneous Amendments) (No.2) 2010 (SSI 2010/416) r.7 (effective January 1, 2011).

[3] Inserted by Act of Sederunt (Ordinary Cause Rules) Amendment (Civil Partnership Act 2004) 2005 (SSI 2005/638), para.3 (effective December 8, 2005).

writ is attached. If you wish to appear as a party, you must lodge a minute with the sheriff clerk (*insert address of sheriff clerk*), for leave to do so. Your minute must be lodged within 21 days of (*insert date on which intimation was given*. N.B. Rule 5.3(2) *relating to postal service or intimation*).

Date (*insert date*)

(*Signed*)
Solicitor for the pursuer
(*insert designation and business address*)

NOTE

If you decide to lodge a minute it may be in your best interests to consult a solicitor. The minute should be lodged with the sheriff clerk together with the appropriate fee of (*insert amount*) and a copy of this intimation.

IF YOU ARE UNCERTAIN WHAT ACTION TO TAKE you should consult a solicitor. You may be entitled to legal aid depending on your financial circumstances, and you can get information about legal aid from a solicitor. You may also obtain advice from any Citizens Advice Bureau or other advice agency.

FORM CP9[1]

Rule 33A.7(1)(h)

Form of intimation in a civil partnership action where the pursuer makes an application for an order under section 18 of the Family Law (Scotland) Act 1985

Court ref. no.

To (*insert name and address as in warrant*)

You are given NOTICE that in this action, the pursuer craves the court to make an order under section 18 of the Family Law (Scotland) Act 1985. A copy of the initial writ is attached. If you wish to appear as a party, you must lodge a minute with the sheriff clerk (*insert address of sheriff clerk*), for leave to do so. Your minute must be lodged within 21 days of (*insert date on which intimation was given*. N.B. Rule 5.3(2) *relating to postal service or intimation*).

Date (*insert date*)

(*Signed*)
Solicitor for the pursuer
(*insert designation and business address*)

NOTE

If you decide to lodge a minute it may be in your best interests to consult a solicitor. The minute should be lodged with the sheriff clerk together with the appropriate fee of (*insert amount*) and a copy of this intimation.

IF YOU ARE UNCERTAIN WHAT ACTION TO TAKE you should consult a solicitor. You may be entitled to legal aid depending on your financial circumstances, and you can get information about legal aid from a solicitor. You may also obtain advice from any Citizens Advice Bureau or other advice agency.

FORM CP10[2]

Rule 33A.7(1)(i)

Form of intimation in an action where an application is made under Chapter 3 of Part 3 of the Civil Partnership Act 2004

Court ref. no

To (*insert name and address as in warrant*)

---

[1] Inserted by Act of Sederunt (Ordinary Cause Rules) Amendment (Civil Partnership Act 2004) 2005 (SSI 2005/638), para.3 (effective December 8, 2005).
[2] Inserted by Act of Sederunt (Ordinary Cause Rules) Amendment (Civil Partnership Act 2004) 2005 (SSI 2005/638), para.3 (effective December 8, 2005).

You are given NOTICE that in this action the pursuer craves the court to make an order under Section (*insert the section under which the order(s) is sought*) of Chapter 3 of Part 3 of the Civil Partnership Act 2004. A copy of the initial writ is attached. If you wish to appear as a party, you must lodge a minute with the sheriff clerk (*insert address of sheriff clerk*), for leave to do so. Your minute must be lodged within 21 days of (*insert date on which intimation was given. N.B. Rule 5.3(2) relating to postal service or intimation*).

Date (*insert date*)

(*Signed*)
Solicitor for the pursuer
(*insert designation and business address*)

NOTE

If you decide to lodge a minute it may be in your best interests to consult a solicitor. The minute should be lodged with the sheriff clerk together with the appropriate fee of (*insert amount*) and a copy of this intimation.

IF YOU ARE UNCERTAIN WHAT ACTION TO TAKE you should consult a solicitor. You may be entitled to legal aid depending on your financial circumstances, and you can get information about legal aid from a solicitor. You may also obtain advice from any Citizens Advice Bureau or other advice agency.

FORM CP11[1]

Rule 33A.7(1)(j)

Form of intimation to person responsible for pension arrangement in relation to an order for payment in respect of pension lump sum under section 12A of the Family Law (Scotland) Act 1985 in a civil partnership action

Court ref. no.

To (*insert name and address as in warrant*)

You are given NOTICE that in this action, the pursuer has applied for an order under section 8 of the Family Law (Scotland) Act 1985 for a capital sum in circumstances where the family property includes rights in a pension arrangement under which a lump sum is payable. The relevant pension arrangement is (*give brief details, including number, if known*). If you wish to appear as a party, you must lodge a minute with the sheriff clerk (*insert address of sheriff clerk*), for leave to do so. Your minute must be lodged within 21 days of (*insert date on which intimation was given. N.B. Rule 5.3(2) relating to postal service or intimation*).

Date (*insert date*)

(*Signed*)
Solicitor for the pursuer
(*insert designation and business address*)

NOTE

If you decide to lodge a minute it may be in your best interests to consult a solicitor. The minute should be lodged with the sheriff clerk together with the appropriate fee of (*insert amount*) and a copy of this intimation.

IF YOU ARE UNCERTAIN WHAT ACTION TO TAKE you should consult a solicitor. You may be entitled to legal aid depending on your financial circumstances, and you can get information about legal aid from a solicitor. You may also obtain advice from any Citizens Advice Bureau or other advice agency.

---

[1] Inserted by Act of Sederunt (Ordinary Cause Rules) Amendment (Civil Partnership Act 2004) 2005 (SSI 2005/638), para.3 (effective December 8, 2005).

FORM CP12[1]

Rule 33A.7(1)(k)

Form of intimation to person responsible for pension arrangement in relation to pension sharing order under section 8(1)(baa) of the Family Law (Scotland) Act 1985 in a civil partnership action

Court ref. no.

To (*insert name and address as in warrant*)

You are given NOTICE that in this action, the pursuer has applied under section 8 of the Family Law (Scotland) Act 1985 for a pension sharing order in circumstances where the family property includes rights in a pension arrangement. The relevant pension arrangement is (*give brief details, including number, if known*). If you wish to appear as a party, you must lodge a minute with the sheriff clerk (*insert address of sheriff clerk*), for leave to do so. Your minute must be lodged within 21 days of (*insert date on which intimation was given. N.B. Rule 5.3(2) relating to postal service or intimation*).

Date (*insert date*)

(*Signed*)
Solicitor for the pursuer
(*insert designation and business address*)

NOTE

If you decide to lodge a minute it may be in your best interests to consult a solicitor. The minute should be lodged with the sheriff clerk together with the appropriate fee of (*insert amount*) and a copy of this intimation.

IF YOU ARE UNCERTAIN WHAT ACTION TO TAKE you should consult a solicitor. You may be entitled to legal aid depending on your financial circumstances, and you can get information about legal aid from a solicitor. You may also obtain advice from any Citizens Advice Bureau or other advice agency.

FORM CP12A[2]

Rule 33A.7(1)(l)

Form of intimation to Board of the Pension Protection Fund in relation to pension compensation sharing order under section 8(1)(bab) of the Family Law (Scotland) Act 1985 in a civil partnership action

Court ref. no.

To (*insert name and address as in warrant*)

You arc given NOTICE that in this action the pursuer has applied under section 8(1)(bab) of the Family Law (Scotland) Act 1985 for a pension compensation sharing order in circumstances where the family property includes rights to Pension Protection Fund compensation. The relevant pension arrangement is (*give brief details, including number, if known*). If you wish to appear as a party, you must lodge a minute with the sheriff clerk (*insert address of sheriff clerk*), for leave to do so. Your minute must be lodged within 21 days of (*insert date on which intimation was given. N.B. Rule 5.3(2) relating to postal service or intimation*).

Date (*insert date*)

(*Signed*)
Solicitor for the pursuer
(*insert designation and business address*)

FORM CP12B[3]

Rule 33.7(1)(m)

---

[1] Inserted by Act of Sederunt (Ordinary Cause Rules) Amendment (Civil Partnership Act 2004) 2005 (SSI 2005/638), para.3 (effective December 8, 2005).

[2] As inserted by the Act of Sederunt (Sheriff Court Rules) (Miscellaneous Amendments) 2011 (SSI 2011/193) r.15 (effective April 6, 2011).

[3] As inserted by the Act of Sederunt (Sheriff Court Rules) (Miscellaneous Amendments) 2011 (SSI 2011/193) r.15 (effective April 6, 2011).

Form of intimation to Board of the Pension Protection Fund in relation to an order under section 12B(2) of the Family Law (Scotland) Act 1985 in a civil partnership action

Court ref. no.

To (*insert name and address as in warrant*)

You arc given NOTICE that in this action the pursuer has applied under section 8(1)(bb) of the Family Law (Scotland) Act 1985 for an order under section 12B(2) of the Act in circumstances where the family property includes rights to Pension Protection Fund compensation. The relevant pension arrangement is (*give brief details, including number, if known*). If you wish to appear as a party, you must lodge a minute with the sheriff clerk (*insert address of sheriff clerk*), for leave to do so. Your minute must be lodged within 21 days of (*insert date on which intimation was given. N.B. Rule 5.3(2) relating to postal service or intimation*).

Date (*insert date*)

(*Signed*)
Solicitor for the pursuer
(*insert designation and business address*)

FORM CP13[1]

Rule 33A.8(3)

Form of intimation to person with whom an association is alleged to have occurred in a civil partnership action

Court ref. no.

To (*insert name and address as in warrant*)

You are given NOTICE that in this action, the defender is alleged to have had an association with you. A copy of the initial writ is attached. If you wish to dispute the truth of the allegation made against you, you must lodge a minute with the sheriff clerk (*insert address of sheriff clerk*), for leave to appear as a party. Your minute must be lodged within 21 days of (*insert date on which intimation was given. N.B. Rule 5.3(2) relating to postal service or intimation*).

Date (*insert date*)

(*Signed*)
Solicitor for the pursuer
(*insert designation and business address*)

NOTE

If you decide to lodge a minute it may be in your best interests to consult a solicitor. The minute should be lodged with the sheriff clerk together with the appropriate fee of (*insert amount*) and a copy of this intimation.

IF YOU ARE UNCERTAIN WHAT ACTION TO TAKE you should consult a solicitor. You may be entitled to legal aid depending on your financial circumstances, and you can get information about legal aid from a solicitor. You may also obtain advice from any Citizens Advice Bureau or other advice agency.

Rules 33A.9(5) and 33A.34(4) **FORM CP13A[2]**

Form of statement of civil partnership property in the cause
SHERIFFDOM OF (*insert name of sheriffdom*)
AT (*insert place of sheriff court*)
[A.B.], (*insert designation and address*, Pursuer against

---

[1] Inserted by Act of Sederunt (Ordinary Cause Rules) Amendment (Civil Partnership Act 2004) 2005 (SSI 2005/638), para.3(effective December 8, 2005).
[2] As inserted by the Act of Sederunt (Sheriff Court Rules) (Miscellaneous Amendments) 2012 (SSI 2012/188) para.4 (effective August 1, 2012).

[C.D..], (*insert designation and address*, Defender Court ref. no:

The [Pursuer] [Defender]'s* financial position at (*insert date*), being the relevant date as defined in section 10(3) of the Family Law (Scotland) Act 1985
Here list all assets owned by you, including assets which are jointly owned (if any) e.g. bank or building society accounts; shares or other investments; houses; land; pension entitlement; and life policies:
Here list your outstanding debts including joint debts with the other party:
Date (*insert date*)
I certify that this information is correct to the best of my knowledge and belief. (*Signed*)
[Pursuer][Defender]*

(*delete as applicable)

FORM CP14[1]

Rule 33A.10

Form of warrant of citation in civil partnership action

Court Ref. No. (*insert*)

(*Insert place and date*)

Grants warrant to cite the defender (*insert name and address of defender*) by serving upon him [*or* her] a copy of the writ and warrant upon a period of notice of (*insert period of notice*) days, and ordains the defender to lodge a notice of intention to defend with the sheriff clerk at (*insert address of sheriff court*) if he [*or* she] wishes to:

   (a)   challenge the jurisdiction of the court;
   (b)   oppose any claim made or order sought;
   (c)   make any claim or seek any order.

[Meantime grants interim interdict, *or* warrant to arrest on the dependence.]

   [*Where a crave for a section 11 order is sought, one of the following must also be included:*

   *Subject to the requirements of rule 33A.7A(6), grants warrant for intimation and the seeking of views in Form F9 to (*insert child(ren)'s name(s) and address(es)*).

   *Dispenses with intimation and the seeking of views in Form F9 to (*insert child(ren)'s name(s) and address(es)*) for the following reason(s): (*insert summary of reasons*).

   Delete as appropriate.]

(*Signed*)
Sheriff

Form of warrant of citation in a civil partnership action

Court ref. no.

(*Insert place and date*)

Grants warrant to cite the defender (*insert name and address of defender*) by serving upon him [*or* her] a copy of the writ and warrant upon a period of notice of (*insert period of notice*) days, and ordains the defender to lodge a notice of intention to defend with the sheriff clerk at (*insert address of sheriff court*), if he [*or* she] wishes to:

[1] As amended by the Act of Sederunt (Rules of the Court of Session 1994 and Ordinary Cause Rules 1993 Amendment) (Views of the Child) 2019 (SSI 2019/123) r.3 (effective 24 June 2019).

(a)   challenge the jurisdiction of the court;
(b)   oppose any claim made or order sought;
(c)   make any claim or seek any order.
[Meantime grants interim interdict, or warrant to arrest on the dependence].

Rule 33A.11(1) and 33A.13(1)(a)   **FORM CP15**[1]

Form of citation in a civil partnership action
CITATION
SHERIFFDOM OF (*insert name of sheriffdom*)
AT (*insert place of sheriff court*)
[A.B.], (*insert designation and address*), Pursuer, against [C.D.], (*insert designation and address*), Defender.
(*Insert place and date*)

Court ref. no.

You [C.D.], are hereby served with this copy writ and warrant, with Form CP16 (notice of intention to defend) [and (*insert details of any other form of notice served, e.g. any of the forms served in accordance with* rule 33A.14.)].

Form CP16 is served on you for use should you wish to intimate an intention to defend the action.

IF YOU WISH TO—
(a)   challenge the jurisdiction of the court;
(b)   oppose any claim made or order sought;
(c)   make any claim; or
(d)   seek any order;

you should consult a solicitor with a view to lodging a notice of intention to defend (Form CP16). The notice of intention to defend, together with the court fee of £ (*insert amount*) must be lodged with the sheriff clerk at the above address within 21 days (*or insert appropriate period of notice*) of (*insert the date on which service was executed. N.B.* Rule 5.3(2) *relating to postal service or intimation*).

IF YOU ARE UNCERTAIN WHAT ACTION TO TAKE you should consult a solicitor. You may be entitled to legal aid depending on your financial circumstances, and you can get information about legal aid from a solicitor. You may also obtain advice from any Citizens Advice Bureau or other advice agency.

PLEASE NOTE THAT IF YOU DO NOTHING IN ANSWER TO THIS DOCUMENT the court may regard you as admitting the claim made against you and the pursuer may obtain decree against you in your absence.

(*Signed*)
[P.Q.], Sheriff officer
[*or*
[X.Y.], (*insert designation and business address*)
Solicitor for the pursuer]

Rules 33A.11(1) and 33A.34(2)(a)   **FORM CP16**[2, 3]

Form of notice of intention to defend in a civil partnership action
Notice of Intention to Defend

---

[1] Inserted by Act of Sederunt (Ordinary Cause Rules) Amendment (Civil Partnership Act 2004) 2005 (SSI 2005/638), para.3 (effective December 8, 2005).
[2] Inserted by Act of Sederunt (Ordinary Cause Rules) Amendment (Civil Partnership Act 2004) 2005 (SSI 2005/638), para.3 (effective December 8, 2005).
[3] As amended by the Act of Sederunt (Rules of the Court of Session 1994 and Ordinary Cause Rules 1993 Amendment) (Views of the Child) 2019 (SSI 2019/123) r.3 (effective 24 June 2019).

Part A

PART A

(This section to be completed by the pursuer's solicitor before service.)

[Insert name and business address of solicitor for the pursuer]

Court ref. No.

In an action brought in Sheriff Court

Pursuer

Defender

Date of service

Date of expiry of period of notice

Part B

(This section to be completed by the defender or defender's solicitor, and both parts of the form to be returned to the Sheriff Clerk at the above Sheriff Court on or before the date of expiry of the period of notice referred to in Part A above.)

(Insert place and date)

[C.D.] *(Insert designation and address)*, Defender, intends to

(a) challenge the jurisdiction of the court;
(b) oppose a crave in the initial writ;
(c) make a claim;
(d) seek an order;

in the action against him [*or* her] raised by [A.B.], *(insert designation and address)*, Pursuer.

Part C

(This section to be completed by the defender or the defender's solicitor where an order under section 11 of the Children (Scotland) Act 1995 in respect of a child is opposed by the defender).

DO YOU WISH TO OPPOSE THE MAKING OF ANY ORDER CRAVED BY THE PURSUER IN RESPECT OF A CHILD?

YES/NO*

*delete as appropriate

If you answered YES to the above question, please state here the order(s) which you wish to oppose and the reasons why the court should not make such order(s).

Part D

(This section to be completed by the defender or the defender's solicitor where an order under section 11 of the Children (Scotland) Act 1995 in respect of a child is sought by the defender).

DO YOU WISH THE COURT TO MAKE ANY ORDER UNDER SECTION 11 OF THE CHILDREN (SCOTLAND) ACT 1995 IN RESPECT OF A CHILD?

YES/NO*

*delete as appropriate

If you answered YES to the above question, please state here the order(s) which you wish the court to make and the reasons why the court should make such order(s).

Part E

IF YOU HAVE ANSWERED YES AT PART D OF THIS FORM AND THE INITIAL WRIT DOES NOT INCLUDE A CRAVE FOR A SECTION 11 ORDER, YOU MUST INCLUDE EITHER CRAVE (1) OR (2) BELOW (*delete as appropriate)

(1)   * Warrant for intimation to the child(ren) (insert full name(s) and date(s) of birth) is sought, by way of Form F9, which also seeks the child(ren)'s views.

(2)   * I seek to dispense with intimation to the child(ren) (insert full name(s) and date(s) of birth) and seeking the child(ren)'s views in Form F9 for the following reasons:—

Signed

[C.D.] Defender [or [X.Y.]

(*add designation and business address*)

Solicitor for Defender]

Rule 33A.11(2)   **FORM CP17**[1]

Form of certificate of citation in a civil partnership action

Certificate of Citation

(*Insert place and date*) I,.......... hereby certify that upon the.......... day of.......... I duly cited [C.D.], Defender, to answer to the foregoing writ. This I did by (*state method of service; if by-officer and not by post, add*: in the presence of [L.M.], (*insert designation*), witness hereto with me subscribing; *and insert details of any forms of intimation or notice sent including details of the person to whom intimation sent and the method of service*).

(*Signed*)

[P.Q.], Sheriff officer

[L.M.], witness

[*or*

[X.Y.] (*add designation and business address*)

Solicitor for the pursuer]

Rule 33A.13(1)(c)   **FORM CP18**[2]

Form of request to medical officer of hospital or similar institution in a civil partnership action

To (*insert name and address of medical officer*)

In terms of rule 33A.13(1)(c) of the Ordinary Cause Rulesof the Sheriff Court a copy of the initial writ at the instance of (*insert name and address of pursuer*), Pursuer, against (*insert name and address of defender*), Defender, is enclosed and you are requested to

(a)   deliver it personally to (*insert name of defender*), and

(b)   explain the contents to him or her,

unless you are satisfied that such delivery or explanation would be dangerous to his or her health or mental condition. You are further requested to complete and return to me in the enclosed stamped addressed envelope the certificate appended hereto, making necessary deletions.

Date (insert date)..........   (*Signed*)..........

---

[1] Inserted by Act of Sederunt (Ordinary Cause Rules) Amendment (Civil Partnership Act 2004) 2005 (SSI 2005/638), para.3 (effective December 8, 2005).

[2] Inserted by Act of Sederunt (Ordinary Cause Rules) Amendment (Civil Partnership Act 2004) 2005 (SSI 2005/638), para.3 (effective December 8, 2005).

Solicitor for the pursuer
(*insert designation and business address*)

Rule 33A.13(1)(d) and 33A.13(2)   **FORM CP19**[1]

Form of certificate by medical officer of hospital or similar institution in a civil partnership action

Court ref. no.

I (*insert name and designation*) certify that I have received a copy initial writ in an action of (*type of civil partnership action to be inserted by the party requesting service*) at the instance of (*insert name and designation*), Pursuer, against (*insert name and designation*), Defender, and that

* I have on.......... day of.......... personally delivered a copy thereof to the said defender who is under my care at (*insert address*) and I have explained the contents or purport thereof to him or her, *or*

* I have not delivered a copy thereof to the said defender who is under my care at (*insert address*) and I have not explained the contents thereof to him or her because (*state reasons*).

Date (*insert date*)

(*Signed*)

Medical officer (*add designation and address*)
* Delete as appropriate.

Rule 33A.14(1)(a)(i)   **FORM CP20**[2]

Form of notice to defender where it is stated that defender consents to granting decree of dissolution of a civil partnership

YOU ARE GIVEN NOTICE that the copy initial writ served on you with this notice states that you consent to the grant of decree of dissolution of your civil partnership.

1. If you do so consent the consequences for you are that—
    [3](a) provided the pursuer establishes the fact that he [*or* she] has not cohabited with you at any time during a continuous period of one year after the date of registration of your civil partnership and immediately preceding the bringing of this action and that you consent, a decree of dissolution of your civil partnership will be granted;
    (b) on the grant of a decree of dissolution of your civil partnership you may lose your rights of succession to the pursuer's estate; and
    (c) decree of dissolution will end your civil partnership thereby affecting any right to such pension as may depend on the civil partnership continuing, or, your right to any state pension that may have been payable to you on the death of your civil partner.

Apart from these, there may be other consequences for you depending upon your particular circumstances.

2. You are entitled, whether or not you consent to the grant of decree of dis-

---

[1] Inserted by Act of Sederunt (Ordinary Cause Rules) Amendment (Civil Partnership Act 2004) 2005 (SSI 2005/638), para.3 (effective December 8, 2005).
[2] Inserted by Act of Sederunt (Ordinary Cause Rules) Amendment (Civil Partnership Act 2004) 2005 (SSI 2005/638), para.3 (effective December 8, 2005).
[3] As amended by Act of Sederunt (Ordinary Cause Rules) Amendment (Family Law (Scotland) Act 2006 etc.) 2006, para.2 (SSI 2006/207) (effective May 4, 2006).

solution of your civil partnership, to apply to the sheriff in this action—

    (a)   to make financial or other provision for you under the Family Law (Scotland) Act 1985;

    (b)   for an order under section 11 of the Children (Scotland) Act 1995 in respect of any child of the family within the meaning of section 101(7) of the Civil Partnership Act 2004; or

    (c)   for any other competent order.

3.   IF YOU WISH TO APPLY FOR ANY OF THE ABOVE ORDERS you should consult a solicitor with a view to lodging a notice of intention to defend (Form CP16).

4.   If, after consideration, you wish to consent to the grant of decree of dissolution of your civil partnership in this action, you should complete and sign the attached notice of consent (Form CP21) and send it to the sheriff clerk at the sheriff court referred to in the initial writ within 21 days of (*insert the date on which service was executed N.B.* Rule 5.3(2) *relating to postal service*).

5.   If, at a later stage, you wish to withdraw your consent to decree being granted against you in this action, you must inform the sheriff clerk immediately in writing.

Date (*insert date*)

(*Signed*)
Solicitor for the pursuer
(*insert designation and business address*)

Rules 33A.14(1)(a)(i) and 33A.18(1)   **FORM CP21**[1]

Form of notice of consent in actions of dissolution of a civil partnership under section 117(3)(c) of the Civil Partnership Act 2004

Court ref. no.

[A.B.], (*insert designation and address*), Pursuer, against [C.D.], (*insert designation and address*), Defender.

I, (*full name and address of the defender to be inserted by pursuer or pursuer's solicitor before sending notice*) have received a copy of the initial writ in the action against me at the instance of (*full name and address of pursuer to be inserted by pursuer or pursuer's solicitor before sending notice*). I understand that it states that I consent to the grant of decree of dissolution of the civil partnership in this action. I have considered the consequences for me mentioned in the notice (Form CP20) sent to me with this notice. I consent to the grant of decree of dissolution of the civil partnership in this action.

Date (insert date)..........   (Signed)

                                    Defender

Rule 33A.14(1)(a)(ii)   **FORM CP22**[2]

Form of notice to defender where it is stated that defender consents to the granting of decree of separation of civil partners

---

[1] Inserted by Act of Sederunt (Ordinary Cause Rules) Amendment (Civil Partnership Act 2004) 2005 (SSI 2005/638), para.3 (effective December 8, 2005).

[2] Inserted by Act of Sederunt (Ordinary Cause Rules) Amendment (Civil Partnership Act 2004) 2005 (SSI 2005/638), para.3 (effective December 8, 2005).

YOU ARE GIVEN NOTICE that the copy initial writ served on you with this notice states that you consent to the grant of decree of separation of you and your civil partner.

1.   If you do so consent the consequences for you are that—

[1](a)   provided the pursuer establishes the fact that he [*or* she] has not cohabited with you at any time during a continuous period of one year after the date of registration of your civil partnership and immediately preceding the bringing of this action and that you consent, a decree of separation of civil partners will be granted;

(b)   on the grant of a decree of separation of civil partners you will be obliged to live apart from the pursuer but the civil partnership will continue to subsist; you will continue to have a legal obligation to support your civil partner and any child of the family within the meaning of section 101(7) of the Civil Partnership Act 2004; and

Apart from these, there may be other consequences for you depending upon your particular circumstances.

2.   You are entitled, whether or not you consent to the grant of decree of separation of civil partners, to apply to the sheriff in this action—

(a)   to make financial or other provision for you under the Family Law (Scotland) Act 1985;

(b)   for an order under section 11 of the Children (Scotland) Act 1995 in respect of any child of the family within the meaning of section 101(7) of the Civil Partnership Act 2004; or

(c)   for any other competent order.

3.   IF YOU WISH TO APPLY FOR ANY OF THE ABOVE ORDERS you should consult a solicitor with a view to lodging a notice of intention to defend (Form CP16).

4.   If, after consideration, you wish to consent to the grant of decree of separation of civil partners in this action, you should complete and sign the attached notice of consent (Form CP23) and send it to the sheriff clerk at the sheriff court referred to in the initial writ and other papers within 21 days of (*insert the date on which service was executed. N.B.* Rule 5.3(2) *relating to postal service or intimation*).

5.   If, at a later stage, you wish to withdraw your consent to decree being granted against you in this action, you must inform the sheriff clerk immediately in writing.

Date (*insert date*)

(*Signed*)

Solicitor for the pursuer (*add designation and business address*)

Rules 33A.14(1)(a)(ii) and 33A.18(1)   **FORM CP23**[2]

Form of notice of consent in actions of separation of civil partners under section 120 of the Civil Partnership Act 2004

Court ref. no

---

[1] As amended by Act of Sederunt (Ordinary Cause Rules) Amendment (Family Law (Scotland) Act 2006 etc.) 2006, para.2 (SSI 2006/207) (effective May 4, 2006).

[2] Inserted by Act of Sederunt (Ordinary Cause Rules) Amendment (Civil Partnership Act 2004) 2005 (SSI 2005/638), para.3 (effective December 8, 2005).

[A.B.], (*insert designation and address*), Pursuer against [C.D.], (*insert designation and address*), Defender.

I, (*full name and address of the defender to be inserted by pursuer or pursuer's solicitor before sending notice*) confirm that I have received a copy of the initial writ in the action against me at the instance of (*full name and address of pursuer to be inserted by pursuer or pursuer's solicitor before sending notice*). I understand that it states that I consent to the grant of decree of separation of civil partners in this action. I have considered the consequences for me mentioned in the notice (Form CP22) sent together with this notice. I consent to the grant of decree of separation of civil partners in this action.

Date (*insert date*)

(Signed)
Defender

Rule 33A.14(1)(b)(i)   **FORM CP24**[1, 2]

Form of notice to defender in an action for dissolution of a civil partnership where it is stated there has been two years' non-cohabitation

YOU ARE GIVEN NOTICE that—

1. The copy initial writ served on you with this notice states that there has been no cohabitation between you and the pursuer at any time during a continuous period of two years after the date of registration of the civil partnership and immediately preceding the commencement of this action. If the pursuer establishes this as a fact and the sheriff is satisfied that the civil partnership has broken down irretrievably, a decree will be granted.

2. Decree of dissolution will end the civil partnership thereby affecting any right to such pension as may depend on the civil partnership continuing or your right to any state pension that may have been payable to you on the death of your civil partner. You may also lose your rights of succession to the pursuer's estate.

3. You are entitled, whether or not you dispute that there has been no such cohabitation during that five year period, to apply to the sheriff in this action—

    (a) to make financial or other provision for you under the Family Law (Scotland) Act

    (b) for an order under section 11 of the Children (Scotland) Act 1995 in respect of any child of the family within the meaning of section 101(7) of the Civil Partnership Act 2004; or

    (c) for any other competent order.

4. IF YOU WISH TO APPLY FOR ANY OF THE ABOVE ORDERS you should consult a solicitor with a view to lodging a notice of intention to defend (Form CP16).

Date (*insert date*)

(Signed)
Solicitor for the pursuer (add designation and business address)

---

[1] Inserted by Act of Sederunt (Ordinary Cause Rules) Amendment (Civil Partnership Act 2004) 2005 (SSI 2005/638), para.3 (effective December 8, 2005).

[2] As amended by Act of Sederunt (Ordinary Cause Rules) Amendment (Family Law (Scotland) Act 2006 etc.) 2006, para.2 (SSI 2006/207) (effective May 4, 2006).

Rule 33A.14(1)(b)(ii)   **FORM CP25**[1, 2]

Form of notice to defender in an action for separation of civil partners where it is
stated there has been two years' non-cohabitation

YOU ARE GIVEN NOTICE that—

1.   The copy initial writ served on you with this notice states that there has been
     no cohabitation between you and the pursuer at any time during a continu-
     ous period of five years after the date of registration of the civil partnership
     and immediately preceding the commencement of this action. If the pursuer
     establishes this as a fact and the sheriff is satisfied that there are grounds
     justifying a decree of separation of civil partners, a decree will be granted.

2.   On the granting of decree of separation you will be obliged to live apart
     from the pursuer but the civil partnership will continue to subsist. You will
     continue to have a legal obligation to support your civil partner and any
     child of the family within the meaning of section 101(7) of the Civil Partner-
     ship Act 2004.

3.   You are entitled, whether or not you dispute that there has been no such
     cohabitation during that two year period, to apply to the sheriff in this ac-
     tion—

     (a)   to make provision under the Family Law (Scotland) Act 1985;

     (b)   for an order under section 11 of the Children (Scotland) Act 1995 in
           respect of any child of the family within the meaning of section
           101(7) of the Civil Partnership Act 2004; or

     (c)   for any other competent order.

4.   IF YOU WISH TO APPLY FOR ANY OF THE ABOVE ORDERS you
     should consult a solicitor with a view to lodging a notice of intention to
     defend (Form CP16).

Date (*insert date*)

                                                                    (*Signed*)
                    Solicitor for the pursuer (*add designation and business address*)

Rule 33A.14(1)(c)   **FORM CP25A**[3]

Form of notice to defender in action of dissolution of civil partnership where an
interim gender recognition certificate has been issued

YOU ARE GIVEN NOTICE that—

1.   The copy initial writ served on you together with this notice states that an
     interim gender recognition certificate has been issued to you [*or* the pursuer].
     If the pursuer establishes this as a fact, decree will be granted.

2.   Decree of dissolution will end the civil partnership thereby affecting any
     right to such pension as may depend on the civil partnership continuing or
     your right to any state pension that may have been payable to you on the
     death of your civil partner. You may also lose your rights of succession to
     the pursuer's estate.

3.   If the pursuer is entitled to decree of dissolution you are nevertheless entitled
     to apply to the sheriff in this action—

---

[1] Inserted by Act of Sederunt (Ordinary Cause Rules) Amendment (Civil Partnership Act 2004) 2005
(SSI 2005/638), para.3 (effective December 8, 2005).

[2] As amended by Act of Sederunt (Ordinary Cause Rules) Amendment (Family Law (Scotland) Act
2006 etc.) 2006, para.2 (SSI 2006/207) (effective May 4, 2006).

[3] Inserted by Act of Sederunt (Ordinary Cause Rules) Amendment (Family Law (Scotland) Act 2006
etc.) 2006, para.2 (SSI 2006/207) (effective 4 May 2006).

   (a)   to make financial or other provision for you under the Family Law (Scotland) Act 1985;

   (b)   for an order under section 11 of the Children (Scotland) Act 1995 in respect of any child of the family within the meaning of section 101(7) of the Civil Partnership Act 2004; or

   (c)   for any other competent order.

  4.   IF YOU WISH TO APPLY FOR ANY OF THE ABOVE ORDERS you should consult a solicitor with a view to lodging a notice of intention to defend (Form CP16).

Date (*insert date*)

(*Signed*)

Solicitor for the pursuer (*add designation and business address*)

Rule 33A.23(2)   **FORM CP26**[1]

Form of intimation to parties of a Child Welfare Hearing in a civil partnership action

Sheriff court (*insert address and telephone number*).......... Court ref. no.

In this action [A.B.], (*design*), Pursuer, against [C.D.] (*design*), Defender

YOU ARE GIVEN NOTICE that a Child Welfare Hearing has been fixed for (*insert time*) on (*insert date*) at (*insert place*).

Date (*insert date*)

Signed....................

Sheriff Clerk (Depute)

Rule 33A.30(1)(b)   **FORM CP27**[2]

Form of minute for decree in a civil partnership action to which rule 33A.29 applies

(*Insert name of solicitor for the pursuer*) having considered the evidence contained in the affidavits and the other documents all as specified in the schedule hereto, and being satisfied that upon the evidence a motion for decree (in terms of the crave of initial writ) [*or in such restricted terms as may be appropriate*] may be properly be made, moves the court accordingly.

In respect whereof

Signed

Solicitor for the Pursuer (*add designation and business address*)

Schedule

(*Number and specify documents considered*)

Rules 33A.65(1) and 33A.65(2)   **FORM CP28**[3, 4]

Form of certificate of delivery of documents to chief constable in a civil partnership action

---

[1] Inserted by Act of Sederunt (Ordinary Cause Rules) Amendment (Civil Partnership Act 2004) 2005 (SSI 2005/638), para.3 (effective 8 December 2005).

[2] Inserted by Act of Sederunt (Ordinary Cause Rules) Amendment (Civil Partnership Act 2004) 2005 (SSI 2005/638), para.3 (effective 8 December 2005).

[3] Inserted by Act of Sederunt (Ordinary Cause Rules) Amendment (Civil Partnership Act 2004) 2005 (SSI 2005/638), para.3 (effective 8 December 2005).

[4] As amended by Act of Sederunt (Ordinary Cause Rules) Amendment (Family Law (Scotland) Act 2006 etc.) 2006, para.2 (SSI 2006/207) (effective 4 May 2006).

[*Omitted by* Act of Sederunt (Ordinary Cause Rules) Amendment (Family Law (Scotland) Act 2006 etc.) 2006, para.2 (SSI 2006/207) *(effective May 4, 2006).*]

Rule 33A.67(1)   **FORM CP29**[1, 2, 3, 4]

Form of simplified dissolution of civil partnership application under section 117(3)(c) of the Civil Partnership Act 2004

Sheriff Clerk

Sheriff Court House

....

....

(Telephone)...............

APPLICATION FOR DISSOLUTION OF A CIVIL PARTNERSHIP WITH CONSENT OF OTHER PARTY TO THE CIVIL PARTNERSHIP (CIVIL PART-NERS HAVING LIVED APART FOR AT LEAST ONE YEAR)

Before completing this form, you should have read the leaflet entitled "Do it yourself Dissolution", which explains the circumstances in which a dissolution of a civil partnership may be sought by this method. If the simplified procedure appears to suit your circumstances, you may use this form to apply for dissolution of your civil partnership. Below you will find directions designed to assist you with your application. Please follow them carefully. In the event of difficulty, you may contact any sheriff clerk's office or Citizen Advice Bureau.

Directions for making application

Write In Ink, Using Block Capitals

Application (Part 1)	1. Complete and sign Part 1 of the form (pages 3-7), paying particular attention to the notes opposite each section.
Consent of civil partner (Part 2)	2. When you have completed Part 1 of the form, attach the (blue) instruction civil partner sheet SP3 to it and send both documents to your civil partner for completion of the consent at Part 2 (page 9).
	NOTE: If your civil partner does **NOT** complete and sign the form of consent, your application cannot proceed further under the simplified procedure. In that event, if you still wish to obtain a dissolution of your civil partnership, you should consult a solicitor.
Affidavit (Part 3)	3. When the application has been returned to you with the consent (Part

---

[1] Inserted by Act of SEderunt (Ordinary Cause Rules) Amendment (Civil Partnership Act 2004) 2005 (SSI 2005/638), para.3 (effective 8 December 2005),

[2] As amended by Act of Sederunt (Ordinary Cause Rules) Amendment (Family Law (Scotland) Act 2006 etc.) 2006, para.2 (SSI 2006/207) (effective 4 May 2006).

[3] As amended by the Act of Sederunt (Rules of the Court of Session 1994 and Sheriff Court Rules Amendment) (Curators ad litem) 2017 (SSI 2017/132) r.2(6)(d) (effective 1 June 2017 subject to saving specified in SSI 2017/132 r.4).

[4] As amended by the Act of Sederunt (Rules of the Court of Session 1994 and Sheriff Court Rules Amendment) (Miscellaneous) 2021 (SSI 2021/75) r.3(4)(d) (effective 1 March 2021).

2) duly completed and signed, you should take the form to a Justice of the Peace, Notary Public, Commissioner for Oaths or other duly authorised person so that your affidavit at Part 3 (page 10) may be completed and sworn.

Returning completed application form to court

4. When directions 1–3 above have been complied with, your application is now ready to be sent to the sheriff clerk at the above address. With it you must enclose:

(i) an extract of the registration of your civil partnership in the civil partnership register (the document headed "Extract of an entry in the Register of Civil Partnerships", which will be returned to you in due course), or an equivalent document, and

(ii) either a cheque or postal order in respect of the court fee, crossed and made payable to "the Scottish Courts and Tribunals Service",

or a completed form SP15, claiming exemption from the court fee.

5. Receipt of your application will be promptly acknowledged. Should you wish to withdraw the application for any reason, please contact the sheriff clerk immediately.

PART 1
WRITE IN INK, USING BLOCK CAPITALS
1. NAME AND ADDRESS OF APPLICANT

Surname ....

Other name(s) in full ....

....

Present address ....

....

Daytime telephone number (if any) ....

2. NAME AND ADDRESS OF CIVIL PARTNER

Surname ....

Other name(s) in full ....

....

Present address ....

....

Daytime telephone number (if any) ....

3. JURISDICTION

Please indicate with a tick (✔) in the appropriate box or boxes which of the following apply:

Please complete both Part A and Part B

PART A

(i)	I am domiciled in Scotland on the date I signed this application	☐
(ii)	My civil partner is domiciled in Scotland on the date I signed this application	☐
(iii)	I was habitually resident in Scotland throughout the period of one year ending with the date I signed this application	☐
(iv)	My civil partner was habitually resident in Scotland throughout the period of one year ending with the date I signed this application	☐

PART B

(i)	I have lived at the address shown above for at least 40 days immediately before the date I signed this application	☐
(ii)	My civil partner has lived at the address shown above for at least 40 days immediately before the date I signed this application	☐
(iii)	I lived at the address shown above for a period of at least 40 days ending not more than 40 days before the date I signed this application and have no known residence in Scotland at that date	☐
(iv)	My civil partner lived at the address shown above for a period of at least 40 days ending not more than 40 days before the date I signed this application and has no known residence in Scotland at that date	☐

4. DETAILS OF PRESENT CIVIL PARTNERSHIP

Place of Registration of Civil Partnership...............(Registration District)
Date of Registration of Civil Partnership: Day..........month..........year..........

5. PERIOD OF SEPARATION

(i) Please state the date on which you ceased to live with your civil partner. (If more than 1 year, just give the month and year)
Day..........Month..........Year..........

(ii) Have you lived with your civil partner since that date?   *[YES/NO]

(iii) If yes, for how long in total did you live together before finally separating again?

..........months

6. RECONCILIATION

Is there any reasonable prospect of reconciliation with your civil partner?   *[YES/NO]

Do you consider that the civil partnership has broken down irretrievably?   *[YES/NO]

7. CONSENT

Does your civil partner consent to a dissolution of the civil partnership being granted?   *[YES/NO]

8. MENTAL DISORDER

As far as you are aware, does your civil partner have any mental   *[YES/NO]
disorder (whether mental illness, personality disorder or learning disability)?

Is your civil partner suffering from any mental disorder   *[YES/NO]
(whether illness or handicap)?(If yes, give details)

9. CHILDREN

Are there any children of the family under the age of 16?   *[YES/NO]

10. Other Court Actions

Are you aware of any court actions currently proceeding in any   *[YES/NO]
country (including Scotland) which may affect your civil
partnership?

(If yes, give details)

* Delete as appropriate

11. REQUEST FOR DISSOLUTION OF THE CIVIL PARTNERSHIP AND DISCLAIMER OF FINANCIAL PROVISION

I confirm that the facts stated in paragraphs 1–10 above apply to my civil partnership.

I do NOT ask the sheriff to make any financial provision in connection with this application.

I request the sheriff to grant decree of dissolution of my civil partnership.

Date ....   Signature of Applicant ....

IMPORTANT

Part 1 MUST be completed, signed and dated before sending the application form to your civil partner.

Part 2

Notice to Consenting Civil Partner

(Insert name and address of consenting civil partner)

CONSENT TO APPLICATION FOR DISSOLUTION OF A CIVIL PARTNER-SHIP (CIVIL PARTNERS HAVING LIVED APART FOR AT LEAST ONE YEAR)

In Part 1 of the enclosed application form your civil partner is applying for dissolution of your civil partnership on the ground the civil partnership has broken down irretrievably because you and he [*or* she] have lived apart for at least one year and you consent to the dissolution being granted.

Such consent must be given formally in writing at Part 2 of the application form. BEFORE completing that part, you are requested to read it over carefully so that you understand the effect of consenting to the dissolution of the civil partnership. Thereafter if you wish to consent—

(a)   check the details given by the Applicant at Part 1 of the form to ensure that they are correct to the best of your knowledge;

(b)   complete Part 2 (Consent by Applicant's civil partner to dissolution) by entering your name and address at the appropriate place and adding your signature and the date; and

(c)   return the whole application form to your civil partner at the address given in Part 1.

Once your civil partner has completed the remainder of the form and has submitted it to the court, a copy of the whole application (including your consent) will later be served upon you formally by the sheriff clerk.

In the event of the dissolution of the civil partnership being granted, you will automatically be sent a copy of the extract decree. (Should you change your address before receiving the copy extract decree, please notify the sheriff clerk immediately.)

If you do NOT wish to consent please return the application form, with Part 2 uncompleted, to your civil partner and advise him or her of your decision.

The sheriff will NOT grant a dissolution of your civil partnership on this application if Part 2 of the form is not completed by you.

CONSENT BY APPLICANT'S CIVIL PARTNER TO DISSOLUTION OF CIVIL PARTNERSHIP

NOTE: Before completing this part of the form, please read the notes opposite (page 8)

I, ...

(Insert full name, in BLOCK letters, of Applicant's civil partner)

residing at ....

....

....

(Insert address, also in BLOCK letters)

HEREBY STATE THAT

(a)   I have read Part 1 of this application;

(b)   the Applicant has lived apart from me for a continuous period of one year immediately preceding the date of the application (paragraph 11 of Part 1);

(c)   I do not ask the sheriff to make any financial provision for me including—

    (i)   the payment by the Applicant of a periodical allowance (i.e. a regular payment of money weekly or monthly, etc. for maintenance);

    (ii)   the payment by the Applicant of a capital sum (i.e. a lump sum payment);

(d)   I understand that dissolution of my civil partnership may result in the loss to me of property rights; and

(e)   I CONSENT TO DECREE OF DISSOLUTION BEING GRANTED IN RESPECT OF THIS APPLICATION

Date ....   Signature ....

NOTE: You may withdraw your consent, even after giving it, at any time before the dissolution of the civil partnership is granted by the sheriff. Should you wish to do so, please contact the sheriff clerk immediately.

Part 3

APPLICANT'S AFFIDAVIT

To be completed by the Applicant only after Parts 1 and 2 have been signed and dated.

I, *(Insert Applicant's full name)* ....

residing at *(insert Applicant's present home address)* ....

....

....

SWEAR that to the best of my knowledge and belief:

(1)   the facts stated in Part 1 of this Application are true; and

(2)   the signature in Part 2 of this Application is that of my civil partner.

Signature of Applicant ....

SWORN at *(insert place)* ....

To be   this..........day of..........20..........

completed by

Justice of the
Peace,

Notary Public   before me (*insert full name*) ....
or Commis-
sioner for

Oaths   (*insert full address*) ....

....

....

Signature ....
*Justice of the Peace/ Notary Public/Commissioner for Oaths
* Delete as appropriate

Rule 33A.67(2)[1, 2, 3]
FORM CP30[4]
Form of simplified dissolution of civil partnership application under section
117(3)(d) of the Civil Partnership Act 2004

Sheriff Clerk
Sheriff Court House

....

....

(Telephone)...............

APPLICATION FOR DISSOLUTION OF A CIVIL PARTNERSHIP (CIVIL
PARTNERS HAVING LIVED APART FOR AT LEAST TWO YEARS)

Before completing this form, you should have read the leaflet entitled "Do it
yourself Dissolution", which explains the circumstances in which a dissolution of a
civil partnership may be sought by this method. If the simplified procedure appears
to suit your circumstances, you may use this form to apply for dissolution of your
civil partnership. Below you will find directions designed to assist you with your
application. Please follow them carefully. In the event of difficulty, you may contact
any sheriff clerk's office or Citizen Advice Bureau.
Directions for making application
WRITE IN INK, USING BLOCK CAPITALS

Application   1. Complete and sign Part 1 of the form (pages 3–7), paying
(Part 1)   particular attention to the notes opposite each section.
Affidavit (Part 2. When you have completed Part 1, you should take the form to
2)   a Justice of the Peace, Notary Public, Commissioner for Oaths
                 or other duly authorised person so that your affidavit at Part 2
                 (page 8) may be completed and sworn.

---

[1] Inserted by Act of Sederunt (Ordinary Cause Rules) Amendment (Civil Partnership Act 2004) 2005 (SSI 2005/638), para.3 (effective 8 December 2005).
[2] As amended by Act of Sederunt (Ordinary Cause Rules) Amendment (Family Law (Scotland) Act 2006 etc.) 2006, para.2 (SSI 2006/207) (effective 4 May 2006).
[3] As amended by the Act of Sederunt (Rules of the Court of Session 1994 and Sheriff Court Rules Amendment) (Curators ad litem) 2017 (SSI 2017/132) r.2(6)(e) (effective 1 June 2017 subject to saving specified in SSI 2017/132 r.4).
[4] As amended by the Act of Sederunt (Rules of the Court of Session 1994 and Sheriff Court Rules Amendment) (Miscellaneous) 2021 (SSI 2021/75) r.3(4)(e) (effective 1 March 2021).

Returning completed application form to court

3. When directions 1–2 above have been complied with, your application is now ready to be sent to the sheriff clerk at the above address. With it you must enclose:

(i) an extract of the registration of your civil partnership in the civil partnership register (the document headed "Extract of an entry in the Register of Civil Partnerships", which will be returned to you in due course), or an equivalent document. Check the notes on page 2 to see if you need to obtain a letter from the National Records of Scotland stating that there is no record of your civil partner having dissolved the civil partnership, and

(ii) either a cheque or postal order in respect of the court fee, crossed and made payable to "the Scottish Courts and Tribunals Service",

or a completed fee exemption form.

4. Receipt of your application will be promptly acknowledged. Should you wish to withdraw the application for any reason, please contact the sheriff clerk immediately.

PART 1

WRITE IN INK, USING BLOCK CAPITALS

1. NAME AND ADDRESS OF APPLICANT

Surname ....

Other name(s) in full...............

....

Present address...............

....

Daytime telephone number (if any)...............

2. NAME OF CIVIL PARTNER

Surname ....

Other name(s) in full ....

3. ADDRESS OF CIVIL PARTNER (If the address of your civil partner is not known, please enter "not known" in this paragraph and proceed to paragraph 4)

Present address ....

....

....

Daytime telephone number (if any) ....

4. Only complete this paragraph if you do not know the present address of your civil partner

NEXT-OF-KIN Name...............

Address ....

....

....

Relationship to your civil partner ....

CHILDREN OF THE FAMILY

Names and dates of birth	Addresses
....	....
	....
....	....

Names and dates of birth   **Addresses**

....

If insufficient space is available to list all the children of the family, please continue on a separate sheet and attach to this form.

5. JURISDICTION

Please indicate with a tick (✔) in the appropriate box or boxes which of the following apply:

Please complete both Part A and Part B

PART A

(i)   I am domiciled in Scotland on the date I signed this application   ☐

(ii)   My civil partner is domiciled in Scotland on the date I signed this application   ☐

(iii)   I was habitually resident in Scotland throughout the period   ☐
        of one year ending with the date I signed this application

(iv)   My civil partner was habitually resident in Scotland   ☐
        throughout the period of one year ending with the date I
        signed this application

PART B

(i)   I have lived at the address shown above for at least 40 days ☐
        immediately before the date I signed this application

(ii)   My civil partner has lived at the address shown above for   ☐
        at least 40 days immediately before the date I signed this
        application

(iii)   I lived at the address shown above for a period of at least   ☐
        40 days ending not more than 40 days before the date I
        signed this application and have no known residence in
        Scotland at that date

(iv)   My civil partner lived at the address shown above for a   ☐
        period of at least 40 days ending not more than 40 days
        before the date I signed this application and has no known
        residence in Scotland at that date

6. DETAILS OF PRESENT CIVIL PARTNERSHIP

Place of Registration of Civil Partnership...............(Registration District)

Date of Registration of Civil Partnership: Day..........month..........year...............

7. PERIOD OF SEPARATION

(i)   Please state the date on which you ceased to live with your civil partner.
        (If more than 2 years, just give the month and year)
        Day..........Month..........Year..........

(ii)   Have you lived with your civil partner since that date?   *[YES/NO]

(iii)   If yes, for how long in total did you live together before finally separating again?

                                                          ....months

8. RECONCILIATION

Is there any reasonable prospect of reconciliation with your civil partner?	*[YES/NO]
Do you consider that the civil partnership has broken down irretrievably?	*[YES/NO]

9. MENTAL DISORDER

As far as you are aware, does your civil partner have any mental disorder (whether mental illness, personality disorder or learning disability)?	*[YES/NO]

(If yes, give details)

10. CHILDREN

Are there any children of the family under the age of 16?	*[YES/NO]

11. OTHER COURT ACTIONS

Are you aware of any court actions currently proceeding in any country (including Scotland) which may affect your civil partnership?	*[YES/NO]
(If yes, give details)	* Delete as appropriate

12. DECLARATION AND REQUEST FOR DISSOLUTION OF THE CIVIL PARTNERSHIP

I confirm that the facts stated in paragraphs 1–11 above apply to my civil partnership.

I do NOT ask the sheriff to make any financial provision in connection with this application.

I request the sheriff to grant decree of dissolution of my civil partnership.

Date............... Signature of Applicant...............

PART 2

APPLICANT'S AFFIDAVIT

To be completed by the Applicant only after Part 1 has been signed and dated.

I, (*Insert Applicant's full name*) ....

residing at (*insert Applicant's present home address*) ....

....

....

SWEAR that to the best of my knowledge and belief the facts stated in Part 1 of this Application are true.

Signature of Applicant....................

	SWORN at (*insert place*)....................
To be completed by Justice of the Peace,	this..........day of..........20 ....
Notary Public or Commissioner for	before me (*insert full name*)...............
Oaths	(*insert full address*)...............
	....
	....
	Signature....................

*Justice of the Peace/ Notary Public/Commissioner for Oaths

* Delete as appropriate

Rule 33A.67(3)[1, 2, 3]

FORM CP31[4]

Form of simplified dissolution of a civil partnership application on grounds under section 117(2)(b) of the Civil Partnership Act 2004

Sheriff Clerk

Sheriff Court House

....

....

(Telephone) ....

APPLICATION FOR DISSOLUTION OF A CIVIL PARTNERSHIP (INTERIM GENDER RECOGNITION CERTIFICATE ISSUED TO ONE OF THE CIVIL PARTNERS AFTER REGISTRATION OF THE CIVIL PARTNERSHIP)

Before completing this form, you should have read the leaflet entitled "Do it yourself Dissolution", which explains the circumstances in which a dissolution of a civil partnership may be sought by this method. If the simplified procedure appears to suit your circumstances, you may use this form to apply for dissolution of your civil partnership. Below you will find directions designed to assist you with your application. Please follow them carefully. In the event of difficulty, you may contact any sheriff clerk's office or Citizen Advice Bureau.

Directions for making application

WRITE IN INK, USING BLOCK CAPITALS

Application (Part 1)	1. Complete and sign Part 1 of the form (pages 3–7), paying particular attention to the notes opposite each section
Affidavits (Part 2)	2. When you have completed Part 1, you should take the form to a Justice of the Peace, Notary Public, Commissioner for Oaths or other duly authorised person so that your affidavit at Part 2 (page 8) may be completed and sworn.
Returning completed Application form to court	3. When directions 1–2 above have been complied with, your application is now ready to be sent to the sheriff clerk at the above address. With it you must enclose:

(i) an extract of the registration of your civil partnership in the civil partnership register (the document headed "Extract of an entry in the Register of Civil Partnerships", which will be returned to you in due course), or an equivalent document. Check the notes on page 2 to see if you need to obtain a letter from the National Records of Scotland stating that there is no

---

[1] Inserted by Act of Sederunt (Ordinary Cause Rules) Amendment (Civil Partnership Act 2004) 2005 (SSI 2005/638), para.3 (effective 8 December 2005).

[2] As amended by Act of Sederunt (Ordinary Cause Rules) Amendment (Family Law (Scotland) Act 2006 etc.) 2006, para.2 (SSI 2006/207) (effective 4 May 2006).

[3] As amended by the Act of Sederunt (Rules of the Court of Session 1994 and Sheriff Court Rules Amendment) (Curators ad litem) 2017 (SSI 2017/132) r.2(6)(f) (effective 1 June 2017 subject to saving specified in SSI 2017/132 r.4).

[4] As amended by the Act of Sederunt (Rules of the Court of Session 1994 and Sheriff Court Rules Amendment) (Miscellaneous) 2021 (SSI 2021/75) r.3(4)(f) (effective 1 March 2021).

record of your civil partner having dissolved the civil partnership,

(ii) either a cheque or postal order in respect of the court fee, crossed and made payable to "the Scottish Courts and Tribunals Service", or a completed fee exemption form, and

(iii) the interim gender recognition certificate or a copy sealed with the seal of the Gender Recognition Panels and certified to be a true copy by an officer authorised by the President of Gender Recognition Panels.

4. Receipt of your application will be promptly acknowledged. Should you wish to withdraw the application for any reason, please contact the sheriff clerk immediately.

PART 1
WRITE IN INK, USING BLOCK CAPITALS
1. NAME AND ADDRESS OF APPLICANT

Surname ....

Other name(s) in full ....

....

Present address ....

....

Daytime telephone number (if any) ....

2. NAME OF CIVIL PARTNER

Surname ....

Other name(s) in full ....

3. ADDRESS OF CIVIL PARTNER (If the address of your civil partner is not known, please enter "not known" in this paragraph and proceed to paragraph 4)

Present address ....

....

....

Daytime telephone number (if any) ....

4. Only complete this paragraph if you do not know the present address of your civil partner

NEXT-OF-KIN

Name ....

Address ....

....

....

Relationship to your civil partner ....

CHILDREN OF THE FAMILY

Names and dates of birth	Addresses
....	....
	....
	....
....	....
	....
	....

If insufficient space is available to list all the children of the family, please continue on a separate sheet and attach to this form.

5. JURISDICTION

Please indicate with a tick (✔) in the appropriate box or boxes which of the following apply:

Please complete both Part A and Part B
PART A

(i)	I am domiciled in Scotland on the date I signed this application	☐
(ii)	My civil partner is domiciled in Scotland on the date I signed this application	☐
(iii)	I was habitually resident in Scotland throughout the period of one year ending with the date I signed this application	☐
(iv)	My civil partner was habitually resident in Scotland throughout the period of one year ending with the date I signed this application	☐

PART B

(i)	I have lived at the address shown above for at least 40 days immediately before the date I signed this application	☐
(ii)	My civil partner has lived at the address shown above for at least 40 days immediately before the date I signed this application	☐
(iii)	I lived at the address shown above for a period of at least 40 days ending not more than 40 days before the date I signed this application and have no known residence in Scotland at that date	☐
(iv)	My civil partner lived at the address shown above for a period of at least 40 days ending not more than 40 days before the date I signed this application and has no known residence in Scotland at that date	☐

6. DETAILS OF PRESENT CIVIL PARTNERSHIP
Place of Registration of Civil Partnership ....(Registration District)
Date of Registration of Civil Partnership: Day..........month..........year..........
7. DETAILS OF ISSUE OF INTERIM GENDER RECOGNITION CERTIFI-
CATE

(i)	Please state whether the interim gender recognition certificate has been issued to you or your civil partner
(ii)	Please state the date the interim gender recognition certificate was issued Day..........Month...........Year..........

8. MENTAL DISORDER

As far as you are aware, does your civil partner have any mental disorder	*[YES/NO]

(If yes, give details)

9. CHILDREN Are there any children of the family under the age of 16?	*[YES/NO]

10. OTHER COURT ACTIONS

Are you aware of any court actions currently proceeding in any country (including Scotland) which may affect your civil partnership?	*[YES/NO]

(If yes, give details)   * Delete as appropriate

11. DECLARATION AND REQUEST FOR DISSOLUTION OF THE CIVIL PARTNERSHIP

I confirm that the facts stated in paragraphs 1-10 above apply to my civil partnership.

I do NOT ask the sheriff to make any financial provision in connection with this application.

I request the sheriff to grant decree of dissolution of my civil partnership.

Date.......... Signature of Applicant...............

PART 2

APPLICANT'S AFFIDAVIT

To be completed by the Applicant only after Part 1 has been signed and dated.

I, (*Insert Applicant's full name*) ....

residing at (*insert Applicant's present home address*) ....

....

....

SWEAR that to the best of my knowledge and belief the facts stated in Part 1 of this Application are true.

Signature of Applicant   ....

SWORN at (*insert place*) ....

To be completed by Justice of the Peace,   this..........day of..........20 ....

Notary Public or Commissioner for   before me (*insert full name*) ....

Oaths   (*insert full address*) ....

....

....

Signature ....

*Justice of the Peace/ Notary Public/Commissioner for Oaths

* Delete as appropriate

Rule 33A.69(3)(a)[1, 2]

FORM CP32

Form of citation in application relying on facts in section 117(3)(c) of the Civil Partnership Act 2004

(*Insert name and address of non-applicant civil partner*)

APPLICATION FOR DISSOLUTION OF A CIVIL PARTNERSHIP (CIVIL PARTNERS HAVING LIVED APART FOR AT LEAST ONE YEAR WITH THE CONSENT OF THE OTHER CIVIL PARTNER)

Your civil partner has applied to the sheriff for dissolution of your civil partnership on the ground that the civil partnership has broken down irretrievably because you and he or she have lived apart for a period of at least one year and you consent to decree of dissolution being granted.

---

[1] Inserted by Act of Sederunt (Ordinary Cause Rules) Amendment (Civil Partnership Act 2004) 2005 (SSI 2005/638), para.3 (effective December 8, 2005).

[2] As amended by Act of Sederunt (Ordinary Cause Rules) Amendment (Family Law (Scotland) Act 2006 etc.) 2006, para.2 (SSI 2006/207) (effective May 4, 2006).

A copy of the application is hereby served upon you.

1. Please note that the sheriff may not make financial provision under this procedure and that your civil partner is making no claim for—

(a) the payment by you of a periodical allowance (i.e. a regular payment of money weekly or monthly, etc. for maintenance);

(b) the payment by you of a capital sum (i.e. a lump sum payment).

2. Dissolution of your civil partnership may result in the loss to you of property rights (e.g. the right to succeed to the Applicant's estate on his or her death) or the right, where appropriate, to a pension.

3. If you wish to oppose the granting of a decree of dissolution of your civil partnership, you should put your reasons in writing and send your letter to the address shown below. Your letter must reach the sheriff clerk before (*insert date*).

4. In the event of the decree of dissolution of your civil partnership being granted, you will be sent a copy of the extract decree. Should you change your address before receiving the copy extract decree, please notify the sheriff clerk immediately.

Signed

Sheriff clerk (depute)

(*insert address and telephone number of the sheriff clerk*)

[*or* Sheriff officer]

NOTE: If you wish to exercise your right to make a claim for financial provision you should immediately advise the sheriff clerk that you oppose the application for that reason, and thereafter consult a solicitor.

Rule 33A.69(3)(b)[1, 2]

FORM CP33

Form of citation in application relying on facts in section 117(3)(d) of the Civil Partnership Act 2004

(*Insert name and address of non-applicant civil partner*)

APPLICATION FOR DISSOLUTION OF A CIVIL PARTNERSHIP (CIVIL PARTNERS HAVING LIVED APART FOR AT LEAST TWO YEARS)

Your civil partner has applied to the sheriff for dissolution of your civil partnership on the ground that the civil partnership has broken down irretrievably because you and he or she have lived apart for a period of at least two years.

A copy of the application is hereby served upon you.

1. Please note:

(a) that the sheriff may not make financial provision under this procedure and that your civil partner is making no claim for—

(i) the payment by you of a periodical allowance (i.e. a regular payment of money weekly or monthly, etc. for maintenance);

(ii) the payment by you of a capital sum (i.e. a lump sum payment);

(b) *[Omitted by Act of Sederunt (Ordinary Cause Rules) Amendment (Family Law (Scotland) Act 2006 etc.) 2006, para.2 (SSI 2006/207) (effective May 4, 2006).]*

2. Dissolution of your civil partnership may result in the loss to you of property rights (e.g. the right to succeed to the Applicant's estate on his or her death) or the right, where appropriate, to a pension.

3. If you wish to oppose the granting of a decree of dissolution of your civil partnership, you should put your reasons in writing and send your letter to the address shown below. Your letter must reach the sheriff clerk before (*insert date*).

---

[1] Inserted by Act of Sederunt (Ordinary Cause Rules) Amendment (Civil Partnership Act 2004) 2005 (SSI 2005/638), para.3 (effective December 8, 2005).

[2] As amended by Act of Sederunt (Ordinary Cause Rules) Amendment (Family Law (Scotland) Act 2006 etc.) 2006, para.2 (SSI 2006/207) (effective May 4, 2006).

4. In the event of the decree of dissolution of your civil partnership being granted, you will be sent a copy of the extract decree. Should you change your address before receiving the copy extract decree, please notify the sheriff clerk immediately.

Signed

Sheriff clerk (depute)

(insert address and telephone number of the sheriff clerk)

[or Sheriff officer]

NOTE: If you wish to exercise your right to make a claim for financial provision you should immediately advise the sheriff clerk that you oppose the application for that reason, and thereafter consult a solicitor.

Rule 33A.69(3)(c)[1]

FORM CP34

Form of citation in application on grounds under section 117(2)(b) of the Civil Partnership Act 2004

(Insert name and address of non-applicant civil partner)

APPLICATION FOR DISSOLUTION OF A CIVIL PARTNERSHIP (INTERIM GENDER RECOGNITION CERTIFICATE ISSUED TO ONE OF THE CIVIL PARTNERS AFTER THE REGISTRATION OF THE CIVIL PARTNERSHIP)

Your civil partner has applied to the sheriff for dissolution of your civil partnership on the ground that an interim gender recognition certificate has been issued to you or your civil partner after your civil partnership was registered.

A copy of the application is hereby served upon you.

1. Please note that the sheriff may not make financial provision under this procedure and that your civil partner is making no claim for—

(a) the payment by you of a periodical allowance (i.e. a regular payment of money weekly or monthly, etc. for maintenance);

(b) the payment by you of a capital sum (i.e. a lump sum payment).

2. Dissolution of your civil partnership may result in the loss to you of property rights (e.g. the right to succeed to the Applicant's estate on his or her death) or the right, where appropriate, to a pension.

3. If you wish to oppose the granting of a decree of dissolution of your civil partnership, you should put your reasons in writing and send your letter to the address shown below. Your letter must reach the sheriff clerk before *(insert date)*.

4. In the event of the decree of dissolution of your civil partnership being granted, you will be sent a copy of the extract decree. Should you change your address before receiving the copy extract decree, please notify the sheriff clerk immediately.

Signed

Sheriff clerk (depute)

(insert address and telephone number of the sheriff clerk)

[or Sheriff officer]

NOTE: If you wish to exercise your right to make a claim for financial provision you should immediately advise the sheriff clerk that you oppose the application for that reason, and thereafter consult a solicitor.

Rule 33A.70(1)(a)[2]

FORM CP35

Form of intimation of simplified dissolution of a civil partnership application for display on the walls of court

---

[1] Inserted by Act of Sederunt (Ordinary Cause Rules) Amendment (Civil Partnership Act 2004) 2005 (SSI 2005/638), para.3 (effective December 8, 2005).

[2] Inserted by Act of Sederunt (Ordinary Cause Rules) Amendment (Civil Partnership Act 2004) 2005 (SSI 2005/638), para.3 (effective December 8, 2005).

Court ref. no.

An application for dissolution of a civil partnership has been made in this sheriff court by [A.B.], (*insert designation and address*), Applicant, naming [C.D.], (*insert designation and address*) as Respondent.

If [C.D.] wishes to oppose the granting of decree of dissolution of the civil partnership he [*or* she] should immediately contact the sheriff clerk from whom he [or she] may obtain a copy of the application.

Date (*insert date*)

Signed

Sheriff clerk (depute)

Rule 33A.70(2)[1]

FORM CP36

Form of intimation to children of the family and next-of-kin in a simplified dissolution of a civil partnership application

Court ref. no.

To (*insert name and address*)

You are hereby given NOTICE that an application for dissolution of a civil partnership has been made against (*insert name of respondent*) your (*insert relationship e.g. father, mother, brother or other relative as the case may be*). A copy of this application is attached.

If you know of his or her present address, you are requested to inform the sheriff clerk (*insert address of sheriff clerk*) in writing immediately. You may also, if you wish, oppose the granting of the decree of dissolution by sending a letter to the court giving your reasons for your opposition to the application. Your letter must be sent to the sheriff clerk within 21 days of (*insert date on which intimation was given. N.B. Rule 5.3(2) relating to postal service or intimation*).

Date (*insert date*)

Signed

Sheriff clerk (depute)

IF YOU ARE UNCERTAIN WHAT ACTION TO TAKE you should consult a solicitor. You may be entitled to legal aid depending on your financial circumstances, and you can get information about legal aid from a solicitor. You may also obtain advice from any Citizens Advice Bureau or other advice agency.

Rule 33A.73(2)[2]

FORM CP37

Form of extract decree of dissolution of a civil partnership in an application for a simplified dissolution of a civil partnership

At (*insert place and date*)

in an action in the Sheriff Court of the Sheriffdom of (*insert name of sheriffdom*) at (*insert place of sheriff court*)

at the instance of (*insert full name of applicant*), Applicant,

against (*insert full name of respondent*), Respondent,

whose civil partnership was registered at (*insert place*) on (*insert date*),

the sheriff pronounced decree dissolving the civil partnership of the Applicant and the Respondent.

Extracted at (*insert place and date*)

---

[1] Inserted by Act of Sederunt (Ordinary Cause Rules) Amendment (Civil Partnership Act 2004) 2005 (SSI 2005/638), para.3 (effective December 8, 2005).

[2] Inserted by Act of Sederunt (Ordinary Cause Rules) Amendment (Civil Partnership Act 2004) 2005 (SSI 2005/638), para.3 (effective December 8, 2005).

by me, sheriff clerk of the Sheriffdom of *(insert name of sheriffdom).*

Signed

Sheriff clerk (depute)

FORM CP38[1, 2]

Rule 33A.21(4)

Form of annex to interlocutor appointing a child welfare reporter

☐ Appointment of Child Welfare Reporter under rule 33A.21(1)(a).

Where this box is ticked the Child Welfare Reporter is required to seek the views of the child [or children] on the issue(s) specified in Part 1 below.

☐ Appointment of Child Welfare Reporter under rule 33A.21(1)(b).

Where this box is ticked the Child Welfare Reporter is required to carry out the enquiries specified in Part 2 below, and to address the issue(s) specified in Part 3 below.

PART 1

Issue(s) in respect of which views of the child [or children] are to be sought *[specify]*

Is a copy of the report to be provided to the parties under rule 33A.21(9)(d)?

☐ Yes

☐ No

PART 2

Enquiries to be undertaken—

☐ Seek views of child
☐ Visit home of *[specify]*
☐ Visit nursery / school / child minder / other *[specify]*
☐ Interview mother / father
☐ Interview other family members *[specify]*
☐ Interview child minder / nanny
☐ Interview teacher / head teacher
☐ Interview child's health visitor / GP / other health professional *[specify]*
☐ Interview a party's GP / other health professional *[specify]*

---

[1] As inserted by the Act of Sederunt (Rules of the Court of Session 1994 and Sheriff Court Rules Amendment) (Miscellaneous) 2016 (SSI 2016/102) para.3 (effective 21 March 2016).
[2] As amended by the Act of Sederunt (Rules of the Court of Session 1994 and Ordinary Cause Rules 1993 Amendment) (Views of the Child) 2019 (SSI 2019/123) para.3 (effective 24th June 2019).

☐ Interview social worker *[specify]*
☐ Interview domestic abuse case worker *[specify]*
☐ Interview other persons *[specify]*
☐ Obtain criminal conviction certificate under section 112 of the Police Act 1997 in respect of *[specify party]*
☐ Observe contact *[specify]*
☐ Observe child in home environment pre/post contact *[specify]*
☐ Obtain record of parties' attendance from contact centre
☐ Other *[specify]*

PART 3

Issues to be addressed in report *[specify]*

Where the views of the child form part of the enquiries to be undertaken, should the views of the child be recorded in a separate report?

☐ Yes
☐ No

If yes, is a copy of that report to be provided to the parties under rule 33A.21(9)(d)?

☐ Yes
☐ No

Rule 34.1(2)[1]
FORM H1
Form of notice informing defender of right to apply for certain orders under the Debtors (Scotland) Act 1987 on sequestration for rent
Rule 34.6(1)

FORM H2
Form of notice of removal
To (*insert name, designation, and address of party in possession*). You are required to remove from (*describe subjects*) at the term of (*or if different terms, state them and the subjects to which they apply*), in terms of lease (*describe it*) [or in terms of your letter of removal dated (*insert date*)] [or otherwise as the case may be].

Date (*insert date*)   Signed
                                         (*add designation and address*)

---

[1] Revoked by the Act of Sederunt (Sheriff Court Rules Amendment) (Diligence) 2008 (SSI 2008/121) r.2(1)(a) (effective April 1, 2008).

Rule 34.6(2)

FORM H3
Form of letter of removal

To (*insert name and designation of addressee*)

(*Insert place and date*) I am to remove from (*state subjects by usual name or short description sufficient for identification*) at the term of (*insert term and date*)

[K.L.] (*add designation and address*).

(*If not holograph, to be attested thus—*)

[M.N.] (*add designation and address*), witness.)

Rule 34.7

FORM H4

Form of notice of removal under section 37 of the 1907 Act

NOTICE OF REMOVAL UNDER SECTION 37 OF THE SHERIFF COURTS (SCOTLAND) ACT 1907

To (*insert designation and address*).

You are required to remove from (*insert description of heritable subjects, land, ground, etc.*) at the term of [Whitsunday or Martinmas], (*insert date*)

Date (*insert date*)   Signed

(*add designation and address*)

FORM H5

Rule 34.11(4)

Form of citation of unnamed occupiers

CITATION

SHERIFFDOM OF (*insert name of sheriffdom*)

AT (*insert place of sheriff court*)

[A.B.] (*insert designation and address*)

Pursuer

against

The Occupier[s] of (*address*)

Defender

An action has been brought in the above Sheriff Court by [A.B.]. [A.B.] calls as a defender the occupier[s] of the property at (*insert address*). If the occupier[s] [or any of them] wish[es] to challenge the jurisdiction of the court or to defend the action, he [or she [or it] [or they]] should contact the sheriff clerk at (*insert address of sheriff court*) immediately and in any event by (*date on which period of notice expires*).

Signed

Sheriff [or Sheriff Clerk]

FORM M1

Rule 35.5

Form of warrant of citation in an action of multiplepoinding

(*Insert place and date*) Grants warrant to cite the defender (*insert name and address*) by serving a copy of the writ and warrant upon a period of notice of (*insert period of notice*) days, and ordains him [or her], if he [or she] intends to lodge:—

(a) defences challenging the jurisdiction of the court or the competence of the action; or

(b) objections to the condescendence on the fund *in medio*; or

---

[1] Inserted by SSI 2000/239 (effective October 2, 2000).

(c) a claim on the fund;

to lodge a notice of appearance with the sheriff clerk at (*insert name and address of sheriff court*) within the said period of notice after such service [and grants warrant to arrest on the dependence].

[*Where the holder of the fund in medio is a defender, insert:* Appoints the holder of the fund in medio to

(a) lodge with the sheriff clerk at (*insert place of sheriff court*) within the said period of notice after such service

(i)   a detailed condescendence on the fund in medio; and

(ii)   a list of parties having an interest in the fund; and

(b) intimate to all parties to the action a copy of the condescendence and list.]

FORM M2

Rule 35.6(1)

Form of citation in an action of multiplepoinding

Citation

SHERIFFDOM OF (*insert name of sheriffdom*) .... Court ref. no. ....

AT (*insert place of sheriff court*) ....

[A.B.]. (*insert designation and address*). Pursuer, against [C.D.], (*insert designation and address*). Defender.

(*Insertplace and date*) You [C.D.] arc hereby served with this copy writ and warrant, together with Form M4 (notice of appearance).

[*Where the defender is the holder of the fund in medio. insert the following paragraph:*— As holder of the fund in medio you must lodge with the sheriff clerk at the above address within (*insert period of notice*) days of (insert date on which service was executed. N. B. Rule 5.3(2) relating to postal service)—

(a) a detailed condescendence on the fund in medio: and

(b) a list of parties having an interest in the fund.

You must at the same time intimate to all other parties to the action a copy of

(a) the detailed condescendence on the fund; and

(b) the list of parties having an interest in the fund.]

FORM M4 is served on you for use should you wish to intimate that you intend to lodge:—

(a) defences challenging the jurisdiction of the court or the competence of the action; or

(b) objections to the condescendence on the fund in medio: or

(c) a claim on the fund.

IF YOU WISH TO APPEAR IN THIS ACTION you should consult a solicitor with a view to lodgng a notice of appearnce (Form M4). The notice of appearance, together with the court fee of £(*insert amount*) must be lodged with the sheriff clerk at the above address within (*insert the appropriat period of notice*) days of (*insert the date on which service was executed. N. B.* Rule 5.3(2) **relating to postal service**).

IF YOU ARE UNCERTAIN WHAT ACTION TO TAKE you should consult a solicitor. You may be eligible for legal aid depending on your income. You can get information about legal aid from a solicitor. You may also obtain advice from any Citizens Advice Bureau or other advice agency.

PLEASE NOTE THAT IF YOU DO NOTHING IN ANSWER TO THIS DOCUMENT the court may regard you as having no interest in the fund in medio and will proceed accordingly.

Signed
[P.O.], Sheriff officer,
or [X.Y.] (*add designation and business address*)
Solicitor for the pursuer

FORM M3

Rule 35.6(2)

Form of certificate of citation in an action of multiplepoinding
Certificate of Citation
(*Insert place and date*) I,.......... hereby certify that upon the..........day of..........
I duly cited [C.D.]. Defender, to answer to the foregoing writ. This I did by (*state method of service; if by officer and not by post, add:* in presence of [L.M.], (*insert designation*), witness hereto with me subscribing *and where service is executed by post state whether made by registered post of the first class recorded delivery service*):

Signed
[P.O.]. Sheriff officer [L.M.], witness
or [X.Y.] (*add designation and business address*)
Solicitor for the pursuer

FORM M4

Rules 35.6(1) and 35.8
Form of notice of appearance in an action of multiplepoinding
NOTICE OF APPEARANCE (MULTIPLEPOINDING)
*PART A Court Ref. No.

(Insert name and business address of solicitor for the pursuer)	In an action raised at Sheriff Court
	Pursuer
Solicitor for the pursuer	Defender

*(This part to be completed by the pursuer before service)
DATE OF SERVICE: DATE OF EXPIRY OF PERIOD OF NOTICE:
....
*PART B
* (This section to be completed by the defender or the defender's solicitor and both parts of this form returned to the sheriff clerk at (insert address of sheriff clerk) on or before the expiry of the period of notice referred to in PART A above)
(*Insert place and date*)
[C.D.] (design), Defender, intends to lodge:

	☐	defences challenging the jurisdiction of the court or the competence of the action.
Tick the appropriate box(es)	☐	objections to the condescendence on the fund *in medio*
	☐	a claim on the fund *in medio*.

Signed
[C.D.] Defender,
or [X.Y.] (*add designation and business address*)

Solicitor for the defender

FORM M5

Rules 35.9(b) and 35.10(5)

Form of intimation of first hearing in an action of multiplepoinding

SHERIFFDOM OF (*insert name of sheriffdom*).............. Court ref. no. ....

AT (*insert place of sheriff court*)

[A.B.] (*insert designation and address*). Pursuer, against [C.D.] (*insert designation and address*), Defender.

You are given notice that in this action of multiplepoinding

Insert date, time and place)

is the date, time and place for the first hearing.

Date (*Insert date*)

Signed

Sheriff clerk (dispute)

Note

If the pursuer fails to return the writ in terms of rule 9.3 of the Ordinary Cause Rules of the Sheriff Court or any party fails to comply with the terms of this notice or to provide the sheriff at the hearing with sufficient information to enable it to be conducted it in terms of rule 35.10 of these rules, the sheriff may make such order or finding against that party so failing as he thinks fit.

NOTE TO BE ADDED WHERE PARTY UNREPRESENTED

Note

IF YOU ARE UNCERTAIN WHAT ACTION TO TAKE you should consult a solicitor. You may be eligible for legal aid depending on your income. You can get information about legal aid from a solicitor. You may also obtain advice from any Citizens Advice Bureau or other advice agency.

FORM M6

Rule 35.10(4)(b)

Form of citation of person having an interest in the fund in an action of multiplepoinding

CITATION

SHERIFFDOM OF (*insert name of sheriffdom*)...............Court ref. no. AT (*insert place of sheriff court*)

[A.B.], (*insert designation and address*), Pursuer, against [C.D.], (*insert designation and address*), Defender.

(*Insert place and date*) In the above action the court has been advised that you (*insert name and address*) have an interest in (*insert details of the fund in medio*). You are hereby served with a copy of the pleadings in this action, together with Form M4 (notice of appearance).

Form M4 is served on you for use should you wish to intimate that you intend to lodge:

(a) defences challenging the jurisdiction of the court or the competence of the action; or

(b) objections to the condescendence on the fund *in medio*; or

(c) a claim on the fund.

IF YOU WISH TO APPEAR IN THIS ACTION you should consult a solicitor with a view to lodging a notice of appearance (Form M4). The notice of appearance, together with the court fee of £ (insert amount) must be lodged with the sheriff clerk

431

at the above address within.......... days of (*insert date on which service was executed* N.B. Rule 5.3(2) *relating to postal service*).

NOTE:

IF YOU ARE UNCERTAIN WHAT ACTION TO TAKE you should consult a solicitor. You may be eligible for legal aid depending on your income. You can get information about legal aid from a solicitor. You may also obtain advice from any Citizens Advice Bureau or other advice agency.

PLEASE NOTE THAT IF YOU DO NOTHING IN ANSWER TO THIS DOCU-MENT the court may regard you as having no interest in the fund *in medio* and will proceed accordingly.

Signed

[P.Q.], Sheriff officer,

or [X.Y.] (*add designation and business address*)

FORM PI1[1]

Form of initial writ in a personal injuries action

Rules 3.1(1) and 36.B1(1)

INITIAL WRIT

(Personal Injuries Action)

SHERIFFDOM OF (*insert name of sheriffdom*)

AT (*insert place of sheriff court; if appropriate, state that the action is for determination in the all-Scotland sheriff court at Edinburgh*)

[A.B.] (*design and state any special capacity in which pursuer is suing*), Pursuer

against

[C.D.] (*design and state any special capacity in which defender is being sued*), Defender

The pursuer craves the court to grant decree—

(a) for payment by the defender to the pursuer of the sum of (*amount of sum in words and figures*);

(b) (*enter only if a claim for provisional damages is sought in terms of* rule 36.12) for payment by the defender to the pursuer of (*enter amount in words and figures*) of provisional damages; and

(c) for the expenses of the action.

STATEMENT OF CLAIM

1. The pursuer is (*state designation, address, National Insurance Number (where applicable), occupation and date of birth of pursuer*). (*In an action arising out of the death of a relative state designation of the deceased and relation to the pursuer*).

2. The defender is (*state designation, address and occupation of the defender*).

3. The court has jurisdiction to hear this claim against the defender because (*state briefly ground of jurisdiction; if the action is raised in the all-Scotland sheriff court, state whether the action is for determination in the exercise of the sheriff's all-Scotland jurisdiction or the sheriff's local jurisdiction*).

4. (*State briefly the facts necessary to establish the claim*).

5. (*State briefly the personal injuries suffered and the heads of claim. Give names and addresses of medical practitioners and hospitals or other institutions in which the person injured received treatment*).

6. (*State whether claim based on fault at common law or breach of statutory duty. If breach of statutory duty, state provision of enactment*).

---

[1] As substituted by the Act of Sederunt (Rules of the Court of Session 1994 and Sheriff Court Rules Amendment) (No.2) (Personal Injury and Remits) 2015 (SSI 2015/227) para.8 (effective September 22, 2015).

(Signed)
[A.B.], Pursuer
or [X.Y.], Solicitor for the pursuer (*insert designation and business address*)
FORM PI2[1]

Rule 36.B1
Form of order of court for recovery of documents in personal injuries action

Court ref. no.

SHERIFFDOM OF (*insert name of sheriffdom*)
AT (*insert place of sheriff court*)
SPECIFICATION OF DOCUMENTS
in the cause
[A.B.] (*designation and address*), Pursuer against
[C.D.] (*designation and address*), Defender

Date: (*date of posting or other method of service*)

To: (*name and address of party or parties from whom the following documents are sought to be recovered*)

You are hereby required to produce to the agent for the pursuer within seven days of the service on you of this Order:

[Insert such of the following calls as are required].

1. All books, medical records, reports, charts, X-rays, notes and other documents of (*specify the name of each medical practitioner or general practitioner practice named in initial writ in accordance with* rule 36.B1 (1)(b)), and relating to the pursuer [*or, as the case may be, the deceased*] from (*insert date*), in order that excerpts may be taken therefrom at the sight of the Commissioner of all entries showing or tending to show the nature, extent and cause of the pursuer's [*or, as the case may be, the deceased's*] injuries when he attended his doctor on or after (*specify date*) and the treatment received by him since that date.

2. All books, medical records, reports, charts, X-rays, notes and other documents of (*specify, in separate calls, the name of each hospital or other institution named in initial writ in accordance with* rule 36.B1 (1)(b)), and relating to the pursuer [*or, as the case may be, the deceased*] from (*insert date*), in order that excerpts may be taken therefrom at the sight of the Commissioner of all entries showing or tending to show the nature, extent and cause of the pursuer's [*or, as the case may be, the deceased's*] injuries when he was admitted to that institution on or about (*specify date*), the treatment received by him since that date and his certificate of discharge, if any.

3. The medical records and capability assessments held by the defender's occupational health department relating to the pursuer [*or, as the case may be, the deceased*], except insofar as prepared for or in contemplation of litigation, in order that excerpts may be taken therefrom at the sight of the Commissioner of all entries showing or tending to show the nature and extent of any injuries, symptoms and conditions from which the pursuer [*or, as the case may he, the deceased*] was suffering and the nature of any assessment and diagnosis made thereof on or subsequent to (*specify date*).

4. All wage books, cash books, wage sheets, computer records and other earnings information relating to the pursuer [*or, as the case may he, the deceased*] (N.I. number (*specify number*)) held by or on behalf of (*specify employer*),

---

[1] As inserted by the Act of Sederunt (Ordinary Cause Rules Amendment) (Personal Injuries Actions) 2009 (SSI 2009/285) r.2 (effective November 2, 2009).

for the period (*specify dates commencing not earlier than 26 weeks prior to the date of the accident or the first date of relevant absence, as the case may be*) in order that excerpts may be taken therefrom at the sight of the Commissioner of all entries showing or tending to show—

    (a)   the pursuer's [*or, as the case may be, the deceased's*] earnings, both gross and net of income tax and employee National Insurance Contributions, over the said period;

    (b)   the period or periods of the pursuer's [*or, as the case may be, the deceased's*] absence from employment over the said period and the reason for absence;

    (c)   details of any increases in the rate paid over the period (*specify dates*) and the dates on which any such increases took effect;

    (d)   the effective date of, the reasons for and the terms (including any terms relative to any pension entitlement) of the termination of the pursuer's [*or, as the case may be, the deceased's*] employment;

    (e)   the nature and extent of contributions (if any) to any occupational pension scheme made by the pursuer [*or, as the case may be, the deceased*] and his employer;

    (f)   the pursuer's present entitlement (if any) to any occupational pension and the manner in which said entitlement is calculated.

5.   All accident reports, memoranda or other written communications made to the defender or anyone on his behalf by an employee of the defender who was present at or about the time at which the pursuer [*or, as the case may be, the deceased*] sustained the injuries in respect of which the initial writ in this cause was issued and relevant to the matters contained in the statement of claim.

6.   Any assessment current at the time of the accident referred to in the initial writ or at the time of the circumstances referred to in the initial writ giving rise to the cause of action (as the case may be) undertaken by or on behalf of the defender for the purpose of regulation 3 of the Management of Health and Safety at Work Regulations 1992 and subsequently regulation 3 of the Management of Health and Safety at Work Regulations 1999 [*or (specify the regulations or other legislative provision under which the risk assessment is required)*] in order that excerpts may be taken therefrom at the sight of the Commissioner of all entries relating to the risks posed to workers [*or (specify the matters set out in the statement of claim to which the risk assessment relates)*].

7.   Failing principals, drafts, copies or duplicates of the above or any of them.

(Signature, name and business address of the agent for the pursuer)

NOTES:

1.   The documents recovered will be considered by the parties to the action and they may or may not be lodged in the court process. A written receipt will be given or sent to you by the pursuer, who may thereafter allow them to be inspected by the other parties. The party in whose possession the documents are will be responsible for their safekeeping.

2.   Payment may be made, within certain limits, in respect of claims for outlays incurred in relation to the production of documents. Claims should be made in writing to the person who has obtained an order that you produce the documents.

3.   If you claim that any of the documents produced by you is **confidential** you must still produce such documents but may place them in a separate sealed

packet by themselves, marked "CONFIDENTIAL". In that event they must be delivered or sent by post to the sheriff clerk. Any party who wishes to open the sealed packet must apply to the sheriff by motion. A party who makes such an application must intimate the motion to you.

4. Subject to paragraph 3 above, you may produce these documents by sending them by registered post or by the first class recorded delivery service or registered postal packet, or by hand to (*name and address of the agent for the pursuer*).

CERTIFICATE

(*Date*)

I hereby certify with reference to the above order in the cause (*cause reference number*) and the enclosed specification of documents, served on me and marked respectively X and Y—

1. That the documents which are produced and which are listed in the enclosed inventory signed by me and marked Z, are all the documents in my possession falling within the specification. OR That I have no documents in my possession falling within the specification.

2. That, to the best of my knowledge and belief, there are in existence other documents falling within the specification, but not in my possession. These documents are as follows: (*describe them by reference to the descriptions of documents in the specification*). They were last seen by me on or about (*date*), at (*place*), in the hands of (*name and address of the person*). OR That I know of the existence of no documents in the possession of any person, other than me, which fall within the specification.

(*Signed*)
(*Name and address*)

FORM PI3[1]

Rule 36.D1

Form of docquet for deemed grant of recovery of documents in a personal injuries action

Court (*insert court*)

Date (*insert date*)

Commission and diligence for the production and recovery of the documents called for in this specification of documents is deemed to have been granted.

(*Signed*)

Sheriff Clerk (depute)

FORM PI4[2]

Form of interlocutor appointing the cause to the procedure in Chapter 36A
Rule 36.C1

(To be inserted on the first page of the initial writ, above the crave(s)

Appointment of cause to Chapter 36A

The sheriff, having considered the application of the pursuer [, having heard parties [*or* parties's solicitors] thereon], and being satisfied, considering the likely complexity of the action, that the efficient determination of the action would be served by doing so, appoints the cause to the procedure in Chapter 36A.

(*Signed*)

---

[1] As inserted by the Act of Sederunt (Ordinary Cause Rules Amendment) (Personal Injuries Actions) 2009 (SSI 2009/285) r.2 (effective November 2, 2009).

[2] As substituted by the Act of Sederunt (Rules of the Court of Session 1994 and Sheriff Court Rules Amendment) (No.2) (Personal Injury and Remits) 2015 (SSI 2015/227) para.8 (effective September 22, 2015).

Sheriff
(*date*)

FORM PI5[1,2]

Rule 36.G1

Form of timetable
TIMETABLE

Court ref. no.

In the cause [A.B.], Pursuer
Against
[C.D.], Defender

This timetable has effect as if it were an interlocutor of the sheriff

1. The diet allocated for the proof in this action will begin on (*date*). Subject to any variation under rule 36.H1, this order requires the parties to undertake the conduct of this action within the periods specified in paragraphs 2 to 9 below.
2. Any motion under rule 20.1 (third party notice) shall be made by (*date*).
3. Where the pursuer has obtained a commission and diligence for the recovery of documents by virtue of rule 36.D1, the pursuer shall serve an order under rule 28.3 not later than (*date*).
4. The pursuer shall lodge a statement of valuation of claim under rule 36.J1 not later than (*date*).
5. For the purposes of rule 36.G1, the adjustment period shall end on (*date*).
6. The pursuer shall lodge a record not later than (*date*).
7. The defender and any third party convened in the action shall lodge a statement of valuation of claim under rule 36.J1 not later than (*date*).
8. Not later than (*date*) parties shall lodge lists of witnesses and productions.
9. Not later than (*date*) the pursuer shall lodge a pre-proof minute under rule 36.K1.

FORM PI6[3]

Rule 36.J1

Form of statement of valuation of claim

Head of claim	Components	Valuation
Solatium	Past	£x
	Future	£x
Interest on past solatium	Percentage applied to past solatium (state percentage rate)	£x
Past wage loss	Date from which wage loss claimed: (date)	£x
	Date to which wage loss claimed: (date)	

---

[1] As inserted by the Act of Sederunt (Ordinary Cause Rules Amendment) (Personal Injuries Actions) 2009 (SSI 2009/285) r.2 (effective November 2, 2009).

[2] As amended by the Act of Sederunt (Rules of the Court of Session 1994 and Sheriff Court Rules Amendment) (No.2) (Personal Injury and Remits) 2015 (SSI 2015/227) para.8 (effective September 22, 2015).

[3] As inserted by the Act of Sederunt (Ordinary Cause Rules Amendment) (Personal Injuries Actions) 2009 (SSI 2009/285) r.2 (effective November 2, 2009).

Head of claim	Components	Valuation
	Rate of net wage loss (per week, per month or per annum)	
Interest on past wage loss	Percentage applied to pas wage loss: (state percentage rate)	£x
Future wage loss	Multiplier: (state multiplier) Multiplicand: (state multiplicand and show how calculated) Discount factor applied (if appropriate): (state factor) Or specify any other method of calculation	£x
Past services	Date from which services claimed: (date) Date to which services claimed: (date) Nature of services:(..........) Person by whom services provided: (..........) Hours per week services provided: (..........) Net hourly rate claimed: (..........) Total amount claimed: (..........) Interest	£x
Future loss of capacity to provide personal service	Multiplier: (insert multiplier) Multiplicand: (insert multiplicand, showing how calculated)	£x
Needs and other expenses	One off Multiplier: (insert multiplier) Multiplicand: (insert multiplicand) Interest	£x

Head of claim	Components	Valuation
Any other heads as appropriate (specify)		

FORM PI7[1]
Form of minute of pre-trial meeting

Rules 36.K1 and 36A.10(3)

SHERIFFDOM OF (*insert sheriffdom*) AT (*insert place*)
JOINT MINUTE OF PRE-TRIAL MEETING
in the cause
[A.B.], Pursuer
against
[C.D.], Defender

[E.F] for the pursuer and [G.H.] for the defender hereby state to the court:

1. That the pre-trial meeting was held in this case at (*place*) [*or* by video conference] on (*date*).
2. That the following persons were present— (*state names and designations of persons attending meeting*)
3. That the following persons were available to provide instructions by telephone— (*state names and designations of persons available to provide instructions by telephone*)
4. That the persons participating in the meeting discussed settlement of the action.
5. That the following questions were addressed—

Section 1

		Yes	No
1.	Is the diet of proof or trial still required?		
2.	If the answer to question 1 is "yes", does the defender admit liability? (If "no", complete section 2) If yes, does the defender plead contributory negligence? If yes, is the degree of contributory negligence agreed? If yes, state % degree of fault attributed to the pursuer.		
3.	If the answer to question 1 is "yes", is the quantum of damages agreed? (If "no", complete section 3).		

Section 2
(*To be inserted only if the proof or trial is still required*)

It is estimated that the hearing will last (*insert number of days*).

N.B. If the estimate differs from the number of days previously allocated for the proof or trial then this should be brought to the attention of the sheriff clerk. This may affect prioritisation of the case.

---

[1] As substituted by the Act of Sederunt (Rules of the Court of Session 1994 and Sheriff Court Rules Amendment) (No.2) (Personal Injury and Remits) 2015 (SSI 2015/227) para.8 (effective September 22, 2015).

During the course of the pre-trial meeting, the pursuer called on the defender to agree certain facts, questions of law and matters of evidence.

Those calls, and the defender's responses, are as follows—

Call	Response	
	Admitted	Denied
1.		
2.		
3.		
4.		

During the course of the pre-trial meeting, the defender called on the pursuer to agree certain facts, questions of law and matters of evidence.

Those calls, and the pursuer's responses, are as follows—

Call	Response	
	Admitted	Denied
1.		
2.		
3.		
4.		

Section 3

Quantum of damages

Please indicate where agreement has been reached on an element of damages.

Head of claim	Components	Not agreed	Agreed at
Solatium	Past		
	Future		
Interest on past solatium	Percentage applied to past solatium (state percentage)		
Past wage loss	Date from which wage loss claimed		
	Date to which wage loss claimed		
	Rate of net wage loss (per week, per month or per annum)		
Interest on past wage loss			
Future wage loss	Multiplier		
	Multiplicand (showing how calculated)		

Head of claim	Components	Not agreed	Agreed at
Past necessary services	Date from which services claimed		
	Date to which services claimed		
	Hour per week services provided		
	Net hourly rate claimed		
Past personal services	Date from which services claimed		
	Date to which services claimed		
	Hour per week services provided		
	Net hourly rate claimed		
Interest on past services			
Future necessary services	Multiplier		
	Multiplicand (showing how calculated)		
Future personal services	Multiplier		
	Multiplicand (showing how calculated)		
Needs and other expenses	One off		
	Multiplier		
	Multiplicand (showing how calculated)		
Any other heads as appropriate (*specify*)			

(Signed by each party/his or her solicitor)
FORM PI8[1]
Form of oath for jurors
Rule 36B.7(1)

The jurors are to raise their right hands and the sheriff clerk will ask them—

"Do you swear by Almighty God that you will well and truly try the issue and give a true verdict according to the evidence?"

The jurors must reply:

"I do".

[1] As inserted by the Act of Sederunt (Rules of the Court of Session 1994 and Sheriff Court Rules Amendment) (No.2) (Personal Injury and Remits) 2015 (SSI 2015/227) para.8 (effective September 22, 2015).

FORM PI9[1]
Form of affirmation for jurors
Rule 36B.7(2)

The jurors must repeat after the sheriff clerk—

"I solemnly, sincerely and truly declare and affirm that I will well and truly try the issue and give a true verdict according to the evidence".

FORM D1

Rule 36.3(2)

Form of intimation to connected person in damages action

SHERIFFDOM OF (*insert name of sheriffdom*) .... Court ref.no. ....
AT (*insert place of sheriff court*) ....

You are given NOTICE that an action has been raised in the above sheriff court by (*insert name and designation of pursuer*) against (*insert name and designation of defender*). A copy of the initial writ is attached.

It is believed that you may have a title or interest to sue the said (*insert name of defender*) in an action based upon [the injuries from which the late (*insert name and designation*) died] [or the death of the late (*insert name and designation*)]. You may therefore be entitled to enter this action as an additional pursuer. If you wish to do so, you may apply by lodging a minute with the sheriff clerk at the above address to be sisted as an additional pursuer within (*insert the appropriate period of notice*) days of (*insert the date on which service was executed N.B. Rule 5.3(2) relating to postal service*).

Signed...............
Solicitor for the pursuer..........

> **NOTE**
> The minute must be lodged with the sheriff clerk with the court fee of (*insert amount*) and a motion seeking leave for the minute to be received and for answers to be lodged. When lodging the minute you must present to the sheriff clerk a copy of the initial writ and this intimation.

> **IF YOU ARE UNCERTAIN WHAT ACTION TO TAKE** you should consult a solicitor. You may be eligible for legal aid depending on your income, and you can obtain information about legal aid from any solicitor. You may also obtain advice from any Citizens Advice Bureau or other advice agency.

FORM D2

Rule 36.17(1)

Form of receipt for payment into court
RECEIPT

In the Sheriff Court of (*insert name of sheriffdom*) at (*insert place of sheriff court*) in the cause, (*state names of parties or other appropriate description*) [A.B.] (*insert designation*) has this day paid into court the sum of (*insert sum concerned*) being a payment into court in terms of rule 36.14 of the Ordinary Cause Rules of the Sheriff Court of money which in an action of damages, has become payable to a person under legal disability.

---

[1] As inserted by the Act of Sederunt (Rules of the Court of Session 1994 and Sheriff Court Rules Amendment) (No.2) (Personal Injury and Remits) 2015 (SSI 2015/227) para.8 (effective September 22, 2015).

[*If the payment is made under* rule 36.15(c) *add*: [the custody of which money has been accepted at the request of *(insert name of court making request)*.]

Date *(insert date)*..............Signed

Sheriff clerk (depute)

FORM P1[1]

Rule 37.2(2)

Form of advertisement in an action of declarator under section 1(1) of the Presumption of Death (Scotland) Act 1977

(insert such facts relating to the missing person as set out in the initial writ as the sheriff may specify).

Sheriff Court *(insert address)*..............Court ref. no. ....

An action has been raised in *(insert name of sheriff court)* by [A.B.], Pursuer, to declare that [C.D.], Defender, whose last known address was *(insert last known address of [C.D.])* is dead.

Any person wishing to defend the action must apply to do so by *(insert date, being [21] days after the date of the advertisement)* by lodging a minute seeking to be sisted a a party to the action with the sheriff clerk at the above address.

A copy of the initial writ may be obtained from the sheriff clerk at the above address.

Date *(insert date)*..............Signed..............

[X.Y.] *(add designation and business address)* Solicitor for the pursuer *or* [P.Q.] Sheriff officer

FORM P2

Rule 37.2(4)

Form of intimation to missing person's spouse and children or nearest known relative

To *(insert name and address as in warrant)*..............Court ref. no. ....

You are given notice that in this action the pursuer craves the court to declare that *(insert the name and last known address of missing person)* is dead. A copy of the initial writ is enclosed.

If you wish to appear as a party, and make an application under section 1 (5) of the Presumption of Death (Scotland) Act 1977 craving the court to make any determination or appointment not sought by the pursuer, you must lodge a minute with the sheriff clerk at *(insert address of sheriff clerk)*.

Your minute must be lodged within [..........] days of *(insert the date on which intimation was given N.B. Rule 5.3(2) relating to postal service or intimation)*.

Date *(insert date)*..............Signed..........

Solicitor for the pursuer
(add designation and business address)

NOTE
The minute must be lodged with the sheriff clerk with the court fee of *(insert amount)* and a motion seeking leave for the minute to be received and for answers to be lodged. When lodging the minute you must present to the sheriff clerk a copy of the initial writ and this intimation.

IF YOU ARE UNCERTAIN WHAT ACTION TO TAKE you should consult a solicitor. You may be eligible for legal aid depending on your income, and you

---

[1] As amended by the Act of Sederunt (Sheriff Court Ordinary Cause Rules Amendment) (Miscellaneous) 2000 (SSI 2000/239) (effective October 2, 2000).

can obtain information about legal aid from any solicitor. You may also obtain advice from any Citizens Advice Bureau or other advice agency.

FORM E1[1]

Rule 38.3(1A)

Form of reference to the European Court

REQUEST

for

PRELIMINARY RULING

of

THE COURT OF JUSTICE OF THE EUROPEAN COMMUNITIES

from

THE SHERIFFDOM OF *insert name of sheriffdom*) at (*insert place of court*)

in the cause

[A.B.] (*insert designation and address*), Pursuer

against

[C.D.] (*insert designation and address*), Defender

[Here set out a clear and succinct statement of the case giving rise to the request for the ruling of the European Court in order to enable the European Court to consider and understand the issues of Community law raised and to enable governments of Member States and other interested parties to submit observations. The statement of the case should include:

(a)   particulars of the parties;

(b)   the history of the dispute between the parties;

(c)   the history of the proceedings;

(d)   the relevant facts as agreed by the parties or found by the court or, failing such agreement or finding, the contentions of the parties on such facts;

(e)   the nature of the issues of law and fact between the parties;

(f)   the Scots law, so far as relevant;

(g)   the Treaty provisions or other acts, instruments or rules of Community law concerned; and

(h)   an explanation of why the reference is being made.]

The preliminary ruling of the Court of Justice of the European Communities is accordingly requested on the following questions:

1, 2, etc. [Here set out the question on which the ruling is sought, identifying the Treaty provisions or other acts, instruments or rules of Community law concerned.] Dated the day of 20 .

Rule 41.5

FORM PA1[2, 3]

Form of certificate of delivery of documents to chief constable

(*Insert place and date*) I, hereby certify that upon the day of I duly delivered to the chief constable of the Police Service of Scotland (*insert details of the documents delivered*). This I did by (*state method of delivery*).

Signed

Solicitor/sheriff officer

---

[1] As substituted by the Act of Sederunt (Sheriff Court Ordinary Cause Rules Amendment) (Miscellaneous) 2000 (SSI 2000/239) (effective October 2, 2000).

[2] As inserted by the Act of Sederunt (Ordinary Cause Rules) (Applications under the Protection from Abuse (Scotland) Act 2001) 2002 (SSI 2002/128), para. 2(3) and Sched.

[3] As amended by the Act of Sederunt (Sheriff Court Rules)(Miscellaneous Amendments) 2013 (SSI 2013/135) para.4 (effective May 27, 2013).

(add designation and business address)
Rule 41A.2(3)

FORM DA1[1, 2]

Form of interlocutor for a determination of a domestic abuse interdict

Court ref no.

SHERIFFDOM OF *(insert name of sheriffdom)*
AT *(insert place of sheriff court)*
[A.B.], *(insert designation and address)*, Pursuer
against
[C.D.], *(insert designation and address)*, Defender
(Date)
The sheriff, in pursuance of section 3(1) of the Domestic Abuse (Scotland) Act 2011, makes a determination that the [interim*] interdict dated *(insert date)* [and to which a power of arrest was attached by interlocutor dated *(insert date)*] is a domestic abuse interdict. [The sheriff appoints *(insert name of person)*] to send forthwith a copy of this interlocutor and a copy of the certificate of service in Form DA2 to the chief constable of the Police Service of Scotland].

(*delete as appropriate)

(Sheriff)..........

Rule 41A.2(4)[3]
FORM DA2

Form of certificate of service

Court ref no.

SHERIFFDOM OF (insert name of sheriffdom)*(insert name of sheriffdom)*
AT *(insert place of sheriff court)*
[A.B.], *(insert designation and address)*, Pursuer
against
[C.D.], *(insert designation and address)*, Defender
(Insert place and date)
I hereby certify that on *(insert date)* I duly served on *(insert name and address of person subject to the interdict)* a copy of Form DA1. This I did by *(state method of service)*.

(Signed)
(Solicitor/sheriff officer)
(add designation and business address)
Rule 41A.2(5)[4, 5]
FORM DA3

Form of interlocutor for recall of a determination of a domestic abuse interdict

Court ref no.

SHERIFFDOM OF *(insert name of sheriffdom)*
AT *(insert place of sheriff court)*
[A.B.], *(insert designation and address)*, Pursuer

---

[1] As inserted by the Act of Sederunt (Sheriff Court Rules) (Miscellaneous Amendments) (No.2) 2011 (SSI 2011/289) para.5 (effective July 20, 2011).
[2] As amended by the Act of Sederunt (Sheriff Court Rules)(Miscellaneous Amendments) 2013 (SSI 2013/135) para.4 (effective May 27, 2013).
[3] As inserted by the Act of Sederunt (Sheriff Court Rules) (Miscellaneous Amendments) (No.2) 2011 (SSI 2011/289) para.5 (effective 20 July 2011).
[4] As inserted by the Act of Sederunt (Sheriff Court Rules) (Miscellaneous Amendments) (No.2) 2011 (SSI 2011/289) para.5 (effective 20 July 2011).
[5] As amended by the Act of Sederunt (Sheriff Court Rules)(Miscellaneous Amendments) 2013 (SSI 2013/135) para.4 (effective 27 May 2013).

against
[C.D.], *(insert designation and address)*, Defender
(Date)

The sheriff, in pursuance of section 3(5)(b) of the Domestic Abuse (Scotland) Act 2011, recalls the determination that the [interim*] interdict dated *(insert date)* is a domestic abuse interdict. [The sheriff appoints *(insert name of person)*] to send forthwith a copy of this interlocutor to the chief constable of the Police Service of Scotland]. *(*delete as appropriate)*

(Sheriff)

FORM DA4[1, 2]

Rule 41A.2(8)

Form of certificate of sending documents to the chief constable

Court ref no.

SHERIFFDOM OF *(insert name of sheriffdom)*
AT *(insert place of sheriff court)*
[A.B.], *(insert designation and address)*, Pursuer
against
[C.D.], *(insert designation and address)*, Defender
(Insert place and date)

I hereby certify that on *(insert date)* I duly sent to the chief constable of the Police Service of Scotland a copy of [the interlocutor in Form DA1 and the certificate of service in Form DA2*] [the interlocutor in Form DA3*]. This I did by *(state method of sending). *delete as appropriate)*

(Signed)
(Solicitor/sheriff officer)
(add designation and business address)[3]

FORM OFT1

Rule 43.1(2)

Form of notice of intimation to the Office of Fair Trading

Date: *(date of posting or other method of intimation)*
To: The Office of Fair Trading
TAKE NOTICE

(Name and address of pursuer or defender) has brought an action against [*or* has defended an action brought by] *(name and address of defender or pursuer)*. The action raises an issue under Article 101 or 102 of the Treaty on the Functioning of the European Union. A copy of the initial writ is [*or* pleadings and interlocutor allowing intimation are] attached.

If you wish to submit written observations to the court, these should be addressed to the sheriff clerk *(insert address of sheriff clerk)* and must be lodged within 21 days of *(insert date on which intimation was given. N.B.* rule 5.3(2) *relating to postal service or intimation)*.

If you wish to submit oral observations to the court, you must lodge a minute with the sheriff clerk *(insert address of sheriff clerk)* for leave to do so. Your minute must be lodged within 21 days of *(insert date on which intimation was given. N.B.* rule

---

[1] As inserted by the Act of Sederunt (Sheriff Court Rules) (Miscellaneous Amendments) (No.2) 2011 (SSI 2011/289) para.5 (effective 20 July 2011).
[2] As amended by the Act of Sederunt (Sheriff Court Rules)(Miscellaneous Amendments) 2013 (SSI 2013/135) para.4 (effective 27 May 2013).
[3] As inserted by Act of Sederunt (Ordinary Cause Rules) Amendment (Causes Relating to Articles 81 and 82 of the Treaty Establishing the European Community) 2006 (SSI 2006/293) (effective 16 June 2006) and amended by the Act of Sederunt (Sheriff Court Rules) (Miscellaneous Amendments) (No.3) 2012 (SSI 2012/271) para.6 (effective 1 November 2012).

5.3(2) *relating to postal service or intimation).*
Date *(insert date)*..........*(Signed)*

Solicitor for pursuer/defender

FORM 48.1A[1]

Rule 48.1A(2)

Form of application for an order restricting the reporting of proceedings

Sheriff Court *(insert address)*

Court ref. no. *(insert)*

[A.B.] *(designation and address)*

Pursuer

Against

[C.D.] *(designation and address)*

Defender

1. The applicant is the pursuer [*or* respondent].

2. The applicant considers it is necessary for the court to make an order restricting the reporting of proceedings in the cause of [A.B.] *(designation and address)* against [C.D.] *(designation and address)* because:

   (state briefly in numbered paragraphs the reasons which, where applicable, should include the following information:

   (a) *details of any person (including their designation and address), or any other matter, in relation to whom or which anonymity is sought,*

   (b) *details of any enactments relied upon to apply for an order and the reasons why the applicant considers an order should be granted, [with reference to enactments and/or authority,]*

   (c) *details of any other legal basis relied upon to apply for an order and the reasons why the applicant consider an order should be granted, [with reference to enactments and/or authority,]*

   (d) *whether anonymity has previously been waived, by the person in respect of whom anonymity is sought, [and/or in relation to any other matter], and if so, the details of that waiver).*

---

[1] As inserted by the Act of Sederunt (Rules of the Court of Session 1994, Sheriff Appeal Court Rules and Sheriff Court Rules Amendment) (Miscellaneous) 2023 (SSI 2023/196) r.5(3), Sch.4 (effective 2 October 2023).

446

Date (*insert date*)   (signed)

[A.B.] [*or* C.D.], Applicant

or [X.Y.], Solicitor for Applicant

(*insert the business address of solicitor*)

FORM 49.6

Rule 49.6(6) and (7)

Form of preliminary act in ship collision action

In the action in which .... is Pursuer

.... and ....

.... is Defender

Preliminary Act

for

Pursuer [*or* Defender]

Court Ref. No:...............

(1) (*State the names of the vessels which came into collision, their ports or registry, and the names of their masters.*)

(2) (*State the date and time of the collision.*)

(3) (*State the place of the collision.*)

(4) (*State the direction and force of the wind.*)

(5) (*State the state of the weather.*)

(6) (*State the state, direction and force of the tidal or other current.*)

(7) (*State the magnetic course steered and speed through the water of the vessel when the other vessel was first seen or immediately before any measures were taken with reference to her presence, whichever was the earlier.*)

(8) (*State the lights (if any) carried by the vessel.*)

(9) (*State the distance and bearing of the other vessel if and when her echo was first observed by radar.*)

(10) (*State the distance, bearing and approximate heading of the other vessel when first seen.*)

(11) (*State what light or combination of lights (if any) of the other vessel when first seen.*)

(12) (*State what other lights or combinations of lights (if any) of the other vessel were subsequently seen, before the collision, and when.*)

(13) (*State what alterations (if any) were made to the course and speed of the vessel after the earlier of the two times referred to in paragraph (7) up to the time of the collision, and when, and what measures (if any), other than alterations of course and speed, were taken to avoid the collision and when.*)

(14) (*State the parts of each vessel which first came into contact and the approximate angle between the two vessels at the moment of contact.*)

(15) (*State what sound signals (if any) were given, and when.*)

(16) (*State what sound signals (if any) were heard from the other vessel and when.*)

---

[1] As inserted by the Act of Sederunt (Sheriff Court Rules) (Miscellaneous Amendments) 2012 (SSI 2012/188) para.10 (effective 1 August 2012).

(Signed by solicitor or Agent)
(Name)
(Address)
(Telephone number)

(Date)[1]

FORM 49.11-A

Rule 49.11(1)(a)(i)

Form of schedule of arrestment of found jurisdiction

Court:...............

Court Ref. No:...............

SCHEDULE OF ARRESTMENT TO FOUND JURISDICTION

Date: *(date of execution)*

Time: *(time arrestment executed)*

To: *(name and address of arrestee)*

I, *(name)*, Sheriff Officer, by virtue of an interlocutor of the Sheriff at *(place)* on *(date)* containing a warrant for arrestment to found jurisdiction, at the instance of *(name and address of pursuer)* against *(name and address of defender)*, arrest to found jurisdiction against *(name of defender)* in your hands: (i) the sum of *(amount)*, more or less, due by you to *(name of defender)* or to any other person on his [*or* her] [*or* its] [*or* their] behalf; and (ii) all moveable subjects in your hands and belonging or pertaining to *(name of defender)*.

This I do in the presence of *(name, occupation and address of witness)*.

(Signed)
Sheriff Officer
(Address)

NOTE

(Do not use this note where arrestment to found jurisdiction is combined with arrestment on the dependence in one schedule.)

(The name, address and twenty-four hour contact telephone number of the agent for the party on whose behalf the arrestment was executed are to be inserted here.)

(Name of agent)
(Address)

(Telephone number)[2]

FORM 49.11-AA

Rule 49.11(1)(a)(ii)

Form of schedule of arrestment of ship to found jurisdiction

Court:...............

Court Ref. No:...............

SCHEDULE OF ARRESTMENT OF SHIP TO FOUND JURISDICTION

Date: *(date of execution)*

Time: *(time arrestment executed)*

I, *(name)*, Sheriff Officer, by virtue of an interlocutor of the Sheriff at *(place)* on *(date)* containing a warrant for arrestment to found jurisdiction, at the instance of *(name and address of pursuer)* against *(name and address of defender)*, arrest to found jurisdiction against *(name of defender)* the ship *(name)* presently lying in *(describe location)* and belonging to the defender.

This I do in the presence of *(name, occupation and address of witness)*.

---

[1] As inserted by the Act of Sederunt (Sheriff Court Rules) (Miscellaneous Amendments) 2012 (SSI 2012/188) para.10 (effective August 1, 2012).

[2] As inserted by the Act of Sederunt (Sheriff Court Rules) (Miscellaneous Amendments) 2012 (SSI 2012/188) para.10 (effective August 1, 2012).

(Signed)
Sheriff Officer
(Address)

NOTE

You should consult your legal adviser about the effect of this arrestment.

(The name, address and twenty-four hour contact telephone number of the agent for the party on whose behalf the arrestment was executed are to be inserted here.)

(Name of agent)
(Address)

(Telephone number)[1]

FORM 49.11-B

Rule 49.11(1)(c)

Form of schedule of arrestment in rem of ship, cargo or other maritime res to enforce maritime hypothec or lien

Court:...............

Court Ref. No:...............

SCHEDULE OF ARRESTMENT IN REM IN ADMIRALTY ACTION IN REM

Date: *(date of execution)*

Time: *(time arrestment executed)*

I, *(name)*, Sheriff Officer, by virtue of an interlocutor of the Sheriff at *(place)* on *(date)* containing a warrant for arrestment in rem of the ship *(name of ship)* [*or* cargo *(describe)*] [*or other maritime res (describe)*] in an Admiralty action in rem at the instance of *(name and address of pursuer)* against *(name and address of defender)*, arrest the ship *(name)* presently lying in *(describe current location e.g. the port of X)* with her float, boats, furniture, appurtenances and apparelling [*or* cargo] [*or other maritime res*] *(describe location)*], to remain in that *(specify more precisely if required)* under arrestment in rem until they are sold or until this arrestment is recalled or other order of the sheriff.

This I do in the presence of *(name, occupation and address of witness)*.

(Signed)
Sheriff Officer
(Address)

NOTE

You should consult your legal adviser about the effect of this arrestment.

(The name, address and twenty-four hour contact telephone number of the agent for the party on whose behalf the arrestment was executed are to be inserted here.)

(Name of agent)
(Address)

(Telephone number)[2]

FORM 49.11-C

Rule 49.11(1)(d)

Form of schedule of arrestment in rem of ship to enforce non-pecuniary claim

Court:...............

Court Ref. No:...............

SCHEDULE OF ARRESTMENT IN REM OF SHIP UNDER THE ADMINISTRATION OF JUSTICE ACT 1956, SECTION 47(3)(b)

Date: *(date of execution)*

---

[1] As inserted by the Act of Sederunt (Sheriff Court Rules) (Miscellaneous Amendments) 2012 (SSI 2012/188) para.10 (effective August 1, 2012).

[2] As inserted by the Act of Sederunt (Sheriff Court Rules) (Miscellaneous Amendments) 2012 (SSI 2012/188) para.10 (effective August 1, 2012).

Time: (*time arrestment executed*)

I, (*name*), Sheriff Officer, by virtue of —

*an interlocutor of the Sheriff at (*place*) on (*date*) granting warrant for arrestment in rem under section 47(3)(b) of the Administration of Justice Act 1956 of the ship (*name of ship*) in an action,

*an interlocutor of the Sheriff at (*place*) on (*date*) containing a warrant for arrestment in rem under section 47(3)(b) of the Administration of Justice Act 1956 of the ship (*name of ship*), at the instance of (*name and address of pursuer*) against (*name and address of defender*), arrest the ship [*or* vessel] (*name*) presently lying in (*describe current location e.g. the port of X*) with her float, boats, furniture, appurtenances and apparelling to remain in that (*specify more precisely if required*) under arrestment in rem until this arrestment is recalled or other order of the sheriff.

This I do in the presence of (*name, occupation and address of witness*).

(*Signed*)
Sheriff Officer
(*Address*)

NOTE

You should consult your legal adviser about the effect of this arrestment.

(The name, address and twenty-four hour contact telephone number of the agent for the party on whose behalf the arrestment was executed are to be inserted here.)

(*Name of agent*)
(*Address*)
(*Telephone number*)

* Delete where not applicable.[1]

FORM 49.11-D

Rule 49.11(1)(e)(ii)

Court:...............

Court Ref. No:...............

Form of schedule of arrestment of ship on the dependence

Court: (*date of execution*)

Time: (*time arrestment executed*)

I, (*name*), Sheriff Officer, by virtue of —

*an interlocutor of the Sheriff at (*place*) on (*date*) granting warrant for arrestment on the dependence of the action at the instance of (*name and address of pursuer*) against (*name and address of defender*),

*a counterclaim containing a warrant which has been granted for arrestment on the dependence of the claim by (*name and address of creditor*) against (*name and address of debtor*) and dated (*date of warrant*),

*an interlocutor dated (*date*) granting warrant [for arrestment on the dependence of the action raised at the instance of (*name and address of pursuer*) against (*name and address of defender*)] [or for arrestment on the dependence of the claim in the counterclaim [or third party notice] by (*name and address of creditor*) against (*name and address of debtor*) [or to arrest in the cause of (*name and address of petitioner*) against (*name and address of respondent*)].

arrest the ship (*name of ship*) presently lying in (*describe current location e.g. the port of X*) to remain in that (*more precisely if required*) under arrestment on the dependence of the action [or claim] until further interlocutor of the sheriff.

This I do in the presence of (*name, occupation and address of witness*).

---

[1] As inserted by the Act of Sederunt (Sheriff Court Rules) (Miscellaneous Amendments) 2012 (SSI 2012/188) para.10 (effective August 1, 2012).

450

(Signed)
Sheriff Officer
(Address)

NOTE

You should consult your legal adviser about the effect of this arrestment.

(The name, address and twenty-four hour contact telephone number of the agent for the party on whose behalf the arrestment was executed are to be inserted here.)

(Name of agent)
(Address)
(Telephone number)

* Delete where not applicable.[1]

FORM 49.11-E

Rule 49.11(1)(a)(i) and (b)

Form of certificate of execution of arrestment

CERTIFICATE OF EXECUTION

I, *(name)*, Sheriff Officer, certify that I executed *(specify the kind of arrestment, whether on the dependence of an action, counterclaim or third party notice, whether on the authority of an interlocutor (specify), or in execution of a decree (specify))*, [obtained] at the instance of *(name and address of party arresting)* against *(name and address of common debtor)* on *(name of person on whom executed)*—

* by leaving the schedule of [arrestment] with *(name of defender or other person]* at *(place)* on *(date)*.

* by leaving the schedule of [arrestment] with *(name and occupation of person with whom left)* at *(place)* on *(date)*. *(Specify that enquiry made and that reasonable grounds exist for believing that the person on whom service is to be made resides at the place but is not available.)*

* by depositing the schedule of [arrestment] in *(place)* on *(date)*. *(Specify that enquiry made and that reasonable grounds exist for believing that the person on whom service is to be made resides at the place but is not available.)*

* by leaving the schedule of [arrestment] with *(name and occupation of person with whom left)* at *(place of business)* on *(date)*. *(Specify that enquiry made and that reasonable grounds exist for believing that the person on whom service is to be made carries on business at the place.)*

* by depositing the schedule of [arrestment] at *(place of business)* on *(date)*. *(Specify that enquiry made and that reasonable grounds exist for believing that the person on whom service is to be made carries on business at that place.)*

* by leaving the schedule of [arrestment] with *(registered office or place of business)* on *(date)*, in the hands of *(name of person)*.

* by leaving [or depositing] the schedule of [arrestment] at *(registered office, official address or place of business)* on *(date)* in such a way that it was likely to come to the attention of *(name of defender or other person on whom served)*. *(Specify how left.)*

* by leaving the schedule of [arrestment] with *(name and occupation of person with whom left)* at the office of the sheriff clerk at *(place)* on *(date)* and sending a copy of the schedule by first class post *(defender's last known address)* on *(date)*.

I did this in the presence of *(name, occupation and address of witness)*.

(Signed)
Sheriff Officer

---

[1] As inserted by the Act of Sederunt (Sheriff Court Rules) (Miscellaneous Amendments) 2012 (SSI 2012/188) para.10 (effective August 1, 2012).

(Address)
(Signed)
Witness

*Delete where not applicable.[1]

FORM 49.11-F

Rule 49.11(1)(a)(ii)

Form of certificate of arrestment of ship to found jurisdiction

CERTIFICATE OF EXECUTION OF ARRESTMENT OF SHIP TO FOUND JURISDICTION

I, *(name)*, Sheriff Officer, certify that I, by virtue of an interlocutor of the Sheriff at *(place)* on *(date)* containing a warrant for arrestment to found jurisdiction, executed an arrestment of the ship *(name)* at the instance of *(name and address of pursuer)* against *(name and address of defender)* by affixing the schedule of arrestment to the mainmast [*or as the case may be*] of the ship *(name)* and marked the initials ER above that affixed schedule at *(place)* on *(date)*.

I did this in the presence of *(name, occupation and address of witness)*.

(Signed)
Sheriff Officer
(Address)
(Signed)

Witness[2]

FORM 49.11-G

Rule 49.11(1)(c) and (d)

Form of certificate of execution of arrestment of ship or cargo in rem

CERTIFICATE OF EXECUTION OF ARRESTMENT OF SHIP [*OR* CARGO] IN REM

I, *(name)*, Sheriff Officer, certify that I executed an arrestment in rem of the ship [*or* vessel] *(name)* [*or* cargo *(describe)*] by virtue of an interlocutor of the Sheriff at *(place)* on *(date)* at the instance of *(name and address of pursuer)* against *(name and address of defender)* by affixing the schedule of arrestment to the mainmast [*or as the case may be*] of the ship [*or* vessel] [*or in the case of cargo landed or transhipped* on *(name)* as custodian for the time being of the cargo [*or as harbourmaster of the harbour where the cargo lies*]] [and delivering a copy of the schedule of arrestment and of this certificate to *(name)* the master of the ship [*or as the case may be*] at *(place)* on *(date)*.

I did this in the presence of *(name, occupation and address of witness)*.

(Signed)
Sheriff Officer
(Address)
(Signed)

Witness[3]

FORM 49.11-H

Rule 49.11(1)(e)

Form of certificate of execution of arrestment of ship or cargo on the dependence

---

[1] As inserted by the Act of Sederunt (Sheriff Court Rules) (Miscellaneous Amendments) 2012 (SSI 2012/188) para.10 (effective August 1, 2012).
[2] As inserted by the Act of Sederunt (Sheriff Court Rules) (Miscellaneous Amendments) 2012 (SSI 2012/188) para.10 (effective August 1, 2012).
[3] As inserted by the Act of Sederunt (Sheriff Court Rules) (Miscellaneous Amendments) 2012 (SSI 2012/188) para.10 (effective August 1, 2012).

CERTIFICATE OF EXECUTION OF ARRESTMENT OF SHIP [*OR* CARGO]
ON THE DEPENDENCE

I, (*name*), Sheriff Officer, certify that I executed an arrestment on the dependence of the ship [*or* vessel] (*name*) [*or* cargo (*describe*)] by virtue of an interlocutor of the Sheriff at (*place*) on (*date*) at the instance of (*name and address of pursuer*) against (*name and address of defender*) by affixing the schedule of arrestment to the mainmast [*or as the case may be*] of the ship [*or* vessel] (*name*) and marked the initials ER above the same [*or by* (*state method of service*)] at (*place*) on (*date*).

I did this in the presence of (*name, occupation and address of witness*).

(Signed)
Sheriff Officer
(Address)
(Signed)
Witness

Rule 51.3(1)[1]
FORM 51.3-A
Form of warrant to place [or renew] a caveat under

Court reference no. (insert reference)

SHERIFFDOM OF (insert name of sheriffdom)
AT (insert place of sheriff court)
WARRANT TO PLACE [or RENEW] CAVEAT
in the cause
[A.B.] (designation and address)

Pursuer

Against
[C.D.] (designation and address)

Defender

Date: (*date of interlocutor*)

To the Keeper of the Registers of Scotland

THE SHERIFF, having considered the application of the pursuer [*or* defender] and being satisfied as to the matters mentioned in section 67(4) [*or* 69(3)] of the Land Registration etc. (Scotland) Act 2012,

GRANTS warrant to place [*or* renew] a caveat on the title sheet of the plot of land—

(a) at (*state description of the plot(s) of land*);
(b) registered under title number (*state title number(s)*);
(c) registered in the name of (*state name and address of proprietor*).

(Signed)

NOTE: append a copy of any plan of the plot(s) of land lodged in accordance with rule 51.2(2)(c).[2]
FORM 51.3-B

Rule 51.3(2)

Form of order restricting a caveat under section 70(2) of the Land Registration etc. (Scotland) Act 2012

Court reference no. (insert reference)

SHERIFFDOM OF (insert name of sheriffdom)
AT (insert place of sheriff court)

---

[1] As inserted by the Act of Sederunt (Rules of the Court of Session and Sheriff Court Rules Amendment No.2) (Miscellaneous) 2014 (SSI 2014/291) para.3 (effective December 8, 2014).
[2] As inserted by the Act of Sederunt (Rules of the Court of Session and Sheriff Court Rules Amendment No.2) (Miscellaneous) 2014 (SSI 2014/291) para.3 (effective 8 December 2014).

ORDER RESTRICTING A CAVEAT
in the cause
[A.B.] (*designation and address*)

Pursuer

against
[C.D.] (*designation and address*)

Defender

Date: (*date of interlocutor*)

To the Keeper of the Registers of Scotland

THE SHERIFF, having considered the application of the pursuer [*or* defender], being satisfied—
  (a)   as to the matters mentioned in section 70(3) of the Land Registration etc. (Scotland) Act 2012; and
  (b)   that it is reasonable in all the circumstances to do so,
ORDERS that the caveat on the title sheet of the plot of land:
  (a)   at (*state description of the plot(s) of land*);
  (b)   registered under title number (*state title number(s)*);
  (c)   registered in the name of (*state name and address of proprietor*),
be restricted as follows:
  (*specify nature and extent of restriction*)
(*Signed*)[1]
FORM 51.3-C

Rule 51.3(3)

Form of order recalling a caveat under section 71(2) of the Land Registration etc. (Scotland) Act 2012

Court reference no. (*insert reference*)
SHERIFFDOM OF (*insert name of sheriffdom*)
AT (*insert place of sheriff court*)
ORDER RECALLING A CAVEAT
in the cause
[A.B.] (*designation and address*)

Pursuer

against
[C.D.] (*designation and address*)

Defender

Date: (*date of interlocutor*)

To the Keeper of the Registers of Scotland

THE SHERIFF, having considered the application of the pursuer [*or* defender] and no longer being satisfied as to the matters mentioned in section 71(3) of the Land Registration etc.(Scotland) Act 2012,
  ORDERS that the caveat on the title sheet of the plot of land—
  (a)   at (*state description of the plot(s) of land*);
  (b)   registered under title number (*state title number(s)*);
  (c)   registered in the name of (*state name and address of proprietor*),
be recalled.
(*Signed*)[2]

---

[1] Inserted by the Act of Sederunt (Rules of the Court of Session and Sheriff Court Rules Amendment No.2) (Miscellaneous) 2014 (SSI 2014/291) para. 3 (effective 8 December 2014).
[2] Inserted by the Act of Sederunt (Rules of the Court of Session and Sheriff Court Rules Amendment No.2) (Miscellaneous) 2014 (SSI 2014/291) para.3 (effective 8 December 2014).

FORM 51.5

Rule 51.5

Form of order for rectification of a document to which section 8A of the Law
Reform (Miscellaneous Provisions) (Scotland) Act 1985 **applies**

SHERIFFDOM OF (*insert name of sheriffdom*)

AT (*insert place of sheriff court*)

ORDER FOR RECTIFICATION OF A DOCUMENT UNDER SECTION 8 OF
THE LAW REFORM (MISCELLANEOUS PROVISIONS) (SCOTLAND) ACT
1985

[Date]

The sheriff, on the motion of the pursuer, orders the rectification of *[insert type of
deed, parties to the deed and date of registration in the Land Register of Scotland]*
registered in the Land Register of Scotland under title number *[state title number
and, if applicable, lease title number]* to the extent of *[insert details of the rectification including, if applicable, a statement in terms of section 8(3A) of the Law Reform
(Miscellaneous Provisions) (Scotland) Act 1985 (i.e. statement of consent)].*

FORM 52.2[1]

Rule 52.2

APPLICATION FOR A CERTIFICATE UNDER ARTICLE 5 OF REGULATION
(EU) NO. 606/2013 OF THE EUROPEAN PARLIAMENT AND OF THE
COUNCIL OF 12TH JUNE 2013 ON MUTUAL RECOGNITION OF PROTEC-
TION MEASURES IN CIVIL MATTERS

[Omitted by Act of Sederunt (Rules of the Court of Session 1994 and Sheriff
Court Rules Amendment) (Civil Protection Measures (EU Exit)) 2022 (SSI 2022/
329) para.3 (effective 1 December 2022).]

FORM 52.5-A[2]

Rule 52.5(2)(a)

NOTICE OF ISSUE OF CERTIFICATE UNDER ARTICLE 5 OF REGULATION
(EU) NO. 606/2013 OF THE EUROPEAN PARLIAMENT AND OF THE
COUNCIL OF 12TH JUNE 2013 ON MUTUAL RECOGNITION OF PROTEC-
TION MEASURES IN CIVIL MATTERS

[Omitted by Act of Sederunt (Rules of the Court of Session 1994 and Sheriff
Court Rules Amendment) (Civil Protection Measures (EU Exit)) 2022 (SSI 2022/
329) para.3 (effective 1 December 2022).]

FORM 52.5-B[3]

Rule 52.5(4)

NOTICE FOR WALLS OF COURT OF ISSUE OF CERTIFICATE UNDER
ARTICLE 5 OF REGULATION (EU) NO. 606/2013 OF THE EUROPEAN
PARLIAMENT AND OF THE COUNCIL OF 12TH JUNE 2013 ON MUTUAL
RECOGNITION OF PROTECTION MEASURES IN CIVIL MATTERS

[Omitted by Act of Sederunt (Rules of the Court of Session 1994 and Sheriff
Court Rules Amendment) (Civil Protection Measures (EU Exit)) 2022 (SSI 2022/
329) para.3 (effective 1 December 2022).]

---

[1] Inserted by the Act of Sederunt (Rules of the Court of Session and Sheriff Court Rules Amendment
No.3) (Mutual Recognition of Protection Measures) 2014 (SSI 2014/371) para.3 (effective 11 January 2015).

[2] Inserted by the Act of Sederunt (Rules of the Court of Session and Sheriff Court Rules Amendment
No.3) (Mutual Recognition of Protection Measures) 2014 (SSI 2014/371) para.3 (effective 11 January 2015).

[3] Inserted by the Act of Sederunt (Rules of the Court of Session and Sheriff Court Rules Amendment
No.3) (Mutual Recognition of Protection Measures) 2014 (SSI 2014/371) para.3 (effective 11 January 2015).

FORM 52.7[1]

Rule 52.7(1)

APPLICATION FOR RECTIFICATION OR WITHDRAWAL OF A CERTIFICATE ISSUED UNDER ARTICLE 5 OF REGULATION (EU) NO. 606/2013 OF THE EUROPEAN PARLIAMENT AND OF THE COUNCIL OF 12TH JUNE 2013 ON MUTUAL RECOGNITION OF PROTECTION MEASURES IN CIVIL MATTERS

[Omitted by Act of Sederunt (Rules of the Court of Session 1994 and Sheriff Court Rules Amendment) (Civil Protection Measures (EU Exit)) 2022 (SSI 2022/329) para.3 (effective 1 December 2022).]

FORM 53.4[2]

Rule 53.4(3)

SHERIFFDOM OF (*sheriffdom*) AT (*place*)
FORM OF MINUTE FOR DECREE

in

UNDEFENDED ACTION OF PROVING THE TENOR

(*insert name of solicitor for the pursuer*), having considered the evidence contained in the affidavits and the other documents as specified in the schedule and being satisfied that on this evidence a motion for decree (in terms of the crave of the initial writ) [*or in such restricted terms as may be appropriate*] may properly be made, moves the court accordingly.

In respect whereof
Signed

Solicitor for the Pursuer (*add designation and business address*)

SCHEDULE

(*numbered list of documents*)
APPENDIX 2

Rule 30.6(1)

FORMS FOR EXTRACT DECREES
FORM 1
Form of extract decree for payment
EXTRACT DECREE FOR PAYMENT

Sheriff Court   Court ref. no.

Date of decree   * In absence

Pursuer(s)   Defender(s)

The sheriff granted decree against the .... for payment to the .... of the undernoted sums.

Sum decerned for £ .... with interest at .... per cent a year from .... until payment and expenses against the .... of £ ....

* A time to pay direction was made under section 1(1) of the Debtors (Scotland) Act 1987.

* The amount is payable by instalments of £ .... per .... commencing within .... of intimation of this extract decree.

* The amount is payable by lump sum within .... of intimation of this extract decree.

---

[1] Inserted by the Act of Sederunt (Rules of the Court of Session and Sheriff Court Rules Amendment No.3) (Mutual Recognition of Protection Measures) 2014 (SSI 2014/371) para.3 (effective 11 January 2015).

[2] Inserted by the Act of Sederunt (Ordinary Cause Rules Amendment) (Proving the Tenor and Reduction) 2015 (SSI 2015/176) (effective 25 May 2015).

This extract is warrant for all lawful execution hereon.
Date .... Sheriff clerk (depute)
* Delete as appropriate.

FORM 2

Form of extract decree ad factum praestandum
EXTRACT DECREE *AD FACTUM PRAESTANDUM*

Sheriff Court   Court ref. no.
Date of decree   * In absence
Pursuer(s)   Defender(s)

The sheriff ordained the defender(s)...............and granted decree against the..........
for payment of expenses of £...........
                    This extract is warrant for all lawful execution hereon.
    Date

                                                    Sheriff clerk (depute)

* Delete as appropriate.

FORM 3

Form of extract decree of removing
EXTRACT DECREE OF REMOVING

Sheriff Court   Court ref. no.
Date of decree   * In absence
Pursuer(s)   Defender(s)

The sheriff ordained the defender(s) to remove* himself/herself/themselves and his/
her/their sub-tenants, dependents and others, and all effects from the premises at the
undernoted address and to leave those premises vacant** [and that after a charge
of.......... days].
    In the event that the defender(s) fail(s) to remove the sheriff granted warrant to
sheriff officers to eject the defender(s), sub-tenants, dependents and others, with all
effects, from those premises so as to leave them vacant.
    The Sheriff granted decree against the.......... for payment of expenses of £...........
    Full address of premises:—
                    This extract is warrant for all lawful execution hereon.
    Date

                                                    Sheriff clerk (depute)

** Delete as appropriate.
** Delete if period of charge is not specified in the decree.

FORM 4

Form of extract decree of declarator
EXTRACT DECREE OF DECLARATOR

Sheriff Court   Court ref. no.
Date of decree   * In absence
Pursuer(s)   Defender(s)

The sheriff found and declared that...............and granted decree against
the...............for payment of expenses of £...........
                    This extract is warrant for all lawful execution hereon.
    Date

                                                    Sheriff clerk (depute)

* Delete as appropriate.

FORM 5
Form of extract decree of forthcoming
EXTRACT DECREE OF FURTHCOMING

Sheriff Court

Date of decree

Date of original decree

Pursuer(s)

Court ref. no.

* In absence

Defender(s)/Arrestee(s)

Common Debtor(s)

The sheriff granted against the arrestee(s) for payment of the undernoted sums.

Sum decerned for £.......... or such other sum(s) as may be owing by the arrestee(s) to the common debtor(s) by virtue of the original decree dated above in favour of the pursuer(s) against the common debtor(s).

Expenses of £.......... * payable out of the arrested fund / payable by the common debtor(s).

This extract is warrant for all lawful execution hereon.

Date

Sheriff clerk (depute)

* Delete as appropriate.

FORM 6
Form of extract decree of absolvitor
EXTRACT DECREE OF ABSOLVITOR

Sheriff Court

Date of first warrant

Pursuer(s)

Court ref. no.

Date of decree

Defender(s)

(Insert the nature of crave(s) in the above action)

The sheriff absolved............... the defender(s) and granted decree against the.......... for payment of expenses of £...........

This extract is warrant for all lawful execution hereon.

Date

Sheriff clerk (depute)

FORM 7
Form of extract decree of dismissal
EXTRACT DECREE OF DISMISSAL

Sheriff Court

Date of first warrant

Pursuer(s)

Court ref. no.

Date of decree

Defender(s)

The sheriff dismissed the action against the............... defender(s) and granted decree against the............... for payment of expenses of £..........

* This extract is warrant for all lawful execution hereon.

Date

Sheriff clerk (depute)

* Delete as appropriate.

FORM 8
[Repealed by the Act of Sederunt (Sheriff Court Ordinary Cause Rules Amendment) (Miscellaneous) 1996 (S.I. 1996 No. 2445) (effective November 1, 1996).]

FORM 9
Form of extract decree
EXTRACT DECREE

Sheriff Court

Date of decree

Pursuer(s)

Court ref. no.

*In absence

Defender(s)

The sheriff and granted decree against the.............. for payment of expenses of
£...........
      This extract is warrant for all lawful execution hereon.
  Date

Sheriff clerk (depute)

*Delete as appropriate.[1]

FORM 10
Form of extract decree of divorce
EXTRACT DECREE OF DIVORCE

Sheriff Court

Date of Decree

Pursuer

Court Ref No

*In absence

Defender

Date of parties marriage...............Place of parties marriage
  The sheriff granted decree
  (1) divorcing the defender from the Pursuer;
  *(2) ordering that the following child(ren):
  ....Full name(s)...............Date(s) of birth
  Reside with the *pursuer/defender and finding the *pursuer/defender entitled to
be in contact with the following child(ren): as follows:
  All in terms of the Children (Scotland) Act 1995.
  *(3) ordaining payment
*(a) by the to the of a periodical allowance of £ per
*(b) by the.......... to the.......... of a capital sum of £
*(c) by the.......... to the.......... of £ per.......... as aliment for each child until that
    child attains years of age, said sum payable in advance and beginning at the
    date of this decree with interest thereon at the rate of per cent a year until
    payment;
*(d) by the.......... to the.......... of £ of expenses;
*(4) finding the.......... liable to the.......... in expenses as the same may be
subsequently taxed.
    This extract is warrant for all lawful execution hereon.
  Date: *(insert date)*

Sheriff Clerk (depute)

* Delete as appropriate.[2]

FORM 11
Form of extract decree of separation and aliment
EXTRACT DECREE OF SEPARATION AND ALIMENT

Sheriff Court

Date of Decree

Court Ref No

*In absence

---

[1] As substituted by the Act of Sederunt (Sheriff Court Ordinary Cause Rules Amendment) (Miscellaneous) 2000 (S.S.I. 2000 No. 239)(effective October 2, 2000).
[2] As substituted by the Act of Sederunt (Sheriff Court Ordinary Cause Rules Amendment) (Miscellaneous) 2000 (SSI 2000/239) (effective 2 October 2000).

Pursuer   Defender

The sheriff found and declared that the pursuer is entitled to live separately from the defender from the date of decree and for all time thereafter.

The Sheriff ordered that the following child(ren):

..........Full name(s)...............Date(s) of birth

Reside with the *pursuer/defender

And found the *pursuer/defender entitled to be in contact with the following child(ren):

as follows:

All in terms of the Children (Scotland) Act 1995.

* The sheriff ordained payment by the .... to the .... of £.......... per ....
as aliment for the ...., said sum payable in advance and beginning at the date of this decree with interest thereon at .... per cent a year until payment.

* The sheriff ordained payment by the .... to the .... of £.......... per ....
as aliment for each child, until that child attains .... years of age, said sum payable in advance and beginning at the date of this decree with interest thereon at .... per cent a year until payment; and granted decree against the .... for payment of £..........

This extract is warrant for all lawful execution hereon.

Date: *(insert date)*

Sheriff Clerk (Depute) *Delete as appropriate.

FORM 12[1]

Form of extract decree: Residence Order/Contact Order and aliment

EXTRACT DECREE OF RESIDENCE ORDER/CONTACT ORDER AND ALIMENT

Sheriff Court   Court Ref No

Date of Decree   *In absence

Pursuer   Defender

The Sheriff granted decree against the *pursuer/defender.

The Sheriff ordered that the following child(ren):

..........Full name(s)...............Date(s) of birth

reside with the *pursuer/defender and found the *pursuer/defender entitled to be in contact with the following child(ren):

as follows:

All in terms of the Children (Scotland) Act 1995.

*The sheriff ordained payment by the .... to the of £.......... per .... as aliment for each child, until that child attains .... years of age, said sum payable in advance and beginning at the date of this decree with interest thereon at .... per cent a year until payment;

and granted decree with interest thereon at per cent a year until payment;and granted decree against the for payment of expenses of £..........

This extract is warrant for all lawful execution hereon.

Date: *(insert date)*

Sheriff Clerk (Depute)

* Delete as appropriate.

Rule 36.G1(1B)

---

[1] As substituted by the Act of Sederunt (Sheriff Court Ordinary Cause Rules Amendment) (Miscellaneous) 2000 (SSI 2000/239) (effective 2 October 2000).

APPENDIX 3[1]

Schedule of Timetable Under Personal Injuries Procedure

Steps referred to under rule 36.G1 (1A)	Period of time within which action must be carried out*
Application for a third party notice under rule 20.1 (rule 36.G1 (1A)(a))	Not later than 28 days after defences have been lodged
Pursuer executing a commission for recovery of documents under rule 36.D1 (rule 36.G1(1A)(b))	Not later than 28 days after defences have been lodged
Parties adjusting their pleadings (rule 36.G1(1A)(c))	Not later than 8 weeks after defences have been lodged
Pursuer lodging a statement of valuation of claim in process (rule 36.G1(1A)(d))	Not later than 8 weeks after defences have been lodged
Pursuer lodging a record (rule 36.G1(1A)(e))	Not later than 10 weeks after defences have been lodged
Defender (and any third party to the action) lodging a statement of valuation of claim in process (rule 36.G1(1A)(f))	Not later than 12 weeks after defences have been lodged
Parties lodging in process a list of witnesses together with any productions upon which they wish to rely (rule 36.G1(1A)(g))	Not later than 8 weeks before the date assigned for the proof
Pursuer lodging in process the minute of the pre-proof conference (rule 36.G1(1A)(h))	Not later than 21 days before the date assigned for the proof

*NOTE: Where there is more than one defender in an action, references in the above table to defences having been lodged should be read as references to the first lodging of defences.

APPENDIX 4[2]

The Personal Injury Pre-action Protocol

Application of the Protocol

1. This Protocol applies to claims for damages for, or arising from personal injuries, unless:
    (a) the claimant reasonably estimates that the total liability value of the claim, exclusive of interest and expenses, exceeds £25,000;
    (b) the accident or other circumstance giving rise to the liability occurred before 28th November 2016;
    (c) the claimant is not represented by a solicitor during the stages of the Protocol; or
    (d) the injuries for which damages are claimed—
        (i)   arise from alleged clinical negligence;
        (ii) arise from alleged professional negligence; or

---

[1] As substituted by the Act of Sederunt (Sheriff Court Rules) (Miscellaneous Amendments) 2010 (SSI 2010/279) Sch.1 App.001 para.1 (effective 29 July 2010) and amended by the Act of Sederunt (Sheriff Court Rules) (Miscellaneous Amendments) (No.3) 2011 (SSI 2011/386) para.5 (effective 28 November 2011).
[2] As inserted by the Act of Sederunt (Sheriff Court Rules Amendment) (Personal Injury Pre-Action Protocol) 2016 (SSI 2016/215) para.2 (effective 28 November 2016).

(iii)   take the form of a disease.

In this paragraph—

"clinical negligence" has the same meaning as in rule 36.C1 of the Ordinary Cause Rules 1993; and

"disease" includes—

(a)   any illness, physical or psychological; and

(b)   any disorder, ailment, affliction, complaint, malady or derangement, other than a physical or psychological injury solely caused by an accident or other similar single event.

Definitions

2.   In this Protocol:

"claimant" means the person who is seeking damages from the defender;

"defender" means the person against whom a claim is made.

"next-day postal service which records delivery" means a postal service which—

(a)   seeks to deliver documents or other things by post no later than the next working day in all or the majority of cases; and

(b)   provides for the delivery of documents or other things by post to be recorded.

Aims of the Protocol

3.   The aims of the Protocol are to assist parties to avoid the need for, or mitigate the length and complexity of, civil proceedings by encouraging:

- the fair, just and timely settlement of disputes prior to the commencement of proceedings; and
- good practice, as regards:
  - early and full disclosure of information about the dispute;
  - investigation of the circumstances surrounding the dispute; and
  - the narrowing of issues to be determined through litigation in cases which do not reach settlement under the Protocol.

Protocol rules

4.   Where, in the course of completing the stages of the Protocol, the claimant reasonably estimates that the total value of the claim, exclusive of interest and expenses, has increased beyond £25,000, the claimant must advise the defender that the Protocol threshold has been exceeded. Parties may agree to continue following the stages of the Protocol on a voluntary basis with a view to facilitating settlement before commencing proceedings.

5.   Anything done or required to be done by a party under this Protocol may be done by a solicitor, insurer or other representative dealing with the claim for, or on behalf of, that party.

6.   Where a party is required under this Protocol to intimate or send a document to another party, the document may be intimated or sent to the solicitor, insurer or other representative dealing with the claim for, or on behalf of, that party.

7.   Documents that require to be intimated or sent under the Protocol, should, where possible, be intimated or sent by email using an email address supplied by the claimant or defender. Alternatively, such documents are to be sent or intimated using a next-day postal service which records delivery.

8.   Where there is a number of days within which or a date by which something has to be done (including being sent or intimated), it must be done or sent so that it will be received before the end of that period or that day.

9. The claimant is expected to refrain from commencing proceedings unless:
- all stages of the Protocol have been completed without reaching settlement;
- the defender fails to complete a stage of the Protocol within the specified period;
- the defender refuses to admit liability, or liability is admitted on the basis that the defender does not intend to be bound by the admission in any subsequent proceedings;
- the defender admits liability but alleges contributory negligence and the fact or level of contributory negligence is disputed by the claimant (see paragraph 18).
- settlement is reached but the defender fails to pay damages and agreed expenses/outlays within 5 weeks of settlement (see paragraph 35 below); or
- it is necessary to do so for time-bar reasons (in which case, proceedings should be commenced and a sist applied for to allow the stages of the Protocol to be followed).

10. Parties are expected to co-operate generally with each other with a view to fulfilling the aims of the Protocol.

The stages of the Protocol

11. *Stage 1 – issuing of Claim Form*

The claimant must send a Claim Form to the defender as soon as sufficient information is available to substantiate a claim. The Claim Form should contain a clear summary of the facts on which the claim is based, including allegations of negligence, breaches of common law or statutory duty and an indication of injuries suffered and financial loss incurred. A suggested template for the Claim Form can be found in Annex A at the end of this Appendix.

12. *Stage 2 – the defender's acknowledgement of Claim Form*

The defender must acknowledge the Claim Form within 21 days of receipt.

13. *Stage 3 – the defender's investigation of the claim and issuing of Response*

The defender has a maximum of three months from receipt of the Claim Form to investigate the merits of the claim. The defender must send a reply during that period, stating whether liability is admitted or denied, giving reasons for any denial of liability, including any alternative version of events relied upon. The defender must confirm whether any admission made is intended to be a binding admission. Paragraph 9 above confirms that the claimant may raise proceedings if a non-binding admission is made.

14. If the defender denies liability, in whole or in part, they must disclose any documents which are relevant and proportionate to the issues in question at the same time as giving their decision on liability.

15. Paragraph 14 does not apply to documents that would never be recoverable in the course of proceedings, or that the defender would not be at liberty to disclose in the absence of an order from the court.

16. A suggested list of documents which are likely to be material in different types of claim is included in Annex B at the end of this Appendix.

17. If an admission of liability is made under this Protocol, parties will be expected to continue to follow the stages of the Protocol, where:
- the admission is made on the basis that the defender is to be bound by it (subject to the claim subsequently being proved to be fraudulent); and
- the admission is accepted by the claimant.

18. *Stage 4 – disclosure of documents and reports following admission of liability*

Where the defender admits liability to make reparation under the Protocol but alleges contributory negligence, the defender must give reasons supporting the allegations and disclose the documents which are relevant and proportionate to the issue of contributory negligence. The claimant must respond to the allegation of contributory negligence before proceedings are raised.

19. Medical reports are to be instructed by the claimant at the earliest opportunity but no later than 5 weeks from the date the defender admits, in whole or part, liability (unless there is a valid reason for not obtaining a report at this stage).

20. Any medical report on which the claimant intends to rely must be disclosed to the other party within 5 weeks from the date of its receipt. Similarly, any medical report on which the defender intends to rely must be disclosed to the claimant within 5 weeks of receipt.

21. Parties may agree an extension to the issuing of medical reports if necessary.

22. *Stage 5 – issuing of Statement of Valuation of Claim*

The claimant must send a Statement of Valuation of Claim to the defender (in the same form as Form P16 in Appendix 1 of the Ordinary Cause Rules), together with supporting documents. The Statement of Valuation of Claim should be sent as soon as possible following receipt of all the other relevant information, including medical reports, wage slips, etc.

23. If the defender considers that additional information is required in order to consider whether to make an offer in settlement, the defender may request additional information from the claimant. Any such request is to be made promptly following receipt of the Statement of Valuation of Claim and supporting documents. The claimant must provide the information requested within 14 days of receipt of the request.

24. *Stage 6 – offer of settlement*

Any offer in settlement to be made by the defender may be made within 5 weeks from the date of receipt of the Statement of Valuation of Claim, medical reports and supporting evidence (including any additional information requested under paragraph 23).

25. Where the claimant's injuries are minor and no formal medical treatment is sought, a settlement offer may be made in the absence of medical evidence; otherwise, settlement offers may only be made following the submission of satisfactory medical evidence of injury.

26. An offer in settlement is only valid for the purposes of this Protocol if it includes an offer to pay expenses in accordance with the expenses provisions (at paragraphs 30-33) in the event of acceptance.

27. *Stage 7 – claimant's response to offer of settlement*

If a settlement offer is made, the claimant must either accept the offer or issue a reasoned response within 14 days of receipt of the offer. Alternatively, if the claimant considers that additional information is required to allow full and proper consideration of the settlement offer, the claimant may make a request for additional information from the defender within 14 days of the receipt of the offer.

28. Where additional information or documentation is requested to allow the claimant to give full and proper consideration to the settlement offer, the claimant must accept the offer or issue a reasoned response within 21 days of receipt of the additional information or documentation.

29. In any reasoned response issued, the claimant must:
- reject the offer outright, giving reasons for the rejection; or
- reject the offer and make a counter-offer, giving reasons.

30. The expenses to be paid to the claimant in the event of settlement comprise—

(a) a payment in respect of the claimant's liability for solicitors' fees calculated in accordance with paragraph 31, and

(b) reimbursement of all other reasonably incurred outlays.

31. The payment in respect of liability for solicitors' fees is the sum of—

(a) £546;

(b) 3.5% of the total amount of agreed damages up to £25,000;

(c) 25% of that part of the agreed damages up to £3,000;

(d) 15% of the excess of the agreed damages over £3,000 up to £6,000;

(e) 7.5% of the excess of the agreed damages over £6,000 up to £12,000;

(f) 5% of the excess of the agreed damages over £12,000 up to £18,000;

(g) 2.5% of the excess of the agreed damages over £18,000; and

(h) a figure corresponding to the VAT payable on the sum of the foregoing.

32. Where an expert report has been instructed, any associate agency fee is not a reasonably incurred outlay for the purpose of paragraph 30(b).

33. Any deduction from damages in accordance with section 7 of the Social Security (Recovery of Benefits) Act 1997 is to be disregarded for the purpose of paragraph 31.

34. *Stage 8 – stocktaking period*

The claimant must not raise proceedings until at least 14 days after the defender receives the claimant's reasoned response (even in cases where the settlement offer is rejected outright). This period allows parties to take stock of their respective positions and to pursue further settlement negotiations if desired.

35. *Stage 9 – payment*

Damages and Protocol expenses must be paid within 5 weeks of settlement (with interest payable thereafter at the judicial rate).

ANNEX A

1. This form is to be used where the details of the defender's insurers are known:

Pre-Action Protocol Claim Form
TO: (*name of insurance company*)
FROM: (*name of solicitor and firm representing claimant*)
DATE: (*date of issue of Claim Form*)
This is a claim which we consider to be subject to the terms of the Personal Injury Pre-Action Protocol as set out in the Act of Sederunt (Sheriff Court Rules Amendment) (Personal Injury Pre-Action Protocol) 2016. **Please acknowledge receipt of this claim within 21 days of the date of this Form.**
CONTACT: (*postal and email address of solicitor representing claimant*)

Claimant's details	
Claimant's Full Name	
Claimant's Full Address	
Claimant's Date of Birth	
Claimant's Payroll or Reference Number	
Claimant's Employer (name and address)	
Claimant's National Insurance Number	

Details of Claim
We are instructed by the above named to claim damages in connection with: [*state nature of accident* an accident at work/road traffic accident/tripping accident] on [Xth] day of [year] at [*state place of accident* – which must be sufficiently detailed to establish location]. The circumstances of the accident are:- [*provide brief outline and simple explanation* e.g. defective machine, vicarious liability]. Your insured failed to:- [*provide brief details of the common law and/or statutory breaches*]. Our client's injuries are as follows:- [*provide brief outline*]. **i.** Our client received treatment for the injuries at [*give name and address of GP/ treating hospital*]. [In cases of road accidents…] **ii.** Our client's motor insurers are:- Our client is still suffering from the effects of his/her injury. We invite you to participate with us in addressing his/her immediate needs by use of rehabilitation. He/she is employed as [*insert occupation*] and has had the following time off work [*provide dates of absence*]. His/her approximate weekly income is [*insert if known*].
Reports
We are obtaining a police report and will let you have a copy of same upon your undertaking to meet half the fee.
At this stage of our enquiries we would expect the undernoted documents to be relevant to this claim. (…)

2. This form is to be used where the details of the defender's insurers are not known:

Pre –Action Protocol Claim Form
TO: (*name of defender*)
FROM: (*name of solicitor and firm representing claimant*)
DATE: (*date of issue of Claim Form*)
This is a claim which we consider to be subject to the terms of the Personal Injury Pre-Action Protocol as set out in the Act of Sederunt (Sheriff Court Rules Amendment) (Personal Injury Pre-Action Protocol) 2016. **You should acknowledge receipt of this claim and forward it to your Insurers as soon as possible, asking them to contact us within 21 days of the date of this Form.**
CONTACT: (*postal and email address of solicitor representing claimant*)
Claimant's details

Claimant's Full Name	
Claimant's Full Address	
Claimant's Payroll or Reference Number	
Claimant's Employer (name and address)	

We are instructed by the above named to claim damages in connection with: [*state nature of accident an accident* at work/road traffic accident/tripping accident] on [Xth] day of [year] at [*state place of accident* – which must be sufficiently detailed to establish location].

The circumstances of the accident are:-

[*provide brief outline and simple explanation* e.g. defective machine, vicarious liability].

You failed to:- [*provide brief details of the common law and/or statutory breaches*].

Our client's injuries are as follows:- [*provide brief outline*].

i. Our client received treatment for the injuries at [*give name and address of GP/ treating hospital*].

[In cases of road accidents...]

ii. Our client's motor insurers are:-

Our client is still suffering from the effects of his/her injury. We invite you to participate with us in addressing his/her immediate needs by use of rehabilitation. He/she is employed as [*insert occupation*] and has had the following time off work [*provide dates of absence*]. His/her approximate weekly income is [*insert if known*].

Reports
We are obtaining a police report and will let you have a copy of same upon your undertaking to meet half the fee.
At this stage of our enquiries we would expect the undernoted documents to be relevant to this claim.
(...)

ANNEX B – STANDARD DISCLOSURE

Road Traffic Cases

1. **Section A – cases where liability is at issue**
   - (i) Documents identifying nature, extent and location of damage to defender's vehicle where there is any dispute about point of impact.
   - (ii) MOT certificate where relevant.
   - (iii) Maintenance records where vehicle defect is alleged or it is alleged by defender that there was an unforeseen defect which caused or contributed to the accident.

   Section B - accidents involving a potential defender's commercial vehicle
   - (i) Tachograph charts or entry from individual control book, where relevant.
   - (ii) Maintenance and repair records required for operators' licence where vehicle defect is alleged or it is alleged by defender that there was an unforeseen defect which caused or contributed to the accident.

   Section C - cases against local authorities where a highway design defect is alleged
   - (i) Documents produced to comply with section 39 of the Road Traffic Act 1988 in respect of the duty designed to promote road safety to include studies into road accidents in the relevant area and documents relating to measures recommended to prevent accidents in the relevant area.

Road/footway tripping claims

2. Documents from the Highway Authority or local authority for a period of 12 months prior to the accident–

    (i)   Records of inspection for the relevant stretch of road/footway.

    (ii) Maintenance records including records of independent contractors working in relevant area.

    (iii) Statement of the Roads Authority's policy under the Code of Practice for Highway Maintenance Management (2005) or alternatively records of the Minutes of Highway Authority or Local Authority meetings where maintenance or repair policy has been discussed or decided.

    (iv) Records of complaints about the state of roads/footway at the accident locus for a 12 month period prior to the accident.

    (v) Records of other accidents which have occurred on the relevant stretch of road/footway within 12 months of the accident.

Workplace claims – general

3.

    (i)   Accident book entry.

    (ii) First aider report.

    (iii) Surgery record.

    (iv) Foreman/supervisor accident report.

    (v) Safety representatives' accident report.

    (vi) RIDDOR (Reporting of Injuries, Disease and Dangerous Occurrences Regulations 2013) report to the Health and Safety Executive (HSE).

    (vii) Other communications between defenders and HSE.

    (viii) Minutes of Health and Safety Committee meeting(s) where accident/matter considered.

    (ix) Report to the Department for Work and Pensions.

    (x) Documents listed above relative to any previous accident/matter identified by the claimant and relied upon as proof of negligence.

    (xi) Earnings information where defender is employer.

Workplace claims -

4. Documents produced to comply with requirements of the Management of Health and Safety at Work Regulations 1991/3242

    (i)   Pre-accident Risk Assessment required by Regulation 3.

    (ii) Post-accident Re-Assessment required by Regulation 3.

    (iii) Accident Investigation Report prepared in implementing the requirements of Regulation 5.

    (iv) Health Surveillance Records in appropriate cases required by Regulation 6.

    (v) Information provided to employees under Regulation 10.

    (vi) Documents relating to the employee's health and safety training required by Regulation 13.

Workplace claims – Disclosure where specific regulations apply

5. Section A – Manual Handling Operations Regulations 1992/2793

    (i)   Manual Handling Risk Assessment carried out to comply with the requirements of Regulation 4(1)(b)(i).

    (ii) Re-assessment carried out post-accident to comply with requirements of Regulation 4(1)(b)(i).

    (iii)   Documents showing the information provided to the employee to give general indications related to the load and precise indications on the weight of the load and the heaviest side of the load if the centre of gravity was not positioned centrally to comply with Regulation 4(1)(b)(iii).

    (iv)   Documents relating to training in respect of manual handling operations and training records.

    (v)   All documents showing or tending to show the weight of the load at the material time.

Section B – Personal Protective Equipment at Work Regulations 1992/2966

    (i)   Documents relating to the assessment of Personal Protective Equipment to comply with Regulation 6.

    (ii)   Documents relating to the maintenance and replacement of Personal Protective Equipment to comply with Regulation 7.

    (iii)   Record of maintenance procedures for Personal Protective Equipment to comply with Regulation 7.

    (iv)   Records of tests and examinations of Personal Protective Equipment to comply with Regulation 7.

    (v)   Documents providing information, instruction and training in relation to the Personal Protective Equipment to comply with Regulation 9.

    (vi)   Instructions for use of Personal Protective Equipment to include the manufacturers' instructions to comply with Regulation 10.

Section C – Workplace (Health Safety and Welfare) Regulations 1992/3004

    (i)   Repair and maintenance records required by Regulation 5.

    (ii)   Housekeeping records to comply with the requirements of Regulation 9.

    (iii)   Hazard warning signs or notices to comply with Regulation 17.

Section D – Provision and Use of Work Equipment Regulations 1998/2306

    (i)   Manufacturers' specifications and instructions in respect of relevant work equipment establishing its suitability to comply with Regulation 4.

    (ii)   Maintenance log/maintenance records required to comply with Regulation 5.

    (iii)   Documents providing information and instructions to employees to comply with Regulation 8.

    (iv)   Documents provided to the employee in respect of training for use to comply with Regulation 9.

    (v)   Any notice, sign or document relied upon as a defence to alleged breaches of Regulations 14 to 18 dealing with controls and control systems.

    (vi)   Instruction/training documents issued to comply with the requirements of Regulation 22 insofar as it deals with maintenance operations where the machinery is not shut down.

    (vii)   Copies of markings required to comply with Regulation 23.

    (viii)   Copies of warnings required to comply with Regulation 24.

Section E – Lifting Operations and Lifting Equipment Regulations 1998/2307

    (i)   All documents showing the weight of any load to establish lifting equipment of adequate strength and stability to comply with Regulation 4.

    (ii)   All notices and markings showing the safe working load of machinery and accessories to comply with Regulation 7.

    (iii)   All documents showing lifting operations have been planned by a competent person, appropriately supervised and carried out in a safe manner to comply with Regulation 8.

    (iv)   All defect reports to comply with Regulation 10.

Section F – Pressure Systems Safety Regulations 2000/128

    (i)   Information and specimen markings provided to comply with the requirements of Regulation 5.

    (ii)   Written statements specifying the safe operating limits of a system to comply with the requirements of Regulation 7.

    (iii)   Copy of the written scheme of examination required to comply with the requirements of Regulation 8.

    (iv)   Examination records required to comply with the requirements of Regulation 9.

    (v)   Instructions provided for the use of operator to comply with Regulation 11.

    (vi)   Records kept to comply with the requirements of Regulation 14.

Section G – Control of Substances Hazardous to Health Regulations 2002/2677

    (i)   Risk assessment carried out to comply with the requirements of Regulation 6.

    (ii)   Reviewed risk assessment carried out to comply with the requirements of Regulation 6.

    (iii)   Copy labels from containers used for storage handling and disposal of carcinogenics to comply with the requirements of Regulation 7.

    (iv)   Warning signs identifying designation of areas and installations which may be contaminated by carcinogenics to comply with the requirements of Regulation 7.

    (v)   Documents relating to the assessment of the Personal Protective Equipment to comply with Regulation 7.

    (vi)   Documents relating to the maintenance and replacement of Personal Protective Equipment to comply with Regulation 7.

    (vii)   Record of maintenance procedures for Personal Protective Equipment to comply with Regulation 7.

    (viii)   Records of tests and examinations of Personal Protective Equipment to comply with Regulation 7.

    (ix)   Documents providing information, instruction and training in relation to the Personal Protective Equipment to comply with Regulation 7.

    (x)   Instructions for use of Personal Protective Equipment to include the manufacturers' instructions to comply with Regulation 7.

    (xi)   Air monitoring records for substances assigned a maximum exposure limit or occupational exposure standard to comply with the requirements of Regulation 7.

    (xii)   Maintenance examination and test of control measures records to comply with Regulation 9.

    (xiii)   Monitoring records to comply with the requirements of Regulation 10.

    (xiv)   Health surveillance records to comply with the requirements of Regulation 11.

    (xv)   Documents detailing information, instruction and training including training records for employees to comply with the requirements of Regulation 12.

(xvi) Labels and Health and Safety data sheets supplied to the employers to comply with the CLP (Classification, Labelling and Packaging) Regulations.

Section H – Control of Noise at Work Regulations 2005/1643

(i) Any risk assessment records required to comply with the requirements of Regulation 5.

(ii) Manufacturers' literature in respect of all ear protection made available to claimant to comply with the requirements of Regulation 7.

(iii) Health surveillance records relating to the claimant to comply with the requirements of Regulation 9.

(iv) All documents provided to the employee for the provision of information to comply with Regulation 10.

Section I – Construction (Design and Management) Regulations 2015/51

(i) All documents showing the identity of the principal contractor, or a person who controls the way in which construction work is carried out by a person at work, to comply with the terms of Regulation 5.

(ii) Notification of a project form (HSE F10) to comply with the requirements of Regulation 6.

(iii) Construction Phase Plan to comply with requirements of Regulation 12.

(iv) Health and Safety file to comply with the requirements of Regulations 4 and 12.

(v) Information and training records provided to comply with the requirements of Regulations 4, 14 and 15.

(vi) Records of consultation and engagement of persons at work to comply with the requirements of Regulation 14.

(vii) All documents and inspection reports to comply with the terms of Regulations 22, 23 and 24.

[THE NEXT PARAGRAPH IS D1.622]

SHERIFF COURTS (SCOTLAND) ACT 1971

(1971 c. 58)

An Act to amend the law with respect to sheriff courts in Scotland, and for purposes connected therewith.

[27th July 1971]

PART I – CONSTITUTION, ORGANISATION AND ADMINISTRATION

General duty of the Secretary of State

Secretary of State to be responsible for organisation and administration of sheriff courts

1. *[Repealed by the Judiciary and Courts (Scotland) Act 2008 (asp 6) Pt 3 s.48 (effective April 1, 2010 subject to transitional provisions and savings specified in SSI 2010/39 art.6).]*   **D1.622**

Sheriffdoms

Power of Secretary of State to alter sheriffdoms
2.—(1)–(2B) *[¹]*   **D1.623**
(3) *[²]*
(4)–(5) *[³]*

Sheriff court districts and places where sheriff courts are to be held

Sheriff court districts and places where sheriff courts are to be held
3.—(1)–(3) *[⁴]*   **D1.624**
(4) *[⁵]*
(5)–(6) *[⁶]*

4.–30. *[⁷]*   **D1.625**

---

[1] Repealed by the Courts Reform (Scotland) Act 2014 (asp 18) Sch.5 Pt 1 para.6 (effective 1 April 2015; as to transitional provisions and savings see SSI 2015/77).

[2] Repealed by the Courts Reform (Scotland) Act 2014 (Consequential Provisions and Modifications) Order 2015 (SI 2015/700) art.2(3) (effective 1 April 2015).

[3] Repealed by the Courts Reform (Scotland) Act 2014 (asp 18) Sch.5 Pt 1 para.6 (effective 1 April 2015; as to transitional provisions and savings see SSI 2015/77).

[4] Repealed by the Courts Reform (Scotland) Act 2014 (asp 18) Sch.5 Pt 1 para.6 (effective 1 April 2015; as to transitional provisions and savings see SSI 2015/77).

[5] Repealed by the Courts Reform (Scotland) Act 2014 (Consequential Provisions and Modifications) Order 2015 (SI 2015/700) art.2(3) (effective 1 April 2015).

[6] Repealed by the Courts Reform (Scotland) Act 2014 (asp 18) Sch.5 Pt 1 para.6 (effective 1 April 2015; as to transitional provisions and savings see SSI 2015/77).

[7] Repealed by the Courts Reform (Scotland) Act 2014 (asp 18) Sch.5 Pt 1 para.6 (effective 1 April 2015; as to transitional provisions and savings see SSI 2015/77).

Civil Jurisdiction

Upper limit to privative jurisdiction of sheriff court to be £5,000

D1.626   **31.** [¹]

D1.627   **32.–34.** [²]

Summary causes

Summary causes

D1.628   **35.**—³(1)   The definition of "summary cause" contained in paragraph (i) of section 3 of the Sheriff Courts (Scotland) Act 1907 shall cease to have effect, and for the purposes of the procedure and practice in civil proceedings in the sheriff court there shall be a form of process, to be known as a "summary cause", which shall be used for the purposes of all civil proceedings brought in that court, being proceedings of one or other of the following descriptions, namely—

    (a)[4]   actions for payment of money not exceeding £5000 in amount (exclusive of interest and expenses);

    (b)[5, 6]   actions of multiple poinding, actions of furthcoming, where the value of the fund in medio , or the value of the arrested fund or subject, as the case may be, does not exceed £5000 (exclusive of interest and expenses);

    (c)[7]   actions ad factum praestandum and actions for the recovery of possession of heritable or moveable property, other than actions in which there is claimed in addition, or as an alternative, to a decree ad factum praestandum or for such recovery, as the case may be, a decree for payment of money exceeding £5000 in amount (exclusive of interest and expenses);

    (d)   proceedings which, according to the law and practice existing immediately before the commencement of this Act, might competently be brought in the sheriff's small debt court or were required to be conducted and disposed of in the summary manner in which proceedings were conducted and disposed of under the Small Debt Acts;

and any reference in the following provisions of this Act, or in any other enactment (whether passed or made before or after the commencement of this Act) relating to civil procedure in the sheriff court, to a summary cause shall be construed as a reference to a summary cause within the meaning of this subsection.

---

[1] Repealed by the Courts Reform (Scotland) Act 2014 (asp 18) Sch.5 Pt 1 para.6 (effective 1 April 2015; as to transitional provisions and savings see SSI 2015/77).

[2] Repealed by the Courts Reform (Scotland) Act 2014 (asp 18) Sch.5 Pt 1 para.6 (effective 1 April 2015; as to transitional provisions and savings see SSI 2015/77).

[3] Prospectively repealed by the Courts Reform (Scotland) Act 2014 (asp 18) Sch.5 Pt 1 para.6 (date to be appointed).

[4] Figure substituted by the Sheriff Courts (Scotland) Act 1971 (Privative Jurisdiction and Summary Cause) Order 2007 (SSI 2007/507) art.3 (effective 14 January 2008: substitution has effect subject to savings specified in SSI 2007/507 art.4)

[5] As amended by the Bankruptcy and Diligence etc. (Scotland) Act 2007 (asp 3) Sch.6(1) para.1 (effective 1 April 2008: as SSI 2008/115).

[6] Figure substituted by the Sheriff Courts (Scotland) Act 1971 (Privative Jurisdiction and Summary Cause) Order 2007 (SSI 2007/507) art.3 (effective 14 January 2008: substitution has effect subject to savings specified in SSI 2007/507 art.4)

[7] Figure substituted by the Sheriff Courts (Scotland) Act 1971 (Privative Jurisdiction and Summary Cause) Order 2007 (SSI 2007/507) art.3 (effective 14 January 2008: substitution has effect subject to savings specified in SSI 2007/507 art.4)

(1A)[1] For the avoidance of doubt it is hereby declared that nothing in subsection (1) above shall prevent the Court of Session from making different rules of procedure and practice in relation to different descriptions of summary cause proceedings.

(2) *[Repealed by the Courts Reform (Scotland) Act 2014 (asp 18) Sch.5(1) para.6 (effective 28 November 2016 subject to transitional provision specified in SSI 2016/291 art.3(2)).]*

(3) *[Repealed by the Courts Reform (Scotland) Act 2014 (asp 18) Sch.5(1) para.6 (effective 28 November 2016 subject to transitional provision specified in SSI 2016/291 art.3(2)).]*

(4) *[Repealed by the Courts Reform (Scotland) Act 2014 (asp 18) Sch.5(1) para.6 (effective 28 November 2016 subject to transitional provision specified in SSI 2016/291 art.3(2)).]*

Procedure in summary causes

36.—[2](1) *[[3]]*

(2) A summary cause shall be commenced by a summons in, or as nearly as is practicable in, such form as may be prescribed by rules under the said section 32. **D1.629**

(3)[4] The evidence, if any, given in a summary cause shall not be recorded.

(4) *[Repealed by the Debtors (Scotland) Act 1987 (c.18), Sch.8.]*

Further provisions as to small claims

36A. *[Repealed by the Courts Reform (Scotland) Act 2014 (asp 18) Sch.5(1) para.6 (effective 28 November 2016 subject to transitional provision specified in SSI 2016/291 art.3(2)).]* **D1.630**

Expenses in small claims

36B. *[Repealed by the Courts Reform (Scotland) Act 2014 (asp 18) Sch.5(1) para.6 (effective 28 November 2016 subject to transitional provision specified in SSI 2016/291 art.3(2)).]* **D1.631**

Remits

37.—[5, 6](1)[7] In the case of any ordinary cause brought in the sheriff court the sheriff— **D1.632**

    (a) shall at any stage, on the joint motion of the parties to the cause, direct that the cause be treated as a summary cause, and in that case the cause shall be treated for all purposes (including appeal) as a summary cause and shall proceed accordingly;

---

[1] As inserted by the Law Reform (Miscellaneous Provisions) (Scotland) Act 1985 (c.73) Sch.2 para.14 with effect from 30 December 1985.

[2] Prospectively repealed by the Courts Reform (Scotland) Act 2014 (asp 18) Sch.5 Pt 1 para.6 (date to be appointed).

[3] Repealed by the Courts Reform (Scotland) Act 2014 (asp 18) Sch.5 Pt 1 para.6 (effective 1 April 2015; as to transitional provisions and savings see SSI 2015/77).

[4] Excluded by the Maintenance Orders (Reciprocal Enforcement) Act 1972 (c.18) s.4(4)(b).

[5] As inserted by the Agricultural Holdings (Scotland) Act 2003 (asp 11) Pt 7 s.86(1).

[6] Prospectively repealed by the Courts Reform (Scotland) Act 2014 (asp 18) Sch.5 Pt 1 para.6 (date to be appointed).

[7] As amended by the Law Reform (Miscellaneous Provisions) (Scotland) Act 1980 (c.55) s.16(a). See the Land Tenure Reform (Scotland) Act 1974 (c.38) s.9(6).

(b)   [¹]

(2)   In the case of any summary cause, the sheriff at any stage—

(a)   shall, on the joint motion of the parties to the cause, and

(b)   may, on the motion of any of the parties to the cause, if he is of the opinion that the importance or difficulty of the cause makes it appropriate to do so,

direct that the cause be treated as an ordinary cause, and in that case the cause shall be treated for all purposes (including appeal) as an ordinary cause and shall proceed accordingly:

Provided that a direction under this subsection may, in the case of an action for the recovery of possession of heritable or moveable property, be given by the sheriff of his own accord.

(2A)   [²]

(2B)   *[Repealed by the Courts Reform (Scotland) Act 2014 (asp 18) Sch.5(1) para.6 (effective 28 November 2016 subject to transitional provision specified in SSI 2016/291 art.3(2)).]*

(2C)   *[Repealed by the Courts Reform (Scotland) Act 2014 (asp 18) Sch.5(1) para.6 (effective 28 November 2016 subject to transitional provision specified in SSI 2016/291 art.3(2)).]*

(2D)   [³]

(3)⁴   A decision—

(a)   to remit, or not to remit, under subsection (2A), (2B) or (2C) above; or

(b)   to make, or not to make, a direction by virtue of paragraph (b) of, or the proviso to, subsection (2) above,

shall not be subject to review; but from a decision to remit, or not to remit, under subsection (1)(b) above an appeal shall lie to the Court of Session.

(4)   In this section "sheriff" includes a sheriff principal.

Appeal in summary causes

D1.633   **38.**⁵,⁶   In the case of—

(a)   any summary cause an appeal shall lie to the sheriff principal on any point of law from the final judgment of the sheriff; and

(b)⁷   any summary cause an appeal shall lie to the Court of Session on any point of law from the final judgment of the sheriff principal, if the sheriff principal certifies the cause as suitable for such an appeal,

but save as aforesaid an interlocutor of the sheriff or the sheriff principal in any such cause shall not be subject to review.

---

¹ Repealed by the Courts Reform (Scotland) Act 2014 (asp 18) Sch.5 Pt 1 para.6 (effective 22 September 2015; as SSI 2015/247).

² Repealed by the Courts Reform (Scotland) Act 2014 (asp 18) Sch.5 Pt 1 para.6 (effective 22 September 2015; as SSI 2015/247).

³ Repealed by the Courts Reform (Scotland) Act 2014 (asp 18) Sch.5 Pt 1 para.6 (effective 22 September 2015; as SSI 2015/247).

⁴ As substituted by the Law Reform (Miscellaneous Provisions) (Scotland) Act 1980 (c.55), s.16(c). As amended by the Law Reform (Miscellaneous Provisions) (Scotland) Act 1985 (c.73), s.18(3)(b).

⁵ As amended by the Law Reform (Miscellaneous Provisions) (Scotland) Act 1985 (c.73), s.18(4). Excluded by the Debtors (Scotland) Act 1987 (c.18), s.103(1).

⁶ Prospectively repealed by the Courts Reform (Scotland) Act 2014 (asp 18) Sch.5 Pt 1 para.6 (date to be appointed).

⁷ As amended by the Courts Reform (Scotland) Act 2014 (asp 18) Sch.5(1) para.6 (effective 28 November 2016 subject to transitional provision specified in SSI 2016/291 art.3(2)).

Miscellaneous and supplemental

39, 40. *[Repealed by the Law Reform (Miscellaneous Provisions) (Scotland)* **D1.634**
Act 1980 (c.55), Sch.3.]

41.–42. *[Repealed by the Courts Reform (Scotland) Act 2014 (asp 18) Sch.5 Pt* **D1.635**
1 para.6 (effective April 1, 2015; as to transitional provisions and savings see SSI
2015/77).]

PART IV – MISCELLANEOUS AND GENERAL

43.–44 *[Repealed by the Courts Reform (Scotland) Act 2014 (asp 18) Sch.5 Pt 1* **D1.636**
para.6 (effective April 1, 2015; as to transitional provisions and savings see SSI
2015/77).]

Interpretation

45. *[Repealed by the Courts Reform (Scotland) Act 2014 (asp 18) Sch.5 Pt 1* **D1.637**
para.6 (effective April 1, 2015; as to transitional provisions and savings see SSI
2015/77).]

46.–47. *[Repealed by the Courts Reform (Scotland) Act 2014 (asp 18) Sch.5 Pt* **D1.638**
1 para.6 (effective April 1, 2015; as to transitional provisions and savings see SSI
2015/77).]

SCHEDULES

SCHEDULE 1

MINOR AND CONSEQUENTIAL AMENDMENT OF ENACTMENTS

General

[Repealed by the Courts Reform (Scotland) Act 2014 (asp 18) Sch.5 Pt 1 para.6 **D1.639**
(effective April 1, 2015; as to transitional provisions and savings see SSI 2015/77).]

SCHEDULE 2

REPEAL OF ENACTMENTS

[Repealed by the Courts Reform (Scotland) Act 2014 (asp 18) Sch.5 Pt 1 para.6 **D1.640**
(effective April 1, 2015; as to transitional provisions and savings see SSI 2015/77).]

[THE NEXT PARAGRAPH IS D1.657]

COURTS REFORM (SCOTLAND) ACT 2014

(2014 ASP 18)

CONTENTS

481

An Act of the Scottish Parliament to make provision about the sheriff courts; to establish a Sheriff Appeal Court; to make provision about civil court procedure; to make provision about appeals in civil proceedings; to make provision about appeals in criminal proceedings; to make provision about judges of the Court of Session; to make provision about the Scottish Land Court; to make provision about justice of the peace courts; to rename the Scottish Court Service and give it functions in relation to tribunals; to provide for assistants to the Judicial Appointments Board for Scotland; and for connected purposes.

The Bill for this Act of the Scottish Parliament was passed by the Parliament on 7th October 2014 and received Royal Assent on 10th November 2014

Part 1 – Sheriff courts

Chapter 1 – Sheriffdoms, sheriff court districts and sheriff courts

Sheriffdoms, sheriff court districts and sheriff courts

1.—(1)   For the purposes of the administration of justice, Scotland is to be divided into areas, each to be known as a "sheriffdom".

D1.657

(2)   A sheriffdom is to comprise one or more areas, each to be known as a "sheriff court district".

(3)   Within each sheriff court district a place is to be designated at which the judiciary of the sheriffdom are to sit and hold court for the purpose of exercising their judicial functions; and such sittings are to be known as a "sheriff court".

(4)   The sheriffdoms and sheriff court districts existing immediately before the date on which this section comes into force are to continue to exist on and after that date, and are accordingly the first sheriffdoms and sheriff court districts for the purposes of subsections (1) and (2).

(5)   On and after the date on which this section comes into force, sheriff courts are to continue to be held at the places at which they were held immediately before that date, and accordingly those places are the first places designated for the holding of sheriff courts for the purposes of subsection (3).

(6)   Subsections (4) and (5) are subject to an order under section 2.

Power to alter sheriffdoms, sheriff court districts and sheriff courts

D1.658   **2.**—(1)   The Scottish Ministers may, following submission of a proposal under subsection (2), by order do any of the following—

(a)   alter the boundaries of sheriffdoms or sheriff court districts,

(b)   abolish sheriffdoms or sheriff court districts,

(c)   form new sheriffdoms or sheriff court districts,

(d)   provide that sheriff courts are to be held, or to cease being held, at any place specified in the order.

(2)   The Scottish Courts and Tribunals Service may, with the agreement of the Lord President of the Court of Session, submit a proposal to the Scottish Ministers for the making of an order under subsection (1).

(3)   Before submitting a proposal to the Scottish Ministers, the Scottish Courts and Tribunals Service must consult such persons as it considers appropriate.

(4)   If, following submission of a proposal, the Scottish Ministers decide to make an order, they must have regard to the proposal in deciding what provision to make in the order.

(5)   The Scottish Ministers may make an order under subsection (1) only with the consent of—

(a)   the Lord President, and

(b)   the Scottish Courts and Tribunals Service.

(6)   An order under subsection (1) may—

(a)   abolish any office in consequence of any provision made under subsection (1),

(b)   modify any enactment (including this Act).

Chapter 2 – Judiciary of the sheriffdoms

Permanent and full-time judiciary

Sheriffs principal

D1.659   **3.**—(1)   For each sheriffdom, there is to continue to be a judicial officer to be known as the "sheriff principal" of the sheriffdom.

(2)   It is for Her Majesty to appoint an individual to the office of sheriff principal.

(3)   The First Minister may, under section 95(4) of the Scotland Act 1998, recommend to Her Majesty the appointment of an individual to the office of sheriff principal only if the individual is qualified for appointment (see section 14).

(4)   Subsection (3) does not affect the operation of section 11 of the Judiciary and Courts (Scotland) Act 2008 (recommendation by the Judicial Appointments Board for Scotland).

(5)   In addition to the jurisdiction and powers that attach specifically to the office of sheriff principal, the sheriff principal of a sheriffdom may also exercise in the sheriffdom the jurisdiction and powers that attach to the office of sheriff.

(6)   Subsection (5) is subject to any provision, express or implied, to the contrary in any other enactment.

Sheriffs

4.—(1)   For each sheriffdom, there are to continue to be judicial officers each to be known as a "sheriff" of the sheriffdom.

(2)   It is for Her Majesty to appoint an individual to the office of sheriff.

(3)   The First Minister may, under section 95(4) of the Scotland Act 1998, recommend to Her Majesty the appointment of an individual to the office of sheriff only if the individual is qualified for appointment (see section 14).

(4)   Subsection (3) does not affect the operation of section 11 of the Judiciary and Courts (Scotland) Act 2008 (recommendation by the Judicial Appointments Board for Scotland).

D1.660

Summary sheriffs

5.—(1)   For each sheriffdom, there are to be judicial officers each to be known as a "summary sheriff" of the sheriffdom.

(2)   It is for Her Majesty to appoint an individual to the office of summary sheriff.

(3)   Her Majesty may appoint an individual only if the individual has been recommended for appointment by the First Minister.

(4)   The First Minister may recommend to Her Majesty the appointment of an individual only if the individual is qualified for appointment (see section 14).

(5)   Before making a recommendation under subsection (3), the First Minister must consult the Lord President of the Court of Session.

(6)   Subsection (4) does not affect the operation of section 11 of the Judiciary and Courts (Scotland) Act 2008 (recommendation by the Judicial Appointments Board for Scotland).

D1.661

Temporary and part-time judiciary

Temporary sheriff principal

6.—(1)   Subsection (2) applies where, in relation to a sheriffdom—

(a)   a vacancy occurs in the office of sheriff principal,

(b)   the Lord President of the Court of Session believes that the sheriff principal is unable to perform all or some of the functions of the office, or

(c)   the sheriff principal rules that he or she is precluded from performing all or some of those functions.

(2)   If the Lord President so requests, the Scottish Ministers must appoint—

(a)   a person holding the office of sheriff (whether of the same or another sheriffdom), or

(b)   a qualifying former sheriff principal (whether of the same or another sheriffdom),

to act as sheriff principal of the sheriffdom.

(3)   A "qualifying former sheriff principal" is an individual who—

(a)   ceased to hold that office other than by virtue of an order under section 25, and

(b)   has not reached the age of 75.

(4)   The appointment may be made for the purposes of the exercise of—

(a)   all of the sheriff principal's functions, or

(b)   only those functions that the sheriff principal is unable to perform or is precluded from performing.

D1.662

(5)   An individual appointed under subsection (2) is to be known as a "temporary sheriff principal".

(6)   The Lord President may request the appointment of a temporary sheriff principal for a sheriffdom in the circumstances specified in subsection (1)(a) only if the Lord President considers such an appointment to be necessary or expedient in order to avoid a delay in the administration of justice in the sheriffdom.

Temporary sheriff principal: further provision

D1.663

7.—(1)   Subject to subsection (3), an individual's appointment as a temporary sheriff principal lasts until recalled under subsection (2).

(2)   The Scottish Ministers must, if requested to do so by the Lord President of the Court of Session, recall the appointment of a temporary sheriff principal.

(3)   A sheriff's appointment as a temporary sheriff principal ceases if the sheriff—

(a)   ceases to hold office as sheriff, or

(b)   is suspended from office as sheriff.

(4)   Subject to section 6(4)(b), a temporary sheriff principal of a sheriffdom may exercise the jurisdiction and powers that attach to the office of sheriff principal of the sheriffdom, and does not need a commission for that purpose.

(5)   The appointment of a sheriff as a temporary sheriff principal does not affect the sheriff's appointment as sheriff.

(6)   Where a sheriff of one sheriffdom ("sheriffdom A") is appointed as temporary sheriff principal of another sheriffdom ("sheriffdom B")—

(a)   the sheriff must not, while remaining temporary sheriff principal of sheriffdom B, act in the capacity of sheriff of sheriffdom A, but

(b)   in addition to the jurisdiction and powers that attach specifically to the office of sheriff principal, the sheriff, by virtue of the appointment as temporary sheriff principal of sheriffdom B, may also exercise in that sheriffdom the jurisdiction and powers that attach to the office of sheriff of that sheriffdom.

Part-time sheriffs

D1.664

8.—(1)   The Scottish Ministers may appoint individuals to act as sheriffs; and individuals so appointed are to be known as "part-time sheriffs".

(2)   The Scottish Ministers may appoint an individual only if—

(a)   the individual is qualified for appointment (see section 14), and

(b)   the Scottish Ministers have consulted the Lord President of the Court of Session before making the appointment.

(3)   Subject to section 20, an appointment as a part-time sheriff lasts for 5 years.

(4)   A part-time sheriff may exercise the jurisdiction and powers that attach to the office of sheriff in every sheriffdom, and does not need a commission for that purpose.

(5)   A part-time sheriff is subject to such instructions, arrangements and other provisions as may be made under this Act by the sheriff principal of the sheriffdom in which the parttime sheriff is for the time being sitting.

(6)   In carrying out their functions under this Act, sheriffs principal must together have regard to the desirability of securing that every part-time sheriff—

(a)   is given the opportunity of sitting on not fewer than 20 days in each successive period of 12 months beginning with the day of the part-time sheriff's appointment, and

(b)   does not sit for more than 100 days in each such successive period.

Reappointment of part-time sheriffs

9.—(1)   A part-time sheriff whose appointment comes to an end by virtue of the expiry of the 5 year period mentioned in section 8(3) is to be reappointed unless—

    (a)   the part-time sheriff declines reappointment,

    (b)   a sheriff principal has made a recommendation to the Scottish Ministers against the reappointment, or

    (c)   the part-time sheriff has sat for fewer than 50 days in total in that 5 year period.

  (2)   Section 8 (apart from subsection (2)) applies to a reappointment under subsection (1) as it applies to an appointment.

  (3)   A part-time sheriff whose appointment comes to an end by resignation under section 20 may be reappointed.

  (4)   Section 8 applies to a reappointment under subsection (3) as it applies to an appointment.

D1.665

Part-time summary sheriffs

10.—(1)   The Scottish Ministers may appoint individuals to act as summary sheriffs; and individuals so appointed are to be known as "part-time summary sheriffs".

  (2)   The Scottish Ministers may appoint an individual only if—

    (a)   the individual is qualified for appointment (see section 14), and

    (b)   the Scottish Ministers have consulted the Lord President of the Court of Session before making the appointment.

  (3)   Subject to section 20, an appointment as a part-time summary sheriff lasts for 5 years.

  (4)   A part-time summary sheriff may exercise the jurisdiction and powers that attach to the office of summary sheriff in every sheriffdom, and does not need a commission for that purpose.

  (5)   A part-time summary sheriff is subject to such instructions, arrangements and other provisions as may be made under this Act by the sheriff principal of the sheriffdom in which the part-time summary sheriff is for the time being sitting.

  (6)   In carrying out their functions under this Act, sheriffs principal must together have regard to the desirability of securing that every part-time summary sheriff—

    (a)   is given the opportunity of sitting on not fewer than 20 days in each successive period of 12 months beginning with the day of the part-time summary sheriff's appointment, and

    (b)   does not sit for more than 100 days in each such successive period.

D1.666

Reappointment of part-time summary sheriffs

11.—(1)   A part-time summary sheriff whose appointment comes to an end by virtue of the expiry of the 5 year period mentioned in section 10(3) is to be reappointed unless—

    (a)   the part-time summary sheriff declines reappointment,

    (b)   a sheriff principal has made a recommendation to the Scottish Ministers against the reappointment, or

    (c)   the part-time summary sheriff has sat for fewer than 50 days in total in that 5 year period.

  (2)   Section 10 (apart from subsection (2)) applies to a reappointment under subsection (1) as it applies to an appointment.

  (3)   A part-time summary sheriff whose appointment comes to an end by resignation under section 20 may be reappointed.

D1.667

(4)   Section 10 applies to a reappointment under subsection (3) as it applies to an appointment.

Re-employment of former holders of certain judicial offices

Re-employment of former judicial office holders

D1.668

12.—(1)   A sheriff principal of a sheriffdom may appoint—

(a)   a qualifying former sheriff principal to act as a sheriff of the sheriffdom,

(b)   a qualifying former sheriff to act as such a sheriff,

(c)   a qualifying former part-time sheriff to act as such a sheriff,

(d)   a qualifying former summary sheriff to act as a summary sheriff of the sheriffdom,

(e)   a qualifying former part-time summary sheriff to act as such a summary sheriff.

(2)   An individual appointed to act as mentioned in any of paragraphs (a) to (e) of subsection (1) may so act only during such periods or on such occasions as the sheriff principal may determine.

(3)   A sheriff principal may make an appointment under subsection (1) only if it appears to the sheriff principal to be expedient as a temporary measure in order to facilitate the disposal of business in the sheriff courts of the sheriffdom.

(4)   A "qualifying former sheriff principal" is an individual who—

(a)   ceased to hold that office other than by virtue of an order under section 25, and

(b)   has not reached the age of 75.

(5)   A "qualifying former sheriff" is an individual who—

(a)   ceased to hold that office other than—

(i)   by virtue of an order under section 25, or

(ii)   by being appointed as a sheriff principal, and

(b)   has not reached the age of 75.

(6)   A "qualifying former part-time sheriff" is an individual who—

(a)   ceased to hold that office other than—

(i)   by virtue of removal under section 25,

(ii)   by virtue of not being reappointed to the office on either of the grounds mentioned in section 9(1)(b) and (c), or

(iii)   by being appointed as a sheriff principal, and

(b)   has not reached the age of 75.

(7)   A "qualifying former summary sheriff" is an individual who—

(a)   ceased to hold that office other than—

(i)   by virtue of an order under section 25, or

(ii)   by being appointed as a sheriff, and

(b)   has not reached the age of 75.

(8)   A "qualifying former part-time summary sheriff" is an individual who—

(a)   ceased to hold that office other than—

(i)   by virtue of removal under section 25,

(ii)   by virtue of not being reappointed to the office on either of the grounds mentioned in section 11(1)(b) and (c), or

(iii)   by being appointed as a sheriff, and

(b)   has not reached the age of 75.

Re-employment of former judicial office holders: further provision

13.—(1) Subject to subsection (4), an individual's appointment under section   **D1.669**
12(1) lasts until the sheriff principal by whom the individual was appointed (or a
successor to that sheriff principal) recalls the individual's appointment.

(2) An individual appointed under section 12(1) to act as a sheriff of a
sheriffdom may exercise in the sheriffdom the jurisdiction and powers that attach to
the office of sheriff, and does not need a commission for that purpose.

(3) An individual appointed under section 12(1) to act as a summary sheriff of a
sheriffdom may exercise in the sheriffdom the jurisdiction and powers that attach to
the office of summary sheriff, and does not need a commission for that purpose.

(4) An individual's appointment under section 12(1) ceases when the individual
reaches the age of 75.

(5) Despite the ending (whether by virtue of subsection (4) or otherwise) of an
individual's appointment under section 12(1)—

(a) the individual may continue to deal with, give judgment in or deal with an
ancillary matter relating to, a case begun before the individual while acting under that appointment,

(b) so far as necessary for that purpose, and for the purpose of any subsequent
proceedings arising out of the case or matter, the individual is to be treated
as acting or, as the case may be, having acted under that appointment.

Qualification and disqualification

Qualification for appointment

14.—(1) An individual is qualified for appointment to a judicial office   **D1.670**
mentioned in subsection (2) if the individual—

(a) immediately before the appointment, held any other judicial office specified in that subsection, or

(b) at the time of appointment—

(i) is legally qualified, and

(ii) has been so qualified throughout the period of 10 years immediately preceding the appointment.

(2) The judicial offices are—

(a) sheriff principal,

(b) sheriff,

(c) summary sheriff,

(d) part-time sheriff,

(e) part-time summary sheriff.

(3) For the purposes of subsection (1), an individual is legally qualified if the
individual is a solicitor or an advocate.

Disqualification from practice, etc.

15.—(1) An individual holding a judicial office mentioned in subsection (2)   **D1.671**
must not, for so long as the individual holds the office—

(a) engage, whether directly or indirectly, in practice as a solicitor or advocate
or in any other business,

(b) be in partnership with, or employed by, a person so engaged, or

(c) act as agent for a person so engaged.

(2) The judicial offices are—

(a) sheriff principal,

(b) sheriff,

(c) summary sheriff.

(3)   A part-time sheriff, or a part-time summary sheriff, who is a solicitor in practice must not carry out any function as a part-time sheriff or, as the case may be, a part-time summary sheriff in a sheriff court district in which his or her place of business as such solicitor is situated.

Remuneration and expenses

Remuneration

D1.672

16.—[1]   Each sheriff principal and sheriff is to be paid such salary as the Treasury may determine.

(1)

(2)   Such salary and such allowances is to be paid quarterly or otherwise in every year, as the Treasury may determine.

(3)   Each summary sheriff is to be paid such remuneration and such allowances as the Scottish Ministers may determine.

(4)   The Scottish Ministers may determine different amounts of remuneration and different amounts of allowances for—

    (a)   different summary sheriffs, or

    (b)   different descriptions of summary sheriff.

(5)   Each judicial officer mentioned in subsection (7) is to be paid such remuneration and such allowances as the Scottish Ministers may determine.

(6)   The Scottish Ministers may determine different amounts of remuneration and different amounts of allowances for—

    (a)   different judicial officers mentioned in subsection (7), or

    (b)   different descriptions of such judicial officers.

(7)   The judicial officers are—

    (za)[2]   (za) a temporary sheriff principal,

    (a)   a part-time sheriff,

    (b)   a part-time summary sheriff,

    (c)   an individual appointed to act as a sheriff or summary sheriff under section 12(1).

(8)   Subsection (9) applies in relation to—

    (a)   a sheriff principal of a sheriffdom authorised under section 30 to perform the functions of a sheriff principal in another sheriffdom, and

    (b)   a sheriff of a sheriffdom ("sheriffdom A") directed under section 31 to perform the functions of sheriff in another sheriffdom in addition to sheriffdom A.

(9)   The sheriff principal or sheriff is to be paid, in respect of the additional functions, such remuneration as appears to the Secretary of State, with the consent of the Treasury, to be reasonable in all the circumstances.

(10)   Subsection (11) applies in relation to a summary sheriff of a sheriffdom ("sheriffdom B") directed under section 31 to perform the functions of a summary sheriff in another sheriffdom in addition to sheriffdom B.

---

[1] As amended by the Public Service Pensions and Judicial Offices Act 2022 (c.7) Sch.2 para.21(2) (effective 10 March 2022 (for the limited purpose of making subordinate legislation or giving directions, or as it otherwise relates to the exercise of a power to make subordinate legislation, or give directions, on or after 10 March 2022); 10 May 2022 (otherwise)).

[2] As inserted by the Courts Reform (Scotland) Act 2014 (Consequential and Supplemental Provisions) Order (SSI 2018/2018) art.5 (effective 1 April 2018).

(11) The summary sheriff is to be paid, in respect of the additional functions, such remuneration as appears to the Scottish Ministers to be reasonable in all the circumstances.

(12) Salaries, allowances and remuneration under subsections (1) to (11) are to be paid by the Scottish Courts and Tribunals Service.

(13) Sums required by the Scottish Courts and Tribunals Service for the payment of a salary or an allowance under subsection (1) or remuneration or an allowance under subsection (3) are charged on the Scottish Consolidated Fund.

Expenses

17.—(1) The Scottish Courts and Tribunals Service may pay to a judicial of-   **D1.673**
ficer mentioned in subsection (3) such sums as it may determine in respect of expenses reasonably incurred by the officer in the performance of, or in connection with, the officer's duties.

(2) The Scottish Courts and Tribunals Service may—

  (a) determine the circumstances in which such sums may be paid, and

  (b) determine different circumstances for—

      (i) different judicial officers, or

      (ii) different descriptions of judicial officers.

(3) The judicial officers are—

  (a) a sheriff principal,

  (b) a sheriff,

  (c) a summary sheriff,

  (d) a temporary sheriff principal,

  (e) a part-time sheriff,

  (f) a part-time summary sheriff,

  (g) individuals appointed to act as a sheriff or summary sheriff under section 12(1).

Leave of absence

Leave of absence

18.—(1) The Lord President of the Court of Session may, for any sheriff   **D1.674**
principal or temporary sheriff principal, approve leave of absence for recreational or other purposes.

(2) The sheriff principal of a sheriffdom may, for any sheriff or summary sheriff of the sheriffdom, approve leave of absence for recreational or other purposes.

(3) The amount of leave for recreational purposes approved under this section for any sheriff principal, temporary sheriff principal, sheriff or summary sheriff must not exceed 7 weeks in any year.

(4) That limit may be exceeded in any case with the permission of the Lord President.

(5) The Lord President may grant permission under subsection (4) only if there are special reasons in the particular case that justify exceeding the limit.

(6) The Lord President may delegate to a judge of the Court of Session a function conferred on the Lord President by this section.

(7) In subsections (1) and (2), the references to leave of absence for purposes other than recreational purposes include (but are not limited to) references to sick leave, compassionate leave and study leave.

Residence

Place of residence

D1.675   **19.**—(1)   The Lord President of the Court of Session may require a judicial officer mentioned in subsection (2) to reside ordinarily at such place as the Lord President may specify.

(2)   The judicial officers are—

(a)   a sheriff principal,

(b)   a sheriff,

(c)   a summary sheriff.

Cessation of appointment

Cessation of appointment of judicial officers

D1.676   **20.**—(1)   A judicial officer mentioned in subsection (3) may resign at any time by giving notice to that effect to the Scottish Ministers.

(2)   An individual's appointment as such a judicial officer ends—

(a)   when the individual resigns in accordance with subsection (1),

(b)   when the individual retires from office,

(c)   if the individual is removed from office as such under section 25, or

(d)   if the individual is appointed as another such judicial officer.

(3)   The judicial officers are—

(a)   a sheriff principal,

(b)   a sheriff,

(c)   a summary sheriff,

(d)   a part-time sheriff,

(e)   a part-time summary sheriff.

Fitness for office

Tribunal to consider fitness for office

D1.677   **21.**—(1)   The First Minister must, if requested to do so by the Lord President of the Court of Session, constitute a tribunal to investigate and report on whether an individual holding a judicial office mentioned in subsection (3) is unfit to hold the office by reason of inability, neglect of duty or misbehaviour.

(2)   Subject to subsection (1), the First Minister may, in such circumstances as the First Minister thinks fit and after consulting the Lord President, constitute such a tribunal.

(3)   The judicial offices are—

(a)   sheriff principal,

(b)   sheriff,

(c)   summary sheriff,

(d)   part-time sheriff, and

(e)   part-time summary sheriff.

(4)   A tribunal constituted under this section is to consist of—

(a)   one individual who is a qualifying member of the Judicial Committee of the Privy Council,

(b)   one individual who holds the relevant judicial office,

(c)   one individual who is, and has been for at least 10 years—

(i)   an advocate, or

(ii)   a solicitor, and

(d)   one individual who—

      (i)   is not and never has been a qualifying member of the Judicial Committee of the Privy Council,

     (ii)   does not hold and never has held a judicial office mentioned in subsection (3), and

   (iii)   is not and never has been an advocate or solicitor.

(5)   In subsection (4)—

"a qualifying member of the Judicial Committee of the Privy Council" means someone who is a member of that Committee by virtue of section 1(2)(a) of the Judicial Committee Act 1833 (that is, someone who holds or has held high judicial office),

"the relevant judicial office" means—

   (a)   in respect of an investigation into whether an individual is fit to hold the office of sheriff principal, that office,

   (b)   in respect of an investigation into whether an individual is fit to hold the office of sheriff or part-time sheriff, the office of sheriff,

   (c)   in respect of an investigation into whether an individual is fit to hold the office of summary sheriff or part-time summary sheriff, the office of summary sheriff.

(6)   It is for the First Minister, with the agreement of the Lord President, to select persons to be members of a tribunal constituted under this section.

(7)   The person who is an individual mentioned in subsection (4)(a) is to chair the tribunal and has a casting vote.

Tribunal investigations: suspension from office

22.—(1)   Subsection (2) applies where the Lord President of the Court of Session has requested that the First Minister constitute a tribunal under section 21.   **D1.678**

(2)   The Lord President may, at any time before the tribunal reports to the First Minister, suspend from office the individual who is, or is to be, the subject of the tribunal's investigation.

(3)   Such a suspension lasts until the Lord President orders otherwise.

(4)   A tribunal constituted under section 21 may, at any time before the tribunal reports to the First Minister, recommend in writing to the First Minister that the individual who is the subject of the tribunal's investigation be suspended from office.

(5)   On receiving such a recommendation, the First Minister may suspend the individual from office.

(6)   Such a suspension lasts until the First Minister orders otherwise.

(7)   Suspension of an individual from the office of sheriff principal, sheriff or summary sheriff under this section does not affect any remuneration payable to, or in respect of, the individual in respect of the period of suspension.

Further provision about tribunals

23.—(1)   A tribunal constituted under section 21 may require any person—   **D1.679**

   (a)   to attend its proceedings for the purpose of giving evidence,

   (b)   to produce documents in the person's custody or under the person's control.

(2)   A person on whom such a requirement is imposed is not obliged—

   (a)   to answer any question which the person would be entitled to refuse to answer in a court in Scotland,

   (b)   to produce any document which the person would be entitled to refuse to produce in such a court.

(3)   Subsection (4) applies where a person on whom a requirement has been imposed under subsection (1)—

    (a)   refuses or fails, without reasonable excuse, to comply with the requirement,

    (b)   refuses or fails, without reasonable excuse, to answer any question while attending the tribunal proceedings to give evidence,

    (c)   deliberately alters, conceals or destroys any document that the person is required to produce.

(4)   The Court of Session may, on an application made to it by the tribunal—

    (a)   make such order for enforcing compliance as it sees fit, or

    (b)   deal with the matter as if it were a contempt of the Court.

(5)   The Court of Session may by act of sederunt make provision as to the procedure to be followed by and before a tribunal constituted under section 21.

(6)   The Scottish Ministers—

    (a)   must pay such expenses as they consider are reasonably required to be incurred to enable a tribunal constituted under section 21 to carry out its functions, and

    (b)   may pay such remuneration to, and such expenses of, the members of such a tribunal as they think fit.

Tribunal report

D1.680   **24.**—(1)   The report of a tribunal constituted under section 21 must—

    (a)   be in writing,

    (b)   contain reasons for its conclusion, and

    (c)   be submitted to the First Minister.

(2)   The First Minister must lay the report before the Scottish Parliament.

Removal from office

D1.681   **25.**—(1)   The First Minister may remove an individual from the office of sheriff principal, sheriff, part-time sheriff, summary sheriff or part-time summary sheriff—

    (a)   if a tribunal constituted under section 21 reports to the First Minister that the individual is unfit to hold that office by reason of inability, neglect of duty or misbehaviour, and

    (b)   only after the First Minister has laid the report before the Scottish Parliament under section 24(2).

(2)   The First Minister may remove a sheriff principal, sheriff or summary sheriff under subsection (1) only by order.

(3)   Such an order is subject to the negative procedure.

Honorary sheriffs

Abolition of the office of honorary sheriff

D1.682   **26.**   The office of honorary sheriff is abolished.

Chapter 3 – Organisation of business

Sheriff principal's general responsibilities

Sheriff principal's responsibility for efficient disposal of business in sheriff courts

D1.683   **27.**—(1)   The sheriff principal of a sheriffdom is responsible for ensuring the efficient disposal of business in the sheriff courts of the sheriffdom.

(2)　The sheriff principal must make such arrangements as appear necessary or expedient for the purpose of carrying out the responsibility imposed by subsection (1).

(3)　In particular, the sheriff principal may—

(a)　provide for the allocation of business among the judiciary of the sheriff-dom,

(b)　make special provision of a temporary nature for the disposal of any business by any member of the judiciary of the sheriffdom in addition to or in place of that member's own duties.

(4)　If, in carrying out the responsibility imposed by subsection (1), the sheriff principal gives a direction of an administrative character to a person mentioned in subsection (5), the person must comply with the direction.

(5)　Those persons are—

(a)　any other member of the judiciary of the sheriffdom,

(b)　a member of the staff of the Scottish Courts and Tribunals Service.

(6)　Nothing in subsections (1) to (4) enables a member of the judiciary of the sheriffdom to dispose of any business which that member could not otherwise competently dispose of in the exercise of the jurisdiction and powers that attach to the member's office.

(7)　Subsections (1) to (4) are subject to section 2(2)(a) and (3) of the Judiciary and Courts (Scotland) Act 2008 (the Head of the Scottish Judiciary's responsibility for efficient disposal of business in the Scottish courts).

Sheriff principal's power to fix sittings of sheriff courts

28.—(1)　The sheriff principal of a sheriffdom may by order prescribe—　　　　**D1.684**

(a)　the number of sittings of sheriff courts to be held at each place designated for the holding of sheriff courts in the sheriffdom,

(b)　the days on which, and the times at which, those sittings are to be held, and

(c)　the descriptions of business to be disposed of at those sittings.

(2)　The sheriff principal must publish notice of the matters prescribed by an order under subsection (1) in such manner as the sheriff principal thinks appropriate in order to bring those matters to the attention of persons having an interest in them.

(3)　Subsection (1) is subject to section 2(2)(a) and (3) of the Judiciary and Courts (Scotland) Act 2008.

Lord President's power to exercise functions under sections 27 and 28

29.—(1)　Subsection (2) applies where in any case the Lord President of the　　　**D1.685**
Court of Session considers that the exercise by the sheriff principal of a sheriffdom of a function under section 27 or 28—

(a)　is prejudicial to the efficient disposal of business in the sheriff courts of the sheriffdom,

(b)　is prejudicial to the efficient organisation or administration of those courts, or

(c)　is otherwise against the interest of the public.

(2)　The Lord President may in that case—

(a)　rescind the sheriff principal's exercise of the function, and

(b)　exercise the function.

(3)　Subsections (1) and (2) apply in relation to a failure to exercise a function mentioned in subsection (1) as they apply to the exercise of such a function, but as if paragraph (a) of subsection (2) were omitted.

(4)   The exercise of a function by the Lord President by virtue of subsection (2)(b) is to be treated as if it were the exercise of the function by the sheriff principal.

Deployment of judiciary

Power to authorise a sheriff principal to act in another sheriffdom

D1.686   **30.**—(1)   Subsection (2) applies where, in relation to a sheriffdom ("sheriffdom A")—

(a)   a vacancy occurs in the office of sheriff principal,

(b)   the Lord President of the Court of Session believes that the sheriff principal is unable to perform all or some of the functions of the office, or

(c)   the sheriff principal rules that he or she is precluded from performing all or some of those functions.

(2)   The Lord President may authorise the sheriff principal of another sheriffdom ("sheriffdom B") to perform the functions of sheriff principal in sheriffdom A (in addition to sheriffdom B) until the Lord President decides otherwise.

(3)   The authorisation may be made for the purpose of the performance of—

(a)   all of the functions of the sheriff principal of sheriffdom A, or

(b)   only those functions that that sheriff principal is unable to perform or is precluded from performing.

(4)   The Lord President may make an authorisation in the circumstances specified in subsection (1)(a) only if the Lord President considers such an authorisation to be necessary or expedient in order to avoid a delay in the administration of justice in sheriffdom A.

(5)   A sheriff principal authorised under this section to perform the functions of sheriff principal in another sheriffdom may exercise the jurisdiction and powers that attach to the office of sheriff principal in the other sheriffdom and does not need a commission for that purpose.

(6)   References in this section to the sheriff principal of a sheriffdom include references to any temporary sheriff principal of the sheriffdom.

Power to direct a sheriff or summary sheriff to act in another sheriffdom

D1.687   **31.**—(1)   The Lord President of the Court of Session may direct a sheriff or summary sheriff of a sheriffdom ("sheriffdom A") to perform the functions of sheriff or, as the case may be, summary sheriff in another sheriffdom ("sheriffdom B") until the Lord President decides otherwise.

(2)   The direction may require the sheriff or summary sheriff to perform the functions in sheriffdom B either in addition to or instead of performing the functions in sheriffdom A.

(3)   The Lord President may at any time give a further direction to the sheriff or summary sheriff directing the sheriff or, as the case may be, summary sheriff to perform the functions of sheriff or, as the case may be, summary sheriff in another sheriffdom until the Lord President decides otherwise.

(4)   Where a further direction is given under subsection (3) requiring functions to be carried out in another sheriffdom, the direction may require the sheriff or summary sheriff to perform the functions in that other sheriffdom in addition to or instead of performing the functions—

(a)   in sheriffdom A, or

(b)   in any other sheriffdom by virtue of—

(i)   a direction under subsection (1), or

(ii)   a further direction under subsection (3).

(5)   A sheriff or summary sheriff directed under this section to perform the functions of sheriff or summary sheriff in another sheriffdom may exercise the jurisdiction and powers that attach to the office of sheriff or, as the case may be, summary sheriff in the other sheriffdom and does not need a commission for that purpose.

Power to re-allocate sheriffs principal, sheriffs and summary sheriffs between sheriffdoms

32.—(1)   The Lord President of the Court of Session may direct that—   **D1.688**
  (a)   the sheriff principal of a sheriffdom is to cease to be the sheriff principal of that sheriffdom and is instead to be sheriff principal of such other sheriffdom as is specified in the direction,
  (b)   a sheriff of a sheriffdom is to cease to be a sheriff of that sheriffdom and is instead to be a sheriff of such other sheriffdom as is specified in the direction,
  (c)   a summary sheriff of a sheriffdom is to cease to be a summary sheriff of that sheriffdom and is instead to be a summary sheriff of such other sheriffdom as is specified in the direction.
(2)   A direction under subsection (1) takes effect on such date as is specified in the direction.
(3)   The reference in subsection (1) to the sheriff principal, a sheriff or summary sheriff of a sheriffdom is to one—
  (a)   appointed for the sheriffdom, or
  (b)   who is the sheriff principal, a sheriff or, as the case may be, summary sheriff of the sheriffdom by virtue of a previous direction under subsection (1).
(4)   A sheriff principal, sheriff or summary sheriff directed under subsection (1) to be the sheriff principal, a sheriff or summary sheriff of another sheriffdom may exercise the jurisdiction and powers that attach to the office of sheriff principal, sheriff or, as the case may be, summary sheriff in the other sheriffdom and does not need a commission for that purpose.

Allocation of sheriffs and summary sheriffs to sheriff court districts

33.—(1)   On the appointment of a sheriff or summary sheriff of a sheriffdom,   **D1.689**
the Lord President of the Court of Session must give the sheriff or summary sheriff a direction designating the sheriff court district or districts in which the sheriff or summary sheriff is to sit and perform the functions of sheriff or, as the case may be, summary sheriff.
(2)   The Lord President may at any time give a further direction to the sheriff or summary sheriff designating a different sheriff court district in which the sheriff or summary sheriff is to sit and perform the functions of sheriff or, as the case may be, summary sheriff.
(3)   A direction given to a sheriff or summary sheriff of a sheriffdom under this section is subject to any direction given under section 27 to the sheriff or summary sheriff by the sheriff principal of the sheriffdom for the purpose of giving effect to special provision made under subsection (3)(b) of that section.
(4)   Subsection (1) applies in the case where a direction under section 32(1) is made in relation to a sheriff or summary sheriff as it applies in the case where a sheriff or, as the case may be, summary sheriff is appointed.

Judicial specialisation

Determination of categories of case for purposes of judicial specialisation

D1.690   **34.**—(1)   The Lord President of the Court of Session may, by direction, determine categories of sheriff court case that the Lord President considers to be suited to being dealt with by judicial officers that specialise in the category of case.

(2)   The Lord President may determine categories of case under subsection (1) by reference to subject matter, value or such other criteria as the Lord President considers appropriate.

(3)   The Lord President may issue different directions under subsection (1) in relation to different types of judicial officer.

(4)   The Lord President may vary or revoke any direction made under subsection (1).

(5)   In this section—

"judicial officer" means—
  (a)   a sheriff,
  (b)   a summary sheriff,
  (c)   a part-time sheriff,
  (d)   a part-time summary sheriff,

"sheriff court case" means any type of proceedings (whether civil or criminal) that may competently be brought in the sheriff court.

Designation of specialist judiciary

D1.691   **35.**—(1)   This section applies where the Lord President of the Court of Session has made a direction under section 34.

(2)   The sheriff principal of a sheriffdom may—
  (a)   in relation to any category of case determined in the direction that may competently be dealt with by a sheriff, designate one or more sheriffs of the sheriffdom as specialists in that category of case,
  (b)   in relation to any category of case determined in the direction that may competently be dealt with by a summary sheriff, designate one or more summary sheriffs of the sheriffdom as specialists in that category of case.

(3)   The sheriff principal may designate the same sheriff or summary sheriff in relation to more than one category of case determined in the direction.

(4)   The sheriff principal of a sheriffdom may at any time withdraw a designation made (whether by that sheriff principal or another) under subsection (2) in relation to any sheriff, or summary sheriff, of the sheriffdom.

(5)   The Lord President may—
  (a)   in relation to any category of case determined in the direction that may competently be dealt with by a part-time sheriff, designate one or more part-time sheriffs as specialists in that category,
  (b)   in relation to any category of case determined in the direction that may competently be dealt with by a part-time summary sheriff, designate one or more part-time summary sheriffs as specialists in that category.

(6)   The Lord President may at any time withdraw a designation made under subsection (5).

(7)   The designation of a sheriff, summary sheriff, part-time sheriff or part-time summary sheriff (a "designated judicial officer") under this section does not affect—
  (a)   the designated judicial officer's competence to deal with any category of case other than the one in relation to which the designation is made, or

(b)   the competence of any other sheriff, summary sheriff, part-time sheriff or parttime summary sheriff to deal with the category of case in relation to which the designation is made.

Allocation of business to specialist judiciary

36.—(1)   Subsection (2) applies where the Lord President of the Court of Session or the sheriff principal of a sheriffdom is exercising any function relating to the allocation of business among the judiciary of a sheriffdom.   **D1.692**

(2)   The Lord President or, as the case may be, the sheriff principal must have regard to the desirability of ensuring that cases falling within a category determined under section 34 are dealt with by sheriffs, summary sheriffs, part-time sheriffs or, as the case may be, part-time summary sheriffs designated under section 35 as specialists in that category of case.

Saving for existing powers to provide for judicial specialisation

37.   Sections 34 to 36 do not affect any power that the Lord President of the Court of Session has apart from those sections to provide for judicial specialisation in the sheriff courts.   **D1.693**

Chapter 4 – Competence and jurisdiction

Sheriffs: civil competence and jurisdiction

Jurisdiction and competence of sheriffs

38.—(1)   A sheriff continues to have the jurisdiction and competence that attached to the office of sheriff in relation to civil proceedings immediately before this section comes into force.   **D1.694**

(2)   Without limiting that generality, a sheriff has competence as respects proceedings for or in relation to—

(a)   declarator,
(b)   aliment or separation,
(c)   recovery of maintenance arising out of an application under section 31(1) of the Maintenance Orders (Reciprocal Enforcement) Act 1972,
(d)   divorce,
(e)   division of commonty and division, or division and sale, of common property,
(f)   questions of heritable right or title, including declarator of irritancy and removing,
(g)   reduction, other than reduction of a decree of any court,
(h)   proving the tenor,
(i)   suspension of charges or threatened charges upon decrees of court granted by a sheriff or upon decrees of registration proceeding upon bonds, bills, contracts or other obligations registered in the books of a sheriff court or the Books of Council and Session,
(j)   all civil maritime proceedings formerly competent in the High Court of Admiralty in Scotland.

(3)   For the purpose of subsection (2)(e), the Division of Commonties Act 1695 has effect as if it conferred the same competence on a sheriff as it confers on the Court of Session.

Exclusive competence

39.—(1)   This section applies to any civil proceedings—   **D1.695**

    (a)   which a sheriff has competence to deal with, and

    (b)   in which—

        (i)   one or more orders of value are sought, and

        (ii)   the aggregate total value of all such orders sought, exclusive of interest and expenses, does not exceed £100,000.

(2)   The proceedings may be brought only in the sheriff court and may not be brought in any other court.

(3)   This section does not apply to family proceedings unless the only order sought in the proceedings is an order for payment of aliment.

(4)   Subsection (2) is subject to section 92(7) (remit of cases in exceptional circumstances to the Court of Session).

(5)   The Scottish Ministers may by order substitute another sum for the sum for the time being specified in subsection (1)(b)(ii).

(6)   For the purposes of this Act, an order is an order of value if it is—

    (a)   an order for payment of money, or

    (b)   an order determining rights in relation to property.

(7)   Provision may be made by the Court of Session by act of sederunt for determining, for the purposes of this Act—

    (a)   the value of an order,

    (b)   the aggregate total value of all the orders of value sought in any proceedings.

(8)   An act of sederunt under subsection (7) may make different provision for different purposes.

Territorial jurisdiction

D1.696   **40.**—(1)   This section applies for the purpose of determining the territorial extent of the jurisdiction of a sheriff of a sheriffdom in relation to matters other than criminal matters.

(2)   The sheriff's jurisdiction extends throughout the sheriffdom and includes all of the following so far as located in or adjoining the sheriffdom—

    (a)   navigable rivers,

    (b)   ports,

    (c)   harbours,

    (d)   creeks,

    (e)   shores,

    (f)   anchoring grounds.

(3)   Where two sheriffdoms are separated by a river, firth or estuary, the sheriffs of each sheriffdom on either side have concurrent jurisdiction over the intervening space occupied by the water.

(4)   This section does not affect any other enactment or rule of law that has effect for the purpose of determining the territorial extent of the jurisdiction of a sheriff of a sheriffdom, whether generally or in relation to a particular case or description of case.

(5)   This section is subject to an order under section 41(1).

Power to confer all-Scotland jurisdiction for specified cases

D1.697   **41.**—(1)   The Scottish Ministers may by order provide that the jurisdiction of a sheriff of a specified sheriffdom sitting at a specified sheriff court extends territorially throughout Scotland for the purposes of dealing with specified types of civil proceedings.

(2)   In subsection (1), "specified" means specified in an order under that subsection.

(3)   An order under subsection (1) may be made only with the consent of the Lord President of the Court of Session.

(4)   An order under subsection (1) does not affect—

(a)   in relation to the sheriffdom specified in the order, the jurisdiction or competence of a sheriff of any other sheriffdom to deal with proceedings of the type specified in the order, or

(b)   in relation to the sheriff court specified in the order, the jurisdiction or competence of a sheriff sitting at any other sheriff court to deal with such proceedings.

(5)   This section does not apply in relation to proceedings under the Children's Hearings (Scotland) Act 2011.

All-Scotland jurisdiction: further provision

42.—(1)   This section applies in relation to a sheriff sitting at a sheriff court specified in an order under section 41(1) (referred to in this section as a "specified sheriff court").   **D1.698**

(2)   The sheriff's all-Scotland jurisdiction is concurrent with, and alternative to, the sheriff's local jurisdiction.

(3)   The sheriff's "all-Scotland jurisdiction" is the extended jurisdiction in relation to specified proceedings that the sheriff has by virtue of the order under section 41(1).

(4)   The sheriff's "local jurisdiction" is the jurisdiction that the sheriff would have in relation to specified proceedings apart from the order under section 41(1).

(5)   A party bringing specified proceedings in the specified sheriff court must indicate, at the time the proceedings are brought, whether they are for determination in the exercise of a sheriff's all-Scotland jurisdiction or a sheriff's local jurisdiction.

(6)   Subsection (5) does not affect any power that a sheriff has to decline jurisdiction in any case.

(7)   In this Act, references to an "all-Scotland sheriff court" are references to a specified sheriff court so far as the court is constituted by a sheriff sitting in the exercise of the sheriff's all-Scotland jurisdiction.

(8)   For the purposes of any provision of this Act, or any other enactment, relating to the transfer or remit of proceedings between courts, a specified sheriff court is, when constituted as an all-Scotland sheriff court, taken to be a separate sheriff court from the court as constituted by a sheriff sitting in the exercise of the sheriff's local jurisdiction.

(9)   In this section, "specified proceedings" means, in relation to a specified sheriff court, civil proceedings of a type that are specified in relation to that court in the order under section 41(1).

Jurisdiction over persons, etc.

43.—(1)   Subsection (2) applies for the purpose of determining the jurisdiction of a sheriff in relation to any civil proceedings that may competently be dealt with by a sheriff.   **D1.699**

(2)   The proceedings may be brought before the sheriff of a particular sheriffdom if—

(a)   the defender (or, where there is more than one defender, one of them) resides in the sheriffdom,

(b)   the defender (or, where there is more than one defender, one of them) formerly resided in the sheriffdom for at least 40 days and the defender—

(i)   has ceased to reside there for fewer than 40 days, and

(ii)   has no known residence in Scotland,

    (c)   the defender—

        (i)   carries on business in the sheriffdom,

        (ii)   has a place of business in the sheriffdom, and

        (iii)   is cited in the sheriffdom, either personally or at the place of business,

    (d)   where the defender is not otherwise subject to the jurisdiction of any court in Scotland, there has been arrested in the sheriffdom—

        (i)   a ship or vessel of which the defender is an owner or part-owner, demise charterer or master, or

        (ii)   goods, debts, money or other moveable property belonging to the defender,

    (e)   any property of which the defender is (either individually or as trustee) the owner, part-owner, tenant or joint tenant is located in the sheriffdom and the proceedings relate to such property or to the defender's interest in it,

    (f)   in proceedings for interdict, the alleged wrong is being committed or threatened to be committed in the sheriffdom,

    (g)   in proceedings relating to a contract—

        (i)   the place of execution or performance of the contract is located in the sheriffdom, and

        (ii)   the defender is personally cited in the sheriffdom,

    (h)   in actions of furthcoming or multiplepoinding—

        (i)   the fund or property that is the subject of the proceedings is located in the sheriffdom, or

        (ii)   the sheriff otherwise has jurisdiction over the arrestee or holder of the fund or property that is the subject of the proceedings,

    (i)   the party sued is the pursuer in any proceedings pending in the sheriffdom against the party suing,

    (j)   where the proceedings are founded in delict, the delict was committed in the sheriffdom,

    (k)   the defender has prorogated the jurisdiction of the sheriff or courts of the sheriffdom.

  (3)   Subsection (2) is subject to—

    (a)   section 8 of, and Schedule 1B to, the Domicile and Matrimonial Proceedings Act 1973,

    (b)   the Civil Jurisdiction and Judgments Act 1982,

    (c)   Chapter 3 of Part 1 of the Family Law Act 1986, and

    (d)   any other enactment or rule of law that applies for the purpose of determining the jurisdiction of a sheriff in relation to persons or subject-matter.

Summary sheriffs: civil and criminal competence and jurisdiction

Summary sheriff: civil competence and jurisdiction

D1.700   **44.**—(1) A summary sheriff may, in relation to civil proceedings in the sheriff court, exercise the jurisdiction and powers that attach to the office of sheriff, but only in relation to the proceedings and other matters listed in schedule 1.

  (2) This section does not affect the jurisdiction and competence of a sheriff in relation to the proceedings and other matters listed in schedule 1.

  (3) The Scottish Ministers may by order modify schedule 1.

Summary sheriff: criminal competence and jurisdiction

45.—(1)   A summary sheriff may, in relation to criminal investigations and   **D1.701**
proceedings (whether summary or solemn proceedings), exercise the jurisdiction
and powers that attach to the office of sheriff.

(2)   Without limiting the generality of subsection (1), the jurisdiction and powers exercisable by a summary sheriff under that subsection include, in particular,
those of a sheriff under the Criminal Procedure (Scotland) Act 1995 ("the 1995
Act").

(3)   Despite subsections (1) and (2), a summary sheriff does not have jurisdiction or power to do any of the following in solemn criminal proceedings—

  (a)   to preside at any of the following diets, other than for the purpose of
        adjourning the diet—
        (i)   a first diet,
        (ii)   a diet under section 76(1) of the 1995 Act,
        (iii) a trial diet,
  (b)   to pass sentence on an offender, or make any other order or disposal in
        respect of the conviction of an offender of an offence,
  (c)   to review, vary, revoke or discharge any sentence or such other order or
        disposal.

(4)   This section does not affect the jurisdiction and competence of a sheriff in
relation to any matter mentioned in subsection (1).

PART 2 – THE SHERIFF APPEAL COURT

Chapter 1 – Establishment and role

The Sheriff Appeal Court

46.—(1)   There is established a court of law to be known as the Sheriff Appeal   **D1.702**
Court.

(2)   The Court consists of judges each to be known as an Appeal Sheriff.

Jurisdiction and competence

47.—(1)   The Sheriff Appeal Court has jurisdiction and competence to hear and   **D1.703**
determine appeals to such extent as is provided by or under—

  (a)   this Act, or
  (b)   any other enactment.

(2)   The Court's jurisdiction and competence is exercisable by one or more of
the Appeal Sheriffs at sittings of the Court.

(3)   The Court has all such powers as are, under the law of Scotland, inherently
possessed by a court of law for the purposes of the discharge of its jurisdiction and
competence and giving full effect to its decisions.

(4)   Subsection (3) is subject to any other provision of this Act or any other
enactment that restricts or excludes any power of the Court in determining or disposing of an appeal.

Status of decisions of the Sheriff Appeal Court in precedent

48.—(1)   A decision of the Sheriff Appeal Court on the interpretation or applica-   **D1.704**
tion of the law is binding—

  (a)   in proceedings before a sheriff anywhere in Scotland,
  (b)   in proceedings before a justice of the peace court anywhere in Scotland,
  (c)   in proceedings before the Sheriff Appeal Court, except in a case where the

Court hearing the proceedings is constituted by a greater number of Appeal Sheriffs than those constituting the Court which made the decision.

(2)   In subsection (1)(a), the reference to proceedings before a sheriff includes, in the case of criminal proceedings, a reference to solemn proceedings before a sheriff and jury.

Chapter 2 – Appeal Sheriffs

Sheriffs principal to be Appeal Sheriffs

D1.705   **49.**—(1)   Each person who holds office as a sheriff principal also holds office as an Appeal Sheriff by virtue of this subsection.

(2)   A person holding office as a sheriff principal ceases to hold office as an Appeal Sheriff if the person ceases to hold office as a sheriff principal.

(3)   If a person holding office as a sheriff principal is suspended from that office for any period, the person is also suspended from office as an Appeal Sheriff for the same period.

Appointment of sheriffs as Appeal Sheriffs

D1.706   **50.**—(1)   The Lord President of the Court of Session may appoint persons holding the office of sheriff to hold office also as Appeal Sheriffs.

(2)   The Lord President may appoint as many Appeal Sheriffs under subsection (1) as the Lord President considers necessary for the purposes of the Sheriff Appeal Court.

(3)   A person may be appointed under subsection (1) only if the individual has held office as a sheriff for at least 5 years.

(4)   The appointment of a sheriff as an Appeal Sheriff does not affect the sheriff's appointment as a sheriff and the sheriff may accordingly continue to act in that capacity.

(5)   A person holding office as an Appeal Sheriff under this section ceases to hold that office if the person ceases to hold office as a sheriff.

(6)   If a person holding office as an Appeal Sheriff under this section is suspended from the office of sheriff for any period, the person is also suspended from office as an Appeal Sheriff for the same period.

(7)   The Lord President may, with the consent of a majority of the sheriffs principal, remove a sheriff from office as an Appeal Sheriff.

(8)   Removal of a sheriff from the office of Appeal Sheriff under subsection (7) does not affect the sheriff's appointment as a sheriff.

Re-employment of former Appeal Sheriffs

D1.707   **51.**—(1)   The Lord President of the Court of Session may appoint a qualifying former Appeal Sheriff to act as an Appeal Sheriff during such periods or on such occasions as the Lord President may determine.

(2)   The Lord President may make such an appointment only if the appointment appears to the Lord President to be expedient as a temporary measure in order to facilitate the disposal of business in the Sheriff Appeal Court.

(3)   A "qualifying former Appeal Sheriff" is an individual who—

(a)   ceased to hold that office other than by virtue of—

(i)   an order under section 25 (as read with sections 49(2) and 50(5)), or

(ii)   removal from office under section 50(7), and

(b)   has not reached the age of 75.

(4)   An individual appointed under subsection (1) is to be treated for all purposes (other than for the purposes of section 50) as an Appeal Sheriff and may exercise the jurisdiction and powers that attach to the office of Appeal Sheriff.

(5)   An individual's appointment under subsection (1) ceases when the individual reaches the age of 75.

(6)   Despite the ending (whether by virtue of subsection (5) or otherwise) of an individual's appointment under subsection (1)—

    (a)   the individual may continue to deal with, give judgment in or deal with an ancillary matter relating to, a case begun before the individual while acting under that appointment,

    (b)   so far as necessary for that purpose, and for the purpose of any subsequent proceedings arising out of the case or matter, the individual is to be treated as acting or, as the case may be, having acted under that appointment.

(7)   An individual appointed under subsection (1) is to be paid such remuneration as the Scottish Ministers may determine.

(8)   The Scottish Ministers may determine different amounts of remuneration for—

    (a)   different individuals so appointed, or

    (b)   different descriptions of individuals so appointed.

(9)   Remuneration under subsection (7) is to be paid by the Scottish Courts and Tribunals Service.

Expenses

52.—(1)   The Scottish Courts and Tribunals Service may pay to an Appeal Sheriff such sums as it may determine in respect of expenses reasonably incurred by the Appeal Sheriff in the performance of, or in connection with, the Appeal Sheriff's duties as such.   **D1.708**

(2)   The Scottish Courts and Tribunals Service may—

    (a)   determine the circumstances in which such sums may be paid, and

    (b)   determine different circumstances for different Appeal Sheriffs.

Temporary provision

53.   Schedule 2 (which makes further provision, for a temporary period, in relation to Appeal Sheriffs) has effect.   **D1.709**

Chapter 3 – Organisation of business

President and Vice President

President and Vice President of the Sheriff Appeal Court

54.—(1)   The Lord President of the Court of Session is to appoint, in accordance with this section—   **D1.710**

    (a)   one of the sheriffs principal to be the President of the Sheriff Appeal Court, and

    (b)   another sheriff principal to be the Vice President of the Court.

(2)   A sheriff principal holds office as President or Vice President for such period as the Lord President may determine.

(3)   The President or Vice President may at any time resign office by giving notice in writing to the Lord President.

(4)   The Lord President may at any time remove a sheriff principal from office as President or Vice President.

(5)   If a person holding office as President or Vice President is suspended from office as a sheriff principal for any period, the person is also suspended from office as President or, as the case may be, Vice President for the same period.

President and Vice President: incapacity and suspension

D1.711   **55.**—(1)   Subsection (2) applies during any period when the President of the Sheriff Appeal Court—

(a)   is unable (for any reason) to carry out the functions of the office, or

(b)   is suspended from office.

(2)   During such a period—

(a)   the functions of the President are to be carried out instead by the Vice President, and

(b)   anything that falls to be done in relation to the President falls to be done instead in relation to the Vice President.

(3)   Subsection (4) applies during any period when—

(a)   subsection (2) would, but for subsection (4), apply, and

(b)   the Vice President of the Sheriff Appeal Court—

(i)   is unable (for any reason) to carry out the functions of the President, or

(ii)   is suspended from office.

(4)   During such a period, subsection (2) does not apply and, instead—

(a)   the functions of the President are to be carried out instead by such sheriff principal (other than the President or Vice President) as the Lord President of the Court of Session may appoint to act in place of the President, and

(b)   anything that falls to be done in relation to the President falls to be done instead in relation to that sheriff principal.

Disposal of business

President's responsibility for efficient disposal of business

D1.712   **56.**—(1)   The President of the Sheriff Appeal Court is responsible for ensuring the efficient disposal of business in the Sheriff Appeal Court.

(2)   The President must make such arrangements as appear necessary or expedient for the purpose of carrying out the responsibility imposed by subsection (1).

(3)   In particular, the President may provide for the allocation of business among the Appeal Sheriffs.

(4)   If, in carrying out the responsibility imposed by subsection (1), the President gives a direction of an administrative character to a person specified in subsection (5), the person must comply with the direction.

(5)   Those persons are—

(a)   an Appeal Sheriff,

(b)   a member of the staff of the Scottish Courts and Tribunals Service.

(6)   This section is subject to section 2(2)(a) and (2A) of the Judiciary and Courts (Scotland) Act 2008 (the Head of the Scottish Judiciary's responsibility for efficient disposal of business in the Scottish courts).

Sittings

Sittings of the Sheriff Appeal Court

D1.713   **57.**—(1)   Sittings of the Sheriff Appeal Court may be held at any place in Scotland designated by virtue of this Act for the holding of sheriff courts.

(2)   More than one sitting of the Court may take place at the same time, and at different places.

(3)   The President of the Sheriff Appeal Court may by order prescribe—

(a)   the number of sittings of the Court that are to be held at each place at which they may be held,

(b)   the days on which, and the times at which, those sittings are to be held, and

(c)   the descriptions of business to be disposed of at those sittings.

(4)   The President must publish notice of the matters prescribed by an order under subsection (3) in such manner as the President thinks appropriate in order to bring those matters to the attention of persons having an interest in them.

(5)   Subsection (3) is subject to section 2(2)(a) and (2A) of the Judiciary and Courts (Scotland) Act 2008.

Rehearing of pending case by a larger Court

58.—(1)   Subsection (2) applies where, in relation to any appeal pending before the Sheriff Appeal Court—   **D1.714**

(a)   the Appeal Sheriff or Appeal Sheriffs constituting the Court consider the appeal to be one of particular difficulty or importance, or

(b)   where the Court is constituted by more than one Appeal Sheriff, they are equally divided on any matter, whether of fact or law.

(2)   The Appeal Sheriff or Appeal Sheriffs may appoint the appeal to be reheard at another sitting of the Court constituted by such larger number of Appeal Sheriffs as may be necessary for the proper disposal of the appeal.

Chapter 4 – Administration

Clerks

Clerk of the Sheriff Appeal Court

59.—(1)   The Scottish Courts and Tribunals Service must appoint a person holding office as a sheriff clerk also to hold the office of Clerk of the Sheriff Appeal Court.   **D1.715**

(2)   A person's appointment as Clerk of the Sheriff Appeal Court does not affect the person's appointment as a sheriff clerk.

(3)   A person holding office as Clerk of the Sheriff Appeal Court ceases to hold that office if the person ceases to hold office as a sheriff clerk.

(4)   Otherwise, a person's appointment as Clerk of the Sheriff Appeal court—

(a)   lasts for such period, and

(b)   is on such other terms and conditions,

as the Scottish Courts and Tribunals Service may determine.

(5)   In this section, "sheriff clerk" does not include sheriff clerk depute.

Deputy Clerks of the Sheriff Appeal Court

60.—(1)   The Scottish Courts and Tribunals Service may appoint individuals to be Deputy Clerks of the Sheriff Appeal Court.   **D1.716**

(2)   The number of Deputy Clerks is for the Scottish Courts and Tribunals Service to determine.

(3)   An individual's appointment as Deputy Clerk—

(a)   lasts for such period, and

(b)   is on such other terms and conditions,

as the Scottish Courts and Tribunals Service may determine.

(4)   An individual may hold office as a Deputy Clerk of the Sheriff Appeal Court at the same time as holding office as clerk, or deputy or assistant clerk, of another court.

Clerk and Deputy Clerks: further provision

D1.717   **61.**—(1)   The Clerk and Deputy Clerks of the Sheriff Appeal Court are also members of staff of the Scottish Courts and Tribunals Service.

(2)   Accordingly, a reference in any enactment to the staff of the Scottish Courts and Tribunals Service includes, except where the context requires otherwise, a reference to the Clerk and Deputy Clerks of the Sheriff Appeal Court.

(3)   The Clerk of the Sheriff Appeal Court may, with the consent of the Scottish Courts and Tribunals Service, delegate the carrying out of any of the Clerk's functions to—

    (a)   a Deputy Clerk of the Sheriff Appeal Court, or

    (b)   any other member of staff of the Scottish Courts and Tribunals Service.

(4)   Subsection (5) applies in relation to any period during which—

    (a)   the office of Clerk of the Sheriff Appeal Court is vacant, or

    (b)   the holder of that office is for any reason unable to carry out the functions of the office.

(5)   The Scottish Courts and Tribunals Service may make arrangements for the functions of the Clerk of the Sheriff Appeal Court to be carried out during the period referred to in subsection (4) by—

    (a)   a Deputy Clerk of the Sheriff Appeal Court, or

    (b)   any other member of staff of the Scottish Courts and Tribunals Service.

(6)   The Scottish Courts and Tribunals Service may give such instructions to the Clerk of the Sheriff Appeal Court, or a person carrying out the Clerk's functions under subsection (5), as it considers necessary for the purposes of this Act; and the Clerk or, as the case may be, such person must comply with any such instructions.

Records

Records of the Sheriff Appeal Court

D1.718   **62.**—(1)   A record of the Sheriff Appeal Court is authenticated by being signed by—

    (a)   an Appeal Sheriff, or

    (b)   the Clerk of the Court.

(2)   A record authenticated in accordance with subsection (1), or a certified copy of such a record or of an extract of such a record, is sufficient evidence of the facts recorded in the record.

(3)   The Sheriff Appeal Court may keep (and produce) records in electronic form.

(4)   For the purposes of this section, a reference to a record or a copy of a record being signed or, as the case may be, certified, includes a reference to the record or copy being authenticated by means of—

    (a)   an electronic signature, or

    (b)   such other means of authentication as may be specified for that purpose by an act of sederunt under section 104(1).

(5)   In this section—

      "certified copy" means a copy certified by the Clerk of the Sheriff Appeal Court as a true copy, "electronic signature" is to be construed in accordance with section 7(2) of the Electronic Communications Act 2000, but includes a version of an electronic signature which is reproduced on a paper document,

"record" means any interlocutor, decree, minute or other document by which the proceedings and decisions of the Sheriff Appeal Court are recorded.

PART 3 – CIVIL PROCEDURE

Chapter 1 – Sheriff court

Civil jury trials

Civil jury trials in an all-Scotland sheriff court

63.—(1) This section applies in relation to relevant proceedings in an all-Scotland sheriff court.

(2) If the proceedings are remitted to probation, they must be tried by jury unless—

    (a) the parties agree otherwise, or

    (b) special cause is shown.

(3) Facts or circumstances constitute special cause for the purposes of subsection (2)(b) only if they would constitute special cause for the purpose of section 9(b) of the Court of Session Act 1988 (allowing of proof by Lord Ordinary).

(4) The questions to be put to the jury are to be—

    (a) approved by the sheriff, and

    (b) specified by the sheriff in an interlocutor.

(5) The jury is to consist of 12 jurors.

(6) Proceedings which are to be tried by jury under this section are referred to in this Chapter as "jury proceedings".

(7) In this section, "relevant proceedings" means proceedings—

    (a) of a type specified in an order under section 41(1), and

    (b) which would be a jury action within the meaning of section 11 of the Court of Session Act 1988 if the same proceedings were (disregarding section 39)—

        (i) taken by an action in the Court of Session, and

        (ii) remitted to probation there.

D1.719

Selection of the jury

64.—(1) The jurors for the trial in jury proceedings are to be selected in open court by ballot.

(2) Each party to the proceedings may challenge the selection of any juror whose name is drawn in the ballot.

(3) A party may, under subsection (2), at any time during the selection of jurors—

    (a) challenge the selection of up to 4 jurors without having to give a reason, and

    (b) challenge the selection of any other juror, provided a reason for the challenge is stated.

D1.720

Application to allow the jury to view property

65.—(1) A party to jury proceedings may apply to the sheriff to allow the jury to view any heritable or moveable property relevant to the proceedings.

D1.721

(2)   Where an application is made under subsection (1), the sheriff may grant the application if the sheriff considers it proper and necessary for the jury to view the property.

Discharge or death of juror during trial

D1.722

66.—(1)   In jury proceedings, the sheriff may, in the course of the trial, discharge a member of the jury from further service on the jury if satisfied that the juror—

    (a)   is, by reason of illness, unable to continue to serve on the jury, or

    (b)   should, for any other reason, be discharged from further service on the jury.

(2)   Subsections (3) and (4) apply where a member of the jury—

    (a)   is discharged under subsection (1), or

    (b)   dies.

(3)   So long as there remain at least 10 members of the jury—

    (a)   the remaining members of the jury are in all respects deemed to constitute the jury for the purpose of the trial, and

    (b)   any verdict returned by the remaining members of the jury, whether unanimous or by majority, is to have the same force and effect as if it were a unanimous or, as the case may be, majority verdict of the whole number of the jury.

(4)   If there remain fewer than 10 members of the jury, the sheriff must—

    (a)   discharge the jury, and

    (b)   order the proceedings to be tried by another jury.

Trial to proceed despite objection to opinion and direction of the sheriff

D1.723

67.—   In jury proceedings, despite any objection being taken in the course of the trial to the opinion and direction of the sheriff—

    (a)   the trial is to proceed, and

    (b)   the jury are to return their verdict and, where necessary, assess damages.

Return of verdict

D1.724

68.—(1)   In jury proceedings, the sheriff must, at the end of the sheriff's charge to the jury, direct the jury to select one of their members to speak for them when returning their verdict.

(2)   The jury may at any time return a verdict by a simple majority of their members.

(3)   Subsection (4) applies if the jury—

    (a)   have been enclosed for at least 3 hours, and

    (b)   at the end of that time are unable to agree a verdict or to return a verdict by majority.

(4)   The sheriff may—

    (a)   discharge the jury without their having returned a verdict, and

    (b)   order the proceedings to be tried by another jury.

(5)   When the verdict is returned, it is to be—

    (a)   declared orally in open court by the juror selected under subsection (1), and

    (b)   taken down in writing by the sheriff clerk before the jury is discharged.

(6)   In jury proceedings containing a claim for damages, where the jury return a verdict for the pursuer, the jury must also assess the amount of damages.

(7)   The verdict of the jury is final so far as relating to the facts found by the jury.

(8)   Subsection (7) is subject to sections 69 and 71.

Application for new trial

69.—(1)   After the jury have returned their verdict in jury proceedings, any party to the proceedings may, on any ground specified in subsection (2), apply to the Sheriff Appeal Court for a new trial. **D1.725**

(2)   The grounds are—

   (a)   the sheriff misdirected the jury,
   (b)   undue admission or rejection of evidence,
   (c)   the verdict is contrary to the evidence,
   (d)   damages awarded are excessive or inadequate,
   (e)   new evidence or information has come to light since the trial,
   (f)   any other ground essential to the justice of the case.

(3)   On an application under subsection (1), the Sheriff Appeal Court may grant or refuse a new trial.

(4)   Subsection (3) is subject to section 70.

(5)   Where the Court grants a new trial—

   (a)   the verdict of the jury is set aside, and
   (b)   the proceedings are to be tried by another jury.

(6)   Subsection (7) applies where—

   (a)   an application is made under subsection (1) on the ground that the verdict is contrary to the evidence, and
   (b)   after hearing the parties, the Sheriff Appeal Court is of the opinion that—
      (i)   the ground is established, and
      (ii)   it has before it all the relevant evidence that could reasonably be expected to be obtained in relation to the proceedings.

(7)   The Court may, instead of granting a new trial—

   (a)   set aside the verdict of the jury, and
   (b)   enter judgment for the party unsuccessful at the trial.

(8)   In a case where the Court is constituted by more than one Appeal Sheriff, the opinion referred to in subsection (6)(b) must be the opinion of all of them.

Restrictions on granting a new trial

70.—(1)   Subsection (2) applies where— **D1.726**

   (a)   an application is made under section 69(1) on the ground of undue admission of evidence, and
   (b)   the Sheriff Appeal Court is of the opinion that exclusion of the evidence in question could not have led to a different verdict from the one actually returned.

(2)   The Court must refuse to grant a new trial.

(3)   Subsection (4) applies where—

   (a)   an application is made under section 69(1) on the ground of undue rejection of documentary evidence, and
   (b)   the Sheriff Appeal Court is of the opinion that the documents in question would not have affected the jury's verdict.

(4)   The Court must refuse to grant a new trial.

(5)   Subsection (6) applies where—

   (a)   an application is made under section 69(1), and
   (b)   the Sheriff Appeal Court is of the opinion that—
      (i)   the only ground for granting a new trial is that damages awarded are excessive or inadequate, and

(ii)   a new trial is essential to the justice of the case.

(6)   The Court may grant a new trial restricted to the question of the amount of damages only.

(7)   On an application under section 69(1), where the Sheriff Appeal Court is constituted by more than one Appeal Sheriff—

(a)   the Court may not grant a new trial except in conformity with the opinion of a majority of the Appeal Sheriffs hearing the application, and

(b)   in the case of equal division, the Court must refuse to grant a new trial.

Verdict subject to opinion of the Sheriff Appeal Court

D1.727   **71.**—(1)   This section applies in relation to any jury proceedings in which the sheriff has directed the jury on any matter.

(2)   A party against whom the verdict of the jury is returned may apply to the Sheriff Appeal Court for the verdict instead to be entered in the party's favour.

(3)   On an application under subsection (2), the Court may—

(a)   set aside the verdict and exercise either of the powers in subsections (4) and (6), or

(b)   refuse the application.

(4)   Where the Court is of the opinion—

(a)   that the sheriff's direction was erroneous, and

(b)   that the party making the application was entitled to the verdict in whole or in part,

it may direct the verdict to be entered in that party's favour.

(5)   The Court may direct the verdict to be so entered—

(a)   either in whole or in part, and

(b)   either absolutely or on such terms as the Court thinks fit.

(6)   Where the Court is of the opinion that it is necessary to do so, it may order the proceedings to be tried by another jury.

Simple procedure

Simple procedure

D1.728   **72.**—(1)   For the purposes of the procedure and practice in civil proceedings in the sheriff court, there is to be a form of procedure to be known as "simple procedure".

(2)   Subject to the provisions of this Part, further provision about simple procedure is to be made by act of sederunt under section 104(1).

(3)   The following types of proceedings may only be brought subject to simple procedure (and no other types of proceedings may be so brought)—

(a)   proceedings for payment of a sum of money not exceeding £5,000,

(b)   actions of multiplepoinding where the value of the fund or property that is the subject of the action does not exceed £5,000,

(c)   actions of furthcoming where the value of the arrested fund or subject does not exceed £5,000,

(d)   actions ad factum praestandum, other than actions in which there is claimed, in addition or as an alternative to a decree ad factum praestandum, a decree for payment of a sum of money exceeding £5,000,

(e)   proceedings for the recovery of possession of heritable property or moveable property, other than proceedings in which there is claimed, in addition or as an alternative to a decree for such recovery, a decree for payment of a sum of money exceeding £5,000.

(4)   Subsection (3) is subject to sections 78 (transfer of cases to simple procedure), 80 (transfer of cases from simple procedure) and 83 (transitional provision: summary cause).

(5)   Subsection (3)(a) is subject to sections 73 and 74.

(6)   The calculation of a sum for the time being mentioned in subsection (3) is to be determined in accordance with provision made by the Court of Session by act of sederunt.

(7)   An act of sederunt under subsection (6) may make different provision for different purposes.

(8)   An act of sederunt under section 104(1) may make provision for the purposes of this Act for determining whether proceedings are of a type mentioned in subsection (3).

(9)   Proceedings that—

    (a)   are subject to simple procedure under subsection (3) or by virtue of any other enactment,

    (b)   are brought subject to simple procedure under section 74, or

    (c)   are continued subject to simple procedure by virtue of section 78 or 79,

are referred to in this Part as a "simple procedure case".

(10)   Subsection (9) is subject to section 80.

(11)   References in subsection (3) to a sum of money is to that amount exclusive of interest and expenses.

(12)   The Scottish Ministers may by order substitute for any sum for the time being specified in this section a different sum.

Proceedings in an all-Scotland sheriff court

73.—(1)   Section 72(3), so far as requiring any relevant proceedings to be brought subject to simple procedure, does not apply to any such proceedings in an all-Scotland sheriff court, and no such proceedings may be brought or continued in such a court subject to simple procedure.

D1.729

(2)   Subsection (1) does not affect the application of section 72(3) in relation to any relevant proceedings brought in any other sheriff court.

(3)   In this section, "relevant proceedings" means proceedings of a type mentioned in section 72(3)(a) so far as they are also of a type specified in an order under section 41(1).

Proceedings for aliment of small amounts under simple procedure

74.—(1)   Subsection (2) applies to a claim for aliment only (whether or not expenses are also sought) under section 2 of the Family Law (Scotland) Act 1985 (actions for aliment).

D1.730

(2)   The claim may be brought subject to simple procedure if the aliment claimed does not exceed—

    (a)   in respect of a child under the age of 18 years, the sum of £100 per week, and

    (b)   in any other case, the sum of £200 per week.

(3)   A provision such as is mentioned in subsection (4) does not apply in relation to a claim brought subject to simple procedure under subsection (2).

(4)   The provision referred to in subsection (3) is provision in any enactment—

    (a)   limiting the jurisdiction of a sheriff in a simple procedure case by reference to any amount, or

    (b)   limiting the period for which a decree granted by a sheriff is to have effect.

(5)   The Scottish Ministers may by order substitute for any sum for the time being mentioned in subsection (2) a different sum.

Rule-making: matters to be taken into consideration

D1.731
75. The power to make provision relating to simple procedure by act of sederunt under section 104(1) is to be exercised so far as possible with a view to ensuring that the sheriff before whom a simple procedure case is conducted—

(a) is able to identify the issues in dispute,

(b) may facilitate negotiation between or among the parties with a view to securing a settlement,

(c) may otherwise assist the parties in reaching a settlement,

(d) can adopt a procedure that is appropriate to and takes account of the particular circumstances of the case.

Service of documents

D1.732
76.—(1) An act of sederunt under section 104(1) may permit a party to a simple procedure case, in such circumstances as may be specified in the act, to require the sheriff clerk to effect service of any document relating to the case on behalf of the party.

(2) In subsection (1)—

(a) the reference to a party to a simple procedure case includes a reference to a description of such a party as may be specified in an act of sederunt mentioned in that subsection,

(b) the reference to any document relating to the case includes a reference to a description of any such document as may be so specified.

Evidence in simple procedure cases

D1.733
77.—(1) Any enactment or rule of law that prevents evidence being led on grounds of admissibility before a court of law does not apply in simple procedure cases.

(2) The evidence, if any, given in simple procedure cases is not to be recorded.

Transfer of cases to simple procedure

D1.734
78.—(1) This section applies to any civil proceedings in the sheriff court that are being conducted otherwise than as a simple procedure case.

(2) The parties to the proceedings may, at any stage, make a joint application for the proceedings to continue subject to simple procedure if the proceedings are of a type that, if brought at the time when the application is made—

(a) would or could be brought subject to simple procedure by virtue of any enactment, or

(b) would or could be so brought but for the fact that a financial limit specified in section 72(3) or 74(2) is exceeded.

(3) Where such a joint application is made, the sheriff must direct that the proceedings are to continue subject to simple procedure for all purposes (including appeal).

Proceedings in an all-Scotland sheriff court: transfer to simple procedure

D1.735
79.—(1) This section applies to any relevant proceedings in an all-Scotland sheriff court.

(2) A party to the proceedings may, at any stage, make an application for the proceedings to continue subject to simple procedure in another sheriff court.

(3) Where such an application is made, the sheriff may, on special cause shown—

(a)   direct that the proceedings are to continue subject to simple procedure for all purposes (including appeal), and

(b)   make an order transferring the proceedings to another sheriff court having jurisdiction in relation to the proceedings.

(4)   Where a sheriff makes a direction under section 78(3) in relation to proceedings to which this section applies, the sheriff must make an order transferring the proceedings to another sheriff court having jurisdiction in relation to the proceedings.

(5)   In this section, "relevant proceedings" has the same meaning as in section 73.

Transfer of cases from simple procedure

80.—(1)   A party to a simple procedure case may, at any stage, make an application for the case not to proceed subject to simple procedure.

D1.736

(2)   Where such an application is made, the sheriff may direct that the proceedings are no longer subject to simple procedure.

(3)   Where a direction is made under subsection (2), the proceedings are to continue for all purposes (including appeal) subject to such procedure as would have been applicable to them had they not been subject to simple procedure.

Expenses in simple procedure cases

81.—(1)   The Scottish Ministers may by order provide that—

D1.737

(a)   in such category of simple procedure cases as may be prescribed in the order, no award of expenses may be made,

(b)   in such other category of simple procedure cases as may be so prescribed, any expenses awarded may not exceed such sum as may be so prescribed.

(2)   The categories of simple procedure cases mentioned in subsection (1) may be prescribed by reference to—

(a)   the value of the claim in the cases,

(b)   the subject matter of the claim in the cases.

(3)   Categories may be prescribed subject to specified exceptions.

(4)   An order under subsection (1) does not apply—

(a)   to simple procedure cases such as those mentioned in subsection (5),

(b)   in relation to an appeal to the Sheriff Appeal Court from any decision in a simple procedure case, or

(c)   to a simple procedure case in respect of which a direction under subsection (7) is made.

(5)   The simple procedure cases referred to in subsection (4)(a) are those in which—

(a)   the defender—

(i)   has not stated a defence,

(ii)   having stated a defence, has not proceeded with it, or

(iii)   having stated and proceeded with a defence, has not acted in good faith as to its merits, or

(b)[1]   a party to the case has behaved in a manner which is manifestly unreasonable in relation to the case.

(6)   Subsection (7) applies where the sheriff in a simple procedure case is of the opinion that a difficult question of law, or a question of fact of exceptional complexity, is involved.

---

[1] As amended by the Civil Litigation (Expenses and Group Proceedings) (Scotland) Act 2018 (asp 10) s.12(2) (effective 30 June 2021 subject to transitional provision specified in SSI 2021/125 reg.3).

(7)   The sheriff may, at any stage, on the application of any party to the case, direct that an order under subsection (1) is not to apply in relation to the case.

Appeals from simple procedure cases

D1.738

82.—(1)   An appeal may be taken to the Sheriff Appeal Court under section 110 on a point of law only against a decision of the sheriff constituting final judgment in a simple procedure case.

(2)   Any other decision of the sheriff in such a case is not subject to review.

Transitional provision: summary causes

D1.739

83.—(1)   Any reference, however expressed, in a pre-commencement enactment to proceedings being subject to summary cause procedure is, on and after the coming into force of this section, to be construed as a reference to proceedings being subject to simple procedure.

(2)   Accordingly, any reference to proceedings being taken by way of summary cause is to be construed as a reference to proceedings being subject to simple procedure.

(3)   In subsection (1), "pre-commencement enactment" means any enactment passed or made before this section comes into force.

Interdicts and other orders: effect outside sheriffdom

Interdicts having effect in more than one sheriffdom

D1.740

84.—(1)   A sheriff has competence to grant an interdict having effect in relation to conduct at places outside the sheriff's sheriffdom as well as at places within the sheriff's sheriffdom.

(2)   In this section, "interdict" includes "interim interdict".

Proceedings for breach of an extended interdict

D1.741

85.—(1)   In this section, "extended interdict" means an interdict granted by a sheriff, by virtue of section 84(1), having effect in relation to conduct at places outside the sheriff's sheriffdom.

(2)   Proceedings for breach of an extended interdict may be brought before a sheriff of the sheriffdom—

(a)   in which the defender is domiciled,

(b)   in which the interdict was granted,

(c)   in which the alleged breach occurred.

(3)   A sheriff before whom proceedings for breach of an extended interdict are brought may make an order transferring the proceedings to a sheriff of another sheriffdom (whether or not one mentioned in subsection (2)) if satisfied that it would be more appropriate for the proceedings to be dealt with by a sheriff of the other sheriffdom.

(4)   A sheriff may make an order under subsection (3)—

(a)   on the application of a party to the proceedings, or

(b)   on the sheriff's own initiative.

(5)   Where an order is made under subsection (3), a sheriff of the sheriffdom to whom the proceedings are to be transferred has jurisdiction and competence to consider and determine the proceedings.

(6)   This section does not affect any power that a sheriff has to decline jurisdiction in any case.

Power to enable sheriff to make orders having effect outside sheriffdom
86.—(1)   In this section, "relevant order" means an order—   **D1.742**
   (a) which a sheriff has competence and jurisdiction to make in civil proceedings, but
   (b) which, apart from this section, the sheriff could make only so as to have effect or be enforceable within the sheriff's sheriffdom.
(2)   The Scottish Ministers may by order provide for a sheriff to have competence to make relevant orders having effect (and being capable of being enforced) outside the sheriff's sheriffdom as well as within that sheriffdom (referred to in this section as "extended competence").
(3)   An order under subsection (2) may—
   (a) make provision in relation to all relevant orders or in relation only to specified categories or descriptions of relevant order,
   (b) make different provision in relation to different categories or descriptions of relevant order,
   (c) provide for a sheriff to have extended competence only—
      (i) in such circumstances,
      (ii) in relation to such civil proceedings, or
      (iii) subject to such conditions,
   as are specified in the order,
   (d) make provision about jurisdiction in relation to proceedings for relevant orders,
   (e) make provision for the transfer of proceedings for relevant orders between different sheriffdoms,
   (f) make provision about the enforcement of orders made in the exercise of extended competence (including provision about jurisdiction in relation to enforcement proceedings).
(4)   Subsection (3) does not affect the generality of section 133(1).
(5)   In subsection (1), "order"—
   (a) includes "interim order", but
   (b) does not include an interdict or an interim interdict.

Execution of deeds relating to heritage

Power of sheriff to order sheriff clerk to execute deed relating to heritage
87.—(1)   This section applies where—   **D1.743**
   (a) an action relating to heritable property is before a sheriff, or
   (b) it appears to a sheriff that an order under this section is necessary to implement a decree of a sheriff relating to heritable property.
(2)   The sheriff may make an order such as is mentioned in subsection (4)—
   (a) on an application by the grantee of any deed relating to the heritable property, and
   (b) if satisfied as to the matters mentioned in subsection (3).
(3)   The matters are that the grantor of any deed relating to the heritable property—
   (a) cannot be found,
   (b) refuses to execute the deed,
   (c) is unable, or otherwise fails, to execute the deed.
(4)   The order is one—
   (a) dispensing with the execution of the deed by the grantor, and
   (b) directing the sheriff clerk to execute the deed.

(5)   A deed executed by the sheriff clerk in accordance with a direction in an order under this section has the same force and effect as if it had been executed by the grantor.

(6)   In this section—

"grantor", in relation to a deed relating to the heritable property, means a person who is under an obligation to execute the deed,

"grantee" means the person to whom that obligation is owed.

Interim orders

Interim orders

D1.744   **88.**—(1)   A sheriff may, on the application of a party to any civil proceedings before the sheriff, make—

(a)   such interim order as the sheriff thinks fit in relation to—

(i)   the possession of any heritable or movable property to which the proceedings relate,

(ii)   the subject matter of the proceedings,

(b)   an interim order ad factum praestandum.

(2)   Subsection (1) does not apply in relation to proceedings under the Children's Hearings (Scotland) Act 2011.

Chapter 2 – Court of Session

Judicial review

D1.745   **89.**   After section 27 of the Court of Session Act 1988, insert—

"Applications to the supervisory jurisdiction of the Court

Time limits

D1.746   **27A.**—(1)   An application to the supervisory jurisdiction of the Court must be made before the end of—

(a)   the period of 3 months beginning with the date on which the grounds giving rise to the application first arise, or

(b)   such longer period as the Court considers equitable having regard to all the circumstances.

(2)   Subsection (1) does not apply to an application to the supervisory jurisdiction of the Court which, by virtue of any enactment, is to be made before the end of a period ending before the period of 3 months mentioned in that subsection (however that first-ending period may be expressed).

Requirement for permission

D1.747   **27B.**—(1)   No proceedings may be taken in respect of an application to the supervisory jurisdiction of the Court unless the Court has granted permission for the application to proceed.

(2)   Subject to subsection (3), the Court may grant permission under subsection (1) for an application to proceed only if it is satisfied that—

(a)   the applicant can demonstrate a sufficient interest in the subject matter of the application, and

(b)   the application has a real prospect of success.

(3)   Where the application relates to a decision of the Upper Tribunal for Scotland in an appeal from the First-tier Tribunal for Scotland under section 46 of the Tribunals (Scotland) Act 2014, the Court may grant permission under subsection (1) for the application to proceed only if it is satisfied that—

(a)   the applicant can demonstrate a sufficient interest in the subject matter of the application,

(b)   the application has a real prospect of success, and

(c)   either—

    (i)   the application would raise an important point of principle or practice, or

    (ii)   there is some other compelling reason for allowing the application to proceed.

(4)   The Court may grant permission under subsection (1) for an application to proceed—

(a)   subject to such conditions as the Court thinks fit,

(b)   only on such of the grounds specified in the application as the Court thinks fit.

(5)   The Court may decide whether or not to grant permission without an oral hearing having been held.

Oral hearings where permission refused, etc.

27C.—(1)   Subsection (2) applies where, in relation to an application to the supervisory jurisdiction of the Court—   **D1.748**

(a)   the Court—

    (i)   refuses permission under subsection 27B(1) for the application to proceed, or

    (ii)   grants permission for the application to proceed subject to conditions or only on particular grounds, and

(b)   the Court decides to refuse permission, or grant permission as mentioned in paragraph (a)(ii), without an oral hearing having been held.

(2)   The person making the application may, within the period of 7 days beginning with the day on which that decision is made, request a review of the decision at an oral hearing.

(3)   A request under subsection (2) must be considered by a different Lord Ordinary from the one who refused permission or granted permission as mentioned in subsection (1)(a)(ii).

(4)   Where a request under subsection (2) is granted, the oral hearing must be conducted before a different Lord Ordinary from the one who refused or so granted permission.

(5)   At a review following a request under subsection (2), the Court must consider whether to grant permission for the application to proceed; and subsections (2), (3) and (4) of section 27B apply for that purpose.

(6)   Section 28 does not apply—

(a)   where subsection (2) applies, or

(b)   in relation to the refusal of a request made under subsection (2).

Appeals following oral hearings

27D.—(1)   Subsection (2) applies where, after an oral hearing to determine whether or not to grant permission for an application to the supervisory jurisdiction of the Court to proceed, the Court—   **D1.749**

(a)   refuses permission for the application to proceed, or

(b)   grants permission for the application to proceed subject to conditions or only on particular grounds.

(2)   The person making the application may, within the period of 7 days beginning with the day on which the Court makes its decision, appeal under this section to the Inner House (but may not appeal under any other provision of this Act).

(3) In an appeal under subsection (2), the Inner House must consider whether to grant permission for the application to proceed; and subsections (2), (3) and (4) of section 27B apply for that purpose.

(4) In subsection (1), the reference to an oral hearing is to an oral hearing whether following a request under section 27C(2) or otherwise.".

Interim orders

D1.750 **90.** In section 47 of the Court of Session Act 1988 (interim interdict and other interim orders), after subsection (2) insert—

"(2A) The power under subsection (2) to make an order includes, in particular, power to make an order ad factum praestandum (including an interim order).".

Warrants for ejection

D1.751 **91.** After section 47 of the Court of Session Act 1988, insert—

Power to grant warrant for ejection

"**47A.** In any proceedings where the Court has competence to grant a decree of removing, it also has competence to grant a warrant for ejection.".

Chapter 3 – Remit of cases between courts

Remit of cases to the Court of Session

D1.752 **92.**—(1) Subsection (2) applies to any civil proceedings before a sheriff that are—

(a) proceedings that the Court of Session also has competence and jurisdiction to deal with,

(b) not proceedings to which section 39 applies, and

(c) not subject to simple procedure.

(2) On the application of any of the parties to the proceedings, the sheriff may, at any stage, remit the proceedings to the Court of Session if the sheriff considers that the importance or difficulty of the proceedings makes it appropriate to do so.

(3) Subsection (4) applies to any civil proceedings before a sheriff that are—

(a) proceedings to which section 39 applies,

(b) proceedings that the Court of Session would (but for that section) also have competence and jurisdiction to deal with, and

(c) not subject to simple procedure.

(4) On the application of any of the parties to the proceedings, the sheriff may, at any stage, request the Court of Session to allow the proceedings to be remitted to that Court if the sheriff considers that the importance or difficulty of the proceedings makes it appropriate to do so.

(5) On receiving a request under subsection (4), the Court of Session may, on cause shown, allow the proceedings to be remitted to the Court.

(6) If the Court of Session allows the proceedings to be remitted to that Court, the sheriff is to remit the proceedings to that Court.

(7) Where the proceedings are remitted to the Court of Session under subsection (6), the proceedings may be dealt with and disposed of by that Court despite section 39(2).

Remit of cases from the Court of Session

D1.753 **93.**—(1) Subsection (2) applies to any proceedings in the Court of Session if—

(a) they are proceedings that a sheriff also has competence and jurisdiction to deal with,

(b) they would be proceedings to which section 39 applies but for the fact that subsection (1)(b)(ii) of that section is not satisfied, and

(c) the Court considers, at any stage, that it is unlikely that the aggregate total value of all the orders of value granted in the proceedings, exclusive of interest and expenses, will be greater than the sum specified in that subsection.

(2) The Court must remit the proceedings to an appropriate sheriff, unless the Court considers, on cause shown, that the proceedings should remain in the Court of Session.

(3) In considering the matter in subsection (1)(c), the Court is to assume—

(a) that liability for the order sought is established, and

(b) that there will, where appropriate, be no deduction for contributory negligence.

(4) Subsection (5) applies to any proceedings in the Court of Session if—

(a) they are proceedings that a sheriff also has competence and jurisdiction to deal with, but

(b) are not proceedings to which paragraph (b) or (c) of subsection (1) applies.

(5) The Court may, at any stage, remit the proceedings to an appropriate sheriff if the Court considers that the nature of the proceedings makes it appropriate to do so.

(6) The Court may remit proceedings under subsection (2) or (5)—

(a) on the application of any party to the proceedings, or

(b) on its own initiative.

(7) In this section, "an appropriate sheriff" means, in relation to proceedings remitted from the Court of Session under this section, a sheriff having competence and jurisdiction to deal with the proceedings sitting at such sheriff court as the Court may, at the time of the remit, specify.

Remit of cases to the Scottish Land Court

94.—(1) Subsection (2) applies to any proceedings before a sheriff where the matter to which the proceedings relate could competently be determined by the Scottish Land Court under— **D1.754**

(a) the Agricultural Holdings (Scotland) Act 1991, or

(b) the Agricultural Holdings (Scotland) Act 2003.

(2) The sheriff may, at any stage, remit the proceedings to the Scottish Land Court if the sheriff considers that it is appropriate to do so.

(3) The sheriff may remit proceedings under subsection (2)—

(a) on the application of any party to the proceedings, or

(b) on the sheriff's own initiative.

(4) A decision of the sheriff to remit, or not to remit, the proceedings under subsection (2) is final and no appeal may be taken against it.

Chapter 4 – Lay representation for non-natural persons

Key defined terms

95.—(1) This section applies for the purposes of the interpretation of this Chapter. **D1.755**

(2) "Non-natural person" means—

(a) a company (whether incorporated in the United Kingdom or elsewhere),

(b) a limited liability partnership,

(c) any other partnership,

(d) an unincorporated association of persons.

(3) "Lay representative" means an individual who is not a legal representative.

(4) "Legal representative" means—

(a) a solicitor,

(b) an advocate, or

(c) a person having a right to conduct litigation, or a right of audience, by virtue of section 27 of the Law Reform (Miscellaneous Provisions) (Scotland) Act 1990.

(5) An individual holds a relevant position with a non-natural person if the individual—

(a) in the case of a company, is a director or secretary of the company,

(b) in the case of a limited liability partnership, is a member of the partnership,

(c) in the case of any other partnership, is a partner in the partnership,

(d) in the case of an unincorporated association, is a member or office holder of the association.

(6) For the purposes of section 96, an individual also holds a relevant position with a non-natural person if the individual is an employee of the non-natural person.

(7) References to conducting proceedings are references to exercising, in relation to the proceedings, a function or right (including a right of audience) that a legal representative could exercise in the proceedings.

Lay representation in simple procedure cases

D1.756   **96.**—(1) This section applies in any simple procedure case to which a non-natural person is a party.

(2) A lay representative may conduct proceedings in the case on behalf of the non-natural person if—

(a) the lay representative holds a relevant position with the non-natural person,

(b) the responsibilities of the lay representative in that position do not consist wholly or mainly of conducting legal proceedings on behalf of the non-natural person or another person,

(c) the lay representative is authorised by the non-natural person to conduct the proceedings,

(d) the lay representative does not have a personal interest in the subject matter of the proceedings, and

(e) the lay representative is not the subject of an order such as is mentioned in section 98(2)(f).

(3) In subsection (2)(d), "personal interest" means an interest other than one that anyone holding the position that the lay representative holds with the non-natural person would have.

(4) Subsection (2) is subject to provision made by an act of sederunt under section 98.

Lay representation in other proceedings

D1.757   **97.**—(1) This section applies in civil proceedings (other than a simple procedure case) to which a non-natural person is a party.

(2) A lay representative may, if the court grants permission, conduct the proceedings on behalf of the non-natural person.

(3) The court may grant permission if satisfied that—

(a)   the non-natural person is unable to pay for the services of a legal representative to conduct the proceedings,

(b)   the lay representative is a suitable person to conduct the proceedings, and

(c)   it is in the interests of justice to grant permission.

(4)   For the purposes of subsection (3)(b), a lay representative is a suitable person to conduct the proceedings if—

(a)   the lay representative holds a relevant position with the non-natural person,

(b)   the responsibilities of the lay representative in that position do not consist wholly or mainly of conducting legal proceedings on behalf of the non-natural person or another person,

(c)   the lay representative is authorised by the non-natural person to conduct the proceedings,

(d)   the lay representative does not have a personal interest in the subject matter of the proceedings, and

(e)   the lay representative is not the subject of an order such as is mentioned in section 98(2)(f).

(5)   In subsection (4)(d), "personal interest" means an interest other than one that anyone holding the position that the lay representative holds with the non-natural person would have.

(6)   For the purposes of subsection (3)(c), in deciding whether it is in the interests of justice to grant permission, the court must have regard, in particular, to—

(a)   the non-natural person's prospects of success in the proceedings, and

(b)   the likely complexity of the proceedings.

(7)   Subsection (2) is subject to provision made by an act of sederunt under section 98.

(8)   In this section—

"civil proceedings" means civil proceedings in—
(a)   the Court of Session,
(b)   the Sheriff Appeal Court, or
(c)   the sheriff court,

"the court", in the case of proceedings in the sheriff court, means the sheriff.

Lay representation: supplementary provision

98.—(1)   The Court of Session may, by act of sederunt, make further provision about—   **D1.758**

(a)   the granting of permission under section 97, and

(b)   the conduct of proceedings by lay representatives by virtue of this Chapter.

(2)   Provision under subsection (1) may include, in particular, provision—

(a)   about the procedure to be followed in considering applications for permission under section 97 (including provision for applications to be considered in chambers and without hearing the parties),

(b)   regulating the conduct of lay representatives in exercising a function or right by virtue of this Chapter,

(c)   about the authorisation of lay representatives for the purposes of this Chapter,

(d)   imposing conditions on the exercise by lay representatives of a function or right by virtue of this Chapter or enabling the court to impose such conditions in particular cases,

(e)   enabling the court, in particular cases, to withdraw a lay representative's right to exercise a function or right by virtue of this Chapter if the representative contravenes provision made by virtue of the act of sederunt,

(f) enabling the court to make an order preventing a lay representative from conducting any proceedings before any court on behalf of non-natural persons,

(g) enabling the court, in awarding expenses against a non-natural person in any case, to find a lay representative jointly and severally liable for the expenses.

(3) An act of sederunt under subsection (1) may make different provision for different purposes.

(4) In this section, "the court", in the case of proceedings in the sheriff court, means the sheriff.

Chapter 5 – Jury service

Jury service

D1.759   **99.**—(1) The Law Reform (Miscellaneous Provisions) (Scotland) Act 1980 is amended in accordance with this section.

(2) In section 1 (qualification of jurors)—

(a) in subsection (1)—

(i) the words "to subsections (2) and (3) below and" are repealed, and

(ii) for paragraph (b) substitute—

"(b) is not less than 18 years of age;",

(b) subsections (1A), (2) and (3) are repealed,

(c) in subsection (5), the words "under subsection (2) or (3) above or" are repealed.

(3) In section 1A (excusal of jurors in relation to criminal proceedings)—

(a) in each of subsections (1), (2) and (3), the words "in relation to criminal proceedings" are repealed,

(b) in subsection (3), for "(a)(iii)" substitute "(ab)",

(c) the title of the section becomes **"Excusal of jurors as of right"**.

(4) In Part III of Schedule 1 (persons excusable from jury service as of right), in Group F, for paragraphs (a) and (aa) substitute—

"(a) persons who have served as a juror in the period of 5 years ending with the date on which the person is cited first to attend;

(aa) persons who have attended for jury service, but have not served as a juror, in the period of 2 years ending with the date on which the person is cited first to attend;

(ab) persons who have attained the age of 71;".

Chapter 6 – Vexatious proceedings

Vexatious litigation orders

D1.760   **100.**—(1) The Inner House may, on the application of the Lord Advocate, make a vexatious litigation order in relation to a person (a "vexatious litigant").

(2) A vexatious litigation order is an order which has either or both of the following effects—

(a) the vexatious litigant may institute civil proceedings only with the permission of a judge of the Outer House,

(b) the vexatious litigant may take a specified step in specified ongoing civil proceedings only with such permission.

(3) In subsection (2)(b)—

(a) "specified ongoing civil proceedings" means civil proceedings which—

      (i)   were instituted by the vexatious litigant before the order was made, and

     (ii)   are specified in the order,

  (b) "specified step" means a step specified in the order.

(4) A vexatious litigation order has effect—

  (a) during such period as is specified in the order, or

  (b) if no period is so specified, indefinitely.

(5) In this section and section 101—

  (a) "the Inner House" means the Inner House of the Court of Session,

  (b) "the Outer House" means the Outer House of the Court of Session,

  (c) "vexatious litigant" means, in relation to a vexatious litigation order, the person to whom the order relates,

  (d) "vexatious litigation order" means an order made under subsection (1).

Vexatious litigation orders: further provision

101.—(1) The Inner House may make a vexatious litigation order in relation to a person only if satisfied that the person has habitually and persistently, without any reasonable ground for doing so—   **D1.761**

  (a) instituted vexatious civil proceedings, or

  (b) made vexatious applications to the court in the course of civil proceedings (whether or not instituted by the person).

(2) For the purpose of subsection (1), it does not matter whether the proceedings—

  (a) were instituted in Scotland or elsewhere,

  (b) involved the same parties or different parties.

(3) A copy of a vexatious litigation order must be published in the Edinburgh Gazette.

(4) A judge of the Outer House may grant permission to a vexatious litigant to institute civil proceedings or, as the case may be, to take a step in such proceedings only if satisfied that there is a reasonable ground for the proceedings or the taking of the step.

(5) The decision of the judge to refuse to grant permission under subsection (4) is final.

(6) Subsection (7) applies in relation to civil proceedings instituted in any court by a vexatious litigant before the Inner House makes a vexatious litigation order in relation to the vexatious litigant.

(7) The court may make such order as it sees fit in consequence of the vexatious litigation order.

(8) In subsection (7), "the court" means—

  (a) the court which is dealing with the proceedings,

  (b) in the case of proceedings in the sheriff court, the sheriff.

Power to make orders in relation to vexatious behaviour

102.—(1) The Scottish Ministers may by regulations confer on the Court of Session, a sheriff or the Sheriff Appeal Court the power to make an order of a kind mentioned in subsection (2) in relation to a person who has behaved in a vexatious manner in civil proceedings before the Court of Session, sheriff or, as the case may be, Sheriff Appeal Court.   **D1.762**

(2) The order referred to in subsection (1) is an order that the person may do any of the following only with the permission of a court or a judge of any court—

  (a) take such a step in those proceedings as is specified in the order,

    (b)   take such a step as is so specified in such other civil proceedings (whether or not those proceedings are before the Court of Session, sheriff or, as the case may be, Sheriff Appeal Court) as are so specified,

    (c)   institute civil proceedings in such a court as is so specified.

(3)   For the purpose of subsection (1), a person behaves in a vexatious manner in civil proceedings if the person—

    (a)   institutes the proceedings and they are vexatious, or

    (b)   makes a vexatious application in the course of the proceedings (whether or not they were instituted by the person).

(4)   Regulations under subsection (1) may include provision for—

    (a)   an order to be made on the application of a party to the proceedings or on the Court's or, as the case may be, sheriff's own initiative,

    (b)   circumstances in which the Court or sheriff may make an order, and the requirements as to permission which may be imposed in an order in those circumstances,

    (c)   the factors which the Court or sheriff may take into account in deciding whether to make an order (including the person's behaviour in other civil proceedings, whether in Scotland or elsewhere),

    (d)   the courts in relation to which an order may have effect,   .

    (e)   the maximum period for which an order may have effect,

    (f)   the effect of an order in any other respects.

(5)   The Scottish Ministers must consult the Lord President of the Court of Session before making regulations under subsection (1).

(6)   Regulations under subsection (1)—

    (a)   are subject to the negative procedure,

    (b)   may make different provision for different purposes,

    (c)   may make incidental, supplemental, consequential, transitional, transitory or saving provision.

PART 4 – PROCEDURE AND FEES

Procedure

Power to regulate procedure etc. in the Court of Session

D1.763   **103.**—(1)   The Court of Session may by act of sederunt make provision for or about—

    (a)   the procedure and practice to be followed in proceedings in the Court,

    (b)   any matter incidental or ancillary to such proceedings.

(2)[1]   Without limiting that generality, the power in subsection (1) includes power to make provision for or about—

    (a)   execution or diligence following on such proceedings,

    (b)   avoiding the need for, or mitigating the length and complexity of, such proceedings, including—

        (i)   encouraging settlement of disputes and the use of alternative dispute resolution procedures,

        (ii)   action to be taken before such proceedings are brought by persons who will be party to the proceedings,

---

[1] As amended by the Civil Litigation (Expenses and Group Proceedings) (Scotland) Act 2018 (asp 10) Pt 2 s.12(3) (effective 30 January 2019).

(c)   other aspects of the conduct and management of such proceedings, including the use of technology,

(d)   simplifying the language used in connection with such proceedings or matters incidental or ancillary to them,

(e)   the form of any document to be used in connection with such proceedings, matters incidental or ancillary to them or matters specified in this subsection,

(f)   appeals against a decision of the Court,

(g)   applications that may be made to the Court,

(h)   time limits in relation to proceedings mentioned in subsection (1), matters incidental or ancillary to them or matters specified in this subsection,

(i)   the steps that the Court may take where there has been an abuse of process by a party to such proceedings,

(j)   expenses that may be awarded in such proceedings,

(k)   other payments such parties or persons representing such parties may be required to make in respect of their conduct relating to such proceedings,

(l)   the payment, investment or application of any sum of money awarded in such proceedings to or in respect of a person under a legal disability,

(m)   the representation of parties to such proceedings, and others, including representation by persons who—

     (i)   are neither solicitors nor advocates, or

     (ii)   do not have the right to conduct litigation, or a right of audience, by virtue of section 27 of the Law Reform (Miscellaneous Provisions) (Scotland) Act 1990,

(n)   the functions and rights of persons appointed by the Court in connection with such proceedings,

(o)   witnesses and evidence, including modifying the rules of evidence as they apply to such proceedings,

(p)   the quorum for a Division of the Inner House considering purely procedural matters and, in the case of an extra Division, as to which judge is to preside and to sign any judgment or interlocutor pronounced by the extra Division,

(q)   such other matters as the Court thinks necessary or appropriate for the purposes of carrying out or giving effect to the provisions of any enactment (including this Act) relating to such proceedings or matters incidental or ancillary to them.

(3)   An act of sederunt under subsection (1) may make—

(a)   incidental, supplemental, consequential, transitional, transitory or saving provision,

(b)   provision amending, repealing or revoking any enactment (including any provision of this Act) relating to matters with respect to which an act of sederunt may be made,

(c)   different provision for different purposes.

(4)   This section is without prejudice to—

(a)   any enactment that enables the Court to make rules (by act of sederunt or otherwise) regulating the practice and procedure to be followed in proceedings to which this section applies, or

(b)   the inherent powers of the Court.

Power to regulate procedure etc. in the sheriff court and the Sheriff Appeal Court

D1.764   **104.**—(1)   The Court of Session may by act of sederunt make provision for or about—

    (a)   the procedure and practice to be followed in civil proceedings in the sheriff court or in the Sheriff Appeal Court,

    (b)   any matter incidental or ancillary to such proceedings.

(2)[1]   Without limiting that generality, the power in subsection (1) includes power to make provision for or about—

    (a)   execution or diligence following on such proceedings,

    (b)   avoiding the need for, or mitigating the length and complexity of, such proceedings, including—

        (i)   encouraging settlement of disputes and the use of alternative dispute resolution procedures,

        (ii)   action to be taken before such proceedings are brought by persons who will be party to the proceedings,

    (c)   other aspects of the conduct and management of such proceedings, including the use of technology,

    (d)   simplifying the language used in connection with such proceedings or matters incidental or ancillary to them,

    (e)   the form of any document to be used in connection with such proceedings, matters incidental or ancillary to them or matters specified in this subsection,

    (f)   appeals against a decision of a sheriff or the Sheriff Appeal Court,

    (g)   applications that may be made to a sheriff or the Sheriff Appeal Court,

    (h)   time limits in relation to proceedings mentioned in subsection (1), matters incidental or ancillary to them or matters specified in this subsection,

    (i)   the steps that a sheriff or the Sheriff Appeal Court may take where there has been an abuse of process by a party to such proceedings,

    (j)   expenses that may be awarded in such proceedings,

    (k)   other payments such parties or persons representing such parties may be required to make in respect of their conduct relating to such proceedings,

    (l)   the payment, investment or application of any sum of money awarded in such proceedings to or in respect of a person under a legal disability,

    (m)   the representation of parties to such proceedings, and others, including representation by persons who—

        (i)   are neither solicitors nor advocates, or

        (ii)   do not have the right to conduct litigation, or a right of audience, by virtue of section 27 of the Law Reform (Miscellaneous Provisions) (Scotland) Act 1990,

    (n)   the functions and rights of persons appointed by a sheriff or the Sheriff Appeal Court in connection with such proceedings,

    (o)   witnesses and evidence, including modifying the rules of evidence as they apply to such proceedings,

    (p)   the quorum for sittings of the Sheriff Appeal Court,

    (q)   determining which Appeal Sheriff is to preside at such sittings where the Court is constituted by more than one Appeal Sheriff,

    (r)   such other matters as the Court of Session thinks necessary or appropriate

---

[1] As amended by the Civil Litigation (Expenses and Group Proceedings) (Scotland) Act 2018 (asp 10) Pt 2 s.12(4) (effective 30 January 2019).

for the purposes of carrying out or giving effect to the provisions of any enactment (including this Act) relating to such proceedings or matters incidental or ancillary to them.

(3)   Nothing in an act of sederunt under subsection (1) is to derogate from the provisions of sections 72 to 82 (simple procedure).

(4)   An act of sederunt under subsection (1) may make—

(a)   incidental, supplemental, consequential, transitional, transitory or saving provision,

(b)   provision amending, repealing or revoking any enactment (including any provision of this Act) relating to matters with respect to which an act of sederunt under subsection (1) may be made,

(c)   different provision for different purposes.

(5)   Before making an act of sederunt under subsection (1) with respect to any matter, the Court of Session must—

(a)   consult the Scottish Civil Justice Council, and

(b)   take into consideration any views expressed by the Council with respect to that matter.

(6)   Subsection (5) does not apply in relation to an act of sederunt that embodies, with or without modifications, draft rules submitted by the Scottish Civil Justice Council to the Court of Session.

(7)   This section is without prejudice to—

(a)   any enactment that enables the Court of Session to make rules (by act of sederunt or otherwise) regulating the practice and procedure to be followed in proceedings to which this section applies, or

(b)   the inherent powers of a sheriff or the Sheriff Appeal Court.

Fees of solicitors etc.

Power to regulate fees in the Court of Session

105.—(1)   The Court of Session may, in relation to any proceedings in the Court (including any execution or diligence following such proceedings), by act of sederunt make provision for or about the fees of—

D1.765

(a)   solicitors,

(b)   messengers-at-arms,

(c)   persons acting under the Execution of Diligence (Scotland) Act 1926,

(d)   witnesses,

(e)   shorthand writers,

(f)   such other persons, or persons of such descriptions, as the Scottish Ministers may by order specify.

(2)   An act of sederunt under subsection (1) may not make any provision for or about the fees that the Scottish Ministers may regulate under or by virtue of section 33 of the Legal Aid (Scotland) Act 1986 (fees and outlays of solicitors and counsel).

(3)   An act of sederunt under subsection (1) and an order under subsection (1)(f) may make—

(a)   incidental, supplemental, consequential, transitional, transitory or saving provision,

(b)   different provision for different purposes.

(4)   Before making an order under subsection (1)(f), the Scottish Ministers must consult the Lord President of the Court of Session.

(5)   An act of sederunt under subsection (1) is subject to the negative procedure.

Power to regulate fees in the sheriff court and the Sheriff Appeal Court

106.—(1)   The Court of Session may, in relation to civil proceedings in the sheriff court or the Sheriff Appeal Court (including any execution or diligence following such proceedings), by act of sederunt make provision for or about the fees of—

    (a)   solicitors,

    (b)   sheriff officers,

    (c)   persons acting under the Execution of Diligence (Scotland) Act 1926,

    (d)   witnesses,

    (e)   shorthand writers,

    (f)   such other persons, or persons of such descriptions, as the Scottish Ministers may by order specify.

    (2)   An act of sederunt under subsection (1) may not make any provision for or about the fees that the Scottish Ministers may regulate under or by virtue of section 33 of the Legal Aid (Scotland) Act 1986 (fees and outlays of solicitors and counsel).

    (3)   An act of sederunt under subsection (1) may make—

    (a)   incidental, supplemental, consequential, transitional, transitory or saving provision,

    (b)   different provision for different purposes.

    (4)   Before making an order under subsection (1)(f), the Scottish Ministers must consult the Lord President of the Court of Session.

    (5)   An act of sederunt under subsection (1) is subject to the negative procedure.

Court fees

Power to provide for fees for SCTS, court clerks and other officers

107.—(1)   The Scottish Ministers may by order make provision for the charging of fees in respect of the carrying out of the functions of the Scottish Courts and Tribunals Service ("the SCTS") or a relevant officer in connection with—

    (a)   proceedings in the Scottish Courts, or

    (b)   any other matter dealt with by a relevant officer.

    (2)   An order under subsection (1) may—

    (a)   in particular include provision—

        (i)   specifying, or for determining, the amount of fees,

        (ii)   specifying, or for determining, the persons or types of person who are to pay the fees,

        (iii)   specifying the times when, places where and persons to whom the fees are to be paid,

        (iv)   for exemptions from the requirement to pay fees,

        (v)   for the remission of fees,

        (vi)   for modification of fees,

    (b)   make different provision for different purposes or circumstances including, in particular, different provision for—

        (i)   different Scottish Courts,

        (ii)   different relevant officers,

        (iii)   different proceedings or types of proceedings.

    (3)   In this section—

    "relevant officer" means—

        (a)   a clerk, deputy clerk or assistant clerk of any of the Scottish Courts,

        (b)   the Accountant of Court,

(c)   the Auditor of the Court of Session,

(ca)[1]   the auditor of the Sheriff Appeal Court,

(d)   the auditor of a sheriff court,

(e)   any other officer who is a member of the staff of the SCTS,

"Scottish Courts" means—

(a)   the Court of Session,

(b)   the High Court of Justiciary,

(c)   the court for hearing appeals under section 57(1)(b) of the Representation of the People Act 1983,

(d)   the election court in Scotland constituted under section 123 of that Act,

(e)   the Scottish Land Court,

(f)   the Lands Valuation Appeal Court,

(g)   the Sheriff Appeal Court,

(h)   sheriff courts,

(i)   justice of the peace courts.

(4)   The Scottish Ministers may by order modify (either or both of) the definitions of "relevant officer" and "Scottish Courts" in subsection (3).

Sanction for counsel

Sanction for counsel in the sheriff court and Sheriff Appeal Court

108.—(1)   This section applies in civil proceedings in the sheriff court or the Sheriff Appeal Court where the court is deciding, for the purposes of any relevant expenses rule, whether to sanction the employment of counsel by a party for the purposes of the proceedings.   **D1.768**

(2)   The court must sanction the employment of counsel if the court considers, in all the circumstances of the case, that it is reasonable to do so.

(3)   In considering that matter, the court must have regard to—

(a)   whether the proceedings are such as to merit the employment of counsel, having particular regard to—

(i)   the difficulty or complexity, or likely difficulty or complexity, of the proceedings,

(ii)   the importance or value of any claim in the proceedings, and

(b)   the desirability of ensuring that no party gains an unfair advantage by virtue of the employment of counsel.

(4)   The court may have regard to such other matters as it considers appropriate.

(5)   References in this section to proceedings include references to any part or aspect of the proceedings.

(6)   In this section—

"counsel" means—

(a)   an advocate,

(b)   a solicitor having a right of audience in the Court of Session under section 25A of the Solicitors (Scotland) Act 1980,

"court", in relation to proceedings in the sheriff court, means the sheriff,

"relevant expenses rule" means, in relation to any proceedings mentioned in subsection (1), any provision of an act of sederunt requiring, or having the effect of requiring, that the employment of counsel by a party for the

---

[1] As inserted by the Courts Reform (Scotland) Act 2014 (Relevant Officer and Consequential Provisions) Order 2016 (SSI 2016/387) art.2 (effective 28 November 2016).

purposes of the proceedings be sanctioned by the court before the fees of counsel are allowable as expenses that may be awarded to the party.

(7) This section is subject to an act of sederunt under section 104(1) or 106(1).

Part 5 – Civil appeals

Appeals to the Sheriff Appeal Court

Abolition of appeal from a sheriff to the sheriff principal

D1.769   **109.**—(1) No appeal may be taken to the sheriff principal against any decision of a sheriff in civil proceedings.

(2) Subsection (3) applies to any provision of any pre-commencement enactment that—

(a) provides for an appeal to the sheriff principal from any decision of a sheriff in civil proceedings, or

(b) restricts or excludes any such appeal.

(3) The provision has effect as if for the reference to the sheriff principal there were substituted a reference to the Sheriff Appeal Court.

(4) In subsection (2), "pre-commencement enactment" means an enactment passed or made before this section comes into force.

Appeal from a sheriff to the Sheriff Appeal Court

D1.770   **110.**—(1) An appeal may be taken to the Sheriff Appeal Court, without the need for permission, against—

(a) a decision of a sheriff constituting final judgment in civil proceedings, or

(b) any decision of a sheriff in civil proceedings—

(i) granting, refusing or recalling an interdict, whether interim or final,

(ii) granting interim decree for payment of money other than a decree for expenses,

(iii) making an order ad factum praestandum,

(iv) sisting an action,

(v) allowing, refusing or limiting the mode of proof, or

(vi) refusing a reponing note.

(2) An appeal may be taken to the Sheriff Appeal Court against any other decision of a sheriff in civil proceedings if the sheriff, on the sheriff's own initiative or on the application of any party to the proceedings, grants permission for the appeal.

(3) In an appeal to the Sheriff Appeal Court, the Court may allow further proof.

(4) This section does not affect any other right of appeal to the Sheriff Appeal Court under any other enactment.

(5) This section does not affect any right of appeal against any decision of a sheriff to the Court of Session under any other enactment.

(6) This section is subject to any provision of this or any other enactment that restricts or excludes a right of appeal from a sheriff to the Sheriff Appeal Court.

Sheriff Appeal Court's powers of disposal in appeals

D1.771   **111.**—(1) In determining an appeal under section 110, the Court has power to—

(a) grant such disposal as the Court sees fit, including by (in whole or in part)—

(i) adhering to the decision that is subject to the appeal,

(ii) recalling the decision,

(iii) varying the decision,

(iv) remitting the case back to the sheriff,

532

      (v)   dismissing the appeal,

  (b)   make such incidental or interim orders as may be necessary, and

  (c)   determine any incidental or other issue that needs to be determined for the purpose of doing justice in the appeal.

  (2)   Subsection (1)—

  (a)   does not affect the generality of section 47(3), but

  (b)   is subject to any other provision of this Act or any other enactment that restricts or excludes any power of the Court in determining or disposing of an appeal.

Remit of appeal from the Sheriff Appeal Court to the Court of Session

112.—(1)   This section applies in relation to an appeal to the Sheriff Appeal Court against a decision of a sheriff in civil proceedings.
          D1.772

  (2)   The Sheriff Appeal Court may—

  (a)   on the application of a party to the appeal, and

  (b)   if satisfied that the appeal raises a complex or novel point of law,

remit the appeal to the Court of Session.

  (3)   Where an appeal is remitted to the Court of Session under subsection (2), the Court of Session may deal with and dispose of the appeal as if it had originally been made direct to that Court.

Appeals to the Court of Session

Appeal from the Sheriff Appeal Court to the Court of Session

113.—(1)   An appeal may be taken to the Court of Session against a decision of the Sheriff Appeal Court constituting final judgment in civil proceedings, but only—
          D1.773

  (a)   with the permission of the Sheriff Appeal Court, or

  (b)   if that Court has refused permission, with the permission of the Court of Session.

  (2)   The Sheriff Appeal Court or the Court of Session may grant permission under subsection (1) only if the Court considers that—

  (a)   the appeal would raise an important point of principle or practice, or

  (b)   there is some other compelling reason for the Court of Session to hear the appeal.

  (3)   This section does not affect any other right of appeal against any decision of the Sheriff Appeal Court to the Court of Session under any other enactment.

  (4)   This section is subject to any provision of any other enactment that restricts or excludes a right of appeal from the Sheriff Appeal Court to the Court of Session.

Appeal from the sheriff principal to the Court of Session

114.—(1)   An appeal may be taken to the Court of Session against a decision of a sheriff principal constituting a final judgment in relevant civil proceedings.
          D1.774

  (2)   This section does not affect any other right of appeal against any decision of a sheriff principal to the Court of Session under any other enactment.

  (3)   This section is subject to any provision of any other enactment that restricts or excludes any right of appeal from a sheriff principal to the Court of Session.

  (4)   In subsection (1), "relevant civil proceedings" means civil proceedings (other than an appeal) under an enactment that provides for the proceedings to be brought before a sheriff principal rather than a sheriff.

Appeals: granting of leave or permission and assessment of grounds of appeal

D1.775   **115.**   In the Court of Session Act 1988, after section 31 insert—

Power to provide for single judge of Inner House to determine leave or permission and assess grounds of appeal

"**31A**(1)   The Court may by act of sederunt provide for any applications to the Court for leave or permission to appeal to the Inner House to be determined by a single judge of the Inner House.

(2)   The Court may by act of sederunt provide for—

    (a)   any appeal proceedings to be considered initially (and, where required, after leave or permission to appeal has been granted) by a single judge of the Inner House, and

    (b)   for the single judge to decide, by reference to whether the grounds of appeal or any of them are arguable—

        (i)   whether the appeal proceedings should be allowed to proceed in the Inner House, and

        (ii)   if so, on which grounds.

(3)   An act of sederunt under subsection (1) or (2)—

    (a)   must include provision—

        (i)   about the procedure to be followed in the proceedings before the single judge, including provision for the parties to be heard before the judge makes a decision,

        (ii)   for review, on the application of any party to the proceedings, of the decision of the single judge by a Division of the Inner House,

        (iii)   about the grounds on which the decision may be so reviewed,

        (iv)   about the procedure to be followed in such a review,

        (v)   about the matters that may be considered in such a review and the powers available to the Division on disposing of the review, and

    (b)   may make different provision in relation to different types of—

        (i)   applications for leave or permission,

        (ii)   appeal proceedings.

(4)   Subject to any provision made in an act of sederunt by virtue of subsection (3)(a)(ii) to (v), the decision of any single judge under an act of sederunt under subsection (1) or (2) is final.

(5)   Subsection (6) applies in appeal proceedings in which—

    (a)   a single judge has granted leave or permission for the appeal by virtue of subsection (1), and

    (b)   the judge's decision is subject to review by a Division of the Inner House by virtue of subsection (3)(a)(ii).

(6)   Where this subsection applies, the reference in subsection (2)(a) to leave or permission to appeal having been granted is a reference to its having been confirmed following review by the Division of the Inner House.

(7)   In subsection (2)(a), "appeal proceedings" means proceedings on—

    (a)   a reclaiming application under section 28 (reclaiming against decisions of a Lord Ordinary),

    (b)   an application under section 29 (application for a new trial),

    (c)   an application under section 31 (application to overturn jury verdict),

    (d)   an appeal from the Sheriff Appeal Court under section 113 of the Courts Reform (Scotland) Act 2014,

    (e)   an appeal from a sheriff principal under section 114 of that Act,

    (f)   any other appeal taken to the Court (whether under an enactment or otherwise).".

Effect of appeal

Effect of appeal

116.—(1) This section applies to—

D1.776

   (a)   an appeal to the Sheriff Appeal Court under section 110 (including such an appeal remitted to the Court of Session under section 112), and

   (b)   an appeal to the Court of Session under section 113 or 114.

(2) In the appeal, all prior decisions in the proceedings (whether made at first instance or at any stage of appeal) are open to review.

(3) Any party to the proceedings may insist in the appeal even though the party is not the one who initiated the appeal.

(4) An appeal to which this section applies does not prevent the immediate execution of any of the following, which may continue to have effect despite the appeal until recalled—

   (a)   a warrant to take inventories,

   (b)   a warrant to place effects in custody for the interim,

   (c)   a warrant for interim preservation,

   (d)   an interim interdict.

Appeals to the Supreme Court

Appeals to the Supreme Court

117. In the Court of Session Act 1988, for section 40 (appeals to the Supreme Court: appealable interlocutors) substitute—

D1.777

Appeals to the Supreme Court

"**40.**(1) An appeal may be taken to the Supreme Court against a decision of the Inner House mentioned in subsection (2), but only—

   (a)   with the permission of the Inner House, or

   (b)   if the Inner House has refused permission, with the permission of the Supreme Court.

(2) The decisions are—

   (a)   a decision constituting final judgment in any proceedings,

   (b)   a decision in an exchequer cause,

   (c)   a decision, on an application under section 29, to grant or refuse a new trial in any proceedings,

   (d)   any other decision in any proceedings if—

      (i)   there is a difference of opinion among the judges making the decision, or

      (ii)   the decision is one sustaining a preliminary defence and dismissing the proceedings.

(3) An appeal may be taken to the Supreme Court against any other decision of the Inner House in any proceedings, but only with the permission of the Inner House.

(4) In an appeal against a decision mentioned in subsection (2)(c), the Supreme Court has the same powers as the Inner House had in relation to the application under section 29, including, in particular, the powers under sections 29(3) and 30(3).

(5) No appeal may be taken to the Supreme Court against any decision of a Lord Ordinary.

(6) But subsection (5) does not affect the operation of subsections (1) and (3) in relation to a decision of the Inner House in a review of a decision of a Lord Ordinary.

(7) In an appeal to the Supreme Court under this section against a decision of the Inner House in any proceedings, all prior decisions in the proceedings (whether made at first instance or at any stage of appeal) are open to review by the Supreme Court.

(8) This section is subject to—

(a) sections 27(5) and 32(5),

(b) any provision of any other enactment that restricts or excludes an appeal from the Court of Session to the Supreme Court.

(9) This section does not affect any right of appeal from the Court of Session to the Supreme Court that arises apart from this section.

(10) In this section—

"final judgment", in relation to any proceedings, means a decision which, by itself or taken along with prior decisions in the proceedings, disposes of the subject matter of the proceedings on its merits, even though judgment may not have been pronounced on every question raised or expenses found due may not have been modified, taxed or decerned for,

"preliminary defence", in relation to any proceedings, means a defence that does not relate to the merits of the proceedings.

Permission for appeal under section 40

40A.—(1) An application to the Inner House for permission to take an appeal under section 40(1) or (3) must be made—

(a) within the period of 28 days beginning with the date of the decision against which the appeal is to be taken, or

(b) within such longer period as the Inner House considers equitable having regard to all the circumstances.

(2) An application to the Supreme Court for permission to take an appeal under section 40(1) must be made—

(a) within the period of 28 days beginning with the date on which the Inner House refuses permission for the appeal, or

(b) within such longer period as the Supreme Court considers equitable having regard to all the circumstances.

(3) The Inner House or the Supreme Court may grant permission for an appeal under section 40(1) or (3) only if the Inner House or, as the case may be, the Supreme Court considers that the appeal raises an arguable point of law of general public importance which ought to be considered by the Supreme Court at that time.".

PART 6 – CRIMINAL APPEALS

Appeals from summary criminal proceedings

Appeals to the Sheriff Appeal Court from summary criminal proceedings

D1.778
118.—(1) There are transferred to and vested in the Sheriff Appeal Court all the powers and jurisdiction of the High Court of Justiciary (whether under an enactment or otherwise) so far as relating to appeals from courts of summary criminal jurisdiction.

(2) Subsection (1) does not apply to the nobile officium of the High Court.

(3) Schedule 3 (which modifies the Criminal Procedure (Scotland) Act 1995 in consequence of subsection (1)) has effect.

Appeals from the Sheriff Appeal Court to the High Court

D1.779
119. In the Criminal Procedure (Scotland) Act 1995, after Part X (appeals from summary proceedings), insert—

"Part 10ZA – Appeals from Sheriff Appeal Court

Appeal from the Sheriff Appeal Court

194ZB.—(1) An appeal on a point of law may be taken to the High Court against any decision of the Sheriff Appeal Court in criminal proceedings, but only with the permission of the High Court.

(2) An appeal under subsection (1) may be taken by any party to the appeal in the Sheriff Appeal Court.

(3) The High Court may give permission for an appeal under subsection (1) only if the Court considers that—

    (a) the appeal would raise an important point of principle or practice, or

    (b) there is some other compelling reason for the Court to hear the appeal.

(4) An application for permission for an appeal under subsection (1) must be made before the end of the period of 14 days beginning with the day on which the decision of the Sheriff Appeal Court that would be the subject of the appeal was made.

(5) The High Court may extend the period of 14 days mentioned in subsection (4) if satisfied that doing so is justified by exceptional circumstances.

Appeals: applications and procedure

194ZC.—(1) An appeal under section 194ZB(1) is to be made by way of note of appeal.

(2) A note of appeal must specify the point of law on which the appeal is being made.

(3) For the purposes of considering and deciding an appeal under section 194ZB(1)—

    (a) three of the judges of the High Court are to constitute a quorum of the Court,

    (b) decisions are to be taken by a majority vote of the members of the Court sitting (including the presiding judge),

    (c) each judge sitting may pronounce a separate opinion.

Application for permission for appeal: determination by single judge

194ZD.—(1) An application to the High Court for permission for an appeal under section 194ZB(1) is to be determined by a single judge of the High Court.

(2) If the judge gives permission for the appeal, the judge may make comments in writing in relation to the appeal.

(3) If the judge refuses permission for the appeal—

    (a) the judge must give reasons in writing for the refusal, and

    (b) where the appellant is on bail and the sentence imposed on the appellant on conviction is one of imprisonment, the judge must grant a warrant to apprehend and imprison the appellant.

(4) A warrant under subsection (3)(b) does not take effect until the expiry of the period of 14 days mentioned in section 194ZE(1) (or, where that period is extended under section 194ZE(2) before the period being extended expires, until the expiry of the period as so extended) without an application for permission having been lodged by the appellant under section 194ZE(1).

Further application for permission where single judge refuses permission

194ZE.—(1) Where the judge refuses permission for the appeal under section 194ZD, the appellant may, within the period of 14 days beginning with the day on which intimation of the decision is given under section 194ZF(2), apply again to the High Court for permission for the appeal.

(2)   The High Court may extend the period of 14 days mentioned in subsection (1), or that period as extended under this subsection, whether or not the period to be extended has expired.

(3)   The High Court may extend a period under subsection (2) only if satisfied that doing so is justified by exceptional circumstances.

(4)   Three of the judges of the High Court are to constitute a quorum for the purposes of considering an application under subsection (1).

(5)   If the High Court gives permission for the appeal, the Court may make comments in writing in relation to the appeal.

(6)   If the High Court refuses permission for the appeal—

    (a)   the Court must give reasons in writing for the refusal, and

    (b)   where the appellant is on bail and the sentence imposed on the appellant on conviction is one of imprisonment, the Court must grant a warrant to apprehend and imprison the appellant.

Applications for permission: further provision

194ZF.—(1)   An application for permission for an appeal under section 194ZB(1) is to be considered and determined (whether under section 194ZD or 194ZE)—

    (a)   in chambers without the parties being present,

    (b)   by reference to section 194ZB(3), and

    (c)   on the basis of consideration of—

        (i)   the note of appeal under section 194ZC(1), and

        (ii)   such other document or information (if any) as may be specified by act of adjournal.

(2)   The Clerk of Justiciary must, as soon as possible, intimate to the appellant or the appellant's solicitor and to the Crown Agent—

    (a)   a decision under section 194ZD or 194ZE determining the application for permission for an appeal, and

    (b)   in the case of a refusal of permission for the appeal, the reasons for the decision.

Restriction of grounds of appeal

194ZG.—(1)   Comments in writing made under section 194ZD(2) or 194ZE(5) may specify the arguable grounds of appeal (whether or not they were stated in the note of appeal) on the basis of which permission for the appeal was given.

(2)   Where the arguable grounds of appeal are specified under subsection (1), the appellant may not, except with the permission of the High Court on cause shown, found any aspect of the appeal on a ground of appeal stated in the application for permission but not specified under subsection (1).

(3)   An application by the appellant for permission under subsection (2) must—

    (a)   be made before the end of the period of 14 days beginning with the date of intimation under section 194ZF(2), and

    (b)   be intimated by the appellant to the Crown Agent before the end of that period.

(4)   The High Court may extend the period of 14 days mentioned in subsection (3) if satisfied that doing so is justified by exceptional circumstances.

(5)   The appellant may not, except with the permission of the High Court on cause shown, found any aspect of the appeal on a matter not stated in the note of appeal (or in a duly made amendment or addition to the note of appeal).

(6)   Subsection (5) does not apply in relation to a matter specified as an arguable ground of appeal under subsection (1).

Disposal of appeals

194ZH.—(1) In disposing of an appeal under section 194ZB(1), the High Court may—

    (a)   remit the case back to the Sheriff Appeal Court with its opinion and any direction as to further procedure in, or disposal of, the case, or

    (b)   exercise any power that the Sheriff Appeal Court could have exercised in relation to disposal of the appeal proceedings before that Court.

(2) So far as necessary for the purposes or in consequence of the exercise of a power by the High Court by virtue of subsection (1)(b)—

    (a)   references in Part X to the Sheriff Appeal Court are to be read as including references to the High Court, and

    (b)   references in Part X to a verdict of or sentence passed by the inferior court are to be read as incuding references to a verdict of or sentence passed by the Sheriff Appeal Court in disposing of the appeal before it.

(3) Subsections (1)(b) and (2) do not affect any power in relation to the consideration or disposal of appeals that the High Court has apart from those subsections.

Procedure where appellant in custody

194ZI.—(1) Section 177 (procedure where appellant in custody) applies in the case where a party making an appeal (other than an excepted appeal) under section 194ZB(1) is in custody as it applies in the case where an appellant making an application under section 176 is in custody.

(2) In subsection (1), "excepted appeal" means an appeal against a decision of the Sheriff Appeal Court in—

    (a)   an appeal under section 32, or

    (b)   an appeal under section 177(3).

Abandonment of appeal

194ZJ. An appellant in an appeal under section 194ZB(1) may at any time abandon the appeal by minute to that effect—

    (a)   signed by the appellant or the appellant's solicitor,

    (b)   lodged with the Clerk of Justiciary, and

    (c)   intimated to the respondent or the respondent's solicitor.

Finality of proceedings

194ZK.—(1) Every interlocutor and sentence (including disposal or order) pronounced by the High Court in disposing of an appeal relating to summary proceedings is final and conclusive and not subject to review by any court whatsoever.

(2) Subsection (1) is subject to—

    (a)   Part XA and section 288AA, and

    (b)   paragraph 13(a) of Schedule 6 to the Scotland Act 1998.

(3) It is incompetent to stay or suspend any execution or diligence issuing from the High Court under this Part, except for the purposes of an appeal under—

    (a)   section 288AA, or

    (b)   paragraph 13(a) of Schedule 6 to the Scotland Act 1998.

Computation of time

194ZL. If any period of time specified in this Part expires on a Saturday, Sunday or court holiday prescribed for the relevant court, the period is extended to expire on the next day which is not a Saturday, Sunday or such a court holiday.".

Power to refer points of law for the opinion of the High Court

D1.780   **120.** In the Criminal Procedure (Scotland) Act 1995, after section 175, insert—

Power to refer points of law for the opinion of the High Court

"**175A**(1) In an appeal under this Part, the Sheriff Appeal Court may refer a point of law to the High Court for its opinion if it considers that the point is a complex or novel one.

(2) The Sheriff Appeal Court may make a reference under subsection (1)—

    (a) on the application of a party to the appeal proceedings, or

    (b) on its own initiative.

(3) On giving its opinion on a reference under subsection (1), the High Court may also give a direction as to further procedure in, or disposal of, the appeal.".

References by the Scottish Criminal Cases Review Commission

D1.781   **121.**—(1) In the Criminal Procedure (Scotland) Act 1995, section 194B (references by the Commission) is amended in accordance with this section.

(2) In subsection (1), after "High Court", in the first place where those words appear, insert "or the Sheriff Appeal Court".

(3) After subsection (3), insert—

"(3A) For the purposes of an appeal under Part X of this Act in a case referred to the High Court under subsection (1)—

    (a) the High Court may exercise in the case all the powers and jurisdiction that the Sheriff Appeal Court would, had the case been an appeal to that Court, have had in relation to the case by virtue of section 118 of the Courts Reform (Scotland) Act 2014, and

    (b) accordingly, Part X of this Act has effect in relation to the case subject to the following modifications—

        (i) references to the Sheriff Appeal Court are to be read as references to the High Court,

        (ii) references to an Appeal Sheriff are to be read as references to a judge of the High Court,

        (iii) references to the Clerk of the Sheriff Appeal Court are to be read as reference to the Clerk of Justiciary.".

Bail appeals

Bail appeals

D1.782   **122.**—(1) Section 32 of the Criminal Procedure (Scotland) Act 1995 (bail appeals) is amended in accordance with this section.

(2) In each of subsections (1), (2), (3H)(a), (3I), (4), (5) and (7) for "High Court" substitute "appropriate Appeal Court".

(3) For subsections (3D) and (3E) substitute—

"(3CA) The clerk of the court from which the appeal is to be taken (unless that clerk is the Clerk of Justiciary) must—

    (a) send the notice of appeal without delay to the clerk of the appropriate Appeal Court, and

    (b)   before the end of the day after the day of receipt of the notice of appeal, send the judge's report (if provided by then) to the clerk of the appropriate Appeal Court.".

(4)   In each of subsections (3F), (3G) and (10), for "Clerk of Justiciary" in each place it occurs substitute "clerk of the appropriate Appeal Court".

(5)   In subsection (3H)—

  (a)   for "Where" substitute "In a case where the Sheriff Appeal Court is the appropriate Appeal Court, if", and

  (b)   for "(3E)" substitute "(3CA)".

(6)   In each of subsections (4) and (5), for "Lord Commissioner of Justiciary" substitute "judge of the appropriate Appeal Court".

(7)   In subsection (7B)(a), for "High Court" substitute "the appropriate Appeal Court".

(8)   After subsection (10), insert—

"(11)   In this section—

"appropriate Appeal Court" means—

    (a)   in the case of an appeal under this section against a bail decision of the High Court or a judge of the High Court, that Court,

    (b)   in the case of an appeal under this section against a bail decision of the Sheriff Appeal Court, the High Court,

    (c)   in the case of an appeal under this section against a bail decision of a sheriff (whether in solemn or summary proceedings) or a JP court, the Sheriff Appeal Court,

"judge of the appropriate Appeal Court" means—

    (a)   in a case where the High Court is the appropriate Appeal Court, judge of that Court,

    (b)   in a case where the Sheriff Appeal Court is the appropriate Appeal Court, Appeal Sheriff,

"the clerk of the appropriate Appeal Court" means—

    (a)   in a case where the High Court is the appropriate Appeal Court, the Clerk of Justiciary,

    (b)   in a case where the Sheriff Appeal Court is the appropriate Appeal Court, the Clerk of that Court.

(12)   In a case where the Sheriff Appeal Court is the appropriate Appeal Court, the references in subsections (3G)(b) and (10) to the Crown Agent are to be read as references to the prosecutor.".

Part 7 – Judges of the Court of Session

Appointment of Court of Session judges, etc.

123.   In the Judiciary and Courts (Scotland) Act 2008, for sections 21 to 23 substitute—   **D1.783**

"Other Court of Session judges

Qualification of certain individuals for appointment as Court of Session judge

20A.—(1)   An individual is qualified for appointment as a judge of the Court of Session if the individual—

(a) immediately before the appointment—
   (i) held the office of sheriff principal or sheriff, and
   (ii) had held office as either sheriff principal or sheriff throughout the period of 5 years immediately preceding the appointment, or
(b) at the time of appointment—
   (i) is a solicitor having a right of audience in the Court of Session or the High Court of Justiciary under section 25A of the Solicitors (Scotland) Act 1980 (rights of audience), and
   (ii) has been such a solicitor throughout the period of 5 years immediately preceding the appointment.

(2) Subsection (1) does not affect an individual's qualification for appointment as a judge of the Court of Session by virtue of article xix of the Union with England Act 1707.

Temporary judges

20B.—(1) The Scottish Ministers may appoint an individual to act as a judge of the Court of Session; and an individual so appointed is to be known as a "temporary judge".

(2) An individual appointed under subsection (1) may also, by virtue of the appointment, act as a judge of the High Court of Justiciary.

(3) The Scottish Ministers may appoint an individual under subsection (1) only if—
(a) the individual is qualified for appointment as a judge of the Court of Session, and
(b) the Scottish Ministers have consulted the Lord President before making the appointment.

(4) Subject to section 20C, an appointment as a temporary judge lasts for 5 years.

(5) Subject to subsection (6), an individual appointed under subsection (1) is, while acting as a judge of the Court of Session or the High Court of Justiciary, to be treated for all purposes as a judge of that Court and may exercise the jurisdiction and powers that attach to that office.

(6) Such an individual is not to be treated as a judge of the Court of Session for the purposes of any enactment or rule of law relating to—
(a) the appointment, tenure of office, retirement, removal or disqualification of judges of that Court (including, without limiting that generality, any enactment or rule of law relating to the number of judges who may be appointed),
(b) the remuneration, allowances or pensions of such a judge.

(7) The appointment of an individual under subsection (1) does not affect—
(a) any appointment of the individual as a sheriff principal or sheriff, or
(b) the individual's continuing with any business or professional occupation not inconsistent with the individual acting as a judge.

Reappointment of temporary judges

20C.—(1) A temporary judge whose appointment comes to an end by virtue of the expiry of the 5 year period mentioned in section 20B(4) is to be reappointed unless—
(a) the temporary judge declines reappointment,
(b) the Lord President has made a recommendation to the Scottish Ministers against the reappointment, or
(c) the temporary judge has sat for fewer than 50 days in total in that 5 year period.

(2)   Section 20B (apart from subsection (3)) applies to a reappointment under subsection (1) as it applies to an appointment.

(3)   A temporary judge whose appointment comes to an end by resignation under section 20D may be reappointed.

(4)   Section 20B applies to a reappointment under subsection (3) as it applies to an appointment.

Cessation of appointment of temporary judges

20D.—(1)   A temporary judge may resign at any time by giving notice to that effect to the Scottish Ministers.

(2)   An individual's appointment as a temporary judge ends—
  (a)   when the individual resigns in accordance with subsection (1),
  (b)   when the individual retires from office, or
  (c)   if the individual is removed from office as such under section 39 (temporary judges: removal from office).

Re-employment of former Court of Session and Supreme Court judges

20E.—(1)   The Lord President may appoint a qualifying former judge to act as a judge of the Court of Session.

(2)   An individual appointed under subsection (1) may also, by virtue of the appointment, act as a judge of the High Court of Justiciary.

(3)   An individual so appointed may act as a judge only during such periods or on such occasions as the Lord President may determine.

(4)   The Lord President may make an appointment under subsection (1) only if it appears to the Lord President to be expedient as a temporary measure in order to facilitate the disposal of business in the Court of Session or the High Court of Justiciary.

(5)   A "qualifying former judge" is an individual who—
  (a)   has ceased to hold the office of—
    (i)   judge of the Court of Session other than by virtue of section 95(6) of the Scotland Act 1998, or
    (ii)   Justice of the Supreme Court or President or Deputy President of that Court and who, at the time of being appointed to the office in question, was eligible for appointment as a judge in the Court of Session, and
  (b)   has not reached the age of 75.

Re-employment of former judges: further provision

20F.—(1)   Subject to subsection (2), an individual's appointment under section 20E(1) lasts until recalled by the Lord President.

(2)   An individual's appointment under section 20E(1) ceases when the individual reaches the age of 75.

(3)   Despite the ending of an individual's appointment under section 20E(1)—
  (a)   the individual may continue to deal with, give judgment in or deal with an ancillary matter relating to, a case begun before the individual while acting under that appointment,
  (b)   so far as necessary for that purpose, and for the purpose of any subsequent proceedings arising out of the case or matter, the individual is to be treated as acting or, as the case may be, having acted under that appointment.

(4)   Subject to subsection (5), an individual appointed under section 20E(1) is, while acting as a judge of the Court of Session or the High Court of Justiciary, to be treated for all purposes as a judge of that Court and may exercise the jurisdiction and powers that attach to that office.

(5) Such an individual is not to be treated as a judge of the Court of Session for the purposes of any enactment or rule of law relating to—

    (a) the appointment, tenure of office, retirement, removal or disqualification of judges of that Court (including, without limiting that generality, any enactment or rule of law relating to the number of judges who may be appointed),

    (b) the oaths to be taken by such judges,

    (c) the remuneration, allowances or pensions of such a judge.

Remuneration and expenses of temporary and former judges

20G.—(1) The Scottish Courts and Tribunals Service ("the SCTS") is to pay to an individual appointed under section 20B(1) or 20E(1) such remuneration as the Scottish Ministers may determine.

(2) The Scottish Ministers may determine different amounts of remuneration for—

    (a) different individuals so appointed, or

    (b) different descriptions of individuals so appointed.

(3) The SCTS may pay to an individual appointed under section 20B(1) or 20E(1) such sums as it may determine in respect of expenses reasonably incurred by the individual in the performance of, or in connection with, the individual's duties.

(4) The SCTS may—

    (a) determine the circumstances in which such sums may be paid, and

    (b) determine different circumstances for different individuals.".

Payment of salaries and allowances of Court of Session judges

D1.784

124.—[1](1) The salaries and allowances of judges of the Court of Session determined under section 9 of the Administration of Justice Act 1973 (judicial salaries) are to be paid by the Scottish Courts and Tribunals Service.

(2) Sums required by the Scottish Courts and Tribunals Service for the payment of such salaries and such allowances are charged on the Scottish Consolidated Fund.

Expenses

D1.785

125.—(1) The Scottish Courts and Tribunals Service may pay to a Senator of the College of Justice such sums as it may determine in respect of expenses reasonably incurred by the Senator in the performance of, or in connection with, the Senator's duties.

(2) The Scottish Courts and Tribunals Service may—

    (a) determine the circumstances in which sums may be paid, and

    (b) determine different circumstances for—

        (i) different Senators,

        (ii) different descriptions of Senators,

        (iii) the different duties of Senators.

Part 8 – Scottish Land Court

Scottish Land Court: remuneration and expenses

D1.786

126.—(1) Schedule 1 to the Scottish Land Court Act 1993 (the Land Court) is amended in accordance with this section.

---

[1] As amended by the Public Service Pensions and Judicial Offices Act 2022 (c.7) Sch.2 para.21(3) (effective 10 March 2022 (for the limited purpose of making subordinate legislation or giving directions, or as it otherwise relates to the exercise of a power to make subordinate legislation, or give directions, on or after 10 March 2022); 10 May 2022 (otherwise)).

(2)   For paragraph 3 substitute—

"**3.**—(1)   The Scottish Courts and Tribunals Service ("the SCTS") is to pay to the Chairman of the Land Court such salary as the Treasury may determine.

(2)   The SCTS is to pay to each of the other members of the Land Court such salary as the SCTS may determine.

(3)   Sums required by the SCTS for the payment of a salary under this paragraph are charged on the Scottish Consolidated Fund.

3A.—(1)   The SCTS may pay to a member of the Land Court such sums as it may determine in respect of expenses reasonably incurred by the member in the performance of, or in connection with, the member's duties.

(2)   The SCTS may—

(a)   determine the circumstances in which sums may be paid, and

(b)   determine different circumstances for different members.".

(3)   For paragraph 18 substitute—

"**18.**—(1)   The Scottish Ministers are to pay to each of the following persons such remuneration as they may determine—

(a)   the principal clerk of the Land Court,

(b)   persons appointed or employed under paragraph 8 of this Schedule.

(2)   The Scottish Courts and Tribunals Service ("the SCTS") is to pay to each of the following persons such remuneration as the SCTS may determine—

(a)   persons nominated under paragraph 7A of this Schedule,

(b)   persons appointed under paragraph 10 of this Schedule.

(3)   The SCTS may pay to each of the following persons such sums as it may determine in respect of expenses reasonably incurred by the person in the performance of, or in connection with, the person's duties—

(a)   persons nominated under paragraph 7A of this Schedule,

(b)   persons appointed under paragraph 10 of this Schedule.

(4)   The SCTS may—

(a)   determine the circumstances in which sums may be paid, and

(b)   determine different circumstances for different persons.

(5)   Expenditure incurred by the Land Court in the performance of its functions may be paid by the Scottish Ministers.".

PART 9 – JUSTICE OF THE PEACE COURTS

Establishing, relocating and disestablishing justice of the peace courts

127.—(1)   Section 59 of the Criminal Proceedings etc. (Reform) (Scotland) Act 2007 (establishing etc. JP courts) is amended in accordance with subsections (2) and (3).   **D1.787**

(2)   In each of subsections (2) and (6), after "may" insert ", following submission of a proposal under subsection (7),".

(3)   For subsections (7) and (7A) substitute—

"(7)   The Scottish Courts and Tribunals Service may, with the agreement of the Lord President, submit a proposal to the Scottish Ministers for the making of an order under subsection (2) or (6).

(7A)   Before submitting a proposal to the Scottish Ministers, the Scottish Courts and Tribunals Service must consult such persons as it considers appropriate.

(7B)   If, following submission of a proposal, the Scottish Ministers decide to make an order, they must have regard to the proposal in deciding what provision to make in the order.

(7C)   The Scottish Ministers may make an order under subsection (2) or (6) only with the consent of—

(a)   the Lord President, and

(b) the Scottish Courts and Tribunals Service.".

(4) In section 81(3)(a) of that Act (orders under the Act that are subject to affirmative procedure), after "56" insert ", 59(2) or (6)".

Abolition of the office of stipendiary magistrate

D1.788
128.—(1) The office of stipendiary magistrate is abolished.

(2) Subsection (3) applies to a person who, immediately before this section comes into force, holds office as a full-time stipendiary magistrate.

(3) The person is to be appointed, by virtue of this subsection, as a summary sheriff unless the person declines the appointment.

(4) Subsection (3) applies regardless of whether the person is qualified for appointment as a summary sheriff.

(5) Subsection (6) applies to a person who, immediately before this section comes into force, holds office as a part-time stipendiary magistrate.

(6) The person is to be appointed, by virtue of this subsection, as a part-time summary sheriff unless the person declines the appointment.

(7) Subsection (6) applies regardless of whether the person is qualified for appointment as a part-time summary sheriff.

(8) A person appointed—

(a) as a summary sheriff by virtue of subsection (3) is to be treated for all purposes as if appointed as such under section 5(2),

(b) as a part-time summary sheriff by virtue of subsection (6) is to be treated for all purposes as if appointed as such under section 10(1).

Summary sheriffs to sit in justice of the peace courts

D1.789
129. A summary sheriff of a sheriffdom may constitute, and exercise the jurisdiction and powers of, any justice of the peace court established for any sheriff court district in the sheriffdom.

PART 10 – THE SCOTTISH COURTS AND TRIBUNALS SERVICE

The Scottish Courts and Tribunals Service

D1.790
130.—(1) The Scottish Court Service is renamed and is to be known as the Scottish Courts and Tribunals Service ("the SCTS").

(2) After section 61 of the Judiciary and Courts (Scotland) Act 2008 insert—

Administrative support for the Scottish Tribunals and their members etc.
"**61A.**—(1) The SCTS has the function of providing, or ensuring the provision of, the property, services, officers and other staff required for the purposes of—

(a) the Scottish Tribunals,

(b) the members of those Tribunals, and

(c) such other tribunals (and their members) as the Scottish Ministers may by order specify.

(2) In carrying out that function, the SCTS must—

(a) take account, in particular, of the needs of members of the public and those involved in proceedings in the tribunals, and

(b) so far as practicable and appropriate, co-operate and co-ordinate activity with any other person having functions in relation to the administration of justice.

(3) In this Part, references to—

(a) the Scottish Tribunals are to the First-tier Tribunal for Scotland and the Upper Tribunal for Scotland,

(b)   the members of the Scottish Tribunals are to be construed in accordance with the Tribunals (Scotland) Act 2014.".

(3)   Schedule 4, which makes further provision in relation to the Scottish Courts and Tribunals Service, has effect.

(4)   Any reference in any enactment to the Scottish Court Service is, unless the contrary intention appears, to be construed as a reference to the Scottish Courts and Tribunals Service.

Part 11 – The Judicial Appointments Board for Scotland

Assistants to the Judicial Appointments Board for Scotland

131.—(1)   In schedule 1 to the Judiciary and Courts (Scotland) Act 2008 (the Judicial Appointments Board for Scotland)—   **D1.791**

(a)   after paragraph 13 insert—

"Appointment of persons to assist the Board

13A.—(1)   The Board may appoint persons (other than Board members) to assist the Board with the carrying out of its functions.

(2)   The Board may appoint persons under sub-paragraph (1) as—
(a)   legal assistants, or
(b)   lay assistants.

(3)   A person may be appointed as a legal assistant if the person is a solicitor or advocate practising as such in Scotland.

(4)   A person may be appointed as a lay assistant if the person is eligible for appointment as a lay member of the Board.

(5)   It is for the Board to determine the number of persons who may be appointed under this paragraph.

(6)   A person who is disqualified from membership of the Board by virtue of paragraph 5 is also disqualified from being a legal assistant or a lay assistant.

(7)   Persons appointed under this paragraph are to be appointed for such period of not more than 3 years as the Board may determine.

(8)   At the end of a period of appointment, a person may be reappointed.

(9)   A person appointed under this paragraph may resign by giving notice in writing to the Board.

(10)   The Chairing Member may, by notice in writing, rescind a person's appointment under this paragraph if satisfied that the person—
(a)   has been convicted of any offence,
(b)   has become insolvent, or
(c)   is otherwise unfit to be a legal assistant or, as the case may be, a lay assistant or unable for any reason to discharge the functions of such an assistant.

(11)   Each person appointed under this paragraph is entitled to such fees and expenses, if any, as the Scottish Ministers may determine.

(12)   It is for the Scottish Ministers to pay those fees and expenses.

Powers and conduct of persons appointed to assist the Board

13B.—(1)   A person appointed under paragraph 13A(1) as a legal assistant may, so far as authorised by the Board, do anything that a legal member of the Board may do, other than take part in a decision of the Board to recommend an individual for appointment.

547

(2) A person appointed under paragraph 13A(1) as a lay assistant may, so far as authorised by the Board, do anything that a lay member of the Board may do, other than take part in a decision of the Board to recommend an individual for appointment.

(3) The Board must issue (and may from time to time revise) a code of conduct for persons appointed under paragraph 13A(1).

(4) Persons appointed under paragraph 13A(1) must have regard to the provisions of the code of conduct while assisting the Board in the carrying out of its functions.",

(b) in paragraph 16A (proceedings relating to the Scottish Tribunals), after sub-paragraph (6) insert—

"(6A) Sub-paragraph (6B) applies if—

(a) the Board is exercising any function under this Act in connection with a position mentioned in section 10(2A),

(b) the Board authorises a person appointed under paragraph 13A(1) to assist it in relation to any proceedings relating to the function, and

(c) the person authorised to assist the Board in relation to the proceedings is a member of the Scottish Tribunals.

(6B) The member of the Scottish Tribunals selected under sub-paragraph (3) may elect not to take part in the proceedings in respect of which the assistant is authorised to assist.".

(2) In paragraph 10(1)(b) of schedule 9 to the Tribunals (Scotland) Act 2014, (transitional provision: making appointments), for "and (3)" substitute ", (3), (6A) and (6B)".

PART 12 – GENERAL

Modifications of enactments

D1.792   132. Schedule 5 makes minor modifications of enactments and modifications consequential on the provisions of this Act.

Subordinate legislation

D1.793   133.—(1) Any power of the Scottish Ministers to make an order under this Act includes power to make—

(a) different provision for different purposes or areas,

(b) incidental, supplemental, consequential, transitional, transitory or saving provision.

(2) The following orders are subject to the affirmative procedure—

(a) an order under section 2(1), 39(5), 44(3), 72(12), 81(1), 107(4) or 135(2) or paragraph 3(5) of schedule 4, or

(b) an order under section 137(1) containing provisions which add to, replace or omit any part of the text of an Act.

(3) All other orders made by the Scottish Ministers under this Act are subject to negative procedure.

(4) This section does not apply to an order under section 138(2).

References to "sheriff"

D1.794   134.—(1) In this Act, references to a sheriff include references to any other member of the judiciary of a sheriffdom, so far as that member has the jurisdiction and competence that attaches to the office of sheriff.

(2) So far as necessary for the purposes, or in consequence, of the exercise by a member of the judiciary of a sheriffdom other than a sheriff of the jurisdiction and

548

competence of a sheriff, references in any other enactment to a sheriff are to be read as including references to any of the members of the judiciary of a sheriffdom.

(3) Subsections (1) and (2) do not apply—

   (a) to references to the office of sheriff,

   (b) to any provision of this Act or any other enactment relating to—

      (i) the appointment, retirement, removal or disqualification of sheriffs,

      (ii) the tenure of office of, and oaths to be taken by, sheriffs,

      (iii) the remuneration, allowances or pensions of sheriffs,

   (c) where the context requires otherwise.

Definition of "family proceedings"

135.—(1) In this Act, "family proceedings" means proceedings for or in rela-tion to—   **D1.795**

   (a) divorce,

   (b) separation,

   (c) declarator of parentage,

   (d) declarator of non-parentage,

   (e) an order under section 11 of the Children (Scotland) Act 1995 (court orders relating to parental responsibilities, etc.) other than an application for the appointment of a judicial factor mentioned in subsection (2)(g) of that section to which Part 1 of the Act of Sederunt (Judicial Factors Rules) 1992 (S.I. 1992/272) applies,

   (f) aliment (including affiliation and aliment),

   (g) financial provision after a divorce or annulment in an overseas country within the meaning of Part 4 of the Matrimonial and Family Proceedings Act 1984 (financial provision in Scotland after overseas divorce, etc.),

   (h) an order under the Matrimonial Homes (Family Protection) (Scotland) Act 1981,

   (i) variation or recall of an order mentioned in section 8(1) of the Law Reform (Miscellaneous Provisions) (Scotland) Act 1966 (variation and recall by the sheriff of certain orders made by the Court of Session),

   (j) declarator of marriage,

   (k) declarator of nullity of marriage,

   (l) declarator of recognition, or non-recognition, of a relevant foreign decree within the meaning of section 7(9) of the Domicile and Matrimonial Proceedings Act 1973,

   (m) an order under section 28(2) (financial provision where cohabitation ends otherwise than by death) or section 29(2) (application by survivor cohabit-ant for provision on intestacy) of the Family Law (Scotland) Act 2006,

   (n) dissolution of civil partnership,

   (o) separation of civil partners,

   (p) declarator of nullity of civil partnership,

   (q) an order under Chapter 3 (occupancy rights and tenancies) or Chapter 4 (interdicts) of Part 3 of the Civil Partnership Act 2004,

   (r) a declarator or other order under section 127 of that Act (attachment),

   (s) financial provision after overseas proceedings as provided for in Schedule 11 to that Act (financial provision in Scotland after overseas proceedings).

(2) The Scottish Ministers may by order modify subsection (1).

[THE NEXT PARAGRAPH IS D1.797]

Interpretation

D1.797   **136.**—(1)   In this Act, unless the context requires otherwise—

"advocate" means a member of the Faculty of Advocates,

"all-Scotland sheriff court" is to be construed in accordance with section 42(7),

"civil proceedings" includes—

(a)   proceedings under the Children's Hearings (Scotland) Act 2011, and

(b)   proceedings for contempt of court where the contempt—

(i)   arises in, or in connection with, civil proceedings, or

(ii)   relates to an order made in civil proceedings,

"decision", in relation to a sheriff, judge or court, includes interlocutor, order or judgment,

"final judgment" means a decision which, by itself, or taken along with previous decisions, disposes of the subject matter of proceedings, even though judgment may not have been pronounced on every question raised or expenses found due may not have been modified, taxed or decerned for,

"sheriff clerk" includes sheriff clerk depute,

"solicitor" means a solicitor enrolled in the roll of solicitors kept under section 7 of the Solicitors (Scotland) Act 1980.

(2)   In this Act, references to the judiciary of a sheriffdom are, in relation to a sheriffdom, references to the following—

(a)   the sheriff principal of the sheriffdom,

(b)   any other sheriff principal so far as authorised under section 30 to perform the functions of the sheriff principal of the sheriffdom,

(c)   any temporary sheriff principal appointed for the sheriffdom,

(d)   the sheriffs and summary sheriffs of the sheriffdom,

(e)   any other sheriffs or summary sheriffs so far as directed under section 31 to perform the functions of sheriff or summary sheriff in the sheriffdom,

(f)   any part-time sheriffs and part-time summary sheriffs for the time being sitting in the sheriffdom,

(g)   any person appointed under section 12(1) to act as a sheriff or summary sheriff of the sheriffdom,

and references to a "member" of the judiciary of a sheriffdom are to be construed accordingly.

(3)   In this Act, references to proceedings in the sheriff court are references to proceedings before any member of the judiciary of a sheriffdom.

Ancillary provision

D1.798   **137.**—(1)   The Scottish Ministers may by order make such incidental, supplemental, consequential, transitional, transitory or saving provision as they consider necessary or expedient for the purposes of, in consequence of, or for giving full effect to, any provision of this Act.

(2)   An order under this section may modify any enactment (including this Act), instrument or document.

Commencement

D1.799   **138.**—(1)   This Part, other than sections 132 and 134(2), comes into force on the day after Royal Assent.

(2)   The remaining provisions of this Act come into force on such day as the Scottish Ministers may by order appoint.

(3) An order under subsection (2) may include transitional, transitory or saving provision.

Short title

139. The short title of this Act is the Courts Reform (Scotland) Act 2014. **D1.800**

SCHEDULE 1

(introduced by section 44(1))

Family proceedings

1. Family proceedings. **D1.801**

Domestic abuse proceedings

2. Proceedings for or in relation to—
  (a) an action of harassment under section 8(2) of the Protection from Harassment Act 1997,
  (b) an exclusion order under section 4(2) of the Matrimonial Homes (Family Protection) (Scotland) Act 1981,
  (c) a matrimonial interdict (within the meaning of section 14 of that Act),
  (d) a domestic interdict (within the meaning of section 18A of that Act),
  (e) an exclusion order under section 104 of the Civil Partnership Act 2004,
  (f) a relevant interdict (within the meaning of section 113 of that Act).

Adoption proceedings

3. Proceedings for or in relation to—
  (a) an adoption order within the meaning of section 28(1) of the Adoption and Children (Scotland) Act 2007,
  (b) an order under section 59(1) of that Act (preliminary order where child to be adopted abroad),
  (c) a permanence order under section 80(1) of that Act.

Children's hearings proceedings

4. Proceedings under the Children's Hearings (Scotland) Act 2011.

Proceedings relating to children under the age of criminal responsibility

Proceedings relating to children under the age of criminal responsibility

4A.[1] Proceedings under the Age of Criminal Responsibility (Scotland) Act 2019.

Forced marriage proceedings

5. Proceedings for or in relation to—
  (a) a forced marriage protection order under section 1(1) of the Forced Marriage etc. (Protection and Jurisdiction) (Scotland) Act 2011,
  (b) an interim forced marriage protection order under section 5(1) of that Act.

---

[1] As inserted by the Age of Criminal Responsibility (Scotland) Act 2019 (asp 7) Pt 7 s.81(2) (effective 31 March 2020).

Warrants and interim orders

6. The granting of—

    (a)   a warrant of citation (including such warrants where the address of the defender is unknown),

    (b)   an interim interdict,

    (c)   an order for the interim preservation of property,

    (d)   an order to recall an interim interdict.

Diligence proceedings

7. Proceedings under—

    (a)   Part 1A of the Debtors (Scotland) Act 1987 (diligence on the dependence) (including proceedings to which that Part is applied by section 15N of that Act), other than proceedings in which there is claimed, in addition or as an alternative to a warrant, a decree for payment of a sum of money exceeding £5,000,

    (b)   Part III of that Act (diligence against earnings),

    (c)   Part 3A of that Act (arrestment and action of furthcoming),

    (d)   Part 8 of the Bankruptcy and Diligence etc. (Scotland) Act 2007 (attachment of money).

8. The receipt of a report of money attachment under section 182(1) of the Bankruptcy and Diligence etc. (Scotland) Act 2007.

9. The granting of authority to begin or continue execution of a decree for removing from heritable property under section 217(2) of the Bankruptcy and Diligence etc. (Scotland) Act 2007.

10. Proceedings for or in relation to—

    (a)   a warrant for the arrest of a ship on the dependence of an action or for the arrest of a ship in rem under section 47 of the Administration of Justice Act 1956, other than proceedings in which there is claimed, in addition or as an alternative to a warrant, a decree for payment of a sum of money exceeding £5,000,

    (b)   an order for the sale of a ship arrested on the dependence of an action under section 47E of that Act, other than an order relating to a decree for payment of a sum of money exceeding £5,000.

Extension of time to pay debts

11. Proceedings for or in relation to—

    (a)   a time to pay direction under section 1 of the Debtors (Scotland) Act 1987,

    (b)   a time to pay order under section 5 of that Act.

Simple procedure

12. A simple procedure case within the meaning of section 72(9).

SCHEDULE 2

Appeal Sheriffs: temporary provision

(introduced by section 53)

The transitional period

D1.802   **1.** In this schedule, "the transitional period" means the period of 3 years beginning with the day on which section 46 comes into force.

Appointment of Senators of the College of Justice to act as Appeal Sheriffs

2.—(1) The Lord President of the Court of Session may appoint persons holding the office of Senator of the College of Justice to act as Appeal Sheriffs for the transitional period.

(2) The Lord President may appoint as many persons under sub-paragraph (1) as the Lord President considers necessary for the purposes of the Sheriff Appeal Court during the transitional period.

(3) A person may be appointed under sub-paragraph (1) only if the person has held office as a Senator of the College of Justice for at least one year.

(4) The appointment of a Senator of the College of Justice to act as an Appeal Sheriff does not affect the Senator's appointment as a Senator and the Senator may accordingly continue to act in that capacity.

(5) A person appointed under sub-paragraph (1) is to be treated for all purposes (other than for the purposes of the enactments specified in sub-paragraph (6)) as an Appeal Sheriff and may exercise the jurisdiction and powers that attach to the office of Appeal Sheriff.

(6) The enactments referred to in sub-paragraph (5) are—

    (a)   sections 50 and 51,

    (b)   section 304(2)(c)(zi) of the Criminal Procedure (Scotland) Act 1995.

Tenure

3.—(1) A person's appointment under paragraph 2(1) ceases—

    (a)   if the person ceases to hold office as a Senator of the College of Justice,

    (b)   on the expiry of the transitional period.

(2) If a person appointed under paragraph 2(1) is suspended from office as a Senator of the College of Justice for any period, the person's appointment under paragraph 2(1) is also suspended for the same period.

(3) The Lord President may, after consulting the President of the Sheriff Appeal Court, recall a person's appointment under paragraph 2(1).

(4) The recall of a person's appointment under sub-paragraph (3) does not affect the person's appointment as a Senator of the College of Justice.

Savings

4. Despite the ending by virtue of paragraph 3(1)(b) of a person's appointment under paragraph 2(1)—

    (a)   the person may continue to deal with, give judgment in or deal with an ancillary matter relating to, a case begun before the person while acting under that appointment,

    (b)   so far as necessary for that purpose, and for the purpose of any subsequent proceedings arising out of the case or matter, the person is to be treated as acting, or having acted, under that appointment.

SCHEDULE 3

Transfer of summary criminal appeal jurisdiction to the Sheriff Appeal Court

(introduced by section 118(3))

[Not reproduced.]   **D1.803**

SCHEDULE 4

THE SCOTTISH COURTS AND TRIBUNALS SERVICE

(introduced by section 130(3))

D1.804   *[Not reproduced.]*

SCHEDULE 5

MODIFICATIONS OF ENACTMENTS

(introduced by section 132)

D1.805   *[Not reproduced.]*

Thomson Reuters™

5 reasons to choose ProView eBooks

1. Always Have Your Publications On Hand
Never worry about an internet connection again. With ProView's offline access, your essential titles are always available, wherever your work takes you.

2. The Feel of a Real Book
ProView's book-like features, including page numbers and bookmarks, offer a seamless transition to digital without losing the touch of tradition.

3. Effortless Library Management
Access previous editions, transfer annotations to new releases, and automatically update your looseleaf materials—all in one place.

4. Tailor Your Reading Experience
With ProView, customize your reading with adjustable display settings, font sizes, and colour schemes. Read your way, effortlessly.

5. Find Information in a Flash
Cut through the clutter with ProView's advanced search. Pinpoint the information you need across your entire library with speed and precision.

Scan the QR code to find out more or contact us at proviewtrial@tr.com for a free trial

Sweet & Maxwell